COMPUTER
SCIENCES

COMPUTER SCIENCES

Second Edition
Volume 2
Software and Hardware

K. Lee Lerner
Editor-in-Chief

Brenda Wilmoth Lerner
Managing Editor

MACMILLAN REFERENCE USA
A part of Gale, Cengage Learning

GALE
CENGAGE Learning

Detroit • New York • San Francisco • New Haven, Conn • Waterville, Maine • London

Computer Sciences
2ⁿᵈ Edition

Editor-in-Chief: K. Lee Lerner

Managing Editor: Brenda Wilmoth Lerner

Product Manager: Douglas A. Dentino

Project Editor: Kimberley A. McGrath

Rights Acquisition and Management: Margaret Chamberlain-Gaston

Composition: Evi Abou-El-Seoud

Manufacturing: Wendy Blurton; Dorothy Maki

Imaging: John Watkins

Product Design: Kristine Julien

For product information and technology assistance, contact us at
Gale Customer Support, 1-800-877-4253.
For permission to use material from this text or product,
submit all requests online at **www.cengage.com/permissions.**
Further permissions questions can be emailed to
permissionrequest@cengage.com

Cover photographs courtesy of the following: Technician working on server rack; © Yurchyks/ShutterStock.com. Screens with program web code; © Taiga/ShutterStock.com. Three business people working at meeting; © Dmitriy Shironosov/ShutterStock.com. Hands holding a tablet or a Pad; © Luis Louro/ShutterStock.com. Computer classroom; © sixninepixels/ShutterStock.com. Wireless computer mouse; © AlexGul/ShutterStock.com.

While every effort has been made to ensure the reliability of the information presented in this publication, Gale, a part of Cengage Learning, does not guarantee the accuracy of the data contained herein. Gale accepts no payment for listing; and inclusion in the publication of any organization, agency, institution, publication, service, or individual does not imply endorsement of the editors or publisher. Errors brought to the attention of the publisher and verified to the satisfaction of the publisher will be corrected in future editions.

LIBRARY OF CONGRESS CATALOGING-IN-PUBLICATION DATA

Computer sciences / K. Lee Lerner, editor-in-Chief, Brenda Wilmoth Lerner, managing editor. -- Second edition.
  v. cm
Summary: "Computer Sciences, 2nd Edition reviews the history of the discipline and concepts, as well as profiles contributors in the field. The impact of computers on the economy and society is explored, with examples in literature, film, and science provided to illustrate and support trends. These illustrated volumes also include sidebars, bibliographies, a timeline, charts, and a glossary. This title is organized in four separate topical volumes, although articles in each volume will be in an A-Z arrangement; the set's comprehensive cumulative index is found in each volume"-- Provided by publisher.
  Includes bibliographical references and index.
  Contents: v. 1. Foundations : ideas and people
  ISBN-13: 978-0-02-866220-6 (set : hardback)
  ISBN-10: 0-02-866220-2 (set : hardback)
  ISBN-13: 978-0-02-866221-3 (v. 1 : hardback)
  ISBN-10: 0-02-866221-0 (v. 1 : hardback)
[etc.]
  1. Computer science. I. Lerner, K. Lee. II. Lerner, Brenda Wilmoth.
QA76.C572 2013
004--dc23
                                                              2012037340

Gale
27500 Drake Rd.
Farmington Hills, MI, 48331-3535

ISBN-13: 978-0-02-866220-6 (set)   ISBN-10: 0-02-866220-2 (set)
ISBN-13: 978-0-02-866221-3 (vol. 1)   ISBN-10: 0-02-866221-0 (vol. 1)
ISBN-13: 978-0-02-866222-0 (vol. 2)   ISBN-10: 0-02-866222-9 (vol. 2)
ISBN-13: 978-0-02-866223-7 (vol. 3)   ISBN-10: 0-02-866223-7 (vol. 3)
ISBN-13: 978-0-02-866224-4 (vol. 4)   ISBN-10: 0-02-866224-5 (vol. 4)

This title is also available as an e-book.
ISBN-13: 978-0-02-866225-1 ISBN-10: 0-02-866225-3
Contact your Gale, a part of Cengage Learning, sales representative for ordering information.

Printed in China
1 2 3 4 5 6 7 17 16 15 14 13

Table of Contents

Volume 1: Foundations: Ideas And People

Preface xi

How To Use This Book xvii

For Your Reference xix

Timeline: Significant Events in the History of Computing xxv

Timeline: The History of Programming, Markup, and Scripting Languages xxxv

A

Abacus. 1

Analog Computing 2

Analytical Engine 6

Animation. 8

Apple Computer, Inc. 17

Artificial Intelligence. 20

Association for Computing Machinery 24

B

Babbage, Charles. 29

Bell Labs 31

Binary Number System 34

C

Census Bureau 39

Computer Fraud and Abuse Act of 1986. 42

Computer Scientists 46

D

Digital Computing 49

E

Early Computers 53

Early Pioneers 61

E-commerce 67

E-mail. 72

Ergonomics. 76

G

Games. 79

Gates, Bill 84

Generations, Computers 86

Generations, Languages. 91

Government Funding, Research 95

H

Hollerith, Herman 99

Hopper, Grace. 101

Hypertext 103

I

IBM Corporation 107

Information Retrieval 112

Information Technology Standards 117

Institute of Electrical and Electronics Engineers (IEEE) 122

Integrated Circuits 125

Intel Corporation 128

Interactive Systems 132

Internet. 138

J

Jacquard's Loom 141

Jobs, Steve 142

K

Keyboard. 147

King, Ada Byron 150

M

Mainframes. 155

Memory 159

Microchip 163

Microcomputers 166

Microsoft Corporation 169

Minicomputers 173

Minitel 177

Mouse. 180

Music 183

N

Napier's Bones. 187

National Aeronautics and Space Administration (NASA). 188

Networks. 193

O

Office Automation Systems. . . . 197

Optical Technology. 201

P

Pascal, Blaise 207

Privacy 209

R

Robotics 212

S

Security. 219

Simulation. 226

Table of Contents

Slide Rule 230

Supercomputers. 232

T

Telecommunications 237

Transistors. 241

Turing, Alan M. 247

Turing Machine. 250

V

Vacuum Tubes. 253

Virtual Reality in Education . . . 256

Viruses 260

W

Watson, Thomas J. 267

Window Interfaces 269

World Wide Web 273

X

Xerox Corporation 276

Glossary 281

*Directory of Computer
  Sciences Organizations* 305

Cumulative Index. 309

Volume 2: Software And Hardware

Preface .xi

How To Use This Book xvii

For Your Reference xix

*Timeline: Significant Events in
  the History of Computing* xxv

*Timeline: The History of
  Programming, Markup,
  and Scripting Languages* xxxv

A

Algol-60 Report 1

Algorithms 4

Assembly Language and
  Architecture 6

Asynchronous and
  Synchronous Transmission 10

ATM Transmission 13

B

Bandwidth Regulation and
  Restriction 17

Bardeen, John, Walter
  H. Brattain, and
  William B. Shockley 20

Bell, Alexander Graham 23

Boole, George 25

Boolean Algebra 27

Bridging Devices 31

C

Cache Memory 35

Cellular Technology 37

Central Processing Unit. 42

Client/Server Technology 45

Codes 50

Coding Techniques 53

Communication Devices. 56

Compatibility (Open
  Systems Design) 60

Compilers 63

Computer System Interfaces 65

D

Design Tools 69

Digital Logic Design 73

Display Devices. 78

Document Processing 85

E

Eckert, Jr., J. Presper, and
  John W. Mauchly 89

F

Fiber Optics 91

G

Game Controllers 95

Graphic Devices 99

H

Hypermedia and
  Multimedia. 103

I

Information Systems 107

Input Devices 112

Invasive Programs 115

J

JPEG, MPEG 119

L

LISP 123

Logo 125

M

Markup Languages 131

Memory Devices. 136

Morse, Samuel. 140

Music, Computer 142

N

Network Design 147

Network Protocols. 150

Network Topologies 154

O

Object-Oriented Languages. . . . 157

Operating Systems 161

Optical Character
  Recognition 166

P

Parallel Processing 171

Pattern Recognition. 176

Personal Digital Assistants 179

Pointing Devices 182

Printing Devices 187

Procedural Languages 192

Programming 200

R

Reading Tools 203

Robots. 207

S

Satellite Technology. 211

Scaling 215

Security Hardware. 217

Security Software. 219

Serial and Parallel
    Transmission. 222

Servers. 225

Simulators. 228

Sound Devices. 232

SQL 238

Storage Devices 240

System Analysis 245

Systems Design 249

T

Touch Screens 253

Transmission Media 256

V

Video Devices 261

Virtual Memory 263

Virtual Private Network 269

Virtual Reality. 272

von Neumann, John 275

W

Wireless Technology 279

Z

Zuse, Konrad 281

Glossary 285

*Directory of Computer
    Sciences Organizations* 309

Cumulative Index. 313

Volume 3: Social Applications

Preface xi

How To Use This Book xvii

For Your Reference xix

*Timeline: Significant
    Events in the History of
    Computing* xxv

*Timeline: The History of
    Programming, Markup,
    and Scripting Languages*. . . . xxxv

A

Accounting Software 1

Agriculture 4

Aircraft Flight Control . . . 8

Aircraft Traffic Management 12

Airline Reservations. 16

Architecture 19

Asimov, Isaac. 23

Astronomy 26

ATM Machines 29

B

Biology 33

C

CAD/CAM, CA
    Engineering 37

Cell Phones. 40

Chess Playing 43

Chip Manufacturing 47

Computer Assisted
    Instruction 50

Computer Professional 54

Computer Supported
    Cooperative Work (CSCW) . . 57

Computerized
    Manufacturing 60

Cormack, Allen, and
    Godfrey Hounsfield 65

Cray, Seymour. 68

D

Data Processing. 71

Data Visualization 73

Database Management
    Software 75

Decision Support Systems 79

Desktop Publishing. 82

Distance Learning 87

E

Economic Modeling 93

Educational Software. 95

Embedded Technology
    (Ubiquitous Computing) 98

Expert Systems 102

F

Fashion Design 107

Film and Video Editing. 109

G

Geographic Information
    Systems. 115

Gross, Alfred J. 117

H

Hacking 121

Hewlett, William. 125

Home System Software 128

I

Image Analysis: Medicine 133

Integrated Software 136

K

Kemeny, John G. 141

Knowledge-Based Systems. 142

Table of Contents

L

Laser Technology. 145

Legal Systems 148

Library Applications 151

M

Magnetic Stripe Cards. 155

Mathematics 157

Medical Systems 160

Molecular Biology. 163

Music Composition. 167

N

Navigation 173

Neural Networks. 177

O

Open Source 183

Organick, Elliot. 187

P

Péter, Rózsa. 189

Physics 191

Process Control. 194

Productivity Software 197

Project Management 202

R

Railroad Applications 205

S

Scientific Visualization 209

Security Applications. 213

Social Media 216

Software Piracy 223

Space Travel and Exploration . . . 226

Speech Recognition. 233

Spreadsheets 236

T

Technology of Desktop
Publishing. 241

Telephony 245

U

User Interfaces. 248

W

Wang, An 253

Weather Forecasting 255

Word Processors 259

Z

Zuckerberg, Mark 262

Glossary 267

Directory of Computer
Sciences Organizations 291

Cumulative Index. 295

Volume 4: Electronic Universe

Preface xi

How To Use This Book xvii

For Your Reference xix

Timeline: Significant Events in
the History of Computing xxv

Timeline: The History of
Programming, Markup,
and Scripting Languages. . . . xxxv

A

Agents. 1

Amdahl, Gene Myron 3

Art 6

Artificial Life. 10

Assistive Computer
Technology for Persons
with Disabilities 13

Asynchronous Transfer
Mode (ATM) 19

Authentication 24

B

Bandwidth 27

Browsers 30

C

Censorship: National,
International 35

Chemistry 37

Computer Vision 41

Cookies. 45

Copyright 47

Credit Online 52

Cryptography 55

Cybercafe 59

Cybernetics 62

D

Data Mining 65

Data Warehousing. 70

Digital Filmmaking. 73

Digital Images. 76

Digital Libraries 79

Digital Photography 83

Digital Signatures 86

E

E-banking 91

E-books. 94

E-commerce: Economic
and Social Aspects. 97

E-journals and E-publishing . . . 100

Electronic Campus 103

Electronic Markets 106

Entrepreneurs 110

Ethics 118

F

Feynman, Richard P. 123

Fiction, Computers in. 125

Firewalls 129

FTP. 132

G

Global Positioning
    Systems. 135

Global Surveillance 139

Glushkov, Victor M. 142

Guru 144

H

Hackers. 147

Home Entertainment 152

Human Factors: User
    Interfaces 155

I

Information Access 159

Information Overload 163

Information Theory 165

Internet: Applications 168

Internet: Backbone 172

Internet Control and
    Cyberwarfare 177

Internet: History 183

Intranet. 188

J

Java Applets. 191

JavaScript 194

Journalism. 199

M

Marconi, Guglielmo 205

Mobile Computing 207

Molecular Computing. 210

N

Nanocomputing 215

Newell, Allen. 219

Nyquist, Harry 222

O

Online Privacy 223

P

Patents 227

Photography 229

Political Applications. 233

R

Routing. 239

S

Search Engines 242

Service Providers 246

Shannon, Claude E. 249

Simon, Herbert A. 252

Social Impact. 254

T

TCP/IP 259

Telnet 262

U

Urban Myths. 264

V

Visual Basic. 267

Glossary 271

*Directory of Computer
    Sciences Organizations* 295

Cumulative Index. 299

Preface

Computer Sciences, 2nd Edition is devoted to providing younger students and general readers with a foundation upon which to build an understanding of modern computer science. Because applications of technology now invigorate almost all fields of study, topics in *Computer Sciences* are carefully selected to present insightful information related to topics in the news. Both updated and new entries, for example, help explain both technical and ethical dimensions of issues related to social media and online privacy. Special entries on digital photography and digital filmmaking highlight applications of computer science that enhance how we view and understand our world.

The articles in *Computer Sciences* are meant to be understandable by anyone with a curiosity about basic computer science. When topics move into highly technical research and development areas, every effort has been taken to explain concepts clearly and simply, without sacrifice of fundamental accuracy. Accordingly, entries in *Computer Sciences* include treatments of topics designed to excite less-experienced students while simultaneously providing a solid reference for students preparing for more specialized studies. The editors have taken special care to provide treatment of topics that foster essential critical thinking skills that will enable students and readers to tackle emerging issues.

We live in an increasingly digital world where an understanding of basic computer science principles and applications is essential. The Internet, for example, is now a global network connecting, with more than a billion computers used by billions of people. Personal information, medical records, opinions, industrial secrets, military communications, financial transactions, messages between conspirators, orders for goods and services, and many other types of communications travel over the Internet. *Computer Sciences* enables students and readers to understand how the digital world works.

Equally as important, however, for citizens of the digital age, *Computer Sciences* enables students and readers to understand how increases in computing capacity relate to the capacity to wage cyberwarfare; how viruses transform from annoyances to instruments of covert operations and computer crime; and how breakthroughs in technology enable online activism that contributes to social and political change.

Contributors and Advisors

In addition to engineers specializing in computer science, *Computer Sciences* contributors include scientists, journalists, artists, teachers, and writers who explain the practical applications of computer science.

In this and the previous edition of *Computer Sciences*, a number of experts have written and advised on topics related to their expertise. We would like to express our sincere appreciation to:

Tom Abel: Penn State University, University Park, PA.

Martyn Amos: University of Liverpool, United Kingdom.

Richard Archer: Pittsburgh, PA.

Pamela Willwerth Aue: Royal Oak, MI.

William Atkins: Independent research consultant, Normal, IL.

Nancy J. Becker: St. John's University, New York.

Mark Bedau: Reed College, Portland, OR.

John Micheal Bell: LMG research associate. Harvard DCE Graduate Professional Program in Journalism. Harvard University, Cambridge MA.

Mercy Bell: LMG research associate. Nashville, TN.

Pierfrancesco Bellini: University of Florence, Italy.

Gary H. Bernstein: University of Notre Dame, Noire Dame, IN.

Anne Bissonnette: Kent State University Museum, Kent, OH.

Kevin W. Bowyer: University of Notre Dame, Notre Dame, IN.

Stefan Brass: University of Giessen, Germany.

Barbara Britton: Windsor Puttie Library, Windsor, Ontario, Canada.

Kimberly Mann Bruch: San Diego Supercomputer Center, University of California, San Diego.

Ivan Bruno: University of Florence, Italy.

Dennis R. Buckmaster: Pennsylvania State University, University Park, PA.

Dan Burk: University of Minnesota, Minneapolis, MN.

Guoray Cai: Pennsylvania State University, University Park, PA.

Shirley Campbell: University of Pittsburgh, Pittsburgh, PA.

Sara V. Castillo: Independent media consultant. Dubai, United Arab Emirates.

Siddharth Chandra: University of Pittsburgh, Pittsburgh, PA.

J. Alex Chediak: University of California, Berkeley, CA.

Kara K. Choquette: Xerox Corporation.

John Cosgrove: Cosgrove Communications, Pittsburgh, PA.

Cheryl L. Cramer: Digimarc Corporation, Tualatin, OR.

Anthony Debons: University of Pittsburgh, Pittsburgh, PA.

Salvatore Domenick Desiano: NASA Ames Research Center (QSS Group, Inc.).

Ken Doerbecker: Perfection Services, Inc.; WeirNet LLC; and FreeAir Networks, Inc.

Judi Effis: KPMG, LLP, Pittsburgh, PA.

Karen E. Esch: Karen Esch Associates, Pittsburgh, PA.

Ming Fan: University of Notre Dame, Notre Dame, IN.

Jim Fike: Ohio University, Athens, OH.

Ida M. Flynn: University of Pittsburgh, Pittsburgh, PA.

Roger R. Flynn: University of Pittsburgh, Pittsburgh, PA.

H. Bruce Franklin: Rutgers University, Newark, NJ.

Thomas J. Froehlich: Kent State University, Kent, OH.

Chuck Gaidica: WDW-TV, Detroit, MI.

G. Christopher Hall: PricewaterhouseCoopers.

Gary Hanson: Kent State University, Kent, OH.

Shaquilla T. Harrigan, Production intern at LernerMedia Global, Summer 2012. Harvard College (Class of 2016), Cambridge, MA.

Karen Hartman: James Monroe Center Library, Mary Washington College, Fredericksburg, VA.

Melissa J. Harvey: Carnegie Mellon University, Pittsburgh, PA.

Albert D. Helfnck: Embry-Riddle Aeronautical University, Daytona Beach, PL.

Angelia Herrin: Harvard Business Publishing, Cambridge, MA.

Stephen Hughes: University of Pittsburgh, Pittsburgh, PA.

Joseph Patterson Hyder: Hyder Law Group, Jacksonville, FL.

Bruce Jacob: University of Maryland, College Park, MD.

Radhika Jain: Georgia State University, Atlanta, GA.

Wesley Jamison: University of Pittsburgh at Greensburg.

Sid Karin: San Diego Supercomputer Center, University of California, San Diego.

Declan P. Kelly: Philips Research, The Netherlands.

Betty Kirke: New York, NY.

Mikko Kovalainen: University of Jyväskylä, Finland.

Paul R. Kraus: Pittsburgh, PA.

Prashant Krishnamurthy: University of Pittsburgh, Pittsburgh, PA.

Marina Krol: Mount Sinai School of Medicine, New York, NY.

Susan Landau: Sun Microsystems Inc., Mountain View, CA.

Nicholas C. Laudato: University of Pittsburgh, Pittsburgh, Pennsylvania.

George Lawton: Eutopian Enterprises.

Cynthia Tumilry Lazzaro: Pinnacle Training Corp., Stonebam, MA.

Joseph J. Lazzaro: Massachusetts Commission for the Blind, Boston, MA.

John Leaney: University of Technology, Sydney, Australia.

Robert Lembersky: Ann Taylor, Inc., New York, NY.

Adrienne Wilmoth Lerner: Hyder Law Group, Jacksonville, FL.

Terri L. Lenox: Westminster College, New Wilmington, PA.

Joyce H-S Li: University of Pittsburgh, Pittsburgh, PA.

Michael R. Macedonia: USA STPJCOM, Orlando,.

Dirk E. Mahling: University of Pittsburgh, Pittsburgh, PA.

Cynthia J. Martincic: St. Vincent College, Latrobe, PA.

Michael J. McCarthy: Carnegie Mellon University, Pittsburgh, PA.

Ann McIver McHoes: Carlow College, Pittsburgh PA.

Genevieve McHoes: University of Maryland, College Park, MD.

John McHugh: CERTTM Coordination Center, Software Engineering Institute, Carnegie Mellon Pittsburgh, PA.

Donald M. McIver: Northrop Grumman Corporation, Baltimore, MD.

Maurice McIver: Integrated Databases, Inc., Honolulu, HI.

William J. McIver, Jr.: University at Albany, State University of New York.

Trevor T. Moores: University of Nevada, Las Vegas.

Christopher Morgan: Association for Computing Machinery, Nero York, NY.

Bertha Kugelman Morimoto: University of Pittsburgh, Pittsburgh, PA.

Tracy Mullen: NEC Research Inc., Princeton, NJ.

Paul Munro: University of Pittsburgh, Pittsburgh, PA.

Stephen Murray: University of Technology, Sydney, Australia.

Carey Nachenberg: Symantec Corporation.

John Nau: Frank R. Rusch.

Paolo Nesi: University of Florence, Italy.

Kai A. Olsen: Molde College and University of Bergen, Norway.

Evan Austin Ott: University of Texas, Austin, TX.

Ipek Ozkaya: Carnegie Mellon University, Pittsburgh, PA.

Bob Patterson: Perfection Services, Inc.

Robert R. Perkoski: University of Pittsburgh, Pittsburgh, PA.

Thomas A. Pollack: Duquesne University, Pittsburgh, PA.

Guylaine M. Pollock: IEEE Computer Society; Sandia National Laboratories, Albuquerque, NM.

Wolfgang Porod: University of Notre Dame, Notre Dame, IN.

Anwer H. Puthawala: Park Avenue Associates in Radiology, P.C., Binghamton, NY.

Mary McIver Puthawala: Binghamton, NY.

Sudha Ram: University of Arizona, Tucson, AZ.

Edie M. Rasmussen: University of Pittsburgh, Pittsburgh, PA.

Robert D. Regan: Consultant, Pittsburgh, PA.

Allen Renear: University of Illinois, Urbana-Champaign.

Sarah K. Rich: Pennsylvania State University, University Park, PA.

Mike Robinson: Sageforce Ltd., Kingston on Thames, Surrey, United Kingdom.

Elke A. Rudensteiner: Worcester Polytechnic Institute, Worcester, MA.

Frank R. Rusch: University of Illinois at Urbana-Champaign.

William Sherman: National Center for Supercomputing Applications, University of Illinois at Urbana-Champaign.

Marc Silverman: University of Pittsburgh, Pittsburgh, PA.

Munindar P. Singh: North Carolina State University, Raleigh, NC.

Cindy Smith: PricewaterhouseCoopers, Pittsburgh, PA.

Barry Smyth: Smart Media Institute, University College, Dublin, Ireland.

Amanda Spink: Pennsylvania State University, University Park, PA.

Michael B. Spring: University of Pittsburgh, Pittsburgh, PA.

Savitha Srinivasan: IBM Almaden Research Center, San Jose, CA.

Maria Stenzel: Photojournalist. *National Geographic*, Washington, D.C.

Igor Tarnopolsky: Westchester County Department of Laboratories and Research, Valhalla, NY.

George A. Tarnow: Georgetown University, Washington, DC.

Lucy A. Tedd: University of Wales, Aberystwyth, Wales, United Kingdom.

Umesh Thakkar: National Center for Supercomputing Applications, University of Illinois at Urbana-Champaign.

Richard A- Thompson: University of Pittsburgh, Pittsburgh, PA.

James E. Tomayko: Carnegie Mellon University, Pittsburgh, PA.

Christinger Tomer: University of Pittsburgh, Pittsburgh, PA.

Upkar Varshney: Georgia State University, Atlanta, GA.

Jonathan Vos Post: Magic Dragon Multimedia, http://magicdragon.com.

Tom Wall: Duke University, Durham, N.

Brett A. Warneke: University of California, Berkeley, CA.

Patricia S. Wehman: University of Pittsburgh, Pittsburgh, PA.

Isaac Weiss: University of Maryland, College Park, MD.

Martin B. Weiss: University of Pittsburgh, Pittsburgh, PA.

Jeffrey C. Wingard: Leesburg, VA.

Victor L. Winter: University of Nebraska, Omaha.

Charles R. Woratschek: Robert Morris University, Moon Township, PA.

Peter Y. Wu: University of Pittsburgh, Pittsburgh, PA.

William J. Yurcik: Illinois State University, Normal, IL.

Gregg R. Zegarelli: Zegarelli Law Group, P.C.

Acknowledgments

The editors offer special thanks to: Angelia Herrin and Maria Stenzel for bringing their expertise in modern practice of journalism and photojournalism to, respectively, the *Computer Sciences*. Herrin, a former Knight Fellow in Journalism at Stanford University reporter for Knight-Ridder newspapers, served as Washington, D.C., editor of *USA Today*. Herrin is now an editor at Harvard Business School

Publishing. Stenzel, a frequent and long-time contributor to *National Geographic* served as a Knight Fellow in Science Journalism at MIT.

Writing on tight deadlines from Dubai in the United Arab Emirates, Sara V. Castillo contributed the article on digital filmmaking.

Evan Ott at the University of Texas offered invaluable assistance in advising and updating topics related to on emerging applications of computer science.

The editors thank Shaquilla T. Harrigan, our summer 2012 production intern at LernerMedia Global. Ms. Harrigan, a member of the class of 2016 at Harvard College in Cambridge, Massachusetts, assisted in photo selection and captioning.

This book would not have been possible without the efforts of project manager Kim McGrath. Her perspectives, patience, and penchant for asking good questions across a broad spectrum of topics added significantly to the quality of all aspects of *Computer Sciences*.

K. Lee Lerner and Brenda Wilmoth Lerner, editors
Cambridge, MA

December, 2012

How To Use This Book

• •

Computer Sciences, 2nd Edition provides an overview of the history and current status of the computer science industry, as well as its economic and cultural impact. This is a broad scope, and for ease of use, entries have been grouped into four subject-based volumes.

Volume 1: Foundations: Ideas and People   This volume discusses the foundation of computer science, including computing history and important innovators. Ranging from Charles Babbage, binary numbers, and slide rule to Steve Jobs, World Wide Web, and windows interfaces, the entries in this volume provide a solid background on the development of the field of computer sciences.

Volume 2: Software and Hardware   Articles in this volume cover topics from system analysis and design (the cornerstone of building a system) to operating systems, compilers, and parallel processing (which discuss some of the technical aspects of computing). Here, too, users will find valuable information on the growing field of telecommunications, including cellular and wireless technologies.

Volume 3: Social Applications   From ATM machines to social media and weather forecasting, the use of computers impacts our everyday lives. For example, computer technology has greatly influence the study of biology, molecular biology, physics, and mathematics, not to mention the large role it plays in air traffic management and aircraft flight control, navigation and geographic information systems. Businesses—large and small—have significantly benefited from applications that track product growth, costs, and the way products are managed. Other articles in this volume include economic modeling, hacking, and home system software.

Volume 4: Electronic Universe   Volume 4 delves into our vastly interconnected, networked society. The Internet is explored in detail, including its history, applications, and backbone. Molecular computing and artificial life are discussed as are mobile computing and encryption technology. The reader will find articles on censorship (national and international), online privacy, digital filmmaking, E-commerce, and search engines. Ethical matters pertaining to the electronic universe are also addressed.

All entries include a bibliography to assist in conducting additional research. Where appropriate, technical terms are defined in the margins of the entries, and photos and charts are used to illustrate most entries.

Entries are arranged in alphabetical order within each volume, with biographies listed by their last names. All four volumes include a comprehensive table of contents and cumulative index that can further assist the reader in locating the information they need. Other features found in every volume are:

■ **Preface** — An essay by editors K. Lee Lerner and Brenda Wilmoth Lerner discussing the importance of computer sciences as it relates to critical thinking and living in the digital age.

■ **For Your Reference** — This section defines scientific units of measurement and supplies conversion charts to customary units of measurement. It also provides examples from various base numbering systems and their equivalents, as well as the relative sizes of objects.

■ **Timeline: Significant Events in the History of Computing** — This chronology lists major events and milestones in the field of computer sciences.

■ **Timeline: The History of Programming, Markup, and Scripting Languages** — This chronology is focused on achievements and milestones as related to computer programming and languages.

■ **Glossary** — The glossary defines over 580 technical terms used throughout the set.

■ **Directory of Computer Sciences Organizations** — This directory provides contact information for over 50 computer sciences-related organizations.

For Your Reference

··

This section provides information that may be of assistance in understanding the entries that make up this book: definitions for SI terms and symbols, and; conversion tables for SI measurements to other measurement systems. Also included are examples from various base numbering systems and their equivalents, as well as the relative sizes of objects.

SI BASE AND SUPPLEMENTARY UNIT NAMES AND SYMBOLS

Physical Quality	Name	Symbol
Length	meter	m
Mass	kilogram	kg
Time	second	s
Electric current	ampere	A
Thermodynamic temperature	kelvin	K
Amount of substance	mole	mol
Luminous intensity	candela	cd
Plane angle	radian	rad
Solid angle	steradian	sr

Temperature

Scientists commonly use the Celsius system. Although not recommended for scientific and technical use, earth scientists also use the familiar Fahrenheit temperature scale (°F). 1°F = 1.8°C or K. The triple point of H_2O, where gas, liquid, and solid water coexist, is 32°F.

- To change from Fahrenheit (F) to Celsius (C):
  °C = (°F-32)/(1.8)
- To change from Celsius (C) to Fahrenheit (F):
  °F = (°C x 1.8) + 32
- To change from Celsius (C) to Kelvin (K):
  K = °C + 273.15
- To change from Fahrenheit (F) to Kelvin (K):
  K = (°F-32)/(1.8) + 273.15

UNITS DERIVED FROM SI, WITH SPECIAL NAMES AND SYMBOLS

Derived Quantity	Name of SI Unit	Symbol for SI Unit	Expression in Terms of SI Base Units
Frequency	hertz	Hz	s^{-1}
Force	newton	N	$m \cdot kg \cdot s^{-2}$
Pressure, stress	pascal	Pa	$m^{-1} \cdot kg \cdot s^{-2}$
Energy, work, heat	joule	J	$m^2 \cdot kg \cdot s^{-2}$
Power, radiant flux	watt	W	$m^2 \cdot kg \cdot s^{-3}$
Electric charge	coulomb	C	$s \cdot A$
Electric potential, electromotive force	volt	V	$m^2 \cdot kg \cdot s^{-3} \cdot A^{-1}$
Electric resistance	ohm	Ω	$m^2 \cdot kg \cdot s^{-3} \cdot A^{-2}$
Celsius temperature	degree Celsius	°C	K
Luminous flux	lumen	lm	Cd
Illuminance	lux	lx	$m^{-2} \cdot cd$

UNITS USED WITH SI, WITH NAME, SYMBOL, AND VALUES IN SI UNITS

The following units, not part of the SI, will continue to be used in appropriate contexts (e.g., angtsrom):

Physical Quantity	Name of Unit	Symbol for Unit	Value in SI Units
Time	minute	min	60 s
	hour	h	3,600 s
	day	d	86,400 s
Plane angle	degree	°	$(\pi/180)$ rad
	minute	'	$(\pi/10,800)$ rad
	second	"	$(\pi/648,000)$ rad
Length	angstrom	Å	10^{-10} m
Volume	liter	l, L	$1\ dm^3 = 10^{-3}\ m^3$
Mass	ton	t	$1\ Mg = 10^3$ kg
	unified atomic mass unit	u	$\approx 1.66054 \times 10^{-27}$ kg
Pressure	bar	bar	$10^5\ Pa = 10^5\ N\ m^{-2}$
Energy	electronvolt	eV (= e X V)	$\approx 1.60218 \times 10^{-19}$ J

CONVERSIONS FOR STANDARD, DERIVED, AND CUSTOMARY MEASUREMENTS

Length

1 angstrom (Å)	0.1 nanometer (exactly) 0.000000004 inch
1 centimeter (cm)	0.3937 inches
1 foot (ft)	0.3048 meter (exactly)
1 inch (in)	2.54 centimeters (exactly)
1 kilometer (km)	0.621 mile
1 meter (m)	39.37 inches 1.094 yards
1 mile (mi)	5,280 feet (exactly) 1.609 kilometers
1 astronomical unit (AU)	1.495979×10^{13} cm
1 parsec (pc)	206,264.806 AU 3.085678×10^{18} cm 3.261633 light-years
1 light-year	9.460530×10^{17} cm

Area

1 acre	43,560 square feet (exactly) 0.405 hectare
1 hectare	2.471 acres
1 square centimeter (cm²)	0.155 square inch
1 square foot (ft²)	929.030 square centimeters
1 square inch (in²)	6.4516 square centimeters (exactly)
1 square kilometer (km²)	247.104 acres 0.386 square mile
1 square meter (m²)	1.196 square yards 10.764 square feet
1 square mile (mi²)	258.999 hectares

MEASUREMENTS AND ABBREVIATIONS

Volume

1 barrel (bbl)*, liquid	31 to 42 gallons
1 cubic centimeter (cm³)	0.061 cubic inch
1 cubic foot (ft³)	7.481 gallons 28.316 cubic decimeters
1 cubic inch (in³)	0.554 fluid ounce
1 dram, fluid (or liquid)	$\frac{1}{8}$ fluid ounce (exactly) 0.226 cubic inch 3.697 milliliters
1 gallon (gal) (U.S.)	231 cubic inches (exactly) 3.785 liters 128 U.S. fluid ounces (exactly)
1 gallon (gal) (British Imperial)	277.42 cubic inches 1.201 U.S. gallons 4.546 liters
1 liter	1 cubic decimeter (exactly) 1.057 liquid quarts 0.908 dry quart 61.025 cubic inches
1 ounce, fluid (or liquid)	1.805 cubic inches 29.573 milliliters
1 ounce, fluid (fl oz) (British)	0.961 U.S. fluid ounce 1.734 cubic inches 28.412 milliliters
1 quart (qt), dry (U.S.)	67.201 cubic inches 1.101 liters
1 quart (qt), liquid (U.S.)	57.75 cubic inches (exactly) 0.946 liter

Units of mass

1 carat (ct)	200 milligrams (exactly) 3.086 grains
1 grain	64.79891 milligrams (exactly)
1 gram (g)	15.432 grains 0.035 ounce
1 kilogram (kg)	2.205 pounds
1 microgram (µg)	0.000001 gram (exactly)
1 milligram (mg)	0.015 grain
1 ounce (oz)	437.5 grains (exactly) 28.350 grams
1 pound (lb)	7,000 grains (exactly) 453.59237 grams (exactly)
1 ton, gross or long	2,240 pounds (exactly) 1.12 net tons (exactly) 1.016 metric tons
1 ton, metric (t)	2,204.623 pounds 0.984 gross ton 1.102 net tons
1 ton, net or short	2,000 pounds (exactly) 0.893 gross ton 0.907 metric ton

Pressure

1 kilogram/square centimeter (kg/cm²)	0.96784 atmosphere (atm) 14.2233 pounds/square inch (lb/in²) 0.98067 bar
1 bar	0.98692 atmosphere (atm) 1.02 kilograms/square centimeter (kg/cm²)

* There are a variety of "barrels" established by law or usage. For example, U.S. federal taxes on fermented liquors are based on a barrel of 31 gallons (141 liters); many state laws fix the "barrel for liquids" as 31½ gallons (119.2 liters); one state fixes a 36-gallon (160.5 liters) barrel for cistern measurment; federal law recognizes a 40-gallon (178 liters) barrel for "proof spirts"; by custom, 42 gallons (159 liters) comprise a barrel of crude oil or petroleum products for statistical purposes, and this equivalent is recognized "for liquids" by four states.

Base 2 (Binary)	Decimal (Base 10) Equivalent	Approximations to Powers of Ten
2^0	1	
2^1	2	
2^2	4	
2^3	8	
2^4	16	
2^5	32	
2^6	64	
2^7	128	10^2; 100; one hundred; 1 followed by 2 zeros
2^8	256	
2^9	512	
2^{10}	1,024	10^3; 1,000; one thousand; 1 followed by 3 zeros
2^{11}	2,048	
2^{12}	4,096	
2^{13}	8,192	
2^{14}	16,384	
2^{15}	32,768	
2^{16}	65,536	
2^{17}	131,072	
2^{18}	262,144	
2^{19}	524,288	
2^{20}	1,048,576	10^6; 1,000,000; one million; 1 followed by 6 zeros
2^{21}	2,097,152	
2^{22}	4,194,304	
2^{23}	8,388,608	
2^{24}	16,777,216	
2^{25}	33,554,432	
2^{26}	67,108,864	
2^{27}	134,217,728	
2^{28}	268,435,456	
2^{29}	536,870,912	
2^{30}	1,073,741,824	10^9; 1,000,000,000; one billion; 1 followed by 9 zeros
2^{31}	2,147,483,648	
2^{32}	4,294,967,296	
2^{33}	8,589,934,592	
2^{34}	17,179,869,184	
2^{35}	34,359,738,368	
2^{36}	68,719,476,736	
2^{37}	137,438,953,472	
2^{38}	274,877,906,944	
2^{39}	549,755,813,888	
2^{40}	1,099,511,627,776	10^{12}; 1,000,000,000,000; one trillion; 1 followed by 12 zeros
2^{50}	1,125,899,906,842,624	10^{15}; 1,000,000,000,000,000; one quadrillion; 1 followed by 15 zeros
2^{100}	1,267,650,600,228,229,401,496,703,205,376	10^{30}; 1 followed by 30 zeros
2^{-1}	1/2	
2^{-2}	1/4	
2^{-3}	1/8	
2^{-4}	1/16	
2^{-5}	1/32	
2^{-6}	1/64	
2^{-7}	1/128	1/100; 10^{-2}; 0.01; 1 hundredth
2^{-8}	1/256	
2^{-9}	1/512	
2^{-10}	1/1,024	1/1000; 10^{-3}; 0.001; 1 thousandth

Base 16 (Hexadecimal)	Binary (Base 2) Equivalent	Decimal (Base 10) Equivalent	Approximations to Powers of Ten
16^0	2^0	1	
16^1	2^4	16	
16^2	2^8	256	2×10^2; 2 hundred
16^3	2^{12}	4,096	4×10^3; 4 thousand
16^4	2^{16}	65,536	65×10^3; 65 thousand
16^5	2^{20}	1,048,576	1×10^6; 1 million
16^6	2^{24}	16,777,216	
16^7	2^{28}	268,435,456	
16^8	2^{32}	4,294,967,296	4×10^9; 4 billion
16^9	2^{36}	68,719,476,736	68×10^9; 68 billion
16^{10}	2^{40}	1,099,511,627,776	1×10^{12}; 1 trillion
16^{-1}	2^{-4}	1/16	
16^{-2}	2^{-8}	1/256	
16^{-3}	2^{-12}	1/4,096	$1/4 \times 10^{-3}$; 1/4-thousandth
16^{-4}	2^{-16}	1/65,536	
16^{-5}	2^{-20}	1/1,048,576	10^{-6}; 1 millionth
16^{-8}	2^{-32}	1/4,294,967,296	$1/4 \times 10^{-9}$; 1/4-billionth
16^{-10}	2^{-40}	1/1,099,511,627,776	10^{-12}; 1 trillionth

Base 10 (Decimal)	Equivalent	Verbal Equivalent
10^0	1	
10^1	10	
10^2	100	1 hundred
10^3	1,000	1 thousand
10^4	10,000	
10^5	100,000	
10^6	1,000,000	1 million
10^7	10,000,000	
10^8	100,000,000	
10^9	1,000,000,000	1 billion
10^{10}	10,000,000,000	
10^{11}	100,000,000,000	
10^{12}	1,000,000,000,000	1 trillion
10^{15}	1,000,000,000,000,000	1 quadrillion
10^{-1}	1/10	1 tenth
10^{-2}	1/100	1 hundredth
10^{-3}	1/1,000	1 thousandth
10^{-6}	1/1,000,000	1 millionth
10^{-9}	1/1,000,000,000	1 billionth
10^{-12}	1/1,000,000,000,000	1 trillionth
10^{-15}	1/1,000,000,000,000,000	1 quadrillionth

Sizes of and Distance to Objects	Equivalent	Additional Information
Diameter of Electron (classical)	5.6×10^{-13} centimeters	5.6×10^{-13} centimeters; roughly 10^{-12} centimeters
Mass of Electron	9.109×10^{-28} grams	roughly 10^{-27} grams (1 gram = 0.0353 ounce)
Diameter of Proton	10^{-15} meters	10^{-13} centimeters
Mass of Proton	1.67×10^{-24} grams	roughly 10^{-24} grams (about 1,836 times the mass of electron)
Diameter of Neutron	10^{-15} meters	10^{-13} centimeters
Mass of Neutron	1.673×10^{-24} grams	roughly 10^{-24} grams (about 1,838 times the mass of electron)
Diameter of Atomic Nucleus	10^{-14} meters	$\sim10^{-12}$ centimeters (10,000 times smaller than an atom)
Atomic Mass (Atomic Mass Unit)	1.66×10^{-27} kilograms	one atomic mass unit (amu) is equal to 1.66×10^{-24} grams
Diameter of Atom (Electron Cloud)	ranges from 1×10^{-10} to 5×10^{-10} meters	$\sim10^{-10}$ meters; $\sim10^{-8}$ centimeters; $\sim3.94 \times 10^{-9}$ inches (roughly 4 billionth of an inch across or 1/250 millionth of an inch across)
Diameter of (standard) Pencil	6 millimeters (0.236 inches)	roughly 10^{-2} meters
Height (average) of Man and Woman	man: 1.75 meters (5 feet, 8 inches) woman: 1.63 meters (5 feet, 4 inches)	human height roughly 2×10^0 meters; 1/804.66 miles; 10^{-3} miles
Height of Mount Everest	8,850 meters (29,035 feet)	~5.5 miles; roughly 10^4 meters
Radius (mean equatorial) of Earth	6,378.1 kilometers (3,960.8 miles)	$\sim6,400$ kilometers (4,000 miles); roughly 6.4×10^6 meters
Diameter (polar) of Earth	12,713.6 kilometers (7,895.1 miles)	$\sim12,800$ kilometers (8,000 miles); roughly 1.28×10^7 meters (Earth's diameter is twice the Earth's radius)
Circumference (based on mean equatorial radius) of Earth	40,075 kilometers (24,887 miles)	$\sim40,000$ kilometers (25,000 miles) (about 8 times the width of the United States) (Circumference = $2 \times \pi \times$ Earth's radius)
Distance from Earth to Sun	149,600,000 kilometers (92,900,000 miles)	$\sim93,000,000$ miles; ~8.3 light-minutes; roughly 10^{11} meters; roughly 10^8 miles
Distance to Great Nebula in Andromeda Galaxy	2.7×10^{19} kilometers (1.7×10^{19} miles)	~2.9 million light-years; roughly 10^{22} meters; roughly 10^{19} miles

Timeline: Significant Events in the History of Computing

•••

The history of computer sciences has been filled with many creative inventions and intriguing people. Here are some of the milestones and achievements in the field.

c. 300-500 BCE	The counting board, known as the ancient abacus, is used. (Babylonia)
1200 CE	The modern abacus is used. (China)
1500	Leonardo da Vinci drafts a design for a calculator. (Italy)
1614	John Napier suggests the use of logarithms. (Scotland)
1617	John Napier produces calculating rods, called "Napier's Bones." (Scotland)
	Henry Briggs formulates the common logarithm, Base 10. (England)
1620	Edmund Gunter devises the "Line of Numbers," the precursor to slide rule. (England)
1623	Wilhelm Schickard conceives a design of a mechanical calculator. (Germany)
1632	William Oughtred originates the slide rule. (England)
1642	Blaise Pascal makes a mechanical calculator which can add and subtract. (France)
1666	Sir Samuel Morland develops a multiplying calculator. (England)
1673	Gottfried von Leibniz proposes a general purpose calculating machine. (Germany)
1777	Charles Stanhope, 3rd Earl of Stanhope, Lord Mahon, invents a logic machine. (England)
1804	Joseph-Marie Jacquard mechanizes weaving with Jacquard's Loom, featuring punched cards. (France)
1820	Charles Xavier Thomas (Tomas de Colmar) creates a calculating machine, a prototype for the first commercially successful calculator. (France)
1822	Charles Babbage designs the Difference Engine. (England)
1834	Charles Babbage proposes the Analytical Engine. (England)
1838	Samuel Morse formulates the Morse Code. (United States)
1842	L. F. Menabrea publishes a description of Charles Babbage's Analytical Engine. (Published, Italy)
1843	Ada Byron King, Countess of Lovelace, writes a program for Babbage's Analytical Engine. (England)
1854	George Boole envisions the Laws of Thought. (Ireland)

1870	William Stanley Jevons produces a logic machine. (England)
1873	William Thomson, Lord Kelvin, devises the analog tide predictor. (Scotland)
	Christopher Sholes, Carlos Glidden, and Samuel W. Soule invent the Sholes and Glidden Typewriter; produced by E. Remington & Sons. (United States)
1875	Frank Stephen Baldwin constructs a pin wheel calculator. (United States)
1876	Alexander Graham Bell develops the telephone. (United States)
	Bell's rival, Elisha Gray, also produces the telephone. (United States)
1878	Swedish inventor Willgodt T. Odhner makes a pin wheel calculator. (Russia)
1884	Dorr Eugene Felt creates the key-driven calculator, the Comptometer. (United States)
1884	Paul Gotlieb Nipkow produces the Nipkow Disk, a mechanical television device. (Germany)
1886	Herman Hollerith develops his punched card machine, called the Tabulating Machine. (United States)
1892	William Seward Burroughs invents his Adding and Listing (printing) Machine. (United States)
1896	Herman-Hollerith forms the Tabulating Machine Company. (United States)
1901	Guglielmo Marconi develops wireless telegraphy. (Italy)
1904	John Ambrose Fleming constructs the diodevalve (vacuum tube). (England)
	Elmore Ambrose Sperry develops the circular slide rule. (United States)
1906	Lee De Forest invents the triode vacuum tube (audion). (United States)
1908	Elmore Ambrose Sperry produces the gyrocompass. (United States)
1910	Sperry Gyroscope Company is established. (United States)
1912	Frank Baldwin and Jay Monroe found Monroe Calculating Machine Company. (United States)
1914	Leonardo Torres Quevado devises an electromechanical calculator, an electromechanical chess machine (End Move). (Spain)
	Thomas J. Watson Sr. joins the Computing Tabulating Recording Company (CTR) as General Manager. (United States)
1919	W. H. Eccles and F. W. Jordan develop the flip-flop (memory device). (England)
1922	Russian-born Vladimir Kosma Zworykin develops the iconoscope and kinescope (cathode ray tube), both used in electronic television for Westinghouse. (United States)
1924	The Computing Tabulating Recording Company (CTR), formed in 1911 by the merger of Herman Hollerith's Tabulating Machine Company with Computing

	Scale Company and the International Time Recording Company, becomes the IBM (International Business Machines).
1927	The Remington Rand Corporation forms from the merger of Remington Typewriter Company, Rand Kardex Bureau, and others. (United States)
1929	Vladimir Kosma Zworykin develops color television for RCA. (United States)
1931	Vannevar Bush develops the Differential Analyzer (an analog machine). (United States)
1933	Wallace J. Eckert applies punched card machines to astronomical data. (United States)
1937	Alan M. Turing proposes a Theoretical Model of Computation. (England)
	George R. Stibitz crafts the Binary Adder. (United States)
1939	John V. Atanasoff devises the prototype of an electronic digital computer. (United States)
	William R. Hewlett and David Packard establish the Hewlett-Packard Company. (United States)
1940	Claude E. Shannon applies Boolean algebra to switching circuits. (United States)
	George R. Stibitz uses the complex number calculator to perform Remote Job Entry (RJE), Dartmouth to New York. (United States)
1941	Konrad Zuse formulates a general-purpose, program-controlled computer. (Germany)
1942	John V. Atanasoff and Clifford Berry unveil the Atanasoff-Berry Computer (ABC). (United States)
1944	The Colossus, an English calculating machine, is put into use at Bletchley Park. (England)
	Howard Aiken develops, the Automatic Sequence Controlled Calculator (ASCC), the Harvard Mark I, which is the first American program-controlled computer. (United States)
	Grace Hopper allegedly coins the term "computer bug" while working on the Mark I. (United States)
1946	J. Presper Eckert Jr. and John W. Mauchly construct the ENIAC (Electronic Numerical Integrator and Computer), the first American general-purpose electronic computer, at the Moore School, University of Pennsylvania. (United States)
	J. Presper Eckert Jr. and John W. Mauchly form the Electronic Control Company, which later becomes the Eckert-Mauchly Computer Corporation. (United States)
1947	John Bardeen, Walter H. Brattain, and William B. Shockley invent the transistor at Bell Laboratories. (United States)
1948	F. C. Williams, Tom Kilburn, and G. C. (Geoff) Tootill create a small scale, experimental, stored-program computer (nicknamed "Baby") at the University of Manchester; it serves as the prototype of Manchester Mark I. (England)

1949	F. C. Williams, Tom Kilburn, and G. C. (Geoff) Tootill design the Manchester Mark I at the University of Manchester. (England)
	Maurice V. Wilkes develops the ED SAC (Electronic Delay Storage Automatic Calculator) at Cambridge University. (England)
	Jay Wright Forrester invents three-dimensional core memory at the Massachusetts Institute of Technology. (United States)
	Jay Wright Forrester and Robert Everett construct the Whirlwind I, a digital, real-time computer at Massachusetts Institute of Technology. (United States)
1950	J. H. Wilkinson and Edward A. Newman design the Pilot ACE (Automatic Computing Engine) implementing the Turing proposal for a computing machine at the National Physical Laboratory (NPL). (England)
	Remington Rand acquires the Eckert-Mauchly Computer Corporation. (United States)
1951	Engineering Research Associates develops the ERA 1101, an American commercial computer, for the U.S. Navy and National Security Agency (NSA). (United States)
	The UNIVAC I (Universal Automatic Computer), an American commercial computer, is created by Remington Rand for the U.S. Census Bureau. (United States)
	Ferranti Mark I, a British commercial computer, is unveiled. (England)
	Lyons Tea Co. announces Lyons Electronic Office, a British commercial computer. (England)
1952	UNIVAC I predicts election results as Dwight D. Eisenhower sweeps the U.S. presidential race. (United States)
	Remington Rand Model 409, an American commercial computer, is originated by Remington Rand for the Internal Revenue Service. (United States)
	Remington Rand acquires Engineering Research Associates. (United States)
1953	The IBM 701, a scientific computer, is constructed. (United States)
1954	The IBM 650 EDPM, electronic data processing machine, a stored-program computer in a punched-card environment, is produced. (United States)
1955	Sperry Corp. and Remington Rand merge to form the Sperry Rand Corporation. (United States)
1957	Robert N. Noyce, Gordon E. Moore, and others found Fairchild Semiconductor Corporation. (United States)
1957	Seymour Cray, William Norris, and others establish Control Data Corporation. (United States)
	Kenneth Olsen and Harlan Anderson launch Digital Equipment Corporation (DEC). (United States)

1958	Jack Kilby at Texas Instruments invents the integrated circuit. (United States)
1959	Robert N. Noyce at Fairchild Semiconductor invents the integrated circuit. Distinct patents are awarded to both Texas Instruments and Fairchild Semiconductor, as both efforts are recognized. (United States)
1960	The first PDP-1 is sold by Digital Equipment Corporation, which uses some technology from the Whirlwind Project. (United States)
	The UNIVAC 1100 series of computers is announced by Sperry Rand Corporation. (United States)
1961	The Burroughs B5000 series dual-processor, with virtual memory, is unveiled. (United States)
1964	The IBM/360 family of computers begins production. (United States)
	The CDC 6600 is created by Control Data Corporation. (United States)
1965	The UNIVAC 1108 from Sperry Rand Corporation is constructed. (United States)
1965	The PDP-8, the first minicomputer, is released by Digital Equipment Corporation. (United States)
	Robert N. Noyce and Gordon E. Moore found Intel Corporation. (United States)
1969	The U.S. Department of Defense (DoD) launches ARP ANET, the beginning of the Internet. (United States)
1970	The PDP–11 series of computers from Digital Equipment Corporation is put into use. (United States)
	The Xerox Corporation's Palo Alto Research Center (PARC) begins to study the architecture of information. (United States)
1971	Ken Thompson devises the UNIX Operating System at Bell Laboratories. (United States)
	Marcian E. (Ted) Hoff, Federico Faggin, and Stanley Mazor at Intel create the first microprocessor, a 4-bit processor, 4004. (United States)
1972	Seymour Cray founds Cray Research Inc. (United States)
	Intel releases the 8008 microprocessor, an 8-bit processor. (United States)
1974	Intel announces the 8080 microprocessor, an 8-bit processor. (United States)
	Motorola Inc. unveils the Motorola 6800, its 8-bit microprocessor. (United States)
	Federico Faggin and Ralph Ungerman co-found Zilog, Inc., a manufacturer of microprocessors. (United States)
1975	Bill Gates and Paul Allen establish the Microsoft Corporation. (United States)

The kit-based Altair 8800 computer, using an 8080 microprocessor, is released by Ed Roberts with MITS (Model Instrumentation Telemetry Systems) in Albuquerque, New Mexico. (United States)

MITS purchases a version of the BASIC computer language from Microsoft. (United States)

The MOS 6502 microprocessor, an 8-bit microprocessor, is developed by MOS Technologies, Chuck Peddle, and others, who had left Motorola, (United States)

1976   Gary Kildall creates the CP/M (Control Program/Monitor or Control Program for Microprocessors) Operating System of Digital Research; this operating system for 8-bit micro-computers is the forerunner of DOS 1.0. (United States)

Steven Jobs and Stephen Wozniak found Apple Computer, Inc. and create the Apple I. (United States)

Seymour Cray devises the Cray-1 supercomputer. (United States)

Commodore Business Machines acquires MOS Technologies. (Canada)

1977   The Commodore PET (Personal Electronic Transactor) personal computer, developed by Jack Tramiel and Chuck Peddle for Commodore Business Machines, features the 6502 8-bit Microprocessor. (Canada)

The Apple II personal computer from Apple Computer, Inc., is released featuring a 6502 microprocessor. (United States)

The TRS-80 personal computer from Tandy Radio Shack, equipped with the Zilog Z80 8-bit microprocessor from Zilog, is unveiled. (United States)

Intel announces the 8086 16-bit microprocessor. (United States)

1978   Digital Equipment Corporation launches the VAX 11/780, a 4.3 billion byte computer with virtual memory. (United States)

1979   Intel presents the 8088 16-bit microprocessor. (United States)

Motorola Inc. crafts the MC 68000, Motorola 16-bit processor. (United States)

1980   Tim Patterson sells the rights to QDOS, an upgrade operating system of CP/M for 8088 and 8086 Intel microprocessors, 16-bit microprocessor, to Microsoft. (United States)

1981   The IBM Corporation announces the IBM Personal Computer featuring an 8088 microprocessor. (United States)

The Microsoft Operating System (MS-DOS) is put into use. (United States)

The Osborne I, developed by Adam Osborne and Lee Felsenstein with Osborne Computer Corporation, invent the first portable computer. (United States)

1982   Scott McNealy, Bill Joy, Andy Bechtolsheim, and Vinod Khosla found Sun Microsystems, Inc. (United States)

1984	The Macintosh PC from Apple Computer Inc., running with a Motorola 68000 microprocessor, revolutionizes the personal computer industry. (United States)
	Richard Stallman begins the GNU Project, advocating the free use and distribution of software. (United States)
1985	The Free Software Foundation is formed to seek freedom of use and distribution of software. (United States)
	Microsoft releases Windows 1.01. (United States)
1986	Sperry Rand and the Burroughs Corporation merge to form Unisys Corporation. (United States)
1989	SPARCstation I from Sun Microsystems is produced. (United States)
1991	Tim Berners-Lee begins the World Wide Web at CERN. (Switzerland)
	Linus Torvalds builds the Linux Operating System. (Finland)
	Paul Kunz develops the first Web server outside of Europe, at the Stanford Linear Accelerator Center (SLAG). (United States)
1993	Marc Andreesen and Eric Bina create Mosaic, a Web browser, at the National Center for Supercomputing Applications (NCSA), University of Illinois-Urbana Champaign. (United States)
1994	Marc Andreesen and James H. Clark form Mosaic Communications Corporation, later Netscape Communications Corporation. (United States)
	Netscape Navigator is launched by Netscape Communications Corporation. (United States)
1995	Java technology is announced by Sun Microsystems. (United States)
1996	World chess champion Garry Kasparov of Russia defeats Deep Blue, an IBM computer, in a man vs. computer chess matchup, four to two. (United States)
1997	IBM's Deep Blue defeats world chess champion Garry Kasparov in a rematch, 3.5 to 2.5. (United States)
	An injunction is filed against Microsoft to prohibit the company from requiring customers to accept Internet Explorer as their browser as a condition of using the Microsoft operating system Windows 95. (United States)
1998	America OnLine (AOL) acquires Netscape. (United States)
	Compaq Computer Corporation, a major producer of IBM compatible personal computers, buys Digital Equipment Corporation. (United States)
	America OnLine (AOL) and Sun form an alliance to produce Internet technology. (United States)

1999	Shawn Fanning writes code for Napster, a music file-sharing program. (United States)
1998	The Recording Industry Association of America (RIAA) files a lawsuit against Napster for facilitating copyright infringement. (United States)
2000	Zhores I. Alferov, Herbert Kroemer, and Jack Kilby share the Nobel Prize in Physics for contributions to information technology. Alferov, a Russian, and Kroemer, a German-born American, share half the prize for their contributions to semiconductor-based technology used in high speed circuits. Kilby is awarded the other half of the prize for invention of the integrated circuit.
	Google becomes the first search engine to index one billion pages. (United States)
2001	Wikipedia, a free online user originated encyclopedia, comes online. (United States)
	Windows XP is introduced. (United States)
	Dell becomes the world's top computer systems provider. (United States)
2002	Hewlett Packard purchases Compaq. (United States)
2003	Apple creates and opens iTunes, an online music-buying application. (United States)
2004	Mark Zuckerberg creates and launches the online social network, Facebook. (United States)
	Google introduces Gmail, an Internet service. (United States)
2005	Video-sharing Web site, YouTube, comes online. (United States)
	Chinese company, Lenovo, acquires IBM's Personal Computing Division, making it the world's third-largest PC purveyor. (China)
2006	Apple switches all computers to Intel core processors. (United States)
	The first Twitter post is posted by co-founder Jack Dorsey at Twitter.com. (United States)
2007	Steve Jobs and Apple release the iPhone.
	Microsoft releases Windows Vista to the public. (United States)
	Apple announces that it will discontinue the use of the word "computer" in its title as it was working with products other than computers. It is now known as Apple, Inc. (United States)
2008	Bill Gates steps down as chairman of Microsoft to focus on philanthropic work. (United States)
2009	Intel unveils the "iA32 processor single-chip cloud computer," a CPU with 48 processing cores on a single chip. (United States)
2010	2010 Cyber-warfare and cyber-counterterrorism goes public: Stuxnet worm disrupts Iran's centrifuges dedicated to uranium enrichment.

2011   Social media, especially Facebook and Twitter, are credited with helping organizers form Arab Spring protests across Middle East. Revolution in Egypt results in resignation of President Hosni Mubarak and first free elections in Egypt's history.

IBM's Watson supercomputer defeats human champions on the game show "Jeopardy."

2012   Facebook begins trading on NASDAQ as a private company (IPO).

Facebook Facebook announces 'Graph Search' tool.

Timeline: The History of Programming, Markup, and Scripting Languages

· ·

The history of computer sciences has been filed with many creative inventions and innovations. Here are some of the milestones and achievements in the field of computer programming and languages.

c. 800   al-Khowarizmi, Mohammed ibn-Musa develops a treatise on algebra, his name allegedly giving rise to the term, algorithm.

1843   Ada Byron King, Countess of Lovelace, programs Charles Babbage's design of the Analytical Engine.

1945   Plankalkul is developed by Konrad Zuse.

1953   Sort-Merge Generator is created by Betty Holberton.

1957   FORTRAN is devised for IBM by John Backus and team of programmers.

   FLOW-MATIC is crafted for Remington-Rand's UNIVAC by Grace Hopper.

1958   LISP is produced by John McCarthy at Massachusetts Institute of Technology.

1959   COBOL is formulated by the CODASYL Committee, initiated by the U.S. Department of Defense (DoD)

1960   ALGOL is the result of work done by the ALGOL Committee in the ALGOL 60 Report.

1961   JOSS is originated by the RAND Corporation.

   GPSS (General Purpose Simulation System) is invented by Geoffrey Gordon with IBM.

   RPG (Report Program Generator) is unveiled by IBM.

   APL (A Programming Language) is designed by Kenneth Iverson with IBM.

1963   SNOBOL is developed by David Farber, Ralph Griswold, and Ivan Polonsky at Bell Laboratories.

1964   BASIC is originated by John G. Kemeny and Thomas E. Kurtz at Dartmouth.

   PL/I is announced by IBM.

   Simula I is produced by Kristen Nygaard and Ole-Johan Dahl at the Norwegian Computing Center.

1967   Simula 67 is created by Kristen Nygaard and Ole-Johan Dahl at the Norwegian Computing Center.

   LOGO is devised by Seymour Papert at the MIT Artificial Intelligence Laboratory.

1971   Pascal is constructed by Niklaus Wirth at the Swiss Federal Institute of Technology (ETH) in Zurich.

1973	C developed by Dennis Ritchie at Bell Laboratories.
	Smalltalk is invented by Alan Kay at Xerox's PARC (Palo Alto Research Center).
1980	Ada is developed for the U.S. Department of Defense (DoD).
1985	C++ is created by Bjarne Stroustrup at Bell Laboratories.
1986	SGML (Standard Generalized Markup Language) is developed by the International Organization for Standardization (ISO).
1987	Perl is constructed by Larry Wall.
1989	HTML (HyperText Markup Language) is proposed by Tim Berners-Lee at CERN (Organization européenne pour la recherche nucléaire).
1991	Visual Basic is launched by the Microsoft Corporation.
1993	Mosaic is created by Marc Andreesen and Eric Bina for the National Center for Computing Applications (TSTCCA) at the University of Illinois-Urbana Champaign.
1994	A written specification of VRML (Virtual Reality Markup Language) is drafted by Mark Pesce, Tony Parisi, and Gavin Bell.
1995	Java is crafted by James Gosling of Sun Microsystems
1996	Javascript is developed by Brendan Eich at Netscape Communications co-announced by Netscape and Sun Microsystems.
1997	VRML (Virtual Reality Modeling Language), developed by the Web3D Consortium, becomes an international standard.
1998	XML (Extensible Markup Language) is originated by a working group of the World Wide Web Consortium (W3C).
2000	Microsoft publicly introduces the programming language C#.
2002	Perl 5.8 is released to the public.
2008	HTML5 is first introduced to the public as a working draft.

A

Algol-60 Report

An important milestone in the history of computer programming was the Algol-60 report. Because of Algol-60, computer scientists and programmers were able to develop many more programming languages, grammars, and theories.

A team of programming language experts consisting of computer scientist Peter Naur (1928–) and several educators and practitioners from Europe and the United States wrote Algol-60 in 1959 and 1960. The purpose of the report was to develop a complete description of an international algorithm*ic language for expressing numerical processes in a form suitable for translation into computer programming languages. It was not intended to be a programming language, although it was subsequently implemented as a language and became popular in Europe.

Many versions of the Algol programming language were implemented in the 1960s and early 1970s. It also led to the development of several other programming languages, such as Pascal, implemented by Niklaus Wirth in the early 1970s, and C.

The report introduced the notions of a reference language, a publication language, and a hardware representation. The reference language was the standard for the report, compiler writers, and hardware implementation. It dictated the form of the language and its syntax*. The publication language used the reference language with minor adjustments for publication variations across countries and printing and writing variations such as the handling of subscripts, superscripts, and other notation. The hardware representation took into consideration the characteristics of the machine. The reference language was the defining language, and the publication language and hardware representation had to be translatable into it.

The purpose of the report and the language was to give an unambiguous representation to various computer concepts—in particular, algorithm design, or ALGOrithmic Language 1960. A subsequent version, Algol68, was not as popular or widely implemented as Algol-60, although it was more powerful.

Algol is a structured language, incorporating while statements, if-then-else-statements, and other constructs that implement selection, iteration, basic statements, block structure, and recursion. Although it was developed only a few years after FORTRAN (FORmula TRANslator), released in 1957 by IBM, it incorporated features missing from FORTRAN—namely the recursion and the structured language—and was a major advance in the programming arena.

* **algorithm** a rule or procedure used to solve a mathematical problem—most often described as a sequence of steps

* **syntax** a set of rules that a computing language incorporates regarding structure, punctuation, and formatting

* **compilers** programs that translate human-readable high-level computer languages to machine-readable code

One of the descendants of Algol and FORTRAN was BASIC (Beginner's All-purpose Symbolic Instruction Code) language, developed by John Kemeny (1926–1992) and Thomas Kurtz (1928–) of Dartmouth University. BASIC was a sort of format-statement-free version of FORTRAN for interactive and beginning computing. BASIC enjoyed a long reign from the 1970s to the 1980s and has recently been implemented in a quite different form, Visual Basic.

Another descendent of Algol was Pascal, which also enjoyed a long reign as a popular language for implementing data structures and studying compilers*. It was not a production language, but a teaching tool. C was a system's language and led to the development of C++, an object-oriented language that is still popular.

The Algol language was described in a notation called Backus normal or Backus-Naur form (BNF). The notation was suggested by John Backus (1924–2007), who based it on a notation by E. L. Post (1897–1954), a famous logician in the 1930s. It was similar to the notation developed by Noam Chomsky (1928–) in 1957 for linguistics, which was used to implement grammars. A grammar is a succinct, unambiguous way of describing languages. The use of a formal notation in language theory was a major advance.

The evolution of programming languages was striking, but not as stunning as the evolution of compiler theory. Shortly after the Algol-60 report, several compiler theorists used the grammar notation to implement compilers in an "automatic" fashion. These compilers were known as compiler-compilers. Similar efforts were the development of Lex, a lexical analyzer, and Yacc ("Yet another compiler-compiler") at Bell Laboratories in the mid-1970s.

Understanding Programming Language

English grammar has certain constructs, such as a noun phrase, which is composed of other constructs, such as a noun and a modifier. Programming languages have constructs such as while-statements, and arithmetic expressions. These constructs are indicated by special symbols called the nonterminal or meta symbols of the language.

The symbols that actually appear in the language are called terminal symbols. The terminology comes from the data structures, or parse trees, used to implement the language.

The basic operational units of the language, known as statements are: assignment statements (formula evaluation), go to statements, dummy statements, and procedure statements (call for execution). More complex structures include conditional statements, compound statements, and blocks.

An example is:

E—>E+T

T

T—>T*F

F

F—>(E)

id

num

This grammar indicates that an arithmetic expression, E, consists of other arithmetic expressions and terms, T, added together (E—>E+T). A term, T, is composed of a term times a factor, F, so that T—>T*F. Finally, a factor, F, is the most basic expression, consisting of parenthesized expressions (the parenthesized E), identifiers (user-defined identifier or variables), id, and numeric constants (num). The grammar gives the form of the arithmetic expressions.

The example gives a flavor of the notation. The items on the left of the arrow are composed of the items on the right. In this case, the E, T, and F are the meta-symbols. The other symbols, +, *, (,), and, in this case, id and num, appear in the language. They are the words of the language. In this case, E is the start symbol or first non-terminal symbol. It is the most general expression being defined. Although the notation may seem awkward at first, it is useful in language design, compiler theory, and implementation.

The development of grammars in computer science gave a great impetus to programming language design and implementation.

 See also **Algorithms • Procedural Languages • Programming**

Resources

Books

Burkowski, Forbes J. *Structural Bioinformatics: An Algorithmic Approach.* Boca Raton, FL: Chapman & Hall/CRC, 2009.

Fleishcer, Rudolf, and Jinhui Xu. *Algorithmic Aspects in Information and Management: 4th International Conference, AAIM 2008, Shanghai, China, June 23–25, 2008: Proceedings.* Berlin: Springer, 2008.

Joux, Antoine. *Algorithmic Cryptanalysis.* Boca Raton, FL: CRC Press, 2009.

Kröning, Daniel, and Ofer Strichman. *Decision Procedures: An Algorithmic Point of View.* Texts in theoretical computer science. Berlin: Springer, 2008.

Wexelblat, Richard L., ed. *History of Programming Languages.* New York: Academic Press, 1981.

Periodicals

Naur, Peter. "Revised Report on the Algorithmic Language Algol-60." *Communications ACM* 6, no. 1 (1963): 1–17.

Algorithms

The word "algorithm" comes from the name of the ninth-century Persian mathematician Mohammed al-Khowarizmi. He wrote a widely read book entitled *Kitab al jabr w'al-muqabala* (*Rules of Restoration and Reduction*). This book describes many procedures for the manipulation of decimal numbers.

Today, the term algorithm* is used to describe a wide variety of procedures, from the sequence of steps executed for the manipulation of integers, to the series of actions involved in searching databases and the Internet.

An algorithm can be described informally or with mathematical rigor. Informally, it might be described as a basic set of steps that must be performed to reach a predetermined result. For example, in grade school, students learn to multiply two integers by carrying out a repetitive sequence of activities. If they proceed carefully according to the directions, they will eventually compute the product.

According to the more rigorous definition of an algorithm, the sequence of steps that are carried out must have five important features: input, output, finiteness, definiteness, and effectiveness.

The New York Stock Exchange uses algorithms to monitor stocks.
© *AP Images/Henny Ray Abrams.*

Input means that zero or more values are available to the algorithm before it begins execution. For example, multiplication of two integers begins with the two integers. Long division begins with the divisor and the dividend. Searching the Internet begins with a collection of web pages and addresses.

Output means that one or more quantities are the result of the algorithm's execution of the inputs. In the case of long division, the results are the quotient and remainder. In the case of an Internet search, the result might be a collection of web pages or addresses.

Finiteness means that an algorithm is guaranteed to terminate after a finite number of steps as long as the algorithm's preconditions (a set of rules for the input) are met. When multiplying two integers, for example, the rules of the procedure will cause one to reach a point where no other steps are possible. For large integers, this might take a long time.

Definiteness means that each step in the sequence is clear and unambiguous. A cake-baking algorithm, for example, usually fails in this regard. Different cooks may define a dash of salt in slightly different ways.

Effectiveness means that each of the steps of the algorithm must be completed in some finite length of time. If effectiveness is combined with finiteness, this guarantees that the algorithm will terminate in a finite amount of time.

All general-purpose digital computers, both past and present, execute algorithms. The algorithm is as central to computer technology as recipes are to the functioning of a gourmet restaurant. Without recipes, whether written on paper or stored in the mind of the chef, nothing gets cooked. Without algorithms, the whole notion of general-purpose digital computers makes little sense and nothing gets computed.

It is difficult to imagine doing multiplication or other tasks without algorithms. For example, try multiplying 3 by 5. Now, without using a calculator, multiply 3,456 by 2,139 without executing a repetitive sequence of steps.

The person or machine executing an algorithm need not be aware of the explanation or mathematical proof of why the algorithm works. Useful computations can be performed mechanically without any understanding of why the sequence of steps is guaranteed to produce the correct result.

History of Algorithms

Algorithms are not new. One of the oldest algorithms known is that of Greek mathematician Euclid (fl. 300 BCE). Euclid's algorithm was designed to compute the greatest common divisor of two positive integers. For example, the greatest common divisor of 40 and 24 is 8 because 8 is the largest integer that divides 40 and 24 evenly. The greatest common divisor of 34,512 and 2,341,200 can also be found by using the repetitive procedure that Euclid's algorithm provides.

In 1937, the British mathematician Alan Turing (1912–1954) wrote a very important paper that introduced a simple mathematical device,

Euclid (fl. 300 BCE)

Euclid, known as a founder of geometry, established a school of mathematics at the great center of education in Alexandria, Egypt, in c.300 BCE. During his lifetime, Euclid proposed, collected, and recorded numerous mathematical postulates and theorems. The most famous of his writings is known as *Elements*, a thirteen-book series that is still the standard text for mathematical principles used in high school education today.

now known as a Turing machine. His intention, in part, was to provide a formal and rigorous definition of algorithm. This mathematical formalization allowed Turing to prove statements about the capabilities and limitations of algorithms. It turns out, for example, that there are well-defined problems that have no algorithmic solution. The theory of algorithms is still an active area of research.

Algorithm discovery, enhancement, and implementation play increasingly important roles in modern life. New algorithms (sometimes called search engines) are being developed to search the Internet in ways that will allow people to gain useful information from a large and broad collection of data. Hardware algorithms are being improved to speed up the rate of instruction execution in modern machines. Software engineers implement algorithms as computer programs, which are used in an ever-widening variety of devices, including smartphones, cars, radios, and desktop computers.

 See also **Boolean Algebra** • **Design Tools** • **Procedural Languages** • **Programming**

Resources

Books

Cormen, Thomas H., Thomas E. Leiserson, Ronald R. Rivest, and Clifford Stein. *Introduction to Algorithms.* 3rd ed. Cambridge, MA: MIT Press, 2009.

Web Sites

Turing, Alan M. "On Computable Numbers, with an Application to the Entscheidungsproblem" http://www.cs.virginia.edu/~robins/Turing_Paper_1936.pdf (accessed October 9, 2012).

Assembly Language and Architecture

When most people hear the term architecture, they automatically visualize a building. However, architecture also refers to a computer system. Architecture can also be defined as an interconnected arrangement of readily available components. A computer systems architect takes a collection of parts and organizes them so that they all work together in an optimal way. More than one way exists to put a computer system together from constituent parts, and some configurations will yield a computer system that is better at a particular task than other configurations, which might be better at something else. For example, consider a computer system for use by human users to support activities in managing their work

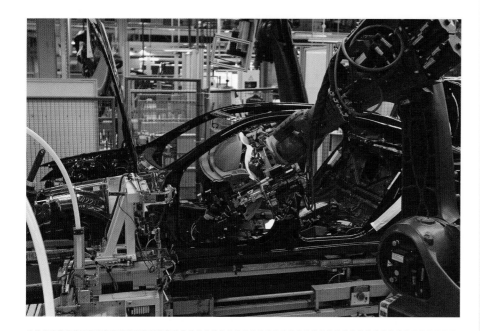

A robot arm installs a dashboard on a vehicle production line. © *Thomas Niedermueller/Getty Images.*

◀

in an office environment—composing documents, storing them, and printing them out. This computer system architecture would be completely different from that of a computer system designed to deal with a task like guiding a rocket in flight.

Even though there are many different ways of structuring computer systems so that they can be matched to the jobs for which they are responsible, there is surprisingly little variation in the nature of the fundamental building blocks themselves. Most conventional computer systems are comprised of a central processing unit (CPU)*, the part of a computer that performs computations and controls and coordinates other parts of the computer; some memory—both random access memory (RAM)* and read only memory (ROM)*; secondary storage to hold other programs and data; and lastly, interconnecting pathways called bus*es. The part that makes a computer different from many other machines is the CPU. Memory devices, storage units, and buses are designed to act in a supporting role, while the principal player is the CPU.

Often people studying the essential nature of a CPU for the first time struggle with some of the concepts because it is not like any other machine they know. A car engine or sewing machine has large moving parts that are easier to analyze and understand, while a CPU does not have moving parts to observe. However, by imagining moving mechanisms, one can gain a better understanding of what happens down inside those black ceramic packages.

The fundamental component of a CPU is an element called a register. A register is an array of flip-flop devices that are all connected and operate in unison. Each flip-flop can store one binary* bit (a 0 or 1) that the CPU

* **central processing unit (CPU)** the part of a computer that performs computations and controls and coordinates other parts of the computer

* **random access memory (RAM)** a type of memory device that supports the nonpermanent storage of programs and data; so called because various locations can be accessed in any order (as if at random), rather than in a sequence (like a tape memory device)

* **read only memory (ROM)** a type of memory device that supports permanent storage of programs

* **bus** a group of related signals that form an interconnecting pathway between two or more electronic devices

* **binary** existing in only two states, such as "on" or "off," "true" or "false," or "one" or "zero"

will use. Registers can be loaded up with bits in a parallel operation and they can then shift the bits left or right if needed. Two registers can be used to hold collections of bits that might be added together, for example. In this case, corresponding bits in each register would be added together with any carried bits being managed in the expected way—just as would be done by a person manually, using pencil and paper.

Registers tend to vary in size from one processor to another, but are usually eight, sixteen, thirty-two, or sixty-four bits in width. This means that each is comprised of that particular number of flip-flop devices. Some registers are set aside to hold specific types of information, like memory addresses or instructions. These are known as special purpose registers. In addition, there are general purpose registers that hold data that are to be used in the execution of a program.

CPUs contain another set of elements that are very similar to registers, called buffers. Buffers, like registers, are constructed from groups of flip-flops, but unlike registers, the information contained within them does not change. Buffers are simply temporary holding points for information while it is being transferred from one place to another in the CPU, whereas registers actually hold information as it is being used to perform an operation.

The part of the CPU that actually carries out the mathematical operations is called the arithmetic and logic unit (ALU). It is more complex than the registers and handles operations like addition, subtraction, and multiplication, as well as operations that implement logic operations, such as logical "or" and "and" operations.

The most complex part of the CPU and the one that requires the most effort in design is the control unit. Registers, buffers, and arithmetic and logic units are all well-documented building blocks, but the control unit is more mysterious. Most manufacturers keep the design of their control units a closely guarded secret, since the control unit manages how the parts of the CPU all work together. This part of the CPU influences the architecture. The control unit is constructed to recognize all of the programming instructions that the CPU is capable of carrying out. When all these instructions are written down in a document that the manufacturer provides, it is known as the instruction set of that particular CPU. All instructions that the processor understands are to be represented as a sequence of bits that will fit into the registers. The control unit responds to the instructions by decoding them, which means that it breaks them down into sub-operations, before getting the ALU and registers to carry them out. Even a relatively simple instruction like subtracting a number in one register from some number in another register, requires the control unit to decode and manage all the steps involved. This would include loading the two registers with the numbers, triggering the ALU to do the subtraction, and finding somewhere to store the difference.

Although it is possible for human users to construct programs as correct sequences of binary bits for the processor to execute, this is very intensive and error-prone. Actually creating a program in this way is known as writing a program in machine code because these sequences of bits are the codes that the CPU machine knows and understands. When programmable computers were first being developed in the mid-twentieth century, this was the only means of programming them. Human programmers were soon looking for a less laborious way of getting the machine code to the CPU. The answer was to represent each of the machine code instructions by shortened words, rather than the sequence of bits. For example, a command to the CPU to add two numbers together would be represented as a short human-readable instruction like "ADD A, B" where A and B are the names of two registers. This can be used instead of a confusing list of binary bits and tends to make programming much easier to comprehend and execute. The short words used to represent the instructions are called mnemonic*s. The programmer can write the program in a computer language known as an assembly language using mnemonics. Another program called an assembler* translates the assembly language mnemonics into the machine code, which is what the CPU can understand.

Other computing languages can be developed that are even more amenable to human use. These languages can be translated to assembly language and then to machine code. That way, human programmers can concentrate more on making sure that their programs are correct and leave all of the drudgery of translation to other programs.

No two assembly languages are exactly alike and most differ markedly from one another in their syntax*. Because assembly languages are quite close to the particular instructions that each particular CPU understands, the programmer, directly using an assembly language must know a great deal about the particular architecture of the processor under study. However, little of this knowledge is transferable directly to processors developed by other manufacturers. The ways in which two different CPUs work might be quite similar, but there will always be some differences in the details that prevent assembly language programs from being transportable to other computers. The advantage of using assembly languages is that the programs constructed in assembly language are usually much smaller than programs constructed in high-level languages, require less memory for storage, and tend to run very fast. Many computer programs that are developed for small-scale but high-market-volume embedded systems environments (like domestic appliances and office equipment) are written in assembly language for these reasons.

Personal computers have their own type of architectures and can be programmed in an assembly language. However, the assembly language on each computer usually is used only in certain parts of the operating system that need to manage the hardware devices directly.

▶ See also **Binary Number System • Central Processing Unit • Object-Oriented Languages • Procedural Languages • Programming**

Assembly Language Lives

Whereas almost no commercial software developer would consider writing programs in assembly language because of the extraordinarily intensive labor it requires, assembly language is not dead. There are groups of dedicated programmers collaborating on projects involving assembly language so as to attain the maximum possible run-time performance from the hardware. For example, the "V2 Operating System" is completely implemented in assembly language.

* **mnemonic** a device or process that aids one's memory

* **assembler** a program that translates human-readable assembly language programs to machine-readable instructions

* **syntax** a set of rules that a computing language incorporates regarding structure, punctuation, and formatting

*address bus a collection of
electrical signals used to transmit
the address of a memory
location or input/output port in
a computer

Resources

Books

Klingman, Edwin E. *Microprocessor Systems Design*, 2 vols. Upper Saddle River, NJ: Prentice Hall, 1977–1982.

Mano, M. Morris, and Charles R. Kime. *Logic and Computer Design Fundamentals.* 4th ed. Upper Saddle River, NJ: Prentice Hall, 2000.

Milutinovic, Veljko M., ed. *High Level Language Computer Architecture.* Rockville, MD: Computer Science Press, 1989.

Stallings, William. *Computer Organization and Architecture: Designing for Performance*, 8th ed. Upper Saddle River, NJ: Prentice Hall, 2000.

Tanenbaum, Andrew S., and Albert S. Woodhull. *Operating Systems Design and Implementation.* 3rd ed. Upper Saddle River, NJ: Prentice Hall, 2006.

Triebel, Walter A., and Avtar Singh. *The 8088 and 8086 Microprocessors.* 4th ed. Upper Saddle River, NJ: Prentice Hall, 1991.

Uffenbeck, John. *The 8086/8088 Family: Design, Programming and Interfacing.* Englewood Cliffs, NJ: Prentice Hall, 1987.

Wakerly, John F. *Digital Design Principles and Practices.* 4th ed. Englewood Cliffs, NJ: Prentice Hall, 2006.

Asynchronous and Synchronous Transmission

Asynchronous and synchronous communication refers to methods by which signals are transferred in computing technology. These signals allow computers to transfer data between components within the computer or between the computer and an external network. Most actions and operations that take place in computers are carefully controlled and occur at specific times and intervals. Actions that are measured against a time reference, or a clock signal, are referred to as synchronous actions. Actions that are prompted as a response to another signal, typically not governed by a clock signal, are referred to as asynchronous signals.

Typical examples of synchronous signals include the transfer and retrieval of address information within a computer via the use of an address bus*. For example, when a processor places an address on the, it will hold it there for a specific period of time. Within this interval, a particular device inside the computer will identify itself as the one being addressed and acknowledge the commencement of an operation related to that address.

In such an instance, all devices involved in ensuing bus cycles must obey the time constraints applied to their actions—this is known as a synchronous operation. In contrast, asynchronous signals refer to operations that are prompted by an exchange of signals with one another, and are not measured against a reference time base. Devices that cooperate asynchronously usually include modems and many network technologies, both of which use a collection of control signals to notify intent in an information exchange. Asynchronous signals, or extra control signals, are sometimes referred to as handshaking signals because of the way they mimic two people approaching one another and shaking hands before conversing or negotiating.

Within a computer, both asynchronous and synchronous protocol*s are used. Synchronous protocols usually offer the ability to transfer information faster per unit time than asynchronous protocols. This happens because synchronous signals do not require any extra negotiation as a prerequisite to data exchange. Instead, data or information is moved from one place to another at instants in time that are measured against the clock signal being used. This signal is usually comprised of one or more high frequency rectangular shaped waveforms, generated by special purpose clock circuitry. These pulsed waveforms are connected to all the devices that operate synchronously, allowing them to start and stop operations with respect to the clock waveform.

In contrast, asynchronous protocols are generally more flexible, since all the devices that need to exchange information can do so at their own natural rate—be they fast or slow. A clock signal is no longer necessary; instead the devices that behave asynchronously wait for the handshaking signals to change state, indicating that some transaction is about to commence. The handshaking signals are generated by the devices themselves and can occur as needed, and do not require an outside supervisory controller such as a clock circuit that dictates the occurrence of data transfer.

Asynchronous and synchronous transmission of information occurs both externally and internally in computers. From its inception in the 1960s, and on through the 1990s, one of the most popular protocols for communication between computers and peripheral devices, such as modems and printers, was the asynchronous Recommended Standard 232 (RS-232) protocol. Designated as the RS-232C by the Electronic Industries Association (EIA), this protocol became so successful at adapting to the needs of managing communication between computers and supporting devices, that it was pushed into service in ways that were not intended as part of its original design. The RS-232C protocol uses an asynchronous scheme that permits flexible communication between computers and devices using byte-sized data blocks each framed with start, stop, and optional parity bit*s on the data line. Other conductors carry the handshaking signals and possess names that indicate their purpose— these include data terminal ready, request to send, clear to send, data set ready, etc.

* **protocol** an agreed understanding for the sub-operations that make up a transaction, usually found in the specification of inter-computer communications

* **bit** a single binary digit, 1 or 0—a contraction of Binary digIT; the smallest unit for storing data in a computer

* **byte** a group of eight binary digits; represents a single character of text

* **bandwidth** a measure of the frequency component of a signal or the capacity of a communication channel to carry signals

The RS-232 protocol is now largely outmoded, but is still used in industrial equipment, specialty equipment (for instance, cash registers), and in older peripheral computer equipment. However, it has largely been replaced in newer computers and peripheral devices by interface standards such as Universal Serial Bus (USB). The first USB protocol version, USB 1.0, was released in the mid–1990s. USB 2.0, which supports higher data rates and other enhanced features, became available at the beginning of the 2000s. USB 3.0 is the latest version; the first commercial products featuring its greatly-enhanced data rates, and other advanced characteristics, appeared in early 2010.

An advantage of asynchronous schemes is that they do not demand complexity in the receiver hardware. As each byte* of data has its own start and stop bits, a small amount of drift or imprecision at the receiving end does not necessarily spell disaster since the device only has to keep pace with the data stream for a modest number of bits. So, if an interruption occurs, the receiving device can re-establish its operation with the beginning of the arrival of the next. This ability allows for the use of inexpensive hardware devices.

Although asynchronous data transfer schemes such as the older RS-232 work well when relatively small amounts of data need to be transferred on an intermittent basis, they tend to be sub-optimal during large information transfers. This is so because the extra bits that frame incoming data tend to account for a significant part of the overall inter-machine traffic, hence consuming a portion of the communication bandwidth*.

An alternative is to dispense with the extra handshaking signals and overhead, instead synchronizing the transmitter and receiver with a clock signal or synchronization information contained within the transmitted code before transmitting large amounts of information. This arrangement allows for collection and dispatch of large batches of bytes of data, with a few bytes at the front-end that can be used for the synchronization and control. These leading bytes are variously called synchronization bytes, flags, and preambles. If the actual communication channel is not a great distance, the clocking signal can also be sent as a separate stream of pulses. This ensures that the transmitter and receiver are both operating on the same time base, and the receiver can be prepared for data collection prior to the arrival of the data.

An example of a synchronous transmission scheme is known as the High-level Data Link Control, or HDLC. This protocol arose from an initial design proposed by the IBM Corporation. HDLC has been used at the data link level in public networks and has been adapted and modified in several different ways since.

A more advanced communication protocol is the Asynchronous Transfer Mode (ATM), which is an open, international standard for the transmission of voice, video, and data signals. Some advantages of ATM include a format that consists of short, fixed cells (53 bytes) which reduce overhead in maintenance of variable-sized data traffic. The versatility of this mode also allows it to simulate and integrate well with legacy technologies, as well as offering the ability to guarantee certain service levels, generally referred to as quality of service (QoS) parameters.

▶ *See also* **ATM Transmission • Networks • Telecommunications**

Resources

Books

Forouzan, Behrouz A. *Data Communications and Networking.* New York: McGraw-Hill, 2006.

ATM Transmission

Asynchronous Transfer Mode (ATM) networking is an outgrowth of efforts during the 1970s and 1980s to develop a broadband Integrated Service Digital Network (ISDN) capability. ATM provides a transport mechanism that allows digital data to be transmitted efficiently over high-speed links. Currently, most of the high-speed backbone networks throughout the world use ATM technology. It is also used to some extent as a local area networks (LANs)* local area networking technology, although the availability of low-cost 100 megabyte and gigabyte Ethernet equipment reduces its appeal for this application.

ATM technology was developed to support a blending of circuit-switching and packet-switching technologies. It is intended to support traffic that requires a fairly constant rate of data delivery, such as voice and video, as well as variable data rate traffic, such as most computer data. ATM is a connection-oriented technology. This means that a fixed path through the network must be established before data can be transmitted. In this respect, ATM is similar to earlier telephone technologies in which physical wires between switching centers were allocated for the duration of each telephone call. Establishing an ATM connection causes a virtual channel connection* (VCC) or virtual circuit* (VC) to be created through the ATM network between the end users of the connection.

Virtual channels can be bundled into virtual paths in much the same way that physical wires were bundled into trunk lines. Virtual channels can be either permanent virtual channels (PVCs), established manually and persisting for long periods of time, or switched virtual channels (SVCs), set up dynamically as needed and torn down when the need no longer exists.

Data traveling over a VC are divided into fixed-length packets called cells. Each cell contains forty-eight byte*s of user data and five bytes of header. Three of the header bytes are used to identify the virtual path (eight bit*s) and virtual channel (sixteen bits). One is used for header error checking, and

local area networks (LANs) high-speed computer networks that are designed for users who are located near each other

virtual channel connection an abstraction of a physical connection between two or more elements (or computers); the complex details of the physical connection are hidden

virtual circuit like a, a virtual circuit appears to be a direct path between two elements, but is actually a managed collection of physical connections

byte a group of eight binary digits; represents a single character of text

bit a single binary digit, 1 or 0—a contraction of Binary digIT; the smallest unit for storing data in a computer

the remaining eight bits are used for flow control (four bits), payload type (three bits), and priority (one bit). The small payload size benefits services such as voice and video, where timely and regular delivery are required.

ATM supports five different classes of service:

■ Constant bit rate (CBR) allows the desired bit rate to be set when the virtual circuit is established; it is used for services such as uncompressed voice and video;

■ Variable bit rate–non-real time (VBR–NRT) allows statistical techniques to be used to optimize network throughput when the rate at which data is available varies;

■ Variable bit rate–real time (VBR-RT) is intended for applications such as compressed speech and video, where data delivery must occur at regular intervals;

■ Available bit rate (ABR) is used for non-time-critical operations such as bulk file transfers that can adjust their rate of input to use available network capacity; minimum acceptable rates can be specified to ensure some service at all times.

■ Unspecified bit rate (UBR) is the residual class with no guaranteed properties; it is used primarily for TCP/IP data traffic.

When an ATM connection is established, a number of parameters may be specified to ensure desired service properties such as acceptable cell loss percentage, maximum delivery time, variation in delivery time, and the variability of variable rate sources, which specify peak and average data rates and the maximum duration of a burst of peak-rate traffic. Not all parameters apply to all classes of service. Variability parameters make no sense for constant-rate connections, for example. The ability to specify both the type of service needed and parameters controlling the quality of service make ATM well suited to deliver data for multimedia applications.

The ATM Forum is a non-profit international organization dedicated to speeding the development and mass-market deployment of ATM broadband communications technologies. The forum is focused on development of interoperability specifications, promotion of industry-wide cooperation, and educational awareness of the technology's capabilities. Among its other activities, the forum defines standards for connecting other networking technologies to ATM systems. This is necessary because few if any applications use the forty-eight byte data cell payloads of ATM as their native format. A number of ATM adaptation layer (AAL) standards exist that specify the methods to be used.

AAL-1 provides for the conversion of voice and video circuits to CBR ATM virtual channels. The use of PVCs emulates fixed physical circuits and is generally wasteful of bandwidth, as few point-to-point circuits carry fixed traffic levels for long periods of time. The use of SVCs for this traffic represents an improvement, but is still far from optimum, because voice traffic is characterized by lengthy periods of silence, such as when one party is listening to the other. AAL-2 provides a VBR–RT trunking mechanism that uses statistical multiplexing techniques to eliminate the cells that would contain silence.

Compressed video in the MPEG-2 format is accommodated by either AAL-1 or CBR AAL-5. The use of AAL-1 provides for forward error correction at the expense of increased bandwidth and delivery delay. It also allows compensation for Cell Delay Variation (CDV) and the replacement of lost cells. AAL-5 does not compensate for CDV or for bit errors, and lost cells cannot be replaced. For these reasons, AAL-1 is recommended when high video quality is needed.

Internet data traffic also travels over ATM circuits. These data typically take the form of Internet Protocol (IP) datagrams that range in length from a few bytes to thousands of bytes. At the lowest levels of the protocol stack, each datagram is treated independently, and delivery is on a best-effort basis where some loss is deemed acceptable. Higher-level protocol*s add additional information to the datagram payloads to ensure that they are delivered reliably and in the proper order, retransmitting lost datagrams as necessary. These functions are provided at the end points and are not part of the network routing structure. It would be possible to set up a VCC for a single datagram and tear it down once the packet had been delivered, but the overheads would be excessive. Instead, ATM connections are established between Internet routers. These connections are treated as equivalent to direct physical links between the routers, with the virtual circuit carrying traffic for multiple users. IP over ATM typically uses UBR AAL-5 connections. A potential problem occurs in mapping IP datagrams into ATM cell payloads, because loss of a single cell necessitates retransmission of the entire datagram.

 See also **Asynchronous and Synchronous Transmission • Network Design • Telecommunications**

Resources

Web Sites

Broadband Forum. "The Broadband Forum" http://www.broadband-forum.org/ (accessed November 3, 2012).

Webtorials. The ATM Forum. "Speaking Clearly with ATM: A Practical Guide to Carrying Voice Over ATM." http://www.webtorials.com/main/resource/papers/atmforum/paper1.htm (accessed November 3, 2012).

Understanding the Terminology

Here is a key to some of the concepts mentioned in this article: 1) Internet Protocol (IP)—specifies the structure and handling of datagrams sent over the Internet. It is defined in RFC (Request for Comments) 791.2) Integrated Services Digital Network (ISDN)—is a system of digital telephone connections that allows voice and/or data to be transmitted over digital circuits. 3) Motion Picture Experts Group (MPEG)—an organization that defines standards for video compression. MPEG-1 provides VCR-quality video at a data rate of about two megabits per second; MPEG-2 provides broadcast audio and video using variable data rates. 4) Request for Comments (RFC)—a series of documents that defines standards for the Internet, which are published by the RFC editor of the Internet Engineering Task Force (IETF). 5) Statistical multiplexing—a technique used in digital telephony to increase the capacity of a multi-channel system by not transmitting channels during periods of silence, such as when a party is listening rather than talking.

* **protocol** an agreed understanding for the sub-operations that make up a transaction, usually found in the specification of inter-computer communications

B

Bandwidth, Regulation, and Restriction

Bandwidth is a measure of the capacity (data rate) of a communication connection or interface to transmit a signal within a given amount of time. In other words, the larger the capacity of a network, the more likely that better performance will be available to its users. Thus, bandwidth is one factor that determines the perceived speed of a network. For instance, a computer's modem is rated at a particular bandwidth, as is the service provided by an Internet Service Provider (ISP).

Measured as a bit rate from an available or consumed communication connection or interface, such measurements are expressed in bits per second (bps, or sometimes as bit/s). They also are measured as multiples of bps, such as kilobits per second (kbps), megabits per second (Mbps), and gigabits per second (Gbps), where kilo stands for one thousand, mega for one million, and giga for one billion. An Internet connection that has a high bandwidth occurs on broadband* connections when compared to slower dial-up connections or cellular telephone speeds.

Bandwidth can be measured in several ways. For instance, for local area networks (LANs), bandwidth is measured with such tools as netperf (short for network performance) and ttcp (test transmission control protocol). To measure the speed of an Internet connection, many free speed programs are available on the Web such as SpeedTest.net (http://www.speedtest.net/) and SpeakEasy.net (http://www.speakeasy.net/speedtest/). However, even with these tools, accurately measuring the speed of the Internet is difficult because its speed varies over time, mostly due to various hardware configurations and software applications.

As of 2012, bandwidth on the Internet is overseen (loosely regulated) by the U.S. Federal Communications Commission (FCC). However, the FCC has made it known that it would like to increase its oversight of broadband Internet service providers (ISPs). The FCC is proposing a compromise in its ability to moderate ISPs, which would allow it to have oversight over Internet transmissions without actually being able to control it. The term Network Neutrality (also called Internet Neutrality or Open Internet) commonly is associated with this proposal. Network neutrality would allow the FCC the authorization to prevent ISPs from restricting customer access to the Internet. Specifically, network neutrality would prevent ISPs from restricting

* **broadband** Internet access through wires or fiber optic cables that provides higher data rate access to the Internet compared to dial-up access

▲

Then FCC Chairman Julius Genachowski
discusses new rules aimed at prohibiting
broadband providers from becoming
gatekeepers of Internet traffic.
© *AP Images/Jacquelyn Martin, file.*

* peer-to-peer technology
abbreviated P2P, a networking
plan that eliminates the need for
central servers because each
computer within the network is
able to act as a server for other
computers in the network, thus
allowing various resources to be
shared easily

consumers' access to Internet networks, including the ability to block
Internet applications and content such as communication modes,
equipment types attached to the Internet, platforms, protocols, services, and Web sites.

The first attempt to enforce its network neutrality policy came when
the FCC issued an order for U.S. cable operator Comcast Communications
to stop interfering with subscribers' use of peer-to-peer technology* (P2P)
technology. The FCC order stated that it had jurisdiction over Comcast's
network management practices. Specifically, it stated that Comcast
impaired the ability of its customers to access applications equally. The
FCC declared that Comcast's method of managing its bandwidth had
violated federal policy.

The U.S. Court of Appeals for the District of Columbia heard
the 2010 lawsuit, *Comcast Corp. v. FCC*, which several subscribers of
Comcast's broadband Internet service brought against the FCC. The
Court concluded that the FCC does not have ancillary jurisdiction over
Comcast's Internet service under the authority of the Communications
Act of 1934. The Act gave the FCC the ability to "perform any and
all acts, make such rules and regulations, and issue such orders, not
inconsistent with [the Act], as may be necessary in the execution of its
functions."

As the lawsuit implies, restricting the Internet is a hotly debated
issue. For instance, the Open Internet Coalition (OIC) is one voice
that stands in support of bandwidth regulation (network neutrality).
Its Web site states, "Internet openness (network neutrality) means that
users are in control of where to go and what to do online, and broadband providers do not discriminate among lawful Internet content or
applications." The OIC states further that, "This is the fundamental
principle of the Internet's design. It shouldn't matter whether you're
visiting a mainstream media website or an individual's blog, sending
emails or purchasing a song. The phone and cable companies that
provide you with access to the Internet should route all traffic in a
neutral manner, without blocking, speeding up, or slowing down particular applications or content." In addition, Web organizations such as
Amazon and Google are in favor of network neutrality so that all ISPs
treat their customers equally.

Internet hardware companies and members of the cable and telecommunications industries, including major telecommunications
providers, are against network neutrality. They feel regulation on the
Internet will restrict its innovation, along with increasing operating costs
and ultimately raising consumer prices. The December 19, 2010, *Wall
Street Journal* article "The FCC's Threat to Internet Freedom" reem-
phasizes this view with, "The Internet has been open and freedom-
enhancing since it was spun off from a government research project in
the early 1990s. Its nature as a diffuse and dynamic global network of
networks defies top-down authority. Ample laws to protect consumers

already exist. Furthermore, the Obama Justice Department and the European Commission both decided this year that net-neutrality regulation was unnecessary and might deter investment in next-generation Internet technology and infrastructure."

Going into effect on November 20, 2011, the FCC issued rules for Preserving a Free and Open Internet. The FCC states that these rules were not issued to regulate Internet content or applications. Its Web site Open Internet states, "To the contrary, the purpose of Open Internet rules is to clarify high-level, flexible rules of the road for broadband to ensure that no one—not the government and not the companies that provide broadband service—can restrict innovation on the Internet." The three basic Open Internet rules are:

- Transparency of network management practices must be allowed: "Broadband providers must disclose information regarding their network management practices, performance, and the commercial terms of their broadband services."

- Blocking of lawful content must not be allowed: "Fixed broadband providers (such as DSL, cable modem, or fixed wireless providers) may not block lawful content, applications, services, or non-harmful devices. Mobile broadband providers may not block lawful websites, or applications that compete with their voice or video telephony services."

- Unreasonable discrimination in transmitting lawful network traffic must not be allowed: "Fixed broadband providers may not unreasonably discriminate in transmitting lawful network traffic over a consumer's broadband Internet access service. Unreasonable discrimination of network traffic could take the form of particular services or websites appearing slower or degraded in quality."

Whether the Internet will be further regulated and restricted with respect to bandwidth is a continuing debate in the United States and around the world, one that is not likely to be settled in the near future.

Resources

Books

Akujuobi, Cajetan M., and Matthew N. O. Sadiku. *Introduction to Broadband Communication Systems.* Boca Raton, FL: Chapman & Hall/CRC, 2008.

Dowling, Jennifer Coleman. *Multimedia Demystified.* New York: McGraw-Hill, 2012.

Web Sites

Federal Communications Commission. "Open Internet." http://www.fcc.gov/topic/open-internet (accessed November 12, 2012).

▲

William B. Shockley. © *AP Images*

* **vacuum tube** an electronic device constructed of a sealed glass tube containing metal elements in a vacuum; used to control electrical signals

* **germanium** a chemical often used as a high performance semiconductor material; chemical symbol Ge

* **semiconductor** solid material that possesses electrical conductivity characteristics that are similar to those of metals under certain conditions, but can also exhibit insulating qualities under other conditions

* **transistor** a contraction of TRANSfer resISTOR; a semiconductor device, invented by John Bardeen, Walter Brattain, and William Shockley, which has three terminals; can be used for switching and amplifying electrical signals

McDowell, Robert M. "The FCC's Threat to Internet Freedom." *The Wall Street Journal*, December 19, 2010. http://online.wsj.com/article/SB10001424052748703395204576023452250748540.html (accessed November 12, 2012).

Open Internet Coalition. "Why an Open Internet Openness Is a Fundamental Principle of the Internet." http://www.openinternetcoalition.org/index.cfm?objectid=8C7857B0-5C6A-11DF-9E27000C296BA163 (accessed November 12, 2012).

John Bardeen, Walter H. Brattain, and William B. Shockley

Inventors of the Transistor
1908–1991, 1902–1987, and 1910–1989

John Bardeen, Walter H. Brattain, and their boss William B. Shockley at AT&T's Bell Labs in Murray Hill, New Jersey, had a job to do. AT&T needed a way to amplify voices, which tended to get "lost" in static when traveling through more than 1,610 kilometers (1,000 miles) of telephone lines. These physicists were intent upon inventing a device to amplify sound in order to replace bulky, fragile, and expensive vacuum tube*s. In December of 1947, after two years of hard work, they succeeded with a piece of V-wedged germanium* and a strip of gold foil. Even though the newly termed semiconductor* transistor was one fiftieth of the size of vacuum tubes and drew one millionth of the electricity, they had no idea their invention would change the face of the twentieth century. The three were awarded a Nobel Prize in Physics in 1956 for their discovery.

John Bardeen

Nicknamed "Whispering John" because of his soft-spoken manner, Bardeen was born in Madison, Wisconsin, on May 23, 1908. He earned a bachelor's degree in electrical engineering in 1928, and his master's degree in 1929, both from the University of Wisconsin. He spent three years researching geophysics at the Gulf Research Laboratories in Pittsburgh, Pennsylvania. Leaving this position, he pursued studies in mathematical physics at Princeton University, receiving his Ph.D. in 1936.

Bardeen then became a junior fellow of the Society of Fellows at Harvard University. An assistant professorship at the University of Minnesota followed. After that, Bardeen worked at the Naval Ordinance Laboratories in Washington, D.C. In the fall of 1943, Bardeen left there to study solid state physics at Bell Labs. Soon after the transistor* discovery, Bardeen and Brattain disputed the implication that their boss, Shockley, was also credited with the invention.

Bardeen left Bell Labs in 1951 to become a professor of electrical engineering of physics at the University of Illinois. Once in Illinois, and along with graduate students L.N. Cooper and J.R. Schrieffer, Bardeen discovered microscopic superconductivity* during 1956 and 1957. He was awarded a second Nobel Prize in 1972, becoming the third Nobel laureate after Marie Curie and Linus Pauling to win the coveted prize a second time.

Experts in the field have compared Bardeen's gift of physics to Wolfgang Mozart's gift of music. Bardeen influenced almost every field of physics and continued publishing papers in his field until his death. He was bestowed with numerous awards and honors representing national and worldwide recognition for his efforts. Bardeen died on January 30, 1991, at age 82, of a heart attack, in Boston, Massachusetts.

Walter H. Brattain

Brattain was born in Amoy, China, on February 10, 1902. His family moved back to the United States soon after his birth. Brattain grew up on a ranch in Washington. He earned a bachelor's degree from Whitman College in 1924 and a master's degree from the University of Oregon. He earned his Ph.D. at the University of Minnesota. His first post-graduate job was at the National Bureau of Standards, but he soon left there to get back into physics. Bell Labs hired Brattain in 1929. He interrupted his stint at Bell Labs to work on ways to detect submarines during World War II, but returned after the war.

Brattain's partnership with Bardeen, whom Brattain met through his brother, was a great success. Brattain had an excellent reputation as an experimenter. Bardeen, the theoretical physicist, watched the experiments. He would then ask Brattain to modify them to test new theories. Together, the two developed the first transistor, while working under the supervision of Shockley. Because of friction, Brattain eventually transferred out of Shockley's department, but he continued to work at Bell Labs until his retirement in 1967.

Brattain also lectured at Harvard University, the University of Minnesota, and the University of Washington. He was also awarded several honorary degrees. He viewed his accomplishments with modesty, saying he was fortunate to be in the right place at the right time. He was a member of the National Inventors Hall of Fame. Brattain died of Alzheimer's disease in Seattle, Washington, on October 13, 1987, at the age of 85.

William Shockley

Born in London, England, on February 13, 1910, Shockley grew up in Palo Alto, California. He received his bachelor's degree from California Institute of Technology and his Ph.D. from Massachusetts Institute of Technology in 1936. Then he began working at Bell Labs in New Jersey. During World War II, he directed research on anti-submarine technology

* **superconductivity** the property of a material to pass an electric current with almost no losses; most metals are superconductive only at temperatures near absolute zero

Oh the Irony

Ironically, the transistor in John Bardeen's automatic garage door malfunctioned as he was preparing to leave for the press conference announcing he had won the Nobel Prize. He had to get a ride to the event.

The Transistor

The transistor allows the miniaturization of electronic equipment and is regarded as the nerve cell of the Information Age. Its first use was in the telephone switching machine in Englewood, New Jersey, in 1952. By the end of the twentieth century, the transistor could be found everywhere, in supercomputers, televisions, radios, toys, greeting cards, and garage door openers.

* **silicon** a chemical element with symbol Si; the most abundant element in the Earth's crust and the most commonly used semiconductor material

* **Silicon Valley** an area in California near San Francisco, which has been the home location of many of the most significant information technology orientated companies and universities

for the U.S. Navy, but like Brattain, returned to Bell Labs. In 1945 he was named the director of solid state physics for Bell Labs.

Although he was not present at the first successful transistor experimentation with Bardeen and Brattain, in the weeks following that discovery, Shockley contributed a series of insights that contributed to the understanding of semiconductor materials, and developed several theories about another type of amplification device, the junction transistor. He also formulated many of the theories that allowed silicon* chips to be mass-produced.

In 1956 Shockley left Bell Labs to form his own company, Shockley Semiconductor Laboratories, with the intent of producing silicon transistors. He established his new company near Palo Alto, California. Eventually, Shockley's abrasive management style led to the departure of several of his employees, including Gordon Moore and Robert Noyce, who then went on to establish Fairchild Semiconductors and later, the Intel Corporation. Because so many of these companies were founded in that area, the region became known as Silicon Valley*.

Later in life, Shockley accepted an appointment at Stanford University, where he formulated several theories about genetics. He withstood substantial criticism regarding his race-based theories, especially since the subject was deemed out of his area of expertise, physics. Shockley died of prostate cancer on August 12, 1989, at the age of 79.

 See also **Bell Labs • Digital Logic Design • Integrated Circuits • Intel Corporation • Transistors • Vacuum Tubes**

Resources

Periodicals

Anderson, Susan Heller. "Walter Brattain, Inventor, Is Dead." *New York Times*, October 14, 1987.

Moore, Gordon E. "Solid State Physicist: William Shockley—He Fathered the Transistor and Brought the Silicon to Silicon Valley but Is Remembered by Many Only for his Noxious Racial Views." *Time*, March 23, 1999, p. 160.

United Press International. "John Bardeen, at Age 82, Was an Electronics Pioneer." *The Record, Bergen Record Corp.*, January 31, 1991.

Web Sites

"John Bardeen." University of Illinois at Urbana-Champaign. http://physics.illinois.edu/people/memorials/bardeen.asp (accessed November 2, 2012).

"Walter Brattain." ScienCentral, Inc., and the American Institute of Physics. http://www.pbs.org/transistor/album1/brattain/brattain2.html (accessed November 2, 2012).

Bell, Alexander Graham

American Inventor
1847–1922

Alexander Graham Bell, best known as the inventor of the telephone, was born in Edinburgh, Scotland, on March 3, 1847. When he died in Baddeck, Nova Scotia, Canada, on August 2, 1922, he was considered one of the most successful inventors of his time.

Bell's interest in communication was stimulated by unique family circumstances. Both his grandfather and father were accomplished speech experts. Many believe Bell's father was the inspiration for Professor Henry Higgins in the 1964 movie *My Fair Lady.* Having a hearing-impaired mother also made Bell conscious of the challenges of being deaf. In 1868 he began using his father's models of visible speech* to teach deaf students phonetics, a career he resumed after emigrating with his family from Scotland to Brantford, Ontario, Canada, in 1870.

The following year he moved to Boston, Massachusetts, and taught at the Boston School for Deaf Mutes (later called the Horace Mann School). Teaching private students supplemented his income. One of these hearing-impaired students, Mabel Hubbard, later became his wife. Bell's passion for helping the disabled, particularly the sight- and hearing-impaired, remained with him throughout his life.

Although Bell experimented throughout his childhood, it was not until he moved to Boston that his interests in inventing became serious. There he decided to work on developing the multiple telegraph, which would allow several telegraphs to be sent over the same line simultaneously instead of one at a time. He received that patent in 1875. He also became fascinated with the concept of sending varying pitches, mimicking the human voice, over a wire via undulating electrical impulses, then reconstructing the pitches at the other end of the wire. After years of experimenting, he and his assistant, Thomas A. Watson, met with success. Bell's patent application for the telephone was submitted only hours before a rival, Elisha Gray, submitted his version.

In July 1877, the Bell Telephone Company was founded. The shares were divided between Bell, Watson, and two other men. As a wedding gift, Bell gave his wife, Mabel, 5,015 shares of Bell Telephone Company, keeping only ten shares for himself. Bell Telephone rapidly expanded throughout the world. While these shares provided Bell with financial security, they made his wife quite wealthy. During Bell's lifetime, Mabel repeatedly provided grants to fund his research.

The photophone, which Bell invented in 1880, worked like a telephone but used light beams instead of wire. Bell considered it one of his greatest inventions. Although the photophone's success was limited because of the lack of technology at that time, Bell's invention used the same principles as modern fiber optic telecommunications.

▲

Alexander Graham Bell makes the first long-distance phone call, between New York and Chicago, 1892. © *AP Images*

* **visible speech** a set of symbols, comprising an alphabet, that "spell" sounds instead of words

Bell's Rival: Elisha Gray

Although most people have heard of Alexander Graham Bell, the name of rival inventor Elisha Gray (1835–1901) is not as recognizable. After growing up on a farm in Ohio, Gray worked as a carpenter to support his studies at Oberlin College, where he became interested in electrical devices. Like Bell, Gray worked on improvements to the telegraph. Bell beat Gray by only two hours when filing the patent for the telephone. Gray went on to create the TelAutograph, which transmitted writing or drawings. He demonstrated his invention at the World's Fair in Chicago in 1893. Shortly before his death, Gray began tests of an underwater signaling device.

While living in Mabel's hometown of Washington, D.C., in 1882, Bell became an American citizen. Later he built a second home in Baddeck and called it Beinn Bhreagh. Much of his inventing was completed there.

After winning the Volta prize of France for the telephone, Bell invested the award money in the creation of the Volta Labs at Beinn Bhreagh. This lab produced the flat-disk record and a floating stylus to improve upon Thomas Edison's phonograph. With earnings from those patents, Bell established the Volta Bureau in 1908, which was dedicated to advancing knowledge of the deaf. He also established the American Association for the Promotion of the Teaching of Speech to the Deaf and continued being instrumental in assisting many deaf children, including Helen Keller, to overcome their disabilities.

Bell also became interested in screening children for hearing impairment. After developing the audiometer, he was honored for his accomplishments in that field with the term used for measuring the level of audible sound: the decibel.

Bell's interests were not confined to matters of speech. His father-in-law, Gardiner Hubbard, was a founding member and the first president of the National Geographic Society. When Hubbard died in 1897, Bell accepted the presidency of the society. He then underwrote the hiring of his future son-in-law to edit the association's monthly publication. Bell influenced many trademark features of the society, including the formation of grants for research expeditions. He also encouraged the inclusion of dynamic multiple-color photographs in *National Geographic Magazine.*

Bell also nurtured a fascination with flight. At Beinn Bhreagh, he experimented with kites and eventually developed and patented the tetrahedron, a four-sided triangle used in his aerial experiments. With Mabel's sponsorship, he formed the Aerial Experiment Association (AEA) with four other men. From 1908 to 1909, after the Wright Brothers flew the first airplane, Bell and his associates built four airplanes. With those machines, the AEA gained patents for improving airplane designs. The AEA then sought to build a craft that could take off and land on water. In 1918 this led to the patent for the fastest watercraft of its time, the hydrofoil HD4, which reached speeds of 114 kilometers (71 miles) per hour.

In tribute to Bell's life and accomplishments, telephones across the United States were silenced for one minute during his funeral in Baddeck in 1922.

 See also **Bell Labs • Internet • Telecommunications**

Resources

Books

Bruce, Robert V. *Bell: Alexander Graham Bell and the Conquest of Solitude.* Boston: Little, Brown, 1973; reprint. Ithaca, NY: Cornell University Press, 1990.

Matthews, Tom L. *Always Inventing: A Photobiography of Alexander Graham Bell.* Washington D.C.: National Geographic Society, 1999; reprint. 2006.

Pasachoff, Naomi. *Alexander Graham Bell: Making Connections.* New York: Oxford University Press, 1996.

Boole, George
English Mathematician
1815–1864

George Boole was a mathematician whose work in symbolic logic laid new foundations for modern algebra, and set the stage for contemporary computer circuitry and database search strategy syntax*. Boole was born in Lincolnshire, England, in 1815, and he died December 8, 1864, in County Cork, Ireland. He received little in the way of formal education, but he was a dedicated reader and self-taught student of languages and mathematics.

At the age of sixteen, Boole became an assistant teacher for elementary school students. By age twenty, Boole had started his own school. Dismayed at what he considered to be inadequate materials available to teach mathematics to young students, Boole undertook the serious study of mathematics on his own. In subsequent years he wrote several seminal papers on the relationship between logic and mathematics. Despite his lack of university training and connections, he managed to get his works published in *The Cambridge Mathematical Journal,* eventually winning the professional respect of other mathematicians and logicians. In 1854 he published *An Investigation of the Laws of Thought, on Which Are Founded the Mathematical Theories of Logic and Probabilities.* Considered his most influential work, this text provides the foundation for what has become known as Boolean algebra*. Other significant works include the *Treatise on Differential Equations* (1859) and the *Treatise on the Calculus of Finite Differences* (1860).

Boole was a deeply religious man. He was influenced by the works of Sir Isaac Newton, Joseph LaGrange, and Pierre-Simon Laplace, as well as the philosopher Gottfried Wilhelm Leibnitz. Also a family man, Boole married Mary Everest, niece of Sir George Everest, for whom Mt. Everest was named. Boole and Everest married in 1855 and eventually had five daughters: Mary, Margaret, Alicia, Lucy, and Ethel.

Boole died of pneumonia at the age of forty-nine, when Alicia was four years old and his youngest daughter was an infant. His widow, Mary Everest Boole, made significant contributions to the field of mathematics herself, carrying on her late husband's work of helping children learn mathematics. She described her work as that of a "mathematical

George Boole. © *SSPL via Getty Images.*

* **syntax** a set of rules that a computing language incorporates regarding structure, punctuation, and formatting

* **Boolean algebra** a system developed by George Boole that deals with the theorems of undefined symbols and axioms concerning those symbols

Like Father, Like Daughter

Alicia Boole Stott continued in the family tradition of mathematics. She later built a reputation in the field of mathematics for her study of the visualization of geometric figures.

* **Venn diagrams** diagrams used to demonstrate the relationships between sets of objects, named after John Venn, a British logician

* **syllogistic statements** the essential tenets of western philosophical thought, based on hypotheses and categories

psychologist," and focused on understanding how children use reason and logic, physical activity, and subconscious processes to learn mathematics.

Boolean Legacies

Many mathematicians consider Boole's most significant contribution to be his Boolean algebra, which articulates a theory of relations. Boolean algebra furnishes laws of possibility among propositions. In the 1940s, early computer pioneer Claude Shannon (1916–2001) applied Boole's principles to electrical wiring and developed a mathematical theory of communication, which led to the connection between the work of George Boole and modern computer circuitry, which Boole of course could not have anticipated.

Boolean algebra is also at the center of symbolic reasoning, which is widely applied in the formation of database search statements. Often called Boolean Logic, Boole's explanation of logical operators of thought provides the foundation of computer search engine syntax. Boolean "operators" are enlisted in search statements to help online searchers to restrict or expand their search results. Boolean Logic separates concepts from each other and examines their properties relative to each other. These properties can be demonstrated through Venn diagrams* and syllogistic statements*.

The pragmatics of Boolean Logic are found in AND, OR, and NOT statements. Unlike in typical mathematics, AND statements limit results. For example, 2 + 3 = 5. However, in Boolean Logic, the combination of Concept A and Concept B yields only results that contain *both* A and B. Thus, the resulting set number is less than either of the two concepts viewed singularly. This concept is often difficult for database searchers to learn to use. Accustomed to the numerical principle that adding units together yields greater results, the most common mistake of novice online searchers is to add too many variables to their search syntax, believing that more variables will provide more results. In fact, the opposite is true.

To get more results with a Boolean search, the OR statement is needed. OR statements can be tricky, however, depending on where they appear in the search statement. For example, A OR B AND C can be interpreted as (A OR B) AND C, which is likely what the searcher intends. If the search engine interprets the statement as A OR (B AND C), very different results are given. Properly placed parentheses are recommended in virtually all cases where the OR operator is employed.

The NOT operator is also a limiter, in that it restricts the search by omitting results that contain the NOT word or concept. For example, A AND B NOT C will retrieve records that contain A and B but exclude all records that contain C, even if they contain A and B.

As is evident from Boolean operators, relationships among objects or ideas may be governed by a logic that is not necessarily congruent with conventional human reasoning. What may be rational in numbers, e.g. addition, does not "add up" when applied to the use of the Boolean "AND" in a search statement.

Boole was drawn to explore the depths of logical and mathematical reasoning, and the ways in which human thought comprehends the relationships among ideas. In ways Boole could never have foreseen, his intellectual interests provided the foundation for future generations of logicians and mathematicians whose work is enhanced by the computing and database searching technology people take for granted today.

 See also **Boolean Algebra • Digital Logic Design**

Resources

Books

Gasser, James, ed. *A Boole Anthology: Recent and Classical Studies in the Logic of George Boole.* Boston: Kluwer Academic Publishers, 2000.

MacHale, Desmond. *George Boole: His Life and Work.* Dublin, Ireland: Boole Press, 1983.

Web Sites

Broadbent, T. A. A. "George Boole." *Complete Dictionary of Scientific Biography.* http://www.encyclopedia.com/topic/George_Boole.aspx (accessed November 2, 2012).

O'Connor, John J., and Edmund F. Robertson. "George Boole." School of Mathematics and Statistics, University of St. Andrews, Scotland. http://www-history.mcs.st-andrews.ac.uk/history/Mathematicians/Boole.html (accessed November 2, 2012).

Boolean Algebra

Boolean algebra is a form of algebra that allows computation and manipulation of binary systems, sometimes derived from predicate logic. In 1847, George Boole (1815–1864), an English mathematician, published one of the works that founded symbolic logic. His combination of ideas from classical logic and algebra resulted in what is called Boolean algebra.

Using variables and symbols, Boole designed a language for describing and manipulating logical statements and determining if they are true or not. The variables stand for statements that are either true or false. The symbols +, * and − represent *and*, *or*, and *not* and are equivalent to the symbols ∧, ∨, and − used in the truth tables in logic. Although truth tables use T and F (for true and false respectively) to indicate the state of the sentence, Boolean algebra uses 1 and 0.

A	B	A ^ B
T	T	T
T	F	F
F	T	F
F	F	F

(a)

A	B	A * B
1	1	1
1	0	0
0	1	0
0	0	0

(b)

 Figure 1. The statement 'mittens and green' is represented using truth tables (a) and Boolean algebra (b). *Reproduced by permission of Gale, a part of Cengage Learning.*

A	B	A ∨ B
T	T	T
T	F	T
F	T	T
F	F	F

(a)

A	B	A + B
1	1	1
1	0	1
0	1	1
0	0	0

(b)

▲

Figure 2. The statement 'mittens or gloves' is represented using truth tables (a) and Boolean algebra (b). *Reproduced by permission of Gale, a part of Cengage Learning.*

* **binary** existing in only two states, such as "on" or "off," "one" or "zero"

The relationship between Boolean algebra, set algebra, logic, and binary* arithmetic has given Boolean algebra a central role in the development of electronic digital computers. Besides its many applications in the design of computers, it forms the foundation of information theory.

Truth Tables

Boolean algebra is based on propositions, which are non-ambiguous sentences that can be either true or false. One can combine these propositions in a variety of ways by using the connectives *and* and *or*, or one can negate them by preceding them with *not*. The results of these operations on propositions are dictated by the rules of Boolean algebra. For example, if one says: "I will buy green mittens," then she is actually saying that she will buy mittens and those mittens will be green. Therefore the properties of "mittens" and "green" will have to be present in all her "hand-covering" purchases. This will exclude gloves and all non-green mittens. How does this work out using truth tables? Let A represent "mittens," B represent "green." Figure 1(a) shows how the statement "mittens and green" is represented using truth tables, while Figure 1(b) shows the same statement using Boolean algebra.

What the tables indicate is that if an item does not possess both the quality of being a mitten and the quality of being green, then it will be discarded. Only those that satisfy both qualities will be selected.

On the other hand, if one says: "I will buy gloves or mittens," then he is actually saying that he will buy mittens, or gloves, or some combination of the two. This means that he will have a great assortment of "hand-covering" garments. Let A represent "mittens" and B represent "gloves." Figure 2(a) shows how the statement "mittens or gloves" is represented using truth tables, while Figure 2(b) shows the same statement using Boolean algebra.

What the tables indicate is that an item will be selected if it possesses both qualities of mitten and glove, or possesses only one quality, either glove or mitten. Only those that satisfy neither quality will be discarded—for example, all red socks.

One can also say: "I will buy something to cover my hands, but not mittens." Let A represent "mittens." Figure 3(a) shows how the statement "not mittens" is represented using truth tables, while Figure 3(b) shows the same statement using Boolean algebra.

The tables indicate that if an item is a mitten then its negation, $-A$, represents a non-mitten (for example, a glove or a sock).

Computer Design

Boolean algebra can be applied to the design and simplification of complex circuits present in computers because computer circuits are two-state devices: they can be either off or on. This corresponds to the general representation of Boolean algebra with two elements, 0 and 1. To show how this works, take a look at two simple circuits, "and," and "or," which correspond to the first two sets of tables presented earlier. These simple circuits consist of a power source—a battery connected by a wire to a destination—and a lamp with two switches that control the flow of electricity. The position of a switch either allows electricity to flow from the power source to the destination, or stops it. For example, if the switch is up, or open, then electricity does not flow, and this condition is represented by a 0. However, if the switch is down, or closed, the electricity will flow, and this is represented by 1.

Figure 4 shows the diagram of a two-switch series circuit, where electricity will flow from the source to the destination only if both switches are closed. This diagram represents the *and* condition of Boolean algebra.

A circuit where electricity flows whenever at least one of the switches is closed is known as a parallel circuit. This corresponds to the *or* condition of Boolean algebra. Figure 5 shows the diagram of a two-switch parallel circuit.

To represent the *not* condition, one must remember that in this system a switch has only two possible positions, open or closed. Its complement is a switch that will have the opposite position. For example, if switch A is open, its complement will be closed and vice versa. Logic designers can use these diagrams to plan complex computer circuits that will perform the needed functions for a specific machine.

Information Theory

Boolean algebra is used in information theory because almost all search engines allow someone to enter queries in the form of logical expressions. The operator *and* is used to narrow a query whereas *or* is used to broaden it. The operator *not* is used to exclude specific words from a query. For example, if one is looking for information about "privacy in computer environments," she could phrase her query as "computer *and* privacy," or "computer *or* privacy," or even "computer *and* privacy *not* mainframes." The amount of information received from each query will be different.

The first query will retrieve fewer documents because it will only select those that contain both terms. The second will retrieve many documents because it will select those that contain "computer," those that contain "privacy," and also those that contain both terms. The last query will retrieve documents that contain both "privacy" and "computer," while anything containing the term "mainframe" will be discarded.

When using search engines, one must realize that each one will access its database differently. Typically the same search performed in more than one database will not return the same result. To do a thorough search, one must become familiar with a few of the different search engines and understand their major features, such as Boolean logic and truncation. In addition, one must check the search engine's documentation often because it can change frequently.

By 2010, Boolean logic was used in a wide diversity of computational search systems, ranging from analysis of genetic databases to comparing

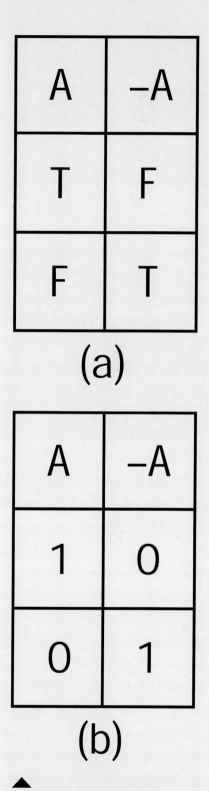

Figure 3. The statement 'not mittens' is represented using truth tables (a) and Boolean algebra (b). *Reproduced by permission of Gale, a part of Cengage Learning.*

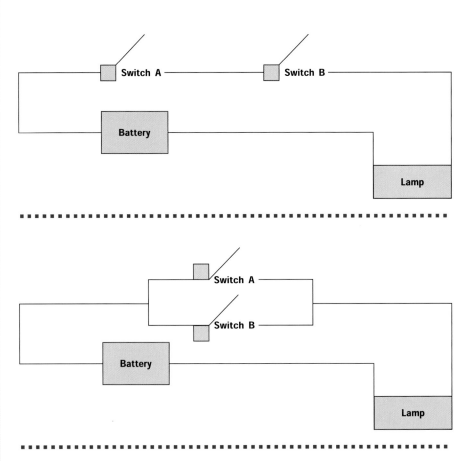

Figure 4. Example of a series circuit. In order for the electricity to flow from the battery to the lamp, both switches must be down or closed. This represents the 'and' condition. *Reproduced by permission of Gale, a part of Cengage Learning.*

Figure 5. Example of a parallel circuit. In order for the electricity to flow from the battery to the lamp, at least one of the switches must be down or closed. This represents the 'or' condition. *Reproduced by permission of Gale, a part of Cengage Learning.*

climate data gathered from geographically scattered sources. For example, Boolean logic can be used to sift data related to stem cell genes involved in various developmental pathways. Using algebraic logic provides rapid identification of genes with asymmetric relationships. For example, assuming evidence that hypothetical gene X is active at the beginning of a developmental process, and gene Z is active later, by using Boolean logic to screen results, scientists can find genes that are inactive when X is active, and active when Z is active, etc. Researchers can then conduct further tests to test to determine the roles these genes might play in the developmental process.

 See also **Algorithms • Binary Number System • Boole, George • Decision Support Systems • Digital Logic Design**

Resources

Books

Cusick, Thomas W., and Pantelimon Stanica. *Cryptographic Boolean Functions and Applications.* Amsterdam and Boston: Academic Press/Elsevier, 2009.

Givant, Steven R., and Paul R. Halmos. *Introduction to Boolean Algebras.* New York: Springer, 2009.

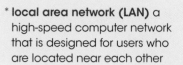

Bridging Devices

The need for bridging devices arises with the need to communicate with computers located beyond a particular local area network (LAN)*. Although all the clients (computers) attached to a LAN need not be located in the same room, there are limitations on the distance between clients as well as on the number of clients that can be attached to a single network segment. Bridging devices are used to overcome these limitations and facilitate communication among machines on different floors, different buildings, different cities, and different countries.

Bridging devices are available in a variety of configurations to interconnect multiple local area network segments. The choice of bridging device depends on distance, traffic volume, and complexity of the communication pathways between sites. Commonly used bridging devices include repeaters, bridges, routers, and gateways.

Repeaters

The simplest bridging device is known as a repeater. As messages travel over increasing distances, their signals become weak and distorted. A repeating device extends the distance over which clear communication can take place by regenerating messages. For example, repeaters can be used to facilitate communication among computers in a LAN that spans several floors of a building.

The LAN cable for each floor is connected to a repeater, which is sometimes called a hub. Additional cabling connects a repeater to other repeaters on adjacent floors. As messages travel from floor to floor, their signal strength is maintained because the repeaters regenerate them.

* **local area network (LAN)** a high-speed computer network that is designed for users who are located near each other

An example of a connectivity kit.
© AP Images/PRNewsFoto/Xilinx, Inc..

Repeaters are limited as bridging devices because they operate at the physical network layer and simply pass on all the bits that they receive. Repeaters do not distinguish between messages intended for clients on the same floor and those intended for clients on different floors. Repeaters also retransmit messages with errors and signals resulting from collisions when clients attempt to send simultaneous messages. If traffic volume is heavy, performance on the network will deteriorate.

Bridges

A device known as a bridge is used to reduce network traffic by filtering messages. Bridges, unlike repeaters, do not retransmit every signal that they receive. Bridges operate at the data link layer of the networking hierarchy. They filter messages using the hardware or medium access control (MAC) addresses of the PCs attached to the local network. A bridge retransmits only correct messages with destination addresses that fall outside the network segment from which the message originated.

A bridge, for example, can be used to connect LAN segments located in two different buildings. Although the two network segments function as a single LAN, the bridge limits traffic between buildings to messages involving client PCs actually located in different buildings. Performance for the entire LAN will be better because a pair of clients in each building will be able to exchange messages without interfering with communications in the other building. Network designers use bridges to improve performance on busy LANs by dividing the network into segments connected by bridges and assigning computers that frequently exchange messages to the same segment.

To filter messages, bridges must "know" the location of the client computers attached to their network segments. When a bridge receives a message, it recovers the hardware address of the sending computer and adds it to a table that associates computers with network segments. After each PC on the network has sent one message, the bridge will have a complete record of PCs and their locations.

This complete table of computers and location addresses is crucial to the operation of the bridge. Bridges compare the destination addresses in messages to their tables to determine when to retransmit a message. If the destination address belongs to the segment over which the message arrived, the destination computer has already received the message and the bridge does not need to forward the message. If the destination address does not belong to the segment over which the message arrived, the bridge will forward a copy of the message to the other network segment.

The great advantage of a bridge is that it is a plug-and-play device that requires no set-up by a network administrator. Bridges are very effective for small networks involving just a few segments. As the number of segments in a network increases, redundant multiple paths between distant LAN segments become an important issue. Redundancy in a network means alternate pathways between network locations are available in case of a failure or congestion in one part of a network. Unfortunately, the rules by which bridges operate restrict the effective pathways between network segments. Consequently, with an increase in both the number of segments in an organization's network and the need to make connections across networks (e.g., the Internet), bridges become less effective than routers as the bridging device of choice.

Routers

A router differs from a bridge because it operates at the network layer of the network model. The addresses used by routers are network addresses such as the familiar "dotted-decimal" addresses found on the Internet. Each message packet must specify a network destination address (e.g., 124.26.112.98). In a complex network with multiple alternate paths between locations, the primary task of the routers on a network is to use the destination address of a message to determine the best path between locations for a message to follow.

Packets traveling through a network are passed from router to router until they reach a router that is attached to the same local network as the destination. When a packet arrives at a router, the router first determines if it is addressed to a device on its local network. If not, the router chooses the next router to receive the packet in its progress across the network.

The data that a router will use to make its forwarding decisions are contained in a routing table. The routing table contains a list of destination addresses and the "next-hop" router appropriate for each of those destinations. The minimum set of entries in a routing table includes an address to identify devices on the router's local network and a default address for forwarding all other packets. More complex tables present alternative pathways so that a router can choose to forward a message along the most direct, the least congested, or the fastest pathway. Routers in a network are able to exchange data to update their routing tables with information about failures, congestion, or new paths in the network.

Gateways

All the routers on the Internet operate according to the Internet Protocol (IP)*. A different kind of bridging device, called a gateway, is needed to interconnect two networks that use different network layer protocols. When an IP router communicates with an adjacent IP router, it is only necessary to package the data for the shared network protocol in a data-link layer frame. However, when an IP router needs to communicate with, for example, an IBM SNA router, it will also be necessary to replace the IP network data with appropriate SNA network data.

The task of translating network layer descriptions for different networks is performed by a gateway. The gateway receives messages from

Network of Networks

The Internet is often described as a network of networks. Bridging devices are the connectors that join one part of the larger network to another. Bridging devices differ in sophistication of the connection they provide, but they all contribute to the rapid movement of data that is the key to the Information Age.

* **Internet Protocol (IP)** a method of organizing information transfer between computers; the IP was specifically designed to offer low-level support to Transmission Control Protocol (TCP)

one network, removes the network layer information, adds network layer information formatted for the second network, packages the message in a data-link layer frame and forwards it to the second network.

▶ *See also* **E-Commerce • Internet • Networks • Telecommunications • World Wide Web**

Resources

Books

Derfler, Frank J., and Les Freed *How Networks Work.* 7th ed. Upper Saddle River, NJ: Que Publishing, 2005.

Cache Memory

Cache memory refers to a fast storage buffer in the central processing unit (CPU)* of a computer, allowing the computer to store data temporarily, making information retrieval faster and more efficient. By storing often-used data in a special memory chip rather than accessing the memory of the computer for the same information each time, cache memory helps maximize the efficiency of the CPU.

Typically, in order to execute a command, the processor in a computer places a numeric address for the instruction it is about to execute on the address bus*. Once the memory subsystem senses the address, it deposits the code representing that instruction onto the data. The processor then collects this code from the data, interpreting it as a command of some sort. The execution of this instruction may involve several operations similar to the one that enabled the processor to fetch the instruction in the first place. For example, the processor may discover that the instruction it just fetched requires it to get some data from memory and then add that data to a register. Whatever the nature of the instruction, once it is complete, the processor must repeat the instruction fetching cycle for the next instruction in the program it is currently executing.

The rate at which the processor can execute instructions partly determines its perceived performance—therefore, it would help tremendously if the next instruction that the processor was going to fetch was located or retrieved for it automatically whilst it was busy executing the previous one. Cache memory allows the processor to do exactly that.

Although the simultaneous functionality discussed earlier introduces a little more complexity into the system, the benefits are significant, and most modern processors incorporate a small amount of memory within them. This block of memory, also called a cache memory, is often built into the processor core itself. Cache memory is managed by another unit, called the cache controller, and is implemented from high-speed, and therefore comparatively expensive, memory devices.

The intent is to increase the average speed at which a program can be executed. This is accomplished when the cache controller tries to pre-fetch blocks of instructions that are to be executed by the processor, storing them in its high-speed cache. Because the instructions are now instantly available, the processor need not wait for each instruction to be fetched in sequence before execution.

Despite their advantages, caches are not completely foolproof. Since the cache cannot know with complete certainty which instruction the

* **central processing unit (CPU)** the part of a computer that performs computations and controls and coordinates other parts of the computer

* **bus** a group of related signals that form an interconnecting pathway between two or more electronic devices

Processors such as this have approximately 37 million transistors. © *AP/MATTHIAS RIETSCHEL.*

processor is going to need next, it selects groups of instructions that happen to be in memory, and close to the last instruction that was executed. The cache relies on a correlation that suggests that when processors execute programs, the instructions tend to be fetched in order in memory. However, it is quite possible that the cache controller will, on some occasions, fetch blocks of instructions from the wrong place. There are several reasons why this would happen. For example, the processor may have just executed an instruction that commands it to jump to another part of the program, which might be quite distant from the current point of execution. Whenever the cache controller correctly predicts the next block of instructions needed by the processor, it is referred to as a cache hit. When the converse happens though, it is described as a miss.

A number of factors can affect the hit rate, and therefore the average speed, of program execution. For example, if the cache is large, it statistically increases the chances of it retrieving the correct pieces of information. However, it also increases the cost and complexity of the cache since it is now somewhat more difficult to manage. Caches tend to work very well when the programs that are being executed are structured as a straightforward sequence of instructions. This can be accomplished by having development tools such as compilers and interpreters take on the responsibility of organizing the memory image.

In addition to blocks of instructions, caches are applied with equal validity to blocks of data needed by programs. Many modern processors incorporate separate instruction and data caches of various sizes, depending on which combination helps optimize the performance of the processor. On a larger scale, but employing exactly the same principle, are data caches for fixed disks and for servers in a distributed network. It is possible to attach special cache units to disk drive controllers. These cache units attempt to speed up the average access time of the disk by predicting what portions might be needed next, pre-loading these into memory set aside on the disk controller based on currently accessed file(s). Similarly, when client computers are accessing a World Wide Web (WWW) server, they might store on their own disk a collection of documents and images that have been recently accessed. Then, if these documents are browsed again soon afterward, they can be reloaded from the local disk cache rather than transferring them from the server again.

Whatever the scale and implementation, caching is a statistically based approach to memory storage that tries to enhance the average performance of a system by attempting to anticipate the information that will be required, and having it ready ahead of time.

 See also **Central Processing Unit • Mainframes • Memory • Minicomputers • Supercomputers • World Wide Web**

Resources

Books

Baron, Robert J., and L. Higbie. *Computer Architecture.* Reading, MA: Addison-Wesley, 1992.

Beck, Michael, H. Bohme, M. Dziadzka, U. Kunitz, R. Magnus, and D. Verworner. *Linux Kernel Internals.* 2nd ed. Harlow, UK: Addison-Wesley, 1998.

Hayes, John P. *Computer Architecture and Organization.* 3rd ed. Boston: WCB/McGraw-Hill, 1998.

Laplante, Philip A. *Real-time Systems Design and Analysis.* 3rd ed. Hoboken, NJ: Wiley, 2004.

Stone, Harold S. *High-Performance Computer Architecture.* 3rd ed. Reading, MA: Addison-Wesley, 1993.

Cellular Technology

The cellular phone is the latest in a long line of mobile, portable, and wireless communications technologies extending back to the 1930s. Military forces were among the first to use mobile radio communications. Early mobile radio equipment for the military consisted of large transmitters aboard military vehicles with bulky antennas and high transmitter power. Robust vehicles were needed to accommodate the massive, power-hungry equipment.

The first use of radio communications for civilian land vehicles was primarily by police departments. The earliest systems were one-way,

---

Cache Memories in Next Generation CPUs

Intel Corporation of Santa Clara, California, has indicated that there will be three levels of cache memories within their "Poulson" Itanium processor, and the largest cache block will be a staggering 32 megabytes in size. This amount of memory constitutes approximately five times the entire memory subsystem of popular microcomputers of only a decade earlier.

A cellular telephone tower in Israel.
© *AP Images/Ariel Schalit.*

* **frequency modulation** a technique whereby a signal is transformed so that it is represented by another signal with a frequency that varies in a way related to the original signal

* **simplex** uni-directional communication over a single communication channel

* **duplex** simultaneous two-directional communication over a single communication channel

where the dispatcher could broadcast to all cars the location and nature of a problem. There was no return communication and thus no verification of a response to the problem, but it was better than nothing.

The first successful installation of a large two-way police radio system was for the Connecticut State Police in 1939. This system used a newly invented type of radio called frequency modulation* (FM). This system set the standard for mobile radio for many years.

Two-way radio installed in automobiles inspired the idea for a mobile telephone service. The first police radio was a simplex*, or one-way, system, meaning that the mobile unit could only receive communications. The two-way police radio was a half duplex* system in which both the mobile and base units could transmit and receive but not at the same time. Proper radio procedures were required, such as saying *over* to invite the other station to transmit, and using radio call signs. The frequency was shared by a number of users and conversations were far from private.

Ideally, a mobile telephone is a full duplex system where both stations transmit and receive simultaneously and the channel is not shared. The first full duplex mobile telephone systems were installed in large cities in the 1950s. The systems used base stations connected to the public switched telephone network (PSTN) and had a range of 60 to 80 kilometers (37 to 50 miles). Mobile telephones had a telephone number, rang like a normal telephone, and were full duplex. Because of the large area covered by the base station and the limited number of available channels or radio frequencies, the mobile phone system (MPS) quickly reached full capacity. Priority for new subscribers was given to physicians and others needing emergency communications, and the waiting lists were very long.

A Texas rancher, Thomas "Tom" Carter, played an important role in mobile telephone history. Carter had made a simple device that would

* **algorithm** a rule or procedure used to solve a mathematical problem—most often described as a sequence of steps

allow his private business two-way radio system to be used with his office telephone when he was out on the ranch. The telephone company refused to allow Carter to connect his device to the PSTN and Carter took the case to court. Although it took fifteen years, the Federal Communications Commission (FCC) in 1968 ruled in favor of Carter in the landmark Carterfone decision. The action opened the PSTN to radio connections as well as those for computer data and other devices.

In the 1970s, Bell Telephone Laboratories began investigating a replacement system for the MPS. After the Carterfone decision, competitors were gearing up to use new technologies to provide alternative mobile telephone service. The FCC reassigned a number of under-used ultra-high frequency (UHF) television channels for a new, advanced mobile phone system (AMPS). The AMPS had considerably more channels than the older MPS and had two sets—one for the local telephone company, and a second set for a competitor.

The concept of the AMPS was to increase the reuse of the communications channels. Frequency reuse occurs when two stations occupy the same frequency or channel but are separated by such a distance that they do not interfere. The MPS used high antennas to provide a 60 to 80 kilometer (37 to 50 mile) range, but no two base stations could be closer than about 150 kilometers (93 miles) to avoid interference. In the AMPS, the height of the base station antenna and the transmitter power are limited so the range of a cell is only about 11 to 15 kilometers (7 to 9 miles). In addition, the base station controls the transmitter powers of the mobile units. This ensures that the least amount of power is used, which limits the interference and allows the channels to be reused by another cell only 20 to 30 kilometers (12 to 19 miles) away.

The cells are interconnected with wire lines or microwave radio links. When a user leaves the coverage of one cell and enters another, the new cell provides continuing communications, a process called handoff. The cell system must determine which cell is most capable of picking up the user, acquire that user, and connect the user to the correct land line. All of this is invisible to the user.

The handoff process involves a number of algorithm*s using various data from the mobile telephone. First, every cell phone handset has a digital address that is continuously transmitted. Any cell site, or base station, can positively identify signals being received even though many of the received signals are not communicating with that cell site. Cell sites continually communicate with neighboring cell sites and compare the signal quality of the mobile units being received. If a particular mobile telephone unit has a superior signal in a neighboring cell site, the handoff process begins. This has to be done with care, as certain situations can cause a signal to fade temporarily in one site while improving at another, perhaps only for a few seconds. If a handoff is initiated prematurely, it will be necessary to quickly restore the mobile phone to the original cell site.

In addition to determining which cell site is capable of providing the best communications to the mobile phone, the computer system must also switch the land lines and keep a tally of the airtime for billing purposes.

Early cell telephone systems only allowed customers to use the system to which the user was a subscriber. Later, roaming, or using another company's cell system, was initiated. This came with very high prices and complicated billing procedures. As the cellular mobile phone system became financially successful, more cell sites were constructed, and now most of the continental United States has cell coverage. Proposed regulations would require the cell system to determine the location of a handset in emergencies. Agreements between cellular telephone companies simplified roaming, and a customer can now travel through much of the country with no loss of service. This is called a seamless system.

AMPS uses frequency modulation (FM), which is the same technology used in the very first mobile two-way radio in 1939. FM has performed well for many years but is inferior to many digital systems. These digital systems opened up the way for more sophisticated applications—especially non-voice communications such as paging, e-mail, and Internet services. Many mobile telephones became not just telephones but personal communications systems or PCSs. These include smartphones, which are phones that use operating systems, have applications, Web-browsing features, and more. The iPhone and Android helped to bring smartphones to a mass user base.

It is important for a global, seamless, wireless cell-phone system to have well thought-out standards to which users adhere. With the advent of the more sophisticated digital cell systems, a large number of new standards have appeared. These include a European standard, global system for mobile, code division multiple access, time division multiple access, and others. The complexity of modern handsets has increased because of the need to operate with a number of different standards. The modern cellular telephone is a sophisticated, cost-effective, and worldwide communications device and promises to become more capable in the future.

Additional Information

Since the beginnings of widespread cell phone use in the 1980s, there has been concern that cell phones might cause brain cancer or other harm. In the 1990s, a number of studies found no tendency for heavy cell phone users to get more brain cancers when compared to other people. However, critics pointed to the short-term nature of these studies, with an average period of cell phone use of only three years. In 2007 and 2008, the debate over cell phones and brain cancer revived when several scientific studies from Israel and Europe tracking 10-year cell-phone use were published. The studies found a correlation between certain rare head cancers and cell-phone use, with the cancers happening more often on the side of the head where the patients habitually held their cell phones. Many experts disputed the results, but others urged caution, especially with regard to children. Because children have thinner skulls than adults, more radio energy from a cell phone held to a child's ear is absorbed in the brain. The MRI 2009 American Kids Study found that 20 percent of children in the United States from the ages of 6 to 11 years of age own a cell phone, which was up from 11.9 percent in 2005. Of children from 10 to 11 years of age, over 80.5 percent owned a cell phone. In the early 2000s, cell-phone use was increasing rapidly among children under age 12, with 10.5 million pre-teen cell-phone users likely in the United States alone by 2010.

Another cell-phone health concern was the possible effect of cell-phone radio signals on brain function: a 2004 study published by the Institute of Electrical and Electronics Engineers found that radio waves from mobile telephones could modify both the waking and sleeping electrical activity of the human brain, with unknown consequences. Using a headset, which allows the phone's radio transmitter to be kept away from the head, is one way of reducing any possible risk from cell phone emissions. The National Cancer Institute (NCI) stated, in 2011, that, "Although there have been some concerns that radiofrequency energy from cell phones held closely to the head may affect the brain and other tissues, to date there is no evidence from studies of cells, animals, or humans that radiofrequency energy can cause cancer." The NCI also commented on the ongoing research being performed on cell phone use and cancer concerns: "The results of these studies have generally not provided clear evidence of a relationship between cell phone use and cancer, but there have been some statistically significant findings in certain subgroups of people."

Although a consistent relationship between cell phone use and cancer has not been established, concern for high-frequency cell phone use continues. The International Agency for Research on Cancer, a part of the World Health Organization, classifies radiofrequency fields as "possibly carcinogenic to humans," based on limited human studies. The American Cancer Society states that some cell-phone risk associated with cancer is possible, but evidence continues to be lacking for it to be considered causal (involving cause). The National Institute of Environmental Health Sciences states more research is necessary since current medical evidence does not support a conclusive relationship between cell phone use and adverse health problems. The U.S. agencies of the Centers for Disease Control and Prevention, the Federal Communications Commission and the Food and Drug Administration support the general consensus that "there is no scientific evidence that proves that wireless phone use can lead to cancer or to other health problems, including headaches, dizziness, or memory loss."

Besides medical problems, other concerns have also been raised concerning cell phone use. A major 2005 medical study found that driving while talking on a cell phone makes a driver four times more likely to be hospitalized by a traffic accident, and that headset use does not alter this statistic. As of 2011, the U.S. Department of Transportation (DOT) defines distracted driving as "any activity that could divert a person's attention away from the primary task of driving." Examples of distracted driving includes texting;

Making Communication Possible

Providing reliable communications for millions of subscribers from portable handsets is not a simple feat. Cellular technology uses sophisticated technologies to achieve this goal.

eating and drinking; talking to passengers; reading (including maps); using a navigational system; and adjusting a radio, CD player, or MP3 player. However, the DOT states that, "because text messaging requires visual, manual, and cognitive attention from the driver, it is by far the most alarming distraction." According to the Virginia Tech Transportation Institute (as reported by the DOT), text messaging is 23 times more likely to cause a collision than driving while not distracted; and sending or receiving a text message while driving takes the eyes of a driver off the road for an average of 4.6 seconds, which is equal to the length of a football field (91 meters/100 yards) while driving at 90 kilometers (55 miles) per hour.

 See also **Cell Phones • Networks • Telecommunications • Wireless Technology**

Resources

Books

Harte, Lawrence, and Steven, eds. *The Comprehensive Guide to Wireless Technologies.* Fuquay-Varina, NC: APDG Publishing, 2000.

Mishra, Ajay R. *Cellular Technologies for Emerging Markets: 2G, 3G, and Beyond.* Chichester, U.K.: Wiley, 2010.

Stetz, Penelope. *The Cell Phone Handbook: Everything You Wanted to Know about Wireless Telephony (But Didn't Know Who or What to Ask).* 2nd ed. La Vergne, TN: Lightning Source, 2006.

Web Sites

Distraction.gov, U.S. Department of Transportation. "What is Distracted Driving?" http://www.distraction.gov/content/get-the-facts/facts-and-statistics.html (accessed November 5, 2012).

National Cancer Institute. "Cell Phones and Cancer Risk." http://www.cancer.gov/cancertopics/factsheet/Risk/cellphones (accessed November 5, 2012).

PC Magazine. "PC Mag.com Encyclopedia." http://www.pcmag.com/encyclopedia_term/0,2542,t=Smartphone&i=51537,00.asp (accessed October 6, 2012).

Central Processing Unit

Computers exist as a collection of interrelated components functioning together under the control of a central processor known as the central processing unit (CPU). The CPU is responsible for manipulating data and coordinating the activities of the computer's other physical components, including memory and peripherals. Instructions gathered from

A teacher demonstrates to students how to clean internal components of a CPU. © *AP Images/Nikki Carlson.*

input interfaces are executed at the CPU, and the results delivered to output interfaces. The CPU, therefore, functions as the heart of the computer, facilitating all data processing activity.

The central processing unit is composed of several internal components needed to retrieve, store, and calculate data in a controlled fashion. Instructions enter the CPU from a computer's random access memory (RAM)* through the bus*. The bus is a grouping of wires that provide a physical medium for data transport between components. The instructions are decoded by the CPU's control unit, which interprets the data and sends control signals to the other components as appropriate. From here, instructions pass to the arithmetic logic unit (ALU), which performs calculations and other logical operations. The control unit and ALU depend on memory registers for the temporary storage of data and internal instructions. These registers, internal to the CPU, are similar to RAM but operate much faster and have far less storage capacity. They are used by the ALU to store calculated results until the end of an operation, and by the control unit to store instructions.

Computer instructions may be for data transfer, data manipulation, or program control. Data transfer instructions cause data to be moved between locations without affecting content, data manipulation instructions request arithmetic or logic operations from the ALU, and program control (branch) instructions facilitate decision operations. The control unit executes these instructions sequentially from consecutive memory locations. Each memory location is represented by a unique address, which permits a program counter to keep track of the last instruction executed. When the control unit retrieves an instruction, the program counter is incremented to reflect the next memory address. Unless the

* **random access memory (RAM)** a type of memory device that supports the nonpermanent storage of programs and data; so called because various locations can be accessed in any order (as if at random), rather than in a sequence (like a tape memory device)

* **bus** a group of related signals that form an interconnecting pathway between two or more electronic devices

* **binary** existing in only two states, such as "on" or "off," "one" or "zero"

* **bit** a single digit, 1 or 0—a contraction of Binary digIT; the smallest unit for storing data in a computer

* **Boolean algebra** a system developed by George Boole that deals with the theorems of undefined symbols and axioms concerning those symbols

* **vacuum tube** an electronic device constructed of a sealed glass tube containing metal elements in a vacuum; used to control electrical signals

* **transistor** a contraction of transfer resistor; a semiconductor device, invented by John Bardeen, Walter Brattain, and William Shockley, which has three terminals; can be used for switching and amplifying electrical signals

control unit is executing a branch instruction that alters this program counter value, that address will be the next instruction retrieved.

As noted earlier, the ALU performs arithmetic and logic operations. Basic arithmetic operations, like addition and subtraction, are performed by an arithmetic circuit; logic operations, such as AND, OR, and XOR (exclusive OR), are performed by a logic circuit. Like all components of the CPU, the ALU operates at the binary* level. AND, OR, and XOR are examples of Boolean operations, whereby bit*s are compared to produce a logical (yes or no) result. A better understanding of ALU operations may be gained through the study of Boolean algebra*.

Memory access is the slowest central processing operation; therefore memory registers are the most important components in determining the performance of a CPU. A register is a group of binary storage cells, or flip-flops, each capable of storing one bit of data. A CPU will often utilize large numbers of small registers because performance and capacity are inversely proportional, meaning that many small registers are faster than fewer larger registers. The smallest memory components are generally placed the closest to central processing components in order to optimize performance for the majority of processing operations.

A clock that sends repetitive pulses throughout the components of the CPU synchronizes all of these operations. Each clock pulse triggers an action—therefore, a CPU's performance can be measured by the frequency of clock pulses. The clock, however, must not exceed the performance of the registers or the CPU cannot function. The frequency of the clock is measured in Hertz (pulses per second).

Early CPUs were constructed from vacuum tube*s, which required a great deal of energy and physical space compared to modern construction. The Electronic Numerical Integrator and Computer (ENIAC), which became operational in 1945 using more than 18,000 vacuum tubes, is largely regarded as the first electronic computer. The transistor* was introduced in 1948, providing a smaller, faster, more efficient and reliable alternative to the vacuum tube. In 1956 the UNIVAC (Universal Automatic Computer) was completed, the first computer to incorporate a transistor-based CPU.

Development of the integrated circuit (IC), or computer chip, began in 1958 when Texas Instruments introduced a single piece of silicon containing multiple components. The integrated circuit provides the physical basis for today's microcomputers. In 1965 Gordon Moore made a prediction, now known as Moore's Law, that the number of transistors contained on a computer chip would double every year. In fact, the number of transistors integrated onto a single chip has doubled about every eighteen months over recent years. The first ICs had less than one hundred transistors, as opposed to the more than eight million transistors now common on a single chip. Continually improving methods in IC manufacturing have led to larger numbers of smaller components, which have in turn led to faster processing.

In 1967 Fairchild Semiconductor introduced an IC that contained all of the ALU functions, but required additional circuitry to provide register storage and data control. Intel Corporation introduced the first fully functioning microprocessor in 1971. The Intel 4004 was capable of four-bit arithmetic operations and was used in a number of handheld calculators.

The 4.77 MHz sixteen-bit Intel 8086 was introduced seven years later, becoming the first generation of the popular x86 series of microprocessors and the basis for the personal computer. This line of microprocessors, including the 80286 (286), 386, 486, and Pentium (586), has evolved to include a robust complement of digital components integrated within the same IC that contains the basic CPU. In 2001 Intel introduced the 32-bit Pentium IV with a clock speed of 1.5 GHz, or 1.5 billion pulses per second. In 2010, IBM introduced the zEnterprise z196, with a system running at 5.2 GHz, and containing a processor with a four-core chip with 1.4 billion transistors. At that point, it was the world's fastest microprocessor.

The integration of CPU and other computer functions on the same microprocessor chip has blurred the distinction between a computer and its CPU. It is not uncommon for computer users to refer to their entire system by the name of its CPU—a practice that is not unfounded since the architecture of a CPU largely determines every other peripheral the computer can support.

 See also **Intel Corporation • Microchip**

Resources

Books

Mano, M. Morris. *Computer Systems Architecture.* 2nd ed. Rockville, MD: Prentice Hall, 1982.

Sclater, Neil. *McGraw-Hill Electronics Dictionary.* New York: McGraw Hill, 1997.

Web Sites

IBM "IBM to Ship World's Fastest Microprocessor" www-03.ibm.com/press/us/en/pressrelease/32414.wss (accessed October 7, 2012)

Moore's Law

Gordon Moore voiced his now famous law in 1965 when he predicted how quickly computer chip technology would advance. He asserted that the number of transistors that could be contained on an integrated circuit would double each year. He was right. It was not until 1995 that Moore revised his projection. Now the number doubles approximately every 18 months to two years. With advances in transistor technology, notably the invention of the molecular transistor, Moore's Law is apt to change once again.

Client/Server Technology

Client server technology (CST), or also called client/server technology, is a term used for a network of distributed or shared computing systems in which the operations, and therefore the computing power, are divided between the clients and the computer servers. That is, software programs (servers) process and store data that is commonly used for and assessed by its users (clients). For example, Web server programs are responsible

* **supercomputer** a very high performance computer, usually comprised of many processors and used for modeling and simulation of complex phenomena, like meteorology

* **input/output (I/O)** used to describe devices that can accept input data to a computer and to other devices that can produce output

* **bus** a group of related signals that form an interconnecting pathway between two or more electronic devices

* **ubiquitous** to be commonly available everywhere

for processing Web content through client software called Web browsers such as Chrome, Firefox, and Internet Explorer. Such a network allows for much more computing power, but the way it works can vary depending on how it is developed and set up.

More computing power can be brought to bear on a problem in three ways. The first way is to build a computer that has a very fast processor. This was the goal of many of the early supercomputer* efforts. The second way is to build a computer that has multiple processors working on different parts of some problem using shared memory, storage, and input/output (I/O)*. These parallel computing systems were the goal of many of the later efforts.

The third way to increase computing power dedicated to solving a problem is to use networks to link many separate computers working on different parts of the same problem. Each of the computers has its own processor, memory, storage, and I/O channels. They use a particular I/O channel—a network connection—to communicate and coordinate with each other.

Collectively, these systems are classified as distributed computing systems. The distinction between parallel and distributed computing is somewhat gray. Generally, a parallel computing system connects the cooperating components within a single system, or box. Distributed computing connects boxes over a network. However, as networks increase in speed, the communications between components comes close to the speed of communication over a slow internal bus*. As networks become ubiquitous* and reliable, the term network computing is frequently used synonymously with distributed computing.

A distributed computing system may be thought of as a loosely coupled parallel system. Although this is true, parallel systems are generally devoted to working on problems where many similar calculations are carried out in parallel by the various components. In distributed computing systems, it is more frequently the case that the various components are optimized for different kinds of functions, which are carried out through a sequential dialog. The dialog generally consists of a series of requests and responses. The dominant paradigm* for this kind of distributed computing system is the client/server model.

In the simplest model for a client/server system, one of the components, a server* process, is started on a given computer and runs in an endless loop waiting for a connection from a client*. The client process is started on another computer, and it makes a request, which is sent across the network and processed by the. A response is formulated. The response is then sent back to the client. The client may then disconnect from the or make another request. At some point, the client terminates its connection to the and the returns to a wait state listening for a connection from another client.

Network and application protocol*s are essential for client/server systems to work. A networking protocol, like a diplomatic protocol, simply defines the conventions that will be used in an interaction. Three classes of protocols are required. The first is an addressing protocol that allows one component to specify the other component with which it wishes to communicate. Although there are numerous addressing protocols, the dominance of the Internet has, for all practical purposes, made the Internet Protocol (IP) the de facto* addressing.

The second class of protocols applies to protecting the quality of networked communication. Since a message from one computer to another must be transmitted as a series of packets, there must be some agreement on what to do if a packet that is part of a message is lost or is corrupted. This protocol must also address how to put the packets back together at the destination should they arrive out of order.

This protocol also addresses issues of synchronization between the two sides—e.g., how many packets should be sent before waiting to see if they have arrived safely, and how long should the sender keep a record of sent packets in the event that one needs to be resent. There are many different ways that this exchange might be managed, but again, the dominance of the Internet has made the Transmission Control Protocol (TCP) the dominant protocol for controlling communications quality.

Finally, the client and the server must have a protocol that governs the nature of the dialog in which they will engage. This third type of protocol defines the nature of the relationship between the client and the server. The names of some of these protocols are well known even if the underlying nature of the dialog they define is not. The relationship between World Wide Web browsers and Web servers is defined by the HyperText Transfer Protocol or HTTP. The process by which files are transferred is defined by the File Transfer Protocol or FTP. The exchange of mail is defined by the Simple Mail Transfer Protocol, or SMTP. These protocols are defined as standards.

* **paradigm** an example, pattern, or way of thinking

* **server** a computer that does not deal directly with human users, but instead handles requests from other computers for services to be performed

* **client** a program or computer often managed by a human user that makes requests to another computer for information

* **protocol** an agreed understanding for the sub-operations that make up a transaction, usually found in the specification of inter-computer communications

* **de facto** as is

Client/Server Paradigms

The preceding section described a simple model for a client server interaction, where a server accepts a connection from a single client, handles the exchange, and then closes the connection to wait for a new one. This is called an iterative* client server model. It is also possible for the server to be constructed to handle multiple requests simultaneously. This model is called a concurrent* client server model.

If the server program is running on a machine with a single processor, it is not really possible to handle requests concurrently. The use of the term concurrent here refers to the overall handling of connections between the clients and the server. In a concurrent model, the server creates copies of the main process. Each copy is dedicated to handling the request from a single client, with the original process returning immediately to listen for additional connections. Depending on the nature of the interaction between the client and the server, this design may be more or less efficient than the iterative design.

For example, if the connection between the client and the server consists of a single request and response, and if the processing of the request by the server is very efficient and quick, the overhead of creating a copy of the server process and then of shutting it down will make the handling of requests less efficient. However, if the exchange between the client and the server involves multiple requests and responses and if the client is operating in conjunction with human input, the server will spend a lot of time waiting for the client to make a request and very little of its time actually handling the request. In this case, the multitasking* capability of the operating system can be used to shift back and forth between the various server processes, handling the requests from the various clients in a timely fashion. Thus, from the point of view of the clients, the server is handling the various requests concurrently.

Other client/server model variations involve the preallocation of server processes such that there are multiple copies of the server listening for a request at the same address. Each request is processed iteratively by one of the servers, but multiple processes can be running in parallel handling these requests. This is the model most frequently employed by Web servers.

It is also possible to design a server that will open multiple connections to a number of different clients. The one server then checks and handles communications from all of these clients in some round-robin fashion. This model is frequently used for applications like chat rooms, where the information presented by one client is then broadcast to all the clients.

Client/server systems may be chained or linked with a server to one client being a client to another server. Additionally, a client may simultaneously connect to multiple servers for different services. As an example of the first model, consider a client that makes a connection to a server to process a purchase order. The server may understand all the rules about who may make orders, and how an order is to be processed, but the actual recording of the order may be handled by another process that would place the order into a database.

* **iterative** a procedure that involves repetitive operations before being completed

* **concurrent** pertaining to simultaneous activities, for example simultaneous execution of many computer programs

* **multitasking** the ability of a computer system to execute more than one program at the same time; also known as multiprogramming

This is the model for most three-tier client server systems. The client handles the user interface that processes requests to a middleware server. This intermediate server applies rules and checks on the data. When satisfied, the middleware server makes a connection as a client to another server, which controls a database. The database server is only responsible for storing the data, assuming that the middleware server has done the necessary checking.

More Sophisticated Models for Clients and Servers

Over the years, it has become clear that the process of defining protocols for clients and servers is a difficult task, and not fully consistent with modern programming techniques. In addition, the process of locating the address at which a server is listening for clients has become more complicated as the number of client/server applications has grown.

These and other problems associated with client/server design and implementation have been addressed by new layers of protocols. The most well-known of these is the Remote Procedure Call (RPC) protocol, which was developed to insure protocol consistency between pairs by automating much of the basic structural code, and by establishing a mechanism for registration and finding of server processes through a shared directory service. While RPC worked for procedural languages, a model was also needed for object-oriented programming languages. Remote Method Invocation (RMI) fills this need in a similar fashion.

Beyond these efforts, more recent developments include mechanisms for standardizing more of the basic functionality of the interaction, allowing for servers to be located across multiple machines, and for managing the various services that are running. These models, generally classified as distributed application servers, include the Common Object Request Broker Architecture (CORBA), Distributed Component Object Model (DCOM), JavaSpaces and JINI, and E'Speak, to name a few.

CST is sometimes divided into two functional categories: thin CST (TCST) and fat CST (FCST). TCST is defined as a computer or computer program that depends primarily on some other computer (server) for its computations, while FCST computers and programs do not have such a high dependence. TCST was developed after FCST primarily due to high costs for upgrading fat computers and programs, along with their increasingly high cost for maintenance. These fat systems often became complicated, and in computer lingo, they were often described as bloated; hence the name fat. Consequently, thin systems may consist of only a simple computer that heavily or totally relies on the server for its processing ability, use of its applications, and most other facets to perform its duties.

Design Issues

Client/server systems endeavor to optimize per-problem performance, multiple-problem throughput, and reliability, among other things. New problems arise for the programmer, however, because techniques used for writing stand-alone serial programs often fail when they are applied to distributed programs.

Computer Sciences, 2nd Edition

data partitioning a technique applied to databases (but not restricted to them) that organizes data objects into related groups

task partitioning the act of dividing up work to be done so that it can be separated into distinct tasks, processes, or phases

parallel debugging specialized approaches to locating and correcting errors in computer programs that are to be executed on parallel computing machine architectures

synchronization the time domain ordering of events; often applied when events repeatedly occur simultaneously

bandwidth a measure of the frequency component of a signal or the capacity of a communication channel to carry signals

In building a system, the programmer must address a variety of issues such as data partitioning*, task partitioning*, task scheduling, parallel debugging*, and synchronization*. In addition, the programmer has to understand that interconnection bandwidth* and message latency dominate the performance of distributed and parallel systems. There is no clear-cut way to predict what the performance of a new system will be. Therefore, it is difficult to predict what the benefits of a distributed or parallel system will be prior to an investment of time and effort. Finally, the design of the server in a client/server system requires particular attention to a number of issues, including process synchronization, global state, reliability, distributed resource management, deadlock, and performance evaluation.

 See also **Assembly Language and Architecture • Information Technology Standards • Networks • Operating Systems**

Resources

Books

Acharya, Vivek. *TCP/IP and Distributed System.* New Delhi: Firewall Media, 2008.

Elmasri, Ramez, and Shamkant B. Navathe. *Fundamentals of Database Systems.* Boston: Pearson/Addison Wesley, 2007.

Kshemkalyani, Ajay D., and Mukesh Singhal. *Distributed Computing: Principles, Algorithms, and Systems.* Cambridge: Cambridge University Press, 2008.

Mahajan, Sunita, and Seema Shah. *Distributed Computing.* New Delhi: Oxford University Press, 2010.

Web Sites

Biohealthmatics.com. "Thin Client/Server Technology (TCST)." http://www.biohealthmatics.com/technologies/networks/thinclient.aspx (accessed September 27, 2012).

Miller School of Medicine, University of Miami. "Clients and Servers." http://it.med.miami.edu/x1057.xml (accessed September 27, 2012).

Codes

A building block of computer programming, codes are a way for people and technology to transmit messages using characters. The first widely used character code was the Morse Code, developed in 1838 by Samuel F. B. Morse (1791–1872). This two-symbol, dot-and-dash code is capable of representing the characters of the alphabet by varying the

▲
Conference participants review lines of code on a laptop. © *Adam Berry/Getty Images.*

* **bit** a single binary digit, 1 or 0—a contraction of Binary digIT; the smallest unit for storing data in a computer

number of symbols between one and four. If one considers the symbols to be similiar to bit*s, then the number character set, 0 to 9, uses 1 to 5 bits.

In 1874 Jean-Maurice Émile Baudot (1845–1903) received a patent for a printing telegraph. He also introduced a code using 5 bits per character. Five bits can be combined in 32 different ways, enough for uppercase letters and a few control characters. To include the number set, Baudot devised a shift to another level, much as the Cap Lock on a keyboard. The shift provides the number set, punctuation symbols, and control character representations for the 32 separate, 5-bit combinations. The control characters include the carriage return and the line feed. All the control characters are present in either letter or figure shift mode. The letters were in the lower shift mode and the figures in the upper shift mode. Early teletype machines punched the messages into paper tapes and read tapes to send messages. Later, machines were designed to print out the messages in character form. Some teletypes for the hearing impaired in use today are based on the Baudot code.

Early computers used a version of Baudot's code called ITA$_2$ a 6-bit code that had more control and format characters in addition to the uppercase letter and the ten numeric characters. The increase to 6 bits, or 64 combinations, eliminated the need for the shift control to switch from letter to numeric characters. There was no urgency to improve the character code by adding lowercase letters and more punctuation symbols, as computers were considered calculation machines. By the late 1950s, computers were used more widely for commercial purposes. The variation in the control character set from system to system was a drawback. The American Standards Association (ASA) developed a standardized code. The ASA was composed of various corporations, including IBM, AT&T, and an AT&T subsidiary, Teletype Corporation—manufacturer of the most widely used communications equipment at that time. The ASA underwent reorganizations and renaming in the 1960s, and is now known as the American National Standards Institute (ANSI).

In 1963 the first version of American Standard Code for Information Interchange (ASCII) was introduced. IBM waited until the 1980s to use it, while AT&T's immediate acceptance of it made ASCII the standard for communications. This new code was based on 7 bits, allowing for 128 characters in the character code table. This initial version did not have a lowercase letter set. It did include all the COmmon Business-Oriented Language (COBOL) graphics characters based on the earlier FIELDATA code used by the military, added more control characters such as a linefeed, and simplified some of the transmission control codes. Collating problems were solved by separating the number set from the letter set in the table, and ordering the letter set to allow collating by letter using simple arithmetic comparisons.

The next version of ASCII in 1967 included the lowercase letter set, FORmula TRANslation (FORTRAN) graphics characters, square bracket, curly braces, and others. Control character changes were made and a small set of international characters was added. The control characters were relocated in the first half of the table. This version of ASCII remained the standard for thirty years.

Meanwhile, back at IBM, a different character code came into use. Why? Perhaps because the origin of IBM goes back to Herman Hollerith (1860–1929), the punched card* and the 6-bit character code. The early IBM mainframes used a 6-bit character code, or Binary Coded Decimal Interchange Code (BCDIC). In 1964 a proprietary* code, Extended Binary Coded Decimal Interchange Code (EBCDIC), was created for use on IBM/360 mainframe* computers. This 8-bit code was an extension of the earlier code. It included most of the characters in the ASCII code but with differing bit-string representations. For example, the ASCII representation of M is 01001101; the EBCDIC representation of M is 11010100.

Multiple versions of EBCDIC character code sets had to be created as the mainframe market spread throughout the world. Another difficulty arose when translating from or into ASCII. Because there was a difference in the character sets, the translation was slow and error-prone. The general trend is to convert EBCDIC data files into ASCII or other non-proprietary code formats.

In the 1980s, the growth of international business generated interest in a multilingual character code. The International Organization for

Standardization (ISO) and a group of American computer firms started work on methods to produce a universal character code set. Unicode, which gives a unique number to each character, resulted from merging the two efforts. Unicode is supported by multiple industries and companies ranging from Apple Computer, Inc., IBM Corporation, and Hewlett Packard to Oracle, Microsoft Corporation, and Sun Microsystems. It is supported by multiple operating systems and browsers. Unicode is capable of transporting data through many platforms without data corruption.

The ever-evolving Unicode standard is controlled by the Unicode Consortium, which is a non-profit organization dedicated to the promotion, development, and maintenance of international code and software standards. The standard specifies the codes representing the various characters employed by every major language currently in use. According to the Unicode Consortium, Unicode Version 6.1 (which was the standard as of late 2012) provides for a character code set consisting of 110,181 characters. That code set encompasses all of the world's presently-used alphabets, as well as many other types of character sets such as symbol collections (for instance, sets of mathematical symbols). As of October 2012, Unicode, Inc. was releasing Unicode 6.2.

▶ See also **Binary Number System • Coding Techniques • Generations, Languages**

Resources

Web Sites

Unicode, Inc. "The Unicode Standard: A Technical Introduction" http://www.unicode.org/standard/principles.html# (accessed October 31, 2012)

Coding Techniques

Representation of information is a fundamental aspect of all communication, from bird songs to human language to modern telecommunications. In the case of digital storage and transmission of information, mathematical analysis has led to principles that drive the design of symbolic representations. For example, it has let a binary code* be defined as a mapping from a set of source symbols, or source *alphabet*, to unique bit strings. A familiar example is the standard American Standard Code for Information Interchange (ASCII) code in which each character from a standard keyboard is represented as a 7-bit sequence.

ASCII is an example of a *block code*, where each symbol is represented by a fixed-length "block" of n bit*s. Given a number of symbols (K) to encode in binary form, a number of bits (n) is chosen such that there are

ISO

The International Organization for Standardization (ISO) began work in 1947. Founded in Geneva, Switzerland, its goal is to create standards to be used in technical and nontechnical fields. For example, it works on issues pertaining to language, measurement, parts and components, and procedures and methods. More than 100 countries belong to the ISO.

* **binary code** a representation of information that permits only two states, such as "on" or "off," "one" or "zero"

* **bit** a single binary digit, 1 or 0—a contraction of Binary digIT; the smallest unit for storing data in a computer

Table 1. The 7-Bit ASCII Code
Reproduced by permission of Gale, a part of Cengage Learning.

TABLE 1. THE 7-BIT ASCII CODE

Symbol	Code	Symbol	Code	Symbol	Code	Symbol	Code
NUL	0000000		0100000	@	1000000	`	1100000
SOH	0000001	!	0100001	A	1000001	a	1100001
STX	0000010	"	0100010	B	1000010	b	1100010
ETX	0000011	#	0100011	C	1000011	c	1100011
EOT	0000100	$	0100100	D	1000100	d	1100100
ENQ	0000101	%	0100101	E	1000101	e	1100101
ACK	0000110	&	0100110	F	1000110	f	1100110
BEL	0000111	'	0100111	G	1000111	g	1100111
BS	0001000	(	0101000	H	1001000	h	1101000
TAB	0001001	)	0101001	I	1001001	i	1101001
LF	0001010	*	0101010	J	1001010	j	1101010
VT	0001011	+	0101011	K	1001011	k	1101011
FF	0001100	,	0101100	L	1001100	l	1101100
CR	0001101	-	0101101	M	1001101	m	1101101
SO	0001110	.	0101110	N	1001110	n	1101110
SI	0001111	/	0101111	O	1001111	o	1101111
DLE	0010000	0	0110000	P	1010000	p	1110000
DC1	0010001	1	0110001	Q	1010001	q	1110001
DC2	0010010	2	0110010	R	1010010	r	1110010
DC3	0010011	3	0110011	S	1010011	s	1110011
DC4	0010100	4	0110100	T	1010100	t	1110100
NAK	0010101	5	0110101	U	1010101	u	1110101
SYN	0010110	6	0110110	V	1010110	v	1110110
ETB	0010111	7	0110111	W	1010111	w	1110111
CAN	0011000	8	0111000	X	1011000	x	1111000
EM	0011001	9	0111001	Y	1011001	y	1111001
SUB	0011010	:	0111010	Z	1011010	z	1111010
ESC	0011011	;	0111011	[	1011011	{	1111011
FS	0011100	<	0111100	\	1011100	|	1111100
GS	0011101	=	0111101	]	1011101	}	1111101
RS	0011110	>	0111110	^	1011110	~	1111110
US	0011111	?	0111111	_	1011111	α	1111111

Table 2. Morse code *Reproduced by permission of Gale, a part of Cengage Learning.*

TABLE 2. MORSE CODE

Symbol	Code	Symbol	Code	Symbol	Code
A	.-	N	-.	0	-----
B	-...	O	---	1	.----
C	-.-.	P	.--.	2	..---
D	-..	Q	--.-	3	...--
E	.	R	.-.	4	....-
F	..-.	S	...	5	.....
G	--.	T	-	6	-....
H	....	U	..-	7	--...
I	..	V	...-	8	---..
J	.---	W	.--	9	----.
K	-.-	X	-..-	period	.-.-.-
L	.-..	Y	-.--	comma	--..--
M	--	Z	--..		

enough binary patterns of that length to encode all *K* symbols. With *n* bits, 2^n unique strings exist, and so we choose the smallest integer *n* that satisfies $K < 2^n$. Thus a 3-bit code can represent up to eight symbols, a 4-bit code can be used for a set of up to 16 symbols, etc.

Because of its universal use, the ASCII code has great advantages as a means of storing textual data and communicating between machines. On the face of it, the ASCII design seems perfectly reasonable. After all, a common language is central to communication. However, ASCII lacks certain properties desirable in a code. One of these is *efficiency* and the other is *robustness*.

Efficiency

Knowledge of symbol probabilities can be exploited to make a code more efficient. Morse code, the system of dots and dashes used for telegraph transmission in the early days of electric communication, made use of such knowledge. By representing the more frequent letters in common English with shorter dash-dot sequences, the average time to transmit a character is reduced in a message whose character statistics are consistent with the assumed frequencies.

Robustness

A principle of redundancy underlies the design of *error correcting codes.* By using more bits than are actually required to represent a set of symbols uniquely, a more robust code can be generated. If the code is designed such that any two legal codewords differ in at least 3 bits, then the result of "flipping" the value of any bit (that is, converting a 1 to a 0 or vice versa) will result in a string that remains closer to the original than it is to any other codeword. Similarly, if the minimum distance is 5 bits, double errors can be reliably corrected, with a 7-bit minimum distance, triple errors can be corrected, etc. A very simple illustration of this principle is the case of two symbols. In each of the four codes in Table 4, the symbol *A* is represented by a set of 0s, and B is represented by a block of 1s. For codes of increasing blocksize, more errors can be tolerated. For example, in the case of the 5-bit double-error correcting code, the received sequence 10100 would be interpreted as an *A*.

The codes noted in Table 4 are *inefficient*, in that they require many bits per symbol. Even the single error correcting code in Table 4 uses three times as many bits than are necessary without error correction. Much more efficient error-correcting codes are possible. The code in Table 5 is an example of a family of codes developed by Richard Hamming. It is a representation of a set of 16 symbols using 7 bits per symbol. While 4 bits would be sufficient to represent each of the symbols uniquely, this 7-bit code designed by Hamming guarantees the ability to correct a single bit error in any 7-bit block. The Hamming code is designed such that any two codewords are different in at least 3 bits. Hence, if one bit is altered by a storage or transmission error, the resulting bit string is still closer to the original codeword

TABLE 3. TWO CODES ON FOUR SYMBOLS

Symbol	Probability	Code I	Code II
a	0.5	00	0
b	0.25	01	10
c	0.125	10	110
d	0.125	11	111
Average Length		2	1.75

Table 3. Two Codes on Four Symbols
Reproduced by permission of Gale, a part of Cengage Learning.

TABLE 4. SIMPLE ERROR CORRECTING CODES

Symbol	Unique encoding	Single error correcting	Double error correcting	Triple error correcting
A	0	000	00000	0000000
B	1	111	11111	1111111

Table 4. Simple Error Correcting Codes
Reproduced by permission of Gale, a part of Cengage Learning.

TABLE 5. A 7-BIT HAMMING CODE

Symbol	Codeword	Symbol	Codeword
A	0000000	I	1000101
B	0001011	J	1001110
C	0010110	K	1010011
D	0011101	L	1011000
E	0100111	M	1100010
F	0101100	N	1101001
G	0110001	O	1110100
H	0111010	P	1111111

▲

Table 5. A 7-Bit Hamming *Reproduced by permission of Gale, a part of Cengage Learning.*

Efficient and Robust

Binary codes for storing and transmitting information can be designed to optimize either efficiency or robustness to noise.

* **twisted pair** an inexpensive, medium bandwidth communication channel commonly used in local area networks

than it is to any of the other 15 symbols. Thus, this code is robust to single errors. Note that if two errors occur in the same block, the code fails.

Conclusion

The primary framework for symbolic representation of information is human language, which has evolved over a period spanning more than 100,000 years. But only the past century has seen the application of mathematical principles to the design of encoding schemes. In combination with high-speed electronic signal transmission, the result is a system that enables communication with efficiency, reliability, and range that would have been inconceivable a few generations ago. Ongoing improvements in high-density magnetic and optical storage media have brought about a tremendous reduction in the physical space required to store information, thus amplifying the utility of these recently developed encoding techniques.

 See also **Bell Labs • Binary Number System • Codes**

Resources

Books

Gallager, Robert G. *Principles of Digital Communication.* Cambridge, UK: Cambridge University Press, 2008.

Communication Devices

The versatility of a computer is enhanced considerably if it can communicate with other computers or a number of users. The very first computers were large machines that occupied an entire room with a control console at the center. The input and output devices for these machines were located at that console and only one user could operate the machine at a time. However, not long after the first computers were made, engineers realized that it would be more efficient if users could access the machine from their desks via a terminal. This was the beginning of the mainframe computer, and some of the first communications devices in the computer industry.

The key to a mainframe computer was a communications network that would allow users to link to the machine. The terminals had no computing power themselves, but were connected to the mainframe computer via copper wire, sometimes called twisted pair*. As computers became larger and faster, developers realized that computing time could be sold to other companies or offered to other offices of the same company. This necessitated gaining access to the computer via long distance communication. In the beginning, during the late 1950s and 1960s, the only available long distance communications device was the telephone line.

However, telephonic communications were designed for voice transmission, while computers require data transmission. Computer data

cannot be applied to a telephone line directly but must be transformed into a signal that is compatible with the telephone system. To enable this compatibility, a signal, usually a sine or cosine function called a carrier, is modulated or modified in some way. This is done via a modulator—a device that produces a signal that can be handled by the telephone system without undue distortion, and without the modulated signal interfering with the operation of the telephone system.

On the receiving end, the modulated signal must be demodulated in order to retrieve the digital data. For two-way communications, the computer must be equipped with a modulator for outgoing data and a demodulator for incoming data. This device is now known as a modem*, a term that was derived from the combination of MOdulator and DEModulator.

The first computer modems modulated the carrier signal by changing the frequency of the sine or cosine function. The frequency of a carrier is the rate at which it repeats. For example, if the function repeats 1,000 times each second, its frequency is 1,000 Hertz or 1,000 Hz, where hertz is the International System of Units (SI) unit of frequency that is defined as the number of cycles per second of any periodic activity. A modem can have two distinct frequencies, called tones, at 1,200 and 2,200 Hz, where 1,200 Hz represents a mark and the 2,200 Hz represents a space. In the early days, the modem would shift between these two frequencies, a method of modulation called frequency shift keying (FSK). This technology was already in place before the invention of computers and was used for teleprinters, better known by their brand name, Teletype machines. It was therefore easy to attach a logic one or zero to the mark and space respectively and use the modem to transmit digital data.

The speed of the modem is expressed in baud, named after French engineer and inventor Jean-Maurice-Émile Baudot (1845–1903), who

modem the contraction of MOdulator DEModulator; a device that converts digital signals into signals suitable for transmission over analog channels, like telephone lines

Computer Sciences, 2ⁿᵈ Edition

* **digital subscriber loop (DSL)** the enabling of high-speed digital data transfer over standard telephone cables and systems in conjunction with normal telephone speech data

invented the fixed-length teleprinter code in 1874. This code was the model on which many computer codes were configured. In modern terminology, baud represents bits per second.

The first computer modems were very slow, at 300 baud. However, the computer input/output devices were Teletype machines, which could not print any faster than 100 baud. When electronic terminals appeared, the 300 baud modem became a major bottleneck, and the speed of the FSK modem (short for frequency shift keying) was increased to 1200, 2400, 4800 and later 9600 baud. Increasing the speed of modems beyond 9600 baud required a modulation scheme more sophisticated than the simple FSK.

Later modulation schemes use much more sophisticated techniques that vary the amplitude, angle, or combinations of both. In addition, improved encoding and error detection techniques are used. With the creation of the Internet, the need for even faster modems increased. The quality of the telephone line, which is the communications channel, now becomes the limiting factor for increased data rates. The highest data rate available from a commercial product for telephone line use is 56,000 baud, 56 kilobaud, or 56kB. When a communications channel is used at speeds beyond its limits, errors occur. These high-speed telephone modems automatically adjust the data rate downward when the errors increase.

Modems faster than 56kB require a higher capacity channel, which is available on cable television systems. The bandwidth of a telephone channel is about 3.5 kilohertz (kHz). In comparison, the bandwidth of one television channel is 6 megahertz (MHz). The cable television system is an inherently broadband system, making it possible to add high-speed data signals to the cable television system without interfering with existing television signals. In these cases as well, modems are used to perform exactly the same function they do when connected to a telephone line. Data rates vary but a typical cable modem data rate is more than 1 million baud, or 1 megabaud (MB).

Another high speed modem is the digital subscriber loop (DSL)* digital subscriber loop, better known as digital subscriber line (DSL). This system uses telephone wires, but not the telephone channel. Just as the cable modem connects to the cable television system while the normal television service is uninterrupted, DSL connects to the telephone system with no effect on normal telephone service.

Special equipment is required by the subscriber and the telephone company to multiplex computer data on the telephone line with normal telephone service. The only difference is that telephone wires being used for the DSL are incapable of being handled by any telephone equipment. Therefore, the digital signals must be separated at the point where the telephone wires enter the telephone network, which is usually a central office.

DSL uses telephone wires that were never intended to handle high speed data. Therefore, the digital signals are quickly reduced in strength, limiting the distance these signals can travel to the central office. Because of this limitation, some telephone customers, who are too distant from the central office, cannot obtain DSL. Other variations on DSL, which allow users to take advantage of the maximum distance and data rate, such as the asymmetric DSL (ADSL), are also available. This system has a higher speed down-link than up-link.

Wireless modems are also available with data rates up to several MB. Large private companies or other organizations usually own these systems. There have been some installations of public access wireless systems but the most common is the cellular telephone system. The most recent cellular telephone systems, called fourth generation or 4G, offer extensive data transmission capability. Fourth-generation transmissions allow Internet users to connect at significantly faster speeds than the previous third-generation (3G) service for their smartphones and other wireless devices. In 2010, the first wireless provider, MetroPCS Communications (headquartered in Richardson, Texas) began offering 4G Long Term Evolution (LTE) service. LTE is the precursor to full 4G cellular service. Since then, several tier-one U.S. companies such as Verizon Wireless began introducing LTE.

The highest performing data links are those based on fiber optics. These links offer data rates measured in the hundreds of MB. These systems are traditionally used within companies or industrial complexes because of their high costs. However, a fiber-optic infrastructure capable of delivering fiber to the home (FTH) is being developed as optical fiber (flexible, transparent fiber made usually of glass) becomes less expensive than electrical copper wires. In 2012, Google announced that it would offer fiber-optic Internet service to the residents of the metropolitan Kansas City area in Missouri and Kansas. Google's Fiber for Communities broadband service would cost $70 per month for service, which the company states is about 100 times faster than a basic cable modem.

 See also **Bridging Devices • Network Design • Network Topologies**

Resources

Books

Blahut, Richard E. *Modem Theory: An Introduction to Telecommunications.* Cambridge: Cambridge University Press, 2010.

Pachnicke, Stephan. *Fiber-optic Transmission Networks: Efficient Design and Dynamic Operation.* Berlin: Springer, 2012.

Web sites

Fox News. "Google Offers Ultra-fast Fiber-optic Internet in Kansas City for $70 a Month." http://www.foxnews.com/tech/2012/07/26/google-set-to-announce-ultra-high-speed-internet-service/ (accessed September 27, 2012).

True Value of Computers

The Internet is a household word. To most, the Internet is associated with computers and is not regarded as a communications system. But, the Internet has more to do with Teletype machines, FAX machines, telephones, and telegraphs than do computers. The value of many computers is based more on their ability to communicate than compute.

Compatibility (Open Systems Design)

Compatibility is the ability to connect things together and have them work, such as connecting a refrigerator to electrical power, a video recorder to a television, or a computer to a printer. Compatibility is an issue that is important in all branches of engineering, especially computer and software engineering. The standard solution to ensuring compatibility is the use of common, well-understood means of defining how to connect things together. These means are commonly called standards. The standards with which compatibility is concerned are the standards at the connection, or the interface*. The is the place where the two devices join, or communicate or interact.

Within any country (for example, the United States of America) a person can move from one house, take all of the electrical appliances, and plug them into the electrical system of another house with confidence that they will work without modification. This is true from city to city, from state to state; people can be assured that the appliances will work. This is because there is a common standard for the electrical interface throughout the U.S. The standard requires that the plugs and wall sockets have the same pins of the same shape, that the voltage is 120 volts (V), and the frequency is 60 hertz (Hz).

In fact, within most countries the electrical systems are built to conform to a common standard. Between countries, however, the standards are often different. The consequence is that very few appliances will work when one moves, for example, from the United States to Australia. One may say that the electrical power systems in the U.S. and Australia are not compatible.

Compatibility is important in the computer industry both on the software side and the hardware side. Hardware compatibility considers the compatibility of the hardware components within a particular

Audiologist Dr. Kurt T. Pfaff shows off a hearing aid that can be programmed with a computer and has Bluetooth compatibility. © *Craig Lassig/Bloomberg via Getty Images.*

* **interface** a boundary or border between two or more objects or systems; also a point of access

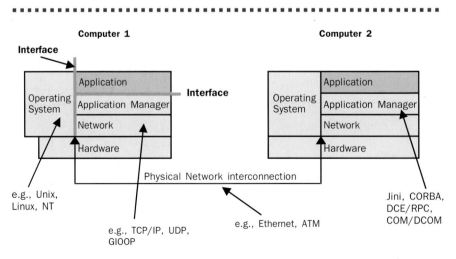

Figure A. *Reproduced by permission of Gale, a part of Cengage Learning.*

* **infrastructure** the foundation or permanent installation necessary for a structure or system to operate

computer's bus, central processing unit (CPU) architecture, motherboard, and operating system. Software compatibility refers to the compatibility of software when it operates on a particular CPU hardware architecture. Most of the time, software is only compatible with one CPU architecture system, while hardware is usually (but not always) compatible with many components. Further, even when hardware and (possibly) software are compatible with various systems, such ability does not mean that all operate equally well. Thus, compatibility has become a major issue in the computing industry. There are a few main suppliers of computer systems (e.g., Microsoft, Intel, Sun, and Apple) and many other companies wishing to supply software and hardware that is compatible with these main suppliers of computer systems. The early lack of compatibility between parts, or components, of computer systems led to the development of open systems. The interfaces of open systems are specified by freely available, publicly controlled standards. An example of a non-computer-specific open system is the electrical system within the United States.

Open systems developed because many organizations discovered that it was difficult to build large and complex computer systems economically and effectively during the 1970s and 1980s. One of the major problems facing large systems was the integration, or joining together, of subsystems to create the whole system. The underlying problem for these early systems was that the desired components were not compatible with each other. The components would not exchange information correctly, and it was difficult to move components from one system to another, in order to reuse components.

The birth of open computer-based systems came from the construction of reliable infrastructure*s, based on standards (see Figure A). This stylized representation shows the elements of an open system with the application sitting on top of the infrastructure. (To return to the electrical system example, the power network that runs throughout the U.S. is an infrastructure.) In a computer, the infrastructure is a computer program that manages the interfaces between components to help ensure that they interface, or interact, correctly.

A critical portion of the infrastructure is the network interface. The Internet is probably the best-known open system. Its development has only been possible because of the standards that exist for the network interface, and for the language used to present the pages on the screen of a user's computer.

Standards are critical to compatibility. Without an agreement shared between two or more component manufacturers that specifies standards for the interfaces, there would be no possibility of compatibility. The issue that arises is whether computer companies are prepared to allow these interface documents to become public, freely available standards. Computer and software companies are concerned that either they will lose money by not keeping the standard to themselves, or, that the bureaucracy of a public standard will destroy the product due to inertia.

Upgradability and portability are important outcomes of using standard infrastructures and open systems. The aim of upgradability is to

Transferring Information

For two systems to transfer information or to interact together, they must have some common basis. If they are hardware systems, then the wiring and the signals must be commonly defined.

Types of Compatibility

Products that effectively interact or transfer information between each other are compatible. A computer and a printer are compatible if information transferred between them results in a correctly printed page. Databases are said to be compatible if they can read each other's files. Products are also said to be compatible if they work within a particular computer system. Software is called Microsoft Windows compatible if it can work within the Microsoft Windows environment. Finally, products are called compatible if they can be substituted for other products—i.e., a personal computer in the past was called IBM-PC compatible if it can run the same software as a brand-name IBM-PC.

allow customers to buy a fast, new computer with the assurance that all of one's software will run on the new computer, or to upgrade a piece of software and have all the surrounding hardware work. That is, if customers upgrade their word processing software, their printers will still work correctly.

The aim of portability is to be able to move software from one computer (e.g., a Windows PC) to another computer (e.g., a Macintosh, or a Linux machine), and have the software work correctly. Standard infrastructures and open systems assist in making upgradability and portability happen because they ensure that the interfaces are managed, and that the manufacturers are aware of the interfaces because they are published as standards.

Manufacturers of computers and operating systems (such as Apple, Intel, and Microsoft) have an interest in compatibility, but not necessarily a commitment to public, freely available standards. Microsoft appears principally interested in having other manufacturers make hardware and software that is compatible with their operating systems. Apple appears to be principally interested in having other manufacturers make software (but not hardware) that is compatible with their operating systems. International Business Machines Corporation (IBM) and Hewlett-Packard (HP) appear to have embraced compatibility, and are focused on the construction of infrastructures as their core business. For the most part, traditional computer manufacturers who are now manufacturing infrastructures do not seem to be interested in open systems—as governed by public, freely available standards—but rather in controlled compatibility that allows them to protect their market niches.

▶ See also **Bridging Devices • Communication Devices • Information Technology Standards**

Resources

Books

Bertolotti, Ivan Cibrario, and Gabriele Manduchi. *Real-time Embedded Systems: Open-source Operating Systems Perspective.* Boca Raton, FL: CRC Press, 2012.

Web Sites

Carnegie Mellon Software Engineering Institute. "Open Systems: What's Old Is New Again." http://www.sei.cmu.edu/library/abstracts/presentations/2010-04-27-sstc-oberndorf-sledge.cfm (accessed September 27, 2012).

TechNewsDaily.com. "How to Fix Compatibility Problems on Your Computer." http://www.technewsdaily.com/237-how-to-fix-compatibility-problems-on-your-computer.html (accessed September 27, 2012).

Compilers

The compiler is a program that translates the source language (in the form of a written program), into machine code, the language of the machine. There are several portions to the compiler, some of the most prominent being the lexical analyzer*, the syntactic analyzer*, the registers, the code generation phase, and a code optimizer, which is optional. The generation of an intermediate code is also optional, but often done to facilitate the portability of the compiler to various machines.

The lexical analyzer finds the words of the source language. It is similar to a dictionary in a natural language such as English. It determines what symbols constitute words, and what types of word they are. In English, this includes words such as cat (N or Noun), ran (V or Verb), or the (Determinant). In programming languages, these are words like +-sign (+), identifiers (user-defined identifiers or variables), and keywords (while, for, read, print). The words are used to form sentences in programming language, such as while (a≤5) do....

The syntactic analyzer checks the form, or organization, of the sentences in programming languages. In other words, it checks to be sure the programming language's grammar is correct. For example, a sentence like "to the store he went" would be considered ungrammatical while "he went to the store" would be considered grammatical. In programming languages, the following statement would be considered grammatical:

```
for(j=0; j<MAXNUM;j+ +)
printf("%d",j);.
```

Compare this to the following statement, which is considered ungrammatical in a language such as C:

```
for(j=0; printf("%d", j);
j<MAXNUM; j+ +).
```

The syntactic analyzer receives the words and their respective types (number, constant, +-sign, keyword, identifier) from the lexical analyzer and sees that they are organized in the proper way according to the rules of the language. The organization, or syntax, of the language is defined by the grammar for the language.

Together, the lexical analyzer and syntactic analyzer determine whether or not a program is well-written. If it is, the code generator generates the code for the program. The code is specific to each type of machine the compiler will run on. An example would be the assignment statement:

```
c = a + b.
```

This adds the values of a and b, and places the result in c. This might be translated as:

```
movl a, R6
addl b, R6
movl R6, c.
```

lexical analyzer a portion of a compiler that is responsible for checking the program source code produced by a programmer for proper words and symbols

syntactic analyzer a part of a compiler that scans program source code ensuring that the code meets essential language rules with regard to structure or organization

* **central processing unit** the part of a computer that performs computations and controls and coordinates other parts of the computer

* **binary code** a representation of information that permits only two states, such as on or off, one or zero

* **mnemonic** a device or process that aids one's memory

This is read as:

"move the value of *a* into register 6"
"add the value of *b* to register 6"
"move the value of register 6 to *c*".

The registers are special locations in the central processing unit* where the arithmetic is done. The previous code is assembly language code. The compiler might also be written to generate machine code directly. This might look like:

70 52,6
72 54,6
70 6,56.

Here, the code 70 would stand for movl, 72 for addl, and 52, 54, and 56 are the addresses of a, b, and c, respectively. The 6 is register 6. Although the example is hypothetical, it is based on the machine language (binary code*) and assembly language (symbolic code) of a real machine, the VAX (Virtual Address eXtension) family of Digital Equipment Corporation. It is because the code is machine-dependent, based on the architecture and mnemonic* (symbols or symbolic language) of the machine, that the compiler must be written differently for different machines in this phase.

The lexical and syntactic analyzers are machine-independent. They base their decisions and actions on the grammar of the language being translated, such as C or Pascal. The code generation phase is machine-dependent. The code generated depends on the architecture of the machine.

A fourth phase that is often implemented is the intermediate code generation. This is a machine-independent code that can be used by the compiler writer to generate the machine code. An example might be:

Add A, B
Store C.

The first instruction indicates that one should add B to A, and the second indicates that the result should be stored in C. The use of the intermediate code allows for a machine-independent code to be optimized, with the final code being translated into the code of the machine.

The machine-independent phases are sometimes referred to as the front end of the compiler, and the final phase as the back end. The front end is the same for all machines, but the back end is machine-dependent. Thus, the front end, which comprises a good portion of the work, can be done once for all machines, while the back end is tailored specifically to the machine at hand. This allows the single compiler for a language, such as C, to be ported, or implemented, to many machines.

See also **Binary Number System • Early Computers • Procedural Languages**

Resources

Books

Cooper, Keith D., and Linda Torczon. *Engineering a Compiler.* Burlington, MA: Morgan Kaufmann, 2012.

Fischer, Charles N., Ron K. Cytron, and Richard J. LeBlanc, Jr. *Crafting a Compiler.* Boston: Addison-Wesley, 2010.

Mogensen, Torben. *Introduction to Compiler Design.* London: Springer, 2011.

Web Sites

Connexions, and Charles Severance and Kevin Dowd. "What a Compiler Does — History of Compilers." http://cnx.org/content/m33686/1.3/ (accessed October 1, 2012).

Slideshare.net and Hirdesh Vishwdewa. "How a Compiler Works?" http://www.slideshare.net/HrideshVishwdewa/how-a-compiler-works (accessed October 1, 2012).

Computer System Interfaces

Computers require a processing unit, some memory, perhaps secondary storage, and interconnecting bus* networks—but computers also need input/output (I/O)* devices. Computers are programmed to execute algorithm*s on data and then make the results of these computations available. If a user cannot supply data to the computer through input devices and then see how the algorithms operate on it through output devices, then the computer is ineffective.

What makes dealing with input and output devices sometimes problematic is that they differ so much in shape and form, and they tend to operate at speeds that are extremely slow compared to the central processing unit (CPU)*. Users prefer that the processor not be continually held up as it waits for tardy I/O devices to catch up with commands. A more satisfactory solution is to have the processor command the I/O devices to begin a lengthy operation of some sort and then busy itself with other activities while it waits for the slow I/O devices to complete their tasks. The I/O devices that are so necessary to make a computer system useful are connected to the rest of the computer by what are known as interface*s.

Strictly speaking, an interface is just a boundary or border line between two different objects. In the context of a computer system, an I/O interface is the physical dividing line between the computer system and its

* bus a group of related signals that form an interconnecting pathway between two or more electronic devices

* input/output (I/O) used to describe devices that can accept input data to a computer and to other devices that can produce output

* algorithm a rule or procedure used to solve a mathematical problem—most often described as a sequence of steps

* central processing unit (CPU) the part of a computer that performs computations and controls and coordinates other parts of the computer

* interface a boundary or border between two or more objects or systems; also a point of access

* **oscilloscopes** measuring instruments for electrical circuitry; connected to circuits under test using probes on leads and having small screens that display the signal waveforms

* **protocol** an agreed understanding for the sub-operations that make up a transaction, usually found in the specification of inter-computer communications

* **resistors** electrical components that slow the flow of current

I/O devices. In order for an interface to connect two pieces of equipment successfully, several requirements must be met. First, the physical interconnections must match—there must be compatible plugs, sockets, cables, and connectors. Beyond this, there must be electrical compatibility across the interface—the electrical signals must be of consistent voltage and current levels. These signals must also be traveling in the correct directions. Lastly, they must also obey timing constraints. This last requirement can be quite an obstacle in practice, as specialized measuring instruments like oscilloscopes* and logic analyzers are the only way to view the time domain characteristics of the electrical signals.

Fortunately, manufacturers of computer systems and input/output devices take care of much of the hard work. The manufacturers of all of the various pieces of equipment select an appropriate standard that is well documented and they build and test their equipment to this standard. The result is a guarantee that their products will inter-operate properly with others that are designed and built to meet the same standards.

Over time, various standards are introduced and adopted to facilitate all sorts of different interconnection schemes. Due to the underlying limitations of the technology, some common characteristics are present across these standards. For example, on a shared communication channel of some sort like a cable or bus, only one device can be permitted to be supplying (or transmitting) information at any one instant. This is because the electrical signals from two or more transmitters will clash, possibly resulting in component damage. Consequently, a standard that documents rules for managing an interface must include a definition of the rules of conversation between devices—otherwise known as a protocol*. Usually, specialized electrical devices are included within the computer system to guarantee that the protocol is adhered to. These devices are called arbiters, or I/O controllers.

One of the most popular standards has been the small computer systems interface (SCSI) standard. This has been used in a variety of personal computers as well as industrial computers. SCSI was originally developed to support the connection of mass storage devices to computer systems—these have traditionally been hard disks and tape drives, but more recently have included compact disc-read only memory (CD-ROM) and digital versatile disc-read only memory (DVD-ROM) drives. Each device with a SCSI interface is connected to a flat ribbon cable with fifty conducting wires. Up to eight SCSI interfaces can share the one cable, although they all cannot be using it at the same instant.

One aspect that often catches the unwary when using SCSI devices is that the last SCSI device attached to the cable must have some special resistors* installed on it. These resistors (often called terminating resistors) are needed to ensure that the electrical signals that pass along the cable are not reflected when they reach the end. If they are permitted to reflect, they can cause problems for the SCSI interfaces that might misinterpret them.

A modern alternative to the SCSI standard is that of the universal serial bus (USB), which permits simultaneous external connection of more than 100 input/output devices. The USB is connectable not only to mass storage devices but also to computer mice and to even more exotic devices like digital cameras, scanners, and games controllers. The USB standard has changed over time as each successive version has featured enhanced performance. The major USB protocol releases (there have also been minor releases in between the major releases) were USB 1.0 in 1996 that supported a data rate of up to 12 megabits per second (Mbit/s); USB 2.0 in 2000, supporting 480 Mbit/s; and USB 3.0 supporting a bit rate of nearly 5,000 Mbit/s, which is equivalent to 5 gigabits per second (Gbit/s)—the first consumer products with USB 3.0 capability were announced on January 5, 2010, at the Las Vegas (Nevada) Consumer Electronics Show, and subsequently released to the consumer.

The preceding descriptions involve the connection of input/output devices to the computer system, which primarily are external to the computer itself. Within the computer system though, the term interfacing takes on a more specialized meaning. It is also necessary to interface the processor to the various memory devices that it needs to access. In addition to this, the processor must be interfaced to various controller devices that manage bus networks internal to the computer.

The physical nature of the interface is usually less of an issue, mainly because the devices are expected to be placed on a printed circuit board, and copper tracks and plastic sockets can be laid out to suit the geometry of the components. However, the electrical and temporal characteristics must be correctly matched—just as before.

SCSI, USB, and other standards applicable to the connection of external devices are not really appropriate here, because those standards are intended for managing input/output devices that are slower in operation than the processor and usually involve comparatively large amounts of data. Instead, other standards are employed that permit high speed operation (at, or near, the natural operating speed of the processor) and usually smaller amounts of information in each transfer.

When the system designer is deciding how to interface networking devices to a processor, for example, then standards like the peripheral components interconnect (PCI) bus protocol might be used (or the more-recent PCI-X or PCI Express). Conversely, an interfacing standard like the accelerated graphics port (AGP) can be used when connecting a graphics device to a processor.

 See also **Central Processing Unit • Microcomputers**

Resources

Books

Patterson, David A., and John L. Hennessy*Computer Organization and Design: The Hardware/software Interface.* Amsterdam: Elsevier/ Morgan Kaufmann, 2012

Elaborate Input Devices

Whereas most users are comfortable with keyboards and conventional mouse pointing devices, there will also continue to be demand for more elaborate input devices. For instance, some companies offer specialized input devices like gloves that are directly connected to the computer. The gloves measure the movement of the user's hand and translate these movements into operations that allow the user to virtually pick up, for example, objects that he or she views on the screen or in a headset/ visor. There are also input devices, such as 3D mice, that can sense their orientation three-dimensionally when moved around by the user.

Web Sites

HowStuffWorks.com. "How USB Ports Work." http://computer. howstuffworks.com/usb.htm (accessed October 1, 2012).

National Aeronautics and Space Administration. "Cyberspace Monitoring System." http://www.nasaimages.org/luna/servlet/detail/NVA2~14~ 14~25059~124336:Cyberspace-Monitoring-System (accessed October 1, 2012).

PC Guide. "Small Computer Systems Interface (SCSI)." http://www. pcguide.com/ref/hdd/if/scsi/index-c.html (accessed October 1, 2012).

D

Design Tools

Computer programming is not easy. The programmer has to be able to think logically and know how to break down a big problem into tiny pieces. To accomplish this, some people like to state the problem and the steps necessary for its solution in their natural language before trying to code the program in a computer language. What they are doing is defining the correct algorithm*—giving the computer the information and process it needs to solve the problem. Writing the program becomes very easy after the has been spelled out. Since the most challenging step is defining the problem and the approach needed for its solution, there are several design tools available to help with this planning process. These include flowcharts, pseudocode, and Nassi-Shneiderman diagrams, which are used specifically with structured programs.

* **algorithm** a rule or procedure used to solve a mathematical problem—most often described as a sequence of steps

Flowcharts

A flowchart represents an algorithm using symbols instead of words. The step-by-step process is shown with lines, arrows, and boxes of different shapes demonstrating the flow of the process. Flowcharts are very useful in program development and provide excellent documentation. Because the steps needed for a solution have been defined, a flowchart can easily be translated into any computer language after it has been tested.

Any process can be articulated with these shapes and some connecting lines and arrows. One should note that the only symbol that allows two exits is the diamond-shaped decision symbol. It is used to indicate that the computer can take either of two paths depending on whether the comparison is true or false. All other flow chart symbols have only one exit line.

The symbols are usually read from top to bottom, and from left to right. Straight lines connect the symbols and represent how the algorithm advances from step to step. Their arrows are used to clarify the direction of flow. To complete the picture, brief instructions are written within each symbol to provide a more detailed description of the tasks represented by the symbols.

Some standard flowchart symbols and their meaning are shown in Figure 1. Flowcharts can be used to provide an overview of the major components of a program or to detail each of the processing steps within a program. Macro flowcharts outline the general flow of a program and are useful when dividing a complex problem into modules, especially

Figure 1. Some standard flowcharting symbols. *Reproduced by permission of Gale, a part of Cengage Learning.*

Start and Stop symbols are used to indicate the beginning and ending of programming modules

Input/Output symbols are used when data are to be read in or displayed

The decision symbol is used when there are branches to be taken depending on the result of a condition

A process symbol is used for any computation

Connectors are used to link different parts of a flowchart

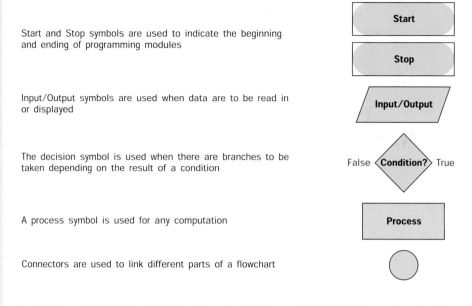

when implementing structured programming techniques. Detail, or micro flowcharts, depict the processing steps required within a particular module and often involve a one-to-one correspondence between flowchart symbols and program statements. Figure 2 shows a flowchart which

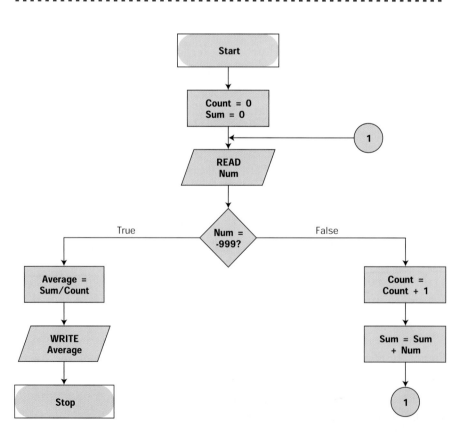

Figure 2. Example of a micro flowchart to compute the average of a list of numbers. *Reproduced by permission of Gale, a part of Cengage Learning.*

```
START
set counter to zero
set sum to zero
read first number
DO UNTIL number = –999
    add number to sum
    add one to counter
    read next number
ENDDO
divide sum by counter to get average
write average
END
```

Figure 3. Example of pseudocode to find the average of a list of numbers. *Reproduced by permission of Gale, a part of Cengage Learning.*

Picture This!

Flowcharts are sometimes called block diagrams or logical diagrams. Why were they developed? Because pictures are usually thought to be easier to understand than text.

computes the average of a list of numbers, in this example an input data value of −999 is used to stop the loop.

Pseudocode

Pseudocode is an English-like description of the processing steps to be performed in a program. The programmer writes these descriptions in the order in which corresponding program statements will appear in the program. Although there are no standards for pseudocode, it usually uses structured programming control structures.

For example, sequence structures are usually written in lowercase, while uppercase START and END are used to denote major blocks of code. In addition, IF, ELSE, ENDIF, DO WHILE and DO UNTIL are always in uppercase, and conditions are indented using lowercase.

The use of pseudocode allows the programmer to focus on the steps needed to perform a specific process without having to worry about how they should be stated in a computer language. Because pseudocode can be easier to update than a flowchart, it is preferred by some programmers. Figure 3 shows an example of a pseudocode used to set up the logic for finding the average of a list of numbers.

Nassi-Shneiderman Diagrams

These charts, an example of which is shown in Figure 4, also are called structured flowcharts or iteration diagrams. They were proposed by Isaac Nassi and Ben Shneiderman as an alternative to flowcharts to help programmers when planning structured programs. Each diagram corresponds to one of the programming control structures: sequence, selection and repetition. For example, a rectangular box is used for sequence, while an "L" or inverted "L" is used for repetition. As shown on page 57, Figure 4 illustrates these and other combinations being used for "if-then-else" and for multiple selections.

The outline of each Nassi-Shneiderman diagram is a rectangle and its subdivision always gives more rectangles that may be subdivided even further. Therefore, these diagrams can be nested within each other, modeling recursion, a feature of structured programming. Programmers like to work with these diagrams because they are easy to follow. They also feel that analyzing an algorithm is made easier because of the simplicity in which the logic is set forth.

All of these design tools can be used in combination to plan and develop accurate and efficient software. Other options may include CASE (computer-aided software engineering) tools, which automate many of the tasks required in developing a system, and structured walkthroughs, which help members of a programming team to review and evaluate the progress of modules in a structured project.

Computer Sciences, 2nd Edition

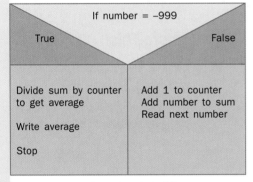

(a) Example of sequence

(b) Example of Do While

(c) Example of Do Until

(d) Example of For

(e) Example of decision

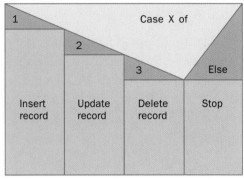

(f) Example of multiple decision (case)

Figure 4. Structured flowcharts. *Reproduced by permission of Gale, a part of Cengage Learning.*

▶ *See also* **Algorithms • Boolean Algebra • Programming**

Resources

Books

Stair, Ralph M., and George W. Reynolds. *Principles of Information Systems*, 10th ed. Boston: Course Technology, Cengage Learning, 2012.

Welburn, Tyler. *Structured COBOL: Fundamentals and Style.* 4th ed. New York: McGraw-Hill, 1995.

Periodical

Swirsky, Robert. "The Art of Flowcharting." *Popular Computing*, September 1982: 75–78.

Web Sites

University of Maryland. "A Short History of Structured Flowcharts (Nassi-Shneiderman Designs)." http://www.cs.umd.edu/hcil/members/bshneiderman/nsd/ (accessed November 5, 2012).

Digital Logic Design

Computers, and other digital systems, are designed using elementary electronic circuits called gates*. In this article, *Inverters, Or,* and *And gate*s are introduced by logical statements justifying the term "logic design." Then, the design procedure is illustrated, and integrated circuits* integrated circuits are discussed.

Gates

Gates are used to regulate electronic flow and to construct devices to process data, as well as to build memory devices. There are three fundamental gates: "And," "Or," and "Not". These fundamental gates can be combined to create "hybrid" gates such as "Nand" (Not-And) and "Nor" (Not-Or).

Not

Consider the logical statement: "The porch light is on ($Z = 1$) when I am *not* home ($A = 0$)." Z is the output; A is the input (I am home). A corresponding binary* function, of one variable* variable, which is also, is called "Complement" or "Not." "Not" is represented by "$Z = {\sim}A$" and its behavior is (see "Not" figure).

The electronic implementation of *Not* is the *inverter,* a one-transistor current amplifier with one input and one output. A high (binary-1) input voltage, typically about +5 Volts, forces current into the amplifier's input. So, the amplifier draws current from its output, pulling its output voltage low (binary-0), typically, close to 0 Volts. A 1 or high input gives a 0 output (the complement of the input). Since a low input voltage provides no current to the amplifier's input, the amplifier draws no current from its output, causing a high voltage there. A low or 0 input gives a 1 output. The output is the opposite or complement (Not) of the input.

Or

Consider the logical statement: "I wear a jacket ($Z = 1$) if it is cold ($A = 1$) *or* if it rains ($B = 1$) *or*..." A corresponding binary function, of two or more binary variables, is called "Or." The behavior of "Or" is tabulated for two and three variables (see "Or" figure).

....

A	Not-A (Z)
0	1
1	0

* **gates** fundamental building blocks of digital and computer-based electric circuits that perform logical operations; for example logical AND, logical OR

* **integrated circuits** circuits with the transistors, resistors, and other circuit elements etched into the surface of a single chip of semiconducting material, usually silicon

* **binary** existing in only two states, such as "on" or "off," "one" or "zero"

* **variable** a symbol, such as a string of letters, which may assume any one of a set of values known as the domain

◀ "Not" *Reproduced by permission of Gale, a part of Cengage Learning.*

AB	Or	ABC	Or
00	0	000	0
01	1	001	1
10	1	010	1
11	1	011	1
		100	1
		101	1
		110	1
		111	1

One or the other or both (or "all" three) of the inputs "on" cause the output to be true. A *Nor gate* is like an inverter, but with N input terminals instead of one. A high input voltage on any of the inputs causes a low output voltage and a low voltage on all inputs causes a high output voltage. Since "Nor" is the complement of "Or," "Or" is implemented in electronics by a "Nor-Not" tandem, giving "Not-Not-Or", or "Or." But, "Nor" has another application.

Consider a pair of two-input "Nor" gates, and let the output of each gate be one of the other gate's inputs. Label the unused inputs as S and R, and assume both these inputs are low. A positive pulse on S causes the corresponding "Nor" gate's output to go low. Since both inputs to the other gate are now low, its output is high. The pair of gates remains in this state even after the pulse on S returns to 0. Similarly, a positive pulse on R causes the output of R's "Nor" gate to go low. Since both inputs to S's gate are low, its output is high. The pair of gates now remains in this opposite state even after the pulse on R returns to 0. This pair of cross-connected "Nor" gates is called a "Set-Reset Flip-Flop" and it is the basic binary storage element used throughout digital design. The memory element is a 1 if S (Set) is 1, 0 if R is 1, and stays at the previous state if R and S are both 0 (R and S cannot both be 1).

AB	And		ABC	And
00	0		000	0
01	0		001	0
10	0		010	0
11	1		011	0
			100	0
			101	0
			110	0
			111	1

"And" *Reproduced by permission of Gale, a part of Cengage Learning.*

And

Consider the logical statement: "I wear a hat ($Z = 1$) when it is cold ($A = 1$) *and* when it is raining ($B = 1$) *and*…" A corresponding binary function of two or more binary variables is called "And." The behavior of "And" is tabulated for two and three variables (see "And" figure).

All inputs must be on for the output to be on.

Like a "Nor" gate, a "Nand gate" also has N input terminals and one output terminal. But, "Nand" is more complicated than "Nor," because a low output voltage is caused by a high voltage on all the inputs, and the output voltage is high if any of the input voltages is low. "And" is implemented in electronics by a "Nand-Not" tandem. Again, "Not-Nand," or "Not-Not-And," hence, "And."

Design Example

Consider a binary circuit, with output X and three inputs. D and E are separate streams of binary data, and C is a control signal so that $X = D$ when $C = 0$ and $X = E$ when $C = 1$. That is, the output is equal to D when C is 0, and equals E when C is 1. C controls the output. This *Binary Multiplexor's* behavior is tabulated (see "Control signal" figure).

Compare the output to D's value when C is 0; compare the output to E's value when C is 1. In the first four rows of the table, $X = D$ because $C = 0$. In the last four rows, $X = E$ because $C = 1$. The device is called a multiplexor*

* **multiplexor** a complex device that acts as a multi-way switch for analog or digital signals

because it switches ("multiplexes") between the data streams D and E under the control of C. It is a "binary multiplexor" because it switches between or "multiplexes" among two devices, D and E. It takes turns servicing them under the control of C. Consider two approaches for implementing this function.

CDE	X
000	0
001	0
010	1
011	1
100	0
101	1
110	0
111	1

▶
"Control signal" *Reproduced by permission of Gale, a part of Cengage Learning.*

Canonic And-Or Implementation Any binary function can be implemented in three layers of logic: (1) a layer of inverters that provides the complement of each input if it is needed; (2) a layer with K different N-input "And" gates where the circuit has N inputs and the circuit's output function has K one-points (one outputs); and (3) one K-input *Or* gate. Since the multiplexor's output function, X, has four one-points, the canonic "And-Or" implementation has four "And" gates, each with three inputs. The different "And" gates' inputs are appropriately inverted so each gate identifies a different one-point (one in the output). For example, an "And" gate whose inputs are ~C, D, and ~E has a 1-output when CDE = 010. A four-input "Or" gate, with an input from each "And" gate, provides the circuit's output. This would be ~(C,D,~E) + (or) (~C,D,E) + (or) (C,D,E) + (or) (C,~D,E) for the four one-points (one outputs) given.

Based on the Logical Description We can design the multiplexor in an ad-hoc manner from its logical description. If the inputs to a two-input "And" gate are ~C and D, this gate's output equals D when C equals 0, and is 0 when C equals 1. If the inputs to another two-input "And" gate are C and E, this gate's output equals E when C equals 1, and equal 0 when C equals 0. The "Or" of these two "And" gates gives X. That is, the output is D (equal to D) when C is off (~C = 1 or C = 0), and the output equals E when C is on.

Obviously this second implementation, with only two two-input "And"-gates and one two-input "Or"-gate, is less expensive than the first. This is one of the issues in design. Cost, a complex issue, is illustrated next.

Integrated Circuits

Integration is the manufacture of more than one gate, an entire binary circuit, or even a whole system, on the same silicon* chip. Transistorized gates and flip-flops were made in the 1950s from discrete resistors and transistors. Then, they were integrated onto a single chip, called a "small-scale" integrated circuit (IC). Often, a chip's complexity is limited by the package's pin-outs. The "7400 series" of integrated circuits, introduced in the late 1960s, is still used today. If a part is popular, its per-chip overhead* is small. Then, its price covers only the cost of materials and manufacturing—about $3 (in quantity). Allowing pins for common battery and ground, a 14-pin package has the following limits (see "Integrated circuits" figure).

As chip manufacturers placed more logic circuits on a single chip of silicon, integration proceeded through three subsequent *scales* of fabrication. Simple binary functions are fabricated on a single chip with up to 100 transistor*s on a chip, in what has come to be called "Medium Scale Integration." For example, the Quad Set-Reset Flip-Flop is a useful digital integrated circuit (IC). But, when fitting four SR-FFs within the pin constraints of a 14-pin DIP (Dual In-Line Package), each SR-FF gets only three pins (14 − 2 (for battery and ground) = 12;

* **silicon** a chemical element with symbol Si; the most abundant element in the Earth's crust and the most commonly used semiconductor material

* **overhead** the expense or cost involved in carrying out a particular operation

* **transistor** a contraction of TRANSfer resISTOR; a semiconductor device, invented by John Bardeen, Walter Brattain, and William Shockley, which has three terminals; can be used for switching and amplifying electrical signals

Port #	Description	Pins/gate	Max# (12 ÷ pins/gate) (14 – 2, battery and ground, = 12)	$/gate ($3 + # of gates)
7404	Inverter	2	Hex (6)	.50
7400	2-input Nand	3	Quad (4)	.75
7410	3-input Nand	4	Triple (3)	1.00
7420	4-input Nand	5	Dual (2)	1.50

12 / 4 (Quad) FF's = 3 pins per SR flip-flop, 2 inputs, 1 output) and only one of each flip-flop's outputs is connected to a pin (the S or the R but not both).

More complicated digital circuits, such as binary counters and shift registers, are fabricated with many hundreds of transistors on a chip in "Large Scale Integration." Finally, modern digital circuits, like 16-and 32-bit CPUs and memory chips with vast amounts of binary storage, are fabricated with thousands of transistors on a chip in "Very Large Scale Integration" (VLSI).

 See also **Boolean Algebra • Integrated Circuits • Transistors**

Resources

Books

Booth, Taylor L. *Digital Networks and Computer Systems.* 2nd ed. New York: Wiley, 1978.

Hill, Fredrick J., and G. R. Peterson. *Introduction to Switching Theory and Logical Design.* 3rd ed. New York: Wiley, 1981.

Display Devices

For as long as computers have existed, they have needed some way to display their output. The first computer display devices were modified typewriters and Teletype machines. These devices were slow, noisy, and expensive, and could handle only text. For graphic output, the devices used an X-Y plotter, a device that pulled a pen over a piece of paper. It shared all the problems of the Teletype machine.

It did not take long before these mechanical machines were replaced with electronic counterparts. The replacement was called a terminal. It consisted of a typewriter-like keyboard, which activated switches, and a display screen, which was a modified television receiver. Thus, the first computer display device was a cathode ray tube or CRT.

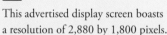

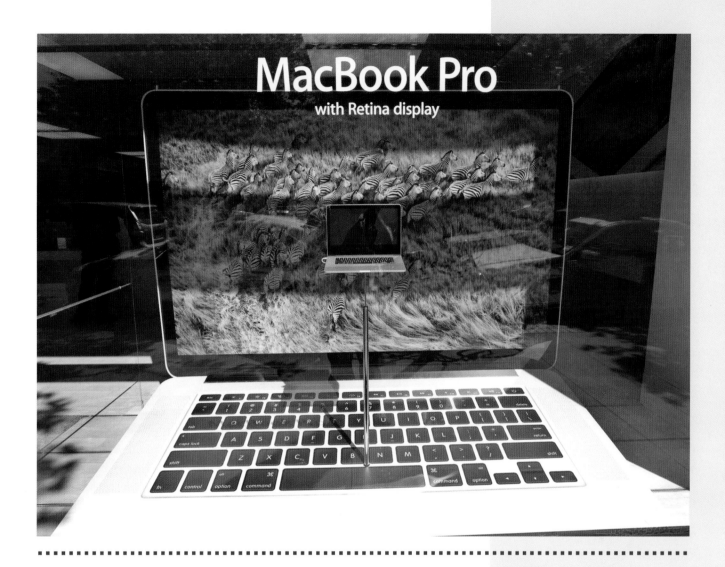

MacBook Pro
with Retina display

Cathode Ray Tubes

A cathode ray tube paints an image on a phosphor* screen using a beam
of electrons. The concept of the CRT was formulated before the nature of
the electron was known. Cathode rays are not rays at all but high-speed
streams of particles called electrons. The CRT is a vacuum tube where
the processing of electrons takes place in an evacuated glass envelope. If
the electron beam passed through air or another gas, the electrons would
collide with the molecules of that gas, making it difficult to manipulate
the electron beam.

    The CRT generates a source of electrons from an electron gun. The
electrons are accelerated in a straight line to a very high velocity using a
high voltage and then deflected from the straight line using a magnetic
field. The beam can be turned on or off with an electrical signal. The
screen of the CRT is coated with a phosphorus compound, which gives
off light energy when it is struck with high-speed electrons. When the
beam hits the face of the CRT, a spot of light results. The beam is scanned

* **phosphor** a coating applied
to the back of a glass screen
on a cathode ray tube (CRT)
that emits light when a beam
of electrons strikes its surface

from left to right and from top to bottom. The beam is turned on when a light area is to be generated and it is turned off when an area is to be dark. This scanning is clearly visible on both computer monitors and television screens.

There are two basic methods of scanning a picture. The first is called "progressive." Every line is scanned beginning at the top left corner and finishing at the lower right. Another method is called "interlace." The picture is scanned twice with half of the lines being scanned each time. This is done to refresh the picture at twice the actual scan rate and reduce the flicker of the display.

From Monochrome to Color Displays

The first CRTs were one color, also called monochrome; the display color was usually green. The first display devices were designed to replace a mechanical printer, so a single color was sufficient. However, the CRT is not limited to only printing text but is capable of producing images and complex graphics where full color is highly desirable. Again, technology was adapted from the television industry, and color monitors were quick to follow the early monochrome versions.

The color CRT is effectively three monochrome CRTs, all in the same glass envelope. There are three electron guns but each gun is individually controlled. The three electron beams are deflected together and strike the face of the CRT. The electron beams must pass through a screen with hundreds of thousands of small holes, called a shadow mask*, before striking the phosphor on the front of the CRT. The holes are arranged in groups of three so that when one electron beam passes through the hole, it strikes a small dot of phosphor that gives off red light. Another beam strikes only a dot of phosphor that gives off green light. The third beam falls on a phosphor dot that gives off blue light.

The mechanics of the color CRT are such that each of the three electron beams produces scanning beams of only one color. These three colors—red, green, and blue, or RGB—are the three additive primary colors. Any color may be generated by using a combination of these three. This shadow mask technology was the first to be used for color television and is still used in most CRTs.

Over the years the shadow mask CRT has been refined. Modern tubes have a nearly flat face, have much improved color, and have very high resolution, which is the ability of a display to show very small detail. One improvement is a shadow mask using stripes rather than round holes. This arrangement is easier to align. These improvements are not only found in computer displays but television receivers as well.

Cathode Ray Tube Disadvantages

Since its inception, the CRT has shown a number of disadvantages. First, the tube is large and heavy. CRT sizes are relative to the diagonal measurement and most CRT displays are deeper than their diagonal measurement. Secondly, the electrons in the tube are accelerated using high voltage. The larger the tube, the higher the accelerating voltage, which reaches to the tens of thousands of volts and requires a large power supply. The tube is made of glass, which is not suited for portable equipment or for applications with significant vibration such as aircraft. Finally, the tube requires significant power.

As hard as it is to believe today, the first "portable" computers actually used CRTs for display devices! In a word, these early portable computers were huge and would have remained so if a suitable replacement for the CRT had not been found. What was needed was a low power display device that had the capability of the CRT yet was small, not as fragile, and required low power and low voltage.

From Cathode Ray Tube to Liquid Crystal Display

The liquid crystal display, or LCD, is a low voltage device. It requires very low power but it was not originally a graphics device or capable of color. The LCD is essentially a light gate, which can be opened to allow light to pass, or closed to shut light off. To use the LCD as a full color graphics display, the display is divided up into picture elements called pixels. Each pixel* represents the color and intensity of a small part of the complete picture. Three LCD light gates are required for each: one for red, green, and blue. Behind each gate is a color filter, which is illuminated by a white light source. Behind one LCD light gate is a red filter, behind another is a green filter, and the third a blue. By adjusting the amounts of the three primaries, as in the CRT, the correct intensity and color can be generated for each.

LCD construction is simple. The liquid crystal material is sandwiched between two flat glass plates. Crystalline materials, which usually are not liquid, have very profound effects on light waves. The liquid crystal can affect the manner in which light energy passes through the material, and this can be changed by the application of an electric field. A thin metal electrode is placed over the area where the LCD is to change from dark to light. The electrode is so thin that it is completely transparent and cannot be seen. An electric field is created when a voltage is applied to the electrodes on the LCD glass.

Most LCDs use the rotation of polarized light to change the intensity of the light. The light entering the pixel is *plane polarized,* meaning that the light waves are in one plane. This is done with a polarizer*, which is the same technique used in sunglasses to reduce glare. A simple way to visualize a polarizer is to think about a venetian blind where the separation of the slats is so close that light waves can only pass through in one plane.

On the front of the LCD there is a second polarizer, which is oriented at a right angle to the first. If these two polarizers were placed together with nothing but vacuum or air between them, no light could pass through. This is because the light is polarized by the first polarizer and is incompatible with the second.

Liquid crystal material has the ability to overcome this by rotating the polarization of light waves, but only when an electric field is placed

* **pixel** a single picture element on a video screen; one of the individual dots making up a picture on a video screen or digital image

* **polarizer** a translucent sheet that permits only plane-polarized light to pass through, blocking all other light

across the liquid crystal. Therefore, if a voltage is placed across the liquid crystal, the light is rotated by 90 degrees and will pass through the front polarizer. The application of a voltage can permit or shut off the light intensity.

In the color LCD display three "sub pixels" are required because the intensity of light from the three primaries must be independently controlled. If one pixel could provide both brightness and color, the LCD could be simplified. An improved LCD display uses a single light valve where the liquid crystal material generates both the color and brightness. This new LCD material is called *cholesteric* because it was originally derived from animal cholesterol.

Display Device Picture Quality

The number of pixels into which an image is divided will directly affect the quality of the picture. As an example, a conventional television picture is generated with 525 scanning lines (the U.S. standard). Of these, only about 484 lines are visible. The aspect ratio of the television picture is 4:3, which means that the width of the picture is four-thirds the height. If the pixels were square, there would be 484 rows and 660 columns of pixels. Because of the interlace scan, the actual number of rows and columns is half of that, or 242 by 330.

When an image is generated with an insufficient number of pixels, the picture lacks resolution and the pixels are very evident. The individual lines of a television picture are clearly visible, particularly in a large screen television. Common computer displays have resolutions of 340 X 680, 680 X 760, and so on. Computer monitors can have a better picture than some television receivers.

An improved television standard is set to replace the older 525 line system; this is called high definition television, or HDTV. In addition to the improved resolution or definition, the aspect ratio is 16:9, which is the same as motion pictures. Because HDTV is a digital system and optical disks are used to store video, the relationship between computer monitors and television receivers will grow closer over the years.

Simplifying LCD Display Technology

In the LCD display, each light gate has to be connected to electronic drivers, which activate or deactivate the gate. An LCD graphics display has a very large number of pixels, which poses a serious challenge in running conductors to each LCD light gate. Thin, transparent conductors can hardly be seen but the sheer number of them would make manufacturing LCD displays difficult, at best. One solution is a method of connecting the LCD segments by mounting electronic circuits right on the glass plate. This arrangement is called an "active matrix" and it significantly reduces the number of interconnects required. The transistors used for the active matrix are made from thin films that are so small they are virtually invisible. This is called a thin film transistor active matrix LCD, or TFTAM LCD or AMLCD.

Even though the AMLCD has simplified the LCD graphics display, a large number of light gates, transistors, and interconnections remain. In the manufacturing process, if one pixel fails, the display must be scrapped. In an LCD graphics display, the number of LCD light gates numbers more than one million. The chances are good that one of those LCD gates or the thin film transistors would be defective in the manufacturing process.

The percentage of good products from a factory production run is called the yield. A poor yield is reflected in a high price of a product. Increasing the yield of the LCD production was the major challenge to the LCD industry in producing a cost-effective display product. The cholesteric LCD can be made with one-third the number of pixels and therefore, one-third the number of LCD light gates. This means the cholesteric LCD will have three times the manufacturing yield, which makes the technology potentially much more cost effective than other options.

Lighting Sources for Display Devices

The AMLCD requires a white light source to operate. Some of the more common light sources are not suited for backlighting an LCD display. The incandescent lamp and LEDs* are point sources of light whereas a distributed source is desired. These two sources are also not energy efficient, which is an important characteristic required for battery power.

For notebook computers, an electroluminescent panel is used. This device generates a low light level with good energy efficiency. The panel is thin and can be sandwiched easily behind the LCD and the display case.

Some portable devices such as small "palm" computers, cellular telephones, and watches must perform in bright sunlight. Displays that reflect, rather than emit, light are used in these devices. LCD displays are well suited to applications where the display operates in the "reflective" mode. When the ambient light is low, a backlight provides the necessary illumination. When backlighting is provided, the LCD is now operating in the "transmissive" mode. LCD displays that operate in both modes are called "transflective."

If the light intensity falling on the front of a transmissive display is greater than the emitted light, the display contrast will be lost and the display will "wash out." Usually, displays are shielded from very bright light such as sunlight but in some applications this is not possible, such as an aircraft instrument panel. Displays used for these applications are called "sunlight readable." This means the display is visible in full sunlight. In these high brightness applications, a thin, serpentine, fluorescent lamp is used for backlighting. This technique provides a high light output but also generates considerable heat. Providing a very high

* **LEDs** the acronym for Light Emitting Diode; a diode that emits light when passing a current and used as an indicating lamp

Talking the Talk

Computing systems that interface with the human operator have to speak the language. This means aural (audio), tactile (touch), or visual means of communication. Of the three, the visual display is the most powerful for most applications.

Putting Cholesterol To Good Use

Cholesteric display is one of several promising display technologies being developed. The phenomenal growth of computer chips has heightened awareness of the limitations of graphics displays. The cholesteric LCD shows the most promise of the low power displays but is not perfect. Most display engineers will readily admit there is no perfect display.

level of backlighting for a color LCD display has become very common as the LCD is used for computer projectors.

The new cholesteric LCD material will also allow for an LCD display that operates with reflected light and will be completely sunlight readable. Improved resolution will result because the cholesteric LCD requires only one light gate per pixel.

Improving LCD Technology

The modern AMLCD display is one of the best display technologies but it still suffers from some weaknesses. The resolution of a good quality AMLCD is not as good as the better CRTs. The cost of AMLCDs, although dropping, is still higher than the equivalent CRT. The AMLCD, or LCD in general, is not well suited for use in harsh environments because it is negatively affected by low temperatures. The response time of an LCD display under these conditions is increased significantly. This would cause moving images to drag and blur. In very cold temperatures, such as those in which military equipment is often operated, the LCD will quit operating completely and could be damaged by the extreme conditions.

A new display technology in the later stages of development is called the field emission display, or FED. The FED uses an array of small, pointed electrodes mounted close to a dot of phosphor. Like the color CRT, the pointed electrode causes an emission of an electron beam, which excites the phosphor to emit light. Essentially, the FED is a flat CRT where the electron beam is not deflected. The FED has all the advantages of the CRT, including good resolution, bright display, full color capability, and sunlight readability, without the major disadvantages, such as low temperature problems. It is not yet clear what direction this new technology will take, but it is likely that FEDs will be used for aircraft instruments and other sunlight readable applications.

 See also **Computer System Interfaces** • **Digital Logic Design**

Resources

Books

Robin, Michael, and Michel Poulin. *Digital Television Fundamentals: Design and Installation of Video and Audio Systems.* 2nd ed. New York: McGraw-Hill, 2000.

Whitaker, Jerry C. *Electronic Displays: Technology, Design and Applications.* New York: McGraw Hill, 1994.

———. *Video Display Engineering.* New York: McGraw-Hill, 2000.

Web Sites

University of Ottawa "LCD vs. CRT Monitors." http://www.ccs.uottawa.ca/pc-purchases/monitor.html (accessed October 31, 2012).

Document Processing

Documents serve to archive and communicate information. Document processing is the activity of operating on information captured in some form of persistent medium. Traditionally, that medium is paper, and documents are bundles of paper with information captured in print or in writing.

Document processing may serve to coordinate and conduct business transactions. When a customer submits an order to purchase a certain product, the order becomes a document for processing. The manufacturing company coordinates the activities of acquiring the raw materials, making the product, and finally delivering it to the customer with an invoice to collect payment—all by passing documents from one department to another, from one party to another.

Humans, endowed with the capacity to read, write, and think, are the principal actors in document processing. The invention of the modern digital computer, supported by various key technologies, has revolutionized document processing. Because information can be coded in other media that is read and written by the computer—from punched card*s in the early 1960s to magnetic tape*, disks, and optical compact discs (CDs) today—it is not always necessary for documents to be on paper for processing.

Automatic Data Processing

If one can implement decision-making into the logic of a computer program, and have the relevant information in the documents coded in some medium for the computer to read and write, the computer running the program can process the documents automatically. Unless the decisions in processing the documents require the intelligence of a human expert, the computer is much faster and more reliable.

The repository for the information is a database. Since the information in the database is readily accessible by the computer, one can generate the paper documents with the desired information any time it is necessary. Automatic data processing and the database technologies for information maintenance and archival have existed since the 1960s. For decisions that require the judgment of a human expert, document processing must bring in the knowledge workers—human users with the expertise in the relevant field of knowledge.

Typographics and Reprographics

The computer is also a versatile tool for the preparation and reproduction of documents. During the early 1980s, as a result of advances in printing technology, text formatting and typesetting tools were available on the computer. People can use these tools to create document content while at the same time specifying the presentation layout, including typesetting details. People can keep all the information in some persistent medium

* **punched card** a paper card with punched holes which give instructions to a computer in order to encode program instructions and data

* **magnetic tape** a way of storing programs and data from computers; tapes are generally slow and prone to deterioration over time but are inexpensive

such as a disk file. This is called a source document, since the computer tool can use it as input to generate the printed document as output.

Commonly the source document contains coded information in a mark-up language—tags that specify typesetting and presentation layout information. Mark-up languages may also incorporate the use of images and graphical drawings supported by the printing technologies. Low-cost laser printers became available in the mid-1980s. Tools such as these greatly enhance one's ability to produce documents readily on demand. It is necessary to keep only the source documents in a computer-readable medium.

Interactive Graphics and Multimedia

A document does not need to be printed on paper in order for people to view it. Since the bit-mapped monitor screen was invented in the 1970s, people can also view a document on the monitor screen. This allows people to interact with the document directly on the screen. The printed document is called a hard copy, and a displayed document on the monitor screen is known as a soft copy. Both copies are generated from the source document.

Using interactive graphics and window interfaces, users can treat the monitor screen as a desktop and retrieve any document for viewing, or interact with one document to bring up another document. Multiple users can easily share documents and view related documents on the computer at the same time. This also means that someone can use the computer to mediate and coordinate the timing and sequencing of people working on documents. A workflow system can implement the business rules of operation to coordinate multiple parties working together in document processing. It is conceivable that an office may have employees working on documents without ever needing to print out the documents on paper. That is the idea of document processing in a paperless office.

Another worthwhile note is the changing concept of a document. The source document kept in a disk file may incorporate document content with graphical drawing, images, and the typesetting and layout information, as well as audio and video scripts. On a computer equipped with the proper hardware, the soft copy of the document can show a video script or play an audio segment. Such a multimedia document is a relatively new concept of the document: It is no longer a physical bundle of papers.

Telecommunications and E-Commerce

Since people can view a document on a monitor screen to work on it, and they can print out the document on paper only when a hard copy is needed, they can easily share documents by sending them across computer networks. Electronic mail (e-mail) is a document sent from one person to another over a network. The Internet was originally proposed in the early 1980s for the purpose of communication between researchers, connecting the computers in research institutions across the nation. But as the Internet has rapidly grown with documents shared by more and more people, the network has become a channel for publishing. The parties involved, however, need to jointly observe certain standards for the communication protocol* and the format for source documents.

▶ *See also* **Input Devices • Markup Languages**

Resources

Books

Harold, Elliotte Rusty and W. Scott Means *XML in a Nutshell.* 3rd ed. Sebastopol, CA: O'Reilly Media, 2004.

Periodicals

Taub, Eric. A "Storing Your Files Inside the Cloud" *The New York Times,* March 3, 2011.

* **protocol** an agreed understanding for the sub-operations that make up a transaction, usually found in the specification of inter-computer communications

EFG

J. Presper Eckert Jr. and John W. Mauchly

Computer Designers
1919–1995 and 1907–1980

The Electronic Numerical Integrator and Computer (ENIAC) fired up its 18,000 vacuum tubes in a large room at the Moore School of Electrical Engineering at the University of Pennsylvania just after the end of World War II. Its youthful designers, (John) Presper Eckert and John Mauchly, looked on with a mixture of pride and anticipation.

Eckert was the chief engineer of the ENIAC. He developed the idea of a reduced electrical load to increase the reliability of the fragile tubes in the machine. Mauchly, effectively the chief scientist, left the hardware problems to Eckert and kept the more fluid software and logic development for himself. Mauchly convinced his younger colleague of the general utility of a perfected model of the machine that they had built for the U.S. Army to calculate tables for firing artillery more accurately and quickly.

Frustrated by the limitations of that machine, these "Wright Brothers of computing" left the university in a patent dispute, and formed what quickly became the Eckert-Mauchly Computer Corporation. Mauchly convinced organizations as diverse as the U.S. Bureau of the Census, Northrop Aircraft, A.C. Neilson, Prudential, and the newly independent U.S. Air Force, to buy a UNIVAC (Universal Automatic Computer), as Eckert and Mauchly called their universal calculator.

Eckert was essentially a prototypical boy genius engineer. He joined the ENIAC project right out of college. He earned both his bachelor's degree (1941) and master's degree (1943) from the Moore School, and started as chief engineer for ENIAC on his twenty-fourth birthday. He stayed close to electrical engineering his entire career. He was an expert on vacuum tubes and mercury delay line memories early in his career. After the ENIAC, he was the chief engineer of the Eckert-Mauchly Computer Corporation. When Remington Rand bought the company, Eckert stayed on as director of engineering. Remington Rand merged with Sperry to form Sperry-Rand in 1955. Eckert became a vice president and retained that rank until they ironically retired him and the UNIVAC brand name the same year, 1982.

Mauchly was a physicist. He taught for most of the 1930s at Ursinis College near Philadelphia, Pennsylvania. He was interested in modeling

John W. Mauchly. © *AP Images/BYRON ROLLINS.*

* **firing tables** precalculated tables that can give an artillery gunner the correct allowances for wind conditions and distance by dictating the elevation and deflection of a gun

the weather and built some crude digital circuits that would have to be part of a machine to do that. He went to a summer program in 1941, sponsored by the Moore School, to learn more about electronic systems. Mauchly hit it off with the staff and was asked to join the school's faculty. This he did. When the U.S. Army developed bottlenecks getting out its firing tables*, he suggested an electronic solution. The army funded his suggestion, and he teamed with Eckert to develop the ENIAC.

During the construction of the ENIAC, mathematician John von Neumann (1903–1957) was brought in to advise the project by Herman H. Goldstine, the army liaison. He facilitated some discussions by Eckert, Mauchly, and other young engineers and scientists who realized ENIAC's shortcomings before it was finished. Von Neumann, in the "Draft Report on the EDVAC," which described a new stored program machine, summarized their discussions. Even though it was only a draft summarizing his own and other people's work, nearly everyone erroneously gave von Neumann complete credit for the insights that led to stored program computers. Von Neumann did nothing to dissuade such beliefs, an omission that embittered both Eckert and Mauchly. When the EDVAC was finally finished in 1951, it, ironically, was put to use by von Neumann to predict the weather.

Mauchly stayed with Eckert until 1959, when he left Sperry-Rand and formed his own consulting firm. While at Sperry-Rand and its predecessors, Mauchly designed logic circuits. Sperry-Rand lost a suit brought in 1968 by Honeywell claiming that John Vincent Atanasoff

(1903–1995) had developed a computer that influenced Mauchly. This obviated previously granted patents. Both Eckert and Mauchly disagreed with the decision, but did not challenge it. As a result, both of them were put on the sidelines and kept from receiving much of the credit for the significant work they had done.

The pair had built a small stored program computer, the BINAC, to raise some money and keep Northrop as a client in the late 1940s. This was the first operational stored program computer in the United States. Therefore, Eckert and Mauchly considered themselves to have designed or suggested ENIAC, the stored program concept, BINAC, and UNIVAC in a little more than five years—a truly major feat of pioneering.

Some involved at the Moore School may have believed that Eckert and Mauchly claimed too much credit. But the facts are clear—without Eckert and Mauchly's contributions, the field of computing would have taken significantly longer to develop.

 See also **Early Computers** • **Early Pioneers** • **von Neumann, John**

Resources

Books

Lee, John A. N. *International Biographical Dictionary of Computer Pioneers.* Chicago: Fitzroy Dearborn, 1995.

Stern, Nancy. *From ENIAC to UNIVAC.* Bedford, Mass.: Digital Press, 1981.

Fiber Optics

Fiber optics is the set of technologies that enables the point-to-point transmission of signals in the form of light—instead of in the form of electricity. The main component is optical fiber, the thread of glass-like material that carries the optical signal. Two related components are: (1) the light emitting diode (LED)* and its advanced cousin, the semiconductor diode laser*, which convert electrical signals to optical signals and couple them into the fiber; and (2) the photodiode, which receives optical signals from the fiber and converts them back to electrical signals.

Although fiber optics has many applications, including its use in sensors*, its greatest impact has been in telecommunications. For millennia, humans used optical technology to send signals over distance—for example, as smoke puffs, reflected sunlight, or flares. Remember American Revolutionary War hero Paul Revere's ride and the warning signal: "one if by land and two if by sea?" But, these techniques are limited to what can be seen by human beings within a finite line of sight. Wired and wireless electrical technologies allow global, even interplanetary, transmission. But, these technologies have high attenuation*, high noise susceptibility, and low bandwidth*. While coaxial cable* helps alleviate these problems, fiber optics provides a better point-to-point transmission medium than any form of wired electronics.

Description

An optical fiber's diameter is typically only one-eighth of a millimeter (0.005 inches), but one rarely sees a bare fiber. When it is covered by protective plastic, an individual fiber looks like an insulated wire. Or, many fibers are incorporated into a cable that includes an internal plastic spine, for strength and rigidity, and a hard outer jacket that protects the fibers from external damage (including bites from gophers or sharks). Like solid metal wires or coaxial cable (co-ax), fibers can be quite long but, unlike wires or co-ax, an 80-kilometer (50-mile) fiber span may not need an intermediate repeater.

Optical fiber is not uniform in its cross-section. A concentric cylindrical* region, called the "core," lies inside the fiber. The core has a slightly different chemistry from the fiber's outer layer, called the "cladding." Light, launched into the fiber's core, travels the length of the fiber, staying inside the core by ricocheting off its walls.

Operation

When an electrical signal moves along a conventional metallic wire, individual electrons move slowly, shifting from atom to atom. But, optical signals are carried by photons, which are launched into the fiber and carry the signal as they traverse the fiber. Electrical signals move along conventional wire or co-ax at a bandwidth-dependent rate, typically around 20 percent of the speed of light. While optical signals, and electrical signals in free space, move at the speed of light, light moves slower in glass than in air. So, optical signals traverse fiber at about two-thirds the speed of light, which is still three times as fast as electrical signals move along wires.

In multi-mode fiber, different ricochet angles (called "modes") have different velocities*—so, a narrow optical pulse spreads as it moves. In more expensive single-mode fiber, the smaller core diameter (eight microns or 0.0003 inches, instead of 62.5 microns or 0.0025 inches) supports only one mode, which eliminates this modal distortion and allows pulses to be more closely spaced, giving a higher data-rate. Since different wavelengths have slightly different within the glass, even single-mode pulses can spread. Using a light source with a narrow range of wavelength reduces this consequence, known as chromatic dispersion*, which allows pulses to be even more closely spaced, resulting in an even higher data-rate. Many commercial long-distance optical fibers carry either 2.5 gigabits per second (Gbps) or 10 Gbps (as of August 2010).

▲

Preparing and checking fiber optic cables in London prior to the 2012 Summer Olympics. © *AP Images/Raphael Satter.*

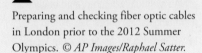

* **attenuation** the reduction in magnitude (size or amplitude) of a signal that makes a signal weaker

* **bandwidth** a measure of the frequency component of a signal or the capacity of a communication channel to carry signals

* **coaxial cable** a cable with an inner conducting core, a dielectric material and an outer sheath that is designed for high frequency signal transmission

* **concentric cylindrical** circles that have coincident centers

* **velocities** vector quantities that have a magnitude or speed and a direction

* **chromatic dispersion** the natural distortion of pulses of light as they move through an optical network; it results in data corruption

Techniques

Since a digitized voice signal requires 64 kilobits per second (Kbps), a single fiber at 2.5 Gbps carries more than 30,000 voice channels, while a 10 Gbps fiber carries well over 120,000 voice channels. A process called "time-division multiplexing" interleaves the individual signals. Another technology, called "wavelength division multiplexing" (WDM), has become practical for supporting higher data rates. WDM allows several channels to use the same fiber by using different wavelengths. These wavelengths must be far enough apart to be practically separable at the receiver, but close enough together to reside within a fiber's low-attenuation wavelength windows.

Fiber optics is highly nonlinear*. When analog* signals (like conventional television channels) are transmitted over fiber, the fiber cannot be pushed to its limits. So, state-of-the-art transmission is digital, because digital signals are not as affected by nonlinearities. One such nonlinearity, which causes light to move faster through a lit fiber than through a dark fiber, imposes practical limits on the number of WDM channels on a single fiber. Data rate and WDM are both being intensely researched.

Characteristics

The maximum span of any transmission link is determined by the signal-to-noise ratio (SNR) at the receiver. Increasing a wire's length increases both the received noise power and the signal's attenuation. So, a wire's SNR is a strong inverse function of length. The property that keeps an optical signal inside a fiber's core also keeps external interference outside it. Since fiber's received noise power is practically independent of length, fiber's SNR depends on attenuation only, making it a relatively weak function of length. This means that fiber spans can be longer than wire spans.

Different wavelengths not only have different velocities within optical fibers, but they also suffer different attenuation. The practical attenuation needed in a short span of optical fiber requires the light source's wavelength to be in the infrared range of 0.7 to 1.6 microns (millionths of a meter). Fortunately, cheap LEDs operate at 0.8 microns. The very low attenuation needed in a long span occurs over two narrow regions of wavelength: around 1.3 and 1.5 microns, where light sources are expensive. The lowest attenuation occurs at 1.5 microns, but chromatic dispersion is minimized at 1.3 microns. Not surprisingly, long-distance optical transmission occurs around these two wavelengths.

Although low attenuation and low noise immunity are important, fiber's most important characteristic is its huge bandwidth. Comparing information transmission to water flow, bandwidth corresponds to pipe diameter. On a scale where a telephone channel (4 kHz) corresponds to 1-centimeter (3/8-inch) copper tubing, a co-ax cable carrying 70 television channels (350 MHz) corresponds to a 2 meter (6-foot) sewer pipe. Fiber's long-span attenuation requirement allows about 15 THz

* **nonlinear** a system that has relationships between outputs and inputs which cannot be expressed in the form of a straight line

* **analog** a quantity (often an electrical signal) that is continuous in time and amplitude

(terahertz) in each of the 1.3- and 1.5-micron windows. This 30 THz of ultimate capacity corresponds to a pipe with 1.6-kilometer (one-mile) diameter. Researchers have continued to research how to use it all.

Cost

Carrying 100 Megabits per second (Mbps) over a short span, where multi-mode fiber and LEDs are used, fiber optics costs only a little more than wired electronics. For high rates over long spans, where single-mode fiber and semiconductor diode lasers must be used, fiber optics is expensive. But, the huge bandwidth makes it cost-effective. While fiber's material (silica) is cheaper than wire's (copper), fiber is more expensive to manufacture—especially single-mode fiber. However, since new installation cost is typically much higher than the cost of the communication lines being installed, it is common practice to include dark fiber* in any wire installation, even if there are no current plans for it.

There are other cost issues, as well. Fiber optics is more difficult to use than wire, and technicians need to be trained. While wire can be soldered or wrapped around a terminal, optical fiber must be carefully spliced. Fiber connectors, especially for single-mode fiber, are more expensive than wire connectors.

Application

Consider Table 1. Users get access (left column) to information signals by several competing media. People access (I) commercial broadcast television signals by local antenna, co-ax, or direct dish, and (II) point-to-point applications, like telephony or connecting to an Internet service provider, by wire or local wireless (cellular). But, the backbone infrastructures (right column), which distribute these signals over wide areas, use an application-dependent medium-of-choice. Commercial television is effectively (III) broadcast using geosynchronous satellites, and the wide-area networks for point-to-point applications, like long-distance networks for telephony and the Internet for data, typically use fiber optics.

Fiber optic networks have risen in popularity as networks have become more sophisticated and customer demand for faster connection speeds and data transfers has increased. This demand has been particularly high in China, which as of 2010, accounted for 40 percent of international demand for fiber optic cable. However, demand for fiber optic connections for homes also has increased in other countries, including Japan, Germany, the Netherlands, and the United States. Researchers speculate that the trend of rising demand for fiber optics will continue in both Europe and North America.

Table 1. *Reproduced by permission of Gale, a part of Cengage Learning.*

	Access Infrastructure	Backbone network
Broadcast application	I	III
Point-to-point apps	II	IV

Future

Because of the nonlinearity that causes light to go faster through a lit fiber than a dark fiber, the photons* at the back of a pulse can actually catch up to the at the front. A *soliton* is a pulse whose shape is retained because this effect carefully balances the effects that widen pulses—and researchers are trying to make them practical. With all that unused potential bandwidth, fiber optics is the logical technology for making networks that must scale easily, like the Internet. If research efforts in photonic switching* and optical computing* are fruitful, there will be wonderful synergies with fiber optic transmission. If researchers learn to master solitons and these other research efforts are fruitful, fiber optics has a promising future.

▶ *See also* **Digital Logic Design • Networks • Telecommunications • Transmission Media**

Resources

Books

DeCusatis, Casimer. *Fiber Optic Essentials.* Amsterdam, Netherlands, and Boston: Elsevier/Academic Press, 2006.

Downing, James N. *Fiber-optic Communications.* Clifton Park, NY: Thomson/Delmar Learning, 2005.

Hecht, Jeff. *Understanding Fiber Optics.* 5th ed. Upper Saddle River, NJ: Pearson/Prentice Hall, 2006.

Web Sites

Integer-Research.com "Fiber Optic Cable Growth Continues in 2012." http://www.integer-research.com/2011/wire-cable/news/fiber-optic-cable-growth-continues-2012/ (accessed October 5, 2012).

Metric Magnitudes

The metric system prefixes are as follows:

ato- 10^{-18}
femto- 10^{-15}
pico- 10^{-12}
nano- 10^{-9}
micro- 10^{-6}
milli- 10^{-3}
kilo- 10^{+3}
mega- 10^{+6}
giga- 10^{+9}
tera- 10^{+12}
peta- 10^{+15}

* **photons** the smallest fundamental units of electromagnetic radiation in the visible spectrum—light

* **photonic switching** the technology that is centered on routing and managing optical packets of digital data

* **optical computing** a proposed computing technology which would operate on particles of light, rather than electric currents

Game Controllers

Game controllers are intricate hardware devices that allow game players to send instructions to a computer, which can range in size from a desktop computer to a handheld proprietary game machine. The wide variety of game controllers includes such devices as game pads, joysticks, paddles, steering wheels, fishing rods, aircraft yokes, light guns, and rifles.

History of Controllers

When Atari game consoles became popular in the 1970s, the standard game controller had a single button in the corner of the four-inch square base, which held a three-inch joystick. Players could maneuver the screen

Shigeru Miyamoto, Nintendo's game creator, plays a violin using Wii Music during a video game display. © *YOSHIKAZU TSUNO/AFP/Getty Images.*

cursor by moving the joystick with one hand, and pressing the button with the thumb of the other hand. The only feedback was an occasional "blip" or "doink" noise from primitive speakers, and relatively slow, jerky movements on the screen.

Joystick design evolved to include a taller, ergonomically shaped handle with a trigger mechanism and a miniature stick at the end, called a *top hat*. With this device, players could squeeze such triggers with their forefingers and maneuver the top hat using one of their thumbs. These controllers often featured additional buttons on both the stick and the base that performed specific actions dictated by the game's software. Games were made more realistic with livelier sound effects from more powerful speakers.

Whereas the one-handed joystick was sufficient for early games, it proved awkward for other sophisticated software. Soon two-handled yokes, simulating a pilot's cockpit, were introduced. Car racing games were made more realistic with the introduction of steering wheel controllers, some of which included brake and gas pedals. Gun fighting games spawned the introduction of light guns and rifles. Even fishing games were enhanced with the introduction of rod-like sticks with buttons to help the player simulate casting and fishing.

Controllers for proprietary games, such as Nintendo's "Game Boy," Sega's "Dreamcast," and Sony's "PlayStation," became special two-handed devices, each with two one-inch joysticks and many multifunction action buttons.

How They Work

Although modern game controllers sport many different features, they operate in essentially the same way as joysticks do. As the stick or indicator is moved from side to side, the position of the handle is converted into a number, known as the "x" coordinate. Likewise, as the stick is moved forward and back, the handle's position is measured with a "y" coordinate. Using these xy coordinates, the computer can precisely track the stick's direction as it moves. If the stick has a rotational capability, the r-axis is tracked as well.

To calculate the distance the stick is moved, the controller's positioning sensor uses a capacitor* and potentiometer*. As electrical current flows through the potentiometer, the current is temporarily collected by the capacitor, which discharges it only when a certain charge is reached, say five volts. When the stick is in the resting position, not pushed from the center, the collects and the capacitor discharges the current rapidly. As the joystick is pushed farther from the center, the capacitor collects and discharges current more slowly. By measuring the number of milliseconds required for the capacitor to charge and discharge, the game adapter card tracks the stick's exact distance from center.

In newer joysticks, the capacitor and potentiometer have been replaced with an optical gray-scale position sensor, which measures the amount of light emitted by an LED (light emitting diode) to track the stick's position. When a button is pushed (to simulate jumping a barrel or hitting a ball), a contact switch sends an electrical signal to the computer's game adapter card and the game software uses the signal to start the intended action. When the button is released, another signal ends the action.

Some controllers, such as those for Sony's "PlayStation 2" and Microsoft's "Xbox," measure the amount of pressure used to push a button. When a button is pushed lightly, the button's curved contact barely touches the conductive strip mounted on the controller's circuit board. But when a button is pressed forcefully, more of the button's contact touches the conductive strip. Therefore, the level of conductivity is greater, signaling to the computer that this is a more intense action than that indicated with a lighter touch.

Force Feedback Controllers

Introduced by several manufacturers in 1997, force feedback controllers allow players to experience tactile stimulation to enhance their gaming experience. In the handgrip of each controller is a built-in electric motor with an unbalanced weight attached to its shaft. When power is supplied to the motor, it spins the unbalanced weight. Ordinarily, such an imbalance would cause the motor to wobble, but since the motor is securely attached to the controller, the wobble is translated into a vibration that shakes the entire handgrip and is felt by the game player.

The force and duration of the wobble in dictated by a waveform*, which is a graph or formula that tells the software when and how to turn on and off the motor. For example, if the game player drives a car that runs into a wall, the wobble will be sudden and will continue for perhaps a second or two. On the other hand, if the game player is a firing

* **capacitor** a fundamental electrical component used for storing an electrical charge

* **potentiometer** an element in an electrical circuit that resists current flow (a resistor) but the value of the resistance can be mechanically adjusted (a variable resistor)

* **waveform** an abstraction used in the physical sciences to model energy transmission in the form of longitudinal or transverse waves

Online Gaming

Video games for the home computer can be costly, especially for avid players. So many players turn to the Internet to take part in games offered online, particularly those that are made available for free. Online gaming piracy has had a significant impact on PC gaming in particular. Anti-piracy measures taken by studios for PC games have created significant controversy. However, online gaming on consoles has skyrocketed in popularity, with all three of the most recent generation of consoles (Nintendo's Wii, Sony's Playstation 3, and Microsoft's Xbox 360) featuring online capabilities.

* **read-only memory (ROM)** a type of memory device that supports permanent storage of programs

* **random access memory (RAM)** a type of memory device that supports the nonpermanent storage of programs and data; so called because various locations can be accessed in any order (as if at random), rather than in a sequence (like a tape memory device)

machine gun, the resulting wobble will rapidly accelerate and decelerate many times a second for as long as the button, the "machine gun trigger," on the controller is pressed. Likewise, if the game player is driving a tank over rough terrain, the controller will experience a series of wobbles that correspond to the ground's bumps and dips.

As microprocessors have become smaller and cheaper, they have been integrated into game controllers, greatly expanding their capabilities. For example, each Microsoft Sidewinder Force Feedback Pro Joystick has a 25-megahertz microprocessor in the base to interpret software commands that dictate the feedback motion. When the command is received, the microprocessor accesses a read-only memory (ROM)* chip, which permanently stores 32 movement effects and unleashes the correct movement on demand. Each movement corresponds to a certain waveform. If the software should dictate a waveform that is not already loaded on the ROM chip, the data can be downloaded to a two-kilobyte random access memory (RAM)* chip for the microprocessor to use.

Motion Sensing Controllers

Nintendo took advantage of motion detection technology and brought it to the forefront of the gaming world with its Wii Remote controller for the Nintendo Wii console. The Wii Remote used a combination of an accelerometer and optical technologies to create a controller that allowed for both side-to-side and three-dimensional motion sensing. Microsoft took motion sensing a step further with its hands-free Kinect controller. Kinect, which relies entirely on the player's physical motions and voice commands, has been hugely successful, with sales of more than 10 million.

 See also **Games • Input Devices**

Resources

Books

White, Ron. *How Computers Work.* 9th ed. Indianapolis: Que, 2008.

Web Sites

Forbes. Their, Dave. "Has the Diablo 3 Launch Damaged PC Gaming?" http://www.forbes.com/sites/davidthier/2012/05/17/has-the-diablo-3-launch-damage-pc-gaming/ (accessed October 20, 2012).

Analog.com. "Analog Devices and Nintendo Collaboration Drives Video Game Innovation with IMEMS Motion Signal Processing Technology" http://www.analog.com/en/press-release/May_09_2006_ADI_Nintendo_Collaboration/press.html/ (accessed October 20, 2012).

Mashable.com. "Microsoft Kinect Sales Top 10 Million, Set New Guinness World Record" http://mashable.com/2011/03/09/kinect-10-million/ (accessed October 20, 2012).

XBox.com. http://xbox.com/ (accessed October 20, 2012).

Graphic Devices

If someone turns on a computer or a smartphone, the screen lights up and interaction is possible through the use of text and images. This data output through graphic devices on computer systems is made possible through techniques that use video generation modules to display images. This differs from text mode output, for which the computer generates horizontal lines of alphanumeric* symbols. Although the technical requirements of both systems overlap, graphic devices use an approach that assumes that every dot on the screen is separately accessible. By contrast, in text mode, the smallest screen element is actually a group of points that together all define a character—a letter, a numeral, or a punctuation mark.

A graphic display is composed of a screen or panel that is made up of a large number of small cells or dots that are called pixel*s. In cathode ray tube (CRT) monitors, these pixels emit light when they are struck by a beam of electrons and switched on. Liquid crystal display (LCD) and plasma display monitors use different technologies to light up, or darken, the individual pixels on a screen. Regardless of the type of monitor used, at any one instant the computer hardware can switch some pixels on fully so that they emit light, skip over others so that they remain dark, and prompt still others to emit an intermediate measure of light. In this way the representation of a picture can be displayed on a graphic device using every pixel as a separate component in the image.

Graphic devices are output devices, but their physical characteristics restrict them from taking data as represented in the computer's memory and displaying the data directly. Instead, they require the assistance of a special device to translate data into electrical signals that are compatible with the display hardware. These devices are called graphics controllers.

One way that data can be formulated for display by the computer is through a technique known as a bitmapped display* or "raster-scan display." Using this approach, the computer contains an area of memory that holds all the data that are to be displayed. The central processor writes data into this region of memory and the video controller collects them from there. The bits of data stored in this block of memory are related to the eventual pattern of pixels that will be used to construct an image on the display.

For example, one could get the central processor to fill the entire video memory region with zeros. This might then correspond to a completely black screen. Then, the processor might selectively fill certain memory

---

* **alphanumeric** a character set which is the union of the set of alphabetic characters and the set of single digit numbers

* **pixel** a single picture element on a video screen; one of the individual dots making up a picture on a video screen or digital image

* **bitmapped display** a computer display that uses a table of binary bits in memory to represent the image that is projected onto the screen

* **vector graphics** graphics output systems whereby pairs of coordinates are passed to the graphics controller, which are interpreted as end points of vectors to be drawn on the screen

* **polygon** a many-sided, closed, geometrical figure

locations in the video memory with data that are non-zero. This would result in an image appearing on the graphics display—perhaps a straight line, for example.

This flexible scheme has been used in many computers. However, it does suffer from performance problems. The central processor is reasonably good at executing instructions that are arithmetic or logical in nature, but it is not very good at handling large blocks of data in single operations. Although the central processor can display a line on the screen, it is a time-consuming operation that compromises processor performance.

For this reason, special devices known as video co-processors are usually incorporated to optimize these sorts of operations and perform them under command from the central processor. This means that the central processor can get on with doing the operations for which it is better suited and the video co-processor can handle the video output. Often the video co-processor is a very complex device, bordering on the same level of complexity as the central processor, complete with its own instruction execution unit and local memory. These devices can draw lines, rectangles, and other shapes very quickly on the graphics display because they are designed specifically for that purpose.

An alternative to the bitmapped display design approach is the vector graphics* display. This design was once popular for engineering workstations since the graphics images produced by these systems are consistent with the diagrams and drawings that are common in engineering analysis and design tasks performed by computer-aided design, manufacturing, and architecture programs, for example.

Instead of sectioning off a large region of computer memory and mapping that to the display device, vector display devices use a variable number of lines to create images—hence the term "vector graphics." Since vector display devices can define a line by dealing with just two points (that is, the coordinates of each end of the line), the device can reduce the total amount of data it must deal with by organizing the image in terms of pairs of points that define lines. The vector graphic display accepts these coordinate pairs, along with other attributes of the line, like color and intensity, and draws the lines directly onto the display.

More advanced graphics systems employ extra specialized devices to help produce more complex images. The presentation of three-dimensional objects on two-dimensional computer screens is an example of an application requiring additional processing. The conventional approach is based on producing a model of the three-dimensional object in a form known as "wire frame," where lines are drawn to represent the object in exactly the same way that a real model might be constructed of it by making a skeletal structure out of wire. Then the wire frame can be filled in with flat, polygon*al panels being attached to the frame.

To represent this on a computer screen, a new step must be introduced in the rendering of the image; this is known as "hidden surface removal," because if the object is solid and opaque, surfaces not directly in the line of sight should not be visible. In addition, the surface of the object can be made to appear smooth if desired, by making the wire frame appear more finely grained and the corresponding polygons smaller. There are also devices available that provide visual effects like shading. Each of these operations can be performed effectively by specialized graphics devices designed for the purpose.

Human beings are much more receptive to high quality graphical displays than any other form of computer output. Consumer-oriented electronic systems including games consoles, conventional computers, hand-held personal digital assistants (PDAs) and smartphones, as well as mobile computers such as laptops and tablet PCs—all feature graphical displays. There will always be a need for sophisticated graphic devices to meet the demand for faster and better processing of these displays.

▶ *See also* **Computer System Interfaces • Games • Input Devices**

Resources

Books

Agoston, Max K. *Computer Graphics and Geometric Modelling: Implementation & Algorithms.* New York: Springer, 2005.

Wearable Graphics Devices

A company in Canada, "tekGear," makes available wearable computer graphics devices. Among the possibilities already at hand are binocular and personal viewing devices that are attached as a visor to the user's head. The devices are lightweight, rugged, and consume little power compared to conventional graphics devices like desktop monitors.

HIJ

Hypermedia and Multimedia

When someone turns on a computer, puts a CD (compact disk) in the drive, uses her MP3 player or music application to listen to her favorite music while she works on a paper, she is experiencing multimedia. Other examples of multimedia usage include looking at pictures taken from a digital camera. In contrast, surfing the internet (or World Wide Web), following links from one site to another, looking for all types of information, is called experiencing hypermedia. The major difference between multimedia and hypermedia is that the user is more actively involved in the hypermedia experience, whereas the multimedia experience is more passive.

Hypermedia is an enhancement of hypertext, the non-sequential access of text documents, using a multimedia environment and providing users the flexibility to select which document they want to view next based on their current interests. The path followed to get from document to document changes from user to user and is very dynamic. This "make your own adventure" type of experience sets hypermedia apart.

Multimedia is defined as the integration of sound, animation, and digitized video with more traditional types of data such as text. It is an application-oriented technology that is used in a variety of ways, for example, to enhance presentations, and is based on the increasing capability of computers to store, transmit, and present many types of information. Some examples of multimedia applications are: business presentations, online newspapers, distance education, and interactive gaming.

Some Examples Business presentations use presentation graphics software to create and display a series of on-screen slides that serve as a visual aid to enhance presentations. These slides may include photographs, drawings, spreadsheets, or tables. Some presentation graphics programs allow the inclusion of animation and video clips along with still images. Others can automatically convert presentations into World Wide Web pages.

Using a web browser, anyone can browse through pages of online newspapers, read articles, and view pictures or audio/video presentations. In addition, readers can locate a specific article by performing index searches, or by typing detailed requests. In some cases, the user may participate in chat groups and provide feedback to the editors. This type of interactivity requires bringing together images, text, audio, and video elements.

The unveiling of a new laptop by Dell.
© *SAJJAD HUSSAIN/AFP/Getty Images.*

* **I/O devices** devices that can accept "input" data to a computer and to other devices that can produce "output"

Distance education allows students at remote locations to participate in live instruction through videoconferencing, to collaborate on projects through shared "whiteboards," or to replay instructional material that has been pre-recorded. Using the World Wide Web as the base, a student can browse through a database consisting of course material in various formats: images, audio and video recordings, and textual information. In addition, the student can request more information while reading text, viewing illustrations, or listening to audio presentations.

Interactive games require multimedia delivery systems that can support real-time, three-dimensional imaging as well as interactions among multiple players. Those who have experienced multi-player multimedia games on the World Wide Web know that they can go on for long periods of time and that the number of players is seldom the same. Systems that support interactive gaming applications need to take care of a large number of interacting players for long periods of time.

Smartphones provide an interesting hybrid of hypermedia and multimedia. These computer-phones offer a host of activities for the user that go far beyond making phone calls and sending texts. Using operating systems similar to those found on computers, smartphones often have fully interactive touch-screens, and the ability to access to the internet, all of which fall into the realm of hypermedia. They also include more passive features such as photos, videos, and music.

Technology

Multimedia applications need computers that support multi-sensory I/O devices*. High-performance computer systems with high-resolution monitors and audio output are the best choice when it comes to multimedia presentation devices. In these systems, the output devices can present visual material in the form of text, graphics, or video, as well as voice and music components. Multimedia computer systems incorporate specialized devices to enter data into the computer system. For example, a scanner can be used to capture still images, voice can be recorded with a microphone and digitizer, and video can be handled with a camera and digitizer. There are many types of devices that can be used to store the large amount of data required by contemporary multimedia files. Multimedia systems may use optical storage, such as CD-ROMs (compact disc-read only memory) or DVDs (digital video discs); magnetic storage media, used in hard disk drives (HDDs); or flash memory, found in memory cards, universal serial bus (USB) flash drives, and solid-state drives.

In early multimedia systems, interaction between users and the computer was through a mouse and a keyboard. Their limited control of spatial manipulation as required by multimedia applications, especially games, soon made them less than ideal multimedia I/O devices. The new generation of devices includes: multiple-axis joysticks, foot pedals, eye motion tracking systems, and "data gloves"—gloves worn by the user to translate finger and hand position to signals that are then interpreted by the application.

Multimedia systems have to be able to compress data files for transmission and storage, especially those containing motion video and sound. Then, the systems have to decompress such files when the user requests it. Standard video display drivers equipped with software decompression can handle different types of video play-out. However, high-end systems accomplish video decompression with add-on boards that continue to decrease in price. Evolving standards for image and video compression include JPEG (Joint Photographic Experts Group)* for still image compression, and MPEG (Motion Picture Coding Experts Group)* for motion picture image compression.

Requirements for multimedia systems continue to increase. For example, this includes the ability to format the data for display, which includes fonts, panning, and zooming across different systems.

Hypermedia

Hypermedia tools focus on the interactive power of computers, which makes it easy for users to explore a variety of paths through many information sources. As opposed to conventional documents, such as books, that one normally reads one page after the other in the order set by the author, hypermedia documents are very flexible and allow one to explore related documents in any order and navigate through them in any direction.

The hypermedia model is fundamental to the structure of the World Wide Web, which is often based on a relational database organization. In this model, documents are interconnected as in a network, which facilitates extensive cross-referencing of related items. Users can browse effectively through the data by following links connecting associated topics or keywords. Object-oriented and hypermedia models are becoming routine for managing very large multimedia systems such as digital libraries.

* **JPEG (Joint Photographic Experts Group)** organization that developed a standard for encoding image data in a compressed format to save space

* **MPEG (Motion Picture Coding Experts Group)** an encoding scheme for data files that contain motion pictures—it is lossy in the same way as encoding

Careers In Multimedia Development

One of the fastest growing careers in the field of technology is in multimedia development. Drawing on artistic, editorial, and computer skills, multimedia developers piece together web sites, CD-ROMs, audio/video presentations, and printed publications. Employment opportunities run the gamut, from education to advertising to web design to publishing.

* **bandwidth** a measure of the frequency component of a signal or the capacity of a communication channel to carry signals

Future

Large-scale multimedia applications require significant advances in high-speed networking and storage servers, as well as the production of low-cost presentation devices for the consumer. Trends indicate that processing units will continue to become faster, display devices will become less expensive, memory devices will become larger, and high-bandwidth* network access will become ubiquitous. An illustration of the rapid advances in computer technology can be seen in the ever-increasing capacity of hard disk drives. In the early 1980s, an HDD capacity of 10 to 20 megabytes was typical. By the mid-1990s, consumer hard disk drives had reached the one gigabyte (GB) mark. In 2007, the first consumer HDDs appeared offering one terabyte (TB) of capacity. And by 2010, HDDs of up to 3 TB were available on the consumer market. Similar rapid increases in capacities and speeds occurred with other electronic components, such as processor clock speeds and communications. Such advances provide improved multimedia computer technology for our use and enjoyment.

 See also **Hypertext • Interactive Systems • World Wide Web**

Resources

Books

Beekman, George. *Computer Confluence: Exploring Tomorrow's Technology.* 6th ed. Upper Saddle River, NJ: Prentice Hall, 2005.

Clark, Ruth Colvin, and Richard E. Mayer. *E-Learning and the Science of Instruction: Proven Guidelines for Consumers and Designers of Multimedia Learning.* 3rd ed. San Francisco: Pfeiffer, 2011.

Havaldar, Parag, and Gerard Medioni. *Multimedia Systems: Algorithms, Standards, and Industry Practices.* Boston: Course Technology Cengage Learning, 2010.

Hwang, Jenq-Neng. *Multimedia Networking: From Theory to Practice.* Cambridge, UK: Cambridge University Press, 2009.

Li, Qing, and Timothy K. Shih, eds. *Ubiquitous Multimedia Computing.* Boca Raton, FL: Chapman & Hall/CRC, 2010.

Li, Wei, and Yang Xiao. *Adaptation Techniques in Wireless Multimedia Networks.* New York: Nova Science Publishers, 2007.

Shi, Yun Q., and Huifang Sun. *Image and Video Compression for Multimedia Engineering: Fundamentals, Algorithms, and Standards.* Boca Raton: CRC Press, 2008.

Sutcliffe, Alistair. *Multimedia and Visual Reality: Designing Usable Multisensory User Interfaces.* Mahwah, NJ: Lawrence Erlbaum, 2003.

Tse, Philip K. C. *Multimedia Information Storage and Retrieval: Techniques and Technologies.* Hershey, PA: IGI Pub, 2008.

Wyeld, Theodor G. Sarah Kenderdine, and Michael Docherty. *Virtual Systems and Multimedia: 13th International Conference, VSMM 2007, Brisbane, Australia, September 23–26, 2007: Revised Selected Papers.* Berlin and New York: Springer, 2008.

Zhang, Zhongfei, and Ruofei Zhang. *Multimedia Data Mining: A Systematic Introduction to Concepts and Theory.* Boca Raton, FL: CRC Press, 2009.

Web Sites

Salon. Murray, Joe. "The Difference between Smartphones and Multimedia Phones." http://techtips.salon.com/difference-between-smartphones-multimedia-phones-3846.html (accessed October 19, 2012).

Information Systems

Before defining information systems, a definition for information is necessary. Information can be regarded as that which is happening in the brain: the questions asked—what, where, when, who—and the answers received. A second approach is to consider information as something that the mind produces, something given to others. Information is something tangible that is constructed from a state of consciousness. What is being read here in this article is information. Thinking makes it possible. That thinking is also information—it is the process that makes the product possible. Information includes, for example, what is written in letters, the subjects studied in school, the articles read in newspapers, or presentations watched on TV or film, and the numbers found printed on pay checks. Information is a material product: something that can be acquired, kept, and given to others.

In addition, each human is a system. There are many components, or subsystems, of the human body—the nervous system, the digestive system, the circulatory system, and numerous others. Almost all things are systems: pens and pencils are systems allowing people to write and express themselves and give ideas and feelings to others. Media entertainment units such as televisions, and computers that help humans do many things—all of these are systems. An organization of people, what they do and produce, is a system. The public transportation used to get to work or school is a system. A system is an environment that includes humans, tools, and ways of doing things for a goal and purpose.

Humans are information systems because of the native capacity of the mind to interact with energy and matter, including the air breathed in and the ground below. All humans have the capacity to be continuously aware or conscious of what is happening in the local and larger environments. This is true from the very moment a human is born to the time that same person dies.

However, humans cannot live without information or the ability to process and respond to it. People are limited as to what their bodies and minds can see, hear, touch, smell, and, in general, do. So, people invent and create tools—technology—that add to their ability and capacity to do things.

The wheel, the carriage, the automobile, and then the airplane are all human-designed technologies—systems—that enable humans to move from one place to another, faster and longer, overcoming the physical limits of their bodies. Information technology (IT) is created to extend the biological ability to think, learn, remember, anticipate, and resolve many of the physical and mental tasks humans face each day.

Human beings invented paper, chalk, and pens and pencils to help record and present their thoughts and experiences. Later, in the 1450s, German printer Johannes Gutenberg's (1398–1468) invention of the printing press made the sharing of written ideas with multiple people more efficient and affordable. The early Chinese invented the abacus, a kind of primitive accounting and adding machine to help facilitate arithmetic computations. Present-day computers are extensions of this early information technology.

There are many kinds of information technologies, including radars, telephones, facsimile (FAX) machines, computers, and satellites, to list a few. These technologies contribute to many forms of information systems such as systems for information retrieval and systems that help to solve problems and make decisions. Some systems help to avoid or reduce paperwork. There are information systems that help manage organizations and there are specialized kinds of information systems such as artificial intelligence (AI)* and expert system*s. Basically, information systems are categorized by the specific work they do and the software that enables them to function as they do. Software consists of instructions that tell the computer what to do, how to do it, and when.

Information Retrieval Systems

An information retrieval system (IRS) is an environment of people, technologies, and procedures (software) that help find data, information, and knowledge resources that can be located in a particular library or, for that matter, anywhere they exist. Information about available resources is acquired, stored, searched, and retrieved when it is needed. An IRS can help users in general ways, such as obtaining data on a subject of general interest, or in more specific ways, such as retrieving information to help them find a good job. Information retrieval software allows a user to formulate and ask a question; then it searches a database to create an appropriate response. A database is a collection of data on a specific subject organized in such a way that a person can locate and acquire chunks of information for specific purposes. Retrieving information is a skill that requires training and experience. Librarians in general, and reference or special librarians in particular, are the professionals who serve this function.

The System for the Mechanical Analysis and Retrieval of Text (SMART) information retrieval system is an example of an IRS. It was developed at Cornell University in the 1960s. Gerard Salton (1927–1995), a professor at Cornell, was an important person in the development of SMART. For more than thirty years, Salton and his students worked on the SMART system, a research environment that allowed them to explore the impact of varying parameters in the retrieval system. Using measures such as precision and recall, he and other researchers found that performance improvements can be made by implementing systems with features such as term weighting, ranked output based on the calculation of query-document similarity, and relevance feedback.

Decision Support Systems

Information systems are particularly important in adding to the capability to solve problems and make decisions. With the huge amount of information being generated each day, solving problems and making decisions can be complicated. Decision support systems (DSS) are information systems with a specific function to help people with the problem-solving and decision-making process. As with all modern information systems, a DSS consists of a collection of people, procedures, software, and databases with a purpose. The computer is the primary technology in such systems; other information technologies may include electronic displays (e.g., a TV monitor) and teletransmission capabilities (e.g., telephone links). DSS systems help identify the factors that are creating the problem, provide ways through which approaches can be established to resolve the problems, and help in the selection of choices that are available to resolve the problem.

Expert Systems

Quite often in solving problems it is wise to benefit from those who know much about a subject—experts in a particular subject area or field. Each of these information systems is referred to as an expert system (ES). An expert system is a specific kind of information system in which computer software serves the same function expected of an expert. The computer, programmed to mimic the thought processes of experts, provides the decision-maker with suggestions as to the best choice of action for a particular problem situation. The hope is that humans can design computers (and generally information systems) that extend their ability to think, learn, and act as an expert.

Artificial intelligence (AI) is a familiar expression of this idea. It is exciting to see if a machine can beat a human in playing chess, or vice versa. During the last years of the twentieth century, information processing technologists began using computer-generated images and *virtual reality (VR)* the use of elaborate input/output devices to create the illusion that the user is in a different environment

sounds, rather than real objects, to explore the relationships between human beings and computer-generated environments known as virtual reality (VR)*. Virtual reality is part of an area in AI where the objective is to explore how the computer can extend the limits of how humans see the world and envision their place in it. Expanding the understanding of reality can enable humans to analyze and design ever better information systems.

Lastly, robots exemplify another perspective on information systems. Robots are machines that are designed to do what humans can do, only more accurately and much faster. An important application of this technology has been to create robots to perform certain functions that are dangerous for human beings, or to do tasks that can be performed more effectively by machine than by people. Although it may not have the physical appearance of a human being, a robot may be thought of as a machine acting as a person while being controlled by a computer.

Management Information Systems

Information systems can be found in homes, schools, workplaces, and places of recreation and relaxation. Information systems are part of all sorts of organizations including schools, the local Young Men's Christian Association (YMCA), worldwide fast food companies, and the governments and military operations of countries around the globe. Within these organizations, resources, both human and technological, require management. A management information system (MIS) is an environment that consists of people, technology (i.e., computers), and procedures that help an organization plan, operate, and control the access and use of resources, both human and material. Resources managed by such systems can include the labor force (executives, line workers, sales people), computer centers, photo and research labs, mailrooms, libraries, and other subsystems of a larger organization. Management information systems help an organization achieve its objectives through the processing and sharing of data and information important to the organization at all levels.

The Internet

Last, but certainly not least, the Internet is an important part of an information system. Since 1950, developments in computer and teletransmission technology (telephone, radio, and FAX, for example) have changed the ways humans communicate with each other. The Internet began as a tool for scientists to discuss their research work over long distances, what was called Advanced Research Projects Agency Network, or ARPANET. As this technology evolved and access expanded to business, industry, education, and personal users, the Internet and the World Wide Web (WWW, or Web) were born. They have changed the way humans work, learn, and stay in touch with others. Through the Internet, a person can locate a long-lost friend or relative; send or receive letters electronically and instantly (without a stamp); purchase products without physically traveling to a store; and quickly locate products and services that may not be available in a local neighborhood. Businesses can be built and networks created without the need for office space and daily commuting.

Computer-based information systems have changed the way information is gathered, processed, and shared. They have enhanced the ability to identify and solve problems and to perform tasks that are beyond human physical ability. Information system technology will continue to provide new horizons to all people.

 See also **Artificial Intelligence • Database Management Software • E-Commerce • Expert Systems • Internet • Intranet • SQL • Virtual Reality**

Resources

Books

Bates, Marcia J. ed. *Understanding Information Retrieval Systems: Management, Types, and Standards.* Boca Raton, FL: CRC Press, Taylor & Francis Group, 2012.

Chowdhury, G. G. *Introduction to Modern Information Retrieval.* 3rd ed. New York: Neal-Schuman, 2010.

Curry, Adrienne, Peter Flett, and Ivan Hollingsworth. *Managing Information and Systems: The Business Perspective.* London and New York: Routledge, 2006.

Davis, Charles H., and Debora Shaw, eds. *Introduction to Information Science and Technology.* Medford, NJ: Information Today, 2011.

Galliers, Robert D., and Dorothy E. Leidner, eds. *Strategic Information Management: Challenges and Strategies in Managing Information Systems.* 4th ed. New York: Routledge, 2009.

Laudon, Kenneth C., and Jane P. Laudon. *Essentials of Management Information Systems.* 10th ed. Boston: Pearson, 2013.

Manning, Christopher D., Prabhaker Raghavan, and Hinrich Schütze. *Introduction to Information Retrieval.* New York: Cambridge University Press, 2008.

Meadow, Charles T., Bert R. Boyce, and Donald H. Kraft. *Text Information Retrieval Systems.* 3rd ed. Amsterdam and London: Academic Press, 2007.

Stair, Ralph M., and George W. Reynolds. *Principles of Information Systems.* 10th ed. Boston: Cengage Learning, 2012.

Zhang, Ping, and Dennis F. Galletta, eds. *Human-Computer Interaction and Management Information Systems: Foundations.* Armonk, NY: Sharpe, 2006.

* **ergonomic** being of suitable geometry and structure to permit effective or optimal human user interaction with machines

* **graphical user interface (GUI)** an interface that allows computers to be operated through pictures (icons) and mouse-clicks, rather than through text and typing

Web Sites

The College of New Jersey, and Eric Thul. "The SMART Retrieval System." http://www.tcnj.edu/~mmmartin/EThul/SMART/smart-pres.pdf (accessed October 8, 2012).

NetHistory. "The Beginnings of the Internet." http://www.nethistory.info/History%20of%20the%20Internet/beginnings.html (accessed October 8, 2012).

Input Devices

The work of a computer can be characterized by an input-process-output model in which a program receives input from an input device, performs some processing on the input, and produces output to an output device. Thus, an input device is any peripheral equipment used to provide data and coordinate access to a computer or other such device. Users employ a variety of input devices to interact with the computer, but most user interfaces today are based upon a keyboard and a mouse pointing input device.

A keyboard consists of a number of switches and a keyboard controller. The keyboard controller is built into the keyboard itself. When a key is pushed, a signal called a scan code is sent to the controller. A different scan code is sent when the key is released. The use of two scan codes allows keys to be used in combination. The controller is able to tell whether a key is being held down while another key is struck, or to determine when a key causes a repeated action. Keyboard scan codes are sent to the computer via a serial port. New keyboards have been designed for ergonomic* reasons.

A mouse is a small device that a computer user pushes across a flat surface, points to a place on a display screen, then clicks on icons and menus. The mouse first became a widely used computer tool when Apple Computer made it a standard part of the Macintosh. Today, the mouse is an integral part of the graphical user interface (GUI)* of any personal computer.

Types of Input Devices

Hundreds of devices can be used as computer input devices, ranging from general-purpose input devices to special-purpose devices used to input specific types of data. Some of more popular ones, from the past to the twenty-first century, are digital cameras, light pens, magnetic stripe readers and magnetic tape, paper tape, punched cards, scanners, and voice recognition devices.

Digital Cameras A digital camera records and stores photographic images in digital form that can be fed to a computer for viewing and printing. First, the impressions are recorded or stored in the camera. The picture can then be downloaded to a computer by removable disk or by parallel port connection.

Light Pens A light pen uses a photodetector in the tip of the pen, which can be moved around the screen to move a corresponding cursor.

Magnetic Stripe Readers and Magnetic Tape Magnetic stripe readers are used to read alphanumeric data from a magnetized stripe on a card, such as a credit card. Magnetic tape can be easily rewritten and stored indefinitely. There are two basic tape mechanisms: reel-to-reel and cartridge. Generally, reel-to-reel tape drives are used with large mainframe computers*. Smaller computers use tape cartridges. Regardless of type, the tape is removable from the tape drive for offline storage. When the tape is in the tape drive ready for operation, it is said to be mounted. Tape heads store bits across tracks in units called frames, with the most common recording densities being 630 frames per centimeter (1,600 frames per inch) and 2,460 frames per centimeter (6,250 frames per inch).

Even though optical and hard disk drive (HDD) technologies continued to dramatically improve throughout the 2010s in terms of maximum data storage, magnetic tape nonetheless continued to be used for data back-up in many computer systems. For instance, in 2012 there were tape drives available to the home and small business user boasting hundreds (even thousands) of gigabytes (GB) of data storage per magnetic tape unit. For data backup and archival purposes, magnetic tape has continued to be attractive to many computer users due to its low cost per bit of data stored. However, in the early 2010s, a shift away from tape storage to online disk-based storage has occurred. Commonly called cloud storage, data commonly is stored in networked on-line storage areas operated by third-party companies. These companies handle large data centers, and customers buy or lease storage capacity from them, accessing their data through the Internet.

Paper Tape Punching paper tape for storage and data input is an old technique dating back to Sir Charles Wheatstone (1802–1875), an English scientist and inventor, who used it in 1857 for the telegraph. Small sprocket holes appear along the length of the tape to feed the tape mechanically. Data are recorded on the paper tape by punching holes in a row across its width. Each row represents one character, and the pattern of holes punched indicates the particular character. Although paper tape is inexpensive, the difficulty of correcting errors and the tape's slow speed have led to its disappearance as a computer input device.

Punched Cards Punched cards, popularly known as IBM (short for International Business Machines) cards, were the dominant input device prior to the introduction of personal computers. Punched cards

* **mainframe computers** large computers used by businesses and government agencies to process massive amounts of data; generally faster and more powerful than desktop computers but usually requiring specialized software

are produced by a keypunch machine off-line from the computer, and then read into it with a high-speed card reader. Punched cards use a Hollerith code, named after its inventor, American statistician Herman Hollerith (1860–1929). Each card has eighty columns with one character per column; therefore each punched card holds eighty characters or exactly one row of text or characters—a unit record. Punched card readers can operate at speeds from 100 cards per minute to 2,000 cards per minute. Like paper tape, punched cards are all but obsolete today.

Scanners Page and hand-held scanners convert black/white and color images into digital data. A bar code scanner uses a laser scanner to read alphanumeric bar-coded labels. Two types of optical data scanners can be used to scan documents: optical mark recognition (OMR) and optical character recognition (OCR). OMR is used in standardized test scoring and surveys where marks are placed in designated boxes. OCR readers use reflected light to convert typed or handwritten documents into digital data. In magnetic ink character recognition (MICR), data are placed on the bottom of a form using special magnetic ink so that they can be scanned by computers.

Voice Recognition Devices Voice recognition devices use microphones and special software to convert a human voice into language that can then be put into digital form. These systems require training the computer to recognize a limited vocabulary of standard words for each user. Formerly, one had to purchase speech recognition software from a software vendor or store. However, some operating systems now incorporate the technology. For instance, Microsoft's Windows Vista, Windows 7 (released for consumer sale in late 2009), and Windows 8 (released in October 2012) all incorporate Windows Speech Recognition software.

Past and Future

Until the advent of stored program computers in the 1950s, punched card machines were the state-of-the-art. Dating back to the U.S. Census Bureau of 1890, Hollerith developed a punched card reader that could repeatedly tabulate and sort. The key event that signaled the end of the punched card era was the launch in 1959 of the IBM 1401 computer, which had magnetic tape and disk storage. The keyboard has dominated interactive personal computing, while voice input devices have yet to gain truly widespread acceptance by computer users, partly due to reliability issues of translating the spoken word into text, and partly because of the ubiquitous availability and acceptance of the keyboard and mouse. Future hands-free wireless infrared input devices may include a wand with a walk-around button, a ring on the index finger, and a reflective dot that sticks to the user's forehead and signals data by eye movement.

See also **Computer System Interfaces • Games • Reading Tools**

Resources

Books

Chavan, Apala Lahiri, and Girish V. Prabhu, eds. *Innovative Solutions: What Designers Need to Know for Today's Emerging Markets.* Boca Raton, FL: CRC Press, 2011.

Dowling, Jennifer Coleman. *Multimedia Demystified.* New York: McGraw-Hill, 2012.

Marmel, Elaine J. *PCs Simplified.* Indianapolis: Wiley, 2011.

White, Ron. *How Computers Work.* 9th ed. Indianapolis: Que Publications, 2008.

Web Sites

The University of Mississippi. "Input Devices." http://home.olemiss. edu/~misbook/hm4.htm (accessed October 8, 2012).

Invasive Programs

Since the late 1990s, outbreaks of malicious computer viruses and worms like LoveLetter have grown increasingly common and have caused billions of dollars in damage and lost productivity. Where do these invasive programs come from? How does the computer industry combat these threats? What are the legal implications of writing or distributing malicious computer software?

Invasive Software Overview

Invasive programs (i.e., viruses, worms, and Trojan horses) are constructed using the same basic computer logic that underlies traditional application programs such as games, word processors, or spreadsheets. Like other programs, invasive software must be written by people, and it must be intentionally designed and programmed to perform specific actions.

Invasive programs act without the computer user's knowledge or permission and may cause a variety of intentional and unintentional damage. Viruses, worms, and Trojan horses that cause intentional damage to computer systems are said to deliver a payload when a certain trigger condition is met. For example, common payloads include sending files or passwords to the originator of the invasive software or deleting the user's files. Common triggers include a certain date on which files may be deleted, or the user's act of logging on to the Internet (at which point the user's password may be sent to the attacker). A specific consecutive computer action could also trigger a payload—for example, the hard disk may be automatically reformatted upon the tenth system reset after infection, thus losing all saved programs and data.

Although virtually all Trojan horses attempt to cause harm or steal information from a computer system, more than 70 percent of all computer viruses and worms are designed only to self-replicate. Although they are not intentionally malicious, such invasive programs are still quite dangerous, because they can cause system crashes, clog the Internet and e-mail systems, and generally compromise productivity.

Currently, all invasive software can be categorized into three broad categories: viruses, worms, and Trojan horses.

Viruses

A virus is a computer program that is designed to replicate itself from one file to another (or one disk to another) on a single computer. Viruses spread quickly to many files within a computer, but typically spread slowly between computer systems because they require people to exchange infected files over a network, external drive, or in e-mail.

The Pakistani Brain virus, discovered in 1986, is widely believed to be the first computer virus. During the late 1990s, the number of viruses skyrocketed to more than 50,000. Despite the thousands of virus strains, few viruses ever find their way out of their developers' computers and on to end-user computers. Based on industry statistics, less than 1,000 of the more than 50,000 known computer viruses are in circulation at any one time.

Viruses are often classified by the type of file or disk that they infect. The most common types are application viruses, which infect common computer application files, and macro viruses, which infect documents and spreadsheet files.

The average computer virus works as follows:

1. The user runs infected program A.
2. Program A executes the virus logic.
3. The virus locates a new program, B, for infection.
4. The virus checks to see if program B is already infected. If infected, the virus goes back to step 3 to locate another program.
5. If B is not infected, the virus inserts a copy of its logic into program B.
6. The virus then runs program A's original logic (so the user does not suspect any malicious activities).

Viruses have been written in numerous computer programming languages including assembly language, scripting languages (such as Visual Basic or JavaScript), C++, Java, and macro programming languages (such as Microsoft's Visual Basic for Applications [VBA]). Some recent computer viruses include Trojan.Flame.A (which was discovered on May 28, 2012), Exploit.CVE-2011-3402.Gen (November 7, 2011), Backdoor.IRCBot.Dorkbot.A (May 15, 2011), Backdoor.Lavandos.A (January 6, 2011), and Trojan.Android.Geinimi.A (January 3, 2011).

Worms

A worm is a computer program that automatically spreads itself over a computer network from one computer to another. While viruses spread from file to file on a single computer, worms infect as many computers as possible over a network. Virtually all modern computer worms spread through e-mail, sending themselves via Internet e-mail programs.

Usually, a worm infects (or causes its logic to run on) a target system only once. After infecting a computer, the worm attempts to spread to other computers on the network. Because computer worms do not rely on humans to spread themselves between computers, they spread much more rapidly than do computer viruses. The infamous Melissa and LoveLetter threats are both categorized as computer worms.

The first computer worms were written at Xerox Palo Alto Research Center in 1982 to understand how self-replicating logic could be leveraged in a corporation. However, a bug in the worms' logic caused computers on the Xerox network to crash. Xerox researchers had to build the world's first anti-virus solution to remove the infections. In 1988, the famous Internet worm spread itself to roughly 10 percent of the fledgling Internet (about 6,000 computers).

Like viruses, computer worms can be written in virtually any computer language. While there have been few script language-based viruses, a high percentage of computer worms have been written in scripting languages like Visual Basic due to the ease of writing self-propagating software with these scripting systems. The stereotypical computer worm works as follows:

1. The user unknowingly runs a worm program.
2. The worm accesses a directory source, such as an e-mail address list, to obtain a list of target computers on the network.
3. The worm sends itself to each of the target computers.
4. A user on the target computer unknowingly receives a copy of the worm in e-mail, unintentionally runs the worm e-mail attachment, and repeats the process.

One of the latest computer worms is called Stuxnet, a computer worm discovered, in July 2010, within the computer system of the Iranian nuclear facility. Stuxnet was found to be able to operate the centrifuges within the nuclear facility and to reprogram its computer systems' files.

Trojan Horses

Trojan horses are programs disguised as normal computer programs that instead cause damage to the host computer when run. Most commonly, Trojan horses either steal information (such as passwords or files) from the computer or damage the contents of the computer (e.g., delete files).

With the increased popularity of the Internet, the latest generation of Trojan horses has been designed to exploit the Internet. Some of these Internet-enabled Trojan horses can be used to control remotely infected

Love Letters

Most people would agree that it is nice to receive a love letter. Computer hackers, however, took advantage of that feeling by creating the LoveLetter worm that was distributed via e-mail attachments. Many computer users received e-mails with the subject line reading "I LOVE YOU" and curiously opened the attachment, which infected their machines. First appearing in May 2001, the LoveLetter (sometimes called the ILOVEYOU) worm tunneled its way into e-mail address books and sent itself to computer users the world over in a matter of days. Since then, more than 80 variations of the worm have been unearthed.

computers or record video/audio from the computer and send it to the attacker. In addition, hackers have used so-called Zombie Trojan horse programs to launch large-scale Denial of Service (DoS) attacks against popular Internet Web sites.

Trojan horses are not classified as viruses or worms because they do not replicate themselves. However, like viruses and worms, Trojan horses can be written in virtually any language. In July 2007, the Trojan horse, now called Zeus, was first identified when it tried to steal data from the U.S. Department of Transportation. Over the next several years, computer investigators discovered that Zeus had compromised tens of thousands of business and governmental accounts in the United States.

Anti-virus Software

Various techniques exist for detecting invasive programs, yet the primary mechanism used by most anti-virus software is called fingerprint scanning. The anti-virus software maintains a database of thousands of known identification characteristics, or fingerprints, from invasive programs, not unlike a police fingerprint database. When scanning a computer for viruses, the anti-virus program compares the fingerprint of each file on the computer to those in its database. If any of the fingerprints match, the anti-virus program reports the infection and can repair any damage. Since new invasive programs are created daily, anti-virus vendors send fingerprint updates to users as often as once per day. According to the June 2012 OPSWAT Market Share Report of worldwide antivirus vendors (as reported by ZDnet.com), Avast leads the anti-virus market with 17.4 percent, followed by Microsoft at 13.2 percent, ESET at 11.1 percent, Symantec at 10.3 percent, AVG at 10.1 percent, Avira at 9.6 percent, Kaspersky at 6.7 percent, McAfee at 4.9 percent, Panda at 2.9 percent, and Trend Micro at 2.8 (with others making up the remaining 11.1 percent; rounding makes the total add to 100.1 percent).

Legality of Writing Intrusive Programs

Although writing malicious software is not illegal in the United States, willfully spreading such programs is considered a crime punishable by fine or imprisonment. In the United States, some virus authors have argued that writing computer viruses is analogous to exercising free speech. In contrast, countries outside the United States have drafted computer crime laws that are far stricter than those in the United States. For instance, Germany has laws restricting mass exchange of computer viruses for any reason and Finland has recently made writing a computer virus an illegal act.

 See also **Privacy • Security • Viruses**

Resources

Books

Aycock, John. *Spyware and Adware.* New York: Springer, 2011.

Johnston, Jessica. *Technological Turf Wars: A Case Study of the Computer Antivirus Industry.* Philadelphia: Temple University Press, 2009.

Onwubiko, Cyril, and Thomas Owens, eds. *Situational Awareness in Computer Network Defense: Principles, Methods, and Applications.* Hershey, PA: Information Science Reference, 2011.

Plotkin, Robert. *Privacy, Security, and Cyberspace.* New York: Facts on File, 2012.

Zalewski, Michal. *The Tangled Web: A Guide to Securing Modern Web Applications.* San Francisco: No Starch Press, 2012.

Web Sites

BitDefender.com. "Virus Encyclopedia." http://www.bitdefender.com/resourcecenter/virus-encyclopedia/ (accessed October 9, 2012).

PCvirusdoctors.com. "Computer Worm List." http://www.pcvirusdoctors.com/virus-terms/computer-worm-list.html (accessed October 9, 2012).

Reuters. "Hackers steal U.S. Government, Corporate Data from PCs." http://www.reuters.com/article/2007/07/17/us-internet-attack-idUSN1638118020070717 (accessed October 9, 2012).

ZD Net. "Worldwide AV Vendors June 2012." http://i.zdnet.com/blogs/antivirus_software_market_share_2012.png (accessed October 9, 2012).

JPEG, MPEG

Joint Photographic Expert Group (JPEG) and Moving Picture Expert Group (MPEG) are compression format standards sanctioned by both the International Organization for Standardization (ISO) and the International Electrotechnical Commission (IEC). JPEG works on the standards for compression of still digital images. MPEG applies to standards for compression of digital movies.

Digital images or video are compressed primarily for two reasons: to save storage space for archival, and to save bandwidth* in communication, which saves time required to send the data. A compressed digital image or video can be drastically smaller than its original size and saves a great deal of storage space. Upon retrieval, the data can be decompressed to get back the original image or video. When one needs to transmit the data through a channel of a certain, the smaller data size also saves transmission time.

There are many different compression algorithm*s, each with its own characteristics and performance. The compressed image or video may be a disk file, or a signal in a transmission channel. People need compression standards for interoperability. As long as the data meet the appropriate

bandwidth a measure of the frequency component of a signal or the capacity of a communication channel to carry signals

algorithm a rule or procedure used to solve a mathematical problem—most often described as a sequence of steps

* **lossy** a nonreversible way of compressing digital images; making images take up less space by permanently removing parts that cannot be easily seen anyway

compression standards, one can display the image or play the video on any system that would observe the same standards.

JPEG

JPEG was proposed in 1991 as a compression standard for digital still images. JPEG compression is lossy*, which means that some details may be lost when the image is restored from the compressed data. JPEG compression takes advantage of the way that human eyes work, so that people usually do not notice the lost details in the image. With JPEG, one can adjust the amount of loss at compression time by trading image quality for a smaller size of the compressed image.

JPEG is designed for full-color or grayscale images of natural scenes. It works very well with photographic images. JPEG does not work as well on images with sharp edges or artificial scenes such as graphical drawings, text documents, or cartoon pictures.

A few different file formats are used to exchange files with JPEG images. The JPEG File Interchange Format (JFIF) defines a minimum standard necessary to support JPEG, is widely accepted, and is used most often on the personal computer and on the Internet. The conventional file name for JPEG images in this format usually has the extension ~.JPG or ~.JPEG (where ~. represents a file name).

Another compression standard issued by the Joint Photographic Expert Group is JPEG 2000, which was published in the year 2000. JPEG 2000 was created with the aim of providing an improved image coding system (as compared to the original JPEG) using the latest compression techniques, which are based on the mathematics of wavelets. The effort has resulted in its use in a wide range of applications, from digital cameras to medical imaging.

Yet another JPEG version was originally created by Microsoft, first under the name Windows Media Photo, and then as HD Photo. In 2009 it was formally recognized (and renamed) as the new ISO/IEC standard JPEG XR. Some of the favorable attributes of the JPEG XR compression standard include higher data compression ratios than JPEG, a "lossless compression" mode, and better color accuracy.

MPEG

MPEG was first released in 1993. It is actually a family of standards for compressed digital movies, and is still evolving. One may think of a digital movie as a sequence of still images displayed one after another at video rate. However, this approach does not take into consideration the extensive redundancy from frame to frame. MPEG takes advantage of that redundancy to achieve even better compression. A movie also has sound channels to play synchronously with the sequence of images.

The MPEG standards actually consist of three main parts: video, audio, and systems. The MPEG systems part coordinates between the video and audio parts, as well as coordinating external synchronization for playing.

MPEG-1 was adopted in video CDs. MP3 audio, which is popular on the Internet, is actually an MPEG-1 standard adopted to handle music in digital audio. It is called MP3 because it is an arrangement for MPEG Audio Layer 3. The MPEG-2 standard was approved in 1994. It is used as the format for many digital television broadcasting applications, and is the basis for digital versatile discs (DVDs), a much more compact version of the video CD with the capacity for full-length movies. The MPEG-4 standard was completed in 1998, and was adopted in 1999. MPEG-4 is designed for transmission over channels with a low bit rate*.

There are several other MPEG standards, and the format continues to evolve with new advances. For example, developers of another video compression format, H.263, joined with MPEG-4 standards to form Advanced Video Coding (AVC), also called H.264 or MPEG-4 Part 10. In 2007, MPEG Surround standards (also known as MPEG-D Part 1 or Spatial Audio Coding (SAC) offered still higher data compression that reduced bit transmission while improving video and audio quality.

> *See also* **Graphic Devices • Music, Computer • World Wide Web**

Resources

Books

Adjeroh, Donald, Timothy C. Bell, and Amar Mukherjee. *The Burrows-Wheeler Transform: Data Compression, Suffix Arrays, and Pattern Matching.* New York: Springer, 2008.

Garrett, Paul B. *The Mathematics of Coding Theory: Information, Compression, Error Correction, and Finite Fields.* Upper Saddle River, NJ: Prentice Hall, 2004.

Hoggar, S. G. *Mathematics of Digital Images: Creation, Compression, Restoration, Recognition.* Cambridge: Cambridge University Press, 2006.

Salomon, David, Giovanni Motta, and D. Bryant. *Handbook of Data Compression.* 5th ed. New York: Springer, 2009.

Sayood, Khalid. *Introduction to Data Compression.* San Francisco, CA: Morgan Kaufmann, 2006.

Shi, Yun Q., and Huifang Sun. *Image and Video Compression for Multimedia Engineering: Fundamentals, Algorithms, and Standards.* Boca Raton: CRC Press, 2008.

** **bit rate** the rate at which binary bits can be processed or transferred per unit time, in a system (often a computer communications system)*

L

LISP

LISP, an acronym for LISt Processing, is a programming language developed by American computer scientist and cognitive scientist John McCarthy (1927–2011) in the late 1950s. Although LISP is a general-purpose language, it is often thought of as a language solely for artificial intelligence (AI) programming, for which it is often used. AI programming often deals with symbolic processing that the standard programming languages are ill-equipped to handle. Symbolic processing focuses on the representation of real-world concepts and on the relationships among the objects rather than numeric processing.

At the time that LISP was under development, other AI programming languages were being developed with rather informal approaches. McCarthy, also a mathematician with a degree from the California Institute of Technology, wanted to establish a firm scientific foundation for LISP. That foundation came from formal logic. American logician Alonzo Church (1903–1995) had developed a clear and unambiguous means of describing the inputs and internal computations of functions. The lambda calculus* notation provided McCarthy, a student of Church's, with a well-defined basis on which to establish this new programming language.

Pure LISP is an example of a functional programming language. In functional programming, functions are applied to arguments and the values that are returned are used as arguments to other functions. Functional programming contrasts with standard or procedural programming, which uses statements that change the program environment in some way, such as assigning a value to a variable. In functional programming, these changes to the environment are minimized by using the values returned by function calls as direct input to other functions without using assignment statements.

As its name implies, the primary data structure in LISP is the list, although it does support a wide variety of data types such as integers, floating point numbers, characters, and strings, as well as user-defined data types. The list is a simple yet flexible data structure. In LISP, a list consists of any number of data elements surrounded by a set of parentheses. For example, a set of integers could be represented by this list: (1 2 3 4 5). However, lists can represent more complicated objects. A list representing a record of a person's name, height in inches, and weight in pounds would be expressed as (John 72 180).

Lists can contain any type of LISP object, even other lists. Several lists, such as the one noted earlier, each containing data for one person,

* **lambda calculus** important in the development of programming languages, a specialized logic using substitutions that was developed by Alonzo Church (1903–1995)

About LISP

LISP (LISt Processing) is a programming language developed primarily for symbolic processing in contrast to other programming languages, which were developed primarily for numeric processing. Symbolic processing is needed in some types of problems encountered in artificial intelligence (AI).

* **syntax** a set of rules that a computing language incorporates regarding structure, punctuation, and formatting

* **artificial intelligence** a branch of computer science dealing with creating computer hardware and software to mimic the way people think and perform practical tasks

* **algorithm** a rule or procedure used to solve a mathematical problem—most often described as a sequence of steps

* **prototypes** working models or experimental investigation of proposed systems under development

could be grouped together in an outer list to represent the height and weight of the members of a sports team, for example. The use of lists in this fashion, along with LISP's list access and retrieval functions, can result in a simple database. Lists can also represent more complicated data structures such as trees and graphs through the use of a more complicated nesting of lists.

The reliance on the list data structure results in a relatively simple syntax*. With a few exceptions, parentheses are the only punctuation needed. This means that all LISP function definitions are written as lists. Since all LISP programs are written as lists, and since LISP contains a myriad of functions that manipulate lists, LISP programs can serve as data to other LISP programs. This means that LISP programs can use other LISP programs as data to produce new programs.

Not only does the syntax of LISP make it easy to do things that are inherently difficult to do in other programming languages, the LISP programming environment is well suited to the exploratory type of programming that artificial intelligence* projects demand. These programming problems are often ill-defined at the outset and are not usually developed in the standard algorithm*ic manner. They require an exploratory approach that involves successively refining a series of prototypes*. The demand for fast prototyping requires an environment that makes it easy for the programmer to develop and revise programs.

Although LISP programs can be compiled in order to speed up program execution, LISP is most often used as an interpreted language. The interpretive environment can considerably shorten development time by allowing programs to be written, debugged, tested, and modified at any time, even while the program itself is running. This avoids the long re-compile time associated with large programs written in other languages and facilitates the development of AI programs.

LISP has long supported facilities that are only recently being incorporated into other programming languages such as a rich object system and function overloading, which is facilitated by run-time type checking. Runtime type checking frees the programmer from declaring a data type for each variable. The type of a variable is one of several pieces of information that LISP maintains about every object in the environment.

 See also **Artificial Intelligence • Procedural Languages**

Resources

Books

Church, Alonzo. "The Calculi of Lambda Conversion." In *Annals of Mathematical Studies*, vol. 6. Princeton, NJ: Princeton University Press, 1941.

Seibel, Peter. *Practical Common Lisp*. Berkeley, CA: Apress, 2005.

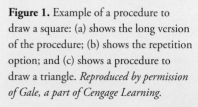

Periodical

McCarthy, John. "Recursive Functions of Symbolic Expressions and Their Computation by Machine, Part I." *Communications of the ACM* 3, no. 4 (1960): 185–195.

Web Sites

The New York Times. "Alonzo Church, 92, Theorist of the Limits of Mathematics." http://www.nytimes.com/1995/09/05/obituaries/alonzo-church-92-theorist-of-the-limits-of-mathematics.html (accessed October 9, 2012).

Oracle ThinkQuest. "The History of Artificial Intelligence." http://library.thinkquest.org/2705/history.html (accessed October 9, 2012).

The Register. "Father of Lisp and AI John McCarthy has Died." http://www.theregister.co.uk/2011/10/24/father_lisp_ai_john_mccarthy_dies/ (accessed October 9, 2012).

The Wall Street Journal. "Computer Scientist Coined 'Artificial Intelligence'." http://online.wsj.com/article/SB10001424052970203911804576653530510986612.html (accessed October 9, 2012).

Logo

The name of the programming language Logo comes from the Greek for word. The first version of Logo (also called LOGO), a dialect of LISP, was developed in 1966 by several researchers and scholars including Wallace "Wally" Feurzeig, a researcher at Bolt Beranek and Newman, a Cambridge, Massachusetts, research firm actively engaged in the study of artificial intelligence (AI)*, and Seymour Papert (1928–), a mathematics and education professor from the Massachusetts Institute of Technology (MIT).

Although it was designed originally for MIT's mainframes and minicomputers, within less than a decade, Logo had found a place in elementary school education curricula across the United States. Logo's

* **artificial intelligence (AI)** a branch of computer science dealing with creating computer hardware and software to mimic the way people think and perform practical tasks

```
TO SQUARE
    FD   30          REPEAT 4 [FD 30 RT 90]      TO SQUARE  TO TRIANGLE
    RT   90          END                          REPEAT 3 [FD 30 RT 120]
    FD   30                                        END
    RT   90                    (b)                            (c)
    FD   30
    RT   90
    FD   30
    RT   90
END
    (a)
```

Figure 1. Example of a procedure to draw a square: (a) shows the long version of the procedure; (b) shows the repetition option; and (c) shows a procedure to draw a triangle. *Reproduced by permission of Gale, a part of Cengage Learning.*

Figure 2. Examples of using variables in procedures to allow different values to be given for the sides of the square and triangle. *Reproduced by permission of Gale, a part of Cengage Learning.* ▶

```
TO SQUARE :SIDE                      TO TRIANGLE :SIDE
   REPEAT 4 [FD :SIDE RT 90]            REPEAT 3 [FD :SIDE RT 120]
END                                  END
```

Figure 3: (a) Example of the SQUARE procedure calling the TRIANGLE procedure to draw a house: a square with a triangle on top. (b) Example of the SQUARE procedure calling itself. *Reproduced by permission of Gale, a part of Cengage Learning.* ▶

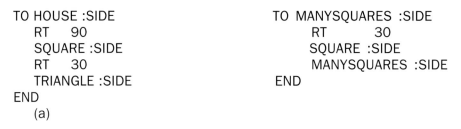

```
TO HOUSE :SIDE                       TO MANYSQUARES :SIDE
   RT   90                              RT        30
   SQUARE :SIDE                         SQUARE :SIDE
   RT   30                              MANYSQUARES :SIDE
   TRIANGLE :SIDE                    END
END
   (a)
```

* **syntax** a set of rules that a computing language incorporates regarding structure, punctuation, and formatting

* **debugging** the act of trying to trace, identify, and then remove errors in program source code

reach into thousands of elementary school classrooms was made feasible by two technological advances of the 1970s: the creation of computer time-sharing and the development of the first high-level conversational programming language. In 1970, Papert founded the Logo Laboratory at MIT. The so-called Logo-based turtles were introduced around 1971, and the use of microcomputers allowed Logo to be used by elementary school students.

The idea of creating a programming language for children grew out of the realization that most existing computer languages were designed to do computation and lacked the ability to handle non-numeric symbols. In addition, most languages had complex syntax* rules and very little support for debugging* and editing. The Logo creators felt that this new language had to satisfy these requirements:

1. Elementary grade students should be able to use it for simple tasks with very little preparation.

2. Its structure should exemplify mathematically-important concepts with minimal intrusion from programming conventions.

3. It should support the expression of mathematically rich numerical and non-numerical algorithms such as changing English into pig Latin, making and breaking secret codes, or determining if words are palindromes.

The plan was to introduce mathematical ideas through experience with familiar problems. The goal was to provide an environment that would encourage mathematical thinking through the completion of concrete projects. Papert and his colleagues felt that this would give students a sense of connectivity between abstract mathematical concepts and everyday practical experiences. For example, when giving directions to someone, a person would likely say: "Go straight for two blocks then turn right," rather than using the words latitude and longitude. In the same way, the commands used in turtle graphics are based on right turns and left turns, rather than on absolute coordinates, making them easy to understand.

The turtle is a triangular object that appears on the computer screen and moves in response to commands typed on the keyboard. If the pen is activated, the turtle will leave tracks on the screen; if the pen is up, it will not. Papert refers to the turtle as "an object to think with." Users learn to create programs that draw simple geometric figures, such as squares or triangles, which can be combined into bigger programs that draw more complex figures, such as houses. The metaphor of "teaching the computer" new things based on what it already knows is the basis of Logo programming.

In an ideal Logo environment, much of the programming is learned through a series of activities. Students can choose many of their own problems and decide how to solve them based on their experience in generating and solving other problems. They teach the computer how to perform a specific action and get immediate feedback. In this environment students learn art, geometry, and computer programming.

Logo Syntax

Logo makes it possible for beginners to learn to program quite quickly because it starts out with a set of words called *primitives* that are easy to understand and can be used to experiment. For example, FORWARD or FD would make the turtle go forward, and RIGHT or RT would make it turn to the right, while HIDETURTLE or HT would hide it from view.

Using those primitives, a user can write a set of instructions, known as a *procedure*, name it, and use it to build other procedures. A procedure is executed by typing its name. Large problems can be broken down into small chunks that are easy to manage. An example of a procedure that draws a square is shown in Figure 1(a) and 1(b), while one to draw a triangle is shown in Figure 1(c).

These procedures use a constant of 30 for the sides of the square and the triangle, which means that if one wanted to draw squares and triangles of different sizes then that person would have to modify the procedures. Logo uses variable*s in the title line of a procedure to allow the use of different values every time the procedure is executed, as shown in Figure 2. The name is separated from the procedure name by a space and a colon (:). To execute procedures using variables, the name of the procedure must be followed by a space and a numerical value. For example, the command SQUARE 60 would draw a square of 60 units.

A procedure can call other procedures, as shown in Figure 3(a), and can also call itself, as shown in Figure 3(b), making Logo a recursive language.

The example in Figure 3(b) shows the occurrence of an infinite loop because the procedure continues to call itself forever; it has no way of

* **recursive** operations expressed and implemented in a way that requires them to invoke themselves

knowing when to stop. All recursive* procedures need to have a condition that will be used to stop the loop after a certain number of calls have been made, as shown in Figure 4.

LEGO-Logo

LEGO-Logo was a unique member of the Logo family in use in American schools through the late 1980s and into the 1990s. LEGO-Logo allowed students to use computers to control the manipulation of special LEGO blocks. Students built LEGO structures that used touch and light sensors, motors, and gears plugged into an interface box, and wrote Logo programs that gave them motion. This expanded the computer's reach into the three-dimensional world in a very dynamic way and provided students with the opportunity to learn the behavior of machines, electronics, and motion.

Students learned to break complex problems and machines into simple ones. For example, they could build and operate moving vehicles of different sizes to observe the relationships between speed and weight. While conducting the experiments, students learned about different types of measurement, standard units of measure, rate-distance-time relationships, and the processes of collecting, representing, and analyzing data. Because these experiments combined the manipulation of concrete materials with symbolic representations, such as the names and definitions of Logo procedures, students learned to connect the concrete with the abstract. LEGO-Logo was eventually superseded by the Lego Mindstorms system, which consists of both hardware (sensors, motors, etc.) and software. In mid-2009, the system was upgraded to Lego Mindstorms NXT 2.0., which, as of October 2012, was the latest version.

Music in Logo

Incorporating music into a program and exploring the development of music can be fun, and one does not need to know music or understand musical notation. In order to program a tune in Logo, one writes a procedure using the PLAY primitive, which requires two lists to designate a musical note. These two lists state its two components, its name, such as A, B, C and its duration, such as eighth, quarter, half. The musical program can be broken down into modules, which are then combined to play the tune.

Developments

Much of the development effort in Logo has gone into discovering new application areas, with new sets of primitive procedures and new peripheral hardware. For example, the modeling and simulation software StarLogo explores massive parallelism with thousands of turtles performing their actions at the same time. This environment can be used to explore how large-scale phenomena emerge from simple small-scale behavior. StarLogo can be used to model a variety of systems, from the foraging behavior of

```
TO MANYSQUARES :SIDE
    IF SIDE <5 STOP
    RT    30
    SQUARE :SIDE
        MANYSQUARES :SIDE-5
END
```

Figure 4: Example of a recursive procedure that will reduce the size of the variable SIDE by 5 each time it is called. When this value becomes less than 5, the procedure will stop executing. *Reproduced by permission of Gale, a part of Cengage Learning.*

◀

ants in a colony to the formation of traffic jams in a highway, and the interaction between antibodies and antigens in an immune system. StarLogo TNG (version 1.5) is the latest generation of StarLogo.

Several versions of Logo have included some form of object-oriented programming, usually with a message-passing syntax in which the first argument is an object and the second is an instruction to be carried out by that object. For instance, the Smalltalk programming language was derived primarily from Logo, as was the Etoys educational programming language, which is written in the Smalltalk-variant called Squeak. Logo also is used as the foundation for Boxer, a multipurpose computational medium; KTurtle, an educational programming environment used for the KDE Desktop (KDE Education Project); and Scratch, a programming language created by members of the MIT Media Laboratory.

 See also **Educational Software • Procedural Languages • Programming**

Resources

Books

Maddux, Cleborne D., and D. LaMont Johnson, eds. *Logo: A Retrospective.* New York: Haworth Press, Inc., 1997.

Noss, Richard, and Celia Hoyles. *Learning Mathematics and Logo.* Cambridge: MIT Press, 1992.

Web Sites

Department of Computer Science, University of Maine. "MicroWorlds." http://www.umcs.maine.edu/~larry/microworlds/microworld.html (accessed October 9, 2012).

KDE Education Project. "KTurtle." http://edu.kde.org/kturtle/ (accessed October 9, 2012).

Lego.com. "8547 LEGO⁻ MINDSTORMS⁻ NXT 2.0." http://mindstorms.lego.com/en-us/products/default.aspx (accessed October 9, 2012).

Massachusetts Institute of Technology. "StarLogo TNG." http://education.mit.edu/projects/starlogo-tng (accessed October 9, 2012).

MIT News. "Creating from Scratch." http://web.mit.edu/newsoffice/2007/resnick-scratch.html (accessed October 9, 2012).

M

Markup Languages

A markup language is a system for noting the attributes of a document. Historically, the term "markup" has been used to refer to the process of marking manuscript copy for typesetting, usually with directions for the use of type fonts and sizes, spacing, indentation, and other formatting features. In the electronic era, "markup" refers to the sequence of characters or other symbols that are inserted within a text or word processing file to describe the document's logical structure or indicate how the document should appear when it is displayed or printed. (Notation entered with the intention of describing logical properties is usually referred to as descriptive markup, whereas notation concerned with formatting is referred to as procedural markup.)

Unlike programming languages, which are dynamic and process data through various calculations, markup languages are static. In essence, a markup language identifies similar units of information within a document, bringing a form of instructed intelligence to a document so that applications may read and process it more effectively.

Efforts to devise electronic markup languages evolved initially along two distinct lines. Proprietary* software developers, such as Microsoft, focused largely on procedural markup schemes, expressed in application-specific language and offering functions similar to printers' marks. Their efforts were concerned mainly with the quality and economy of presentation. Interest in descriptive markup languages was motivated by several factors, including the realization that the extent to which electronic documents may be manipulated depends largely on the extent and sophistication of the treatment of logical structures. There was also an awareness that common methods of treatment enhance communication, and the recognition that it will be simpler and less expensive to build backward compatible systems if archived documents have been marked under a standardized system.

This interest grew dramatically, with the advent and rapid expansion of the World Wide Web, a system in which publication and information exchange are based largely on the Hypertext Markup Language (HTML), an open, application-neutral markup language. Application-neutral markup languages have become increasingly important in the design of network-aware applications in recent years. This is in part because proprietary developers have begun to accommodate the interests of users who want to create web documents and take advantage of the other capabilities inherent in application-neutral schemes, and because increasing bandwidth* has allowed programmers to consider the Internet as a computational environment.

* **proprietary** a process or technology developed and owned by an individual or company, and not published openly

* **bandwidth** a measure of the frequency component of a signal or the capacity of a communication channel to carry signals

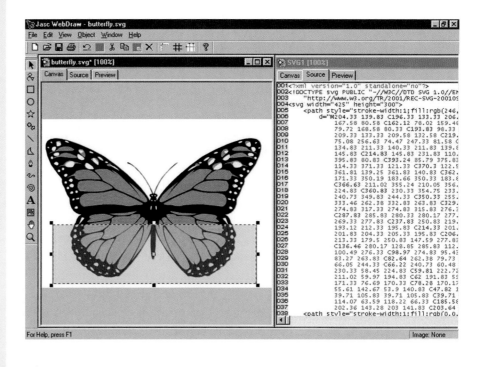

Extensible markup language
© *AP Images/Jasc.*

Today, the most important markup languages are the Standard Generalized Markup Language (SGML), the Hypertext Markup Language (HTML), and the Extensible Markup Language (XML).

SGML

The Standard Generalized Markup Language (SGML) is "a set of rules for defining and expressing the logical structure of documents, thereby enabling software products to control the searching, retrieval, and structured display of those documents," as noted on the *Encoded Archival Description Official Web Site*. SGML was developed at IBM in the late 1960s by a group of programmers charged with the development of an integrated information system. Led by Charles Goldfarb, the team rejected the idea of application-specific coding, opting instead for an open scheme of descriptive tags capable of accommodating the requirements of different types of documents and different computer platforms. Known first as the Generalized Markup Language (GML), SGML was expanded in its scope and further developed under the auspices of the American National Standards Institute (ANSI) and the International Organization for Standardization (ISO). It was adopted as an international standard (ISO 8879) in 1986.

Originally intended to be a method for creating interchangeable, structured documents, SGML became instead a framework for developing more specific markup languages, based largely on its implementation of the concept of a formally defined document type definition (DTD), with an explicit, nested element structure.

```
<!doctype html public "-//W3C//DTD WWW HTML 3.2 Final//EN">
<html>
<head>
<title>Crash Landing in Roswell</title>
<meta name="keywords" content="Roswell, New Mexico, aliens, Air Force">
</head>
<body>
<h1>Space Invaders; Or, Weather Balloon Gone Astray?<h1>
<p>In the summer of 1947, in the desert of central New Mexico, a local rancher found some
unusual debris on his property. After authorities began to investigate the nature of the strange,
metallic material, the U.S. Air Force quickly ruled that the debris was a remnant of a downed
weather balloon. Then and today, many believe the government was trying to hide the
truth<em>that the debris was actually part of a extraterrestrial spacecraft that had crash
landed in the desert, with aliens onboard.<p>
<img src="roswell.jpg" alt="Roswell in 1947" height="350" width="500">
<p><a href="home.html">Home</a></p>
</body>
</html>
```

An example of HTML coding.
Reproduced by permission of Gale, a part of Cengage Learning.

HTML

The Hypertext Markup Language is an SGML Document Type Definition (DTD) that was designed specifically for the World Wide Web. In essence, HTML is a set of markup codes inserted in a file that note logical structures and instruct a web browser how to display a web page's words and images.

Under HTML, markup elements are expressed in pairs to indicate when a structure or display effect begins and ends. For example

<p>Now is the time for all good men to come to the aid of their country. </p>

instructs a web browser to treat the sentence as a paragraph. Under the HTML 4.01 version of the Hypertext Markup Language, the paragraph may be formatted through an enhancement known as "inline styling." The expression below

<p STYLE = "font:Garmond; font-size: 12pt; text-align:justify"> Now is the time for all good men…

renders the paragraph as a line of justified text, using the font and point size specified for display.

The original goal of the World Wide Web was to create an information space in which hypertext links could be made from one document to another without the need to navigate any hierarchical organization of documents. HTML was devised because the Web's designers wanted to create a system that would facilitate communication among users, and that would do so whether the user had a dumb terminal* or a workstation running a graphical user interface (GUI)*. They concluded that a common and simple descriptive language was needed, deciding early on that the creation of an SGML DTD incorporating a limited and basic syntax* would be the most effective way to manage documents under their system.

Over the years HTML was expanded and refined, culminating in HTML 4.01, which included enhancements for greater support of forms, tables, and style sheets. But as the World Wide Web has grown in size and

* **dumb terminal** a keyboard and screen connected to a distant computer without any processing capability

* **graphical user interface (GUI)** an interface that allows computers to be operated through pictures (icons) and mouse-clicks, rather than through text and typing

* **syntax** a set of rules that a computing language incorporates regarding structure, punctuation, and formatting

in the sophistication of the demands it attempted to support, the limitations of HTML became increasingly evident and problematic.

The main problem is that HTML provides a single way of describing the information in a document. It is not extensible, it has many formatting limitations, and it cannot be customized, so it cannot be adapted to meet special needs such as: mathematical notation, chemical formulas, or proprietary, vendor-specific tags that would extend capabilities. Most important of all, HTML does not deal with content or semantics*.

Developers concluded that the best way to solve these problems was to abandon the continued improvement of HTML and create a new markup language. The result is the Extensible Markup Language (XML).

XML

The Extensible Markup Language (XML) is a subset of SGML, whose purpose is "to enable generic SGML to be served, received, and processed on the web" through a system of notation that is unlimited and self-defining. Although XML has been designed to be compatible with HTML (as well as SGML), it is not another single, predefined markup language. It is a meta-language* for designing markup.

From a functional perspective, the most significant difference between HTML and XML is that although HTML can describe a logical structure within a document by document, such as the <p> tag above, XML permits a notation indicating the content of the structure, such as an <author> tag, because XML enables authors and editors to create DTDs that conform to the more specific requirements of a document. This capability means that, in addition, an XML document or a portion of its contents can be processed purely as data by a program or stored with similar data on another computer.

Coordinated mainly by the World Wide Web Consortium (W3C), XML existed in two versions as of mid-2010. By far the most widely-used version is XML 1.1, which was published in its fifth edition in late 2008. Owing to its extensibility, XML has engendered a substantial number of adjunct specifications, including:

- Document Object Model, which is a platform-and language-neutral interface that allows programs and scripts to dynamically access and update the content, structure, and style of documents;

- XML Query, which is intended to provide flexible query facilities to extract data from real and virtual documents on the web and support full interaction between the web and server-side databases, including databases of XML files;

- XPath, which is a language for addressing parts of an XML document;

- XSL, which is a language for stylesheets intended to support the presentation of XML documents and the specification of formatting semantics.

A number of important XML applications were previously developed. Of them, the most important was XHTML, which itself was a reformulation of HTML 4.01 in XML that effectively treated HTML as an XML application. Its main purpose was to build a bridge for web designers from HTML to XML. It was also intended to establish a modular standard capable of supporting the provision of "richer web pages" to the increasing wide range of browser platforms including cellular phones, televisions, cars, wireless communicators, and kiosks, as well as desktop computers.

XHTML 1.0 was formulated in three variant DTDs. *XHMTL Strict* supported strictly structural markup, with formatting available through the use of the World Wide Web Consortium's Cascading Style Sheet (CSS) language that set the font, color, and other layout effects. *XHTML Transitional* enables authors to retain some of HTML's presentation features, so that documents may be successfully addressed by older browsers without support for CSS. *XHTML Frameset* replaced HTML Frames for partitioning a browser window into two or more frames.

Both HTML 4.01 and XHTML have been revised. For instance, XHTML 1.1 was published in January 2000, while HTML 5 was published as a so-called "working draft" by the W3C in early 2008. However, WAC has not scheduled HTML 5.0 for release in its final form until 2014. In tandem with the development of HTML 5, XHTML 5 also is being produced.

Another important XML application is the Mathematical Markup Language (MathML). MathML, which can be used to encode both mathematical notation and mathematical content, provides a rich vocabulary with 30 tags to describe abstract notational structures, and another 150 tags to provide the means of specifying the intended meaning of a particular expression, and allows for documents with sophisticated mathematical content. Yet another important XML application is the Synchronized Multimedia Integration Language (SMIL). SMIL defines an XML-based language that allows authors to write interactive multimedia presentations. Using SMIL, an author can describe the temporal behavior of a multimedia presentation, associate hyperlinks with media objects, and describe the layout of the presentation on a screen.

Future Directions

A few things about the future of markup languages are clear. First, extensible languages will be dominant, owing to the extent to which they may be enhanced and customized. Second, in order to accommodate the increasing number of portable devices connected to the web and their computational and display capabilities, markup languages will be necessarily modular. And third, because XML's data description capabilities affords the opportunity to replace web browsers with more powerful applications, such as the applications that make up Microsoft Office, it seems likely that XML and its successors will shift the principal motif of web-based computing from the browser to productivity suites and other client-based applications.

▶ *See also* **Document Processing** • **E-Commerce** • **Hypermedia and Multimedia** • **Hypertext** • **World Wide Web**

Markup Language Cost Considerations

Economics plays an important role in how and to what extent electronic documents are marked. Although formatting for presentation is relatively inexpensive, until recently formatting documents for both content and presentation represented a significant additional expense in the production of electronic documents. Although the production of "neutrally coded" text, based on the Standard Generalized Markup Language (SGML) and its derivatives, has diminished in cost, the limited number of suppliers able to produce logical markup of sufficiently high quality for complex text contributes significantly to the interest in presentation-oriented systems, most notably the Portable Document Format (PDF) of Adobe Systems.

* **bit** a single binary digit, 1 or 0—a contraction of Binary digIT; the smallest unit for storing data in a computer

* **polarity** the positive (+) or negative (−) state of an object, which dictates how it will react to forces such as magnetism or electricity

* **ASCII** an acronym that stands for American Standard Code for Information Interchange; assigns a unique 8- binary number to every letter of the alphabet, the digits (0 to 9), and most keyboard symbols

* **EBCDIC** the acronym for Extended Binary Coded Decimal Interchange Code, which assigns a unique 8- binary number to every letter of the alphabet, the digits (0 to 9), and most keyboard symbols

* **byte** a group of eight binary digits; represents a single character of text

Resources

Books

Aronson, Larry. *HTML Manual of Style: A Clear, Concise Reference for Hypertext Markup Language (including HTML5)*. 4th ed. Reading, MA: Addison-Wesley Professional, 2011.

Goldfarb, Charles F., and Paul Prescod. *The XML Handbook*. 5th ed. Upper Saddle River, NJ: Prentice Hall, 2004.

Memory Devices

Digital computers must convert the information that the user enters into them; that is, from documents, graphics, videos, or sound, into digital data. These data are really a series of 1s and 0s. Each 1 or 0 is called a binary digit (bit*). The determination of whether a bit is a 0 (off) or a 1 (on) is made by the electronics in the computer hardware. Some computers make this determination by the polarity* of magnetized material, while others determine the status of a by whether or not electricity is flowing along a circuit. Using these binary digits and a coding scheme such as ASCII* or EBCDIC*, eight bits are grouped into a byte* with each byte representing one character (e.g., letter, punctuation mark, or number). These bytes are sent from one area of the computer to another and stored in various areas of the computer.

In order for data to be processed by a computer, they must first be stored in main computer storage. Over the years, different memory devices have been used to store data (as 1s and 0s) in main computer storage. One of the first devices for storing data was the vacuum tube. Vacuum tubes were light bulb-sized electronic tubes with glowing filaments. Although they worked, vacuum tubes generated a tremendous amount of heat, used a large amount of electric power, and were delicate, bulky, unreliable, and expensive.

In the early 1950s, American computer scientist and systems scientist Jay W. Forrester (1918–) and his group at Massachusetts Institute of Technology (MIT) developed magnetic core storage, which replaced vacuum tubes and was the most popular device for storing data in main computer storage for two decades. Magnetic cores consisted of small ring-shaped pieces of metal that could be polarized or magnetized in either of two directions to represent a 1 or a 0.

Invented in 1948, transistors become the memory device of choice by the 1960s. Transistors can be thought of as tiny electrically operated switches that can alternate between On (1) and Off (0) many millions of times per second.

Integrated Circuits

Integrated circuits (IC) are entire collections of electrical circuits etched onto very thin slices of silicon. (Silicon, with chemical symbol Si, is a natural element found in sand that is purified.) A single integrated circuit is less than a quarter-inch square and is often called a chip or microchip. Integrated circuits are housed within ceramic containers of various types including single in-line memory module (SIMM), dual in-line pin (DIP), dual in-line memory module (DIMM), pin-grid array (PGA), or single edge contact (SEC).

At the start of the twenty-first century, integrated circuit-based semiconductor* memory was the primary memory device used for main computer storage. Semiconductor memory is an integrated circuit made up of millions of tiny transistors printed on small chips of silicon. Data that were stored in magnetic core memory could be accessed in microseconds, but data stored in memory are accessed even more quickly, in nanosecond*s. The use of memory devices has increased the speed and decreased the price of main computer storage. The disadvantage to using some memory devices is that they are volatile*; that is, whenever the current no longer flows to the device, the stored data are lost. Magnetic cores did not have this problem.

There are several different categories of semiconductor memory, including: RAM, SRAM, DRAM, ROM, PROM, EPROM, and EAPROM. Each type of memory is characterized by the technology it uses to hold the data and the type of data it stores.

RAM, SRAM, and DRAM

Random Access Memory (RAM) is used when program instructions or data are temporarily stored in the computer before and after they are processed. RAM is also called primary storage or main computer storage. RAM is very important to computer systems. When the computer starts, the operating system is loaded from storage into RAM, and when the user opens an application software package, the instructions for it are also loaded into RAM. As someone uses that software to write a letter to his mother, for example, the characters he types are held in RAM until the software is told to perform some action such as print the document. RAM is the kind of memory referred to when computers are said to be 2 GB (pronounced gig or gigabyte) computers. Having enough RAM is important because it affects how quickly the user can perform certain tasks. In some cases, the user will not be able to use certain software programs if he does not have enough RAM.

Random Access Memory can be static* or dynamic*. In random-access memory (SRAM), a small current is used to maintain the stored data values without further manipulation while the power is on. CMOS memory (complementary metal oxide semiconductor), pronounced *SEE moss*, is a type of SRAM that is used to hold data concerning someone's computer configuration. The most common type of device used for main memory is a paired transistor and capacitor, which holds an electric charge. Because capacitors slowly lose their charges, they must be recharged about every 4 milliseconds. This type of memory is called dynamic random access memory (DRAM). DRAM is cheaper, but slower, than SRAM.

* **semiconductor** solid material that possesses electrical conductivity characteristics that are similar to those of metals under certain conditions, but can also exhibit insulating qualities under other conditions

* **nanosecond** one-thousand-millionth (one billionth, or 10^{-9}) of a second

* **volatile** subject to rapid change; describes the character of data when current no longer flows to a device (that is, electrical power is switched off)

* **static** without movement; stationary

* **dynamic** changing; possessing volatility

*robotics the science and engineering of building electromechanical machines that aim to serve as replacements for human laborers

One major problem with RAM is that it is volatile. That is, its contents will be lost when the computer's power is lost. Thus, other means of permanently storing data and instructions must be used, including other types of memory such as ROM and external storage devices such as magnetic tapes, magnetic disks, CD-ROMs (compact disc-read only memory), and DVDs (digital versatile discs).

ROM, PROM, EPROM, and EAPROM

ROM, or read-only memory, is a type of semiconductor memory that is permanent and cannot be erased. The Central Processing Unit (CPU) can read data stored in ROM, but cannot write to ROM. With ROM, the data are recorded when the memory is manufactured. The data are activated when the computer is turned on. ROM is normally used to store data and programs, such as language interpreters (BASIC, short for Beginner's All-purpose Symbolic Instruction Code), display controllers, or the storage of manufacturer-specific micro codes such as Basic Input Output System (BIOS). Unlike RAM, ROM is not volatile.

PROM, or programmable read-only memory, is a subclass of ROM. Like ROM, it can be read, but it cannot be altered. PROM differs from ROM in that the stored data are not recorded when the chip is manufactured. Rather, the data to be stored in PROM are recorded by the manufacturer of the computer using special high-current devices to burn fuses on the devices. Thus, PROM is programmed once and the manufacturer of the computer can use this memory device to control a specific product. PROM is non-volatile.

EPROM, or erasable programmable read-only memory, is a special kind of PROM. EPROM allows the user to erase the data stored in this memory device by using special ultraviolet devices and then reprogram it. An example of where EPROM is used is in the field of robotics*. Because a robot may have to be re-programmed on a routine basis, an EPROM memory device is used.

Another type of PROM is called electrically alterable programmable read-only memory (EAPROM). This type of memory can be changed by the computer using special high-current operations. Programming these devices repeatedly (more than 1,000 times) tends to destroy them, so they are used to hold data that rarely changes.

Managing Memory for Data Retrieval

The type and quantity of memory available in a computer system is important, and so is the user's ability to store and retrieve data. The management of memory is a very significant function of a computer's operating system. A part of the operating system called the Memory Manager controls how programs access memory to store necessary instructions and data before and after processing by the CPU. When a program needs to use RAM, the Memory Manager checks for an unused portion and allocates it. The Memory Manager tracks which portions of memory are being used and by whom. One major task of the Memory Manager is to protect the portion of RAM that contains the operating system. It cannot be altered or deleted. The Memory Manager also deallocates memory when a program is finished.

There have been many schemes developed to allow the operating system to allocate and manage memory. Early computer systems were single-user and had simple algorithm*s. As computer systems and operating systems have become more sophisticated, the memory management schemes have had to become more sophisticated, too. One of the latest schemes allows programs or data files that are larger than the available memory space to be brought into memory in segments. This is called virtual memory. Using virtual memory is slower than if the entire program was small enough to be stored in RAM in one piece.

The cost of memory has decreased rapidly and the speed of memory has increased quickly since the days of the vacuum tube. These trends are expected to continue, partly due to the fact that integrated circuits are packing more and more technology into a very small space. The decrease in memory cost allows programmers to use more and more memory for application programs while the increasing speed of memory makes these programs run faster and faster.

Additional Information

In April 2008, International Business Machines Corporation (IBM) researcher Stuart Parkin announced a demonstration of a new memory technology, namely a working 3-bit register (unit of digital memory) built using racetrack memory. Racetrack memory stores information as domains of magnetization in a microscopic metal wire. Short lengths of a wire are magnetized one way to represent a 0 and the other to represent a 1. To read or write data, a whole string of domains is pushed back and forth at high speed by running a current through the wire. Racetrack memory chips could keep their data even with the power off. Flash memory chips can do this, but store data slowly and wear out after a limited number of reads and writes. A racetrack memory chip could in theory store as much data as a hard drive, be as fast as or faster than a random-access memory chip (which cannot keep its data without power), have no moving parts, and endure an unlimited number of reads and writes. Parkin, already famous for applying the phenomenon known as giant magnetoresistance to hardware, making today's high-density computer hard drives possible, said that racetrack memory chips might be ready for market in 10 years or less. Many details of device design and manufacturing would have to be resolved before this could happen. Racetrack memory, under the broader field called Spintronics, is being developed and tested to provide the high reliability and performance of flash memory and the high capacity and low cost of hard disks. However, as of 2012, this technology had yet made it to the commercial market.

▶ See also **Assembly Language and Architecture • Central Processing Unit • Operating Systems • Storage Devices**

Computer Sciences, 2ⁿᵈ Edition

Is Silicon Found In Silicon Valley?

Yes. In fact, silicon is found in 25 percent of earth's crust. First discovered in 1822 by Swedish chemist Jöns Jacob Berzelius (1779–1848), silicon is an element found in many mineral compounds, including mica, quartz, and talc. In its natural state, it appears metallic in luster and has a reddish- brown or black color. It is used mostly in metal alloys such as cast iron and steel, as well as in lubricants and glass. A small amount of silicon is mined each year to be purified and used in the manufacturing of semiconductors and integrated circuits.

* **algorithm** a rule or procedure used to solve a mathematical problem—most often described as a sequence of steps

Resources

Books

Clements, Alan. *Principles of Computer Hardware.* 4th ed. Oxford and New York: Oxford University Press, 2007.

Harris, David Money, and Sarah L. Harris. *Digital Design and Computer Architecture.* Boston: Morgan Kaufmann, 2013.

Laudon, Kenneth C., and Jane Price Laudon. *Essentials of Management Information Systems.* 9th ed. Upper Saddle River, NJ: Pearson Prentice Hall, 2011.

McHoes, Ann McIver, and Ida M. Flyn. *Understanding Operating Systems.* 6th ed. Boston: Course Technology/Cengage Learning, 2011.

Null, Linda, and Julia Lobur. *The Essentials of Computer Organization and Architecture.* 3rd ed. Sudbury, MA: Jones & Bartlett Learning, 2012.

Parsons, June Jamrich, and Dan Oja. *New Perspectives on Computer Concepts.* 13th ed. Boston: Course Technology/Cengage Learning, 2010.

Zelkowitz, Marvin V. *Advances in Computers, Volume 78: Improving the Web.* Amsterdam: Elsevier, 2010.

Web Sites

The Register. "'Spintronics' Brings IBM's Racetrack Memory Closer to Reality." http://www.theregister.co.uk/2012/07/26/spintronics_advances_racetrack_memory/ (accessed October 10, 2012).

Morse, Samuel

American Inventor
1791–1872

Samuel Finley Breese Morse was responsible for creation of the Morse Code, an electronic alphabet that carries messages via electric wires. Morse was born in 1791 in Charlestown, Massachusetts. At a young age, he began to display artistic talent that he developed throughout his life. While attending college lectures in natural philosophy, Morse studied electricity. Although formal academics did not initially interest Morse, his studies inspired him to construct models of batteries.

To supplement his college income, Morse began to paint portraits of fellow students and faculty members. He considered painting professionally and in 1811 went abroad to study painting, returning home in 1815. During a European trip in 1829 to expand his artistic horizons, he became aware of the French telegraph, a semaphore system. Morse quickly realized that an electric spark could transmit a message more rapidly than the semaphore. His interest again turned toward potential uses for electricity.

As he returned from Europe in 1831, Morse began efforts to develop what would become the American telegraph. In conversations with fellow passengers, Morse learned about sparking properties of an electromagnet and the fact that wires can carry current. These two factors would allow the transmission of coded messages, and Morse started developing a numerical based code.

The digits from one to five were represented by one to five dots, the digits from six to nine by a combination of dots and dashes. The next step was to translate the coded numbers to words. Each group of numbers translates to a word, for example, dots representing 215 would translate to the word "war" and fifteen to "Belgium." Morse started to develop a conversion dictionary for translating the number groups to words. Another problem was how to record the transmissions. Morse's early drawings show an electromagnet causing a pencil to contact a moving paper strip when the electrical circuit closed and another magnet to raise the pencil when the circuit was broken. The pencil marks would record the code dots.

▲

Samuel Morse. © *Three Lions/Stinger/ Hulton Archive/Getty Images.*

Although he was an art professor, Morse continued working on the telegraph, experimenting with various ways for recording the message and trying various methods to extend the distance over which the message could travel. His art studio doubled as a laboratory where he demonstrated working models of the telegraph to students and visitors. Some changes in the model resulted from discussing ideas and problems with the visitors. He determined that an electronic message could be sent any distance by relaying the signals. There had to be a way to increase the signal distance between relays. Morse needed more than casual advice; he needed partners with expertise.

In 1835 Leonard Gale, a professor of geology and mineralogy, became the first partner. Gale provided the techniques needed to solve the distance/relay problem based on professor Joseph Henry's scientific articles. The second partner, Alfred Vail, joined in 1837 to design and supervise the production of the instruments. Vail's major contributions were replacing the pencil with a blunt stylus and designing a key for transmitting the message. In 1837 the fourth partner, Maine congressman F.O.J. Smith was enlisted to help with obtaining financial support from Congress and to contact for the services necessary to construct the communications network.

As the telegraph came closer to reality, it became apparent that the number to letter code was too cumbersome. By 1838 the first version of dots and dashes representing letters appeared. The code uses combinations of dots and dashes from one to a set of four. The most frequently occurring letters have the shortest code. For example an E is one dot; the Q is

Translation Problems

The Morse Code was adapted for use in Europe when used to transmit non-English-language text. One problem encountered was that many non-English languages use diacritical marks that the Morse Code was not designed to handle. In 1851, a group of European nations agreed on an International Morse Code, which made diacritical translation possible

two dots, one dash, one dot. There are two versions of the code: American Morse and International Morse. "What hath God wrought!" was the first intercity telegraph message, which was sent from Washington, D.C., to Baltimore, Maryland, on May 24, 1844. Telegraphed reports of events and votes at the 1844 Democratic Convention in Baltimore proved the usefulness of the telegraph for transmitting information.

Morse viewed the telegraph as source of financial security and a means to obtain resources to support education. He served as a charter trustee of Vassar College and donated gifts to Yale University, the Cleveland Female Seminary, and other educational institutions. His other ventures included developing improvements in Daguerreotype, an early form of photography using silver and copper plates; running twice for mayor of New York City; and cofounding and serving as first president of the National Academy of Design. At the end of his life, Morse attained international stature as the inventor of the American telegraph. Today he is also recognized as an important American artist. Morse died in April 1872.

▶ *See also* **Codes • Coding Techniques • Internet • Telecommunications**

Resources

Books

Mabee, Carleton. *The American Leonardo.* New York: Alfred A. Knopf, 1944.

Periodicals

Bird, D. "Morse Code Examined Using Modern Communication Theory: Morse Is Remarkably Efficient." *RADCOM -POOLE.* 2011. 87, no. 1: 79–82.

Music, Computer

The term "computer music" encompasses a wide range of compositional activities, from the generation of conventionally notated scores using data calculated by the computer, to the direct synthesis of sound in a digital form within the computer itself, ready for conversion into audio signals.

There are three basic techniques for producing sounds with a computer: sign-bit extraction, the use of hybrid digital-analog systems, and digital-to-analog conversion. Sign-bit extraction has occasionally been used for compositions of serious musical intent. Little interest persists in building hybrid digital-analog facilities because some types of signal processing, such as reverberation and filtering, are time-consuming even in the fastest of computers. Digital-to-analog conversion has become the standard technique for computer sound synthesis because it is the most

Creating music electronically.
© *AP Images/MUHAMMED MUHEISEN.*

versatile method of computer sound generation. Because the sound wave is constructed directly, there are almost no restrictions on sound properties.

To use a computer for music production, the composer or performer first "calls up" from the computer memory the appropriate precompiled program. The program includes various "instruments," i.e., digitally stored musical waveforms, and the operator selects the instruments to use before indicating to the computer in detail—note by note, correct in pitch and timbre—the musical composition to be reproduced.

The computer then translates the instrument definitions into a machine language program, and, if necessary, puts the score into the proper format for processing. After that, the program actually "plays" the score on the instruments, thus creating the sound. The processing of a note of the score consists of two stages: initialization and performance. At the initialization of a note, the values that are to remain fixed throughout the duration of the note are set. During the performance of a note, the computer calculates the actual output corresponding to the sound.

The advantage of digital-to-analog conversion is that the computer can be called upon to assemble the individual sounds into a composition so that the composer need only be concerned with the conception of the piece and the preparation of that conception for the computer. Other advantages are that almost any computer may be used for sound generation, and the devices of a synthesizer can be simulated by a computer program.

As early as 1843, it was suggested that computers might be suitable for the production of music. Referring to Charles Babbage's "Analytical Machine" (a precursor of the modern computer), Ada Byron King, Countess of Lovelace, suggested that the engine could be used for making music if the necessary information could be understood and properly expressed.

The Vocoder

Much of today's pop music involves synthesized sounds. Many performers—including Cher, Madonna, Britney Spears, and T-Pain—have tried to incorporate this distinct sound into their voices, by using voice-coding devices. The Vocoder was one of the first voice-coding devices. Although the sound is very high-tech, the Vocoder originally was developed in the 1940s to improve telephone service. Inventor Homer Dudley of Bell Laboratories designed a way to break speech patterns into modules that could be transmitted over a narrow bandwidth. The Vocoder was also used during World War II to enhance poor-sounding trans-Atlantic messages between British Prime Minister Winston Churchill and U.S. President Franklin Roosevelt. Similarly, many music artists also use Auto-Tune, a proprietary audio processor created by Antares Audio Technologies in 1997.

In 1950 or 1951, CSIRAC, the first digital computer in Australia, produced the world's first computer-generated music, including a public performance of "Colonel Bogey March" in 1951. CSIRAC merely played programmed music and did not engage in computer-aided composition. In 1957, Max Mathews (1926–2011), an engineer at Bell Labs, began working on computer generation of music and speech sounds. Together with John Pierce (1910–2002) and Joan E. Miller, Mathews wrote several computer music programs, the best known of which is MUSIC V. This program was more than just a software system because it included an "orchestration" program that simulated many of the processes employed in the classical electronic music studio. It specified unit generators for the standard waveforms, adders, modulators, filters, and reverberators. It was sufficiently generalized that users could freely define their own generators. Thus, MUSIC V became the software prototype for music production installations all over the world.

One of the most notable successors of MUSIC V was designed by Barry Vercoe at the Massachusetts Institute of Technology during the 1970s. His program, MUSIC XI, ran on a PDP-11 computer and was a tightly designed system that incorporated many new features, including graphic score output and input. MUSIC XI was significant not only for these advances, but also for its direct approach to synthesis, thanks to improvements in the efficient use of memory space. Thus, MUSIC XI became accessible to a family of much smaller machines that many studios were able to afford. Another major advance was discovered in 1973 by John Chowning (1934–) of Stanford University, who pioneered the use of digital FM (frequency modulation) as a source of musical timbre.

The most advanced digital sound synthesis is conducted in large institutional installations, most of them in American universities, followed by European facilities. Examples of American installations are Columbia University, University of Illinois, Indiana University, University of Michigan, State University of New York at Buffalo, and Queens College, New York. European facilities include the Instituut voor Sonologie in Utrecht, the Netherlands; LIMB (Laboratorio Permanente per l'Informatica Musicale) at the University of Padua, Italy; and IRCAM (Institut de Recherche et de Coordination Acoustique/Musique), part of the Centre Georges Pompidou in Paris, France.

Computer technology has led to a tremendous expansion of music resources by offering composers a spectrum of sounds ranging from pure tones to random noise. Computers have enabled the rhythmic organization of music to a degree of subtlety and complexity never before attainable. They have allowed composers complete control over their work, if they so choose, even to the point of bypassing the performer as an intermediary between the creators of music and their audience. Perhaps computers' greatest contribution to music is that they have brought about the acceptance of the definition of music as "organized sound."

See also **Codes • Film and Video Editing • Graphic Devices • Music • Music Composition**

Resources

Books

Collins, Nick. *Introduction to Computer Music.* Hoboken, NJ: John Wiley &amp Sons, 2009.

Dean, Roger T., ed. *The Oxford Handbook of Computer Music.* Oxford, UK: Oxford University Press, 2009.

N

Network Design

Network design is a category of systems design that deals with data transport mechanisms. As with other systems' design disciplines, network design follows an analysis stage, where requirements are generated, but it precedes implementation, where the system (or relevant system component) is constructed. The objective of network design is to satisfy data communication requirements while minimizing expense. Requirement scope can vary widely from one network design project to another based on geographic particularities and the nature of the data requiring transport.

Network analysis may be conducted at an inter-organizational, organizational, or departmental level. The requirements generated during the analysis may therefore define an inter-network connecting two or more organizations, an enterprise network that connects the departments of a single organization, or a departmental network to be designed around specific divisional needs. Inter-networks and enterprise networks often span multiple buildings, some of which may be hundreds or thousands of miles apart. The distance between physical connections often dictates the type of technology that must be used to facilitate data transmission.

Components that exist within close physical proximity (usually within the same building) and can be connected to each other directly or through hubs or switches using owned equipment are considered part of a local area network (LAN)*. It is generally impractical and often impossible to connect the equipment of multiple buildings as a single LAN; so individual LANs are instead interconnected to form a greater network, such as a metropolitan area network (MAN) or wide area network (WAN).

MANs may be constructed where buildings are located close enough to each other to facilitate a reliable high-speed connection (usually less than 50 kilometers or 30 miles). Greater distances generally result in much slower connections, which are often leased from common carriers to create WANs. Due to the close proximity of equipment, LAN connections offer the best performance and control (usually with speeds around 100 megabits per second [Mbps]) and WAN connections the worst (with many machines often sharing a single connection of less than 2 Mbps).

Toward the end of the 2000s, several competing technologies were touted as offering greatly increased LAN speeds for homes and small businesses. For instance, the HomePlug Powerline Alliance is an industry-led group with sixty-five member companies (as of October 2012) promoting high-speed LAN capabilities with technology that utilizes

* **local area network (LAN)** a high-speed computer network that is designed for users who are located near each other

* **binary** existing in only two states, such as on or off, one or zero

* **bitstream** a serialized collection of bits; usually used in transfer of bits from one system to another

a home's existing power lines. First released in 2001 as HomePlug 1.0, the system was initially rated at 14 Mbps. Later versions increased the data rate substantially, with the Alliance touting home LAN data rates of 200 Mbps in 2010. A newer standard aiming to achieve one gigabits per second (Gbps) data rates, dubbed HomePlug AV2, was released in January 2012, with consumer products compatible with the new standard projected to go on sale later in the year. On March 12, 2012, the HomePlug Powerline Alliance announced that the Digital Living Network Alliance (DLNA) had approved the HomePlug AV and HD-PLC Powerline networking standards. These HomePlug standards will be incorporated into the Networked Device Interoperability Guidelines, improvements that will increase the network speeds at which homes will be connected digitally in the future.

Besides HomePlug, there are other recently-developed technologies for increased home network speeds, such as the G.hn standard developed by the International Telecommunication Union (ITU). The G.hn technology, which is an alternative to Wi-Fi (the trademarked name of the Wi-Fi Alliance), would allow data rates of 1 Gbps, and is appealing because it is designed to be able to utilize the existing power, phone, or cable TV lines of a home or business for data transfer.

Networks connect machines—which may be computers, computer peripherals, digital telephones, or other digital communication equipment—to each other for the purpose of exchanging data. The data carried by a network may represent voice, video, text, numeric values, or computer-readable code. Regardless of its context at the machines that send and receive the data, the data are handled by the physical network as an uninterpreted series of Boolean values or binary* digits called a bitstream*. At this lowest logical level, these values of zero and one are represented on the physical network as discrete electronic pulses (baseband) or frequency modulations (broadband) depending on the physical transmission method chosen for a given network segment.

The physical network is responsible for delivering the bitstream to its destination without regard to the high-level meaning of the data. In this sense, all computer networks are responsible for performing the same function. Because the bitstream must include data from many different machines, however, the network needs to define a method for sharing the physical resources. This method, referred to as network architecture, determines the means by which data from competing machines are introduced to the network and delivered to the appropriate destinations.

Common network architectures for LANs and MANs, also called Media Access Control (MAC) protocols, include Ethernet, Token Ring, Fiber Distributed Data Interface (FDDI), and Asynchronous Transfer Mode (ATM). Most network architectures dictate specific physical topologies, including the type of medium to be used and its configuration. Token passing methods, such as FDDI and Token Ring for instance, require physical rings of a specified cable. The various MAC protocols and physical mediums—including copper wire, glass fiber, and radio frequency—all possess relative advantages and limitations in terms of speed, consistency, security, expense, and many other important attributes. The combination of these characteristics means that, although all networks can carry all varieties of data, some network architectures are better suited for certain types of data than others. A primary planning function in network design is the determination of which network architecture best suits the type of data the network is being built to support.

Using inter-networking protocols, such as Transmission Control Protocol/Internet Protocol (TCP/IP), MANs, and WANs, one can connect many local area networks incorporating a variety of different LAN architectures. This capability affords the network designer some flexibility to choose MAC protocols that best accommodate the needs of a given network segment without jeopardizing connectivity to the rest of the enterprise or inter-organizational network.

A network planning effort, therefore, may conclude that a segment with requirements focused around multimedia use ATM for its consistent performance, while another segment of the same enterprise network with less demanding performance requirements use Ethernet for its low cost and compatibility with existing hardware. Such network segments are interconnected using routers*, which strip MAC-specific addressing from data packages, or packets, and rebuild the addresses at the destination segment using the appropriate MAC protocol.

So although many different MAC configurations can interconnect seamlessly, a common inter-networking protocol must be chosen and adhered to across the network in order to realize data communication between all machines. Increasingly, and especially for organizations wanting to connect to the public Internet, that choice is TCP/IP.

Network design is an ongoing effort at most organizations because new applications and business growth create new requirements, which can be fulfilled with ever improving network technology. Network engineering, of which network design is a component, is a balance between performance and expense. So as communication technology continues to improve, resulting in higher data speeds and lower costs, network analysis and redesign is continually necessary to maintain that balance effectively.

▶ See also **Internet • Network Protocols • Network Topologies • Security • Telecommunications**

Resources

Books

Donoso, Yezid. *Network Design for IP Convergence.* Boca Raton, FL: CRC Press, 2009.

Iannone, Eugenio. *Telecommunication Networks.* Boca Raton, FL: CRC Press, 2012.

* **routers** network devices that direct packets to the next network device or to the final destination

Stallings, William. *Business Data Communications.* 6th ed. Upper Saddle
River, NJ: Prentice Hall, 2008.

Web Sites

Digital Living Network Alliance. "Discover the Possibilities." http://
www.dlna.org/consumer-home/The-Possibilities (accessed
October 15, 2012).

HomePlug Powerline Alliance. "DLNA® Approves HomePlug AV
Powerline Networking for Increased Digital Home Connectivity."
https://www.homeplug.org/news/pr/view?item_key=a4a2b475cfae3
07bc9cc4d3f58933fe8d139415f (accessed October 15, 2012).

International Telecommunication Union. "Overview." http://www.itu.
int/en/about/Pages/default.aspx (accessed October 15, 2012).

Network Protocols

Most modern computers are interconnected with other computers in
one way or another, whether by a dialup connection or over a local area
network (LAN)*. For interconnections that cover distances greater than a
few meters, *serial* connections are economical. In serial communications,
the information bits are sent one at a time over a single communications
channel. This stands in contrast to *parallel* communications, where information is sent one byte (or word) at a time over eight or more communications channels between the machines.

As in all communications, the problem normally focuses on establishing ways for the receiver (meaning the destination computer) to interpret and decode correctly the transmitted information. Communications
protocol*s are designed to facilitate this in serial communications; they
are especially important in this case because the receiver must be able to
process correctly each bit that it receives.

Protocol Functions

For serial communications to take place correctly, several functions have
to be possible. First, the receiving and sending computers must be able to
coordinate their actions, to enable flow control, error control, addressing,
and connection management. *Flow control* manages the rate of information
flow between machines (note that this may be different than the data rate
of the network connecting the machines); *error control* enables transmission errors to be corrected; *addressing* allows information to be routed to
the correct destination; and *connection management* is the set of functions
associated with setting up and maintaining connections (where needed).

Second, the receiver must be able to determine when a message (or
data packet) begins and ends and distinguish control information from
the information that the user is transmitting.

---

* **local area network (LAN)** a
high-speed computer network
that is designed for users who
are located near each other

* **protocol** an agreed
understanding for the sub-
operations that make up a
transaction, usually found in the
specification of inter-computer
communications

Protocol Mechanisms

These functions are implemented through communications protocols. These protocols are a strict set of rules that both the sending and the receiving computers follow when communicating. These rules include the format of information to be sent, as well as rules defining how a machine (sender or receiver) is to behave when an event occurs. An event can be externally created (such as the occurrence of an error) or internally generated (such as a connection request). These behaviors are written into the communications software that runs in both the sender and receiver.

Generally, protocols break the information that the user wishes to send into packets*. These normally consist of a *header,* the user information (message), and often a *trailer.* The trailer is most commonly a checksum* generated by a *cyclical redundancy check* (CRC) coder and is used for error detection. The header carries information fields that the sender and receiver use to communicate with each other so that they can implement the necessary functions as defined by the protocol.

Network Architectures

Although the general functions of protocols are as stated earlier, it turns out to be convenient and efficient to optimize specific protocols for specific classes of functions, and then to use multiple protocols to get the overall job done rather than designing a *one size fits all* system. To aid in this task, protocol developers created an approach to classify and organize the different functions that have to be performed in data communications. The most common approach to this is called the Open Systems Interconnection Reference Model (OSI Reference Model) that was developed and standardized by the International Organization for Standardization (ISO). The OSI Reference Model is a seven-layer model, with each layer representing a particular set of functions, and for which specific protocols have been developed.

The layers and their functions are outlined below:

- The *physical* layer is concerned with moving bits, and includes physical and electrical connections.
- The *link* layer is concerned with reliable bit transfer, as well as local (as opposed to global) addressing. This involves synchronization, error control, and some flow control.
- The *network* layer is concerned with routing packets through network elements (called nodes) interconnected by reliable links. This layer deals with addresses that are global in scope. Examples of global addresses are a telephone number or a postal address, whereas a local address might be an office telephone extension or mailbox.
- The *transport* layer ensures end-to-end reliability, connection control, and flow control. Its task is to make a network meet the special

* **packets** collections of digital data elements that are part of a complete message or signal; packets contain their destination addresses to enable reassembly of the message or signal

* **checksum** a number that is derived from adding together parts of an electronic message before it is dispatched; it can be used at the receiver to check against message corruption

requirements of end user machines. *End-to-end* means that network elements are not involved in implementing transport layer functionality.

- The *session* layer is concerned with the establishment and maintenance of connections for the communicating end nodes.

- The *presentation* layer is concerned with ensuring that information can be transmitted between different types of computer systems (for example, Apple Macintosh computers and Windows PCs).

- Finally, the *application* layer is concerned with providing the functions needed by networked applications. A networked application may be a mail program (such as Eudora or Microsoft Outlook), and the application layer function would be the mail transport protocols.

Quite a number of protocols have been developed under the guidelines of the OSI reference model. Many of these have not met with commercial success, so they are most often used to provide the basis for new protocols today. Still, the OSI reference model serves as a convenient way to organize the necessary functionality of data communications systems.

TCP/IP Protocols

The effort to garner commercial support of OSI protocols has been undermined in large part by the protocols that are used in the Internet, which are called the Transport Control Protocol (TCP) and the Internet Protocol (IP). These protocols were developed outside of the OSI effort, and were designed to provide minimal services. This design strategy moved much of the intelligence (i.e., the processing requirements) needed to implement networked applications to the user machines. TCP/IP was developed and debugged before similar OSI protocols got off the ground so many users adopted them as an interim measure until the OSI protocols were available. They took hold, and users never saw the need to switch protocols, which is a costly procedure that often results in unreliable systems for a time.

Two principal protocols exist in this system. The Internet Protocol (IP) was designed to provide an adaptive (though it is sometimes unreliable) network that could interconnect independently owned and managed subnetworks. It is unreliable because the network makes no assurances that packets are delivered to their destinations, though they do their best to try. Allowing independently owned and managed networks is also important because different organizations have different local requirements, yet they still might want to communicate with other users. IP corresponds fairly closely to the OSI network layer in functionality.

To provide some confidence to end users, the Transport Control Protocol (TCP) was developed to work with IP. TCP provides end-to-end error control as well as flow control. Thus, if IP loses some packets along the way, TCP will recover them transparently to the user, so the network will seem reliable. TCP also performs some session management functions. Thus, it is a mix between OSI's transport and session layers (though it does not contain all session layer functions).

By pushing the processing requirements for services out of the network, TCP/IP has set the stage for rapid innovation in applications and services. Adding a new service means developing the necessary application protocol, constructing a server*, and advertising the services. What is significant is that no network changes are necessary for new services, which supports the rate of innovation. Thus, TCP/IP networks can carry electronic mail, images, worldwide web traffic, even video images and telephone calls, all without changes to the underlying network systems (with the exception, of course, of the capacity increases needed to handle all of the packets that are generated by these services).

* **server** a computer that does not deal directly with human users, but instead handles requests from other computers for services to be performed

Future Evolution of TCP/IP

Despite its success, TCP/IP faces some challenges. One of the challenges is that the available IP addresses are being exhausted, due to its success. Another is that many of the new services are making demands on the network that would be best served if some additional capabilities existed; for example, telephone calls and interactive video would benefit from real time capabilities to minimize network delays.

To address these concerns, a new version of IP was developed, version 6 (called IPv6, or Internet Protocol version 6). It was deployed on June 6, 2012, with what was called the World IPv6 Launch. On that day, major Web sites had IPv6 permanently enabled, while participating Internet Service Providers (ISPs) offered connectivity of IPv6 to their customers and participating router makers had IPv6-enabled devices available for distribution. IPv6 supports a much larger number of addresses and offer a broader range of services to network users, including real-time support and security services. For instance, IPv4, which is being replaced by IPv6, allowed only 4,294,967,296 unique addresses worldwide. However, IPv6 allows many more; in fact, it provides for 3.4×10^{38} unique addresses. Conversion to IPv6 will require that all network elements and all end-user machines be converted to this new protocol. To ease this pain, a transition strategy exists that calls for parallel (but interconnected) networks to be operated for a number of years.

▶ *See also* **Bridging Devices • Internet • Network Design • Network Topologies • Telecommunications**

Resources

Books

Casad, Joe. *Sams Teach Yourself TCP/IP in 24 Hours.* 5th ed. Indianapolis: Sams/Pearson Education, 2012.

Zalewski, Michal. *The Tangled Web: A Guide to Securing Modern Web Applications.* San Francisco: No Starch Press, 2012.

Web Sites

International Organization for Standardization. "Standards Catalogue." http://www.iso.org/iso/products/standards/catalogue_ics_browse. htm?ICS1=35&ICS2=100&ICS3=01& (accessed October 15, 2012).

The Internet Society. "World IPv6 Launch." http://www.worldipv6launch. org/ (accessed October 15, 2012).

Network Topologies

The topology of a network is the geometric representation of all links and nodes of a network—the structure, consisting of transmission links and processing nodes, which provides communications connectivity between nodes in a network. A link is the physical transmission path that transfers data from one device to another. A node is a network addressable device.

Graph theory describes certain characteristics of a network topology such as the average node degree for robustness (average number of links terminating at a node in a network), network diameter for size (the longest/shortest path between any two nodes in a network), number of paths for complexity (total number of paths between all node pairs), and cutsets for flow (minimum number of removed links to partition a network). However, the most dominant characteristic of a network topology is its shape.

Mesh, Star, Tree, Bus, Ring

The most general shape characteristics are symmetry and regular/irregular shape. There are five basic network topology regular shapes: mesh, star, tree, bus, and ring. The bus is a special case of a tree with only one trunk. The mesh has the highest node degree; the bus has the lowest node degree.

Mesh Topology   In a mesh topology, every node has a dedicated point-to-point link to every other node that requires $n(n-1)/2$ links to connect n nodes. The original telephone network started this way in major East Coast cities of the United States. Before long, the sky was not visible on certain downtown intersections due to the amount of overhead wire! The mesh topology allows for robustness in presence of faults because the loss of links or nodes can be routed around due to the amount of connectivity. However, this comes at the cost of complex network management due to the number of links and expensive resource usage because each n node must have $n-1$ ports to connect in the mesh.

Star Topology   In a star topology, each node has a dedicated point-to-point link to a central hub. If one node wants to send data to another, it sends to the central hub, which then relays the data to the destination node. A star provides centralized control but also represents a performance bottleneck and single-point-of-failure.

Tree Topology   A tree topology occurs when multiple star topologies are connected together such that not every node is directly connected to a central hub. Thus, a tree extends a star topology, allowing for community clustering around local hubs. The two fundamental trees upon which topologies are built are: the minimum spanning tree, which is the least-cost tree connecting all nodes in a graph; and the Steiner Tree (ST), which is the least-cost tree connecting a subset of member nodes in a graph. (The ST may contain non-member nodes also, which are called Steiner points). Cost is determined by placing weights on links and nodes based on predetermined metrics such as distance, supply/demand, economic cost, delay, or bandwidth*.

Bus Topology   In a bus topology, a shared medium connects all nodes in the network. This shared medium may be a single wire or radio frequency. The shared medium provides ease-of-installation and flexibility, since it initially consists of a single cable run alongside targeted computers or computers broadcasting on specific frequencies. However, the shared medium also creates two problems: collisions when two nodes broadcast simultaneously, and fault management, since any network problems affect all connected computers. Isolating the problem requires physically separating the shared medium in a methodological manner.

Ring Topology   The ring topology is a series of unidirectional, dedicated point-to-point links connecting in a physical ring. This topology provides inherent reliability since a signal from a source travels around the ring to the destination and back to the source as an acknowledgement. Least-cost rings may approach the cost of a least-cost tree but are generally more expensive and have more delay. In addition, a ring is not a flexible topology—adding and deleting links and nodes is disruptive.

Usage Tradeoffs

Protocol*s are matched to these topologies to enable computer network usage. The bus topology requires a shared medium access based on sensing transmission to avoid collisions with probabilistic retransmission (that is, retransmission after a probabilistically determined time). The ring topology requires a token-passing where a node needs to have a token in order to transmit. At high loads, the bus topology with a shared medium access experiences collisions, and thus offers diminished performance beyond a particular usage threshold. The ring topology with a token-passing has unnecessary overhead at low loads but its performance does not degrade at high loads.

   In general, there are two alternatives for operation of a star: (1) the central hub broadcasts all traffic it receives (physically a star but logically a bus), or (2) the central hub selectively switches incoming traffic only to destination nodes. The performance of a star depends on the processing

* **bandwidth** a measure of the frequency component of a signal or the capacity of a communication channel to carry signals

* **protocol** an agreed understanding for the sub-operations that make up a transaction, usually found in the specification of inter-computer communications

More About Mesh

Mesh topologies can exist in two states: full or partial mesh. Full mesh means that every node has a connection to every other node in the network. Partial mesh occurs when not all nodes are connected to the others; only some have a full connection. Partial mesh costs less but the results with full mesh are better.

capability of the central hub as well as the capacity of the spoke links, and beyond a threshold connections may be blocked. The tree topology is used for multipoint or group communications and thus depends on the slowest link or node with lowest processing capability in the tree connecting the group.

Examples

Examples of networks matched to these topologies include local area network (LAN) standard ETHERNET, which is a bus topology using a shared media access protocol, and LAN standard TOKEN RING, which is a ring topology using a token-passing protocol. The star is the topology of the local loop, circuit-switched telephone network with the central hub being the local central office. The tree topology is the basis of emerging group communication applications that are not yet standardized.

 See also **Bridging Devices • Internet • Network Design • Network Protocols • Office Automation Systems • Telecommunications**

Resources

Books

Estrada, Ernesto. *The Structure of Complex Networks: Theory and Applications.* New York: Oxford University Press, 2012.

Stallings, William. *Data and Computer Communications*, 9th ed. Boston and London: Pearson, 2011.

Web Sites

Florida Center for Industrial Technology. "Topology." http://fcit.usf.edu/network/chap5/chap5.htm (accessed October 15, 2012).

How Stuff Works. "Network Topologies." http://computer.howstuffworks.com/lan-switch2.htm (accessed October 15, 2012).

Object-Oriented Languages

An object-oriented language is a computer programming language that revolves around the concept of an object. Object-oriented languages were developed to make it easier to develop, debug, reuse, and maintain software than is possible with earlier languages. Understanding objects, and object-oriented languages, requires knowledge of the evolution of computer programming languages and data structures.

Evolution of Computer Programming Languages

Computer programming languages have evolved continually over the years. This evolution is detailed in the following examples.

Assembly Language The first computer programs were written in assembly language. This is a primitive type of language in which each statement corresponds to a single machine instruction; it is the most basic computer operation possible. Accomplishing anything useful takes many machine instructions. Assembly language is specific to a particular type of computer; moving the program to a different type of computer requires writing a whole new program. Assembly language programs are difficult to write, debug, and maintain. Although other languages are now used for most computer applications, assembly language is still used today as the first language when a new chip is developed.

High Order Languages After assembly language, higher order languages were developed; among the early ones were FORTRAN and BASIC. One statement in a high order language corresponds to a sentence in English. A program called a compiler reads the statements from a source file and generates a file containing machine instructions, which is called an object file. The object file can then be loaded and executed by the computer. A high order language is more portable than an assembly language program; the same source file can be compiled for any computer as long as a suitable compiler exists.

Early high order languages only allowed for simple data types such as integer, floating point number, or string (a sequence of letters). The only data structure available was the array. An array is a list of elements that are all the same data type; for example, a list of numbers or a list of strings. A database was created using a group of arrays. For example, a product database might contain three arrays called Product Number, Product Description, and Product Price. It was up to the programmer to keep the

Computer Sciences, 2ⁿᵈ Edition

Focus on FORTRAN

Short for FORmula TRANslator, FORTRAN was the first widely used high-level language. The high costs associated with programming in the mid-1950s spurred the development of FORTRAN, which was intended to make programming easier. A team, led by John Backus, created the language. FORTRAN I was released in 1957, followed closely by FORTRAN II, released in the spring of 1958.

arrays aligned; for example, to make sure the third element of each array corresponded to the same product.

Structured Languages   The next step in the evolution of computer programming languages was the development of structured languages, like C and PASCAL, and the introduction of data structures. A data structure is an assembly of simpler data types into a single record. For example, a product database could be constructed as an array of product records, each record containing Product Number, Product Description, and Product Price fields. Now one record could contain all necessary information about a single item. Structures also became more defined in the procedural part of the language. A function or procedure is a small part of a larger program that could be written to provide some basic operation on a data structure such as a record.

Object-Oriented Languages   The next step in the evolution of computer programming languages, object-orientation, was introduced in the Smalltalk language. Object-orientation takes the concepts of structured programming one step further. Now, instead of data structures and separate program structures, both data and program elements are combined into one structure called an object. The object data elements are called attributes, while the object program elements are called methods. Collectively, attributes and methods are called the object's members. Usually, an object's methods are the only programs able to operate on the object's attributes.

With object-orientation, a fundamental change came in the way programs are viewed. The earlier view was that data must be manipulated in some way to achieve a final result, and a program was viewed as a sequential means of performing the manipulations. From an object-orientation perspective, a program is viewed as a group of objects that react to messages from the user, other programs, or other objects. This view led to the idea of event-driven programming; i.e., when event A happens, this object performs action B. A message is sent to an object by calling one of its methods.

Characteristics of Object-Oriented Programming

Key characteristics of object-oriented programming include encapsulation and data hiding, inheritance, and polymorphism.

Encapsulation and Data Hiding   The central idea in object-oriented programming (OOP) is that the object attributes and the methods that operate on the attributes are bound together, or encapsulated, in the object. The object's methods provide the only interfaces between the object and other parts of the program. This is different from earlier languages, where any part of a program could operate on any piece of data at any time. Although this seems restrictive, the restrictions result in a more modular program that is easier to develop and less likely to contain errors. It also means it is easier to move an object to a different environment and still have it function correctly.

* **syntax** a set of rules that a computing language incorporates regarding structure, punctuation, and formatting

A software object is somewhat similar to a physical object. For example, an engine can be used to power a car. It has internal components, corresponding to attributes, but one does not have to be concerned with what they are or how they work. The engine must interface with the throttle, fuel system, transmission, intake, and exhaust manifolds, all of which correspond to methods. It is inconceivable that fuel would get into the engine by any means other than by way of the fuel system. As long as the correct interfaces are maintained, the engine will work. So it is with software objects. The object attributes are hidden from the outside. The object interacts with its environment through its methods.

Inheritance Another important concept to object-oriented programming is inheritance. An object class is defined in a hierarchy, and is said to inherit the behavior of its ancestors (those objects above it in the hierarchy). For example, a drawing program might include three object classes: Shape, Rectangle, and Circle. They could be defined so that Rectangle and Circle are both descendents of Shape.

Shape includes attributes common to any shape, such as the location of the shape on a drawing surface. Shape also provides methods for manipulating those attributes. For example, a move method would change the shape's location. Additionally, Shape would provide a definition for methods to which all shapes must be able to respond, for example, a draw method to display the shape on a drawing surface. The draw method in this case is said to be abstract; it does not do anything other than create a requirement that descendent classes must implement it.

Since Rectangle is a descendent of Shape, it inherits attributes (location) and methods (move) from Shape. It provides the additional attributes it needs (width and height) and new methods that manipulate those attributes (setWidth, setHeight). Rectangle must also provide a draw method that paints a rectangle on the drawing surface, because every descendent of Shape must implement a draw method. Likewise, Circle provides a new attribute (radius), methods for manipulating it (setRadius), and a draw method of its own.

With this kind of arrangement, the drawing manager program would have a list of shapes on the drawing surface. To move an object, it would call the object's move method. To draw an object, the manager calls the object's draw method. The manager neither knows nor cares how the object moves or draws itself, as long as the job gets done. In fact, it may not even know what kind of Shape a particular object really is. It could be a Rectangle, a Circle, or any other object descendent from Shape. It only needs to know that it is descendent from Shape, so it can send to it any message that a Shape can receive.

The inheritance capability of an object-oriented language added a whole new dimension to programming. Learning an earlier high order language was mainly involved with learning the language syntax* (how the

* **Hypertext Markup Language (HTML)** an encoding scheme for text data that uses special tags in the text to signify properties to the viewing program (browser) like links to other documents or document parts

language statements are constructed), which is not that difficult. In an object-oriented language, learning the is still necessary, but becoming familiar with the standard class hierarchies is a much larger task, since the hierarchies may include thousands of classes, each class with its own methods. It is worthwhile, however, because an object inherits the attributes and behavior of its parent. A programmer can avoid unnecessary work by finding an existing object that already does most of what is needed. Then new capability can be added incrementally. The result is lower cost, higher quality software.

This characteristic also led to the inclusion of automatic documentation features in several object-oriented languages. In earlier languages, documentation (if generated at all) was done separately, almost as an afterthought. Now documentation information can be included in the object source code and used to generate a Hypertext Markup Language (HTML)* document automatically, complete with hyperlinks up and down the class hierarchies, which may be viewed with an Internet browser. This makes it much easier to maintain accurate, up-to-date documentation.

Polymorphism The next important characteristic of object-oriented language is polymorphism, which means that a descendent object does not have to respond to a message exactly like its ancestor does. A new object can override its parent's methods, which causes the new object to react to a message differently. For example, a common class in a windowing system is a Component, which represents a visible object. A Component is an ancestor class for every visible object on the screen: icons, buttons, menus, slide bars, check boxes, radio buttons, even windows. All of these descendent classes override some of Component's methods to change behavior. For example, an Icon object needs to display itself as a small picture. Icon overrides Component's draw method to show the picture.

Common Object-Oriented Languages

Common object-oriented languages include C++, Java, and other languages such as BASIC and PASCAL.

Smalltalk Smalltalk was the original object-oriented language, developed in the early 1970s by Xerox. Since then, several variations have been introduced. It is still being used, but widespread acceptance has been hampered by the lack of a universal standard.

C++ C++ is an extension of the C language that provided OOP capabilities. It is probably the most widespread object-oriented language currently in use. C++ is a hybrid language because it compiles standard C programs; it does not require the use of objects. This enables it to take advantage of existing C software, while using object orientation for new software. C++ is controlled by ANSI standards.

Java Java is the most widely accepted pure object-oriented language. It was developed by Sun Microsystems originally as a control language for small appliances. However, it proved ideal for use with the Internet. A Java applet* can be embedded in a Web page. When a browser loads the Web page, it also loads and displays the. Sun still maintains strict control of the language standard.

To facilitate cross-platform operability (working on entirely different computer types without recompiling), Java is implemented in two parts. The compiler produces an object file that can only be executed by a Java Virtual Machine (JVM). A separate JVM is available for each supported operating system (Windows, Unix/Linux, or Solaris). This makes Java programs able to run on any of those systems without recompiling.

Other Languages Most languages commonly used today allow some form of object orientation. BASIC has evolved into object-oriented Visual BASIC; PASCAL into object-oriented DELPHI. Generally these are hybrid languages, like C++, that support object-orientation without requiring it.

▶ *See also* **Compilers • Mouse • Procedural Languages**

Resources

Books

Deitel, Harvey M., and Paul J. Deitel. *Java: How to Program*, 9th ed. Upper Saddle River, NJ: Prentice Hall, 2012.

Voss, Greg. *Object-Oriented Programming, An Introduction.* Berkeley, CA: Osborne McGraw-Hill, 1991.

Web Sites

Oracle. "The Java Tutorials." http://docs.oracle.com/javase/tutorial/ (accessed October 27, 2012).

An Object or a Class?

What is the difference between an object and a class? A class is a definition of an object type. For example, say Rectangle is a class. The Rectangle (with a capital "R") class defines what a rectangle (lowercase "r") object is and how it behaves. However, a rectangle *object* does not actually exist until the user instructs the drawing program to create one. Each rectangle object created (or *instantiated*) is said to be an *instance* of the Rectangle class. Because object-oriented languages are frequently case-sensitive, class names usually have the first letter capitalized, while instance names and member names have a lowercase first letter.

* **applet** a program component that requires extra support at run time from a browser or run-time environment in order to execute

* **nanosecond** one-thousand-millionth (one billionth, or 10^{-9}) of a second

Operating Systems

The operating system is software that manages every part of a computer system—all hardware and all other software. To be specific, it controls every file, every device, every section of main memory, every nanosecond* of processing time, and every network connection. It controls who can use the system and how. In short, it is the boss—without it, nothing can happen.

When a computer user sends a command by typing it from the keyboard or clicking with the mouse, the operating system must make sure

OSX Mountain Lion and iOS6 are popular operating systems. © *Justin Sullivan/Getty Images.*

* **interface** a boundary or border between two or more objects or systems; also a point of access

that the command is executed. If it is not executed, the operating system must arrange for the user to receive a message, usually on the monitor, explaining the error. This does not necessarily mean that the operating system executes the command or sends the error message, but it does control the parts of the system that do.

Every operating system, regardless of its size and complexity, can be represented by a pyramid showing how its five major functions (called managers) work together. The memory manager, the processor manager, the device manager, and the file manager form the pyramid's base; network operating systems add a network manager as well. The user interface*— the part of the operating system that communicates with the user—is supported by the other four or five managers.

Responsibilities and Relationships

These virtual managers must do more than perform their individual tasks. They must also be able to work harmoniously with every other manager. For example, they must be able to monitor their resources continuously, enforce the policies that determine who gets what, when, and how much, allocate their resources when it is appropriate, and de-allocate their resources—reclaim them—when appropriate.

The *memory manager* is in charge of main memory, also known as random access memory (RAM)*. It checks the validity of each request for memory space and, if it is a legal request, the memory manager allocates a portion that is not already in use. In a multi-user environment, the memory manager sets up a table to keep track of who is using which section of memory. Finally, when the time comes to reclaim the memory, the memory manager de-allocates the memory space. One of the manager's primary responsibilities is to preserve the part of main memory that is occupied by the operating system itself—it cannot allow any part of it to be altered accidentally or intentionally.

The *processor manager* decides how to allocate the central processing unit (CPU)*, and also keeps track of the status of each executable step of every program (called a process or task). For example, the processor manager monitors whether the CPU is executing a process or waiting for a *READ* or *WRITE* command to finish execution. Later, when the process is finished, or the maximum amount of time has expired, the processor manager reclaims the processor so it can be allocated again.

The *device manager* chooses the most efficient way to allocate all of the system's devices, including printers, disk drives, compact disc (CD) and/or digital versatile disc (DVD) drives, keyboard, monitor, and so forth. The device manager makes these decisions based on a scheduling policy chosen by the system's designers. The device manager allocates a device, starts its operation, and, finally, de-allocates it.

The *file manager* keeps track of every piece of software in the system, including application programs, data files, directories, etc. The file manager allocates the file by opening it and de-allocates it by closing it. It is based on predetermined access policies to enforce the correct security for each file so that files can be accessed only by individual or group users that have permission to do so. The file manager also controls the amount of flexibility each user is allowed with that file (such as read-only, read-and-write-only, or the authority to create and/or delete records).

Operating systems with networking capability have a fifth element called the *network manager*, which provides a convenient way for users to share resources. Network resources usually include both hardware (such as CPUs, memory areas, printers, disk drives, modems, and tape drives) and software (such as application programs and data files).

User Interfaces

Most modern operating systems feature a menu-driven graphical user interface (GUI)*, which is pronounced "gooey," with menus, icons, and task bars. The Macintosh was the first widely-used computer with a GUI, which in turn was based on a desktop created by Xerox. Microsoft introduced Windows version 1.0 in 1985, but it was not a real operating system because it acted merely as an interface between the user and the real operating system. Instead, it was called an "environment" that ran only on computers with the MS-DOS operating system. Later PC operating

* **random access memory (RAM)** a type of memory device that supports the nonpermanent storage of programs and data; so called because various locations can be accessed in any order (as if at random), rather than in a sequence (like a tape memory device)

* **central processing unit (CPU)** the part of a computer that performs computations and controls and coordinates other parts of the computer

* **graphical user interface (GUI)** an interface that allows computers to be operated through pictures (icons) and mouse-clicks, rather than through text and typing

Linux Beginnings

When Linus Torvalds completed an early version of Linux in 1991, he sent the following message to other programmers in an Internet user group: "Hello everybody out there using minix. I'm doing a (free) operating system (just a hobby, won't be big and professional like gnu) for 386(486)AT clones." Torvalds' message proved only partly correct. His hobby did produce a new operating system, but it turned out to be a very big and highly professional piece of software.

systems, including Microsoft's Windows 95, Windows 98, Windows 2000, Windows Millennium Edition (Me), Windows XP, Windows Vista, and Windows 7 are all true operating systems. Windows 8—the successor to Windows 7—was released in October 2012.

As of 2012, Windows 7 was the most widely used operating system, with 40 percent of the Windows OS market share. Windows XP, the predecessor to Windows Vista, was second with 37 percent, or more than seven times as many users as the oft-criticized Vista.

Operating systems without GUIs (such as early versions of UNIX and Linux) are called command-driven systems. They accept commands that are typed into the system (menus are not available). Command-driven systems are cumbersome for some new users to learn. Therefore, since the late-1990s, most operating systems (including UNIX and Linux) have been converted from command-driven to menu-driven interfaces, which feature GUIs that allow users to click on menus to make the system run.

Adding GUIs was a popular move for anyone who had trouble working with brief or mysterious-looking command lines. For example, the UNIX command to list all subdirectories (but not files) found in the root directory looks cryptic (ls -l / | grep '^d'). Today, users can achieve a similar result by choosing an option from a menu.

Linux

Linux is an operating system that has been widely adopted in commercial and academic markets around the world. Linux is unique among the most-used operating systems because it is an open-source program, which means the source code is freely available to anyone for improvement.

Programmers from around the world are encouraged to submit improvements to the programming code. If the new code is accepted as a universal improvement to the operating system, it is added to the next version, which is then made available to the computing world for further improvement. This development technique has resulted in a powerful, stable, inexpensive operating system, which is constantly being improved by a variety of people who may never meet in person.

Linux was created in Finland by 21-year-old Linus Torvalds who wanted to build a new operating system for the Intel 80386 microprocessor. Torvalds started with Minix, a miniature version of the well-known UNIX operating system, and rewrote certain parts to add more functionality. The first version of Linux, which was named for Torvalds and UNIX, had much of the basic functionality of the then-popular MS-DOS operating system with UNIX-like power and flexibility. It has been enhanced considerably in the years since.

Although there are similarities between the two systems, Linux is not UNIX. (UNIX is a legal trademark, registered with the federal government. Before a developer can use the term UNIX to describe an operating system, it must demonstrate that it can meet certain certification criteria.)

Policies and Design Considerations

One of the biggest differences among operating systems is the set of policies on which each one is based. These policies, in turn, drive design considerations, which dictate the inner workings of the system, including the following:

- Processor time—the amount of uninterrupted time the processor is allocated to a certain job.
- Memory space—the amount of memory area that a given job is allowed to monopolize at any time.
- Printers—the number of printers that one job is allowed to use.
- User access—the number of users who are allowed to log into the system.
- File access—the identity of the files that a given user can read, write, modify, or delete.
- System resources—the number of system resources that can be allocated to one job before it has to share them.

Before writing an operating system, these issues are examined by system designers who make choices that ideally will optimize the system's day-to-day operations. The goal is to minimize downtime, system crashes, wasted overhead, security breaches, overloaded printers, and other operational problems.

For example, if the designers want to create a simple operating system that would process each job in the order it arrives, without giving a higher priority to any of them, then the team might choose policies that would:

- Assign the processor to one job when it is received;
- Never interrupt processing once the job begins;
- Give it access to all files in the system, just in case they are needed later;
- Give the job all available disk space, printers, and network resources.

This would be a fair, unbiased system, but a very inefficient one. For example, if one big job was printing out thousands of pages for a large report, even if the printing required several days, then all other jobs would sit idle as they waited for it to finish. In the meantime, most of the available memory space, processor time, disk space, and other resources would also sit idle, waiting for the next job to begin.

Therefore, most modern operating systems feature complex formulas, which allow resources to be allocated wisely. Some systems allow multiple tasks, multiple jobs, multiple users, and even multiple processors, to work together so available resources can be shared without causing the system to crash routinely.

No single operating system can be considered the best for every situation because each one is based on policies that favor certain jobs or

* **optophone** a system that uses
artificial intelligence techniques
to convert images of text into
audible sound

certain circumstances. That is why one operating system might be chosen to run an architect's computer and another might be preferred to operate a writer's computer.

▶ *See also* **Compatibility (Open Systems Design)** • **Memory** • **Networks** • **Security**

Resources

Books

Flynn, Ida M., and Ann M. McHoes. *Understanding Operating Systems.* 6th ed. Boston: Course Technology, 2011.

White, Ron, and Timothy Edward Downs. *How Computers Work.* 9th ed. Indianapolis, IN: Que Publications, 2008.

Web Sites

Net MarketShare. "Operating System Market Share." http://marketshare. hitslink.com/operating-system-market-share.aspx?qprid=10 (accessed October 8, 2012).

Optical Character Recognition

Optical Character Recognition (OCR) uses a device that reads handwritten (such as with pencil or pen) or typewritten (such as from a newspaper story) text and electronically converts them into a computer-usable form. OCR technology recognizes characters on a source document using the optical properties of the equipment and media. OCR improves the accuracy of data collection and reduces the time required by human workers to enter the data.

Although OCR is used for high-speed data entry, it did not begin with the computer industry. The beginnings of OCR can be traced back to 1809 when the first patents for devices to aid the blind were awarded. In 1912, Russian-born Israeli chemist and inventor Emmanuel Goldberg (1881–1970) patented a machine that read characters, converted them into standard telegraph code, and then transmitted telegraphic messages over wires without human intervention. In 1914, Irish physicist and chemist E. E. Fournier D'Albe (c. 1868–1933) invented an OCR device called the optophone* that produced sounds. Each sound corresponded to a specific letter or character. After learning the character equivalent for various sounds, visually impaired people were able to interpret (read) the printed material. Developments in OCR continued throughout the 1930s, becoming more important with the beginnings of the computer industry in the 1940s. OCR development in the 1950s attempted to address the needs of the business world.

Methods for Recording Data

OCR requires hardware, in the form of a scanning device, and software to convert the images and character data from the source document into a digital form. Three primary methods are used to record data on a source document to be read by an OCR device. These include optically readable marks, bar codes, and optically readable characters, including handwritten characters.

Optical mark recognition (OMR) uses OMR paper, sometimes called a mark sense form. This paper has a series of rectangular shapes that are filled in using a pencil. The completed form is then fed through a scanning device that reads the filled-in rectangles. The software of the OMR scanning device can perform an elementary statistical analysis of the data. OMR technology is commonly used to score standardized tests, such as the Scholastic Aptitude Test (SAT) and Graduate Management Aptitude Test (GMAT), quickly and accurately.

Bar codes are zebra-striped marks of various widths that appear on, or are attached to, most manufactured retail products. The most common use of the bar code is the 10-digit Universal Product Code (UPC)*. Other kinds of bar code systems are used in a variety of places—from overnight mail packages to airplane luggage tags. The width and combination of the stripes on the bar code represent data. A bar code reader consists of a scanner and decoder. The scanner emits a beam of light that is swept past the bar code and senses light reflections to distinguish between the bars and spaces. A photo detector converts the spaces into an electrical signal and the bars into the absence of an electrical signal. The decoder analyzes the signal patterns to validate and interpret the corresponding data.

Some OCR readers can convert typed and handwritten documents into digital data. These readers scan the shape of a character within a document, compare the scanned character with a pre-defined shape, and convert the character into its corresponding bit* pattern for storage in main computer memory.

Handwriting recognition is enabled by a combination of hardware and software. Devices such as Personal Data Assistants (PDAs) or tablet personal computers (PCs) typically possess touch screen technology that can display the handwritten characters that a user inputs. A tablet PC is a small laptop computer that normally combines a touch screen with input from a stylus or the user's fingers. The Apple iPad tablet computer is a prime example—it was introduced in April 2010. Software programs installed on tablet computers or PDAs can convert the user's handwriting into a standard document form. For instance, Microsoft's Windows 7 operating system, released in 2009, and Windows 8, released in October 2012, has built-in handwriting character recognition.

A special type of OCR, magnetic ink character recognition (MICR), is used by several industries, including banks. The enormous amount of paper in the form of checks, loans, and bank statements, combined with the need for accurate and quick processing, prompted the banking

* **Universal Product Code (UPC)** the first barcode standard developed in 1973 and adopted widely since

* **bit** a single binary digit, 1 or 0—a contraction of Binary digIT; the smallest unit for storing data in a computer

industry to seek new ways to manage the flow of paper. In 1956, the American Bankers Association recommended adopting magnetic ink for high-speed automatic character recognition, resulting in MICR. With MICR, data are recorded using a magnetic ink that is readable by either a scanning device or a person. On bank checks, which represent the most common use of MICR, characters in magnetic ink detail the bank's identification number, the individual's account number, and the check number. Checks can be scanned and the data are quickly and accurately read into a computer for further processing.

Another use of OCR allows printed documents—such as text, images, or photographs—to be stored in a computer. Either hand-held scanners or page scanners are used to convert physical documents into computer-readable forms. Page scanners are stationary. The page is typically placed face down on the glass plate of the scanner and then scanned. Handheld scanners are manually moved over the document. Both types of scanners can convert monochrome or color pictures, forms, text, and other images into machine-readable digital data. The data can then be modified, saved, and distributed over computer networks.

In 2007, Google began to create its own OCR process called Google Docs, which supported the scanning of documents imported to the Google Web site. When documents are uploaded to Google, Google Docs extracts text and formats them from the scans. The Optical Character Recognition system was provided by Google Books, and was functional, as of 2010, with the languages of English, French, Italian, German, and Spanish. In April 2012, Google Docs was replaced with Google Drive, a cloud storage system that provides all the features of Docs with improved storage functionality. However, Docs is still available from Google, only under the direction of Drive.

 See also **Artificial Intelligence • Input Devices • Pattern Recognition • Virtual Reality • Virtual Reality In Education**

Resources

Books

Cheriet, Mohamed, Nawwaf Kharma, Cheng-Lin Liu, and Ching Suen. *Character Recognition Systems: A Guide for Students and Practitioners.* New York: Wiley-Interscience, 2007.

Schantz, Herbert F. *The History of OCR, Optical Character Recognition.* Manchester Center, VT: Recognition Technologies Users Association, 1982.

Web Sites

Google. "Google Docs." https://accounts.google.com/ServiceLogin?service=writely&passive=1209600&continue=http://docs.google.com/%23&followup=http://docs.google.com/&ltmpl=homepage (accessed October 16, 2012).

Google. "Google Drive." https://www.google.com/intl/en_US/drive/start/index.html (accessed October 16, 2012).

IMT Magazine. "The History Of OCR Technology." http://www.imtmagazine.com/imtnewswire/?c=117&a=1048 (accessed October 17, 2012).

P

Parallel Processing

Parallel processing is information processing that uses more than one computer processor simultaneously to perform work on a problem. This should not be confused with multitasking*, in which many tasks are performed on a single processor by continuously switching between them, a common practice on serial machines. Computers that are designed for parallel processing are called parallel processors or parallel machines. Many parallel processors can also be described as supercomputers, a more general term applied to the class of computer systems that is most powerful at any given time.

The need to coordinate the work of the individual processors makes parallel processing more complex than processing with a single processor. The processing resources available must be assigned efficiently, and the processors may need to share information as the work progresses. Parallel processors are used for problems that are computationally intensive, that is, they require a very large number of computations. Parallel processing may be appropriate when the problem is very difficult to solve or when it is important to get the results very quickly.

Some examples of problems that may require parallel processing are image processing, molecular modeling, computer animations and simulations, and analysis of models to predict climate and economics. Many problems, such as weather forecasting, can be addressed with increasingly complex models as the computing power is developed to implement them, so there is always an incentive to create newer, more powerful parallel processors. Although early work in parallel processing focused on complex scientific and engineering applications, current uses also include commercial applications such as data mining* and risk evaluation in investment portfolios. In some situations, the reliability added by additional processors is also important.

Parallel processors are one of the tools used in high-performance computing, a more general term that refers to a group of activities aimed at developing and applying advanced computers and computer networks. In 1991, a U.S. federal program, the High Performance Computing and Communications (HPCC) program, was introduced to support the development of supercomputing, gigabit networking*, and computation-intensive science and engineering applications. The HPCC program uses the term Grand Challenges to identify computationally intensive tasks with broad economic and scientific impact that will only be solved with high performance computing technologies.

* **multitasking** the ability of a computer system to execute more than one program at the same time; also known as multiprogramming

* **data mining** a technique of automatically obtaining information from databases that is normally hidden or not obvious

* **gigabit networking** the construction and use of a computer network that is capable of transferring information at rates in the gigahertz range

A small military version of of the ICL Distributed Array Processor, an early example of the parallel processing computer. © *SSPL via Getty Images.*

* **taxonomy** the classification of elements or objects based on their characteristics

* **algorithm** a rule or procedure used to solve a mathematical problem—most often described as a sequence of steps

As of June 2012, many of the world's fastest computers (as cited by the Top 500 Supercomputers list, which is published on the Internet: http://www.top500.org/) were parallel processors. For instance, at number six on the Top 500 is the Jaquar by Cray, which is located at Oak Ridge National Laboratory, in Oak Ridge, Tennessee. The Jaguar has a top performance of just above 1,750 terafloating-point operations per second (teraflops, or 10^{12} flops), or 1.75 petaflops (10^{15} flops). The number of processors within each parallel processor may be from fewer than fifty to hundreds of thousands. Companies manufacturing these machines include International Business Machines Corporation (IBM), Silicon Graphics International Corporation (SGI), Cray, Hitachi, Fujitsu, Bull SA, and National University of Defense Technology (NUDT).

Parallel Architecture

There are many possible ways of designing a parallel computer, and American professor Michael J. Flynn (1934–), from Stanford University (California), in 1966 developed a taxonomy* for parallel processors, a way of thinking about these alternatives. Flynn categorized them based on two parameters: the stream of instructions (the algorithm*) and the stream of data (the input). The instructions can be carried out one at a time or concurrently, and the data can be processed one at a time or in multiples. In Flynn's scheme, SISD—the acronym for Single Instruction stream, Single Data stream—refers to a traditional sequential computer in which a single operation can be carried out on a single data item at a time.

The two main categories of parallel processor are SIMD and MIMD. In a SIMD (Single Instruction, Multiple Data) machine, many processors operate simultaneously, carrying out the same operation on many different pieces of data. In a MIMD (Multiple Instruction, Multiple Data) machine, the number of processors may be fewer but they are capable of acting independently on different pieces of data. The remaining category, MISD (Multiple Instruction, Single Data) is rarely used since its meaning is not clearly defined. Since it implies that several instructions are being applied to each piece of data, the term is sometimes used to describe a vector supercomputer* in which data pass through a pipeline of processors each with a different instruction.

Sometimes Flynn's taxonomy is augmented with the SPMD category, which refers to Single Program, Multiple Data to describe a system in which there are many instances of a single type of process, each executing the same code independently. This is equivalent to implementing a SIMD operation in a MIMD machine.

Different parallel architectures have varying strengths and weaknesses depending on the task to be performed. SIMD machines usually have a very large number of simple processors. They are suited to tasks that are massively parallel, in which there are relatively simple operations to be performed on huge amounts of data. Each data stream is assigned to a different processor and the processors operate in lockstep (synchronous*ly), each performing the same operation on its data at the same time. Processors communicate to exchange data and results, either through a shared memory and shared variables or through messages passed on an interconnection network between processors, each of which has its own local memory. Array processors such as the International Computers Limited (ICL) Distributed Array Processor (DAP), which was later taken over by Cambridge Parallel Processors (CPP), and the Connection Machine, produced by Thinking Machines Corporation (which was eventually secured by Sun Microsystems), are well-known examples of SIMD machines.

There is greater variety in the design of MIMD machines, which operate asynchronously with each processor under the control of its own program. In general, MIMD machines have fewer, more powerful processors than SIMD machines. They are divided into two classes: multiprocessors (also called tightly coupled machines) which have a shared memory, and multicomputers (or loosely coupled machines), which operate with an interconnection network. Although many of the earlier, high-performance parallel processors used in government research were very large, highly expensive SIMD machines, MIMD machines can be built more easily and cheaply, often with off-the-shelf components. Many different experimental designs have been created and marketed.

Parallel Algorithms and Languages

In a serial algorithm, each step in the algorithm is completed before the next is begun. A parallel algorithm is a sequence of instructions for solving a problem that identifies the parts of the process that can be

* **vector supercomputer** a highly optimized computing machine that provides high performance using a vector processing architecture

* **synchronous** synchronized behavior

carried out simultaneously. To write a program for a parallel processor, the programmer must decide how each sub-task in the algorithm will be assigned to processors and in what order the necessary steps will be performed, and at what points communication is necessary. There can be many algorithms for a particular problem, so the programmer needs to identify and implement the one best suited for a particular parallel architecture.

Sometimes software inertia, the cost of converting programming applications to parallel form, is cited as a barrier to parallel processing. Some systems automatically adapt a serial process for parallel processing but this may not result in the best performance that can be obtained for that problem. In general, it is difficult to write parallel programs that achieve the kind of high-speed performance of which parallel processors are theoretically capable. Programming languages have been developed specifically for use on parallel processors to handle parallel data structures and functions, scheduling, and memory management. In some cases, these are extensions of existing programming languages, such as parallel versions of C and Lisp; in other cases, they are new languages developed for use on specific parallel architectures.

Performance of Parallel Processors

Designers of parallel processors would like to be able to compare the performance of different machines. The usual measure is the number of floating point operations* per second, or FLOPS (sometimes written as flops), which is the rate at which a machine can perform single-precision floating point calculations. Many parallel machines are capable of TeraFLOPS (trillions of per second; Tera is sometimes also written as tera) performance and, by the early 2010s, newer machines were performing in the low PetaFLOPS range (quadrillions of per second; peta is sometimes used instead of Peta).

As a performance measure, FLOPS refers to the maximum performance of which the machine may be capable. However, performance on most problems is dependent on the extent to which they can be parallelized, or broken down into concurrent activities. Another factor is the suitability of the task for a particular parallel architecture. Some problems may be better suited to a SIMD machine, others to some variant of a MIMD machine. A measure of performance relative to the problem to be solved is *speedup,* which is the ratio of two programs' execution times, usually on a single node and on P nodes of the same computer.

The speedup that can be obtained on a parallel machine depends on the number of processors available, and also on the size of the problem and the way in which it can be broken into parts. Ideally, speedup would be linear* so that five processors would give a speedup of five, or ten processors a speedup of ten. However, a number of factors contribute to sub- speedup, including additional software overhead in the parallel implementation, load balancing to prevent idle processors, and time spent communicating data between processors. A critical limitation is the amount of parallel activity that the problem allows. Amdahl's (1922–) Law, which was named after American computer architect Gene Amdahl (1922–), states that the speedup of a parallel algorithm is limited by the fraction of the problem that must be performed sequentially.

In June 2008, scientists at the Los Alamos National Laboratory, a facility in New Mexico operated by the U.S. government, announced that they had built a new supercomputer named Roadrunner that performed over 1 PetaFLOP, or 1 quadrillion (1×10^{15}) numerical operations per second. Like many other recent supercomputers, Roadrunner was built using off-the-shelf technology, in this case 12,960 IBM microprocessors similar to those found in the Playstation 3 video game. To achieve high computation speeds using these unremarkable chips, Roadrunner's designers used a parallel computing architecture. The previous computing speed record, 0.596 PetaFLOPS, had been held since 2007 by IBM's BlueGene/L supercomputer. In late 2009, Oak Ridge National Laboratory's Jaguar XT5 supercomputer took the top spot with a performance of 1.75 PetaFLOPS. As of June 2012, the fastest computer in the world, according to Top500.org, is the IBM Sequoia – BlueGene/Q, (Power BQC 16C 1.60 GHz, Custom), which performs at 20.132 PetaFLOPS.

 See also **Algorithms • Procedural Languages • Supercomputers • Virtual Memory**

Resources

Books

Gabali, Fayez. *Algorithms and Parallel Computing*. Hoboken, NJ: Wiley, 2011.

Herlihy, Maurice, and Nir Shavit. *The Art of Multiprocessor Programming*. revised 1st ed. Burlington, MA: Morgan Kaufmann Publishing, 2012.

Kirk, David B., and Wen-mei W. Hwu. *Programming Massively Parallel Processors: A Hands-on Approach*. Burlington, MA: Morgan Kaufmann Publishers, 2010.

Web Sites

How Stuff Works. "How Parallel Processing Works." http://computer. howstuffworks.com/parallel-processing.htm (accessed October 17, 2012).

Top500.org. "June 2012." http://www.top500.org/lists/2012/06 (accessed October 17, 2012).

Why Parallel?

Parallel processing, in which multiple computers work on a problem simultaneously, is complex because the problem must be broken down into subproblems on which work can be carried out independently. It requires a parallel architecture, through which processors can communicate and share data, a parallel algorithm or method for solving the problem in concurrent steps, and a parallel programming language to implement the algorithm for a specific parallel architecture.

Pattern Recognition

Pattern recognition is a branch of science that helps develop classifiers, which can recognize unknown instances of objects. In this context, to recognize an object means to classify it, or to assign it to one of a set of possible classes or labels. This class assignment of objects is based on an analysis of the values of one or more features of the object. Pattern recognition techniques are used in a wide variety of commercial applications. Common examples include character recognition, such as the scanning of a printed page of text into a word processor; natural language recognition, such as using voice commands to relay a set of possible responses to a computer system over the phone; analysis of fingerprint, face, or eye images in order to verify a person's identity; analysis of images taken from airplanes or satellites, perhaps in order to detect and track oil spills in the ocean; or analysis of medical images in order to scan for abnormalities, such as cancer versus normal tissue.

Humans have a powerful ability to classify objects based on sensory input. They can easily read documents printed in a wide variety of type fonts, including handwritten documents. Such ability is amazing because

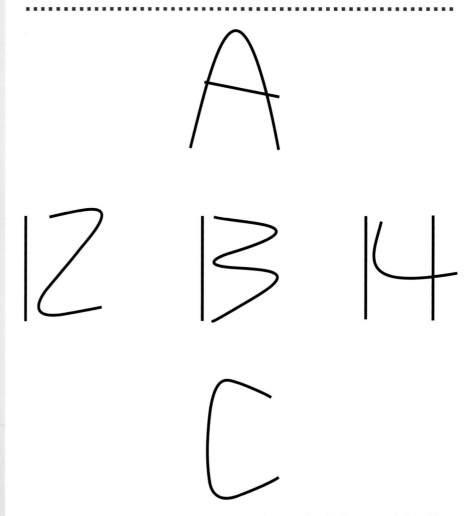

Figure 1. Note how the middle object can be interpreted as a "B" or as the number 13, depending on the context in which it is read. Such ambiguities are key difficulties for pattern recognition. *Reproduced by permission of Gale, a part of Cengage Learning.*

it often seems to require little conscious effort. Although humans have the ability to read patterns, there are at least two potential advantages to using computer systems for pattern recognition. Even if a person with minimal training could perform a certain task, he or she might not be able to handle the volume of work in a timely fashion, or without becoming bored and error-prone. For example, reading handwritten addresses on pieces of mail is a simple task in principle, but is made difficult by the repetitive nature of handling a large number of pieces of mail. In other cases, such as recognizing signs of cancer in x-ray images, the task requires specialized training, and there simply may not be as many human experts as needed.

Another difficulty in pattern recognition is ambiguity*. That is, a particular pattern may have multiple possible interpretations, each of which is equally reasonable. Sometimes this problem can be resolved by considering the local context of the pattern. A common illustration of and context is presented in Figure 1. The interpretation of the middle object is ambiguous. In the context of the column, the object could reasonably be interpreted as the letter B, and yet in the context of the row, it could reasonably be interpreted as the number 13.

Construction of a classifier typically requires the use of some examples whose class label is already known by some other means. The examples used in constructing the classifier are referred to as labeled data* because their classification is already known. They may also be referred to as training data* because they will be used to train the classifier. Acquiring the appropriate amount and type of training data is one of the secrets to building a successful pattern recognition system.

Consider the example of labeling regions in an x-ray image—each region is classified as either cancerous or normal tissue. The following example of an x-ray (mammogram) image shows a cancerous region. Note that many different regions in the image could be identified as possibly representing an abnormality. The cancerous region is distinguished from the other possible regions by being larger, brighter overall, and having an irregular boundary.

This suggests that useful features for classifying a region might include its size, average brightness, and degree of smoothness of its boundary. To construct the classifier, some example image regions would be identified and their class label determined. The true class label for a region might be determined, for example, by performing a lab test on a tissue sample corresponding to the region. The values of some features of the training samples would be computed. Then the classifier would be constructed by finding some rule for examining the feature values to separate the normal samples from the cancer samples. Then, in use, the classifier would compute the feature values for an unknown region and assign it to either the normal class or the cancer class using the rule learned from the training samples. Commercial systems that recognize signs of cancer or other diseases in

* **ambiguity** the quality of doubtfulness or uncertainty; often subject to multiple interpretations

* **labeled data** a data item whose class assignment is known independent of the classifier being constructed

* **training data** data used in the creation of a classifier

* **Gaussian classifiers** classifiers constructed on the assumption that the feature values of data will follow a Gaussian distribution

* **k-nearest neighbors** a classifier that assigns a class label for an unknown data item by looking at the class labels of the nearest items in the training data

* **decision trees** classifiers in which a sequence of tests are made to decide the class label to assign to an unknown data item; the sequence of tests can be visualized as having a tree structure

* **neural networks** pattern recognition systems whose structure and operation are loosely inspired by analogy to neurons in the human brain

medical images are more complex than this simple example suggests, but the basic idea is the same.

The essence of constructing a good classifier for a given problem is generally to:

1. Select the pattern recognition approach whose assumptions best match the characteristics of the problem;

2. Use a set of training data that is large enough and representative of the problem;

3. Decide on the right features.

Deciding which pattern recognition approach best matches the characteristics of the problem requires an understanding of both the assumptions implicitly made by each approach and a characterization of the problem. Acquiring a set of training data that is large enough, and that is representative of the examples the classifier will see in operation, requires experimental and statistical expertise. Deciding on the right features tends to rely on good intuition about the important properties of objects, and also on experimental analysis to select the better-performing features.

At the highest level, pattern recognition techniques can be divided into structural techniques and statistical techniques. A simplified explanation is that structural techniques assume that the parts of an object are known and subsequently restricts itself to how the parts fit together to form the whole, whereas statistical approaches simply assume that some properties of the whole can be measured and that the values of properties vary between classes. Of the two approaches, statistical pattern recognition techniques are perhaps more widely used. A few of the many possible approaches under the general umbrella of statistical pattern recognition are Gaussian classifiers*, k-nearest neighbors*, and decision trees*. The approach known as neural networks* is also sometimes considered as a part of statistical pattern recognition. Neural networks have come to be widely used. The use of the word neural tends to invoke the idea that the classifier is working like a human brain. However, the structure and operation of the typical neural network classifier are only very loosely inspired by the structure and operation of neurons in the human brain.

Pattern recognition technology has many important uses beyond those already mentioned. It can be used in the area of data mining to sift through large amounts of data and spot important trends. For example, pattern recognition techniques might be used to spot credit card fraud, or to detect attempts to break into computer systems. Pattern recognition techniques can also be used in the area of robotics to help robots interpret visual input and move from one place to another. In summary, it should be clear that pattern recognition technology lies at the core of many applications that involve advanced decisions made by the computer. To help coordinate such work in pattern recognition, the Open Pattern Recognition (OpenPR) project has been established. Supported by the National Laboratory of Pattern Recognition, the

Institution of Automation, and the Chinese Academy of Sciences, the OpenPR Web site states that the organization "is intended to be an open source platform for sharing algorithms of image processing, computer vision, natural language processing, pattern recognition, machine learning and the related fields."

▶ *See also* **Artificial Intelligence • Computer Vision • Data Mining • Neural Networks • Robotics • Robots**

Resources

Books

Davies, E. R. *Computer and Machine Vision: Theory, Algorithms, and Practicalities.* 4th ed. Waltham, MA: Elsevier, 2012.

Goshtasby, A. Ardeshir. *Image Registration: Principles, Tools and Methods.* London and New York: Springer, 2012.

Theodoridis, Sergios, and Konstantinos Koutroumbas. *Pattern Recognition.* 4th ed. Amsterdam and Boston: Academic Press, 2009.

Vacca, John R. *Biometric Technologies and Verification Systems.* Amsterdam and Boston: Butterworth-Heinemann/Elsevier, 2007.

Wolpaw, Jonathan R., and Elizabeth Winter Wolpaw, eds. *Brain-computer Interfaces: Principles and Practice.* Oxford and New York: Oxford University Press, 2012.

Web Sites

OpenPR.org. "Open Pattern Recognition Project." http://www.openpr. org.cn/ (accessed October 17, 2012).

Personal Digital Assistants

Personal digital assistants (PDAs) are small, hand-held computers. They incorporate a form of touch screen technology, using a light pen, stylus, and/ or fingers as an input device rather than a keyboard. In addition, a detachable keyboard or a voice recorder could serve as a form of input. A versatile information processing device, the PDA frequently functions as a personal information manager (PIM) to record telephone numbers, addresses, appointments, and to-do lists. Also, PDAs can synchronize with microcomputers to transfer e-mail, text documents, spreadsheets, files, or databases.

The vast majority of PDAs use wireless communications technology, providing great mobility. Often, wireless-capable PDAs are referred to as smartphones. Smartphones incorporate many of the functions of traditional PDAs, such as information management, with cellular telephone and texting, Web and email capability, digital cameras, and customized applications.

Biometrics For Human Identification

In many security applications, it is valuable to recognize a person automatically, or to confirm his/her claimed identity. The field of biometrics uses pattern recognition techniques for this purpose. For example, an image of the eye can be used to obtain features that describe the pattern in someone's iris. Banks are testing the technique to confirm customer identity at automated teller machines (ATMs).

PDAs are frequently used in the classroom. © *AP Images/Kelli Cardinal.*

In 1993 Apple Computer introduced the first PDA, which was called the Newton MessagePad. Rather than just storing handwritten words, Newton converted them into typescript. Early versions of Newton had limited success with this difficult process. Three years later, 3Com's Palm Computing introduced the revolutionary PalmPilot. IBM's Simon Personal Communicator, which was released in 1994, was the first commercially-available device to feature a cellular telephone with PDA features. In 1997, Ericsson coined the term "smartphone" to describe its GS 88 phone.

PDA Features

By the close of the first decade of the 2000s, the functions originally performed by PDAs, such as organizing information, had been merged with the functions performed by cellular phones, such as calling or texting. Indeed, by 2010 the vast majority of PDAs were marketed as smartphones. Typically, a smartphone can connect wirelessly to the Internet, place cell phone calls and perform instant messaging like a basic cell phone, and perform the traditional tasks of the PDA as well, including the management of all sorts of disparate information, from video clips and audio files to legal documents and shopping lists. Smartphones may have many other features, such as built-in cameras that can take pictures or video along with audio recording; they may contain handwriting recognition software that can convert the user's handwritten memo into a standard text document.

Many PDAs, and particularly smartphones, are now equipped with Global Positioning System (GPS) receivers. The GPS capability can be put to use in a variety of situations, but probably the most widely-used pertains to driving. The GPS feature in the PDA can help in navigating through traffic by displaying current traffic conditions and suggesting alternative routes that avoid traffic jams, road construction, and the like. In addition to a PDA's built-in GPS capabilities, several companies offer their own proprietary GPS navigation software (applications, or "apps") that consumers can upload into their PDA.

Older versions of personal digital assistants could recognize only one touch to their touchscreen at a time. However, most contemporary smartphones—for instance, the Apple iPhone and Google Android-based phones—tout touchscreens with the capability of accepting multiple touches simultaneously. This so-called "multi-touch" capability means that the user can utilize multi-fingered gestures interactively with the screen; for example, by touching one's thumb and forefinger close together (in an almost pinching position) on top of, or next to, a tiny picture on the screen, a widening of the two digits (i.e., thumb and forefinger) results in the picture being enlarged.

Specialty Types of PDAs

There are a variety of purpose-built PDAs that are aimed at meeting the needs of particular users. Specialized uses include the disciplines of medicine, science, recreation, and business applications. For instance, medical care providers can use their PDA to access stored databases that provide information on a variety of medically-related information, including treatment options and lists of medications. Some PDAs are used by medical professionals to access patient records while visiting patients in a variety of locations, such as hospital rooms or nursing homes. Doctors can also create new entries in a patient's file concerning their condition, as well as any recommended follow-up treatment. PDAs have also gained wide use in a variety of business applications, including retailing, warehousing, and inventory control. For all these applications—medicine, business, science, and recreation—the latest news and database-updates pertinent to each field can be continuously updated by downloading new information via the Internet.

Primary Smartphone/PDA Manufacturers

According to industry analysts at International Data Corporation (IDC), as of late 2012, the top producers of smartphones worldwide included Samsung, Apple, Research in Motion (RIM), ZTE, and HTC. Nokia dropped out of IDC's list of the top five smartphone manufacturers for the first time since IDC began compiling its list in 2004. The higher connection speeds are essential for supporting data-intensive applications, such as those involved with video streaming. The faster Internet speeds are supported by the so-called 3G and 4G wireless cellular communication standards; smartphones are sometimes referred to in terms of their 3G or 4G capabilities.

 See also **Microcomputers • Telecommunications • Wireless Technology • World Wide Web**

Medical Uses

In health care, PDAs are frequently used for identifying patients, charting the administration of medication, tracking laboratory specimens, monitoring a patient's vital signs, and maintaining overall management of patient information.

* **graphical user interface (GUI)**
an interface that allows
computers to be operated
through pictures (icons) and
mouse-clicks, rather than
through text and typing

Resources

Books

Poslad, Stefan. *Ubiquitous Computing: Smart Devices, Environments and Interactions.* Chichester, UK: Wiley, 2009.

Saylor, Michael. *The Mobile Wave: How Mobile Intelligence Will Change Everything.* New York: Vanguard Press, 2012.

Pointing Devices

In the early days of computers, commands and data were input via a keyboard. On early computer monitor screens, the text entry position was denoted by a blinking underscore or vertical bar, called a cursor. At first, users had no control over the location of this cursor; later, directional arrow keys and key commands allowed users to select text entry points. In more recent operating systems that utilize a graphical user interface (GUI)*, the cursor still indicates the point where text may be

An astronomer uses a laser pointer.
© *AP Images/Petar Petrov.*

entered, but it is also a visible and moving on-screen pointer controlled with an input device, such as a mouse. The computer operator uses the *pointing cursor* to establish where the *position indicator cursor* should be placed, or to select a program to run or file to view. Typically, the pointing cursor appears on the screen as an arrow.

Since early computer user keyboard commands were difficult to learn and cryptic to non-computer specialists, computer manufacturers and software developers quickly embraced the point-and-click interface*s first popularized by the Apple Macintosh. However, keyboard arrows were no longer adequate as a way to move a cursor around the screen. The point-and-click concept required the user to move something that would cause a corresponding movement on the screen. This led to the development of input devices such as the mouse, the joystick, and other tools for controlling on-screen movement of the cursor. Although the mouse and its descendants are not replacements for the keyboard, they do supplement the keyboard in tasks for which it is ill suited.

Common Pointing Devices

Common pointing devices used to control on-screen movement include computer mice, touchpads, touch screens, joysticks, graphics tablets, and trackballs. Some of these devices, including the mouse and the joystick, can be added to a computer system according to the needs of a user. Other devices, such as touch screens, are integrated into specialized computer systems designed for particular purposes.

Computer Mouse A computer mouse is a small, hand-held, interactive input pointing device that, when rolled or pushed over a flat surface, controls placement of the cursor on a computer display. A computer mouse is analogous* to a live mouse in that it is palm-size and mouse-shaped, with rounded corners. Originally, all mice were connected to computers with a wire suggestive of a tail; however, cordless (wireless) mice are also available.

A mouse can be a one-, two-, or three-button device. After a user positions the cursor on the computer display by moving the mouse, screen action can be controlled by single or multiple clicks of the mouse buttons. Screen icons can be activated with one click, or dragged across the computer display by a single click that is held as the mouse is moved from one location to another.

Traditionally, computer mice were electromechanical devices. A rubber-coated steel ball that protrudes from the bottom is detected by two orthogonal* rollers, which also touch the ball, inside the plastic housing. These rollers act as transducers* to convert the speed and direction of the rolling ball to electrical signals that are sent to a software driver* to move the screen cursor. To provide better traction for the rolling ball, an electromechanical mouse is generally operated on a flat, cushioned pad of foam.

* **interface** a boundary or border between two or more objects or systems; also a point of access

* **analogous** a relationship of logical similarity between two or more objects

* **orthogonal** elements or objects that are perpendicular to one another; in a logical sense this means that changes in one have no effect on the other

* **transducers** devices that sense a physical quantity, such as temperature or pressure, and convert that measurement into an electrical signal

* **driver** a special program that manages the sequential execution of several other programs; a part of an operating system that handles input/output devices

* **light emitting diode (LED)** a discrete electronic component that emits visible light when permitting current to flow in a certain direction; often used as an indicating lamp

* **byte** a group of eight binary digits; represents a single character of text

* **dielectric** a material that exhibits insulating properties, as opposed to conducting properties

There are also several other kinds of mice available to consumers: optical, optomechanical, and laser mice. An optical mouse has no wheels or balls but instead depends on a light emitting diode (LED)* and a photodetector. As the mouse moves across a surface, the photodetector senses movement by changes in reflected light. An optomechanical mouse combines characteristics of the optical mouse and the standard electromechanical mouse: it is built with a moving ball and shafts with slits through which light can pass. As the mouse moves, the shafts rotate and light pulses strike the photodetector through the slits. The amount of cursor motion is proportional to the number of light pulses detected. No special mouse pad is required with optomechanical mice, and they are less vulnerable to dust and dirt-related failure than are mechanical mice.

As the name implies, a laser mouse utilizes a laser beam to gauge movement. Both laser and optical mice use light as the basic mechanism for tracking movements; but the laser mouse is generally capable of achieving much higher resolution in tracking its movements—while an optical mouse can typically resolve movements corresponding to 400 to 800 dots per inch (dpi), a laser mouse can achieve up to 2,000 dpi resolution. For most ordinary tasks performed on a personal computer (such as word processing and Web browsing), this difference in precision is unimportant. However, for some purposes, like gaming and computer-aided design (CAD), the higher precision of the laser mouse is very helpful. Another advantage of the laser mouse over electromechanical and optical mice is that it can be used on almost any surface; by contrast, electromechanical mice often perform best on a specialized mouse pad, and optical mice sometimes return erroneous readings to the computer when used on black or glossy surfaces, or on glass.

Besides the ubiquitous 2D mice—meaning the typical mice designed to move two-dimensionally over a flat surface—there are also 3D (three-dimensional) mice available. Such mice are designed to be held and moved in three dimensions; that is, in addition to the familiar back-and-forth and side-to-side movements, these devices can be moved up-and-down as well. 3D mice find use in applications such as computer games.

Common to all types of mice are the serial communications sent back to the computer every time the mouse moves a certain distance (e.g., 0.25 millimeters or 0.01 inch or a *mickey*)—one byte* for x-movement, one for y-movement, and one or two bytes for button status. Low-level software in the computer converts the relative mouse movements to absolute cursor position on the display.

Touchpads Where using a mouse would be awkward, such as in a laptop computer configuration, or cursor movement is more important than characters, touchpads have become popular. These are generally built into a computer unit, and they often include clickable buttons that correspond to the buttons of a mouse. Beneath the top layer of the touchpad are two or more layers separated by a non-conducting dielectric*; each layer contains a grid of electrode rows and columns. The different layers create a capacitance (electric field) between them that may be drastically changed by the electric field of a human finger either touching or moving near the touchpad. Changes in capacitance are measured 100 times a second and translated into cursor movement.

Touch Screens   A touch screen is a computer display screen that is sensitive to human touch, allowing the screen to function as an input pointing device. The user touches the screen itself to cause some action to take place.

As of 2012, there exists a variety of touch screen technologies. Three of the more common types are *resistive touch screen*, *surface wave*, and *capacitive.*

A *resistive touch screen panel* is coated with a thin, metallic, electrically conductive and resistive layer that causes a change in the electrical current that is registered as a touch event and sent to the controller for processing. A *surface wave touch screen* uses ultrasonic waves that pass over the touch screen panel. When the panel is touched, a portion of the wave is absorbed and this change in the ultrasonic waves registers the position of the touch event and sends this information to the controller for processing. A *capacitive touch screen panel* is coated with a material that stores electrical charges. When the panel is touched, a small amount of charge is drawn to the point of contact. Circuits located at each corner of the panel measure the charge and send the information to the controller for processing.

Resistive touch screen panels are generally the most affordable but they offer only 75 percent clarity and the layer can be damaged by sharp objects. Resistive touch screen panels are not affected by outside elements such as dust or water. Surface wave touch screen panels are the most advanced of the three types, but they can be damaged by outside elements.

Touch screens are especially popular in very small computers and electronic devices, including tablet personal computers (PCs), Personal Digital Assistants (PDAs), and smartphones, in order to eliminate the requirement of a keyboard space. They are also commonly used in retail situations such as gas stations, automated teller machine (ATM) bank machines, restaurants, and information kiosks.

Joysticks   Joysticks are similar to mice in that they transmit X-Y (x-coordinate and y-coordinate) hand coordinates to the computer to position a cursor on the screen. A joystick is connected to a yoke that pivots freely in all directions. Sensors detect movement and generate corresponding electric currents that are interpreted by a microcontroller as movement of the cursor. Later model joysticks also have a tophat button or contact switch that can be pressed to trigger screen activity. Joysticks are most commonly used in computer games and simulations to provide users with flexibility and quick response time when interacting with on-screen events.

Computer Sciences, 2ⁿᵈ Edition

Invention of the Mouse

The creation of the earliest mouse is attributed to American inventor Douglas Engelbart (1925–) and his colleagues at the Stanford Research Institute in 1965. The idea was further developed at Xerox Corporation's Palo Alto Research Center (PARC). Engelbart's first mouse—so named because of its tail of wire attaching it to the computer—was a wooden, box-like housing with wheels placed at right angles along the top. The user moved the wheels to regulate cursor movement.

Graphics Tablets   Digitizing graphics tablets give artists the flexibility to translate precise pen movements into lines on a display. They can also interpret (read) a user's handwriting through the use of specialized software. Graphics tablets use a variety of technologies, including pressure-sensitive sensors, optical sensors, magnetic sensors, and capacitive sensors, to determine the location of a pen on the pad. Some tablets require the use of a special pen that is attached to the tablet while others allow the use of any pointed object, including a wooden pencil. The resolution and accuracy of a graphics tablet depends on the technology employed. Graphics tablets can be used as mouse replacements but they are particularly suited for drawing.

Trackballs   A trackball is a computer cursor control device usually built into the front of the keyboard, close to the user. Essentially, the trackball is an upside-down mouse that rotates in place within a socket. The user first rolls the ball to direct the cursor to the desired place on the screen and then clicks one of two buttons (identical to mouse buttons) near the trackball to select desktop objects or position the cursor for text entry. Like a touchpad, this pointing device is used in laptop computers and other applications where a mouse would be inconvenient or awkward to use.

Other Pointing Devices

Less commonly used pointing devices include eraser-like pointer sticks built into some laptop keyboards, as well as hand-held units such as light pens, which were among the earliest input units, and pen input devices. Pointing sticks, or eraserhead pointing devices, are so called because they look like a pencil eraser; they are typically located near the middle of the keyboard, between the G and K keys. When a user's finger puts pressure on the eraserhead, the pressure is passed to contacts underneath the keyboard which varies electric current; a microcontroller translates the variable electric current to cursor movement on the computer display.

Pen input devices and light pens allow users to bypass a keyboard and instead use the familiar hand movements of writing or drawing to control action on a computer screen or input graphics or text information. A photodetector in the tip of a light pen responds to points of light on the screen so when a point of light on the screen is lit, the light pen notifies the program that the current location is correct. By moving a pen around the screen, a cursor can be made to follow the pen. Pen input devices and light pens make it possible to activate a command, execute a task, or draw. Handwriting recognition software is available to convert on-screen handwriting into text. The consumer can purchase a handwriting recognition program to install on their personal computer, laptop, or tablet PC; alternatively, many operating systems now incorporate handwriting recognition software, such as Microsoft Windows 7 (released in late 2009) and Microsoft Windows 8 (released in October 2012).

▶ *See also* **Game Controllers • Games • Input Devices • Mouse**

Resources

Books

Clements, Alan. *Principles of Computer Hardware.* 4th ed. New York: Oxford University Press, 2006.

Marmel, Elaine. *PCs Simplified.* Indianapolis, IN: Wiley, 2011.

White, Ron, and Timothy Edward Downs. *How Computers Work.* 9th ed. Indianapolis, IN: Que Publishing, 2007.

Web Sites

The Centre for Computing History. "A Visual History of the Computer Mouse." http://www.computinghistory.org.uk/det/613/The-History-of-the-Computer-Mouse/ (accessed October 17, 2012).

DVICE. "The History of the Computer Mouse." http://dvice.com/archives/2011/04/a-visual-histor.php (accessed October 17, 2012).

Printing Devices

The prediction that the computer would create a paperless office could not have been further from reality. More paper is being consumed as computer printing has become available to the masses. In fact, computers, along with printing devices, have created a new category of computing—desktop publishing—that produces printed paper of near-publication quality.

◀

Computer printer. © *PC Plus Magazine via Getty Images.*

* **bit maps** images comprised of bit descriptions of the image, in black and white or color, such that the colors can be represented by the two values of a binary bit

* **pixel** a single picture element on a video screen; one of the individual dots making up a picture on a video screen or digital image

Printing devices, or printers, provide a permanent paper record of computer output data, graphics, or text and are available in a wide variety of different speeds, features, and capabilities. Printers can also be used with different types of paper forms to print labels, stamps, bank checks, and a wide range of business forms. All printers have some level of variable recurring cost in toner cartridges that must be replaced when the toner is completely used. Printers have both a built-in character set and can download new character set fonts. The output of many printers takes the form of graphical bit maps* that represent image dots exactly. Some printers have built-in processing capability to accept data in the form of a page description language, usually Adobe Postscript or Adobe Portable Document Format. The controller in the printer then processes the page description language to a bit map image within the printer itself. Memory is provided within the printer to store temporarily the bit-mapped image while it is being printed.

The performance of a printer is measured in speed and quality. The speed of a printer is measured by the number of pages printed per minute (ppm). Like a display screen, the quality or resolution of a printer's output is measured by the number of dots printed per inch (dpi). There are, however, two major differences between the dots used in printers and the pixel*s used in computer displays. The number of dots per inch in a printer is generally much higher (300–1200 dpi) than the number of pixels per inch in a monitor (70–100 dpi). While some printers can slightly vary the size of dots, in general the dots created by a printer are fixed in intensity, as opposed to pixels in a display, which can take an infinite range of intensities. To create an intermediate intensity, referred to as a half-tone, printers cluster groups of dots together in close proximity so that the human eye will perceive a gray or intermediate color.

Types of Printers

Regardless of the size of the system, quantity of printing, or capacity of the printer, modern printers use one of three technologies to print dots: dot matrix, inkjet, or laser.

Dot matrix technology results from physical impact of the print head onto paper. The print head on a dot matrix printer consists of a number of printing pins, usually between seven and twenty-four, whose positions can be controlled by individual electromagnets. When a current is applied, the corresponding pin is forced to strike the paper through an inked ribbon to form a dot. Using more pins and overlapping dots by multiple passes over the same line can increase print quality. Most dot matrix printers can operate in several modes offering different tradeoffs between print quality and speed.

Over many years of development, better print heads and more intelligent controllers have improved the size and accuracy of the dots so that dot matrix printers, originally only intended for character printing, can now print high-quality graphics with resolutions that rival laser printers.

Multiple inked ribbons can be used to produce color. However, dot matrix color is not considered acceptable for most purposes. Dot matrix printers are inexpensive in terms of ink ribbon and are reliable, but they are slow, noisy, and poor at graphics. They have all but disappeared from the home and office printer markets, but are still used in certain business applications. Nowadays, dot matrix printers have three major uses: printing on large preprinted forms; printing on small pieces of paper (such as cash register receipts, ATM machine receipts, credit card transactions, and airline tickets); and multi-part, continuous forms with carbon paper in between.

Inkjet printers use nonimpact printing by spraying heated ink from a tiny nozzle onto paper. The tiny nozzle is smaller than the width of a human hair and the volume of each sprayed droplet is about one-millionth the volume of an eye-drop. Inside each nozzle, an ink droplet is electrically heated to its boiling point until it explodes so that the only place the ink can go is out the front of the nozzle. The nozzle is then cooled and the resulting vacuum sucks in another droplet of ink. The speed of the printer is thus limited by the length of the boil/cool cycle.

Inkjets have resolutions ranging from 300 dots per inch (dpi) to 1440 dpi. Some inkjet printers use a vibrating piezo-crystal* instead of heat to produce ink droplets. In ink jet printers, the electric current causes a deformation of the crystal that squeezes out the drop of ink. Mechanically the inkjet printer works similarly to a dot matrix printer. It moves across a page to print a row, and mechanical rollers move the paper downward to print successive rows. Multiple reservoirs of ink may be available to print multiple colors. Inkjet printers are popular for low-cost home printing because they are small and economical. However, they can sometimes produce ink-soaked output that can be messy.

Laser printing is derived from xerography* with the difference that the image is produced electronically from the computer using a laser or light-emitting diode rather than scanned with a bright light. There are four steps in the operation of a laser printer. First, a laser illuminates the dots to be printed on a photosensitive drum that becomes electrically charged wherever a dot is to be printed. Second, the photosensitive drum rotates the charged dots into a tank of black toner where the toner sticks to the drum wherever a charge is present. Third, a sheet of paper is fed toward the drum, coated with electrical charges, and contacts the drum, picking up the toner image from the drum. Finally, the toner image on the paper is heated in a fusing system that melts the toner into the paper while the drum has its charge erased by the corona wire in preparation for the next page.

Other Printing Devices

The complete set of colors that a printer can produce is called its gamut. No printer has a gamut that matches the real world. It is limited by colors, discrete intensities, imperfections, non-uniform spacing across the color spectrum, and human perception. Transferring a color image

* **piezo-crystal** an electronic component that when subjected to a current will produce a waveform signal at a precise rate, which can then be used as a clock signal in a computer

* **xerography** a printing process that uses electrostatic elements derived from a photographic image to deposit the ink

that looks perfect on a computer display to an identical printed page is difficult for the following reasons:

- Display monitors use transmitted light, while color printers use reflected light;
- Display monitors produce 256 intensities per color, while color printers use half-tones;
- Display monitors have a dark background, paper has a light background;
- Display monitors have a red, green, blue (RGB) gamut and printers have a cyan, yellow, magenta, black (CYMK) gamut.

Common ways to print color images include the use of special inks and paper. Inkjet printers can use dye-based inks or pigment-based inks. Dye-based inks consist of colored dyes dissolved in a fluid carrier. They provide bright colors and flow easily. Pigment-based inks contain solid particles of pigment suspended in a fluid carrier that evaporates from the paper leaving the pigment behind. They do not fade in time like dye-based inks, but they are also not as bright, and the pigment particles tend to clog nozzles requiring periodic cleaning. Coated or glossy paper, specially designed to hold ink droplets and not let them spread, is required for printing photographs.

Solid ink printers are slightly higher quality than inkjet printers. These printers accept solid blocks of special waxy ink that is then melted in hot ink reservoirs. Startup times of these printers are long (typically ten minutes) while the ink blocks are melting. The hot ink is sprayed onto the paper, where it solidifies and is fused with the paper by forcing it between two hard rollers.

A step up from solid ink printers is a color laser printer. A color laser printer works exactly like a black and white laser printer, except an image is transferred to the roller using four different toners (the CYMK gamut) instead of just one. Because the full bit map of an image is generally produced in advance, the memory requirements make this type of printer expensive, but printing is fast, high quality, and images are stable over time. A 1200 by 1200 dpi image for a page containing 516 square centimeters or 80 square inches needs 115 million pixels. At 4 bits per pixel, the printer needs 55 megabytes (MB) just for the bit map, exclusive of memory for the internal processors and fonts.

For highest-quality color images, more specialized methods such as thermal wax transfer or dye sublimation are required. Sublimation is the scientific name for a solid changing into a gas without passing through a liquid state. The mechanisms for both methods are similar. The paper is fed into the printer and clamped against a drum with a print head providing a row of dot-sized heating elements. Between the paper and the print head, a roll of impregnated film is exposed. The heat from the print head melts the wax or dye onto the paper. The film is impregnated with either colored wax or dye in page-sized sections of cyan, yellow, magenta, and black.

For thermal wax transfer, the input paper is pre-coated with clear wax to compensate for slight paper imperfections and so that the wax may be applied more uniformly. For dye sublimation, the dyes diffuse and actually blend in the paper. Although dye sublimation can print continuous color tones without half toning, it also requires high temperatures and expensive specialized paper. The colors fade when exposed to ultraviolet light, such as that contained in sunlight. Small snapshot printers often use the dye sublimation process to produce highly realistic photographic images.

Organizations that produce and store significant copies of paper documents sometimes use computer output microfilm (COM) devices to place data from a computer directly onto microfilm, thus eliminating the need for photographic conversion.

Evolution of Printing and Plotters

English mathematician and inventor Charles Babbage (1791–1871) is considered to have been the first person to invent a printer (although it was never actually assembled). The printer was a mechanically driven device for use with his mechanical computer, the difference engine. Early printers were derived from typewriters using daisywheel printers—form characters that were mounted at the ends of arms attached to wheels shaped like a daisy. Like typewriters, printing resulted from the wheel rotating to the proper position and an energized magnet forcing the wheel through an inked ribbon onto paper. These printers were difficult to maintain and incapable of generating any graphical images or foreign words that could not be formed by the given set of formed characters. Most formed-character impact printers have disappeared from use. Nearly all modern computer printers produce their output as a combination of dots.

Plotters are hard-copy printing devices consisting of one or multiple independently maneuverable ink pens that are used for general design work such as blueprints, schematics, drawings, and plotting mathematical functions. Standard plot widths are 61 centimeters by 91.5 centimeters or 24 inches by 36 inches, but the attractive feature of plotters is limitless size when necessary for uses such as graphic arts.

 See also **Input Devices • Pointing Devices • Serial and Parallel Transmission**

Resources

Books

Clements, Alan. *Principles of Computer Hardware.* 4th ed. Oxford and New York: Oxford University Press, 2006.

Marmel, Elaine. *PCs Simplified.* Indianapolis: Wiley, 2011.

Rosen, Mitchell, and Noboru Ohta, eds. *Color Desktop Printer Technology.* Boca Raton, FL: CRC Press, 2006.

A Paperless Society?

Many industry experts believed that paper sales would decrease as more and more people and businesses turned to electronic documents, networked filing systems, and e-mail. However, the paper industry is not suffering lost sales. Industry forecasts show that the demand for home paper use is on the rise.

Family Histories

Home printers and scanners have revolutionized the way in which people can recreate their family's genealogical history. Instead of having costly reproductions made by professional photography studios, people can scan their family photos, resize them, enhance the color or black and white imagery, and make their own copies for use in family history albums. With a high-quality scanner, printer, and photo paper, a family genealogist can reproduce images that are hard to distinguish from the source photo.

Shelly, Gary B., Thomas J. Cashman, and Misty E. Vermaat. *Discovering Computers: Fundamentals.* 8th ed. Mason, Ohio: Shouth-Western, 2011.

White, Ron, and Timothy Edward Downs. *How Computers Work.* 9th ed. Indianapolis: Que Publications, 2008.

Web Sites

Softpedia, and Georgiana Bobolicu. "History of Computer Printers." http://gadgets.softpedia.com/news/History-of-Computer-Printers-032-01.html (accessed October 18, 2012).

Procedural Languages

Procedural languages are computer languages used to define the actions that a computer has to follow to solve a problem. Although it would be convenient for people to give computers instructions in a natural language, such as English, French, or Chinese, they cannot because computers are just too inflexible to understand the subtleties of human communication. Human intelligence can work out the ambiguities of a natural language, but a computer requires a rigid, mathematically precise communication system: each symbol, or group of symbols, must mean exactly the same thing every time.

Computer scientists have created artificial languages that enable programmers to assemble a set of commands for the machine without dealing directly with strings of binary digits. The high-level form of a procedural language frees a programmer from the time-consuming chore of expressing algorithm*s in lower-level languages such as assembly and machine language. Additionally, procedural language instructions are expressed in a machine-independent form that facilitate portability, thus increasing the lifetime and usefulness of a program.

Higher-level languages work for people because they are closer to natural language, but a computer cannot carry out instructions until that communication has been translated into zeros and ones. This translation may be done by compilers or interpreters, which are special programs custom-made to fit both the language and the machine being used. A compiler reads the entire program, makes a translation, and produces a complete binary code version, which is then loaded into the computer and executed. Once the program is compiled, neither the original program nor the compiler is needed. On the other hand, an interpreter translates and executes the program one instruction at a time, so a program written in an interpreted language must be interpreted each time it is run. Compiled programs execute faster, but interpreted programs are generally easier to correct or modify.

A procedural language is either compiled or interpreted, depending on the use for which it was created. FORTRAN, for example, is usually implemented with a compiler because it was created to handle large programs for scientific and mathematical applications where speed of execution is very important. On the other hand, BASIC is typically implemented with an interpreter because it was intended for use by novice programmers.

Each programming language has a special vocabulary of keywords, which correspond to specific operations or sequences of operations to be performed by the computer. Some of them act as verbs, or commands, others act as nouns, modifiers, or punctuation marks. By using them to form sentences, a programmer tells a computer exactly what to do with each item of information being processed. Typical commands include: input and output, conditions, and repetition. Because they are indispensable to programmers, these commands are common to all computer languages, but they are written differently in each language because the sentences must follow the syntax* of the language.

Many of the hundreds of programming languages also have dialects. A dialect is a variation of the main language. While people can understand one another even if they speak different dialects of their language, a computer cannot understand a program written in a different dialect from its own. Dialects present problems when a program using the same data set gives different answers when run on two different machines. This means that the program cannot be ported from one machine to the other. Asking several programmers to name the best computer language will most likely give you several different answers, because there is no best computer language, any more than one natural language is better than all the rest. Theoretically, most programming tasks could be accomplished with any language, but writing a program for a given job is actually considerably easier in some languages than in others. None can claim all-around utility.

This section covers, in some historical order, procedural languages that were popular or significant during the period of their development: FORTRAN, ALGOL, COBOL, BASIC, Pascal, C, and Ada.

FORTRAN

It can safely be stated that FORTRAN (FORmula TRANslating System) was the first true high-level language. A factor that influenced the development of FORTRAN was the amount of money spent on programming in 1954. The cost of programming heavily impacted on the cost of operating a computer, and as computers got cheaper, the situation got worse. American computer scientist John Backus (1924–2007) was able to convince IBM's directors that a language could be developed with a compiler that would produce very efficient object code. He was put in charge of the group that developed FORTRAN, which included Irving Ziller, Roy Nutt, David Sayre, and Peter Sheridan. One of their goals was to design a language that would make it possible for engineers and scientists to write programs on their own for the IBM 704.

* **syntax** a set of rules that a computing language incorporates regarding structure, punctuation, and formatting

The first FORTRAN compiler took about twenty-five person-years to complete and proved to be as efficient as the then-current assemblers, making it a striking achievement in the history of programming languages. FORTRAN I was released in 1957 and was followed in the spring of 1958 by FORTRAN II. It included function statements and better diagnostic messages. A more advanced version, FORTRAN III, depended heavily on the architecture of the IBM 704, and was not made into a commercial product. However, many of its features were incorporated into FORTRAN IV, which was released in 1962 and had a life of almost fifteen years. It added COMMON storage, double-precision and logical data types, and relational expressions as well as the DATA statements, which provided a simple facility to initialize variables. Programs written using versions subsequent to FORTRAN III were machine independent, which meant that they could be run on any scientific machine. For the first time, one single language was used by many manufacturers for many different machines.

By the mid-1970s, FORTRAN IV was no longer a modern language, and although the investment in FORTRAN programs was immense, it was time to bring the language up to speed. In 1967, work began on what was later called FORTRAN 77, which became the official standard in April of 1978. By 1981, the demand for FORTRAN 77 compilers was very high, making it clear that it was a success. However, it did not have all the features needed to implement modern control structures, so work on its successor began in 1978. It was to include if-then-else control structures, case selection, do/enddo structure, and recursion, among other things. Work on this project ended in 1990 and FORTRAN 90 was published in 1991. FORTRAN 95, an extension of FORTRAN 90, was published in December 1997, and work on FORTRAN 200x was underway in 2001. It is an upward compatible extension of FORTRAN 95 adding support for exception handling, object-oriented programming, and improved interoperability with C.

ALGOL

Because many languages and dialects were developed between 1956 and 1959 creating portability problems, various computer groups petitioned the Association for Computing Machinery (ACM) to recommend action for the creation of a universal programming language. Representatives from industry and universities were appointed to a committee that met three times, starting in January 1958, and agreed that the new language would be an algebraic language similar to FORTRAN. However, FORTRAN could not be used as a universal language because, in those days, it was a creation of IBM and closely tied to IBM hardware. Some members of the group, including John Backus and Alan Perlis, were chosen to represent the American viewpoint at the meetings that would shape this international language.

ALGOL 58 was really a group effort. It was the first formal attempt to address issues of portability, and integrated the best features of programming languages available at the time. It introduced new terms such as: type, formal versus actual parameter, for statement, the *begin end* delimiters*, and three levels of language description. This effort was considered as a draft and was not commercially implemented. However, many recommendations for its improvement were considered at a Paris meeting in June 1959.

* **delimiters** special symbols that mark the beginnings and/ or endings of other groups of symbols (for example to mark out comments in program source code)

In January 1960, seven representatives of European countries, including Peter Naur and Fritz Bauer, and six from the United States, including Backus and Perlis, met in Paris to develop ALGOL 60, which was expected to become a universal tool with the addition of the following features: block, call by value and call by name, dynamic arrays, *own* variables, global and local variables, *until, while, if then else,* and recursion. ALGOL was used more in Europe than in the United States by computer scientists conducting research. ALGOL 60 became the standard for the publication of algorithms and was a great influence on future language developments.

In 1962, a new international committee of computer scientists was formed to develop an enhanced version of ALGOL 60. The meetings began in 1965 and lasted until 1968 when ALGOL 68 was released. Although it allowed non-English-speaking programmers to write programs in their own language, it proved to be too cumbersome to be readily accepted. Proficient programmers had trouble understanding the document that defined it and very few institutions had an actual ALGOL 68 compiler in use.

However, out of this effort arose a new language, Pascal, developed by Niklaus Wirth who began work on it in 1968.

COBOL

In April of 1959, two years after the introduction of FORTRAN, a group of academics, computer manufacturers, and computer users, including American programming pioneer Grace Hopper (1906–1992), met to discuss the feasibility of designing a programming language that would satisfy the needs of the business community and would become a standard. FORTRAN did not suit their needs because business programs deal with large quantities of data but do not perform complicated calculations. Existing programming languages were not portable as they could only function in one type of computer: scientific or business. Since large organizations sometimes had different types of computers, their programmers had to know several languages, thus increasing the cost of software. For example, the U.S. Department of Defense (DoD) had more than 1,000 computers and it was costing the DoD close to $500 million a year to program them and keep them operating smoothly.

A meeting of forty representatives from the government, users, consultants, and manufacturers met at the Pentagon in May 1959 to discuss the need of a common business language. They formed three committees and proceeded to analyze existing business programming

BASICally Speaking

It is estimated that by the mid-1980s, several million school children in the United States and abroad had learned BASIC. Currently, the most popular version is Visual BASIC. It uses data typing and structuring and was first introduced in 1991.

languages: FLOWMATIC, AIMACO, and Commercial Translator. They sought to learn if the best features of each could be merged into one. By December of 1959, the group had completed the specifications for COBOL, which were made public in 1960.

COBOL programs are composed of four divisions, each one serving a specific purpose. The IDENTIFICATION division serves to identify the program and programmer. The ENVIRONMENT division is used to identify the actual computer, compiler, and peripheral devices that will be used by the program and it is the most machine dependent. The DATA division describes the files, records, and fields used by the program, and the PROCEDURE division contains the instructions that will process the data. COBOL commands are written using English words and syntax, and its variable names can be up to 30 characters long, making them very descriptive. These features make programs easy to read and understand for nonprogrammers, and it also makes them easier to debug and maintain. COBOL programs are highly portable, therefore COBOL was readily accepted by the American business community.

The 1961 revision of COBOL included the Report Writer and Sort features, and was the first to be widely implemented. COBOL was revised again in 1965 and 1968, the latter was the first American National Standards Institute (ANSI) standard compiler.

COBOL 74 improved indexed file handling, specifically, ISAM (Indexed Sequential Access Method). During the growth of the microcomputer market, several versions of microcomputer COBOL became available and were used in the business community as well as in universities and colleges. COBOL 85 reflected the efforts of making it more compatible with structured programming by providing END IF, END PERFORM, a direct case structure, and an in-line PERFORM. The next revision appeared in 2002 and includes object-oriented features.

BASIC

In the early 1960s, there were no personal computers. If you wanted to ompute, you had to punch your program on cards, carry them to the nearest computer center, and then wait hours for the results. John G. Kemeny and Thomas E. Kurtz, professors at Dartmouth College, believed that computer programming was too important to be relegated exclusively to engineering students and professional programmers. So in 1963, they designed and built a time-sharing system and developed the Beginners All-purpose Symbolic Instruction Code (BASIC). Their goals included ease of learning for the beginner, hardware and operating system independence, the ability to accommodate large programs, and sensible error messages in English. BASIC became available in 1964. Although Kemeny and Kurtz implemented it to run with a compiler, current versions run under interpreters.

BASIC can be classified as a general-purpose language because it can handle business applications as well as scientific and educational applications. Unfortunately, the language has been modified widely and extensively by computer manufacturers and software companies. Numerous dialects of BASIC, each with its own syntax and special features, make it difficult to port programs from one computer to another.

The original version was revised and expanded by Kemeny and Kurtz to include graphic statements in 1975. The following year, in order to comply with the requirements of structured programming, they dropped the GOTO statement; this version was called SBASIC and was taught to Dartmouth undergraduates. In 1983 they developed "true BASIC," a more powerful and versatile form that follows the proposed ANSI standards. Some of its features were optional line numbers, long variable names, array-handling statements, Do loops, a SELECT case structure, and independent subprograms. BASIC was widely accepted in the educational community because it was an easy language to teach and learn.

Pascal

Pascal was developed by Niklaus Wirth, a Swiss computer scientist who was part of the ALGOL 68 committee. He felt that ALGOL was too complex and wanted to design a computer language that could easily be taught to college students. The new language, which is a derivative of ALGOL, was published in 1971 and was later called Pascal.

Pascal incorporates the ideas of structured programming that started to appear in the 1960s, redefining ALGOL's concept of breaking down a program into modules, procedures, and functions, and also expanding on some of ALGOL's features by adding new data types and control structures. Its structure makes programs easier to read and maintain by people other than the original programmer. Although there are variations among Pascal compilers, the language has a fairly standard form, so programs are portable between different computers.

Wirth's idea found its most important audience at the University of California at San Diego, where in late 1974, Kenneth Bowles worked out a Pascal operating system and compiler to be used on mini- and microcomputers. He went on to develop an entire system containing a compiler, text editor, an assembler, a linker, a file-handling utility, and a set of utility programs. This package, ready for distribution by 1977, was known as UCSD Pascal. By 1978, it began to receive national attention. The growth of personal computers helped it achieve wide acceptance in the educational community, and for almost two decades it was the language of choice for most introductory computer science courses.

Because Pascal was meant to be used as a teaching tool, its input and output functions were limited, making it impractical for writing commercial applications. However, several languages including Modula-2 and Ada were based on it.

C

C is one of the descendants of ALGOL 60. It was developed in 1972 by Ken Thompson and Dennis Ritchie, both of Bell Laboratories. Their goal was to create a language that would combine high-level structured language features with those that control low-level programming. This makes C well suited for writing operating systems, compilers, and also business applications. C compilers can basically run on all machines, and since a standard for C was defined in 1988, most C programs are portable. Conversely, C has been defined as a programming language written by a programmer, which means that novices find it difficult to learn.

C supports structured programming and provides for several data types. For example, pointer arithmetic is an integral part of C, as is the use of functions that may be called recursively. Although input and output statements are not part of the language, they are functions found in a "library" ready to be used when needed. Some of the functions found in a standard UNIX C library include string manipulation, character functions, and memory allocation. In addition to external, automatic and static variables, C provides register variables, which shorten execution time because they use registers.

C makes it possible to work on bit data using the bit operators for AND, OR, Exclusive OR, One's complement, SHIFT LEFT, and SHIFT RIGHT, giving programmers great control over data manipulation.

When compared to other programming languages such as FORTRAN or Pascal, C has remained quite stable. Its success in the early 1980s was due in part to its close ties with UNIX and its availability on personal computers. Additionally, it satisfied the needs of both system and application programmers alike. Several languages such as C++, Perl, and Javascript are based on C's syntax.

Ada

Development of Ada started in 1975 under the direction of the U.S. Department of Defense (DoD) for use in its military computer systems. This action was necessary because the expense of developing and maintaining DoD programs was becoming very high due to the variety of programming languages being used. In the early 1970s, the DoD used at least 450 different computer languages and dialects.

The DoD uses most of its programming efforts to guide military equipment, such as tanks, airplanes, and nuclear bombs. Those programs execute in *real time,* at the same time as a tank is moving or an airplane is flying. For example, to perform its mission, a fighter pilot cannot wait for the computer to send back the results later in the day. Although real-time systems can operate outside of the device they are controlling, they can also be embedded within a larger system, for example a robot.

Usually real-time systems are large and multifaceted, so the task of coordinating the programming effort is key to the success of the system. These systems have to respond to outside events, which happen in the real world, within a specific amount of time. They must be able to communicate with typical computer peripherals, such as printers and modems, as well as non-typical input and output devices like patient monitoring devices. Most importantly, real-time systems have to be reliable because in certain cases, an error in the program could result in a loss of human lives. These conditions dictate that programming languages for real-time systems must be robust. That means that the compiler must detect programming errors automatically before any damage is done, and the language must provide for recovery from undetected errors.

In 1975, the High Order Language Working Group (HOLWG) was formed to find the exact language for DoD's needs. After careful study, the committee decided that none of the existing languages would be appropriate and a new one had to be developed. The foundations for the definition and design of this language were: PL/I, ALGOL 68, and Pascal. It came to be called Ada. Its development was carefully monitored; it took five years before the first reference manual was published in 1980. A revision came out in 1982, and in 1995, ANSI adopted a new standard for Ada.

Ada was developed to reduce the cost of software development and maintenance, especially for large, constantly changing programs that will be used for a long period of time. A fundamental idea of this language is the "package," which is used to divide a program into modules that can be compiled, tested separately, and stored in a library until needed. This makes large programs easier to write, debug, and maintain by teams of programmers. Another feature of Ada is that it supports parallel processing*, including concurrently executable code segments called "tasks," which can execute independently of each other or can be synchronized to relay information between themselves.

Although Ada is not very difficult to learn at the basic level, using it to its full capacity requires programming knowledge and experience. Therefore, Ada is considered a language for advanced programmers, especially suited for large projects, real-time systems, and systems programming.

Because it is a very good language for large critical systems, Ada has achieved a high level of acceptance and is used by many organizations worldwide. Not only is most DoD code written in Ada, but the language has been used to write important non-military applications such as international air traffic control, railways, and commercial satellites. For example, programs for the French TGV rail system, Channel Tunnel, and many Global Positioning System projects are mostly written in Ada.

 See also **Algol-60 Report • Algorithms • Compilers • Programming**

Resources

Books

Baron, Naomi S. *Computer Languages: A Guide for the Perplexed.* Garden City, NY: Anchor Books, 1986.

Hsu, Jeffrey. *Microcomputer Programming Languages.* Hasbrouck Heights, NJ: Hayden Book Co., 1986.

Wexelblat, Richard, ed. *History of Programming Languages.* New York: Academic Press, 1981.

Computer Sciences, 2nd Edition

Ada's Namesake

The Ada programming language was named after Ada Byron King, Countess of Lovelace (1815–1852). The daughter of English poet Lord George Gordon Byron, King is considered to be the first computer programmer. King worked closely with British mathematician Charles Babbage (1791–1871) in the programming of his hypothetical Analytical Engine.

* **parallel processing** the presence of more than one central processing unit (CPU) in a computer, which enables the true execution of more than one program

Programming

Award-winning computer designer and engineer W. Daniel Hillis (1956–) captured the essence of programming when he said: "The magic of a computer lies in its ability to become almost anything you can imagine, as long as you can explain exactly what that is. The hitch is in explaining exactly what you want. With the right programming, a computer can become a theater, a musical instrument, a reference book, a chess opponent. No other entity in the world except a human brain has such an adaptable, universal nature."

Computer programming has many facets: It is like engineering because computer programs must be carefully designed to be reliable and inexpensive to maintain. It is an art because good programs require that the programmer use intuition and a personal sense of style. It is a literary effort because programs must be understood by computers, and this requires mastery of a programming language. That is not all: Programs must be analyzed to understand how they work and usually must be modified periodically to accommodate changing requirements. Therefore, as programs are written, programmers should care about how elegant they are, and they should understand how they arrived at the solution of a problem.

Techniques

Telling a computer what to do is not as easy as it sounds. Every detail of the computer's desired operation must be precisely described, and plans must be made for all possible occurrences. For example, if a store has a billing program set up to send monthly bills to all customers, then the computer will send out a bill for $0 to those who owe nothing. If one tells a computer to send a threatening letter to customers who have not paid, then those who owe nothing will receive menacing letters until they send in payments of $0! Avoiding this kind of mix-up is one aspect of computer programming. The programmer's art is stating exactly what is desired. In this example, it means making a distinction between customers who have not sent any money because they do not owe anything, and those who actually still owe money.

A combination of thorough problem definition and straightforward programming techniques lead to precise and effective programs. Therefore, programmers should observe the following steps:

- Define the problem exactly, because this constitutes about 80 percent of the difficulty of programming;
- Design the program simply because simple programs are easier to develop and maintain, and they result in more reliable, secure, robust, and efficient code;
- Execute the program with different sets of data. If possible, test the program by hand with just one input; this is a great way to find bugs, and is easy to use and understand.

The task of writing a computer program requires great attention to detail. Computers demand absolute completeness and precision in their instructions: they do only what they are told and their instructions cannot contain any ambiguity*. This is true of all software. It applies equally to a simple program that makes a computer play a tune and to a huge program that monitors traffic at an airport.

In programming, nothing can be left to chance. Non-programmers tend to forget that actions they take for granted must be spelled out in great detail for the machine. Every action must be broken down into its most elementary parts to produce an algorithm*. No detail, however self-evident to the human mind, can be omitted or taken for granted in a computer program. A good programmer must be capable of thinking about the big-picture that generates useful algorithms, and paying attention to the details that convert those algorithms into unambiguous computer code.

In its simplest form, an algorithm is like a recipe, but a computer programmer must specify extra steps that a cook would usually skip over. For example, a recipe might call for two eggs, without specifying that the eggs must be fresh, uncooked, and added to the mixture without the shell. If such criteria were assumed and not detailed precisely in a computer program, the recipe would fail. When hundreds or thousands of instructions covering every contingency have to be spelled out for the computer, expense naturally rises and bugs* creep in.

There are several ways programmers can approach the problem systematically. Two of them are flowcharts* and pseudocode*. A flowchart is a graphic representation of the algorithm using standard symbols that can then be translated into computer language instructions. Pseudocode involves refining the problem in several stages starting with English sentences, which are then restated in subsequent steps with more computer-like words and statements.

Structured Programming

Structured programming, championed in 1968 by Dutch computer scientist Edsger W. Dijkstra, has exerted a major influence on the development of software ranging from small personal computer programs to multimillion-dollar defense projects. Only three control structures are required to turn out useful structured programs:

- Simple sequencing or instructing the computer to do one thing after another;

- Looping, or telling the computer to perform the same set of instructions while a condition holds or until a condition is met;

- Decision making, or enabling the computer's ability to branch in one of two directions depending on the outcome of a condition.

In addition, structured programs are typically divided into modules*, which each perform one function, and do it well. The algorithms are easy

* **ambiguity** the quality of doubtfulness or uncertainty; often subject to multiple interpretations

* **algorithm** a rule or procedure used to solve a problem, most often described as a sequence of steps

* **bugs** errors in program source code

* **flowcharts** techniques for graphically describing the sequencing and structure of program source code

* **pseudocode** a language-neutral, structural description of the algorithms that are to be used in a program

* **modules** a generic term that is applied to small elements or components that can be used in combination to build an operational system

The Heart of Programming

The hardest part of programming is not learning the programming language, but figuring out how to cast a problem into statements the computer can follow. It is not unlike solving word problems on math tests. The hardest part is not solving the problem; for many students, the most difficult aspect is restating the problem in the form of an equation.

---

* **debug** the act of trying to trace, identify, and then remove errors in program source code

to follow because there is only one logic entry into each module and one logic exit from it. Since the are small, usually not exceeding one page of code, they are easy to debug*.

Programmers

A programmer's goal is not to solve a problem but to map out instructions that will let the computer find the solution. Performing rapid calculations is a job tailor-made for a computer, but designing the step-by-step algorithm that tells the computer exactly how to proceed with a given assignment is better left to human intelligence. To make the algorithm as clear as possible, a programmer always starts by assembling the known facts and setting out a clear statement of the problem. Then the programmer begins devising a logical progression of steps for the computer to follow en route to the solution. Often the programmer will use an extreme version of the problem just to see if the logic of the algorithm holds up. This test often discovers missing steps or inaccurate instructions that would cause the computer to flash error messages.

Finally, the programmer has to consider the types of data the computer will be handling and decide on the best method for storing and retrieving the data for processing. By making the right decision regarding language, logic, and programming techniques, programmers can harness the power of the computer with maximum effectiveness.

The computer programmer is the link between a problem and its computer solution. Good programmers write well-structured and clear programs that others can read and modify. Writing good programs requires creativity, but it must be tempered with great patience and intense discipline so that the resulting programs will be correct and efficient.

 *See also* **Algorithms • Compilers • Design Tools • Logo • Procedural Languages**

Resources

Books

Bentley, Jon. *Programming Pearls.* 2nd ed. Reading, MA: Addison-Wesley, 2000.

Hillis, W. Daniel. *The Pattern on the Stone.* New York: Basic Books, 1998.

Time-Life Books. *Understanding Computers: Software.* Alexandria, VA: Time-Life Books, 1986.

R

Reading Tools

Systems for recognizing printed text and images, what are called reading tools, originated in the late 1950s and have been in widespread use on desktop and laptop computers, and other such devices, since the early 1990s. Examples of such reading tools include bar code technology, optical character recognition, optical mark readers, and smart card technology.

* **prototype** a working model or experimental investigation of proposed systems under development

Bar Code Technology

A bar code is a printed series of black parallel bars or lines of varying width on a white background that is used for entering data into a computer system. The bars represent the binary digits 0 and 1, sequences of which, in turn, can represent numbers from 0 to 9. The numbers presented by a bar code are also printed out at its base. Bar code information is read by an optical scanner such as a handheld wand or a bar code pen that is moved across the code or vice versa. The computer then stores or immediately processes the data in the bar code.

History of the Bar Code As a graduate student at Drexel Institute of Technology, American inventor Bernard Silver (1924–1963) overheard the president of a local food chain asking one of the deans to develop a system that would automatically read product information during checkout. The problem intrigued Silver so much that he and another Drexel student, Joseph Woodland (1921–), invented the bull's eye symbol, the prototype* of the bar code, which was patented on October 7, 1952.

Bar code technology was first used commercially in 1966. Soon afterward, consumers and industry leaders realized that bar code standardization was needed. Thus, by 1970, Logicon, Inc. introduced the Universal Grocery Products Identification Code (UGPIC). The first company to produce bar code equipment for the retail sector using UGPIC was Monarch Marking, and for the industrial sector, Plessey Telecommunications. In 1973, UGPIC gave way to the Universal Product Code (UPC), which has been used in the United States ever since. The first UPC scanner (made by National Cash Register Compny, now NCR Corporation) was installed at a Marsh's supermarket in Troy, Ohio, in June 1974. The first product to bear a bar code was a pack of Wrigley's Juicy Fruit chewing gum, which is now on display at the Smithsonian Institution's National Museum of American History.

Electrodes planted in the man's brain connect to a camera that is mounted onto a pair of glasses allowing him to read large letters. © *AP Images/ STEPHEN CHERNIN.*

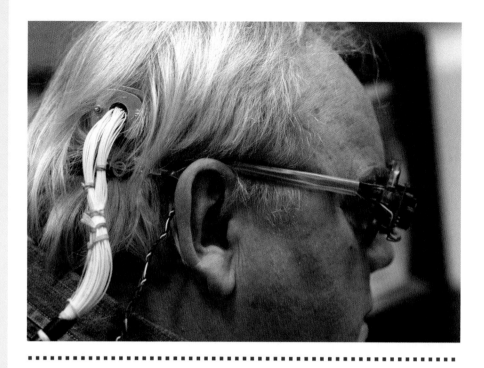

Uses of Bar Codes   In retail, bar codes are used to obtain price information and other data about goods at the point of purchase by customers. At ski resorts, tags with codes are affixed to skiers' jackets and scanned as people enter ski lifts in order to monitor patterns of slope use. In industry, bar codes are used to track products as they are manufactured, distributed, stored, sold, and serviced.

Optical Character Recognition (OCR)

Optical character recognition is the method for the machine-reading of type-set, type, and hand-printed letters, numbers, and symbols using an optical scanner and optical character software. The light reflected by a printed text or image is recorded as patterns of light and dark areas by photoelectric cells in the scanner. A computer program then analyzes the patterns and identifies the characters they represent. OCR is also used to produce text files from computer files that contain images of alphanumeric characters such as those produced by fax transmissions.

History of OCR   Engineering attempts at automated recognition of printed characters began before World War II. However, it was not until the early 1950s that a commercial venture justified funding for research and development of such technology. The American Bankers Association and the financial services industry challenged major equipment manufacturers to develop a common language to process checks automatically. Although the banking industry eventually favored Magnetic Ink Character Recognition (MICR)—a branch of character recognition involving the sensing of characters containing magnetic particles to determine the character's most probable identity—some vendors had proposed the use of OCR technology.

Uses of OCR Any standard form or document with repetitive variable data is suitable for OCR—for example, credit card sales drafts and invoices. Perhaps the most innovative use of OCR can be found in the Kurzwell scanners that read for the blind by scanning pages and converting the text into spoken words.

Optical Mark Reader (OMR)

An Optical Mark Reader (OMR) unit scans for either the presence or absence of a mark in a particular location on a page, as specified by the user. The technology is also known as mark sense, and it is familiar to students and teachers at all levels because it is widely used for standardized and classroom testing purposes.

OMR technology was pioneered in the United States and was first used for student assessments in the 1950s. Its introduction was related to advances in behavioral and child psychology as well as to the development of tests designed to measure various aspects of human performance. Since that time, OMR has become commonplace throughout the American education system. Although OMR has a variety of administrative applications, its major use is to score multiple-choice tests such as the SAT (formally called Scholastic Aptitude Test) and Graduate Record Examinations (GRE). Other uses include the recording of responses for surveys and questionnaires.

Smart Card Technology

Unlike the magnetic swipe card (a plastic card with a magnetic strip containing encoded data), a smart card is a plastic card containing a chip that holds a microprocessor and data storage unit. Such cards have standardized electrical contacts for drawing power and for communicating with external devices.

History of Smart Cards The first smart card-related research began in 1968 when German inventors Jürgen Dethloff (1924–2002) and Helmut Grötrupp (1916–1981) patented their idea of using plastic cards as a carrier for microchips. In 1973, French inventor Roland Marino developed and patented the first smart card. The first commercial field trial did not occur until 1981 when a banking chip card was tested in several French cities. In 1984, France Télécom introduced the first phone chip card. This led to widespread use in that country, followed by adoption in Germany, where patients have health records stored on such cards. In the United States, field trials were conducted for identification cards, and a pilot for an electronic purse (also known as the stored value card) took place in Atlanta, Georgia, in conjunction with the 1996 Summer Olympics.

Computer Sciences, 2ⁿᵈ Edition

Uses of Smart Cards Smart card technology is used in a variety of applications, including building access systems, electronic payment schemes, and public transportation. Smart cards are also used to provide conditional access for satellite television users, and to store and retrieve information about customers and their purchases through grocery or retail loyalty cards.

Radio-Frequency Identification (RFID)

Radio-Frequency Identification (RFID) refers to the use of a device affixed onto or within an object for the purpose of identifying that object (and/or its characteristics) using radio waves. The RFID device is often referred to as a RFID tag. RFID tags most often incorporate a very compact radio antenna, as well as an integrated circuit chip for processing and modulating the radio signal. RFID tags can be broadly categorized as being passive or active. Active tags possess a battery and can transmit a signal using their own power. By contrast, passive tags lack batteries or other internal power source, and only transmit in response to an external radio signal. The signals produced by either active or passive tags are intercepted and interpreted by devices called interrogators or readers.

RFID technology has found use in a variety of applications, including implantation into pets for identification if the animal becomes lost; in passports; and for automated payments on toll roads. In the case of toll charges, the motorist places an RFID tag in his car so that whenever he drives through a toll area, the RFID tag is activated and a debit charge is automatically placed on his account, thus relieving the motorist of the necessity of having to stop at a toll both to pay.

Perhaps the greatest potential for RFID tags relates to consumer purchases and company inventories. The idea is that a consumer could load their shopping cart with products and simply walk out the store—the entire purchase would be accomplished all at once with RFID tags, without the need to individually scan each product. A helpful step in enabling widespread use of RFID tags for consumer shopping was reported by Rice University (Houston, Texas) researchers and their Korean colleagues in 2010. The researchers infused ink with carbon nanotubes and then used an inkjet printer to printout small, flexible antennae for use in tags. The researchers predicted that the capability to printout antennae using low-cost, mass-printing methods could help bring the per-cost price of RFID tags down considerably, which is a necessary requirement for their use on products in grocery stores and other retail stores. In 2012, French researchers successfully created a paper-thin RFID tag from aluminum that reduces the amount of metal needed for such tags, which lowers their cost dramatically. Consequently, the new process allows many more uses for RFID tagging. In fact, Dr. Camille Ramade led the French team from the University of Montpellier in showing how RFID tags could be made by applying an aluminum coil antenna onto paper in an inexpensive process called thermal evaporation. The Ramade team suggests that their process could reduce prices to a fifth of the current price necessary for RFID tagging.

There is an overlap between smart card and RFID technology; for instance, some smart cards use radio waves to communicate at a distance with other electronic devices. However, it is important to note that smart cards and RFID are not necessarily used together: many types of smart cards do not communicate information using radio waves (i.e., they do not use RFID); likewise, RFID technology can be used without being incorporated within a smart card platform.

▶ See also **Input Devices • Optical Character Recognition • Video Devices**

Resources

Books

Mayes, Keith, ed. *Smart Cards, Tokens, Security and Applications.* New York and London: Springer, 2009.

Rankl, Wolfgang, and Wolfgang Effing. *Smart Card Handbook.* 4th ed. New York: John Wiley & Sons, 2010.

Periodical

Ramade, Camille, et al. "Thin Film HF RFID Tag Deposited on Paper by Thermal Evaporation." *International Journal of Radio Frequency Identification Technology and Applications* 4, no. 1 (2012): 49–66.

Web Sites

ScienceDaily.com. "Playing RFID Tag With Sheets of Paper." http://www.sciencedaily.com/releases/2012/02/120206102952.htm (accessed October 18, 2012).

Robots

The traditional romantic portrayal of the robot is as an anthropomorphic*, autonomous* entity that possesses intelligence and walks and talks in a way that mimics human behavior. The truth is not quite so glamorous. Robots are electromechanical machines that rarely resemble the human form. Instead, the overwhelming majority of robots are often anchored to one point and consist of a single flexible arm.

The purpose of robotics technology is essentially to carry out repetitive, physically demanding and potentially dangerous manual activities so that humans are relieved from these tasks. Examples of these chores include working on a factory production line assembly, handling hazardous materials, and dealing with hostile environments like underground mines, underwater construction sites, and explosives plants. Industrial robots can also be scheduled to work twenty-four hours a day to maximize productivity in manufacturing environments—something that human workers have never been able to do.

* **anthropomorphic** having human form, or generally resembling human appearance

* **autonomous** self governing, or being able to exist independently

The robot, Asimo, performs at a showroom ath the headquarters of the Honda Motor Company, Tokyo, Japan. © *AP Images/Koji Sasahara.*

* **end-effector** the end piece of a robotic arm that can receive various types of grippers and tools

* **hydraulic** motion being powered by a pressurized liquid (such as water or oil), supplied through tubes or pipes

* **pneumatic** powered by pressurized air, supplied through tubes or pipes

Conventional robots possess a base which is usually anchored to the floor, but may also be attached to a rail or gantry (platform) that permits sliding movement. An arm called a manipulator, which is flexible and is one of the main features of the robot, is connected to the base. On the tip of the arm is an attachment called the end-effector*—this is the mounting point for interchangeable grippers or tools. The arm is moved about by using either hydraulic* or pneumatic* actuators, or by gears, linkages, and cables driven by electric motors. The motors used are usually of the servo or stepper type. Servo motors rotate at a required speed under command, whereas stepper motors rotate through a given angular displacement (in steps of a certain number of degrees) before stopping. In this way, controlled movement of the arm can be affected within a region known as the workspace or workcell.

Depending on the number of limbs and the type and number of joints that the arm possesses, the robot will be described as having a certain number of degrees of freedom of movement. This indicates the dexterity with which the robot can work using tools and workpieces. A typical robot of moderate complexity will have three degrees of freedom including translational movement and a rotating wrist at the end-effector. The term "payload" is used to refer to the mass that the robot is capable of lifting at the end-effector—a payload of more than 100 kilograms (220.5 pounds) is not uncommon, and loads that would be beyond the capabilities of most human laborers are no trouble for a suitably structured robot. In addition to handling massive payloads, some specialized robots are able to work with a high degree of precision—many guarantee accuracy of placement to within a fraction of a millimeter.

Another type of robot is the mobile robot. These offer features that are uncommon to standard industrial robots used on production lines. Instead, mobile robots often propel themselves on wheels or tracks and carry telemetry* equipment like video cameras, microphones, and sensors of other types. The information they collect is then encoded and transmitted to a remote receiving station where human operators interpret the information and guide the mobile robot. Mobile robots are often used to handle dangerous goods like explosives, but perhaps the finest example of this type of robot was the Sojourner rover from the Mars Pathfinder Mission of 1997. This small robot demonstrated that it was possible to guide reliably and accurately a small robotic vehicle over the vast distance between Earth and Mars.

In 2012, NASA launched their most advanced robotic rover yet. In addition to being mobile, the Mars rover, named Curiosity, sends high-resolution, full color images of the Martian landscape, as well as atmospheric data that has increased scientists' understanding of the planet's history significantly.

Beyond the source of power that is needed to animate the robot, a computer system of some sort is generally employed to control its actions. This system acts in real-time to both command the robot's movements and to monitor its actions to ensure that it is complying with instructions. Command signals are sent to the motors to initiate a movement, and special sensing devices called transducers* are used to measure the amount of actual movement. If the actual movement does not correspond to the requested movement, then the computer system is notified and can make further adjustments. This continual measurement of the robot's activities is called feedback and is of the utmost importance in guaranteeing precise control over its movements. Three-dimensional geometry is the primary mathematical approach that is used to specify the dynamics of robots. Matrix representations of rotational and translational motion are the favored way of programming the required movements of the manipulator and the end-effector.

Frequently, one reasonably small computer is responsible for managing the movements of one robot. However, in large installations that contain many robots, it is also necessary to coordinate their collective operations effectively. This means that other computers need to be used in a supervisory role. The supervisory computer system works at a more abstract level, ensuring that overall production processes can be carried out efficiently. It passes down commands to the individual computers linked to the robots, leaving them to carry out the details of each allotted job. As an example, the supervisory computer might take a computer-aided design (CAD)* drawing of a complex assembly and separate out various parts from the drawing, for fabrication by a collection of individual robots. The robots can be retooled for these new tasks and then the supervisory computer can dispatch to their computers the various coordinates and commands for grasping, moving, cutting, milling or whatever else is required—directly from the CAD drawings.

* **telemetry** the science of taking measurements of something and transmitting the data to a distant receiver

* **transducers** devices that sense a physical quantity, such as temperature or pressure, and convert that measurement into an electrical signal

* **computer-aided design (CAD)** the use of computers to replace traditional drawing instruments and tools for engineering or architectural design

Robotic Surgery

Throughout the world, computer scientists are working to perfect robots to assist in and ultimately perform surgery. With the help of such robots, surgeons have more control and precision in performing operations. The first robotic surgical system was approved for use by the U.S. Food and Drug Administration in 2000. Called the da Vinci Surgical System, it was developed by Intuitive Surgical in California. The company reports that by the end of 2009 it had sold a total of 1,395 da Vinci Surgical System units—1,028 units had been sold within the United States, while 367 units had been shipped to other nations.

* **nanotechnology** the design and construction of machines at the atomic or molecular level

The future offers a great deal for robotics technology. Established areas of research are making significant strides toward becoming mainstream. Artificial intelligence and robot vision become closer to being standard features each year. It is also proposed that microscopic robots could be developed using the results of advances in nanotechnology*, expanding their current role in medical science, where they already assist in performing surgery.

 See also **Artificial Intelligence • Digital Logic Design • Nanocomputing • Robotics**

Resources

Books

Craig, John J. *Introduction to Robotics: Mechanics and Control.* 3rd ed. Upper Saddle River, New Jersey: Prentice Hall, 2005.

Web Sites

NASA. "Mars Science Laboratory." http://www.nasa.gov/mission_pages/msl/index.html (accessed September 24, 2012).

S

Satellite Technology

The world changed on October 4, 1957, when the Soviet Union launched the Earth's first artificial satellite* (the Moon is a natural). Sputnik, a Russian word meaning "fellow traveler," was an 83-kilogram (183-pound) the size and shape of a basketball. It did little except orbit the Earth every 98 minutes and emit a simple radio signal. Yet, this simple event started what was to be known as "The Space Race" that eventually led to the lunar landings as well as space shuttle missions, and weather and direct broadcast television s.

* **satellite** an object that orbits a planet

Although the satellite concept is theoretically simple—an object placed high enough above Earth's atmosphere to ameliorate air resistance, while moving at a speed of eight km/sec (17,280 miles/hour)—the successful launch, orbital insertion, and control of any satellite is extremely complex. This is evidenced by the many failures that occurred before Sputnik (and since). In spite of the complexity of the task, according to the U.S. National Aeronautics and Space Administration (NASA) there were approximately 3,000 useful satellites orbiting Earth in 2012. In addition to these, NASA and the U.S. Space Command currently track more than 500,000 pieces of space debris that could pose a threat to piloted spacecraft or satellites. This demonstrates that humans have not only mastered satellite technology, but also succeeded in extending their well-developed littering tendencies into space.

A satellite's orbit around Earth is described in one or more of three dimensions: the *perigee,* its closest distance from the Earth; the *apogee,* its furthest distance from the Earth; and, its *inclination,* the angle the orbit makes with the equator. Satellites are put into particular types of orbit depending on their mission. In a geostationary orbit, the satellite speed is synchronized with the Earth's rotation in order for the satellite to maintain the same relative position. A polar orbit is characterized by its 90-degree inclination to Earth's equator. A typical trajectory for a satellite in Low Earth Orbit (LEO) is approximately circular (rather than elliptical, for which perigee and apogee are different), with the apogee and perigee each only about 483 kilometers (300 miles) above Earth's surface.

Types of Satellites

Most satellites are in orbit for communication, environmental monitoring, or navigational purposes. There are both government and commercial satellites in space.

* **protocol** an agreed understanding for the sub-operations that make up a transaction, usually found in the specification of inter-computer communications

* **ubiquitous** to be commonly available everywhere

Communication Of all satellite technologies, communication technology has probably had the greatest impact on our world. It has been called one of the greatest forces for the "super-tribalization" of the human species. Communication satellites have also proven to be one of the most successful commercial applications of space technology. At even given time there are several hundred functioning communications satellites orbiting the Earth.

The first telephone communication satellites, ECHO and Telstar, were launched in 1960 and 1962, respectively. These and many subsequent satellites carried analog signals to all parts of the world. The computer resources in such satellites were minimal: for the most part, the satellites were simple passive transceivers.

However, the demands of the Internet and personal communication devices such as cellular phones, Global Positioning System (GPS) devices, and smartphones have resulted in radically changed communication satellite technologies. Present satellites not only utilize digital signals and processing but also, in some systems, provide satellite-to-satellite communications. Perhaps this was nowhere more evident than in the Iridium system, a constellation of 66 LEO communication satellites that features sophisticated computer resources and protocol*s for inter-satellite communication.

Television broadcast or, more precisely, relay, from satellite also began in 1962 with the launch of the Relay satellite. This technology has similarly improved, as is evidenced by the size of the ubiquitous* home satellite "dishes" that, owing to greater satellite transmission power and other advances in technology, are now almost unnoticeable.

Environmental Monitoring The view from a geostationary environmental satellite often is shown during televised weather broadcasts. The Geostationary Operational Environmental Satellites (GOES) orbit simultaneously with the Earth's rotation at an altitude of just under 36,000 kilometers (about 22,300 miles). As of 2012, there were four GOES satellites available for observations—GOES–12 through GOES–15—two of which are positioned so that they can deliver views of the of the entire United States (one views the eastern half of the country, while the other views the western half). The GOES are true environmental satellites: In addition to images of the clouds, they also provide information on water vapor, land and sea temperatures, winds, and estimates of precipitation.

Landsat is also an environmental, as well as a natural resource, series of satellites. Since the early 1970s, seven Landsat satellites have been launched and, as of late 2012, two remained operational in polar, sun-synchronous orbits. A sun-synchronous orbit is one in which the satellite passes over points on the ground at the same local time. Landsat's multi-spectral scanner (MSS) and thematic mapper imaging systems provide digital imagery over discrete sections of the visible and infrared portions of the electromagnetic spectrum. Such multi-spectral imagery and its analyses are used routinely in environmental studies such as deforestation, water pollution, tracking oil spills, and monitoring forest fires and droughts. It is also utilized in natural resource studies such as land use classification, vegetation and soil mapping, and geological, hydrological, and coastal resource studies.

The Landsat program is a joint endeavor involving NASA and the U.S. Geological Survey (USGS). In August 2012, the USGS announced that it had reached the milestone of providing nine million images from Landsat for public download at no charge. The USGS plans to launch the next-generation Landsat satellite, dubbed the Landsat Data Continuity Mission (LDCM), in 2013.

Navigation Lines of latitude and longitude have been noted on maps since ancient times. Yet, the accurate determination of one's exact position on the Earth has always been a vexing problem. Perhaps at no time was this more evident than during the eighteenth century when scholars and inventors vied to solve the problem of accurately determining longitude at sea. Such a determination required a highly accurate (and stable) clock, since it was necessary to know simultaneously the time on the ship and at a land-based point of known longitude. It is interesting to note that the problem of determining accurate time was the basis of accurate position determination then, as it is also the basis of today's most accurate worldwide satellite navigation and position system. Indeed the navigation satellites of the twenty-first century have precise clocks that are accurate to within three nanoseconds, or three billionths of a second.

As of 2012, the navigational system known as the Global Positioning System (GPS) consisted of a satellite constellation of at least thirty NAVSTAR (NAVigation Satellite Timing And Ranging) satellites orbiting at 20,278 kilometers (12,600 miles) altitude in six orbital planes. Each orbital plane is spaced at an inclination of approximately 55 degrees with respect to adjacent planes. Within each of the six orbital planes, there are at least four equally-spaced satellites. This arrangement of satellites within distinct orbital planes was designed so that a minimum of five satellites would be visible from any location on the planet at any given moment (unless the view to one or more of the orbiting satellites happens to be locally obstructed by buildings, mountains, etc). Each satellite broadcasts time and orbit information. Receivers on the ground also contain internal clocks. The difference in time between when a signal was sent and when it was received from each observable satellite is used to solve a spherical trigonometry* problem to determine the location of the observer.

Different signals are sent from the GPS satellites for use by the military and by the general public. The accuracy of a consumer GPS receiver is dependent in large part upon the sophistication (and hence cost) of the particular receiver. Depending upon the sophistication of the receiver and other factors (such as whether or not the device employs techniques such as "differential GPS" to improve accuracy) the consumer can typically

* **trigonometry** a branch of mathematics founded upon the geometry of triangles

Leica, The Space Dog

When the Soviet Union launched *Sputnik II* into space on November 3, 1957, there was one sole passenger aboard. Leica (also transliterated as Laika), most likely a mixed breed, was intended to orbit the Earth for seven days aboard the spacecraft. Scientists believed that by monitoring Leica, they could learn about radiation and weightlessness on animals in space. The *Sputnik II* spacecraft was not designed to return to Earth intact, so Leica was slated to die at the end of the seven-day mission, either from a lack of oxygen, or by being euthanized on directions from ground control. Unfortunately, the temperature control system aboard the spacecraft failed, and Leica expired after less than a half day in orbit.

expect accuracy to approximately 10 meters (33 feet). More sophisticated (and generally expensive) consumer GPS devices can increase the accuracy to within a few meters (yards). According to federal regulations, the U.S. government strives to provide a "worst case" accuracy for civilian use within 7.8 meters at a 95 percent confidence level. However, even more sophisticated receiver systems (such as those used for scientific research or for surveying), are able to determine an exact position on the surface of the Earth to within one centimeter (four-tenths of an inch)!

Space Junk

The amount of debris orbiting Earth continues to increase, posing a risk to both manned and unmanned spacecraft. This ongoing increase of space litter is due not only to the ever-increasing number of old, defunct satellites that remain in orbit, but also from satellites that have disintegrated into numerous smaller pieces. The first-ever collision between two intact satellites took place on February 10, 2009, when a functioning Iridium satellite (Iridium 33) impacted a Russian satellite, the obsolete Kosmos 2251. A shower of debris resulted from the high-speed collision, increasing the risk of future impacts with other spacecraft.

Debris from wrecked satellites is not always accidental: As of late 2012, China, Russia, and the United States all possessed anti-satellite weapons systems. In 2010, India claimed to have the technology to use anti-satellite missiles against satellites in a low Earth or polar orbit. The United States was the first nation to destroy an Earth-orbiting spacecraft when it annihilated a malfunctioning scientific satellite in 1985 using an air-launched missile. In January 2007 the Chinese government destroyed a defunct weather satellite it owned (also using a missile) in a low Earth, polar orbit; a little over a year later (in February 2008) the U.S. military fired a missile at an inoperative U.S. spy satellite, destroying it.

 See also **Communication Devices • Telecommunications • Wireless Technology**

Resources

Books

Maini, Anil K., and Varsha Agrawal. *Satellite Technology: Principles and Applications.* 2nd ed. Chichester, UK, and Hoboken, NJ: Wiley, 2011.

Maral, Gérard, and Michel Bousquet. *Satellite Communications Systems: Systems, Techniques and Technology.* 5th ed. Chichester, UK: Wiley, 2009.

Web Sites

European Space Agency. "Homepage." http://www.esa.int (accessed November 5, 2012).

Japan Aerospace Exploration Agency (JAXA). "Homepage." http://www. jaxa.jp/index_e.html (Accessed November 5, 2012).

National Aeronautics and Space Administration (NASA). "NOAA Environmental Satellites." NOAA-N http://www.nasa.gov/mission_ pages/noaa-n/main/index.html (Accessed November 5, 2012).

National Aeronautics and Space Administration (NASA). "Small Satellite Missions." http://www.nasa.gov/mission_pages/smallsats/ (Accessed November 5, 2012).

Scaling

Scaling is defined as the ability of a computer system to expand in order to meet growing demand. The scalability of such computer hardware or software is founded in its inherent capability to handle an increasing amount of work or its ability to be enlarged to accommodate that increased workload. Scaling is exceptionally important when dealing with computers, databases, operating systems, networks, routers, and servers. For instance, a server may be able to handle twenty clients but when an additional two hundred of them are added, it may fail unless it is readily scalable. When scaling is able to be performed successfully within such computer hardware or software, then it is said to be a scalable system.

The scale of a system consists of three important factors: administrative, geographical and numerical. The administrative factor comprises the number of organizations that exert control over the various parts of the system. Obviously, more complication is introduced when organizations become larger. As more administration of a system is brought on-board, a highly scalable system will meet the challenge and function normally as the system grows. The geographical factor consists of the distance over which the system is scattered. As a system expands physically outward, more risk is possible to degrade that system, unless that system is able to handle that outward expansion, i.e., is geographically scalable. The numerical factor consists of the number of users within the system, and the number of objects and services it contains. As the number of users increases, the likelihood that a part of the system will be disrupted increases, unless that system is very numerically scalable.

All three of these scaling factors were no doubt in play at Facebook and MySpace late in the first decade of the 2000s. On June 17, 2009, the *Los Angeles Times* reported in the article "How MySpace Fell Off the Pace" that MySpace stayed with its portal strategy of numerous entertainment applications while Facebook developed its social networking strategy. Unable to meet its customers' needs, MySpace lost its lead to Facebook with respect to the number of U.S. users. Charlene Li, the founder of the social networking research company Altimeter Group, stated within the article, "The speed with which a company like Facebook is able to innovate and keep things fresh is the key to survival in this space." Thus, Facebook maintained a much more responsive Web site than MySpace on the three key scalable factors of administrative, geographical, and numerical, which turned it into a much more successful company.

One example of a scalable system is when computer networks use the transmission control protocol/Internet protocol (TCP/IP). Such networks are very scalable because TCP/IP has been designed to allow the overall volume of data that is handled to be increased in proportion to the number of computers on the network. Thus, highly scalable networks can be adjusted without much difficulty and cost, enabling them to grow larger easily with increased demand. This ability to increase in size—its scalability—has allowed the Internet to be a very effective network around the world.

A computer's operating systems is also another example of a system that can be scalable. For instance, the operating system was first developed by Finnish American software engineer Linus Torvalds (1969–) in 1991. Currently in the 2010s, Linux continues to be highly scalable because it continues to be effective in a variety of devices: from tiny devices, such as global positioning system (GPS) devices, to the largest of computers, the supercomputers. The ability of Linux to remain scalable is due largely to the upgradability of its algorithms, data structures, and other critical components to accommodate the large amount of memory and storage needed for many of the most advanced computing devices.

Scalability is an important factor for organizations in the first quarter of the twenty-first century. When preparing to buy new computer hardware or software, these systems must be highly scalable so growth can be accomplished seamlessly by updating these systems rather than having to replace them. For instance, a highly scalable operating system can mean that it will be able to handle a vast expansion in the variety of computers within the organization. This means that the communications of employees and the exchange of data between these employees and the company's customers will not be disrupted when the new system is placed in operation.

As of the middle of 2012, there are about 1 billion active Facebook users on the social networking site, whereas Twitter has about 500 million users. These may seem to be very large numbers but the world's population, as of November 2012, is just over 7 billion. Thus, only one out of about seven people is using Facebook on a regular basis. A fully scalable system for the entire planet Earth has yet to be accomplished, although some may think Google is close to it. Scalability in the future will extend itself to a planet-wide basis as connectivity among the world's peoples increases even more than is the case 2012. Companies are preparing for this global scalability so their Web sites can handle several times more traffic than they currently handle. This global expansion for computing systems, databases, and networks, such as the Internet, makes scalability a very important feature for supporting future planet-wide applications.

Resources

Books

Dubitzky, Werner, Krzysztof Kurowski, and Bernard Schott, eds. *Large-scale Computing*. Oxford, UK, and Hoboken, NJ: Wiley, 2012.

Zhou, Qing, et al. *Network Robustness under Large-Scale Attacks*. New York: Springer 2012.

Web Sites

Chmielewski, Dawn C., and David Sarno. "How MySpace Fell Off the Pace." *Los Angeles Times*. http://articles.latimes.com/2009/jun/17/business/fi-ct-myspace17 (accessed November 8, 2012).

HighScalability.com. "High Scalability." http://highscalability.com/ (accessed November 8, 2012).

Linux Information Project. "Scalable Definition." http://www.linfo.org/scalable.html (accessed November 8, 2012).

Security Hardware

The use of hardware to provide or enhance security dates from the early days of shared or multi-user computing systems. The Multics system (Multiplexed Information and Computing Service), developed in the 1960s and 1970s, was one of the first to use hardware mechanisms to isolate user processes from each other and from the operating system core and utility functions, and to permit sharing of information according to a well-defined security policy. In 1985, Multics was given a highly coveted B2 Orange Book security rating by the National Computer Security Center (NCSC)*, the first such designation granted by the government to a computer security system. The Multics system was in operation in many organizations and institutions from the mid-1960s until the last Multics installation was decommissioned in 2000.

The history of Multics and subsequent systems has demonstrated that it is difficult to design and implement software to provide security, even with adequate hardware support in the central processing unit (CPU)*. The LOCK (short for Logical Coprocessing Kernel) by Secure Computing Corporation used a security coprocessor, a secondary CPU with its own address space, which controlled the memory and device accesses of user processes that run in the primary CPU. This isolated the security enforcement mechanism from potentially hostile user code. Most present day hardware processors support memory management systems and multiple CPU privilege modes that can be used to provide process isolation. However, few operating systems take full advantage of them.

Hardware authentication* tokens are frequently used to reduce the risks associated with transmitting passwords over lines that might be

* National Computer Security Center (NCSC) a branch of the National Security Agency responsible for evaluating secure computing systems; the Trusted Computer Systems Evaluation Criteria (TCSEC) were developed by the NCSC

* central processing unit (CPU) the part of a computer that performs computations and controls and coordinates other parts of the computer

* authentication the act of ensuring that an object or entity is what it is intended to be

subject to interception. These tokens establish security systems that are a combination of "Something you have (the token), plus something you know (a password or PIN [personal identification number])." The first such system, Polonius, was developed in the mid-1980s by Ray Wong, Tom Berson, and Rich Feiertag of Sytek, Inc.

In the Polonius system, each token contains a keypad, an encryption device with a key, and a display. The key is protected with a PIN (personal identification number)* known only to the user. Authentication is done as follows: When the user is identified to the remote computer with a user identification (ID) or account name, the computer uses this information to look up its copy of the key shared with the Polonius device. The computer then generates a random number, which is sent to the user as a challenge, and encrypts the number with its copy of the user's key. The user enters both a PIN and the challenge number into the Polonius device. The Polonius device uses its copy of the key, modified if an incorrect PIN is given, to encrypt the challenge and display the result. The user sends the result to the remote computer, which compares it with its own result. The user is granted access only if the results agree. Because the challenge is a large, randomly generated number, an observer who captures both the challenge and the response is unlikely to be able to use them again.

A number of similar devices exist. Some simply display a password that changes every minute or so, based on a key associated with the token and an internal clock that must be synchronized with the remote computer. In this case, the PIN is transmitted along with the token, placing the user at risk should the token be stolen after the PIN has been intercepted. On other tokens, the user enters the PIN into the token where it is combined with a time-dependent value before encryption, giving a password that is valid for a minute or so.

Authentication tokens represent a simple example of a cryptographic processor. Specialized cryptographic hardware can be combined with general purpose computers to enhance security in a number of ways. It is increasingly common to provide encryption as a part of communications devices, such as wireless cards or wired network links. Encryption hardware can also be incorporated into disk controllers or disk drives. Although encryption algorithm*s can be implemented in software, they are computationally intensive. In addition, the encryption keys used are likely to appear in the computer's memory and can often be recovered from the swap files* maintained on disk by the operating system.

Certain cryptographic coprocessors such as Dallas Semiconductor's Crypto iButton (commonly known as the Dallas Key) can be used to generate and maintain cryptographic keys that are extremely difficult for unauthorized users to extract. (As of 2001, Dallas Semiconductor was a subsidiary of Maxim Integrated Products.) These devices also contain general purpose processors that can be used with the cryptographic hardware. The iButton is about the size and shape of a watch battery and is extremely durable and tamper-resistant. The processor contains a Java virtual machine that complies with recent Java smart card* standards. The iButton has been used to develop a variety of security-related applications such as secure postage meters for the issuance of postage from a home computer and the management of certificates for a public key infrastructure (PKI).

▶ *See also* **Privacy • Security • Security Software**

Resources

Books

Dube, Roger. *Hardware-based Computer Security Techniques to Defeat Hackers: From Biometrics to Quantum Cryptography.* Hoboken, NJ: Wiley, 2008.

Organick, Elliott I. *The Multics System: An Examination of Its Structure.* Cambridge, MA: MIT Press, 1972.

Sadeghi, Ahmad-Reza, and David Naccache, eds. *Towards Hardware-intrinsic Security: Foundations and Practice.* New York: Springer, 2010.

Periodicals

Saydjari, O. Sami, Joseph M. Beckman, and Jeffrey R. Leaman. "LOCK Trek: Navigating Uncharted Space." *Proceedings of the 1989 IEEE Symposium on Security and Privacy*, May 1989, pp. 167–175.

Wong, Raymond M., Thomas A. Berson, and Richard J. Feiertag. "Polonius: An Identity Authentication System." *Proceedings of the 1985 IEEE Symposium on Security and Privacy*, April 1985, pp. 101–107.

Web Sites

Federation of American Scientists. "Department of Defense Trusted Computer System Evaluation Criteria." http://www.fas.org/irp/nsa/rainbow/std001.htm (accessed October 22, 2012).

Information Services and Technology, Massachusetts Institute of Technology. "Multics." http://web.mit.edu/multics-history/ (accessed October 22, 2012).

Multicians.org. "Multics." http://www.multicians.org/ (accessed October 22, 2012).

Security Software

Computer security involves making sure the good guys (those with the right to access a computer or computer system) get in and the bad guys (those without such a right) stay out. Throughout the development of the computer, security has been an increasingly important consideration. Software has evolved to include security functions, and with the advent of

The Orange Book

Called the Orange Book, the TCSEC (or Trusted Computer Systems Evaluation Criteria) contained the basic criteria for evaluating computer systems intended to handle sensitive or classified material. It divided the systems into four classes: D (no security features), C (user-based access controls), B (mandatory access controls based on information classification and user clearance), and A (the same as B, with formal assurance arguments). Class B2 systems enforce security based on a clearly defined and documented formal security policy model. The security enforcement must be carefully structured into protection-critical and non-protection-critical elements. Multics' hardware isolation mechanisms played a key role in meeting these requirements.

Public Key Infrastructure (PKI)

A public key infrastructure (PKI) is a system designed to facilitate the use of public/ private keys in encryption. The public keys are published but a private one is held securely by each individual in the network. A message can be sent to individuals using the public key to encrypt it, but only the holder of the private key can decipher it.

There are a number of security software systems available to users. © *Carla Gottgens/Bloomberg via Getty Images.*

the Internet, the World Wide Web (or simply the Web), and large networks, security has become a daily issue. In fact, security software is considered by many in the computer industry to be a necessary evil (that is; something that is absolutely necessary but is viewed widely as being unacceptable, or evil).

At the core of any security software process is the fundamental proposition that the level of risk associated with electronic data (often called an information asset) is the product of the data's value, threats, and vulnerabilities. Understanding this risk and being able to determine its relative rating are key components of security. As the significance of any of these factors increases, the risk also increases. Conversely, reducing any of these factors will significantly reduce the relevant risk. All three factors must be understood before it is possible to assess risk in a reliable manner.

- *Asset Value* is measured in terms of importance of data to the organization's business, operations, or ongoing support.
- *Threats* are measured in terms of events or actions that could have a negative impact on the availability, integrity, or confidentiality of an information asset. Threats are typically evaluated in terms of the source (internal or external), nature (structured or unstructured), and agents (hostile or non-hostile).
- *Vulnerabilities* are measured in terms of the absence, inadequacy, or inconsistency of facilities and processes that are deployed to protect the asset's value from the identified threats.

Basic Structure

Security software has been incorporated into large computer systems for many years. The basic proposition is to lock up and protect computing resources (data and programs) from unauthorized use and access.

Large computing systems typically use the following three-part scheme: (1) Identification; (2) Authentication; (3) Authorization.

Identification is usually done with a user identification (userid) indicator. The userid can be similar to the person's name (i.e., JOHN1) or it can be a totally arbitrary indicator (i.e., WX99RCA).

Authentication is the process of proving that a person is really who they say they are. It is typically accomplished using a password or secret phrase. The password is known only to the user and allows the security software to ensure (with a limited degree of comfort) that users are, in fact, who they purport to be.

Authorization, the last step, assigns the userid the appropriate privileges within the system once identification and authentication have been completed.

While these steps sound easy enough, it can be difficult to provide assurance that the person attempting to gain access is actually an authorized user. Userids tend to be publicly known or easily guessed. Passwords are often guessed or not changed with sufficient frequency. Further, creative people can come up with new ways to circumvent the process. As a result, security software has become more sophisticated. For instance, according to ZDnet (as of June 2012), Microsoft owns the most popular antivirus software in North America, followed by Symantec and AVG.

A Brief History

Before networks and the Web-based Internet, security software was much easier to create, manage, and even understand. Individual machines and their software could be protected from unauthorized use through the use of protection programs that ensured that only one authorized user could gain entry to the machine's capabilities. In most cases, this involved a userid tied to the individual machine. Some software systems also allowed the user to restrict access to the data and software housed in the individual machine.

Once local area networks (LANs)* and other connection capabilities (i.e., the Internet) appeared, security software became a top priority. From the smallest to the largest network, it was necessary to make sure that the system was secure from attack, theft, or other malicious use. This required security software functionality to increase. In addition, the number of system components to be protected multiplied as people added capabilities to their networks. The advent of business transactions over the Internet (e-commerce) has led to great advances in security software. For instance, Amazon.com is one of the largest electronic commerce companies (e-retailers) on the Web. As of 2011, its total revenue was just over $48 billion.

Summary

Security software has evolved as the systems it protects have grown in complexity and capabilities. There are basic activities that any security software performs. Specialized needs can be accommodated with more complex software programs.

Computer Sciences, 2ⁿᵈ Edition

* **local area networks (LANs)** high-speed computer networks that are designed for users who are located near each other

bus a group of related signals that form an interconnecting pathway between two or more electronic devices

bit serial mode a method of transferring binary bits one after another in a sequence or serial stream

interface a boundary or border between two or more objects or systems; also a point of access

Selecting the appropriate security software requires a careful analysis of several criteria including degrees of risk and vulnerability; types of assets to be protected; budget considerations; the security policy underlying the system; implementation resources; and auditing processes to test system security. As computing technology grows, security software will continue to develop in sophistication and function.

▶ *See also* **Invasive Programs • Privacy • Security • Security Hardware • Viruses**

Resources

Books

Beekman, George, and Ben Beekman. *Digital Planet: Tomorrow's Technology and You*, 10th ed. Boston: Prentice Hall, 2012.

Cowley, John. *Communications and Networking: An Introduction*. 2nd ed. New York and London: Springer, 2013.

Whitman, Michael E., and Herbert J. Mattord. *Principles of Information Security*. 4th ed. Boston: Course Technology, Cengage Learning, 2012.

Web Sites

Information Systems Audit and Control Association. "About ISACA." http://www.isaca.org/about-isaca/Pages/default.aspx (accessed October 22, 2012).

Information Systems Security Association. "About ISSA." http://www.issa.org/?page=AboutISSA (accessed October 22, 2012).

ZDnet.com. "Which is the Most Popular Antivirus Software?" http://www.zdnet.com/blog/security/which-is-the-most-popular-antivirus-software/12608 (accessed October 22, 2012).

Serial and Parallel Transmission

Digital data transmission can occur in two basic modes: serial or parallel. Data within a computer system is transmitted via parallel mode on bus*es with the width of the parallel matched to the word size of the computer system. Data between computer systems is usually transmitted in bit serial mode*. Consequently, it is necessary to make a parallel-to-serial conversion at a computer interface* when sending data from a computer system into a network and a serial-to-parallel conversion at a computer interface when receiving information from a network. The type of transmission mode used may also depend upon distance and required data rate.

Parallel Transmission

In parallel transmission, multiple bit*s (usually 8 bits or a byte/character) are sent simultaneously on different channels (wires, frequency channels) within the same cable, or radio path, and synchronized* to a clock. Parallel devices have a wider data bus than serial devices and can therefore transfer data in words of one or more bytes at a time. As a result, there is a speedup in parallel transmission rate over serial transmission rate. However, this speedup is a tradeoff versus cost since multiple wires cost more than a single wire, and as a parallel cable gets longer, the synchronization timing between multiple channels becomes more sensitive to distance. The timing for parallel transmission is provided by a constant clocking signal sent over a separate wire within the parallel cable; thus parallel transmission is considered synchronous*.

Serial Transmission

In serial transmission, bits are sent sequentially* on the same channel (wire), which reduces costs for wire but also slows the speed of transmission. Also, for serial transmission, some overhead time is needed since bits must be assembled and sent as a unit and then disassembled at the receiver.

Serial transmission can be either synchronous or asynchronous*. In synchronous transmission, groups of bits are combined into frames and frames are sent continuously with or without data to be transmitted. In transmission, groups of bits are sent as independent units with start/stop flags and no data link synchronization, to allow for arbitrary size gaps between frames. However, start/stop bits maintain physical bit level synchronization once detected.

Applications

Serial transmission is performed between two computers or from a computer to an external device located some distance away. Parallel transmission either takes place within a computer system (on a computer bus) or to an external device located a close distance away.

A special computer chip known as a universal asynchronous receiver transmitter (UART) acts as the interface between the parallel transmission of the computer bus and the serial transmission of the serial port. UARTs differ in performance capabilities based on the amount of on-chip memory they possess.

Examples

Examples of parallel mode transmission include connections between a computer and a printer (parallel printer port and cable). Most printers are within 6 meters (about 20 feet) of the transmitting computer and the slight cost increase for extra wires is offset by the added speed gained through parallel transmission of data.

Examples of serial mode transmission include a connection between a computer and a modem using the (rather outdated) RS-232 protocol*.

* **bit** a single binary digit, 1 or 0—a contraction of Binary digIT; the smallest unit for storing data in a computer

* **synchronized** events occurring at specific points in time with respect to one another

* **synchronous** synchronized behavior

* **sequentially** operations occurring in order, one after another

* **asynchronous** events that have no systematic relationship to one another in time

* **protocol** an agreed understanding for the sub-operations that make up a transaction, usually found in the specification of inter-computer communications

Kbps a measure of digital data transfer per unit time—one thousand (kilo, K) bits per second

fiber optics transmission technology using long, thin strands of glass fiber; internal reflections in the fiber assure that light entering one end is transmitted to the other end with only small losses in intensity; used widely in transmitting digital information

Although an RS-232 cable can theoretically accommodate 25 wires, all but two of these wires are for overhead control signaling and not data transmission; the two data wires perform simple serial transmission in either direction. In this case, a computer may not be close to a modem, making the cost of parallel transmission prohibitive—thus speed of transmission may be considered less important than the economic advantage of serial transmission.

Tradeoffs

Serial transmission via RS-232 is officially limited to 20 Kbps* for a distance of 15 meters (about 50 feet). Depending on the type of media used and the amount of external interference present, RS-232 can be transmitted at higher speeds, or over greater distances, or both. Parallel transmission has similar distance-versus-speed tradeoffs, as well as a clocking threshold distance. Techniques to increase the performance of serial and parallel transmission (longer distance for same speed or higher speed for same distance) include using better transmission media, such as fiber optics* or conditioned cables, implementing repeaters, or using shielded/multiple wires for noise immunity.

Technology

The RS-232 protocol is now largely outmoded, but is still used in older computer equipment (especially peripheral devices), in industrial equipment, and in certain types of specialty equipment. To resolve the speed and distance limitations of serial transmission via RS-232, several other serial transmission standards were developed including RS-449, V.35, IEEE-1394 (Firewire), and Universal Serial Bus (USB). The first USB protocol version, USB 1.0, was released in the mid-1990s. USB 2.0, supporting higher data rates and other enhanced features, became available at the beginning of the 2000s. USB 3.0 is the latest version, with the first commercial products featuring its greatly-enhanced data rates, and other advanced characteristics, appearing in early 2010. For instance, USB 3.0 is capable of transmission speeds of up to 5 gigabits per second, which is about ten times faster than USB 2.0.

Each of the above-mentioned standards has different electrical, mechanical, functional, and procedural characteristics. The electrical characteristics define voltage levels and timing of voltage level changes. Mechanical characteristics define the actual connector shape and number of wires. Common mechanical interface standards associated with parallel transmission are the DB-25 and Centronics connectors. The Centronics connector is a 36-pin parallel interface that also defines electrical signaling. Functional characteristics specify the operations performed by each pin in a connector; these can be classified into the broad categories of data, control, timing, and electrical ground. The procedural characteristics or protocol define the sequence of operations performed by pins in the connector.

▶ *See also* **Asynchronous and Synchronous Transmission • ATM Transmission • Internet • Telecommunications**

Resources

Books

Iannone, Eugenio. *Telecommunication Networks.* Boca Raton, FL: CRC Press, 2012.

Saha, Debashis, and Varadharajan Sridhar, eds. *Next Generation Data Communication Technologies: Emerging Trends.* Hershey, PA: IGI Global, 2012.

Stallings, William. *Data and Computer Communications.* 9th ed. Boston: Prentice Hall, 2011.

Web Sites

InetDaemon.com. "Serial vs. Parallel." http://www.inetdaemon.com/ tutorials/basic_concepts/parallel_vs_serial.shtml (accessed October 22, 2012).

Scottish Qualifications Authority. "Serial and Parallel Communication." http://www.sqa.org.uk/e-learning/NetTechDC01BCD/page_02.htm (accessed October 22, 2012).

WiseGeek.com. "What Is the Difference Between a Serial and Parallel Port?" http://www.wisegeek.com/what-is-the-difference-between-a-serial-and-parallel-port.htm (accessed October 22, 2012).

Servers

A server computer, usually called a server, is a computer system that has been designated to run a specific application for computer users within a network or through the same computer system. As the name suggests, a server is meant to serve other computers; that is, it provides service to all the computers in its network or computer system. For instance, to use the Internet a Web server and associated server program must be utilized so users are able to connect to the server through an application, or client, program. Many server programs are available: Three examples are Apache for Unix, Microsoft Information Interchange Server (IIS) for Windows, and WebStar for Apple. Common client programs, also called operating systems (OSs), include Microsoft's Internet Explorer, Google's Chrome, Mozilla's Firefox, and Apple's Safari. For these server and client programs, all of the information is formatted in a language called hypertext markup language (HTML).

Servers are physically similar to other computers. However, their hardware configuration has been upgraded to meet their specific assigned role.

They often are distinguished from regular computers because they contain faster processing speeds, more random access memory (RAM), and larger hard drives. In addition, they are built more reliably, along with having better serviceability, redundant power supplies and hard drives, and many other important features. Because servers are different from regular computers, their hardware and software is called a server platform to distinguish it from the operating system within a normal computer. All of these enhanced abilities enable them to handle better the needs of their clients. These enhancements also allow servers to be left running unattended for long periods of time while doing exceptionally intense work.

Servers were first manufactured in the middle part of the 1960s. However, they were very bulky and complex, with only skilled technicians able to operate them. When the Internet was born in the late 1980s, programming engineers created local area networks (LANs). These networks made servers very important because users at remote sites needed to be able to talk with each another. British computer scientist Tim Berners-Lee (1955–) and Belgium engineer and computer scientist Robert Cailliau (1947–) wrote the first server software in 1990. Server computers became popular in the early 1990s as businesses began to use personal computers (PCs) to provide services formerly performed on larger mainframe computers or minicomputers. This popularity also coincided with the increased use of computer networks, which allowed multiple systems to communicate simultaneously with each other. In the first quarter of the twenty-first century, the job of servers is similar to what microcomputers did in the latter quarter of the twentieth century. As such, each server is assigned a specific job but this assignment does not limit the server to just this job—it can also be used for other jobs simultaneously. As networks such as the Internet in homes and offices continue to grow, so does the need for servers.

Some of the major server manufacturers are Cybertron International (http://www.cybertronpc.com/), Compucase UK (http://www.compucase-hec.co.uk/), Hewlett Packard (http://www8.hp.com/us/en/home.html), iStarUSA (http://www.istarusa.com/), and Visionman (http://www.visionman.com/).

There are many types of servers. Often they are classified by functionality, hardware, and operating system. With regard to functionality, some of more common server types are:

- application server: often called middleware because such servers are used for running various software applications that are not otherwise connected
- catalog server: for information accessed from a central search point across a distributed network
- chat server: for the use of many people to share information and provide real-time discussions within an Internet newsgroup or chat room
- communications server: for the use of communications networks
- database server: for the providing of database services to other computer programs or computers
- e-mail server: for the use of e-mail programs
- fax server: for the running of facsimile (fax) services, when the actual document needs to be sent
- file server: for storage and retrieval of files that need remote access
- gaming server: for access of numerous clients to play video games online
- groupware server: for the ability of users to work from remote sites through Internet or Intranet systems
- home server: for users needing a server at home
- IRC server: short for Internet relay chat, for the use of various independent networks of servers, which allows users to connect real-time through an IRC network
- list server: for the management of mailing lists that deliver advertisements, announcements, newsletters, and other information
- print server: for printing services
- proxy server: for clients needing resources from other servers; such servers work from a client program (such as a Web browser) and one or more external servers in order to share connections, filter requests, and other needed tasks
- sound server: for multimedia broadcasting and streaming
- standalone server: for client-server Web-based programs that need a computer emulator
- Web server: for hypertext transfer protocol (HTTP) clients that need to send commands and receive responses, along with data

With regards to type of hardware, servers are categorized as rack units and blade units. Blade units have a small modular design to minimize their size. They are generally about one-third the thickness of rack units. Servers are also differentiated by their distinct operating systems. Two of the most popular operating systems for servers are Microsoft's Windows 2008 Server and Apple's Mac OS X Server. Other operating systems include International Computers Limited's Virtual Machine Environment (ICL VME), Novell's Netware, and Microsoft's Windows NT Server.

Servers also are classified by their server file systems and the platform on which the operating system resides. Two common types of server file systems are Microsoft Window's New Technology File System (NTFS) and Unix/Linux's Network File System (NFS). Three platforms on which a server's operating system can be hosted are Unix/Linux, Mac OS X, and Microsoft Windows.

Resources

Books

Johnson, Steven. *Mastering Microsoft Windows Small Business Server 2008.* Indianapolis: Wiley, 2010.

Yadav, Subhash Chandra, and Sanjay Kumar Singh. *An Introduction to Client/Server Computing.* New Delhi: New Age International, 2009.

Web Sites

TigerDirect.com. "Servers." http://www.tigerdirect.com/applications/Category/guidedSearch.asp?CatId=30 (accessed November 8, 2012).

Tuffil, Steve. "About Computer Servers." eHow.com. http://www.ehow.com/about_5120951_computer-servers.html (accessed November 8, 2012).

WiFiNotes.com. "What is Server." http://www.wifinotes.com/computer-networks/server-types.html (accessed November 9, 2012).

Simulators

One area experiencing rapid growth in the use of computers in recent years is simulation. A computer simulation is a program that runs on a single computer or a network of computers, which uses a mathematical model to reproduce the characteristics of a particular phenomenon, process, system, or other activity. Simulations are used for training in procedures that would be too dangerous or expensive to perform in real life. For instance, the National Aeronautics and Space Administration (NASA) runs simulations of its crewed space missions to help familiarize

▲

A simulator in the virtual reality center. © *MEHDI FEDOUACH/AFP/Getty Images.*

its astronauts and flight controllers with the mission's objectives and to practice many problems that may occur during actual missions. Some simulations are even used for routine and repetitious tasks. As computers become more powerful, the variety of things that they can imitate becomes larger, and the accuracy of the simulations is better.

Aviation was among the first fields to use simulation. In the early twenty-first century, military and airline pilots spend much of their time interacting with the computers that are flying the airplane. Computers have taken over both the mundane and the most difficult piloting tasks. The mundane tasks are automated because in many cases they are more distracting than they are worth. The difficult tasks are automated to increase efficiency and safety. The pilot of an aircraft approaching a runway with a low, thick cloud cover need not hand-fly using an instrument landing procedure when, instead, a computer is on board carrying all the information necessary for the task and programmed to follow all the steps in order to land the plane successfully without making a mistake.

Even with good autopilots and computers, human pilots must still monitor the systems and be ready to recognize failures and take over the controls. Pilots of highly automated aircraft have training that involves all of the computer systems. They must be placed into situations where

interface a boundary or border
between two or more objects or
systems; also a point of access

events occur that might not happen in years of routine flight so that they can see how they and their systems react. Most of these situations are dangerous: engine fires, hail storms, and electrical failures, for example. It is not sensible or possible to put pilots and multi-million dollar aircraft at risk for training purposes. Fortunately, for every computer advance that makes the cockpit more automated, other advances make it easier to create an artificial environment for training that is closer to reality. Simulations of real airplanes are now of such high fidelity that a pilot training on them can legally log actual flying time.

Simulators of aircraft are of two types: fixed-base and motion-base. The main purpose of a fixed-base simulator is to enable a student to practice complex procedures in a specialized environment. Many part-task trainers exist for the trainee to concentrate on one set of events or components, such as the interface* to the computer systems. At the high end of the scale of fixed-base simulators is a stationary version of the forward area of an airliner cockpit.

As desktop computers become more powerful and graphics capability increases, both procedures and trainers can be created out of one computer system. The simulator can configure itself to be a different airplane in a few seconds. In contrast, some simulators, both fixed-and motion-base, would have to be rebuilt to represent a different airplane. There is research underway to take advantage of improved hardware and software by enabling a larger simulator to simulate several cockpits using very big displays to show instruments graphically.

Motion-base simulators are much different than fixed-base. The hallmark of the very best motion-base simulators is the complete cockpit. Every instrument, lever, and control in the cockpit is the same as on the aircraft. In most cases, the equipment is on the same maintenance and replacement schedule as that in real airplanes. This means that when an airline pilot comes to his airline's simulator center for transition or recurrent training, there is complete carryover back to operations.

From the outside, a motion-base simulator looks like a box on stilts. The box contains the cockpit and the instructor's stations. The stilts are hydraulically actuated pistons that can move the box in response to control inputs by the pilot. In the earlier days of these simulators, they only operated on three axes. Therefore, the feel was close, but not quite right. Currently, most motion-base simulators move with six degrees of freedom. They can mix roll and yaw, pitch and roll, and so on, in order to give the pilots a more realistic feel. This improvement is due to advances in computer technology.

On top of the front of the cockpit are image generators connected to computers in an adjacent machine room. The image generators place scenes on the windows of the cockpit. Full-color, daylight imaging is available, but expensive. Many airlines opt for dusk/dark imaging. The outside scene appears to be well after sunset. Buildings are in ghostly light, cars have their lights on, and forests are shades of gray. Aside from

* **bus** a group of related signals that form an interconnecting pathway between two or more electronic devices

making the simulator less costly, it also forces pilots to practice in what is the most common time of day for accidents: twilight.

Inside the cockpit, the flight deck from the forward bulkhead (where the door to the cabin would be in a real airplane) to the nose is a precise copy of the actual aircraft. A rectangular room containing a workstation for the instructor and a maintenance terminal for the software and hardware technicians is located just off the flight desk. These technicians work in three shifts. The simulators are in use twenty-four hours per day. Time not used by the owner airline can be rented out to another airline's crews and instructors. A typical motion-base simulator has several different computer systems to create artificial reality. The main computer is often a 32-bit word-size machine, like the average desktop. Fortran (previously called FORTRAN, the acronym for Formula Translating System) programs reside in this computer to analyze control inputs and send commands to the hydraulics and the instruments. The commands travel on an ARINC 429 (the acronym is short for Aeronautical Radio Inc.) serial data bus*—the standard in actual commercial aircraft. Another system drives displays and handles input and output to the instructor's station. Three large cabinets of image generation hardware—one for the front generators, one for each side—complete the system.

The best characteristic about the simulator is that it can perform actions that would be impossible in real life. It can return the simulation to a marked point for repetitive practice, say at 2,438 kilometers (8,000 feet) and 24 kilometers (15 miles) from the runway. After a few keystrokes, the entire airplane is transported from the landing point back up into the air. The movement of the simulation can be frozen at any point and then resumed at that point. An approach to landing in instrument conditions can be run a few feet at a time for teaching purposes.

The pilots who do the training emphasize to their students that they should treat the simulator just like a real airplane. That way they can get the maximum benefit from the training. In fact, the simulator makes it easy to maintain the illusion. Sitting on the simulated ramp in Indianapolis, Indiana, for example, pilots can see the terminal building and the lights of cars going by on Interstate 70 in the distance. Beginning to taxi to the active runway, the building moves out of view and the taxiway lights pass by the windows. The runway is a dark ribbon bordered by its rows of lights.

Besides professional flight simulators—usually involving specialized software and hardware, such as aircraft cockpit mockups—commercial versions of flight training software has been available for many years for use on home or office personal computers (PCs). Perhaps the most successful, and also one of the longest-running, PC-based flight simulator programs has been Microsoft's *Flight Simulator*, often abbreviated MSFS. The earliest version of Flight Simulator (version 1.0) was released in the early 1980s by Microsoft; the latest version (as of this writing) was *Microsoft Flight*; its release was announced in August 2010. Released on February 29, 2012, *Microsoft Flight* was intended to replace

Is it Live or is it a Simulation?

Modern simulators can be made to seem like the real thing thanks to computers and software programs. Such simulators can train people in complex tasks far more cheaply than having someone perform the real task. Safety, also a factor in training, is greatly increased by using simulators instead of real equipment in actual situations.

Flight Simulator. On July 25, 2012, Microsoft announced that further development of *Microsoft Flight* would end; however, the company would continue to support the software.

Pilots are not the only ones trained for complex tasks using simulation. Nuclear reactor operators, air traffic controllers, and astronauts are all able to take advantage of computer power to create a virtual world that allows them to practice their occupation safely and cheaply.

 See also **Artificial Intelligence • Robotics • Simulation • Virtual Reality • Virtual Reality In Education**

Resources

Books

Jentsch, Florian, Michael Curtis, and Eduardo Salas, eds. *Simulation in Aviation Training.* Farnham, UK: Ashgate, 2011.

Lee, Alfred T. *Flight Simulation: Virtual Environments In Aviation.* Burlington, VT: Ashgate Publishing, 2005.

Williams Bruce. *Scenario-based Training with X-plane and Microsoft Flight Simulator: Using PC-based Flight Simulations Based on FAA and Industry Training Standards.* Indianapolis, IN: John Wiley & Sons, 2012.

Web Sites

Microsoft. "Flight Simulator." http://www.microsoft.com/games/fsinsider/ (accessed October 22, 2012).

Figure 1. An electronic (analog) sound signal. *Reproduced by permission of Gale, a part of Cengage Learning.*

Sound Devices

Sound devices are computer peripherals that produce, manipulate, or record sound or electronic signals representing sound. Virtually all modern music and movie sound production is done digitally using computer sound devices.

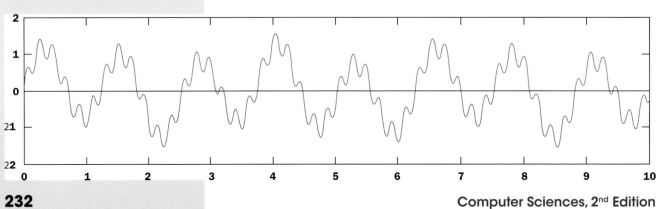

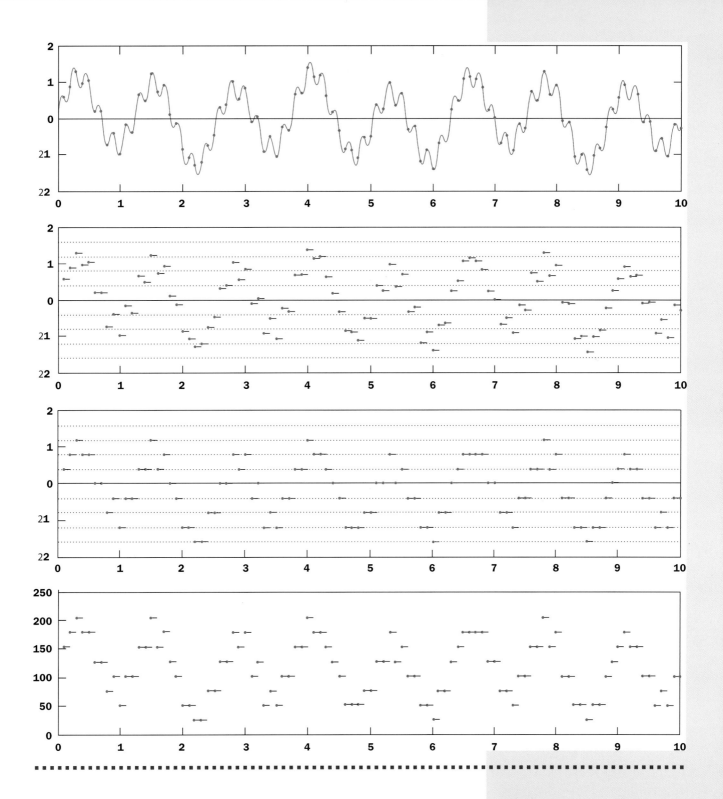

Speakers and Signals

Whether it is in a computer, a pair of headphones, or a stereo system, a speaker produces sound by causing the cone (external surface) to vibrate. The cone, often made of paper, is attached to the voice coil, an electromagnet. Behind the voice coil is a second magnet. By sending a positive

Figures 2 & 3. (Top) An analog sound signal with sample points. (Bottom) A sampled analog sound signal. *Reproduced by permission of Gale, a part of Cengage Learning.*

or negative electrical signal to the voice coil, it is alternatively attracted to and repelled from the second magnet. By continuously alternating the signal between positive and negative, the voice coil, and therefore the cone, can be made to vibrate. The faster the material vibrates, the higher the frequency of the sound; the larger the vibration, the louder the sound.

Digital Sound

Instead of directly recording or manipulating a continuous, continuously varying (analog) signal, sound devices record a digital signal, which is a series of whole numbers, represented in binary notation, at regular intervals. For example, a compact disc records a number between 0 and 65,535 at a rate of 44,100 times per second. In order to move from the analog world of speakers and microphones to the digital one, a device must sample (measure), quantize (divide), and compand (renumber) the signal.

First, the analog signal is sampled once in each interval (in this example, every 1/44,100 of a second). Any changes that happen between samples are lost. Second, the entire range of the signal, from zero volume to full volume, is quantized into sections (in this example, 65,535 of them) and the value of each sample is moved to the closest quantization level (dividing line). Third, each dividing line is renumbered, or companded, to be a whole number (in this example, between 0 and 65,535).

These samples can now be easily converted into binary data (in this example, 16 bits per sample) and recorded to a digital medium such as a hard drive, floppy drive, or compact disc. In order to reconstruct (play back) the sound, the binary data are read from the media, companded back to the original range (no volume to full volume), and each sample is played until a new sample is found (in this example, every 1/44,100 of a second).

Encoding and Compression

Converting an analog signal to a digital one is called encoding. The encoding method described earlier is Linear Pulse Coding Modulation, often abbreviated LPCM. This means that the quantization levels are equally spaced (linear), the signal is sampled regularly (pulse), the signal is encoded (coding), and the signal is being converted from an analog signal (modulation). The human ear, however, is better at detecting changes in quiet sounds than those in loud sounds. In linear encoding, then, the ear often cannot distinguish between two adjacent levels in loud sound.

Most encoding methods take advantage of this by placing the levels very close together at low volumes and further apart for high volumes. Every sound format (e.g., WAVE [Waveform Audio File Format] from Microsoft and International Business Machines [IBM], AIFF [Audio Interchange File Format] from Apple, μ-law (short for μ-law algorithm) from NeXT and Sun Microsystems) has its own method of nonlinear quantization, though most space the levels logarithmically.

With carefully chosen quantization levels, sound can take roughly four fewer bits per sample than a linearly encoded sound of the same quality.

In general, if the digital signal is changed to contain less information (e.g., fewer bits per sample), then the signal has been compressed.

Compression is important because it takes an extraordinary amount of binary code to represent high-quality digital sound. A three-minute song, recorded accurately enough for the human ear, requires 30 megabytes of storage. A compact disc, though it can store more than 700 megabytes of data, can only hold 74 minutes of music.

Many encoding techniques compress the data after they have been digitized (sampled) and companded. Though these techniques are lossy* (they degrade the quality of the recording), like non-linear encoding, they take advantage of characteristics of human hearing to minimize the audible effect of those losses. No matter what method is used, however, there is always a trade-off between the quality of the sound and the amount of compression.

Like companding, there are many methods of compression. The MPEG-2 Layer III (MP3) format is particularly popular because it can compress sound by a factor of ten while reliably reproducing popular music. It also allows the user to trade off compression for quality by explicitly specifying the number of bits per second of music.

There are many other methods of encoding and compression, both public (e.g., differential pulse code modulation, adaptive differential pulse code modulation) and proprietary (e.g., RealAudio from RealNetworks, Advanced Systems Format from Microsoft). The Musical Instrument Digital Interface (MIDI) is a method for electronic instruments to communicate and is also a form of encoding. Instead of encoding analog signals, it encodes the length, pitch, volume, and instrument of each note.

Sound Cards

In a computer, digital sound data are read from a medium and decoded or uncompressed by the central processing unit, but the sound card*, sometimes also called an audio card, performs the signal processing (companding, quantization, mixing, etc.). It is the that digitizes the signal from the microphone or other input device or converts it to analog for the speakers.

In the case of MIDI encoding, the digital data only includes qualitative data about notes, but no actual recorded sound. For MIDI, sound cards have methods for emulating specific instruments. In wave table synthesis, the sound card itself contains a short recording of each instrument, and is very accurate because it is based upon recordings of real instruments. In frequency modulation synthesis (FM synthesis), the sound card contains information about how to simulate each instrument. This method is less realistic because the simulation is not exact. In either case, by shifting the frequency of samples and combining them according to the MIDI data, the sound card can reproduce an entire piece of music. By using polyphony (imitating more than one instrument at the same time), the sound card can simulate entire groups of instruments.

* **lossy** a nonreversible way of compressing digital images; making images take up less space by permanently removing parts that cannot be easily seen anyway

* **sound card** a plug-in card for a computer that contains hardware devices for sound processing, conversion, and generation

Sound cards have other techniques for enhancing sound or making it more realistic. Head-related transfer functions allow the device to warp the music in order to make the sound seem to originate from somewhere other than the speakers. Digital filters can boost or change components of the sound (e.g., boost the bass) in ways that are difficult and expensive on analog equipment. Digital devices also rarely lose accuracy over time as all analog devices do.

One of the most popular sound cards used in computers has been the Sound Blaster family of sound cards, made by Creative Technology (Singapore), with its U.S. subsidiary called Creative Labs. In the 2010s, some of the most popular sound card manufacturers are Ad Lib, Inc., ASUS, Aureal Semiconductor, Auzentech, and C-Media, along with Creative Technology.

Social Issues

Music, like any artistic work, is copyrighted under U.S. law. Like patents, copyrights were created so that people could make their work public without losing the right to protect and profit from their work. Copyright law dictates that the copyright holder has control over the distribution of the work, for profit or otherwise.

Though making audiotape mixes for other people is illegal, the labor-intensive quality of making them and the degradation of quality associated with copying from one tape to another has limited its popularity. Digital technology created new ways for users to share music widely without the sound quality problems associated with tape recordings. During the late 1990s, the speed of modern computers, the availability of high-speed Internet connections for private use, the low price of computer compact disc players and recorders, and the wide availability of compression techniques like MP3, turned computers into tools for obtaining and storing enormous amounts of music. These collections, like taped mixes, are only legal if their owner purchased the original tape or compact disc as well.

By the end of the twentieth century, the illegal copying and distribution of music became so widespread that the music industry feared such actions were substantially infringing on the rights of the copyright holders. The music industry began experimenting with cryptographic methods for ensuring that music is not copied. Industry watchers know that any solutions are likely to be temporary, since digital security is always vulnerable to the efforts of technologically savvy programmers who seek ways to break through new digital boundaries.

Even with the restrictions placed on MP3, it remains a popular medium for music in the early twenty-first century. Other similar formats also exist, including AAC (Advanced Audio Coding), mp3PRO, and MP2 (MPEG-2 Audio Layer II). Free (open-source) formats also exist, including FLAC (Free Lossless Audio Codec), Opus, and Vorbis.

In the 2010s, streaming media is a popular way to listen to audio recordings, along with videos. The process of streaming is performed when media, such as audio and video presentations, are constantly received and presented to a customer while being simultaneously delivered by a provider. RealNetworks was a pioneer in streaming media when it launched its RealPlayer streaming video technology in 1997. Since then, Microsoft entered the streaming media market with its Windows Media Player 6.4 in 1999, as did Apple with its Quick Time 4 media player.

At the beginning of the 2000s, Adobe introduced its Flash video streaming format. Popular video hosting sites such as YouTube use the Flash format, which also provides live streaming video, as of 2008. Live streams are generally provided by what is called true streaming, where data is sent directly into a computer or other device without it being saved to a hard disk. The movie service Netflix is an example of live streams. The other type of streaming, called on-demand streaming, is provided by a process called progressive streaming, which saves the data on a hard disk or server so it can be played back from that source. Some movie services, such as satellite television broadcaster Disk Network, provides both live and on-demand streams through its Pay-Per-View movies.

In addition, another company that provide streaming media include Pandora Media, which operates Pandora Internet Radio (sometimes called simply Pandora), an automated music recommendation service in the United States, Australia, and New Zealand. As of June 2011, Pandora possessed a collection of about 800,000 tracks from around 80,000 artists, and a customer base of approximately 80 million. Further, Spotify is a streaming music service headquartered in Stockholm, Sweden. It streams music from records labels, such as EMI, Sony, and Universal, to about 15 million customers (4 million paying ones), as of August 2012, in Australia, Austria, Belgium, Denmark, Faroe Islands, Finland, France, Germany, the Netherlands, New Zealand, Norway, Spain, Sweden, Switzerland, the United Kingdom, and the United States.

 See also **Codes • Coding Techniques • Music, Computer**

Resources

Books

Alten, Stanley R. *Working with Audio.* Boston: Course Technology, 2012.

Berg, Richard E., and David G. Stork. *The Physics of Sound.* 3rd ed. Upper Saddle River, NJ: Prentice Hall, 2005.

Pohlmann, Ken. *Principles of Digital Audio.* 6th ed. New York: McGraw-Hill, 2011.

Winer, Ethan. *The Audio Expert: Everything You Need to Know about Audio.* Waltham, MA: Focal Press, 2013.

Web Sites

BrightHub.com, and John Garger. "A Brief History of the Evolution of Computer Sound Cards." http://www.brighthub.com/computing/hardware/articles/60555.aspx (accessed October 23, 2012).

MP3 and Napster

The popularity of MP3 as a format gave rise to audio file- sharing services on the Internet such as Napster and mp3.com. Some of these services ran afoul of the music and entertainment industries in the late 1990s and early 2000s because they allegedly facilitated unauthorized sharing of copyrighted music. Settlements of the copyright claims were expensive and caused major changes in the file-sharing services, but listeners continued to seek sources of music files while the music industry developed secure ways of selling music to audio consumers.

* **concurrency control** the management and coordination of several actions that occur simultaneously; for example, several computer programs running at once

SQL

Databases are designed, built, and populated with data for a specific purpose and for an intended group of users. Databases are built for many different users, including banks, hospitals, high schools, government agencies, and manufacturing companies. The data contained in databases vary and can include account, patient, student, employee, planning, or product data. Users of a database can add new records, insert or change data in existing records, retrieve data from existing records, or delete records from the database.

Databases are designed, built, maintained, and queried using a set of tools called a database management system (DBMS). Often, the DBMS is considered the user interface to the database system because everything else is invisible to the user. The DBMS defines the data in a database using the Data Definition Language (DDL) and handles requests to retrieve, update, or delete existing data or add new data to the database using the Data Manipulation Language (DML). In addition, the DBMS must monitor user requests and reject any attempts to violate integrity or security constraints defined for the data. The DBMS must be able to recover the data in case of problems. The DBMS also performs a function called concurrency control*. Finally, the DBMS provides a tool called the data dictionary that stores data about the data. One language used with the DBMS to provide this functionality is called Structured Query Language (SQL). It is the industry standard adopted by many database vendors for relational databases.

Database architecture can be configured in one of three basic ways:

■ Host-based, where users are connected directly to the same computer on which the database resides;

Microsoft CEO, Steve Ballmer unveils a new SQL server. © *AP Images/Matt Sayles.*

- Client/server, where a user accesses the data from a microcomputer (client) via a network and the database sits on a separate computer (server);

- Distributed processing, where users access a database that resides on more than one computer. The database is distributed across these computers in various ways.

In the client/server architecture, the server supports all basic DBMS functions (data definition, data manipulation, data security, and integrity). The clients are the various applications that run on top of the DBMS. These applications are provided by the DBMS vendor or a third party to query the database, write reports, produce graphics and spreadsheets, and many other functions. The server machine in a client/server architecture can be tailored to the DBMS function and thus provide better performance. Typically, several clients share the same server.

When more than one person can access a database, several SQL commands can be given at the same time. Each of these commands is called a transaction. A transaction is simply a logical unit of work. Since many transactions can access the same database at the same time, some means of controlling them is necessary. This is called concurrency control. One way to understand the need for concurrency control is to consider what would happen if Emily and Christopher both wish to modify a particular record for Jon Vogler from the SCHOOL table at the same time. Emily wishes to change the grade point average (GPA) for Jon, and Christopher wishes to change Jon's address, as the two SQL commands that follow show.

UPDATE STUDENT **SET** GPA = 3.9 **WHERE** LNAME = 'Vogler' **AND** FNAME = 'Jon'; **UPDATE** STUDENT **SET** ADDRESS = '3 Soccer Lane' **WHERE** LNAME = 'Vogler' **AND** FNAME = 'Jon';

If both retrieve the record at approximately the same time but Emily updates the record before Christopher does, Emily's modifications are lost and only Christopher's changes are made to the record, so Jon's address changes, but his GPA does not. This situation is called the lost update problem and it can reduce the quality of the data in a database.

Locking is the most common method of concurrency control: whenever a transaction needs to access a part of the database (typically a database record), the DBMS locks other transactions out of that part of the database. The first transaction can perform its processing without being affected by any other changes that might be made to the record. In our SCHOOL example, if Emily is the first to request Jon's record, Christopher is prevented from requesting that record until Emily finishes. This is a type of locking called exclusive locking. However, if another type of locking called shared locking is used for concurrency control, Christopher would be permitted to see Jon's record, but not change it.

▶ See also **Database Management Software** • **Information Systems** • **Storage Devices**

Fast Facts

SQL is short for Structured Query Language. It is fast becoming the standard dialect for accessing database management systems. Some people pronounce SQL as "sequel," while others pronounce each letter separately.

* **random access memory (RAM)** a type of memory device that supports the nonpermanent storage of programs and data; so called because various locations can be accessed in any order (as if at random), rather than in a sequence (like a tape memory device)

* **central processing unit (CPU)** the part of a computer that performs computations and controls and coordinates other parts of the computer

* **volatile** subject to rapid change; describes the character of data when current no longer flows to a device (that is, electrical power is switched off)

Resources

Books

Elmasri, Ramez A., and Shamkant B. Navathe. *Fundamentals of Database Systems.* 6th ed. Reading, MA: Addison-Wesley, 2010.

Web Sites

W3Schools. "SQL Tutorial." http://www.w3schools.com/sql/default.asp (accessed November 3, 2012).

Storage Devices

A computer storage device is any device that records (stores) information. Data and programs are stored in main memory, as random access memory (RAM)*, before and after processing by the central processing unit (CPU)*. However, RAM is volatile*—its contents disappear when a computer's power is turned off. So, what does one do with data that will be reused, stored on a long-term basis, or is simply too large to fit into the main memory of a computer? Mechanical storage devices, called secondary storage or external storage, are used to store data externally. Secondary storage is non-volatile—that is, data and programs are permanent.

Types of Storage Devices

There are many secondary storage devices, including magnetic drums, magnetic tapes, magnetic disks, and optical disks. These devices vary with respect to their versatility, durability, capacity, and speed.

▶

The LaCie FastKey 120 GB, USB 3.0, PC and Mac-compatible solid-state drive (SSD) device capable of data transfer speeds of up to 260 MB/s. © *ROBYN BECK/AFP/Getty Images.*

Magnetic Drums These are very early high-speed, direct access storage devices used in the 1950s and 1960s. The magnetic drum is a metal cylinder coated with a sensitive magnetic material. The cylinder has tracks around its circumference. Each track has its own read/write head, and data are stored as magnetic spots on the tracks. Like the magnetic disk, which was introduced later, the read/write head can move quickly to any track, providing direct access to the data stored on the drum.

Magnetic Tape This is one of the oldest secondary storage devices. It was first used for storing data in the early 1950s. At that time, the tape was made of a flexible metal and was stored on reels. The metal tape was plated with a thin film of iron, which allowed data to be stored as a series of small, magnetized spots. Although the tape provided a compact form of storage, it was extremely heavy and not universally accepted. It was not until a very thin, flexible material called mylar* was developed that tape processing gained wide acceptance. This plastic was coated with an iron oxide that could be magnetized to store data. In the 1950s and 1960s, magnetic tape was the primary means for storing large amounts of data.

Data are stored on magnetic tape in columns. Each byte* of data (eight bit*s) utilizes one column across the width of the tape. Data are stored on the magnetic tape at different densities*. Low density is 1,600 bytes per inch (bpi). Densities of 6,250 bpi and greater were common in the 1980s.

The old reel-to-reel magnetic tapes are being replaced by tape cartridges, which are used to back up or archive data. A tape backup is a copy of the data used to restore lost data. If one loses the data on a hard disk, he can copy the data from the tape backup. Tape cartridges used on microcomputers are similar to audiocassettes and can hold up to 35 gigabytes (GB) of data. There are several different types of tape cartridges, including quarter-inch cartridge (QIC), digital audio tape (DAT), digital linear tape (DLT), Travan, and advanced digital recording (ADR).

Magnetic tapes are an inexpensive and relatively stable way to store large volumes of data. Tapes can be used repeatedly, although time and environmental factors such as heat and humidity do affect them. The principle disadvantage of magnetic tape is that it stores data sequentially—that is, one record is stored right after another. Retrieving data from the tape is slow since the tape must be read from the beginning up to the location of the desired record. Thus, magnetic tapes are not a good choice when one needs to find information rapidly.

Magnetic Disk Currently, the most widely used secondary storage device is the magnetic disk. There are two kinds of magnetic disks: hard disks and floppy disks. Hard disks are thin, metallic platters developed in the 1950s. Each hard disk contains one or, more commonly, a series of platters that rotate on a shaft at a high rate of speed. The platters have

Mylar

Data storage devices—compact disks, floppy disks, and magnetic tapes—come in all shapes and sizes. The first magnetic tapes were made of thin strips of metal. In the early 1950s, DuPont patented a thin, polyester film that revolutionized the magnetic tape market. Called Mylar, this plastic material is chemically stable and is virtually as strong as metal, yet heat-resistant and lightweight. Mylar has a myriad of uses and is used in the manufacturing of numerous plastic products, including photo negative sleeves, food wraps, and magnetic tape.

* **mylar** a synthetic film, invented by DuPont (formally called E. I. du Pont de Nemours and Company), used in photographic printing and production processes, as well as disks and tapes

* **byte** a group of eight binary digits; represents a single character of text

* **bit** a single binary digit, 1 or 0—a contraction of Binary digIT; the smallest unit for storing data in a computer

* **densities** measures of the density of a material; defined as the mass of a sample of material, divided by its volume

* **concentric circles** circles that have coincident centers

a top and bottom surface where data can be recorded as magnetic spots. The platters have concentric circles* called tracks where the data are actually stored. Access arms containing read/write heads move across the spinning platters to read or write data on the tracks. There is a read/write head for each platter surface. These read/write heads float on a cushion of air and do not actually touch the surface of the disk. When reading data from the disk, the read head senses the magnetic spots on the surface and transfers the data to main memory. When writing, the data are transferred from main memory and are stored as magnetic spots on the recording surface.

The speed of access to data on a disk is based on both the rotational speed of the disk and the speed of the access arm. The read/write heads must position themselves over the platter at the proper address and the disk pack must rotate until the proper data are located. The time it takes the read/write heads to position themselves to the correct address is referred to as access motion time. Rotational delay time is the time needed for the disk to rotate the data under the read/write head.

The read/write heads move horizontally (from left to right) to any of 200 positions, called cylinders, on the platter surface. The cylinder represents the circular tracks on the same vertical line within the disk pack. To find data on the disk, an address is used. This address consists of a cylinder number, the recording surface number, and the data record number. The computer's operating system figures out how to fit data into the fixed spaces on the disk.

The microcomputer utilizes a hard disk, but it also uses floppy disks, also called floppy diskettes. Floppy disks are the second kind of magnetic disk and are removable. The two common standard sizes of floppy disks are 8.9 centimeters (3.5 inches) and 13.3 centimeters (5.25 inches). It is difficult in the 2010s to find a microcomputer that uses either size of floppy disk. Floppy disks are made up of one platter constructed from polyester film rather than metal. This polyester film is covered with a magnetic coating. Data are stored on the floppy disk in much the same manner as on a hard disk—in the form of magnetic spots on tracks. However, floppy disks use sectors to store data rather than cylinders. In this method of storing data, the disk is divided into pie-shaped pieces called sectors. Each sector is assigned a unique address to locate data. Sectors are created on a floppy disk by formatting it. Floppy disks have a much lower data storage capacity (usually 1.44 megabyte [MB] for a 3.5-inch floppy disk) and a much slower data access rate than hard disks.

As software packages such as Microsoft Office became popular, the need for larger data capacity for items such as text and graphics in a portable form became necessary. The zip drive and zip disk were introduced by Iomega in the 1990s as a relatively inexpensive large-storage-capacity floppy disk. The zip disk is 8.9 centimeters (3.5 inches), removable, and provides about 100 megabytes (MB) of data storage. In late 1998, a 250 MB version of the zip disk was introduced. While this zip disk had double the storage capacity of its predecessor, it was still only 8.9 centimeters (3.5 inches) in size. Still later, a 750-MB capacity version was introduced. However, zip drives decreased in popularity in the early years of the decade of the 2000s.

About the time that zip drives were losing their appeal, the USB flash drive became popular. In 2000, Trek Technology initially sold the ThumbDrive brand name flash drive, while IBM marketed its DiskOnKey. The IBM product, which was designed and manufactured by M-Systems, had storage capacities of 8 MB, 16 MB, and 32 MB. These data storage devices, which include flash memory (a non-volatile computer chip that is electrically erased and reprogrammed) with an integrated Universal Serial Bus (USB) interface, weighed less than 30 grams. As of 2012, flash drives contained up to 256 GB of data.

The main advantages of using a magnetic disk as a secondary storage device are its speed and direct access capability. Data can be easily and rapidly read, written, or accessed. Floppy disks provide the added advantage of portability. Disadvantages of using a magnetic disk as a secondary storage device include cost, environmental factors, user misuse and abuse, head crashes, and update problems.

Magnetic disks, both hard and floppy, are also susceptible to environmental factors such as dust, dirt, and smoke. Any of these factors will cause a hard disk to fail. Because of this, hard disks are sealed. Floppy disks are also vulnerable to environmental factors. Also, because of their portability, the floppy disk is vulnerable to misuse or abuse by users.

Head crashes can occur with any magnetic disk technology. This is when the read/write head touches the surface of the disk platter, destroying it and all of the stored data. Head crashes are normally caused by misalignment of the platter and the read/write head. A head crash renders a magnetic disk unusable. Another disadvantage of any magnetic disk is that when updating data, the old data are written over, destroying them instantly and permanently. Unless proper precautions are taken, data may be written over by mistake.

Optical Disks These are the newest secondary storage devices. Originally optical disks were called optical disk-read-only memory (OD-ROM) and are now called compact disk-read-only memory (CD-ROM). Data are not recorded on optical disks magnetically, but with a laser device that burns microscopic holes on the surface of the disk. Binary information (0s and 1s) is encoded by the length of these bumps and the space between them. Optical disks can store much more data than floppy disks. Data can be stored in the form of text as well as pictures, sound, and full-motion video. The disks are not as sensitive to dust, dirt, and smoke as magnetic disks are, and they are portable.

CD-ROM is read-only storage. No new data can be written to it. Once recorded, the CD can be read an indefinite number of times. This

The DVD

Watching a favorite film on VHS (video home system) has become as antiquated as listening to a favorite song on vinyl albums. DVD technology has been popular, especially in the movie rental market, along with the growing market for Blu-ray Disk (BD) technology. In addition to providing a clearer picture, films on DVD and BD are enhanced with many extras, which can include director commentaries, deleted scenes, cast bios and interviews, and games.

Recent Trends

In the 2010s, cloud storage is becoming increasingly popular. Cloud storage is data storage that resides online, managed by organizations that sell or lease storage capacity. Normally, users access cloud storage services through an application programming interface (API), which can be either a Web-based user interface or a cloud storage gateway. Amazon Simple Storage Service (S3) is an example of a Web-based storage service. Begun in 2006, S3 is managed by Amazon Web Services.

is commonly referred to as write once/read many (WORM). CD-ROM has been used for storage of large financial, legal, educational, or demographic databases, and by the music industry. Encyclopedias and multimedia applications are also stored using CD-ROM technology.

Individuals and organizations can now record their own CD-ROMs using compact disk-recordable (CD-R) technology. CD-ReWritable (CDRW) is a newer technology that has been developed to allow users to create rewritable optical disks.

Another optical storage medium is the digital video disk or digital versatile disk (DVD). This optical disk is the same size as a CD-ROM, but has much higher storage capacity. DVDs can store large amounts of data, video, graphics, digitized text, and audio, and are portable.

 See also **Codes • Computer System Interfaces • Memory**

Resources

Books

Abou-Zeid, El-Sayed, ed. *Knowledge Management and Business Strategies: Theoretical Frameworks and Empirical Research.* Hershey, PA: Information Science Reference, 2008.

Laudon, Kenneth C., and Jane P. Laudon. *Essentials of Management Information Systems*, 10th ed. Boston: Pearson, 2013.

Parsons, June Jamrich, and Dan Oja. *New Perspectives on Computer Concepts.* 10th ed. Boston: Thomson/Course Technology, 2008.

Shelly, Gary B., and Thomas J. Cashman. *Introduction to Computers and Data Processing.* Brea, CA: Anaheim Publishing Company, 1980.

Spencer, David D. *Data Processing: An Introduction.* Columbus, Ohio: Charles E. Merrill Publishing Company, 1978.

Stair, Ralph M., and George W. Reynolds,. *Principles of Information Systems: A Managerial Approach.* 10th ed. Boston: Course Technology, Cengage Learning, 2012.

Zhang, Ping, and Dennis Galletta, eds. *Human-computer Interaction and Management Information Systems.* Armonk, NY: M. E. Sharpe, 2006.

Web Sites

Amazon. "Amazon Simple Storage Service (Amazon S3)." http://aws.amazon.com/s3/ (accessed October 23, 2012).

eHow.com. "History of Data Storage Devices." http://www.ehow.com/facts_6791448_history-data-storage-devices.html (accessed October 23, 2012).

System Analysis

System analysis is a broad, technical area focused on the creation, enhancement, and trouble-shooting of systems for users. These can be data, information, or knowledge systems. The purpose of these systems is to provide an understanding of what is going on in a particular environment. Sensors, including radar*, sonar*, and satellite*s, for example, are components of systems that provide specific knowledge about the physical world. Sensors in the home can warn residents that someone is breaking in. Telephones are part of a system that brings police assistance when one dials 911. People have computers they use to perform a number of tasks—from writing term papers or diaries to communicating with people they have never met via messaging software programs. There are decision support systems that help people use computers to solve problems, and communication systems that tell people what is happening around them. System analysis is used to design, enhance, and fix problems in all of these systems.

System Analysis Methods

System analysis is creative work. The systems analyst can be considered an artist, an information scientist, and an engineer, all in one. The work begins with thinking about how to accomplish something. System analysis can be considered to have three primary functions, each of which is related to the others. First, system analysis is done to fix something that has gone wrong and to help one understand why there is a problem. Second, analysis is used to figure out how to do something more easily and less expensively as new technologies become available. Third, system analysis is done to help design a system that can accommodate future circumstances, such as anticipated events that are not being experienced now, but that might need to be dealt with in the future.

Troubleshooting Systems Each system has components that perform certain functions and, when put together, do a particular job, or serve a specific purpose. System analysts are trained to ensure that each component or function of a system—whether people, tools (technology), or procedures—is acting properly. If a system fails, the system analyst tries to find out how and why. The systems analyst then communicates with the designer about the factors found to be related to the failures in order to find a solution and avoid future problems. One way to consider system analysis is that it is a process that first identifies the factors that influence and lead to system breakdown, and then identifies ways to repair or avoid breakdowns.

Retrofitting Systems Systems have a life cycle. They become operational, they age, and they become obsolete. Typewriters have given way to computers. People still use telephone booths but cell phones are replacing them because they allow people to make phone calls and do many other

* **radar** the acronym for RAdio Direction And Ranging; a technique developed in the 1930s that uses frequency shifts in reflected radio waves to measure distance and speed of a target

* **sonar** the science and engineering of sound propagation in water

* **satellite** an object that orbits a planet

things better and faster. As new tools and technologies become available, people want to use them. The system analyst examines and studies how technology and people can be placed and used in current systems, and figures out how existing systems could benefit from all the new ideas and inventions that are coming to market. System analysis is a process for updating or retrofitting systems, replacing old technology with new, and installing new ways of doing things.

Creating Systems System analysis also considers situations or events where no existing system may yet be available to deal with them, such as biological warfare, or global warming, and analysts work to find ways to better address other large-scale events that affect the fabric of human life. Systems do exist that can respond to events such as hurricanes, tornadoes, floods, and health epidemics. Yet the need to anticipate unpredictable global circumstances—economic, political, medical, or environmental—demands new, creative approaches to minimize the potential damage to lives and property. System analysis is a way to explore how new situations or challenges can be met.

The Relationship Between Analysis and Design

A system analyst investigates; whereas a system designer specifies. The analyst asks questions such as who, what, when, where, why, and how. The system designer finds the best procedures, tools, and human skills to meet the needs and requirements of people and organizations. System analysis and system design work best when analyst and designer work together. The analysis component helps reduce the likelihood that design and technology will drive and influence the problem-solving process. If design precedes and directs analysis, there is a good chance that a given system may not be what the user needs or requires. Basements are full of technologically interesting gadgets that people buy and rarely use because they never needed them in the first place—no matter how intriguing the design, they were not designed specifically to meet the identified needs or requirements of the user!

Needs and Requirements

People are born with needs and requirements. A need is a state of being. Requirements are the things that meet these needs. People are hungry or thirsty; they need to feel well; they need shelter from environmental conditions and circumstances. They need to make a living; they need to feel as if their actions have some meaning. To address these varied needs, they require food, water, air, shelter, and other resources. However, the resources, or requirements, applied to address these needs in a tropical environment, for example, would be inappropriate in an arctic climate. Individual human characteristics such as personality or physical limitations can also influence the appropriateness of certain resources being applied to meet these needs. Requirements to meet needs vary from situation to situation. The same logic applies to system analysts. They must learn how to match up needs and requirements so that a system will actually function effectively in its particular environment.

Human needs may be physical, psychological, intellectual, emotional, or social. They can generally be identified only through a careful process of examination and investigation. Needs and requirements can be difficult to sort out and obtain from users because dictionaries and people's language habits lead them to ignore the distinctions. But the success of any system depends on the skills of a system analyst to recognize these distinctions and gather the correct needs and requirements information before trying to engineer a system.

The System Development Cycle

The system development cycle consists of the steps taken for the conceptualization* and engineering of a system. There are several ways to represent or describe the system development cycle. One is to show the analysis process in a series of blocks in hierarchical (top-down) or horizontal line (timeline) form. Another way is to show the system analysis process as a circle of operations, namely, requirement analysis, specifications, design, implementation, testing, and maintenance. Another approach is to regard the process as representing a waterfall cycle—one step flowing into another in a continuous stream. All share a common property of sequencing. System analysis is a step-by-step procedure: each step follows or interacts with the others, and all are directed toward meeting the objectives stated by the intended user of the system.

The Conceptual Stage

Once the initial information gathering stage is completed—that is, user needs and requirements have been identified, and the parties involved in a system design process have agreed on certain parameters of time, money investment, and expected outcomes—the system analyst begins conceptualizing the problems to be solved and the possible solutions to be applied.

One of the first steps is known as event analysis. The system analyst will engage in a detective-like process of investigating the properties and attributes of an event, or of a series of events that make up the problem to be solved. For each event, the system analyst creates a model, which is a tool in the analytical process. A model provides a view, a mental and physical picture, of the total system, explaining how the various parts of the system are structured and how they work together.

A prevailing model for system analysis is to consider three functions: namely, input, throughput, and output. What goes into the system? What happens to it? What is the outcome? These three dimensions of the analysis are applied to each component or event within the system and to the total system, as well, in its final configuration.

Input refers to the data that are acquired, through human or machine means, as part of an event in which the system is engaged. At the *throughput* stage, these data are transmitted to a processor, which can again be human, machine, or both. The data may then be modified, organized,

* **conceptualization** a creative process that is directed at envisaging a structure or collection of relationships within components of a complex system

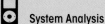

Job Prospects

The U.S. Bureau of Labor Statistics (BLS) indicated in 2010 that the median pay for computer system analysts was $77,740, when attaining an entry-level education with a bachelor's degree. The job outlook for such majors, according to the BLS, was 22 percent better when compared to the average college graduate in 2010. With 544,000 jobs in the market in 2010, the BLS expected an increase of 120,400 jobs over the next ten years. According to a 2012 report by the *U.S. News and World Report*, the BLS projected a 22.1 percent growth in employment for computer system analysts during this ten-year period; making the position the seventh in rank of The Best Jobs of 2012.

The Bureau of Labor Statistics projects 22.1 percent employment growth for computer system analysts between 2010 and 2020. During that time period, about 120,400 jobs will need to be filled. The profession's strong growth prospects helped boost computer systems analyst to the No. 7 spot in the ranking of The Best Jobs of 2012, behind Web developer.

* **prototype** a working model or experimental investigation of proposed systems under development

* **documentation** literature in a human-readable form that is referred to in support of using a computer or computer system

stored for retrieval, or used in problem-solving and decision-making activities; whatever happens to it during processing is part of the through-put function. The *output* of a system, or of an event within the system, is the result of the processing steps being applied to the data originally entered into the system. The system analyst's model should account for everything that happens from the time data enters the system to the point at which the end results are achieved.

Throughout the system analysis process, analysts test the ideas and conclusions that arise. Often the model of the system provides the basis for creating a prototype* of what is being studied. Although prototyping is a common exercise of designers, who use s to test system configurations and hardware-software specifications, it is also a method for the system analyst to refine the conclusions of the analysis before design decisions are made.

Documentation

Documentation* is a necessary part of system analysis. Documentation means that all actions taken in the process of analyzing a system are recorded. This provides an enduring record of everything that has taken place and all the thoughts or ideas generated throughout the process. This includes both the individual work and testing done by a particular system analyst, and the group work, such as brainstorming, that is usually part of the overall process of analyzing and designing a system. Documentation objectifies the system analysis process. Thorough can help reduce the amount of guessing that goes into solving certain system problems. It helps analysts keep track of what has been tried, and when, and under what specific circumstances. It can be useful in future work on a particular system, and it is a practice through which the process and outcomes of system analysis can be improved and validated.

 See also **Decision Support Systems • Design Tools • Information Systems • Office Automation Systems • Systems Design**

Resources

Books

Booch, Grady, et al. *Object-oriented Analysis and Design with Applications.* 3rd ed. Upper Saddle River, NJ: Addison-Wesley, 2007.

Elleithy, Khaled, and Tarek Sobh, eds. *Innovations and Advances in Computer, Information, Systems Sciences, and Engineering.* London and New York: Springer, 2012.

Kusic, George L. *Computer-aided Power Systems Analysis..* 2nd ed. Boca Raton, FL: CRC Press, 2009.

Ravindran, A. Ravi, ed. *Operations Research and Management Science Handbook.* Boca Raton, FL: CRC Press, 2008.

Sage, Andrew P., and William B. Rouse, eds. *Handbook of Systems Engineering and Management.* Hoboken, NJ: John Wiley & Sons, 2009.

Satzinger, John W., Robert B. Jackson, and Stephen D. Burd. *Systems Analysis and Design in a Changing World.* 6th ed. Boston: Course Technology, Cengage Learning, 2012.

Web Sites

Bureau of Labor Statistics, U.S. Department of Labor. "Computer Systems Analysts." http://www.bls.gov/ooh/computer-and-information-technology/computer-systems-analysts.htm (accessed October 24, 2012).

U.S. News and World Report. "Computer Systems Analyst: Job Profile & Salary." http://money.usnews.com/careers/best-jobs/computer-systems-analyst (accessed October 24, 2012).

Systems Design

Systems design is a component of the systems engineering process. Typically, it follows systems analysis, precedes implementation, and is driven by the requirements generated during the earlier phases of the project. Within the context of computer sciences, systems design includes the specification of hardware and software architecture granulated to the necessary components, modules, and interfaces.

The systems design process may include such subcategories as network design, software design, and data design. The scope of the project is a primary determinant of the degree to which any of these and potentially other sub-processes factor into the overall system design effort. Organizational standards and budgetary constraints may also limit design activity.

The sequence of design events relative to other processes in a system's life cycle is largely determined by the systems methodology chosen for the project. This is often based upon the nature of the system being considered. The traditional systems engineering methodology, often referred to as the waterfall paradigm*, assumes that all planning, business analysis, risk assessment, and requirements definition occur before any of the design activity begins. All systems design activity must then be completed and verified against requirements before any implementation can begin. Implementation may include constructing a network, developing software, or a combination of such activities, depending on the scope of the system. When implementation is complete, the system is evaluated and ultimately introduced to the operational environment.

Often, such a strict serial methodology is impractical. Increasingly, and especially for the development of software, an iterative* approach is chosen. The most evolutionary of the models, often preferred for

* **paradigm** an example, pattern, or way of thinking

* **iterative** a procedure that involves repetitive operations before being completed

* **prototype** a working model or experimental investigation of proposed systems under development

object-oriented software construction, is the spiral methodology. Under this paradigm, a prototype* is rapidly constructed through much shorter phases of analysis, design, development, and testing. The cycle is then repeated many times until the original prototype is adequately refined and ready for operation.

While the waterfall paradigm is structurally confining, the spiral approach has the potential for lack of structure and initial planning. For this reason, a compromise is often chosen between the two models. For instance, project managers may choose an approach that is predominately sequential, but with review and refinement iterations planned between each phase. Or they may choose an incremental model, which is closer to the spiral methodology but defines a limited number of structured iterations.

Regardless of the scope or chosen methodology, systems engineering activities occur in the same functional sequence: Analysis is followed by design, which is followed by implementation. The scope of design activities changes on a per-project basis, but effective design practices apply to all engineering projects regardless of scope or chosen methodology.

The design phase deals with decisions regarding the specific architecture of the system so that it meets all of the stated requirements when constructed. During the first round of an iterative project, requirements may be few and vague. A large-scale waterfall-based project, by contrast, may present many specific requirements. Regardless of scope or methodology, stated requirements must be addressed and verified before the design can be considered complete.

A well-designed system will operate efficiently, providing maximum value given its use of resources. Surplus resources sometimes permit the designer to incorporate features or performance in excess of basic requirements. Such decisions must be carefully evaluated because improving one aspect generally diminishes another. Most systems design decisions involve some degree of compromise, so effective evaluation methods are an important part of the design process.

Decision models, often constructed as tables or trees, may be incorporated to assist designers in quantifying alternatives. Decision tables assist in translating actions and conditions into a tabular format, while tree models generally break a high-level decision into alternatives, each of which is further aggregated into individual consequences and further alternatives. Decision models may extend into several layers of conditions and actions. If systems and their associated decisions are complex enough to justify it, decision support systems may be implemented to assist the decision process. Decision support systems are often computer-based and built specifically to help evaluate both objective and subjective considerations of much larger independent systems. Decision models may be used to help the designer evaluate high-level decisions about the system's construct as well as to demonstrate the internal decision processes that occur within a system.

Other models that assist designers in visualizing system processes include flowcharts and data flow diagrams (DFDs). Both models graphically depict process flows through a system using shapes to represent processes or entities. The shapes are connected by arrows that direct flow.

Flowcharts primarily depict the sequence of decisions internal to a system, based on logical conditions. By convention, boxes indicate processing steps and diamonds depict conditions. This simple set of constructs was originally proposed in the late 1960s and is most effective for designing procedural programs. Object-oriented software development projects may benefit from a program design language such as the Unified Modeling Language (UML), which defines a robust set of notational conventions.

Data flow diagrams provide a means to depict the movement of data through a system or organization. They were introduced in 1979 in the book *Structured Analysis and System Specification* by American software engineer and author Tom DeMarco (1940–). The DFD depicts data flow between processes, external agents, and data stores. DFD convention defines an oval to be a process, a rectangle to be an external agent, and two horizontal lines to represent a data store. Other tools for modeling data include entity-relationship diagrams and state-transition diagrams.

Systems design that is complete, based upon solid decisions, and well-documented produces a valuable blueprint for the remaining phases of the engineering project. This is especially important under the waterfall approach, since all subsequent activity is reliant on the product of the design effort, and previous project phases are not easily revisited. An effective design product provides measurable deliverables and verifies that, in concept, the finished system will satisfy all requirements.

 See also **Design Tools • Office Automation Systems • System Analysis**

Resources

Books

Laplante, Phillip A., and Seppo J. Ovaska. *Real-time Systems Design and Analysis: Tools for the Practitioner.* 4th ed. Hoboken, NJ: Wiley-IEEE Press, 2012.

O'Docherty, Mike. *Object-oriented Analysis and Design: Understanding System Development with UML 2.0.* Chichester, UK, and Hoboken, NJ: Wiley, 2005.

Pfaffengerger, Bryan. *Webster's New World Computer Dictionary.* 9th ed. Indianapolis: Wiley, 2003.

Pressman, Roger S. *Software Engineering: A Practitioner's Approach.* 7th ed. New York: McGraw-Hill Higher Educaton, 2010.

Summers, Boyd L. *Effective Methods for Software and Systems Integration.* Boca Raton, FL: Auerbach Publications, 2012.

More About Flowcharts

A flowchart represents an algorithm—which is a rule or procedure used to solve a mathematical problem. However, the flowchart uses symbols rather than words. In addition to their use in program development, flowcharts are also used to enhance documentation.

Job Prospects

According to the *Occupational Outlook Handbook*, which is published by the Bureau of Labor Statistics (BLS), the positions of computer software engineer and application designer are among the top job prospects for the early 2010s. Requiring a bachelor's degree in computer science or software engineering or a master's degree in mathematics or systems design, these positions have a median annual salary of $79,780. In addition, as of 2012, the BLS states that computer network architects have a median annual salary of $75,660, whereas software developers are at $90,530.

Web Sites

Bureau of Labor Statistics, Department of Labor. "Computer and Information Technology Occupations." http://www.bls.gov/ooh/computer-and-information-technology/home.htm (accessed October 24, 2012).

Cutter Consortium. "Tom DeMarco." http://www.cutter.com/meet-our-experts/tdbio.html (accessed October 24, 2012).

Investopedia.com. "10 Careers With Great Job Prospects." http://www.investopedia.com/financial-edge/0709/16-careers-with-great-job-prospects.aspx#axzz2AFnGMn4r (accessed October 24, 2012).

T

Touch Screens

Touch screens, sometimes also spelled as touchscreens, are devices that enable a user to provide input to a computer or electronic system by making physical contact or near-contact with the system's display. Often seen in Automated Teller Machines (ATMs), information kiosks, and other public computers, touch screens are also widely used in computer graphics and animation, and play a role in assistive technology for users with special needs. In addition, the popularity of smartphones, tablet computers, and other such mobile devices is driving the demand for touch screens. For instance, the Apple iPad is one such device that uses touch screen technology.

Applications

Public computer systems are often designed around a touch screen, which is often the only visible component. Automated Teller Machines (ATMs) are the most common application, but falling prices for touch screen technology are making it available for other applications such as museum exhibits, ticket sales in airports and movie theaters, and public information kiosks. Touch screens are ideal for these applications because they provide input and output capabilities. They are often the only part of the system contacted by the user and are sturdier than many other input devices because they have no moving parts. These qualities make touch screen-based systems easy and inexpensive to maintain and repair.

Touch screens are used, like mice, as pointing devices. Instead of moving a mouse to activate and relocate the cursor, the user touches the screen to position the cursor. For specifying precise location, a touch screen often works with a stylus—a device like a pencil that has a rubber or plastic point. The user modifies what is seen on the screen by touching it, rather than by manipulating a cursor or other on-screen component with a mouse, keyboard, or joystick. Touch screens are invaluable to artists who have been trained to use pencils, brushes, and other implements that effect change wherever they touch the canvas.

Touch screens have revolutionized personal digital assistants (PDAs)*. Older PDAs required the user to enter data using an extremely small keyboard. Modern PDAs consist almost entirely of a touch screen, which makes them substantially smaller and easier to use because the user can write information directly into the device.

* **personal digital assistants (PDAs)** small-scale hand-held computers that can be used in place of diaries and appointment books

Using a mobile phone touch screen keypad to write a text message. © *ROSLAN RAHMAN/AFP/Getty Images.*

▶

* **computer peripheral** a device that is connected to a computer to support its operation; for example, a keyboard or a disk drive unit

* **liquid crystal display (LCD)** a type of crystal that changes its level of transparency when subjected to an electric current; used as an output device on a computer

In the late twentieth century, companies began to integrate touch screen technology with dry-erase boards (wall-mounted surfaces that allow the user to write with markers and erase the markings with a cloth). With these devices, whatever a user writes on the board can be simultaneously recorded and saved in a computer file.

Development

The touch screen was derived from the digitizing tablet, which is still in use as a computer peripheral*. The digitizing tablet, developed by American physicist and inventor George Samuel Hurst (1927–2010) in 1971 at the University of Kentucky, was designed to allow scientists to record data from graphs by placing the graph on the tablet and pressing the paper against the tablet with a stylus. In 1977, Elographics (now Elo Touch Solutions), the first commercial producer of digitizing tablets, paired with Siemens Corporation to develop a transparent version of the tablet on curved glass so that it could fit over a CRT (cathode ray tube) screen, which was then the predominant display technology. The first touch screens were built by hand, but advances soon allowed all of the layers to be produced by machine.

Touch Screen Technologies

Touch screens consist of a display component, typically a liquid crystal display (LCD)* or CRT covered or surrounded with a transparent sensor device that allows the screen to detect the contact or proximity of an object. There is a wide variety of sensor devices. Some devices are not entirely transparent or create glare that makes the screen behind the device difficult to see. The amount of pressure or types of contact needed to detect a touch varies from device to device. Devices also vary widely in accuracy (determining exactly where the touch occurred), durability (reliability with repeated use or in inclement circumstances), expected lifetime (time before failure of the device or parts of it), and response time (how long it takes the screen to detect a touch).

A 4-wire resistive (pressure sensitive) screen is made of two thin sheets separated by a grid of plastic dots. Each sheet, though clear, conducts electricity. When the user touches the screen, the sheets contact each other only at the spot where the user touched it. The screen measures the amount of electricity flowing between the two sheets to determine where the user touched. The term 4-wire comes from the four wires used to provide and measure the currents on the screen. These are the cheapest and most common touch screens. A 5-wire screen increases durability by adding a sheet so that the surface touched by the user is not one carrying the current. An 8-wire screen is the same as a 4-wire screen except that it uses an extra set of wires to measure the currents and has increased durability.

Capacitive screens use a single thin sheet. The screen is connected to electric oscillator*s. A signal of a specific frequency is broadcast through the sheet creating an oscillating electric field around it. When the user comes near the screen with a conductive object, such as a finger, the electric field is changed, which changes the signal in the sheet. The screen can determine the location of the conductive object by measuring the signal in the sheet. Although these screens are much clearer and transparent than those covered with resistive sheets, they lose accuracy over time and do not detect the presence of non-conductive objects, such as gloved fingers.

Wave interruption screens send a wave of some kind over the surface of the screen. When the user puts a finger into the wave, the screen can detect where the interference occurred. An infrared screen has a row of infrared lights along two adjacent sides. The opposite sides have infrared detectors. When a finger interrupts the light wave, the screen can determine where the interruption is by measuring which detectors went into the shadows. With surface acoustic wave (SAW) screens, an inaudible sound wave is played over the surface of the screen. A finger near the screen will absorb some of the sound wave, even if it is gloved, and the screen can determine the location by the change in frequency and strength of the sound wave. With near-field imaging, an object changes the frequency and strength of an electric (radio) wave. As with capacitive screens, the object interfering with the wave must be capacitive. Unlike with capacitive screens, the object can be covered with thin non-conductive covering, like a glove.

For applications that require more accuracy in terms of screen sensitivity, there are touch screens that respond to a stylus. The stylus triggers the sensors in the same manner as a finger does, but allows the user to specify a more precise location for software action.

▶ See also **Animation** • **Information Retrieval** • **Personal Digital Assistants**

* **oscillator** an electronic component that produces a precise waveform of a fixed known frequency; this can be used as a time base (clock) signal to other devices

* **random access memory (RAM)**
a type of memory device that supports the nonpermanent storage of programs and data; so called because various locations can be accessed in any order (as if at random), rather than in a sequence (like a tape memory device)

Resources

Books

Chen, Kevin Y., and H. K. Lee, eds. *Mobile Computing Research and Applications.* New York: Nova Science Publishers, 2009.

Kurkovsky, Stan, ed. *Multimodality in Mobile Computing and Mobile Devices: Methods for Adaptable Usability.* Hershey, PA: IGI Global, 2010.

Web Sites

AbilityHub. "Touch Screens." http://www.abilityhub.com/mouse/touchscreen.htm (accessed October 25, 2012).

About.com, and Mary Bellis. "Who Invented Touch Screen Technology?" http://inventors.about.com/od/tstartinventions/a/Touch-Screen.htm (accessed October 25, 2012).

Elo Touch Solutions. "Fast Facts." http://www.elotouch.com/AboutElo/default.asp (accessed October 25, 2012).

Tributes.com. "George Samuel Hurst: Obituary." http://www.tributes.com/show/George-Samuel-Hurst-88860237 (accessed October 25, 2012).

Transmission Media

Communication is one of the most important functions performed by computers. It is easy to understand that a computer must calculate, compare, and store data. It is also easy to see that the computer must input and output data used to communicate with the input and output devices. Also, within the computer, data must be transferred from one location—for example, from read only memory to random access memory (RAM)*, or from permanent storage such as a compact disc (CD) to temporary memory. Transferring data, therefore, is just another way of referring to communication. The communication of data is accomplished through various forms of transmission media, which is defined as the physical pathways that connect computers and other devices, along with people, through networks. Examples of such media include twisted-pair wire and fiber-optic cable, along with wireless devices such as satellites.

Communicating from one device to another within the computer is usually done through a bus, which is essentially a set of printed circuit board traces or wires within the computer. Buses are usually local to the device. Very special wire arrangements, called transmission lines, must be used when the required communications travel a significant distance or are executed at a very high speed. For high-speed computers, these transmission line techniques are even used for the internal computer buses.

To understand transmission lines, it is helpful to appreciate what makes a very poor transmission line. When Italian inventor Guglielmo Marconi (1874–1937) first spanned the Atlantic Ocean with radio waves in 1901, he erected a very long wire as an antenna at both the transmitter site and the receiver site. It was Marconi's goal to radiate energy in the form of radio waves and receive the energy on the other side of the Atlantic. When one desires to transmit signals *through long wires*, one does not want the radiation and reception of radio waves. A transmission line is the opposite of an antenna; it transmits data from one place to another with no loss of energy by radiating radio waves, called egress*, and receives no energy from external radio waves, called ingress*.

A very simple transmission line consists of a pair of wires that are kept precisely side by side. Because the wires often are twisted to keep them together, they have earned the title twisted pair. The twisted pair was one of the first transmission lines originally used, and remains in use for telephone systems. The twisted pair is inexpensive to manufacture and is also used extensively for computer communications.

Twisted pairs are used in many local area networks (LANs)*. There is a large selection of standard cable for use in LANs. Some twisted pairs include a shield, which reduces the amount of egress and ingress. The two basic types of twisted pairs are unshielded twisted pair (UTP) and shielded twisted pair (STP).

Although twisted pairs can have very little ingress and egress, they are not perfect, particularly at higher frequencies and data rates. The imperfections in transmission lines become more pronounced when the data rates are very high. One transmission line topology that reduces the amount of egress and ingress for very high data rates, extending to the gigabit per second range, is the coaxial transmission line, commonly called coaxial cable* or co-ax. In this transmission line design, one conductor is actually a hollow cylinder and the other conductor is placed in the center of the cylinder. Egress and ingress can be reduced to very low levels but is much more expensive than unshielded twisted pairs. Coaxial cable is used for television distribution despite the increased cost because of the very broad frequency range of television signals.

The loss of energy due to radiation and from other losses within the transmission line subtracts from the signal energy in the line. This means that the signal has to be amplified or restored if the transmission line is long. Since there are more losses at higher frequencies, more amplification is required for the higher frequencies. Very high-speed data communications systems will require more amplifiers or repeaters for the same length of cable.

The best transmission line for very high-speed data or wide bandwidth is a glass fiber. It is often difficult to view the glass fiber as a transmission line because the signals within the fiber are not electrical but light waves. However, light waves are electromagnetic waves just like radio. The glass fiber has characteristics exactly like a wire transmission line. However, the transmission rate is generally higher.

* **egress** to move out of an object, system, or environment

* **ingress** the act of entering a system or object

* **local area networks (LANs)** high-speed computer networks that are designed for users who are located near each other

* **coaxial cable** a cable with an inner conducting core, a dielectric material and an outer sheath that is designed for high frequency signal transmission

* **modem** the contraction of MOdulator DEModulator; a device which converts digital signals into signals suitable for transmission over analog channels, like telephone lines

Many computer communications applications require a wireless communications medium. Of course, in modern terminology it must be understood that wireless also implies fiber optic-less. Clearly, this is the only communications solution for portable and vehicle-mounted devices. Wireless transmission is accomplished through electromagnetic waves, radio, and light. These electromagnetic waves require no physical medium because they are able to flourish through a vacuum better than through any substance. In fact, wireless signals can be partially blocked by common building materials causing difficulties with wireless systems used indoors.

For transmission through short distances, wireless modems are used. These modem*s are low powered radio transmitters and receivers that require no government license. Long distance data communications using radio waves include terrestrial microwave links and satellite data links. These applications involve much higher power transmitters and require government licensing to insure that users do not interfere with other users. Microwave links propagate in straight lines. Depending on the height of the transmitting and receiving antennas, the microwave links are seldom more than 100 kilometers (approximately 62 miles) apart because of the curvature of earth. As with wired communications, repeaters are required to extend microwave communications.

There are two basic types of satellite links; one type pertains to satellites in low earth orbit (LEO), while the other type pertains to satellites in geostationary earth orbit (GEO). LEO satellites orbit earth in less than two hours and are visible to the user on earth for only 20 minutes or so. To provide continuous communications, a number of satellites called a constellation is required. Thus, when one satellite sets beneath the horizon, or is no longer in view, another satellite can be used for communications. Because the satellites are relatively close to earth, typically only 800 kilometers (about 500 miles) or so, a modest antenna and transmitter power will provide reliable communications. However, because the user must switch from one satellite to another, a complex system must be employed to switch the communications channel between satellites much like a cellular telephone system in space.

A satellite in geostationary orbit rotates around earth at the same rate as earth spins on its axis—therefore, the GEO satellite is always in view and the user's ground-based antenna is pointed at the satellite. Because the satellite never sets, only one satellite is suffcient. Large organizations use most GEO satellite systems. This is because the uplink transmitter must employ a rather large antenna and needs to be licensed by the government. For small users and individuals desiring Internet access, especially in more remote regions, some satellite systems are available where the uplink is provided via a conventional telephone line and the downlink is via the satellite. Generally, the uplink data rate required by the individual user is much less than the downlink and this arrangement is acceptable. There are also two-way satellite systems in which both the uplink (from the user's home computer to the satellite) and downlink (from the satellite to the user's computer) are via a satellite connection. Both LEO and GEO satellites are used for Internet communications.

For short distance communications, such as from a large room of computers to a LAN, infrared radiation may be used. Low-powered infrared radiation from a light emitting diode (LED) provides the transmitter while the receiver is a phototransistor or diode. This type of infrared technology has been used for many years for remote control devices for consumer entertainment equipment such as television. The range of these systems can be as much as 30 meters (98.5 feet), but the light energy can be blocked easily.

▶ *See also* **Bridging Devices • Satellite Technology • Telecommunications • Wireless Technology**

Resources

Books

Blahut, Richard E. *Modem Theory: An Introduction to Telecommunications.* Cambridge, UK, and New York: Cambridge University Press, 2010.

Horak, Ray. *Telecommunications and Data Communications Handbook.* Hoboken, NJ: Wiley-Interscience, 2007.

Pachnicke, Stephan. *Fiber-optic Transmission Networks: Efficient Design and Dynamic Operation.* Berlin: Springer, 2012.

Web Sites

InformIT.com, Kitty Wilson Jarrett, and Lillian Goleniewski. "Traditional Transmission Media for Networking and Telecommunications" http://www.informit.com/articles/article.aspx?p=683070 (accessed October 26, 2012).

Perplexing Situation

Signals for communicating must travel through some medium. The idea that energy could travel through total emptiness, a total vacuum, perplexed scientists for centuries. To satisfy their theories, scientists invented a medium called aether. Modern science knows there is no aether and signals can pass through a vacuum as well as wires, and fiber optics.

V

Video Devices

Video devices are peripherals, such as printers and monitors, added to a computer to enable it to work with visual images. Video is defined as any technology that is able to electronically record, process, store, transmit, and view a series of still images through moving scenes. In computer science, a video capture card provides a way to input video to the computer from conventional sources such as a camera, digital versatile disk (DVD), or a television (TV) cable or antenna. A video output card allows video to be output from the computer to a monitor. It is also possible to get video output cards that output video via a cable that can be connected directly to a television, allowing video to be played from a computer and watched on a television.

All information stored on a computer is stored in digital form as a sequence of numbers. Sometimes when video is received from a source outside the computer, such as a (now obsolete) videocassette recorder (VCR), it is in analog format and must be converted into digital form that can be stored in the computer. This used to be one of the key functions of the video capture card. However, by June 2009 all full-power TV broadcasts in the United States were required to be transmitted in digital format; hence the conversion from analog-to-digital is no longer necessary for most consumers (unless they are capturing a video signal from an older analog device, such as a VCR).

To record a video sequence in digital form with the quality of a standard TV program would require approximately ninety gigabytes (GB, where one gigabyte is equal to 1 billion bytes) for one hour, equivalent to the capacity of approximately 140 compact discs (CDs), around six to twenty standard DVDs (depending on whether the DVD is single- or double-sided), or two to four Blu-ray optical discs (again, depending on whether they are single- or dual-layered). A significant reduction in the required disc space, without a noticeable loss of quality, can be achieved by compressing the video. Instead of 90 GB to store one hour of TV-quality video, the same information can be compressed to approximately 2 GB. Because video almost always is stored on a computer in compressed form. Most video capture cards also include hardware to perform video compression.

In the same way that a video capture card can compress incoming video, the video output card can include hardware for decompression of the video signal. However, software running on the computer can also perform the decompression, but if the computer is not fast enough, the video will not play back smoothly.

Texas Instruments vice president, Greg Delagi, holds a video microchip board. © *AP Images/LM Otero.*

Advertising Nightmare

In 1975, Sony introduced the Betamax home videocassette recorder (VCR), enabling television viewers to tape their favorite shows to watch at a later date and time. In a 1984 study conducted by Nielsen, television advertisers and network executives were shocked to learn that 49 percent of TV watchers were not only using their VCRs to watch their favorite shows at a later time but also to fast-forward through commercials.

Modern video camera recorders (often referred to as camcorders) record images in digital form. The digital information is usually recorded onto a particular medium or device, such as video tape, miniature optical discs, mini hard disks, or flash memory cards. Sometimes a camcorder is designed so that it can record onto multiple types of recording media. Digital camcorders can be connected directly to a computer without the need to use a video capture card because the video is already in a compressed digital video form.

One reason to transfer video to a computer is to allow for editing. Once the video is stored on the computer, sophisticated editing software can be used to manipulate the video. For example, holiday camcorder recordings typically contain much unwanted material. After transferring the video from the camcorder to a computer, the video can be edited to remove the unwanted parts. When the editing is finished, the holiday video can be transferred back to the camcorder tapes or to a standard DVD. Or, the edited video can be kept on the computer and played from the computer to a monitor or television.

If a computer is equipped with both a camera and a video output card, it can be used for video conferencing. In video conferencing, two or more people in different locations communicate with each other using both sound and video through their computers. The camera captures a digital video signal of the person, and the computer transmits it through a network to the other participants. Similarly, the other participants have cameras so that video is transmitted to them also. Each person also needs a video output card to display the video received from the other video conference participants. Video conferencing allows people to both see and hear each other while in remote locations.

When a computer is equipped to handle video, it can be used to perform functions normally done by consumer electronics devices. If a computer includes a DVD read-only memory (ROM) drive and a suitable video output card, it is possible to play DVD videos on the computer. Or, the output from the video card can be connected to a television and the DVDs can be watched on the television instead of the computer monitor.

 See also **Animation • Games • Interactive Systems • Virtual Reality**

Resources

Books

Jack, Keith. *Video Demystified: A Handbook for the Digital Engineer.* 5th ed. Maryland Heights, MO: Newnes, 2007.

Wong, Yue-Ling. *Digital Media Primer: Digital Audio, Video, Imaging and Multimedia Programming.* 2nd ed. Boston: Pearson, 2013.

Web Sites

About.com. "The History of Video and Related Innovations." http://inventors.about.com/library/inventors/blvideo.htm (accessed October 26, 2012).

Virtual Memory

Virtual memory is a model—one of many possible models—for managing the resource of physical memory, or main memory. Such management is necessary because a microprocessor, the heart of a computer, has direct access only to main memory, while all programs and data are stored on permanent media such as hard disks.

Reading or writing main memory is as simple as executing a single computer instruction. In contrast, any access to hard disks, digital versatile discs (DVDs), compact discs-read only memory (CD-ROMs), or flash

Figure 1: Memory management models. There are at least three ways to manage physical memory. The first, *physical addressing,* uses physical addresses in the program itself. The second, *base+offset addressing,* uses relative offsets in the program and adds the physical base address at runtime. The third, *virtual addressing,* uses any appropriate naming scheme in the program (usually relative offsets) and relies upon the operating system and hardware to translate the references to physical addresses at runtime. Tradition virtual memory is therefore a small subset of the virtual addressing model of memory management. *Reproduced by permission of Gale, a part of Cengage Learning.*

▼

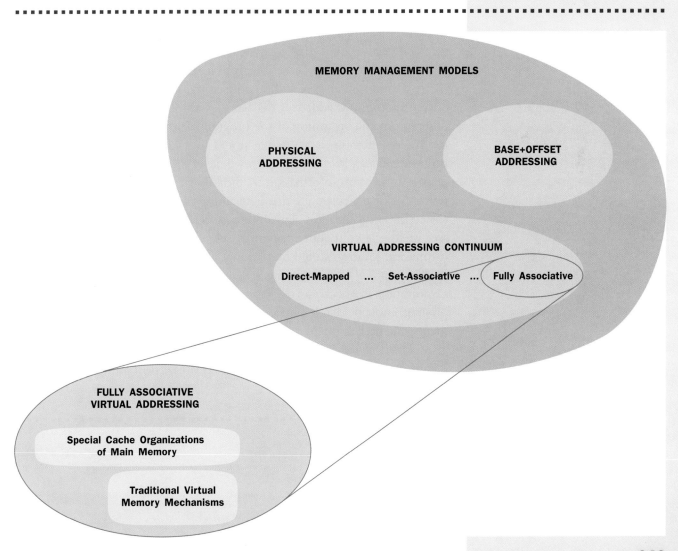

* **protocol** an agreed understanding for the sub-operations that make up a transaction, usually found in the specification of inter-computer communications

drives is indirect and requires relatively complex communication protocol*s involving dozens to thousands of computer instructions. Therefore, accessing a file or running a program requires that the data on disk first be moved into main memory. Virtual memory is one method for handling this management of data. To illustrate what it is and how it differs from other possibilities, this discussion will compare several memory alternatives.

Memory-Management Alternatives

In the simplest model of program creation and execution, physical addressing, a programmer determines what physical memory is available, reserves it so that no one else uses it, and writes a program to use the reserved memory locations. This allows the program to execute without any runtime support required from the operating system. However, because a program is not likely to use the same physical location on every invocation, this requires a rewrite of the program every time it runs—a tedious task, but one that could be left to the operating system. At process start-up, the operating system could modify every pointer reference in the application (including loads, stores, and absolute jumps such as function calls) to reflect the physical address at which the program is loaded. The program as it resides in main memory references itself directly and so contains implicit knowledge about the structure and organization of the physical memory. This model is depicted in Figure 2. A program sees itself exactly as it resides in main memory.

A second model, base+offset addressing, involves writing the program once using pointer addresses that are not absolute but are instead relative offsets from the beginning of the program. If the location of the program in physical memory is a variable stored in a known hardware register, at runtime one can load the program wherever it fits in physical memory and place this location information in the known register so that all memory references first incorporate this base address and are then redirected to the correct physical location. This model is depicted in Figure 3. The process sees itself as a contiguous region or set of contiguous regions, each with its physical location stored in a known hardware register. The advantage is that, as opposed to the previous scheme, knowledge of the memory-system organization is not exposed to the program. The disadvantage is that the program must be divided into a relatively small number of contiguous segments, and each segment must fit entirely in main memory if it is to be used.

A third model, virtual addressing, involves writing the program as if it is loaded at physical memory location zero, loading the program

Figure 2: The Physical Addressing model of program creation and execution. In this model, a program's view of itself in its environment (physical memory) is equivalent to reality; a program contains knowledge of the structure of the hardware. A program can be entirely contiguous in memory, or it can be split into multiple pieces, but the locations of all parts of the program are known to the program's code and data. *Reproduced by permission of Gale, a part of Cengage Learning.*

Program's View of the World:
Physical Memory: | | Program | | Program | |

Reality:
Physical Memory: | | Program | | Program | |

Program's View of the World:

Region 1: Program

Region 2: Program

Reality:

Physical Memory: Program   Program

Figure 3: The Base+Offset Addressing model of program creation and execution. In this model, a program's view of itself in its environment is not equivalent to reality, but it does see itself as a set of contiguous regions. It does not know where in physical memory these regions are located, but the regions must be contiguous; they cannot be fragmented. *Reproduced by permission of Gale, a part of Cengage Learning.*

* **granularity** a description of the level of precision that can be achieved in making measurements of a quantity; for example coarse granularity means inexpensive but imprecise measurements

wherever it fits (not necessarily location zero), and using some as-yet-undefined mechanism to translate the program's addresses to the equivalent physical addresses while it is running. If the translation granularity* is relatively small (that is, the program is broken down into smaller pieces that are translated independently of each other), the program can even be fragmented in main memory. Bits and pieces of the program can lie scattered throughout main memory, and the program need not be entirely resident to execute. This model is depicted in Figure 4. The advantage of this scheme is that one never needs to rewrite the program. The disadvantage is the potential overhead of the translation mechanism.

Physical addressing can be implemented on any hardware architecture; base+offset addressing can be implemented on any architecture that has the appropriate addressing mode or address-translation hardware; and virtual addressing is typically implemented on microprocessors with memory-management units (MMUs). The following paragraphs discuss the relative merits of the three models.

Physical Addressing In physical addressing, program execution behaves differently every time the program is executed on a machine with a different memory organization, and it is likely to behave differently every time it is executed on the same machine with the same organization, because the program is likely to be loaded at a different location every time. Physical addressing systems outnumber virtual addressing systems. An example of a physical addressing system is the operating system for the original Macintosh, which did not have the benefit of a memory-management unit. Though later Macintosh systems added an optional virtual memory implementation, many applications require that the option be disabled during their execution for performance reasons. The newest

Figure 4: The Virtual Addressing model of program creation and execution. In this model, a program's view of itself in its environment has virtually nothing to do with reality; a program can consider itself a collection of contiguous regions or a set of fragments, or one large monolithic program. The operating system considers the program nothing more than a set of uniform virtual pages and loads them as necessary into physical memory. The entire program need not be resident in memory, and it need not be contiguous. *Reproduced by permission of Gale, a part of Cengage Learning.*

Program's View of the World:

"Virtual" Memory: Program   Program

Reality:

Physical Memory:

amortized phasing out something in until it is gradually extinguished, like a mortgage loan

version of the Macintosh operating system (OS), Mac OS X, is based on a UNIX core and has true high-performance virtual memory at its heart.

The advantages of the physically addressed scheme are its simplicity and performance. The disadvantages include slow program start-up and decreased flexibility. At start-up, the program must be edited to reflect its location in main memory. While this is easily amortized* over the run-time of a long-running program, it is not clear whether the speed advantages outweigh this initial cost for short-running programs. Decreased flexibility can also lead to performance loss. Since the program cannot be fragmented or partially loaded, the entire program file must be read into main memory to execute. This can create problems for systems with too little memory to hold all the running programs.

Base+Offset Addressing In base+offset addressing, like physical addressing, program execution behaves differently every time the program is executed. However, unlike physical addressing, base+offset addressing does not require a rewrite of the program every time it is executed. Base+offset systems far outweigh all other systems combined: an example is the Disk Operating System (DOS)/Windows system running on the Intel x86. The Intel processor architecture has a combined memory management unit that places a base+offset design on top of a virtual addressing design. The architecture provides several registers that hold segment offsets, so a program can be composed of multiple regions, each of which must be complete and contiguous, but which need not touch each other.

The advantages of this scheme are that the code needs no editing at process start-up, and the performance is equal to that of the physical addressing model. The disadvantages of the scheme are similar to physical addressing: A region must not be fragmented in main memory because this can be problematic when a system has many running programs scattered about main memory.

Virtual Addressing In virtual addressing, program execution behaves identically every time the program is executed, even if the machine's organization changes, and even if the program is run on different machines with wildly different memory organizations. Virtual addressing systems include nearly all academic systems, most UNIX-based systems such as Mac OS X, and many UNIX-influenced systems such as Windows NT, Windows 2000, Windows, XP, Windows Vista, Windows 7, and Windows 8. The advantages of virtual memory are that a program needs no rewrite on start-up, one can run programs on systems with very little memory, and one can easily juggle many programs in physical memory because fragmentation of a program's code and data regions is allowed. In contrast, systems that require program regions to remain contiguous in physical memory might be unable to execute a program because no single unused space in main memory is large enough to hold the program, even if many scattered unused areas together would be large enough. The disadvantage of the virtual addressing scheme is the increased space required to hold the translation information and the performance overhead of translating addresses. These overheads have traditionally been no more than a few percent.

Now that the cost of physical memory, DRAM*, has decreased significantly, the schemes that use memory for better performance—physical and base+offset addressing—have become better choices. Because memory is cheap, perhaps the best design is now one that simply loads every program entirely into memory and assumes that any memory shortage will be fixed by the addition of more . However, the general consensus is that virtual addressing is more flexible than the other schemes, and its overhead is accepted as reasonable. Moreover, it seems to provide a more intuitive and bug-free paradigm* for program design and development than the other schemes.

How Are Virtual Addresses Translated?

In the virtual addressing model, programs execute in imaginary address spaces that are mapped onto physical memory by the operating system and hardware. Executing programs generate instruction fetches, loads, and stores using imaginary or virtual addresses for their instructions and data. The ultimate home for the program's address space is backing store, usually a disk drive. This is where the program's instructions and data originate and where all of its permanent changes go. Every hardware memory structure between the central processing unit (CPU) and the backing store is a cache—temporary storage—for the instructions and data in the program's address space. This includes main memory. Main memory is nothing more than a cache for a program's virtual address space. Everything in the address space initially comes from the program file stored on disk or is created on demand and defined to be zero. Figure 5 illustrates this.

In Figure 5(a), the program view is shown. A program simply makes data loads stores, and implicit instruction fetches to its virtual address space. The address space, as far as the program is concerned, is contiguous and held completely in main memory, and any unused holes between objects in the space are simply wasted space.

Figure 5(b) shows a more realistic picture. There is no linear storage structure that contains a program's address space, especially since every address space is at least several gigabytes when one includes the unused holes. The address space is actually a collection of fixed-sized pages that are stored piecemeal on disk or conjured up out of thin air. The instructions and initialized data can be found in the program file, and when the running program needs extra workspace, the operating system can dynamically allocate new pages in main memory. The enabling mechanism is the page table. This is a database managed by the operating system that indicates whether a given page in a program's address space is found on disk, needs to be created from scratch, or can be found in physical memory at some location. Every virtual address generated by the program is translated according to the page table before the request is sent

Managing Memory

Virtual memory is a technique for managing memory resources in which one uses physical memory as a cache for program code and data stored on disk. Because it provides such an intuitive model, all modern systems support virtual memory, even though the problem for which is was originally invented—running a program on memory systems smaller than the program itself—is no longer an issue.

* **DRAM** the acronym for Dynamic Random Access Memory; high density, low cost and low speed memory devices used in most computer systems

* **paradigm** an example, pattern, or way of thinking

Figure 5: Caching the process address space in main memory. In the first view (a), a program is shown referencing locations in its virtual address space. All loads, stores, and fetches use virtual addresses to reference objects. The second view (b) shows that the address space is not a linear object stored on some device, but is instead scattered across main memory and hard drives and even dynamically allocated when necessary. The page table handles the translation from virtual address space to physical location. Note that it has the same shape as the address space in figure (a), indicating that for every chunk of data in the virtual address space (each chunk is called a "virtual page"), there is exactly one translation entry in the page table. *Reproduced by permission of Gale, a part of Cengage Learning.*

▶

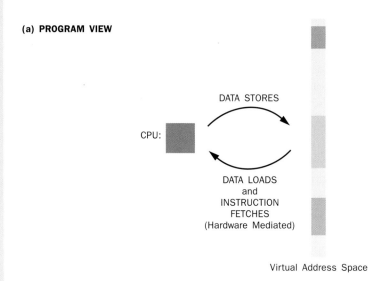

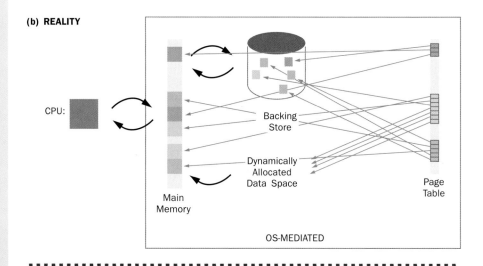

to the memory system. To speed access to the page table, parts of it are held temporarily in hardware. This is one of the functions of a memory-management unit.

Virtual memory is but one of many models of program creation and execution and one of many techniques to manage one's physical memory resources. Other models include base+offset addressing and physical addressing, each of which offers performance advantages over virtual addressing but at a cost in terms of flexibility. The widespread use of virtual memory in contemporary operating systems is testimony to the fact that flexibility is regarded as a valuable system characteristic, outweighing any small amount of performance loss.

▶ *See also* **Generations, Computers • Memory • Operating Systems**

Resources

Books

Bott, Ed, Carl Siechert, and Craig Stinson. *Windows 7 Inside Out.* Redmond, WA: Microsoft Press, 2011.

Duncan, Ray, et al. *Extending DOS—A Programmer's Guide to Protected-Mode DOS.* 2nd ed. Reading, MA: Addison-Wesley, 1994.

Hart-Davis, Guy. *Mac OS X System Administration.* New York: McGraw-Hill, 2010.

Williams, Robin. *The Little Mac Book.* Berkeley, CA: Peachpit Press, 2012.

Web Sites

Department of Computer Science, George Mason University. "Virtual Memory: History." http://www.cs.gmu.edu/cne/itcore/virtualmemory/vmhistory.html (accessed October 29, 2012).

How Stuff Works. "How Virtual Memory Works." http://www.howstuffworks.com/virtual-memory.htm (accessed October 29, 2012).

* **bandwidth** a measure of the frequency component of a signal or the capacity of a communication channel to carry signals

* **wide area network (WAN)** an interconnected network of computers that spans upward from several buildings to whole cities or entire countries and across countries

* **TCP/IP protocol suite** Transmission Control Protocol/Internet Protocol; a range of functions that can be used to facilitate applications working on the Internet

Virtual Private Network

Corporations have traditionally leased transmission capacity or contracted bandwidth* services from common carriers to create their own private-wide area network (WAN)*. However, a WAN is expensive to create and maintain. The economics and technology justifying a WAN drastically changed in the 1990s due to the following factors:

- Decreasing costs for Internet connectivity;
- Increasingly higher connections to the Internet; and
- Mature encryption technology for secure Internet communications.

These changes made feasible a new type of network called a Virtual Private Network (VPN) which provides all the features of a private WAN for a fraction of the cost.

A Virtual Private Network is simply a secure system of connectivity over a public network—a private network on a public network infrastructure (the Internet). A VPN is virtual in the sense that it has no corresponding physical network but rather shares physical circuits with other traffic. A VPN is private in the sense that it isolates and secures Internet traffic using routing and encryption, respectively.

How Does It Work?

There are different types of VPNs corresponding to the different layers within the TCP/IP protocol suite*: Data Link, Network, Transport, and Application Layers. The most common VPN in use provides secure

* **Internet Service Provider (ISP)** a commercial enterprise which offers paying subscribers access to the Internet (usually via modem) for a fee

* **tunneling** a way of handling different communication protocols, by taking packets of a foreign protocol and changing them so that they appear to be a locally known type

* **cryptography** the science of understanding codes and ciphers and their application

* **digital certificates** certificates used in authentication that contain encrypted digital identification information

* **software-defined networks (SDNs)** the same as virtual private networks (VPNs), where the subscriber can set up and maintain a communications system using management software, on a public network

dial-up (data link) access. Here, a remote user connects to the Internet through an Internet Service Provider (ISP)*. Software on the user's computer creates a secure, virtual circuit or tunnel to the company's VPN gateway. The benefits include lower costs through the elimination of long distance telephone charges, improved security through the integration of the latest security technology, and unparalleled flexibility, since any Internet connection from dial-up can be used as a VPN connection.

The key to a VPN is tunneling*. VPN traffic is logically routed separately from other traffic by mechanisms that repackage data from one network to another. Tunneling at the network layer between a source and a destination wraps (encapsulates) packets with a new header and forwards them into a tunnel with a destination address of the tunnel endpoint. When the packet reaches the tunnel endpoint, the header is unwrapped (unencapsulated) and the packet is forwarded to its original destination. A VPN can thus be created by a collection of tunnels.

Tunneling does not ensure privacy since even encapsulated IP packets are typically transported in plain text. This is clearly a problem if a corporation wants to use the Internet to transmit important business information. Privacy is ensured by cryptography*. End-to-end encryption to individual end systems provides for the highest level of security. Tunnel mode encryption is performed between intermediate routers leaving traffic between the end system and the first hop router in plain text. Any corruption of operation or interception of traffic at tunnel endpoints will compromise the entire VPN. Hackers foiled in attempts to crack network traffic may instead target client machines. To help maintain security and privacy, a Certificate Authority (CA) is needed to issue and manage digital certificates* to VPN devices and users.

Applications

VPNs have been implemented for both data and voice. The idea of using a public network to create the illusion of a private network devoted exclusively to VPN subscribers is not new. The first packet network VPN was created in 1975 when the Bolt, Beranek, and Newman (BBN) company delivered the first Private Line Interface (PLI) packet encryption devices to protect classified data for transmission over the U.S. Department of Defense's Advanced Research Projects Agency NETwork (ARPANET). Another example is the CENTRal EXchange (CENTREX) service, which has been offered for many years by local telephone companies as a central office switch service providing private data and voice networks. In 1985, AT&T began offering software-defined networks (SDNs)* for private voice networks based on dedicated and later switched connections; users were billed differently for on-net and off-net calls.

There are several strong motivations for building VPNs: (1) to make a standard corporate computing environment transparent to users; (2) to secure communications; and (3) to take advantage of the cost efficiencies of a common public infrastructure versus building and operating a private WAN. A VPN also increases flexibility since global Internet connections can be established and released on-demand. Internet connectivity is also a VPN's major disadvantage: it is difficult to guarantee quality-of-service (QoS)* over the Internet since aggregate* traffic flows can be unpredictable. Service Level Agreements (SLAs) between ISPs and corporations are an evolving contractual solution designed to guarantee QoS based upon throughput, availability, and response time thresholds. One example of a large VPN is the U.S. State Department, which has implemented a VPN to connect all its embassies around the world.

Mobile virtual private networks (mobile VPNs or mVPNs) are becoming increasingly popular as mobile communications spreads around the world. These mVPNs provide wireless devices, such as smartphones, with uninterrupted access to the Internet on their local network when they connect through another wireless or wired network. They commonly are used in such work environments as public safety, medicine (especially in hospitals), and utilities.

 See also **E-Commerce • Network Design • Networks • Security • Telecommunications • World Wide Web**

Resources

Books

Comer, Douglas E. *The Internet Book: Everything You Need to Know about Computer Networking and How the Internet Works.* 4th ed. Upper Saddle River, NJ: Pearson Prentice Hall, 2007.

Dodd, Annabel Z. *The Essential Guide to Telecommunications.* 5th ed. Upper Saddle River, NJ: Prentice Hall, 2012.

Estrada, Ernesto. *The Structure of Complex Networks: Theory and Applications.* Oxford: Oxford University Press, 2012.

Iannone, Eugenio. *Telecommunication Networks.* Boca Raton, FL: CRC Press, 2012.

Stallings, William. *Data and Computer Communications.* 9th ed. Upper Saddle River, NJ: Prentice Hall, 2011.

Zalewski, Michal. *The Tangled Web: A Guide to Securing Modern Web Applications.* San Francisco: No Starch Press, 2012.

Web Sites

How Stuff Works. "How VPNs Work." http://www.howstuffworks.com/vpn.htm (accessed October 29, 2012).

Microsoft. "Virtual Private Networks." http://technet.microsoft.com/en-us/network/bb545442.aspx (accessed October 29, 2012).

Computer Sciences, 2nd Edition

Global VPN

The U.S. State Department has a Virtual Private Network (VPN) to coordinate the government's numerous agencies with overseas offices. This network enables Internet access to e-mail and other communications between agencies, as well as the distribution of information—unclassified, of course.

* **quality-of-service (QoS)** a set of performance criteria that a system is designed to guarantee and support as a minimum

* **aggregate** a numerical summation of multiple individual scores

Virtual Reality

The terms virtual reality (VR) and virtual environment (VE) refer to an artificial reality created by computer technology that provides the user with a first-person, interactive view into the simulated (hypothetical) world that has been created. This interactive capability distinguishes VR from other systems based on computer graphics such as the extremely realistic computer animations that are increasingly being used by the filmmaking industry. Actors do not actually interact with the computer animations that will ultimately appear in a film. Instead, they interact with an imaginary scene or animation that is then added later to provide realism for the moviegoer. This provides the audience with a third-person view of a virtual world. Such a view is in sharp contrast to VR, in which the environment is centered around the perspective of the user who will also typically have the ability to interact dynamically with it.

Although its origins date back to the 1950s, the phrase virtual reality first became widely known in the mid–1980s, when mainstream computer technology finally become powerful enough to perform the calculations necessary to create a minimally realistic virtual environment. However, in spite of earlier technological limitations, VR ideas were envisioned long before the 1980s. In 1957, Mort Heilig filed a patent for a head-mounted "stereoscopic television apparatus for personal use." Thus, the head-mounted display (HMD) was born, though at the time, applying this technology to view a virtual world created by a computer was not considered or envisioned.

In 1965, American Internet pioneer Ivan Edward Sutherland (1938–) published an article called "The Ultimate Display," which described how a computer someday could be used to provide a window into virtual worlds.

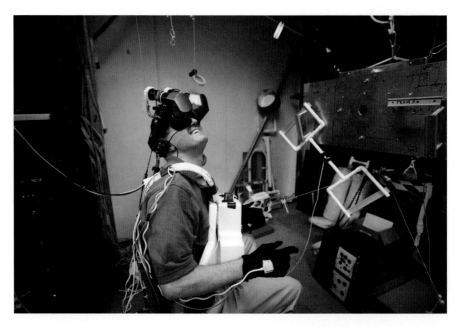

▶

Astronaut trains with virtual reality program. © *AP Images/Houston Chronicle, Smiley N. Pool.*

Then in 1968, Sutherland combined these ideas together with head tracking and built a head-mounted display providing a stereoscopic view into a simple three-dimensional (3D) world that remained stationary despite viewer head movements! Virtual reality was born.

Today VR consists of much more than just head-mounted displays. Gloves containing strain gauges or fiber optics* can be used to allow a user to interact with a virtual world through hand gestures. Force feed-back information, such as the weight of a virtual object, can be provided via haptic* devices, and a virtual reality modeling language, called VRML, has even been developed to allow Internet browsers to interact with 3D environments.

The Theory Behind VR

Philosophically speaking, the objective of VR is to create an environment that is believable to the user, but which does not exist in the physical world. The understanding of the world, human reality, is derived ulti-mately from the senses. Humans have five major senses: sight, hearing, touch, smell, and taste. These senses provide the brain with information that enables people to understand their surroundings—what is termed the human reality. The most important sense for understanding the phys-ical world is sight, followed by sound and touch.

At the present time, computer technology has enabled the development of sophisticated means to stimulate the senses of sight and hearing. To a lesser degree, the technology for stimulating touch has also been developed. A virtual environment that the brain can easily interpret as being real is created when these technologies are integrated into a system where the sensory data that are produced are consistent with (i.e., conforms to) what has been observed in the physical world.

Anyone who has experienced motion sickness while sitting perfectly still and watching a plane fly in a 360-degree theater will attest to the fact that the brain can be decisively tricked through visual stimulus alone. Recognizing that a large part of human understanding of reality is based on visual stimulus has led significant effort in VR research to be devoted to visual-based stimulus such as image generation and animation.

Concepts such as perspective, reflection of light, texturing, and rota-tion of 3D images form the basis of constructing stationary images and provide people with a way to navigate through such images. These con-cepts are well understood and have been precisely defined by mathemati-cal equations. Manipulating these mathematical equations has allowed computers to generate images that are exceedingly real.

The next piece of the visual puzzle is animation, that is, making objects in the virtual world move. Animation is based on kinetics* and kinematics*. These fields of study are essentially concerned with how things move and react to forces.

A complementary technique that can be used to amplify the realism of a virtual word is called immersion. A user can be immersed in a virtual

* **fiber optics** transmission technology using long, thin strands of glass fiber; internal reflections in the fiber assure that light entering one end is transmitted to the other end with only small losses in intensity; used widely in transmitting digital information

* **haptic** pertaining to the sense of touch

* **kinetics** a branch of physics or chemistry concerned with the rate of change in chemical or physical systems

* **kinematics** a branch of physics and mechanical engineering that involves the study of moving bodies and particles

world by removing the conflicting stimulus associated with the physical world. In other words, it is easier for someone to imagine she is in a virtual world if she is only allowed to see that virtual world and nothing else. Immersion is what makes 360-degree theaters so realistic.

Applications

As with all technologies, the use of virtual reality is often limited only by the imagination of the user. In movies such as *Tron Legacy* (2010), *The Matrix Reloaded* (2003), and *The Matrix Revolutions* (2003), Hollywood shows a more sinister look at how VR might be abused. The series of *Matrix* movies, for instance, describes how the world has been turned into a virtual reality environment by intelligent machines. However, the ability to create realistic virtual environments has the potential to benefit society significantly. This stems from the fact that a virtual environment is a model of reality. Models typically do not contain every aspect of the thing they are modeling. What this means in the context of VR is that in a virtual environment, the rules of the physical world can be broken or bent!

For example, a pilot can learn to fly a commercial airliner in a virtual environment, without having to worry about experiencing the consequences associated with an actual crash. Fly-by-wire systems or new airplane designs can be tested without the cost or worry of crashing an aircraft. Surgeons can master complex operations without having to worry about accidentally killing a patient. The effects of a nuclear reactor meltdown can be studied without any risk to the environment. New designs for supertankers that minimize oil spillage in the event of a collision can be studied without the cost associated with physical testing.

There are also many military applications of VR technology. For instance, soldiers can simulate the conditions of combat, including the landscape, buildings, and inhabitants of a foreign land, as well as the sights and sounds of explosions and weapons, all without leaving the security and safety of their own training camp. Besides combat training, VR also has the potential of meeting many other defense-related needs. In 2010, the U.S. Defense Advanced Research Projects Agency (DARPA) announced funding opportunities to interested companies willing to develop VR-based therapies for troops traumatized by their wartime experiences. One application of VR would be for the treatment of post-traumatic stress syndrome (PTSD). The VR proposals form one segment of the larger Healing Heroes (HH) program designed to help meet the needs of returning troops and their families.

Another application employs VR technology to treat people with phobias and various other psychological problems. The physician exposes a patient to a virtual reality that introduces the phobia in a controlled manner. Patients are much more willing to try such therapy because they know it is not real, and the medical professional likes it because it is more convenient than traditional methods of treatment. Dr. Barbara Rothbaum, Emory University, and Dr. Larry Hodges, Georgia Institute of Technology, have pioneered the use of virtual reality environments for the treatment of people with phobias and other related conditions. The list of interesting and useful applications of VR—such as in military defense, medicine, entertainment, and scientific visualization—is long and growing rapidly.

▶ *See also* **Interactive Systems** • **Optical Technology** • **Simulation** • **Simulators** • **Virtual Reality In Education**

Resources

Books

Gutiérrez, Mario, Frédéric Vexo, and Daniel Thalmann. *Stepping into Virtual Reality.* New York: Springer, 2008.

Yang, Harrison Hao, and Steve Ci-Yin Yuen, eds. *Handbook of Research on Practices and Outcomes in Virtual Worlds and Environments.* Hershey, PA: Information Science Reference, 2012.

Web Sites

Healing Heroes Network. "About Us." http://www.healingheroes.org/about-us.html (accessed October 29, 2012).

How Stuff Works. "How Virtual Reality Works." http://electronics.howstuffworks.com/gadgets/other-gadgets/virtual-reality6.htm (accessed October 29, 2012).

von Neumann, John
Hungarian Computer Scientist and Mathematician
1903–1957

John Louis von Neumann was one of the great pioneers of computer science and mathematics during the twentieth century. Known for his concept of the stored computer program, he performed work that paved the way for the powerful and ubiquitous* electronic computers of the early twenty-first century. His work on the Institute for Advanced Studies (IAS) computers built the foundation for what is now known as the "von Neumann Architecture." This architecture resulted in the development of powerful supercomputer*s employed by government, universities, and other institutions.

Von Neumann was born December 28, 1903, in Budapest, Hungary, and died February 8, 1957, in Washington D.C. During his youth, he was often referred to as a prodigy, having published his first technical paper at the age of eighteen. He began attending the University of Budapest in 1921, where he studied chemistry, receiving his diploma in chemical engineering in 1925.

* **ubiquitous** to be commonly available everywhere

* **supercomputer** a very high performance computer, usually comprised of many processors and used for modeling and simulation of complex phenomena, like meteorology

John von Neumann. © *Stock Montage/ Getty Images.*

In 1930 von Neumann was invited to Princeton University in the United States, and he was one of the original professors when the university established the Institute for Advanced Studies in 1933. He recognized the importance of computers in the field of applied mathematics and other disciplines and was involved in several strategic government research projects during World War II. Indeed, one of the cornerstones of von Neumann's philosophy was to apply computers to fields of study that interested him. His work in the fields of statistics, ballistics, meteorology, hydrodynamics, and game theory was invaluable during World War II.

He contributed his scientific expertise to the Manhattan Project, the first attempt to develop an atomic bomb for military purposes. At the time, it was feared that Nazi Germany would be the first to develop and deploy the atomic bomb and thus win the war. Von Neumann played an important role as an adviser to the U.S. government, and his talent for finding solutions to complex problems proved invaluable on the projects with which he was involved. He also played an important part as a trusted conduit between groups of scientists working on separate projects that were sequestered from one another due to wartime needs of security. Thus, he brought together the talents of scientists working at Los Alamos National Laboratory, the scientists working on the Manhattan Project, and the scientists and engineers working on the first digital computer, Electronic Numerical Integrator and Computer (ENIAC).

After World War II, von Neumann continued to work on government research projects with military applications. His work with supercomputers helped perform the calculations necessary for developing the next generation hydrogen bomb. His ongoing research also led to increasingly capable supercomputers used by the U.S. national laboratories. These proved important for both military and peacetime scientific applications. Hired as a consultant by the IBM Corporation in the 1950s, von Neumann performed duties that involved reviewing proposed and ongoing projects for the company.

Von Neumann is also considered the father of "self replicating systems," systems that could reproduce themselves in a manner not greatly dissimilar from biological life. Von Neumann's concept consisted of two central components: a universal computer and a universal constructor. The universal computer contained the software that directed the universal constructor, and was essentially the central brain of the system. Guided by the universal computer, the constructor was a machine that was fully capable of creating copies of the universal computer and of itself. Once the constructor built another copy of itself, the control software was copied from the original universal computer.

The newly created constructors would then begin to execute the control software, and the process would repeat. The system as a whole is thus self-replicating. The self-replicating concept has been extended to constructors capable of building other objects, depending on the control software employed by the universal computer. The self-replicating machine concept has been explored by scientists at the National Aeronautics and Space Administration (NASA) for building inexpensive and self replicating probes for future space exploration.

One of von Neumann's most famous quotes illustrates the brilliance and depth of his intelligence and personality: "If people do not believe that mathematics is simple, it is only because they do not realize how complicated life is."

▶ *See also* **Babbage, Charles • Early Computers • Early Pioneers • Government Funding, Research • Hollerith, Herman • Turing, Alan M**

Resources

Books

Goldstine, Herman H. *The Computer from Pascal to von Neumann.* Princeton, NJ: Princeton University Press, 1972; reprint. 1993.

Vonneumann, Nicholas A. *John von Neumann as Seen by His Brother.* Meadowbrook, PA: N.A. Vonneumann, 1988.

The Manhattan Project

In 1939 scientist Albert Einstein wrote a letter to U.S. President Franklin Roosevelt encouraging government funding for atomic and nuclear fission research for use in atomic weapons. His letter was prompted by rumors that Adolf Hitler and the Nazis were close to creating an atomic bomb. Roosevelt agreed and placed General Leslie Groves and physicist J. Robert Oppenheimer in charge of the Manhattan Project two years later. The name "Manhattan Project" was the code word for the development of the atomic bomb. On July 16, 1945, the first atomic bomb was tested at the Trinity Site in New Mexico. The weapon was later used against the Japanese to end World War II.

WZ

Wireless Technology

Wireless technology provides the ability to communicate between two or more entities over distances without the use of wires or cables of any sort. This includes communications using radio frequency (RF) as well as infrared (IR) waves*.

The birth of wireless technology started with the discovery of electromagnetic waves by Heinrich Hertz (1857–1894). Guglielmo Marconi (1874–1937) established the very first commercial RF communications, the wireless telegraph, in the late 1890s—more than fifty years after the first commercial wired telegraph service that was demonstrated in 1832 by Samuel F. B. Morse (1791–1872). Marconi was also the first to transmit radio signals to a mobile receiver on ships in the early 1900s. Wireless technology has always been preceded by wired technology and is usually more expensive, but it has provided the additional advantage of mobility, allowing the user to receive and transmit information while on the move.

Another major thrust of wireless technology has been in the area of broadcast communications like radio, television, and direct broadcast satellite. A single wireless transmitter can send signals to several hundreds of thousands of receivers as long as they all receive the same information. Today, wireless technology encompasses such diverse communication devices as garage-door openers, baby monitors, walkie-talkies, and cellular telephones, as well as transmission systems such as point-to-point microwave links, wireless Internet service, and satellite communications.

Wireless technology involves transmitting electromagnetic signals over the air. Interference and obstacles that block RF signals are common problems with wireless technology. Wireless technology allows users to communicate simultaneously over the same medium without their signals interfering with one another. This is made possible because of two physical phenomena—the weakening of electromagnetic signals with distance, and the electromagnetic spectrum*. While listening to a radio station as one drives along a highway, one can observe how an RF or IR signal rapidly loses its strength as it travels away from the transmitter. Thus, two people can transmit at the same time if they are sufficiently far apart. If there are no obstacles, signals fall as the square of the distance. This is called freespace loss.

RF and IR signals can also be generated at different frequencies that do not interfere with each other. The range of frequencies is from a few cycles per second—called hertz (Hz)* in honor of the scientist who discovered electromagnetic waves—to trillions of hertz, and is called the electromagnetic spectrum. Visible light is included on this spectrum.

* **infrared (IR) waves** radiation in a band of the electromagnetic spectrum within the infrared range

* **electromagnetic spectrum** a range of frequencies over which electromagnetic radiation can be generated, transmitted, and received

* **hertz (Hz)** a unit of measurement of frequency, equal to one cycle per second; named in honor of German physicist Heinrich Hertz (1857-1894)

An engineer inspects wireless connectivity antennas. © *JOSEPH EID/AFP/Getty Images.*

The 3 kilohertz (kHz)* to 300 gigahertz (GHz)* frequency range is the RF spectrum. The IR spectrum corresponds to frequencies beyond 300 GHz. There are strict government regulations on the usage of chunks of the RF spectrum (called frequency bands*) in all nations of the world. In the United States, the Federal Communications Commission (FCC) decides who uses what frequency bands and for what purpose. They also set limitations on transmit power and on how much interference can be caused between frequency bands.

Frequency bands are either licensed or unlicensed. Licensed bands are owned by certain companies or facilities for specific purposes and cannot be used by anyone else. Unlicensed bands are free and anyone can use them, subject to certain etiquettes. Licensed bands are usually free from interference and more reliable, since there is control over who can transmit in them.

Numerous applications of wireless technology exist. There are wireless keyboards and mice for computers, wireless speakers and headphones, and wireless smart sensors now available on the market. In addition to point-to-point microwave links and broadcast radio, wireless appliances and devices are becoming increasingly common. Wireless technology is often employed to provide communications in places where it is difficult to run cables, for mobile communications, as extensions to wired communications, and for emergency deployment. Bluetooth is a new cable replacement wireless technology that can connect almost any appliance that can be networked to any other appliance—a digital camera to a laptop, or a coffee machine to the Internet, for example. Bluetooth applications include cordless telephones, laptops, and other devices.

Wireless technology can also be classified based on voice or data applications or based on mobility—fixed, stationary, portable, and mobile. Cordless and cellular telephones are common examples of voice applications. Cordless telephones operate in unlicensed bands, and cell phones in licensed bands, at frequencies around 1,000 megahertz (MHz)*. Satellites have been used for a long time to provide voice communications. Pagers are examples of data applications.

Today, it is also possible to access the Internet using wireless technology. Cellular digital packet data (CDPD) service is available for accessing the Internet in the same licensed frequency bands as cell phones. It is possible to buy a CDPD modem for handheld computers and palmtops and to browse the web and send e-mail without connecting via a cable to the Internet. Wireless local area networks (WLANs)* in unlicensed bands are also very popular, both in companies and for residential networking, for shared access to the Internet.

Modern fixed wireless technology applications include wireless local loops (WLLs) that provide local telephone service using rooftop antennas, and local multipoint distribution service (LMDS), a digital wireless transmission at 28 GHz that can provide several megabits per second of data for access to the Internet. Stationary wireless technology includes desktop computers that connect to the Internet using WLANs. Cordless phones, laptops, and palmtop computers with wireless connectivity fall into the portable category, while cell phones are the most common example of mobile wireless technology.

Wireless access to the Internet is expected to exceed wired access in the next few years, and the prospects for the future are exciting.

▶ *See also* **Network Topologies • Networks • World Wide Web**

Resources

Books

Carr, Joseph J. *Microwave & Wireless Communications Technology.* Boston: Butterworth-Heinemann, 1997.

Gralla, Preston. *How Wireless Works.* 2nd ed. Indianapolis, IN: Que Publishing, 2006.

Zuse, Konrad

German Engineer
1910–1995

Konrad Zuse was a German engineer who designed and built a binary computer during the 1930s. He is thought to have created the first functioning program-controlled computer, however his earliest efforts were destroyed during World War II. By the end of his life, Zuse had received

* **megahertz (MHz)** a unit or measure of frequency, equivalent to a million (or 10^6) hertz, or cycles per second

* **Wireless local area networks (WLANs)** an interconnected network of computers that uses radio and/or infrared communication channels, rather than cables

Konrad Zuse holding piece of his Z1 computer. © *AP Images/KARSTEN THIELKER.*

* **vacuum tube** an electronic device constructed of a sealed glass tube containing metal elements in a vacuum; used to control electrical signals

* **electromagnetic relays** switches that have a high current carrying capacity, which are opened and closed by an electromagnet

* **punched card** a paper card with punched holes which give instructions to a computer in order to encode program instructions and data

many honors for his contributions to the development of the computer, and he was recognized as one of the pioneers of electromechanical computing.

Zuse was born in Berlin, Germany, in 1910. During his youth he showed talent in art and engineering. As an artist, he created block prints, drawings, and cartoons; as an engineer, he built mechanical devices such as grab cranes and model train rail networks. He graduated from high school at the age of sixteen and entered the Technical University of Berlin, having made the decision to study civil engineering. While he was a university student, he built a vending machine that delivered selected items, accepted money, and returned change.

Zuse completed his degree in 1935 and worked for a brief time as a structural engineer for the Henschel Aircraft Company. He left this position to work independently on building a computer. His parents' living room served as his laboratory, his assistants were unpaid college friends, and his funding was raised from friends and family members. His goal was to create a mechanical calculating machine based on a binary system rather than on the decimal system used in calculators. The machine would consist of a memory unit and an arithmetic unit, and it would be programmable.

Zuse's Z1 computer was operational by 1938. Helmut Schreyer, a friend and electronic engineer, suggested replacing the mechanical relay system with vacuum tube*s and telephone relay switches to shorten the processing time. Zuse rejected the idea but considered using the telephone relay switches. The design of the Z2 incorporated this idea.

In 1939 Adolf Hitler and the Nazis invaded Poland, beginning World War II. The war interrupted Zuse's work and he was soon drafted into the German army. To no avail, both Zuse and Schreyer tried to interest the German military in the computer project. However, Zuse was transferred from active duty to work as a structural engineer for Henschel Aircraft. His assignment was related to the development of unmanned flying bombs, or cruise missiles. This transfer allowed him time to complete construction of the Z2, which used telephone relays for the arithmetic unit. In 1940 Zuse successfully demonstrated the Z2 to the German Aeronautics Research Institute or DLV.

As a result, he received partial funding for the next generation model, the Z3, which was constructed from recycled materials. Once again he relied on the support of family and friends. The telephone relays were used equipment rescued by associates who worked for the state telephone and postal system. The Z3 used electromagnetic relays* for the memory and arithmetic units, was based on a binary number system, and was programmable. Discarded film strips were used in place of punched card*s for input. The Z3 was destroyed during a bombing raid over Berlin.

Construction of the Z4 began in 1942. This model was moved from Berlin to southern Germany when the Allied bombing became intense. At the end of the war in 1945, Zuse, his family, and the Z4 were refugees in

Hinterstein, a small alpine village in southern Germany. For the next two years Zuse worked on theoretical problems, developing Plankalkül, an algorithmic language, and formalizing the game of chess. To support his family, he painted and sold alpine scenes to vacationing American troops.

In 1947 Zuse and Harro Stucken, an engineer from the Henschel Aircraft Company, founded Zuse Engineering Company to build computers for science and industry. Later the company became ZUSE KG. The company contracted with Remington Rand to build punched card devices. In 1950 the company leased the Z4 to the Swiss Federal Institute of Technology, where it remained in use until 1955. The company's first German contract was with Leitz Camera to build computers to determine lens specifications.

As the company grew, Zuse began to receive honorary degrees and awards for his work. In 1962 Howard H. Aiken, who designed the MARK I computer (the first American-built programmable computing system) acknowledged Zuse's claim to being one of the first to build a program-controlled computer. During this time a copy of model Z3 was built for display in the German Museum. By the late 1960s the company had been sold to Seimans, and Zuse turned his attention to other areas. He continued to work on problems related to computers and developed a prototype* for a CAD, or computer-aided design, machine.

The claim that Zuse built the first computer will remain unresolved, due in part to the destruction of both the Z1 and the Z3 computers in wartime bombings. What is clear, however, is that he developed his machines without knowledge of or interaction with others in the field, without proper funding, and using scavenged materials while always in danger from the war. At the time of his death in 1995, he had gained recognition for his contribution to computer science.

▶ *See also* **Early Computers • Early Pioneers**

Resources

Books

Zuse, Konrad. *The Computer: My Life.* New York: Springer-Verlag, 2010.

Working Independently

When Konrad Zuse began his experiments developing computer technology, he was unaware of the work done by Charles Babbage more than 100 years earlier. Babbage envisioned the Analytical Engine, an early calculating machine. Zuse ultimately carried on that work.

* **prototype** a working model or experimental investigation of proposed systems under development

Glossary

· ·

3D printing a manufacturing process in which machines lay down successive layers of materials to create three-dimensional products from digital information. Also known as additive manufacturing.

4G shorthand for fourth generation mobile communication and mobile Internet standards, including LTE and Mobile WiMAX networks.

abacus an ancient counting device that probably originated in Babylon around 2400 BCE.

acuity sharpness or keenness, especially when used to describe vision.

additive manufacturing an additive manufacturing process in which machines lay down successive layers of materials to create three-dimensional products from digital information. Also known as 3D printing.

address bus a collection of electrical signals used to transmit the address of a memory location or input/output port in a computer.

aerodynamics the science and engineering of systems that are capable of flight.

agents systems (software programs and/or computing machines) that can act on behalf of another, or on behalf of a human.

aggregate a numerical summation of multiple individual scores.

ailerons control surfaces on the trailing edges of the wings of an aircraft—used to manage roll control.

ALGOL a language developed by the ALGOL committee for scientific applications—acronym for ALGOrithmic Language.

algorithm a rule or procedure used to solve a mathematical problem—most often described as a sequence of steps.

all-points-addressable mode a technique for organizing graphics devices where all points (pixels) on the screen are individually accessible to a running program.

alpha beta pruning a technique that under certain conditions offers an optimal way to search through data structures called "trees."

alphanumeric a character set which is the union of the set of alphabetic characters and the set of single digit numbers.

ambient pertaining to the surrounding atmosphere or environment.

ambiguity the quality of doubtfulness or uncertainty; often subject to multiple interpretations.

amortized phasing out something in until it is gradually extinguished, like a mortgage loan.

amplitude the size or magnitude of an electrical signal.

analog a quantity (often an electrical signal) that is continuous in time and amplitude.

analogous a relationship of logical similarity between two or more objects.

analytic simulation modeling of systems by using mathematical equations (often differential equations) and programming a computer with them to simulate the behavior of the real system.

Analytical Engine Charles Babbage's vision of a programmable mechanical computer.

animatronics the animation (movement) of something by the use of electronic motors, drives, and controls.

anthropomorphic having human form, or generally resembling human appearance.

anti-aliasing introducing shades of gray or other intermediate shades around an image to make the edge appear to be smoother.

app short for application or application software, apps are software features designed to perform specific tasks or improve the user interface with Internet-based resources in a mobile operating system. Apps are common to smartphones, tablets, and other Internet-enabled portable devices.

applet a program component that requires extra support at run time from a browser or run-time environment in order to execute.

approximation an estimate.

arc tangent the circular trigonometric function that is the inverse of the tangent function; values range from $-\Pi/2$ to $\Pi/2$.

artificial intelligence (AI) a branch of computer science dealing with creating computer hardware and software to mimic the way people think and perform practical tasks.

ASCII an acronym that stands for American Standard Code for Information Interchange; assigns a unique 8-bit binary number to every letter of the alphabet, the digits (0 to 9), and most keyboard symbols.

assembler a program that translates human readable assembly language programs to machine readable instructions.

assembly language the natural language of a central processing unit (CPU); often classed as a low level language.

asynchronous events that have no systematic relationship to one another in time.

attenuation the reduction in magnitude (size or amplitude) of a signal that makes a signal weaker.

authentication the act of ensuring that an object or entity is what it is intended to be.

automata theory the analytical (mathematical) treatment and study of automated systems.

automaton an object or being that has a behavior that can be modeled or explained completely by using automata theory.

autonomous self-governing, or being able to exist independently.

autonomy the capability of acting in a self-governing manner; being able to exist independently or with some degree of independence.

axioms statements that are taken to be true, the foundation of a theory.

Bakelite an insulating material used in synthetic goods, including plastics and resins.

ballistics the science and engineering of the motion of projectiles of various types, including bullets, bombs, and rockets.

bandwidth a measure of the frequency component of a signal or the capacity of a communication channel to carry signals.

bar code a graphical number representation system where alphanumeric characters are represented by vertical black and white lines of varying width.

base-2 a number system in which each place represents a power of 2 larger than the place to its right (binary).

base-8 a number system in which each place represents a power of 8 larger than the place to its right (octal).

base-10 a number system in which each place represents a power of 10 larger than the place to its right (decimal).

base-16 a number system in which each place represents a power of 16 larger than the place to its right (hexadecimal).

batch processing an approach to computer utilization that queues non-interactive programs and runs them one after another.

Bayesian networks structures that describe systems in which there is a degree of uncertainty; used in automated decision making.

Bernoulli numbers the sums of powers of consecutive integers; named after Swiss mathematician Jacques Bernoulli (1654–1705).

binary existing in only two states, such as "on" or "off," "one" or "zero."

binary code a representation of information that permits only two states, such as "on" or "off," "one" or "zero."

binary coded decimal (BCD) an ANSI/ISO standard encoding of the digits 0 to 9 using 4 binary bits; the encoding only uses 10 of the available 16 4-bit combinations.

binary digit a single bit, 1 or 0.

binary number system a number system in which each place represents a power of 2 larger than the place on its right (base-2).

binary system a machine or abstraction that uses binary codes.

binomial theorem a theorem giving the procedure by which a binomial expression may be raised to any power without using successive multiplications.

bit a single binary digit, 1 or 0—a contraction of Binary digIT; the smallest unit for storing data in a computer.

bit mapped display a computer display that uses a table of binary bits in memory to represent the image that is projected onto the screen.

bit maps images comprised of bit descriptions of the image, in black and white or color, such that the colors can be represented by the two values of a binary bit.

bit rate the rate at which binary bits can be processed or transferred per unit time, in a system (often a computer communications system).

bit serial mode a method of transferring binary bits one after another in a sequence or serial stream.

bitstream a serialized collection of bits; usually used in transfer of bits from one system to another.

Boolean algebra a system developed by George Boole that deals with the theorems of undefined symbols and axioms concerning those symbols.

Boolean logic a system, developed by George Boole, which treats abstract objects (such as sets or classes) as algebraic quantities; Boole applied his mathematical system to the study of classical logic.

Boolean operators fundamental logical operations (for example "and" and "or") expressed in a mathematical form.

broadband access a term given to denote high bandwidth services.

browsers programs that permit a user to view and navigate through documents, most often hypertext documents.

bugs errors in program source code.

bus a group of related signals that form an interconnecting pathway between two or more electronic devices.

bus topology a particular arrangement of buses that constitutes a designed set of pathways for information transfer within a computer.

byte a group of eight binary digits; represents a single character of text.

C a programming language developed for the UNIX operating system; it is designed to run on most machines and with most operating systems.

cache a small sample of a larger set of objects, stored in a way that makes them accessible.

calculus a method of dealing mathematically with variables that may be changing continuously with respect to each other.

Callback modems security techniques that collect telephone numbers from authorized users on calls and then dial the users to establish the connections.

capacitates fundamental electrical components used for storing electrical charges.

capacitive touch one of the two primary types of touch screen technology, it detects touches utilizing the conductive electrical properties of human skin. This systems, common on many popular smartphones, allows for user control of the device with very light touches.

capacitor a fundamental electrical component used for storing electrical charge.

carpal tunnel syndrome a repetitive stress injury that can lead to pain, numbness, tingling, and loss of muscle control in the hands and wrists.

cartography map-making.

cathode ray tube (CRT) a glass enclosure that projects images by directing a beam of electrons onto the back of a screen.

cellular automata a collection or array of objects that are programmed identically to interact with one another.

cellular neural networks (CNN) a neural network topology that uses multidimensional array structures comprised of cells that work together in localized groups.

central processing unit (CPU) the part of a computer that performs computations and controls and coordinates other parts of the computer.

certificate a unique electronic document that is used to assist authentication.

chaos theory a branch of mathematics dealing with differential equations having solutions which are very sensitive to initial conditions.

checksum a number that is derived from adding together parts of an electronic message before it is dispatched; it can be used at the receiver to check against message corruption.

chromatic dispersion the natural distortion of pulses of light as they move through an optical network; it results in data corruption.

cipher a code or encryption method.

client a program or computer often managed by a human user, that makes requests to another computer for information.

client/server technology computer systems that are structured using clients (usually human-driven computers) to access information stored (often remotely) on other computers known as servers.

cloud computing the use over a network of remote hardware and software computing resources.

cloud storage a remote network of computing resources accessible over the Internet that hosts user files. Also called a cyberlocker or file hosting service and popular as a location for remote computer back-ups or storing media, cloud storage allows users to access files stored "in the cloud" from other computers, tablets, or smartphones.

coaxial cable a cable with an inner conducting core, a dielectric material and an outer sheath that is designed for high frequency signal transmission.

cognitive pertaining to the concepts of knowing or perceiving.

collocation the act of placing elements or objects in a specific order.

commodity raw material or service marketed prior to being used.

compiled a program that is translated from human-readable code to binary code that a central processing unit (CPU) can understand.

compiled executable code the binary code that a central processing unit (CPU) can understand; the product of the compilation process.

compilers programs that translate human-readable high-level computer languages to machine-readable code.

computer-aided design (CAD) the use of computers to replace traditional drawing instruments and tools for engineering or architectural design.

computer-assisted tomography the use of computers in assisting with the management of X-ray images.

computer peripheral a device that is connected to a computer to support its operation; for example, a keyboard or a disk drive unit.

concatenates the joining together of two elements or objects; for example, words are formed by concatenating letters.

concentric circles circles that have coincident centers.

conceptualization a creative process that is directed at envisaging a structure or collection of relationships within components of a complex system.

concurrency control the management and coordination of several actions that occur simultaneously; for example, several computer programs running at once.

concurrent pertaining to simultaneous activities, for example simultaneous execution of many computer programs.

configuration files special disk files containing information that can be used to tell running programs about system settings.

cookie a small text file that a Web site can place on a computer's hard drive to collect information about a user's browsing activities or to activate an online shopping cart to keep track of purchases.

copyrights the legal rules and regulations concerning the copying and redistribution of documents.

cord cutting a term that refers to forging traditional cable and satellite-based television subscription services in favor of online streaming media.

cosine a trigonometric function of an angle, defined as the ratio of the length of the adjacent side of a right-angled triangle divided by the length of its hypotenuse.

counterfeiting the act of knowingly producing non-genuine objects, especially in relation to currency.

crawls severe weather warnings that are broadcast on the bottom of TV screens.

creative commons licensing a free, easy-to-understand, rights management scheme that allows creators to reserve or waive some of their intellectual property rights in the interest of sharing and using works in public forums such as the Internet.

cross-platform pertaining to a program that can run on many different computer types (often called hardware platforms).

CRT the acronym for cathode ray tube, which is a glass enclosure that projects images by directing a beam of electrons onto the back of a screen.

cryptanalysis the act of attempting to discover the algorithm used to encrypt a message.

cryptanalyst   a person or agent who attempts to discover the algorithm used to encrypt a message.

cryptography   the science of understanding codes and ciphers and their application.

cryptosystem   a system or mechanism that is used to automate the processes of encryption and decryption.

cuneiform   in the shape of a wedge.

cybercafe   a shop, cafe, or meeting place where users can rent a computer for a short time to access the Internet.

cybernetics   a unified approach to understanding the behavior of machines and animals developed by Norbert Wiener (1894–1964).

cycloids   pertaining to circles, in either a static way or in a way that involves movement.

dark fiber   a fiber optic network that exists but is not actively in service, hence the darkness.

data mining   a technique of automatically obtaining information from databases that is normally hidden or not obvious.

data partitioning   a technique applied to databases (but not restricted to them) which organizes data objects into related groups.

data reduction technique   an approach to simplifying data, e.g. summarization.

data warehousing   to implement an informational database used to store shared data.

de facto   as is.

de jure   strictly according to the law.

debug   the act of trying to trace, identify, and then remove errors in program source code.

decimal system   a number system in which each place represents a power of 10 larger than the place to its right (base-10).

decision trees   classifiers in which a sequence of tests are made to decide the class label to assign to an unknown data item; the sequence of.

deformations   mechanical systems where a structure is physically misshapen, e.g., dented.

degrade   to reduce quality or performance of a system.

delimiters   special symbols that mark the beginnings and/or endings of other groups of symbols (for example to mark out comments in program source code).

demographics   the study of the statistical data pertaining to a population.

densities   measures of the density of a material; defined as the mass of a sample of material, divided by its volume.

deregulation   the lowering of restrictions, rules, or regulations pertaining to an activity or operation (often commercial).

die   the silicon chip that is the heart of integrated circuit fabrication; the die is encased in a ceramic or plastic package to make the completed integrated circuit (IC).

dielectric   a material that exhibits insulating properties, as opposed to conducting properties.

Difference Engine   a mechanical calculator designed by Charles Babbage that automated the production of mathematical tables by using the method of differences.

differential analyzer   a computer constructed in the early 1930s by Vannevar Bush at Massachusetts Institute of Technology (MIT); it solved differential equations by mechanical integration.

digital   a quantity that can exist only at distinct levels, not having values in between these levels (for example, binary).

digital certificates certificates used in authentication that contain encrypted digital identification information.

digital divide imaginary line separating those who can access digital information from those who cannot.

digital library distributed access to collections of digital information.

digital media receiver any device that connects to a network to locate, download, or stream digital media files from a server so that users can broadcast them to their television. They are also known as media streaming devices or digital media hubs.

digital signature identifier used to authenticate the sender of an electronic message or the signer of an electronic document.

digital subscriber line (DSL) a technology that permits high speed voice and data communications over public telephone networks; it requires the use of a DSL modem.

digital subscriber loop (DSL) the enabling of high-speed digital data transfer over standard telephone cables and systems in conjunction with normal telephone speech data.

digital watermarks special data structures permanently embedded into a program or other file type, which contain information about the author and the program.

digitizes converts analog information into a digital form for processing by a computer.

diode a semiconductor device that forces current flow in a conductor to be in one direction only, also known as a rectifier.

diode tube an obsolete form of diode that was made of metal elements in a sealed and evacuated glass tube.

direction buttons buttons on a program with a graphical user interface that provide a way of navigating through information or documents.

discrete composed of distinct elements.

disintermediation a change in business practice whereby consumers elect to cut out intermediary agencies and deal directly with a provider or vendor.

distance learning the form of education where the instructor and students are separated by either location or time (or both), usually mediated by some electronic communication mechanism.

distributed denial of service (DDoS) an attack in which large numbers of messages are directed to send network traffic to a target computer, overloading it or its network connection; typically, the attacking computers have been subverted.

distributed systems computer systems comprising many individual computers that are interconnected and act in concert to complete operations.

documentation literature in a human readable form that is referred to in support of using a computer or computer system.

domain a region in which a particular element or object exists or has influence; (math) the inputs to a function or relation.

doping a step used in the production of semiconductor materials where charged particles are embedded into the device so as to tailor its operational characteristics.

dot.com a common term used to describe an Internet-based commercial company or organization.

dragged to have been moved by the application of an external pulling force; quite often occurring in graphical user interfaces when objects are moved with a mouse.

DRAM the acronym for Dynamic Random Access Memory; high density, low cost and low speed memory devices used in most computer systems.

driver a special program that manages the sequential execution of several other programs; a part of an operating system that handles input/output devices.

drop-down menu a menu on a program with a graphical user interface that produces a vertical list of items when activated.

dumb terminal a keyboard and screen connected to a distant computer without any processing capability.

duplex simultaneous two-directional communication over a single communication channel.

dynamic changing; possessing volatility.

dynamic links logical connections between two objects that can be modified if the objects themselves move or change state.

EBCDIC the acronym for Extended Binary Coded Decimal Interchange Code, which assigns a unique 8-bit binary number to every letter of the alphabet, the digits (0-9), and most keyboard symbols.

e-books short for electronic books; books available for downloading onto an e-book reader.

e-reader an electronic device that displays and stores books and other texts.

egress to move out of an object, system, or environment.

electromagnetic a piece of metal that becomes magnetic only when electricity is applied to it; in general, the more electricity applied to metal, the stronger its magnetism.

electromagnetic relays switches that have a high current carrying capacity, which are opened and closed by an electromagnet.

electromagnetic spectrum a range of frequencies over which electromagnetic radiation can be generated, transmitted, and received.

embedded computers computers that do not have human user orientated I/O devices; they are directly contained within other machines.

embedded systems another term for "embedded computers"; computers that do not have human user orientated input/output devices; they are directly contained within other machines.

emoticons symbols or key combinations used in electronic correspondence to convey emotions.

enciphered encrypted or encoded; a mathematical process that disguises the content of messages transmitted.

encryption also known as encoding; a mathematical process that disguises the content of messages transmitted.

end-effector the end piece of a robotic arm that can receive various types of grippers and tools.

end users computer users.

enterprise information system a system of client and server computers that can be used to manage all of the tasks required to manage and run a large organization.

entropy a measure of the state of disorder or randomness in a system.

ephemeris a record showing positions of astronomical objects and artificial satellites in a time-ordered sequence.

ergonomic being of suitable geometry and structure to permit effective or optimal human user interaction with machines.

esoteric relating to a specialized field of endeavor that is characterized by its restricted size.

ether a highly volatile liquid solvent; also, the far regions of outer space.

ethernets a networking technology for mini and microcomputer systems consisting of network interface cards and interconnecting coaxial cables; invented in the 1970s by Xerox corporation.

Euclidean geometry the study of points, lines, angles, polygons, and curves confined to a plane.

expert system a computer system that uses a collection of rules to exhibit behavior which mimics the behavior of a human expert in some area.

fiber optics transmission technology using long, thin strands of glass fiber; internal reflections in the fiber assure that light entering one end is transmitted to the other end with only small losses in intensity; used widely in transmitting digital information.

field searching a strategy in which a search is limited to a particular field; in a search engine, a search may be limited to a particular domain name or date, narrowing the scope of searchable items and helping to eliminate the chance of retrieving irrelevant data.

file transfer protocol (FTP) a communications protocol used to transfer files.

filter queries queries used to select subsets from a data collection, e.g., all documents with a creation date later than 01/01/2013.

firewall a special purpose network computer or software that is used to ensure that no access is permitted to a sub-network unless authenticated and authorized.

firing tables precalculated tables that can give an artillery gunner the correct allowances for wind conditions and distance by dictating the elevation and deflection of a gun.

flashdrive a small, typically portable, solid state drive (SSD) utilizing flash memory for storing or transferring computer data.

floating point operations numerical operations involving real numbers where in achieving a result, the number of digits to the left or right of the decimal point can change.

flowcharts techniques for graphically describing the sequencing and structure of program source code.

fluid dynamics the science and engineering of the motion of gases and liquids.

Freedom of Information Act (FOIA) permits individuals to gain access to records and documents that are in the possession of the government.

freon hydrocarbon based gases used as refrigerants and as pressurants in aerosols.

frequency bands ranges of signal frequencies that are of particular interest in a given application.

frequency modulation a technique whereby a signal is transformed so that it is represented by another signal with a frequency that varies in a way related to the original signal.

full-text indexing a search engine feature in which every word in a document, significant or insignificant, is indexed and retrievable through a search.

fuzzy logic models human reasoning by permitting elements to have partial membership to a set; derived from fuzzy set theory.

gallium arsenide a chemical used in the production of semiconductor devices; chemical symbol GaAs.

gates fundamental building blocks of digital and computer based electric circuits that perform logical operations; for example logical AND, logical OR.

Gaussian classifiers classifiers constructed on the assumption that the feature values of data will follow a Gaussian distribution.

gbps acronym for gigabits per second; a binary data transfer rate that corresponds to a thousand million (billion, or 109) bits per second.

Geographic Information Systems (GIS) computing systems that capture, compare, create, analyze, organize, and display geographical data in a searchable and visually useful ways.

geometric relating to the principles of geometry, a branch of mathematics related to the properties and relationships of points, lines, angles, surfaces, planes, and solids.

germanium a chemical often used as a high performance semiconductor material; chemical symbol Ge.

gestural interface technologies designed to use mathematical algorithms to interpret or respond to human gestures.

GIF animation a technique using Graphic Interchange Format where many images are overlaid on one another and cycled through a sequence to produce an animation.

GIF image the acronym for Graphic Interchange Format where a static image is represented by binary bits in a data file.

gigabit networking the construction and use of a computer network that is capable of transferring information at rates in the gigahertz range.

gigabytes units of measure equivalent to a thousand million (billion, or 109) bytes.

gigahertz (GHz) a unit or measure of frequency, equivalent to a thousand million (billion, or 109) hertz, or cycles per second.

Global Positioning System (GPS) a method of locating a point on the Earth's surface that uses received signals transmitted from satellites to accurately calculate position.

granularity a description of the level of precision that can be achieved in making measurements of a quantity; for example coarse granularity means inexpensive but imprecise measurements.

graphical user interface (GUI) an interface that allows computers to be operated through pictures (icons) and mouse-clicks, rather than through text and typing.

groupware a software technology common in client/server systems whereby many users can access and process data at the same time.

gyros a contraction of gyroscopes; a mechanical device that uses one or more spinning discs which resist changes to their position in space.

half tones black and white dots of certain sizes, which provide a perception of shades of gray.

ham radio a legal (or licensed) amateur radio.

haptic pertaining to the sense of touch.

Harvard Cyclotron a specialized machine (cyclotron) developed in 1948 at Harvard University; it is used to carry out experiments in sub-atomic physics and medicine.

head-mounted displays (HMD) helmets worn by a virtual reality (VR) participant that include speakers and screens for each eye, which display three-dimensional images.

hertz (Hz) a unit of measurement of frequency, equal to one cycle per second; named in honor of German physicist Heinrich Hertz.

heuristic a procedure that serves to guide investigation but that has not been proven.

hexadecimal a number system in which each place represents a power of 16 larger than the place to its right (base-16).

high-bandwidth a communication channel that permits many signals of differing frequencies to be transmitted simultaneously.

high precision/high recall a phenomenon that occurs during a search when all the relevant documents are retrieved with no unwanted ones.

high precision/low recall a phenomenon that occurs when a search yields a small set of hits; although each one may be highly relevant to the search topic, some relevant documents are missed.

high-speed data links digital communications systems that permit digital data to be reliably transferred at high speed.

hoaxes false claims or assertions, sometimes made unlawfully in order to extort money.

holistic looking at the entire system, rather than just its parts.

hydraulic motion being powered by a pressurized liquid (such as water or oil), supplied through tubes or pipes.

hydrologic relating to water.

hyperlinks connections between electronic documents that permit automatic browsing transfer at the point of the link.

Hypertext Markup Language (HTML) an encoding scheme for text data that uses special tags in the text to signify properties to the viewing program (browser) like links to other documents or document parts.

Hypertext Transfer Protocol (HTTP) a simple connectionless communications protocol developed for the electronic transfer (serving) of HTML documents.

I/O the acronym for input/output; used to describe devices that can accept input data to a computer and to other devices that can produce output.

I/O devices devices that can accept "input" data to a computer and to other devices that can produce "output."

icon a small image that is used to signify a program or operation to a user.

illiquid lacking in liquid assets; or something that is not easily transferable into currency.

ImmersaDesks large 4 x 5 foot screens that allow for stereoscopic visualization; the 3-D computer graphics create the illusion of a virtual environment.

ImmersaWalls large-scale, flat screen visualization environments that include passive and active multi-projector displays of 3-D images.

immersive involved in something totally.

in-band pertaining to elements or objects that are within the limits of a certain Local Area Network (LAN).

inference a suggestion or implication of something based on other known related facts and conclusions.

information theory a branch of mathematics and engineering that deals with the encoding, transmission, reception, and decoding of information.

infrared (IR) waves radiation in a band of the electromagnetic spectrum within the infrared range.

infrastructure the foundation or permanent installation necessary for a structure or system to operate.

ingot a formed block of metal (often cast) used to facilitate bulk handling and transportation.

ingress the act of entering a system or object.

init method a special function in an object oriented program that is automatically called to initialize the elements of an object when it is created.

input/output (I/O) used to describe devices that can accept input data to a computer and to other devices that can produce output.

Inquisition the establishment of a religious court (1478–1834) where Christians as well as non-Christians were prosecuted for heresy.

intangible a concept to which it is difficult to apply any form of analysis; something which is not perceived by the sense of touch.

integrated circuit a circuit with the transistors, resistors, and other circuit elements etched into the surface of a single chip of semiconducting material, usually silicon.

integrated modem a modem device that is built into a computer, rather than being attached as a separate peripheral.

intellectual property the acknowledgement that an individual's creativity and innovation can be owned in the same way as physical property.

interconnectivity the ability of more than one physical computer to operate with one or more other physical computers; interconnectivity is usually accomplished by means of network wiring, cable, or telephone lines.

interface a boundary or border between two or more objects or systems; also a point of access.

Internet Protocol (IP) a method of organizing information transfer between computers; the IP was specifically designed to offer low-level support to Transmission Control Protocol (TCP).

Internet Service Provider (ISP) a commercial enterprise which offers paying subscribers access to the Internet (usually via modem) for a fee.

interpolation estimating data values between known points but the values in between are not and are therefore estimated.

intranet an interconnected network of computers that operates like the Internet, but is restricted in size to a company or organization.

ionosphere a region of the upper atmosphere (above about 60,000 meters or 196,850 feet) where the air molecules are affected by the sun's radiation and influence electromagnetic wave propagation.

isosceles triangle a triangle that has two sides of equivalent length (and therefore two angles of the same size).

iterative a procedure that involves repetitive operations before being completed.

Jacquard's Loom a weaving loom, developed by Joseph-Marie Jacquard ((1752–1834), controlled by punched cards; identified as one of the earliest examples of programming automation.

Java applets applets written in the Java programming language and executed with the support of a Java Virtual Machine (JVM) or a Java enabled browser.

joysticks the main controlling levers of small aircraft; models of these can be connected to computers to facilitate playing interactive games.

JPEG (Joint Photographic Experts Group) organization that developed a standard for encoding image data in a compressed format to save space.

k-nearest neighbors a classifier that assigns a class label for an unknown data item by looking at the class labels of the nearest items in the training data.

Kbps a measure of digital data transfer per unit time—one thousand (kilo, K) bits per second.

keywords words that are significant in some context or topic (often used in searching).

kilohertz (kHz) a unit or measure of frequency, equivalent to a thousand (or 103) hertz, or cycles per second.

kinematics a branch of physics and mechanical engineering that involves the study of moving bodies and particles.

kinetics a branch of physics or chemistry concerned with the rate of change in chemical or physical systems.

labeled data a data item whose class assignment is known independent of the classifier being constructed.

lambda calculus important in the development of programming languages, a specialized logic using substitutions that was developed by Alonzo Church (1903–1995).

LEDs the acronym for Light Emitting Diode; a diode that emits light when passing a current and used as an indicating lamp.

lexical analyzer a portion of a compiler that is responsible for checking the program source code produced by a programmer for proper words and symbols.

Library of Congress Classification the scheme by which the Library of Congress organizes classes of books and documents.

light-emitting diode (LED) a discrete electronic component that emits visible light when permitting current to flow in a certain direction; often used as an indicating lamp.

linear pertaining to a type of system that has a relationship between its outputs and its inputs that can be graphed as a straight line.

Linux operating system an open source UNIX operating system that was originally created by Linus Torvalds in the early 1990s.

liquid crystal display (LCD) a type of crystal that changes its level of transparency when subjected to an electric current; used as an output device on a computer.

local area network (LAN) a high-speed computer network that is designed for users who are located near each other.

logarithm the power to which a certain number called the base is to be raised to produce a particular number.

logic a branch of philosophy and mathematics that uses provable rules to apply deductive reasoning.

lossy a nonreversible way of compressing digital images; making images take up less space

by permanently removing parts that cannot be easily seen anyway.

low precision/high recall a phenomenon that occurs during a search when a large set of results are retrieved, including many relevant and irrelevant documents.

lumens a unit of measure of light intensity.

magnetic tape a way of storing programs and data from computers; tapes are generally slow and prone to deterioration over time but are inexpensive.

mainframe large computer used by businesses and government agencies to process massive amounts of data; generally faster and more powerful than desktop computers but usually requiring specialized software.

malicious code program instructions that are intended to carry out malicious or hostile actions; e.g., deleting a user's files.

mammogram an X-ray image of the breast, used to detect signs of possible cancer.

Manhattan Project the U.S. project designed to create the world's first atomic bomb.

mass spectrometers instruments that can identify elemental particles in a sample by examining the frequencies of the particles that comprise the sample.

mass spectrometry the process of identifying the compounds or elemental particles within a substance.

media streaming device a device that enables users to connect to a network or server and view digital media files on their television; also known as a digital media receiver or digital media hub.

megahertz (MHz) a unit or measure of frequency, equivalent to a million (or 106) hertz, or cycles per second.

memex a device that can be used to store personal information, notes, and records that permits managed access at high speed; a hypothetical creation of Vannevar Bush.

menu label the text or icon on a menu item in a program with a graphical user interface.

metadata data about data, such as the date and time created.

meteorologists people who have studied the science of weather and weather forecasting.

metropolitan area network (MAN) a high-speed interconnected network of computers spanning entire cities.

microampere a unit of measure of electrical current that is one-millionth (10^{-6}) amperes.

microchip a common term for a semiconductor integrated circuit device.

microcomputer a computer that is small enough to be used and managed by one person alone; often called a personal computer.

microprocessor the principle element in a computer; the component that understands how to carry out operations under the direction of the running program (CPU).

millisecond a time measurement indicating one-thousandth (or 10^{-3}) of a second.

milliwatt a power measurement indicating one-thousandth (or 10^{-3}) of a watt.

minicomputers computers midway in size between a desktop computer and a mainframe computer; most modern desktops are much more powerful than the older minicomputers.

minimax algorithm an approach to developing an optimal solution to a game or contest where two opposing systems are aiming at mutually exclusive goals.

Minitel network used in France that preceded the Internet, connecting most French homes, businesses, cultural organizations, and government offices.

mnemonic a device or process that aids one's memory.

Mobile device management (MDM) software that aids in standardizing settings, managing programs, protecting confidential information, and securing mobile devices.

mobile operating system (MOS) the software that allows smartphones, tablets, other portable devices to run programs and apps.

modalities classifications of the truth of a logical proposition or statement, or characteristics of an object or entity.

modem the contraction of MOdulator DEModulator; a device which converts digital signals into signals suitable for transmission over analog channels, like telephone lines.

modulation a technique whereby signals are translated to analog so that the resultant signal can be more easily transmitted and received by other elements in a communication system.

modules a generic term that is applied to small elements or components that can be used in combination to build an operational system.

molecular modeling a technique that uses high performance computer graphics to represent the structure of chemical compounds.

motherboard the part of the computer that holds vital hardware, such as the processors, memory, expansion slots, and circuitry.

MPEG (Motion Picture Coding Experts Group) an encoding scheme for data files that contain motion pictures—it is lossy in the same way as JPEG (Joint Photographic Experts Group) encoding.

multiplexes operations in ATM communications whereby data cells are blended into one continuous stream at the transmitter and then separated again at the receiver.

multiplexor a complex device that acts as a multi-way switch for analog or digital signals.

multitasking the ability of a computer system to execute more than one program at the same time; also known as multiprogramming.

mylar a synthetic film, invented by the DuPont corporation, used in photographic printing and production processes, as well as disks and tapes.

nanocomputing the science and engineering of building mechanical machines at the atomic level.

nanometers one-thousand-millionth (one billionth, or 10^{-9}) of a meter.

nanosecond one-thousand-millionth (one billionth, or 10^{-9}) of a second.

nanotechnology the design and construction of machines at the atomic or molecular level.

narrowband a general term in communication systems pertaining to a signal that has a small collection of differing frequency components (as opposed to broadband which has many frequency components).

National Computer Security Center (NCSC) a branch of the National Security Agency responsible for evaluating secure computing systems; the Trusted Computer Systems Evaluation Criteria (TCSEC) were developed by the NCSC.

Network Control Protocol (NCP) a host-to-host protocol originally developed in the early 1970s to support the Internet, which was then a research project.

network packet switching the act of routing and transferring packets (or small sections) of a carrier signal that conveys digital information.

neural modeling the mathematical study and the construction of elements that mimic the behavior of the brain cell (neuron).

neural networks pattern recognition systems whose structure and operation are loosely inspired by analogy to neurons in the human brain.

Newtonian view an approach to the study of mechanics that obeys the rules of Newtonian physics, as opposed to relativistic mechanics; named after Sir Isaac Newton (1643–1727).

nonlinear a system that has relationships between outputs and inputs which cannot be expressed in the form of a straight line.

O-rings 37-foot (11-meter) rubber circles (rings) that seal the joints between the space shuttle's rocket booster segments.

OEM the acronym for Original Equipment Manufacturer; a manufacturer of computer components.

offline the mode of operation of a computer that applies when it is completely disconnected from other computers and peripherals (like printers).

Open Systems Interconnections (OSI) a communications standard developed by the International Organization for Standardization (ISO) to facilitate compatible network systems.

operands when a computer is executing instructions in a program, the elements on which it performs the instructions are known as the.

operating system a set of programs which control all the hardware of a computer and provide user and device input/output functions.

optical character recognition the science and engineering of creating programs that can recognize and interpret printed characters.

optical computing a proposed computing technology which would operate on particles of light, rather than electric currents.

optophone a system that uses artificial intelligence techniques to convert images of text into audible sound.

orthogonal elements or objects that are perpendicular to one another; in a logical sense this means that changes in one have no effect on the other.

oscillator an electronic component that produces a precise waveform of a fixed known frequency; this can be used as a time base (clock) signal to other devices.

oscilloscopes measuring instruments for electrical circuitry; connected to circuits under test using probes on leads and having small screens that display the signal waveforms.

out-of-band pertaining to elements or objects that are external to the limits of a certain local area network (LAN).

overhead the expense or cost involved in carrying out a particular operation.

packet-switched network a network based on digital communications systems whereby packets of data are dispatched to receivers based on addresses that they contain.

packet-switching an operation used in digital communications systems whereby packets (collections) of data are dispatched to receivers based on addresses contained in the packets.

packets collections of digital data elements that are part of a complete message or signal; packets contain their destination addresses to enable reassembly of the message or signal.

paradigm an example, pattern, or way of thinking.

parallel debugging specialized approaches to locating and correcting errors in computer programs that are to be executed on parallel computing machine architectures.

parallel processing the presence of more than one central processing unit (CPU) in a computer, which enables the true execution of more than one program.

parametric modeling a system using variables or parameters that can be observed to change as the system operates.

parity a method of introducing error checking on binary data by adding a redundant bit and using that to enable consistency checks.

pattern recognition a process used by some artificial-intelligence systems to identify a variety of patterns, including visual patterns, information patterns buried in a noisy signal, and word patterns imbedded in text.

PDF the acronym for Portable Document Format, developed by Adobe Corporation to facilitate the storage and transfer of electronic documents.

peer-to-peer services the ways in which computers on the same logical level can interoperate in a structured network hierarchy.

permutations significant changes or rearrangement.

personal area networking the interconnectivity of personal productivity devices such as computers, mobile telephones, and personal organizers.

personal digital assistants (PDA) small-scale hand-held computers that can be used in place of diaries and appointment books.

phosphor a coating applied to the back of a glass screen on a cathode ray tube (CRT) that emits light when a beam of electrons strikes its surface.

photolithography the process of transferring an image from a film to a metal surface for etching, often used in the production of printed circuit boards.

photonic switching the technology that is centered on routing and managing optical packets of digital data.

photons the smallest fundamental units of electromagnetic radiation in the visible spectrum—light.

photosensitive describes any material that will change its properties in some way if subjected to visible light, such as photographic film.

picoseconds one-millionth of a millionth of a second (one-trillionth, or 10^{12}).

piezoelectric crystal an electronic component that when subjected to a current will produce a waveform signal at a precise rate, which can then be used as a clock signal in a computer.

PIN (personal identification number) a password, usually numeric, used in conjunction with a cryptographic token, smart card, or bank card, to ensure that only an authorized user can activate an account governed by the token or card.

ping sweeps technique that identifies properties belonging to a server computer, by sending it collections of "ping" packets and examining the responses from the server.

piracy the unlawful copying and redistribution of computer software, ignoring the copyright and ownership rights of the publisher.

pixel a single picture element on a video screen; one of the individual dots making up a picture on a video screen or digital image.

pixilation the process of generating animation, frame by frame.

plug-in a term used to describe the way that hardware and software modules can be added to a computer system, if they possess interfaces that have been built to a documented standard.

pneumatic powered by pressurized air, supplied through tubes or pipes.

polarity the positive (+) or negative (–) state of an object, which dictates how it will react to forces such as magnetism or electricity.

polarizer a translucent sheet that permits only plane-polarized light to pass through, blocking all other light.

polygon a many-sided, closed, geometrical figure.

polynomial an expression with more than one term.

polypeptide the product of many amino acid molecules bonded together.

population inversion used in quantum mechanics to describe when the number of atoms at higher energy levels is greater than the number at lower energy levels—a condition needed for photons (light) to be emitted.

port logical input/output points on computers that exist in a network.

port scans operations whereby ports are probed so that information about their status can be collected.

potentiometer an element in an electrical circuit that resists current flow (a resistor) but the value of the resistance can be mechanically adjusted (a variable resistor).

predicate calculus a branch of logic that uses individuals and predicates, or elements and classes, and the existential and universal quantifiers, all and some, to represent statements.

privatized to convert a service traditionally offered by a government or public agency into a service provided by a private corporation or other private entity.

progenitor the direct parent of something or someone.

propositional calculus a branch of logic that uses expressions such as "If … then …" to make statements and deductions.

proprietary a process or technology developed and owned by an individual or company, and not published openly.

proprietary software software created by an individual or company that is sold under a license that dictates use and distribution.

protocol an agreed understanding for the sub-operations that make up a transaction, usually found in the specification of inter-computer communications.

prototype a working model or experimental investigation of proposed systems under development.

proxy server a server, system, or application in a computer network that acts as an intermediary for clients needing to mask a computer's location or identity on the network, get around network access restrictions, or that otherwise cannot access information on other servers directly.

pseudocode a language-neutral, structural description of the algorithms that are to be used in a program.

public key information certain status and identification information that pertains to a particular public key (i.e., a key available for public use in encryption).

public key infrastructure (PKI) the supporting programs and protocols that act together to enable public key encryption/decryption.

punched card a paper card with punched holes which give instructions to a computer in order to encode program instructions and data.

quadtrees data structures resembling trees, which have four branches at every node (rather than two as with a binary tree); used in the construction of complex databases.

quality-of-service (QoS) a set of performance criteria that a system is designed to guarantee and support as a minimum.

quantification to quantify (or measure) something.

quantum-dot cellular automata (QCA) the theory of automata as applied to quantum dot architectures, which are a proposed approach for the development of computers at nano-technology scales.

quantum mechanical something influenced by the set of rules that govern the energy and wave behavior of subatomic particles on the scale of sizes that are comparable to the particles themselves.

queue the ordering of elements or objects such that they are processed in turn; first-in, first-out.

radar the acronym for RAdio Direction And Ranging; a technique developed in the 1930s that uses frequency shifts in reflected radio waves to measure distance and speed of a target.

radio telescopes telescopes used for astronomical observation that operate on collecting electromagnetic radiation in frequency bands above the visible spectrum.

random access memory (RAM) a type of memory device that supports the nonpermanent storage of programs and data; so called because various locations can be accessed in any order (as if at random), rather than in a sequence (like a tape memory device).

raster a line traced out by a beam of electrons as they strike a cathode ray tube (CRT).

raster scan pattern a sequence of raster lines drawn on a cathode ray tube such that an image or text can be made to appear.

read-only memory (ROM) a type of memory device that supports permanent storage of programs.

real-time a system, often computer based, that ensures the rates at which it inputs, processes, and outputs information meet the timing requirements of another system.

recursive operations expressed and implemented in a way that requires them to invoke themselves.

recursive functions functions expressed and implemented in a way that requires them to call themselves.

relational database a collection of records that permits logical and business relationships to be developed between themselves and their contents.

relay contact systems systems constructed to carry out logic functions, implemented in relays (electromechanical switches) rather than semiconductor devices.

resistive touch one of the two primary types of touch screen technology, it detects variously applied pressure as device-controlling touches.

resistors electrical components that slow the flow of current.

retinal scan a scan of the retina of the eye, which contains a unique pattern for each individual, in order to identify (or authenticate) someone.

robotics the science and engineering of building electromechanical machines that aim to serve as replacements for human laborers.

routers network devices that direct packets to the next network device or to the final destination.

routing the operation that involves collecting and forwarding packets of information by way of address.

satellite an object that orbits a planet.

scalar a quantity that has magnitude (size) only; there is no associated direction or bearing.

scalar processor a processor designed for high-speed computation of scalar values.

schematic a diagrammatic representation of a system, showing logical structure without regard to physical constraints.

scripting languages modern high level programming languages that are interpreted rather than compiled; they are usually cross-platform and support rapid application development.

search engine optimization (SEO) takes advantage of the way search engines crawl and index the Internet to increase visibility and prominence of a Web site among search engine results.

Secure Sockets Layer (SSL) a technology that supports encryption, authentication, and other facilities and is built into standard UNIX communication protocols (sockets over TCP/IP).

semantics the study of how words acquire meaning and how those meanings change over time.

semiconductor solid material that possesses electrical conductivity characteristics that are similar to those of metals under certain conditions, but can also exhibit insulating qualities under other conditions.

semiconductor diode laser a diode that emits electromagnetic radiation at wavelengths above about 630 nanometers, creating a laser beam for industrial applications.

sensors devices that can record and transmit data regarding the altitude, flight path, attitude, etc., so that they can enter into the system's calculations.

sequentially operations occurring in order, one after another.

server a computer that does not deal directly with human users, but instead handles requests from other computers for services to be performed.

SGML the acronym for Standard Generalized Markup Language, an international standard for structuring electronic documents.

shadow mask a metal sheet behind the glass screen of a cathode ray tube (CRT) that ensures the correct color phosphor elements are struck by the electron beams.

shareware a software distribution technique, whereby the author shares copies of his programs at no cost, in the expectation that users will later pay a fee of some sort.

Sherman Antitrust Act the act of the U.S. Congress in 1890 that is the foundation for all American anti-monopoly laws.

signaling protocols protocols used in the management of integrated data networks that convey a mix of audio, video, and data packets.

SIGs short for "Special Interest Group," SIGs concentrate their energies on specific categories of computer science, such as programming languages or computer architecture.

silica silicon oxide; found in sand and some forms of rock.

silicon a chemical element with symbol Si; the most abundant element in the Earth's crust and the most commonly used semiconductor material.

silicon chip a common term for a semiconductor integrated circuit device.

Silicon Valley an area in California near San Francisco, which has been the home location of many of the most significant information technology-related companies and universities.

silver halide a photosensitive product that has been used in traditional cameras to record an image.

simplex uni-directional communication over a single communication channel.

simputers simple to use computers that take on the functionality of personal computers, but are mobile and act as personal assistants and information organizers.

sine wave a wave traced by a point on the circumference of a circle when the point starts at height zero (amplitude zero) and goes through one full revolution.

single-chip a computer system that is constructed so that it contains just one integrated circuit device.

slide rule invented by Scotsman John Napier (1550–1617), it permits the mechanical automation of calculations using logarithms.

smart card a credit-card style card that has a microcomputer embedded within it; it carries more information to assist the owner or user.

smart devices devices and appliances that host an embedded computer system that offers greater control and flexibility.

smart matter materials, machines, and systems whose physical properties depend on the computing that is embedded within them.

smartphone an Internet-enabled cellular phone with computing ability that utilizes a mobile operating system and apps.

social informatics a field of study that centers on the social aspects of computing technology.

social media online sites or communities—such as Facebook or Twitter—where users share information, photos, video, music, and other media with other users.

softlifting the act of stealing software, usually for personal use (piracy).

software-defined networks (SDNs) the same as virtual private networks (VPNs), where the subscriber can set up and maintain a communications system using management software, on a public network.

solid-state drive (SSD) a data storage device without moving mechanical parts that utilizes an array of circuit assemblies as memory.

sonar the science and engineering of sound propagation in water.

SONET the acronym for Synchronous Optical NETwork, a published standard for networks based on fiber optic communications technology.

sound card a plug-in card for a computer that contains hardware devices for sound processing, conversion, and generation.

source code the human-readable programs that are compiled or interpreted so that they can be executed by a computing machine.

speech recognition the science and engineering of decoding and interpreting audible speech, usually using a computer system.

spider a computer program that travels the Internet to locate Web documents and FTP resources, then indexes the documents in a database, which are then searched using software the search engine provides.

spreadsheet an accounting or business tool that details numerical data in columns for tabulation purposes.

static without movement; stationary.

stellar pertaining to the stars.

streaming media audio or video that are viewable without delay or completely downloading because they are received over the Internet or other computer network by the user as a constant stream of data packets.

streaming media media such a music, videos, movies, and television shows available over the Internet.

subnet a logical section of a large network that simplifies the management of machine addresses.

supercomputer a very high performance computer, usually comprised of many processors and used for modeling and simulation of complex phenomena, like meteorology.

superconductivity the property of a material to pass an electric current with almost no losses; most metals are superconductive only at temperatures near absolute zero.

swap files files used by an operating system to support a virtual memory system, in which the user appears to have access to more memory than is physically available.

syllogistic statements the essential tenets of western philosophical thought, based on hypotheses and categories.

synchronization the time domain ordering of events; often applied when events repeatedly occur simultaneously.

synchronized events occurring at specific points in time with respect to one another.

synchronous synchronized behavior.

synergistic relating to synergism, which is the phenomenon whereby the action of a group of elements is greater than their individual actions.

syntactic analyzer a part of a compiler that scans program source code ensuring that the code meets essential language rules with regard to structure or organization.

syntax a set of rules that a computing language incorporates regarding structure, punctuation, and formatting.

T1 digital circuitry a type of digital network technology that can handle separate voice and/ or digital communications lines.

tablet (or tablet computer) is an Internet-enabled portable computing device with a touch screen user interface.

tangible of a nature that is real, as opposed to something that is imaginary or abstract.

task partitioning the act of dividing up work to be done so that it can be separated into distinct tasks, processes, or phases.

taxonomy the classification of elements or objects based on their characteristics.

TCP the acronym for Transmission Control Protocol; a fundamental protocol used in the networks that support the Internet (ARPANET).

TCP/IP networks interconnected computer networks that use Transmission Control Protocol/Internet Protocol.

TCP/IP protocol suite Transmission Control Protocol/Internet Protocol; a range of functions that can be used to facilitate applications working on the Internet.

telegraph a communication channel that uses cables to convey encoded low bandwidth electrical signals.

telemedicine the technology that permits remote diagnosis and treatment of patients by a medical practitioner; usually interactive bi-directional audio and video signals.

telemetry the science of taking measurements of something and transmitting the data to a distant receiver.

teleoperation any operation that can be carried out remotely by a communications system that enables interactive audio and video signals.

teletype a machine that sends and receives telephonic signals.

terabyte one million million (one trillion, or 10^{12}) bytes.

thermal ignition the combustion of a substance caused by heating it to the point that its particles have enough energy to commence burning without an externally applied flame.

thermodynamic relating to heat energy.

three-body problem an intractable problem in mechanics that involves the attempts to predict the behavior of three bodies under gravitational effects.

thumbnail an image which is a scaled down copy of a much larger image; used to assist in the management of a large catalog of images.

time lapse mode to show a sequence of events occurring at a higher than natural speed so it looks like it is happening rapidly rather than in real time.

title bar the top horizontal border of a rectangular region owned by a program running in a graphical user interface (GUI); it usually contains the program name and can be used to move the region around.

tomography the process of capturing and analyzing X-ray images.

topographic pertaining to the features of a terrain or surface.

topology a method of describing the structure of a system that emphasizes its logical nature rather than its physical characteristics.

touch screen an interface that allows users to control the computing device by touching its screen.

trademark rights a trademark is a name, symbol, or phrase that identifies a trading organization and is owned by that organization.

trafficking transporting and selling; especially with regard to illegal merchandise.

training data data used in the creation of a classifier.

transaction processing operations between client and server computers that are made up of many small exchanges that must all be completed for the transaction to proceed.

transducers devices that sense a physical quantity, such as temperature or pressure, and convert that measurement into an electrical signal.

transistor a contraction of TRANSfer resIS-TOR; a semiconductor device, invented by John Bardeen, Walter Brattain, and William

Shockley, which has three terminals; can be used for switching and amplifying electrical signals.

translational bridges   special network devices that convert low-level protocols from one type to another.

Transmission Control Protocol (TCP)   a stream-orientated protocol that uses Internet Protocol (IP); it is responsible for splitting data into packets, transferring it, and reassembling it at the receiver.

transmutation   the act of converting one thing into another.

trigonometry   a branch of mathematics founded upon the geometry of triangles.

triodes   nearly obsolete electronic devices constructed of sealed glass tubes containing metal elements in a vacuum; triodes were used to control electrical signals.

Trojan horse   potentially destructive computer program that masquerades as something benign; named after the wooden horse employed by the Acheans to conquer Troy.

tunneling   a way of handling different communication protocols, by taking packets of a foreign protocol and changing them so that they.

Turing machine   a proposed type of computing machine that takes inputs off paper tape and then moves through a sequence of states under the control of an algorithm; identified by Alan Turing (1912–1954).

twisted pair   an inexpensive, medium bandwidth communication channel commonly used in local area networks.

ubiquitous   to be commonly available everywhere.

ultrasonic   the transmission and reception of sound waves that are at frequencies higher than those audible to humans.

Uniform Resource Locator (URL)   a reference to a document or a document container using the Hypertext Transfer Protocol (HTTP); consists of a hostname and path to the document.

Universal Product Code (UPC)   the first barcode standard developed in 1973 and adopted widely since.

UNIX   operating system that was originally developed at Bell Laboratories in the early 1970s.

uplinks   connections from a client machine to a large network; frequently when information is being sent to a communications satellite.

vacuum tube   an electronic device constructed of a sealed glass tube containing metal elements in a vacuum; used to control electrical signals.

valence   a measure of the reactive nature of a chemical element or compound in relation to hydrogen.

variable   a symbol, such as a string of letters, which may assume any one of a set of values known as the domain.

vector graphics   graphics output systems whereby pairs of coordinates are passed to the graphics controller, which are interpreted as end points of vectors to be drawn on the screen.

vector processing   an approach to computing machine architecture that involves the manipulation of vectors (sequences of numbers) in single steps, rather than one number at a time.

vector supercomputer   a highly optimized computing machine that provides high performance using a vector processing architecture.

velocities   vector quantities that have a magnitude or speed and a direction.

Venn diagrams   diagrams used to demonstrate the relationships between sets of objects, named after John Venn, a British logician.

venture capitalists persons or agencies that speculate by providing financial resources to enable product development, in the expectation of larger returns with product maturity.

video capture cards plug-in cards for a computer that accepts video input from devices like televisions and video cameras, allowing the user to record video data onto the computer.

video compression algorithms special algorithms applied to remove certain unnecessary parts of video images in an attempt to reduce their storage size.

virtual channel connection an abstraction of a physical connection between two or more elements (or computers); the complex details of the physical connection are hidden.

virtual circuit like a virtual channel connection, a virtual circuit appears to be a direct path between two elements, but is actually a managed collection of physical connections.

Virtual Private Networks (VPNs) a commercial approach to network management where privately owned voice and data networks are set up on public network infrastructure.

virtual reality (VR) the use of elaborate input/output devices to create the illusion that the user is in a different environment.

virtualization as if it were real; making something seem real, e.g., a virtual environment.

visible speech a set of symbols, comprising an alphabet, that "spell" sounds instead of words.

visualization a technique whereby complex systems are portrayed in a meaningful way using sophisticated computer graphics systems; e.g., chemical molecules.

voice over Internet protocol (VoIP) communication technology that delivers telephone calls, video calls, and voice communications via Internet Protocol.

volatile subject to rapid change; describes the character of data when current no longer flows to a device (that is, electrical power is switched off).

waveform an abstraction used in the physical sciences to model energy transmission in the form of longitudinal or transverse waves.

Web surfers people who "surf" (search) the Internet frequently.

wide area network (WAN) an interconnected network of computers that spans upward from several buildings to whole cities or entire countries and across countries.

wireless lavaliere microphones small microphones worn around the speakers' necks, which attach to their shirts.

wireless local area network (WLAN) an interconnected network of computers that uses radio and/or infrared communication channels, rather than cables.

workstations computers (usually within a network) that interact directly with human users (much the same as "client computers").

xerography a printing process that uses electrostatic elements derived from a photographic image to deposit the ink.

XML the acronym for eXtensible Markup Language; a method of applying structure to data so that documents can be represented.

Directory of Computer Sciences Organizations

A

Apple, Inc.
1 Infinite Loop
Cupertino, CA, 95014
USA
Telephone: (408) 996-1010
Email: media.help@apple.com
Web site: www.apple.com

Argonne National Laboratory: Mathematics and Computer Science Division
9700 South Cass Avenue, Building 240
Argonne, IL, 60439-4844
USA
Telephone: (630) 252-8808
Web site: http://www.mcs.anl.gov

Association for the Advancement of Artificial Intelligence
2275 East Bayshore Road, Suite 160
Palo Alto, CA, 94303
USA
Telephone: (650) 328-3123
Fax: (650) 321-4457
Web site: http://www.aaai.org

Association for Computer Machinery
2 Penn Plaza, Suite 701
New York, NY, 10121-0701
USA
Telephone: (800) 342-6626
Email: acmhelp@acm.org
Web site: http://www.acm.org

Association for Information Systems
PO Box 2712
Atlanta, GA, 30301-2712
USA
Telephone: (404) 413-7445
Email: onestop@aisnet.org
Web site: https://ais.site-ym.com

B

Bell Laboratories
600-700 Mountain Avenue
Murray Hill, NJ, 07974
USA
Telephone: (908) 508-8080
Email: execoffice@alcatel-lucent.com
Web site: http://www.alcatel-lucent.com/belllabs

Bletchley Park
The Mansion, Bletchley Park
Milton Keynes, MK3 6EB
UK
Telephone: +44 (0) 1908 640404
Fax: +44 (0) 1908 274381
Email: info@bletchleypark.org.uk
Web site: http://www.bletchleypark.org.uk

C

Cisco Systems, Inc.
170 West Tasman Drive
San Jose, CA, 95134
USA
Telephone: (408) 526 4000
Web site: www.cisco.com

Computer History Museum
1401 North Shoreline Boulevard
Mountain View, CA, 94043
USA
Telephone: (650) 810-1010
Fax: (650) 810-1055
Web site: http://www.computerhistory.org

Computing and Information Technology Interactive Digital Educational Library (CITADEL)
Web site: http://citidel.villanova.edu

Cray, Inc.
901 Fifth Avenue, Suite 1000
Seattle, WA, 98164
USA
Telephone: (206) 701-2000
Fax: (206) 701-2500
Email: crayinfo@cray.com
Web site: www.cray.com

D

Defense Advanced Research Projects Agency
675 North Randolph Street
Arlington, VA, 22203-2114
USA
Telephone: (703) 526-6630
Email: outreach@darpa.mil
Web site: http://www.darpa.mil

E

Electronic Frontier Foundation
454 Shotwell Street
San Francisco, CA, 9411-1914
USA
Telephone: (415) 436-9333
Fax: (415) 436-9993
Email: info@eff.org
Web site: https://www.eff.org

G

GE Global Research
1 Research Circle
Niskayuna, NY, 12309
USA
Telephone: (518) 387-7914
Web site: http://ge.geglobalresearch.com

Google Developers Academy
Web site: https://developers.google.com/academy/

Google, Inc.
1600 Amphitheatre Parkway
Mountain View, CA, 94043
USA

Telephone: (650) 253-0000
Fax: (650) 253-0001
Web site: www.google.com/about/company

H

Hewlett-Packard Co.
3000 Hanover St.
Palo Alto, CA, 94304
USA
Telephone: (650) 857-1501
Fax: (650) 857-5518
Web site: www.hp.com

Hon Hai Precision Industry Co., Ltd. (Foxconn)
105 S. Puente Street
Brea, CA, 92821
USA
Telephone: (714) 626-6900
Fax: (714) 626-6901
Email: foxconn-service@foxconn.com
Web site: www.foxconnchannel.com

I

Institute of Electrical and Electronics Engineers (IEEE) Computer Society
2001 L Street NW, Suite 700
Washington, DC, 20036-4928
USA
Telephone: (202) 371-0101
Fax: (202) 728-9614
Email: help@computer.org
Web site: http://www.computer.org

Intel Corp.
2200 Mission College Boulevard
Santa Clara, CA, 95952
USA
Telephone: (408) 765-8080
Web site: www.intel.com

International Business Machines Corp.
1 New Orchard Road
Armonk, NY, 10504
USA
Telephone: (800) 426-4968
Web site: www.ibm.com

International Standards Organization
1, ch. de la Voie-Creuse, CP 56
Geneva, CH-1211 Geneva 20
Switzerland
Telephone: +41 22 749 01 11
Email: central@iso.org
Web site: http://www.iso.org

Internet Society
1775 Wiehle Avenue, Suite 201
Reston, VA, 20190-5108
USA
Telephone: (703) 439-2120
Fax: (703) 326-9881
Email: isoc@isoc.org
Web site: https://www.internetsociety.org

L

Los Alamos National Laboratory
PO Box 1663
Los Alamos, NM, 87545
USA
Telephone: (505) 667-7000
Email: community@lanl.gov
Web site: http://www.lanl.gov

M

Massachusetts Institute of Technology (MIT) Computer Science and Artificial Intelligence Laboratory (CSAIL)
The Strata Center, Building 32, 32 Vassar Street
Cambridge, MA, 02139
USA
Telephone: (617) 253-5851
Fax: (617) 258-8682
Web site: http://www.csail.mit.edu

Microsoft Corp.
1 Microsoft Way
Redmond, WA, 98052
USA
Telephone: (425) 882-8080
Web site: www.microsoft.com

Microsoft Research (MSR)
1 Microsoft Way
Redmond, WA, 98052
USA

Telephone: (800) 642-7676
Web site: http://research.microsoft.com

N

NASA Advanced Supercomputing (NAS) Division
Ames Research Center
Moffett Field, CA, 94035
USA
Telephone: (650) 604-4377
Email: contact-nas@nas.nasa.gov
Web site: http://www.nas.nasa.gov

National Center for Supercomputing Applications
1205 West Clark Street, Room 1008
Urbana, IL, 61801
USA
Telephone: (217) 244-0710
Email: help@ncsa.illinois.edu
Web site: http://ncsa.illinois.edu

The National Museum of Computing
Block H, Bletchley Park
Milton Keynes, MK3 6EB
UK
Telephone: +44 (0)1908 374708
Email: lin.jones@tnmoc.org
Web site: http://www.tnmoc.org

O

Oak Ridge Leadership Computing Facility
PO Box 2008
Oak Ridge, TN, 37831-6161
USA
Telephone: (865) 241-6536
Fax: (865) 241-2850
Email: help@olcf.ornl.gov
Web site: http://www.olcf.ornl.gov

Oracle Corp.
500 Oracle Parkway
Redwood Shores, CA, 94065
USA
Telephone: (650) 506-7000
Web site: www.oracle.com

P

Palo Alto Research Center (PARC)
3333 Coyote Hill Road
Palo Alto, CA, 94304
USA
Telephone: (650) 812-4000
Web site: www.parc.com

S

Samsung Electronics Co., Ltd.
85 Challenger Road
Ridgefield Park, NJ, 07660
USA
Telephone: (800) 726-7864
Fax: (864) 752-1632
Web site: www.samsung.com

SAP
3999 West Chester Pike
Newton Square, PA, 19073
USA
Telephone: (610) 661-1000
Web site: www.sap.com

SRI International
333 Ravenswood Ave.
Menlo Park, CA, 94025
USA
Telephone: (650) 859-2000
Web site: www.sri.com

T

Texas Instruments, Inc.
12500 TI Boulevard
Dallas, TX, 75243
USA

Telephone: (972) 995-2011
Web site: www.ti.com

Thomas J. Watson Research Center
1101 Kitchawan Road
Yorktown Heights, NY, 10598
USA
Telephone: (914) 945-3000
Web site: http://www.research.ibm.com/labs/watson

W

World Wide Web Consortium (W3C)
32 Vassar Street, Room 32-G515
Cambridge, MA, 02139
USA
Telephone: (617) 253-2613
Web site: http://www.w3.org

Cumulative Index

Page numbers referring to illustrations are in *italic* type. Volume numbers are included.
Bold page numbers refer to the main entry on the subject.

A

A. M. Turing Award, 1:24, 25, 248, 251

AALs (ATM adaptation layers), 2:14–15, 4:20, 22–23

Abacuses, 1:**1–2**, *2*, 49–50

ABR (available bit rate) service, 2:14

Abu Ghraib prison, 4:86

Acceptor impurities, 1:243, 244

Access motion time, 2:242

Accessibility technology. *See* Assistive computer technology for persons with disabilities

Accounting software, 3:**1–4**, *2*, 5

Accounts payable software, 3:1

Accounts receivable software, 3:1–2

ACM. *See* Association for Computing Machinery (ACM)

Acrobat Reader, 3:130

Activation of software, 3:225

Active matrix liquid crystal displays, 2:82–84

ADA (Americans with Disabilities Act), 4:13–14, 18

Ada computer language, 1:153, 2:198–199

Adams, Michael, 3:45

Adaptive technology. *See* Assistive computer technology for persons with disabilities

Adding machines, 1:2, 3

Additive sound synthesis, 3:171

Address buses, 2:10

Addressing protocols, 2:47, 150
   See also Internet Protocol (IP); TCP/IP (Transmission Control Protocol/Internet Protocol)

Adleman, Leonard, 1:221, 4:58

Administrative factors, scaling, 2:215

Adobe Systems
   Flash plug-in, 1:15, 2:237
   founding, 3:244
   PDF file format, 2:135, 3:130, 4:102
   PhotoShop software, 3:22, 4:232
   Postscript page description language, 3:82, 85, 243, 244

ADS-B (automatic dependent surveillance-broadcast), 3:11

ADSLs (asymmetric digital subscriber lines), 2:59, 4:29

Advance phase, hacking, 3:122

Advanced Encryption Standard algorithms, 4:57

Advanced mobile phone system (AMPS), 2:39–40

Advanced Networks and Services (ANS), 4:175

Advanced Research Projects Agency Network. *See* ARPANET

Advanced Video Coding (AVC), 2:121

Adventure video games, 1:15

Advertising
   cookies and, 4:46
   data mining and, 4:65–66
   e-commerce, 1:70, 71
   fast-forwarding through commercials, 2:262
   free e-mail providers, 1:73, 74–75
   journalism Web sites, 4:202
   search engines, 4:243

AEA (Aerial Experiment Association), 2:24

AECL (Atomic Energy of Canada Limited), 4:119

Aerial Experiment Association (AEA), 2:24

AFCS (Automated Facer Cancelor System), 1:*197*

AFNOR (Association Francais de Normalization), 1:120

Africa
   abacuses, 1:1
   digital divide, 4:162

Agents, 1:136–137, 4:**1–3**, 12, 156

Agents on the Web (online column), 4:3

Agreement on Trade Related Aspects of Intellectual Property Rights (TRIPS), 4:228–229

Agriculture, 3:*4*, **4–8**

AI. *See* Artificial intelligence (AI)

AIEE (American Institute of Electrical Engineers), 1:122

Aiken, Howard, 1:54, 62, 66, 268, 2:283, 3:253

AIM (AOL Instant Messenger), 4:169

Aircrack network security program, 3:214

Aircraft flight control, 3:*8*, **8–12**

Aircraft navigation systems, 3:173–175, 176–177

Aircraft traffic management, 3:*12*, **12–15**

Airline reservation systems (ARSs), 1:33, 3:*16*, **16–19**

AirPlay mirroring, 1:19

AirPort technology, 1:144

AITP (Association for Information Technology Professionals), 4:118, 119

Akers, John, 1:110

Al Jazeera network, 3:221

al-Khowarizmi, Mohammed, 2:4

Alcatel-Lucent, 1:34

Alcatel-Lucent Bell Labs, 1:*32*, 2:*226*

Alcom, Al, 1:79

Aldus Publishing, 3:82, 85, 242

Algol-60 Report, 2:**1–3**

Algol programming language, 2:1–3, 194–195, 3:187, 188

Algorithms, 2:*4*, **4–6**
   Algol programming language, 2:1–2
   encryption, 4:55–56, 57
   music composition, 3:170
   parallel processing, 2:173–174, 175
   programming, 2:201, 202
   Turing Machine, 1:251

Alife. *See* Artificial life

Allen, George, 4:234

Allen, Paul, 1:84, 169, 172, 4:112

Alliance for Telecommunications Industry Solutions (ATIS), 1:120

Alpha beta pruning, 3:44

Altair computers, 1:84, 169, 4:112

Alternative Museum, 4:9

Alto computer, 1:251, 272, 278, 4:184

ALUs (arithmetic logic units), 2:8, 43, 44

Amadeus Global Travel Distribution SA, 3:17

Amazon Simple Storage Service (S3), 2:244

Amazon.com, 1:69–70, 4:95–96, 97, 111–112

Amdahl Corporation, 4:4

Amdahl, Gene Myron, 2:175, 4:**3–6**

Amdahl's law, 2:175, 4:4

Amelio, Gil, 1:18

America Online (AOL), 1:82, 274, 3:131, 4:172

American Airlines, 3:16–17

American Civil Liberties Union, 4:37

American Folklore (Dorson), 4:265

American Imago (journal), 4:265

American Institute of Electrical Engineers (AIEE), 1:122

American Mathematical Society, 4:102

American Memory project, 4:81

American National Standards Institute (ANSI), 1:120, 2:52

American Registry for Internet Numbers (ARIN), 4:179

American Standard Code for Information Interchange. *See* ASCII code

American Standards Association (ASA), 2:52

American Telephone & Telegraph Company. *See* AT&T

Americans with Disabilities Act (ADA), 4:13–14, 18

Ameritech, 4:175

Amplification
    assistive computer technology, 4:17
    discovery, 1:253
    operational amplifiers, 1:4
    transistors, 1:126, 245
    See also Repeaters

Amplitude modulation, lasers, 3:147

AMPS (advanced mobile phone system), 2:39–40

Analog computing, 1:**2–5,** *3,* 49, 53, 164

Analog music synthesis, 1:184

Analog simulation, 1:228
    See also Simulation

Analog systems
    bandwidth, 4:27
    defined, 1:36
    early video games, 1:80
    linear integrated circuits, 1:126

Analog-to-digital conversion
    chip-based, 1:51
    digital cameras, 4:230–231
    magnetic stripe cards, 3:156
    mixed systems, 1:49
    music synthesis, 1:184
    overview, 1:36–37
    sampling rates, 4:222–223
    sound data, 2:234–235
    time lags, 1:50–51

Analysis-oriented music models, 3:169

Analytical engines, 1:*6,* **6–7**
    Babbage, Charles development, 1:6–7, 20, 29–30, 50, 95–96, 151, 152, 184, 3:191
    music applications, 1:184, 2:143

Ancestors, in object-oriented programming, 2:159–160

"and" gates, 1:34, 127, 2:75, *75,* 77

AND statements, 2:26, 27–29, *27–30*

Anderson, Paul Thomas, 4:75

Andor Systems, 4:5

Andreessen, Marc, 1:274, 4:33

Android mobile operating system, 4:208

Animation, 1:*8,* **8–16**
    fashion design, 3:109
    history, 1:11–13
    principles, 1:14
    simulation and, 1:228
    story creation, 1:8–9
    types, 1:9–11, 14–16
    virtual reality use, 2:273

Animatronics, 1:9, 11

Anodes, in vacuum tubes, 1:253, 255

Anomaly-based intrusion detection systems, 3:213–214

Anonymous FTP, 4:133, 186

Anonymous (hacker organization), 4:*36,* 147–148, 182

Anonymous reposting servers, 1:223

ANS (Advanced Networks and Services), 4:175

ANSI (American National Standards Institute), 1:120, 2:52

ANSNET, 4:175

Answering machines, 1:74

Antarctic ice flow, 4:140

Antares Audio Technologies, 2:144

Anthrax scare (2001), 3:36

Anthropomorphism, robotics, 1:216

Anti-aliasing, in video games, 1:82

Anti-satellite weapons systems, 2:214

Anti-virus software
    defined, 3:124
    detection avoidance techniques, 1:264
    first programs, 1:261
    home systems, 3:129–130
    overview, 2:118

Anticipation (animation), 1:14

Antitrust (film), 4:128

Antitrust litigation
    Bell Labs, 1:246
    Bell Telephone Company, 4:246
    IBM, 1:109
    Intel, 1:131
    Microsoft Corporation, 1:85, 172, 274, 4:172
    National Cash Register Company, 1:268

Antonelli, Kathleen McNulty Mauchly, 1:66

AOL (America Online), 1:82, 274, 3:131, 4:172

AOL Instant Messenger (AIM), 4:169

AOL Time Warner, 4:172

Apache OpenOffice software, 3:200

Apache Project, 3:185–186

Apache Web server program, 2:225

Apogees (satellites), 2:211

Apollo moon missions, 1:189–190, 191, 3:227–228

Apollo Reservation System, 3:17

Appeal (animation), 1:14

Appelbaum, Jacob, 4:*148*

Apple Computer, Inc., 1:*17,* **17–20**
    collaboration with rivals, 1:172, 2:62
    founding, 1:17, 143
    G4 series, 3:69
    GarageBand software, 3:169
    HyperCard introduction, 1:105
    initial public offering, 1:143
    iPads, 1:19, 146
    iPhones, 1:19, 145, 146
    iPods, 1:19, 145, 146
    Laserwriter printer, 3:82, 85
    magic mouse, 1:183

mobile computing operating systems, 4:208

name change, 1:145

PDA/smartphone production, 2:180, 181

Quick Time media player, 2:237

Safari browser, 1:274, 2:225, 4:170, 225

stock options controversy, 1:145–146

Visi-Calc software integration, 3:239

See also Jobs, Steve

Apple I computer, 1:143

Apple II computer, 1:143, 261

Apple Inc., 1:145

See also Apple Computer, Inc.

Apple TV, 1:19, 145

Applets, Java, 1:223, 2:161, 4:191–194

Application layer
firewall implementation, 4:130, 131–132

OSI Reference Model, 2:152

Application protocols, client/server systems, 2:47

Application servers, 2:227

See also Servers

Application service providers (ASPs), 4:247

Application viruses, 1:262

See also Viruses

Application wizards, 1:271–272

Approximations, physics applications, 3:192, 193

Arab Spring, 3:219–222, 4:85–86

Arbiters, 2:66

Archie (Internet index), 4:186

Architecture, 3:**19–23**, *20*

Archiving utilities, 3:130

Arcs (animation), 1:14

Ariane rocket, 3:229

ARIN (American Registry for Internet Numbers), 4:179

ARINC 429 serial data bus, 2:231

Arithmetic
abacuses, 1:1

analog computer calculations, 1:4

binary number system, 1:35–36

Pascaline calculating machine, 1:208

Arithmetic logic units (ALUs), 2:8, 43, 44

ARPANET
FTP development, 4:132–133

Internet backbone connections, 4:174

as Internet precursor, 1:138, 273, 4:184–185

library applications, 3:152–153

packet encryption devices, 2:270

security measures, 1:221

TCP/IP development, 4:260, 261

Arrays, early high order language development and, 2:157–158

ARSs (airline reservation systems), 1:33, 3:*16*, 16–19

Art, 4:**6–10**, *7*

The Art of 3-D Computer Animation and Imaging (Kerlow), 1:13

Artificial intelligence (AI), 1:*20*, **20–23**
artificial life *vs.*, 4:12

Berners-Lee, Tim contributions, 4:111

cybernetics groundwork, 4:63–64

as fifth generation of computers, 1:90

geographic information systems integration, 3:117

IBM research, 1:111

industrial robots, 3:63

LISP programming language, 2:123–125

neural networks, 3:177–181, *179*

Newell, Allen contributions, 4:219–221

personalization capabilities, 4:164

political event simulation, 4:237

railroad applications, 3:208

robotics research, 1:213–214

Shannon, Claude contributions, 4:251

Simon, Herbert A. contributions, 4:253

Stanford open course, 3:90

Turing test, 1:22–23, 249

ubiquitous computing and, 3:101

video game contributions, 1:79

See also Expert systems

Artificial Intelligence: AI (film), 1:23

Artificial life, 4:*10*, **10–13**

Artillery firing charts
early programming, 1:65–66

ENIAC calculations, 1:254, 2:90, 3:71

wartime needs, 1:61–62

Artzt, Russ, 4:115

ASA (American Standards Association), 2:52

ASCII code, 2:54*t*
as block code, 2:53–55

defined, 1:113

e-text use, 4:94

in searches, 1:113

as standard, 1:120–121, 2:52

ASDLs (asymmetric digital subscriber lines), 2:59, 4:29

Asimo (robot), 2:*208*

Asimov, Isaac, 1:15, 216, 3:**23–26**, *24*, 4:127

Asimov's Three Laws of Robotics, 3:25, 4:127

ASK Computer Systems, Inc., 4:114–115

ASPs (application service providers), 4:247

ASs (Autonomous Systems), 4:173–174

Assad, Bashar al-, 3:221–222

Assembler programs, 1:92, 175, 2:9

Assembly language and architecture, 1:91–92, 2:**6–10**, *7*, 63–64, 157, 3:10

Asset value, security software and, 2:220

Assignment statements, 2:2

Assistive computer technology for persons with disabilities, 4:**13–19**, *14*, 33, 34, 43

Association for Computing Machinery (ACM), 1:*24*, **24–28**
Algol development, 2:194

Amdahl, Gene Myron honors, 4:5–6

digital library conference, 4:80

e-journals, 4:102

ethics code, 4:118, 119

Organick, Elliot contributions, 3:188

Turing Award, 1:24, 25, 248, 251

Association for Information Technology Professionals (AITP), 4:118, 119

Association Francais de Normalization (AFNOR), 1:120

Association models, data mining, 4:69

"Asteroids" (video game), 1:79, 81

Astronomy, 3:**26–29**, *27*

Asymmetric digital subscriber lines (ADSLs), 2:59, 4:29

Asynchronous and synchronous transmission, 2:**10–13**, 223

Asynchronous transfer mode (ATM), 4:**19–23**, *20, 22t*
    See also ATM transmission
Atanasoff-Berry Computer (ABC), 1:55–56, 63, 66
Atanasoff, John V., 1:50, 55–56, 62–63, 66, 2:90–91
Atari, Inc.
    early video games, 1:82, 2:95–96
    founding, 1:79, 4:154
    Jobs, Steve employment, 1:142
    video game development, 1:15
ATIS (Alliance for Telecommunications Industry Solutions), 1:120
Atlantis (space shuttle), 3:229
ATM adaptation layers (AALs), 2:14–15, 4:20, 22–23
ATM Forum, 2:14
ATM layers, 4:20, 22
ATM machines (automated teller machines), 2:253, 3:*29*, **29–32**
ATM transmission, 1:194–195, 2:12, **13–15,** 4:173
Atomic bomb development. *See* Manhattan Project
Atomic Energy of Canada Limited (AECL), 4:119
AT&T
    Bell Labs, 1:31–32, 33–34
    frequency division multiplexing, 3:41
    software-defined networks, 2:270
    as top-tier backbone, 4:176
AT&T Labs, 1:33–34
Attenuation, fiber optics, 2:93
Auction sites, 4:108
    See also eBay
AUDEO voice synthesizer, 3:*234*
Audio books, 4:97
Audio files, 2:121, 3:113–114
Audio oscillators, 3:126
Audio synthesis. *See* Music, computer
Audiometer invention, 2:24
Augment interactive multimedia system, 1:105
Authentication, 4:**24–26**
    digital signatures, 4:86–89, *87, 88*
    distributed, 1:222
    e-banking, 4:93
    e-commerce, 4:99
    e-journals, 4:101, 102
    FTP, 4:133
    with HTTPS, 1:67

    password protection, 1:220
    security software processes, 1:219, 2:221
    tokens, 2:217–218, 4:25, 107
Authorization, 1:219, 2:221
Auto-pilots, 3:9–11
Auto-Tune audio processor, 2:144
AutoCAD, 3:22
AutoDesk 3D Studio Viz, 3:22
AutoDesk Inc., 3:22
AutoDesSys Inc., 3:22
Automata (short story), 4:126–127
Automata theory, 1:32
Automated Facer Cancelor System (AFCS), 1:*197*
Automated teller machines (ATMs), 2:253, 3:*29*, 29–32
Automatic data processing, 2:85
    See also Data processing; Document processing
Automatic dependent surveillance-broadcast (ADS-B), 3:11
Automation, 3:*194*, 194–197
Automatons, 1:212–213, 4:126–127, 143, 144
    See also Robotics
Automobile industry
    driverless vehicles projects, 4:44
    onboard navigation systems, 3:176
    robotics use, 1:213, 214, 3:62–63
Autonomous Systems (ASs), 4:173–174
Autonomous vehicles, 4:44
Available bit rate (ABR) service, 2:14
Avatar (film), 4:8
AVC (Advanced Video Coding), 2:121
Aviation simulation. *See* Flight simulation
Aztec abacuses, 1:1

B

Babbage, Charles, 1:*29*, **29–31**
    analytical engines, 1:6–7, 20, 29–30, 50, 181, 182, 184, 3:191
    funding sources, 1:95–96
    King, Ada Byron collaboration, 1:30, 96, 151
    music applications, 1:184, 2:143
    printer concept, 2:191
    Royal Astronomical Society medal, 3:26–27
    Zuse, Konrad connection, 2:283
Baby Bells, 1:33

Backbone, Internet, 4:172–176, 186
Backgrounds, animation, 1:9, 10
Backlighting, LCDs, 2:83–84
Backpropagation, 3:180–181
BackTrack network security program, 3:214
Backup devices
    cloud storage, 2:113, 244
    magnetic disks, 2:241–243
    tape drives, 1:158, 2:113, 241
Backus, John, 2:2, 157, 193–194, 195
Backus-Naur form (BNF), 2:2
Bacteria research, 3:34–35
Bacteriorhodopsin, 3:166
Baer, Ralph, 1:79
Ballard, Robert, 3:136
Ballistics charts. *See* Artillery firing charts
Ballmer, Steve, 1:85, 170, 172, 2:*238*
Bandwidth, 1:155, 156, 2:92, 93–94, 4:**27–30**, *28*
    See also Data rates
Bandwidth regulation and restriction, 2:**17–20**
Banking, online. *See* E-banking
Bar codes, 2:167, 203–204, 207, 3:206
Baran, Paul, 4:184
Barbera, Joseph, 1:13
Bardeen, John, 2:**20–22**
    Bell Labs involvement, 1:34, 2:20
    superconductivity research, 1:128
    transistor invention, 1:66, 88, 125, 126, 241, 2:20
Barnes & Noble Nook e-reader, 4:95–96
Bartik, Jean Jennings, 1:66
Base-2 number system, 1:34
    See also Binary number system
Base-8 number system, 1:50, 91
Base-10 number system, 1:34, 35, 36, 50
Base-16 number system, 1:35, 36
Base stations, cellular networks, 3:40–41
Base terminals, transistors, 1:126, 245
Base+offset addressing, 2:*263*, 264, 265, *265*, 266
Basic Input Output System (BIOS), 1:161
BASIC programming language
    Algol origins, 2:2
    Gates, Bill contributions, 1:84, 169, 4:112

as high-level language, 1:93

history, 2:196–197

Kemeny, John G. contributions, 3:141, 4:267

Kurtz, Thomas E. contributions, 3:141, 142, 4:267

Visual Basic, 2:196, 4:267–269

Basketball, data mining application, 4:69

Batch fabrication, 3:47–48

Batch processing

early laser printers, 3:243

information retrieval systems, 1:113

mainframes, 1:156–157

Baud rates, 4:28

Baud (unit), 2:57–58

Baudot, Jean-Maurice-Émile, 2:51, 57–58

Bauer, Fritz, 2:195

Baughman, Ernest, 4:265

Baum, L. Frank, 4:126

BBB (Better Business Bureau), 4:53–54

BBSs (bulletin board systems), 3:216

BCDIC (Binary Coded Decimal Interchange Code), 2:52

Be The Reds (cybercafe), 4:59, 62

Bear, Greg, 4:128

Beardsley, Richard K., 4:265

Beginner's All-purpose Symbolic Instruction Code. *See* BASIC programming language

BeiDou-2 Navigation System (BNS), 4:138

Bell, Alexander Graham, 1:122, 240, 2:*23*, **23–25**

Bell Communications Research (Bellcore), 1:33

Bell Labs, 1:**31–34**, *32*

cell phone research, 2:39

compiler research, 2:2

Model 1, 1:53–54

Multics development, 3:188

music synthesis, 1:185

telephone system history, 3:247

transistor research, 1:88, 246

Bell Telephone Company, 2:23, 3:245, 4:246

Benjamin, Joel, 3:45

Bennett, Gillian, 4:265

Bentley Inc., 3:22

Berkshire Hathaway Inc., 1:108

Berne Convention, 4:51

Berners-Lee, Tim, 1:*138, 275*

biographical overview, 4:111

browser development, 1:274, 4:32–33, 169–170

as guru, 4:145

net neutrality concerns, 1:140, 4:162, 187

server software, 2:226

World Wide Web development, 2:226, 4:32–33, 111, 145, 186

Bernoulli, Jacques, 1:30

Bernoulli numbers, 1:30

Berry, Clifford, 1:50, 55–56, 63

Berson, Tom, 2:218

Berzelius, Jöns Jacob, 2:139

Best Buy, 4:49

Betamax videocassette technology, 2:262

Better Business Bureau (BBB), 4:53

Bezos, Jeff, 4:111–112

Bill and Melinda Gates Foundation, 1:85–86, 172, 4:113

Billings, John Shaw, 1:99

Bina, Eric, 4:33

BINAC (Binary Automatic Computer), 1:102, 2:91

Binary code, 1:6

Binary Coded Decimal Interchange Code (BCDIC), 2:52

Binary number system, 1:**34–37,** *35*

defined, 1:2, 34

digital computing use of, 1:49, 50

machine language use, 1:91

Binary operations, 1:35–36

Bing, 4:245

Biocomputers. *See* Molecular computing

Bioengineering, 3:35

Bioinformatics, 3:34–35, 57, 165

Biology, 3:**33–36,** *34*

mathematical, 3:158

molecular, 3:163–167, *164*

Biomedical engineering, 3:35

Biometrics, 2:179, 4:25, 26

BIOS (Basic Input Output System), 1:161

Bioterrorism, 1:75, 3:36

See also Terrorism

Bipolar Junction Transistors (BJTs), 1:245–246

Bitmapped display, 2:99–100

BITNET, 1:263, 4:174, 185

Bits, 1:2–3, 34

Bits per pixel, of color images, 4:77

Bits per second (bps), 2:17, 4:28

BJTs (bipolar junction transistors), 1:245–246

Black and white images, 1:36–37, 4:76

Black Hat hackers, 4:148

Blackberry mobile operating system, 4:208

Blade units, 2:228

Blindness, assistive technology, 4:15, 33, 34

Block diagrams. *See* Flowcharts

Blocking software. *See* Filtering software

Blocks, in programming, 2:2

Blood Music (Bear), 4:128

Blu-ray disc technology, 1:204–205, 2:244

Blue Box (hacking device), 4:148

Blue Gene P supercomputer, 3:46

Blue Horizon supercomputer, 1:234

Blue Origin, 4:112

BlueGene/L supercomputer, 2:175

Bluetooth wireless technology, 2:280, 4:209

BNF (Backus-Naur form), 2:2

BNS (BeiDou-2 Navigation System), 4:138

Bolt, Beranek, and Newman (BBN) company, 2:270

Bomb development. *See* Manhattan Project

Bombe (cryptographic machine), 1:56

Bonaparte, Marie, 4:265

Booker, Cory, 3:264

Boole, George, 1:20, 2:*25*, **25–27**

Boolean algebra, 2:25, 26, *27–30*, **27–30**

Boolean information retrieval, 1:114–115, 116

Boolean operators, 4:245

Boolean searches, 2:26–27

Boot viruses, 1:262, 264

See also Viruses

Boron, in semiconductors, 1:125–126

Bosnia and Herzegovina, cybercafes, 4:61

Boston Dynamics Inc., 4:44

Botkin, B. A., 4:265

Botvinnik, Mikhail, 3:45

Bouazizi, Mohamed, 3:219

Boulez, Pierre, 3:169

Bounded rationality concept, 4:253

Bowles, Kenneth, 2:197

Boyle, Danny, 4:75

Bps (bits per second), 2:17, 4:28

Braille output, 4:15

The Brain (play), 4:127

Brain research, 4:63

Brattain, Walter H., 2:**20–22**

    Bell Labs involvement, 1:34, 2:21

    semiconductor research, 1:128

    transistor invention, 1:66, 88, 125, 126, 241, 2:20

Braun, Karl Ferdinand, 4:206

Brick and click enterprises, 4:99

Bricklin, Daniel, 1:168, 3:198, 239

Bridges, 2:32–33

Bridging devices, 2:*31*, **31–34**

Brin, Sergey, 4:115–116

British Standards Institute (BSI), 1:120

British Telecommunications, 4:64

Britton, Lionel, 4:127

Broadband connections, 2:17, 4:28–29, 159–160

Broadcast telecommunications, 1:193, 238–239, 2:212, 3:113

Brown, Gordon, 4:235

Browsers, 4:**30–34**, *31*

    automatic teller machine interfaces, 3:30

    Berners-Lee, Tim development, 1:274, 4:32–33, 169–170

    cookies, 4:45–47

    digital library access, 4:80

    information access and, 4:160–161

    intranets, 4:188

    Java applets, 1:223, 2:161, 4:191–194

    JavaScript embedded programs, 4:194–199

    overview, 1:274, 3:131

    as primary Internet application, 4:169–170, 172

    See also specific types

Brute-force inference engines, 3:104

BSA (Business Software Alliance), 3:224–225

BSI (British Standards Institute), 1:120

Buchanan, Bruce, 3:102–103

Budgeting software, 3:3

Buffers, CPUs, 2:8

Buffett, Warren, 1:85, 108

Bugs. *See* Debugging

Bugzilla, 3:204–205

Bulletin board systems (BBSs), 3:216

Bunny suits, 4:212

Bus topology networks, 1:193–194, 2:155

Buses

    in CPUs, 2:43

    internal computer communication, 2:256

Bush, George W., 1:224, 4:120, 180, 237

Bush, Vannevar, 1:53, 61, 103–104, 3:191, 4:32, 250

Bushnell, Nolan, 1:79, 4:154

Busicom, 1:129

Business Software Alliance (BSA), 3:224–225

Busy tones (telephone system), 3:246

Bytes, 1:34, 160

C

C programming language, 1:33, 93, 2:197–198

C++ programming language, 1:33, 2:160

C-T-R (Computing-Tabulating-Recording Company), 1:101, 107, 268

CA (Certificate Authority), 1:67–68, 2:270, 4:25, 99

CAAD (Computer-aided architectural design), 3:21–22

Cable modems, 2:58

Cable television, 1:239

Cable transmission, 4:28–29, 30

Cable & Wireless, 4:176

Cache controllers, 2:35–36

Cache hits, 2:36

Cache memory, 1:89, 2:**35–37**, *36*

Caching, 2:267–268, *268*

CAD. *See* Computer-aided design (CAD)

CAD/CAM, CA Engineering, 3:*37*, **37–40**

    See also Computer-aided design (CAD); Computer-aided engineering (CAE); Computer-aided manufacturing (CAM)

Caesar cipher, 4:56

Cafe Cyberia, 4:59, 62

CAI (computer assisted instruction), 3:50–53

Cailliau, Robert, 2:226

Cain and Abel network security program, 3:214

Calculating machines

    abacuses, 1:1–2, *2*, 49–50

    adding machines, 1:2, 3

    analog devices, 1:2–5

    astronomy needs, 3:26–28

    Difference Engine, 1:20, 29–30, 95, 151, 152, 2:191, 3:191

    fictional depictions, 4:126

    mechanical calculators, 1:61

    neural networks, 3:177–180

    Pascaline, 1:208

    Turing Machine, 1:248, 250–252, 2:6, 4:11, 62

    See also Analytical engines

Calculators

    Asimov, Isaac prediction, 3:24

    Hewlett-Packard Company, 3:127

    history, 1:4–5

    Intel microprocessor invention, 1:129, 167

    Wang developments, 3:254

Calculus, lambda and predicate, 1:21

Calendars, electronic, 3:150

California Digital Library, 4:81

Callahan, Michael, 3:*234*

Callback modems, 1:222

Calm computing, overview, 3:99–100

CAM (computer-aided manufacturing), 3:38–39, 60–65, 4:255

Cambridge Journals Online, 4:102

Camcorders. *See* Video cameras

Cameras

    computer vision, 4:42–43

    document cameras, 4:104

    as input device, 2:112–113

    multiplane animation, 1:12

Cameron, James, 4:8, 74

Campaigns, political, 4:234–235, 236

Campbell, John, 3:25

Canada

    cybersecurity attacks, 1:225

    ING Direct bank cafes, 4:91

    Positive Train Control project, 3:208

Cancer

    biocomputer applications, 3:166

    cell phone concerns, 2:40–41, 3:42

    pattern recognition applications, 2:177

Canon, 4:75, 229
Canonic And-Or implementation, 2:77
CANs (controller area networks), 3:6
Capacitive touch screens, 2:185, 255
Capacitors, 1:160
Capek, Karel, 1:216, 3:24–25
CAPP (computer-aided process planning), 3:63–64
Carbon nanotubes, 3:49
Card readers
    ATMs, 3:30
    punched cards, 1:55, 58, 2:114
Card, Stuart, 4:221
Careers
    computer professionals, 3:54–57
    distance learning, 3:91
    multimedia development, 2:106
    system analysts, 2:248
    systems designers, 2:251
Carlson, Chester, 1:276, 278
Carnegie Institute of Technology, 3:79
Carnegie Mellon University, 3:90, 4:81, 185
Carpal tunnel syndrome, 1:66, 149–150
Carter, Thomas ("Tom"), 2:38–39
Case-based design tools, architecture, 3:22
Cash, digital, 1:69, 4:107
CAT scans, 3:65–67, 134
Catalog servers, 2:227
    See also Servers
Cataloging, electronic, 3:152
Catastrophe insurance market, 4:108–109
Catastrophe Risk Exchange (CATEX), 4:109
Cathode ray tube (CRT) displays, 1:255, 2:78–81, 254–255
Cathodes, in vacuum tubes, 1:253, 255
CATV (Community Antenna Television) systems, 1:239
Cave Automated Virtual Environments (CAVEs), 1:256, 257–258
The Caves of Steel (Asimov), 3:25, 4:127
CB radio, 3:118
CBR (constant bit rate) service, 2:14
CC (Creative Commons) licensing, 4:51–52
CCDs (charge-coupled devices), 4:231
CCTV (closed circuit television) systems, 4:141

CD drives, 3:131
CD-R (compact disk-recordable) technology, 2:244
CD-ROM (compact disk-read only memory), 1:171, 2:243–244
CD-RW (compact disk-rewritable) technology, 2:244
CDC. See Control Data Corporation (CDC); U.S. Centers for Disease Control and Prevention (CDC)
CDC 160/160-A minicomputers, 1:175
CDC 6600 supercomputer, 3:68
CDC 7600 supercomputer, 3:68
CDMA (Code Division Multiple Access) networks, 1:119, 3:41, 42
CDMA2000/WCDMA technologies, 3:41, 4:209
CDPD (cellular digital packet data) service, 2:281
CDS2000E Enterprise Server, 4:5
CDV (cell delay variation), 2:15
Cedeno, Judy, 4:115
Cel animation, 1:9–10
Cell Delay Variation (CDV), 2:15
Cell header generation/extraction, 4:22
Cell Loss Priority (CLP), 4:20
Cell multiplex and demultiplex function, 4:22
Cell phone towers, 2:38
Cell phones, 3:40, 40–42
    authentication functions, 4:26
    e-mail capabilities, 4:168
    encryption needs, 4:58
    history, 2:38–41, 3:40–42
    phreaker hackers, 4:148
    social media access, 3:216, 217
    telephone system interactions, 3:246–247
    touch screens, 2:254
Cells (data packets), 4:19, 20
Cells, spreadsheets, 3:236–238, 237
Cells, virtual circuits, 2:13–14
Cellular automata, 4:11, 13
Cellular digital packet data (CDPD) service, 2:281
Cellular networks
    base stations, 3:40–41
    generations of, 1:240
    increasing data transmission capabilities, 2:59
    overview, 1:238
    varying standards, 1:119

Cellular neural networks (CNNs), 4:217
Cellular technology, 2:37–42, 38
Censorship: national, international, 4:35–37, 36
    Arab Spring Internet blockage, 3:219–220
    Internet control and, 4:178–179
    social media protests, 3:222
Census Bureau, 1:39–42, 40, 96, 100, 101, 107, 4:236
Centaur Records, 1:185
Center for Democracy and Technology, 4:37
CENTRal EXchange (CENTREX) service, 2:270
Central processing units (CPUs), 2:42–45, 43
    assembly language and architecture, 2:7–9
    cache memory, 2:35–37, 36
    mainframes, 1:155, 156, 157
    security measures, 2:217
    supercomputers, 1:232, 233
    vector processing, 1:233–234, 3:68
    See also Microprocessors; Parallel processing
Centronics connectors, 2:224
Century Optics, 4:74
CenturyLink, 4:176
Cerf, Vinton, 1:25, 4:260
CERN (European Council for Nuclear Research), 3:193, 4:32, 111
CERT (Computer Emergency Response Team), 4:87–88, 185
Certificate Authority (CA), 1:67–68, 2:270, 4:25, 99
Challenge-response password systems, 1:222
Challenger (space shuttle), 3:228, 4:125
Character-based interfaces, 3:249
Character codes. See Codes
Charge-coupled devices (CCDs), 4:231
Chat servers, 2:227
    See also Servers
Check out (e-commerce), 1:68
Checks, digital, 4:109
Checksums, 2:151
Chemistry, 4:37–41, 38
Chemometrics, 4:40
Chen, Steve, 3:69
Chess, computer, 1:83

Chess playing, 3:*43*, **43–47**, *44*, 4:253

China
abacuses, 1:1
Compass global positioning system, 4:138
copyright concerns, 4:51
cybersecurity allegations, 1:224, 4:150, 178
e-banking, 4:*92*
nationwide intranet, 4:189
National People's Congress Web site, 4:*233*
Qzone social media site, 4:257
software piracy, 3:*224*, 225
space program, 3:230

Chip manufacturing, 3:*47*, **47–50**

Cholesteric liquid crystal displays, 2:82, 83, 84

Chomsky, Noam, 2:2

Chowning, John, 1:185, 2:144, 3:168

CHRISTMAS.EXE worm, 1:263

Chromatic dispersion, 2:92

Church, Alonzo, 1:21, 248, 251, 2:123, 3:141

CICS (Customer Information Control System), 1:157

CIM (computer integrated manufacturing), 3:64
See also Manufacturing

Ciphers, 4:56
See also Cryptography

Circuit-switched networks, 1:193, 2:13

Circular slide rules, 1:230

Cisco Systems, 4:189

Citibank, 4:91

Citizens Band (CB) radio, 3:118

Citizens Radio Corporation, 3:118

CIX (Commercial Internet Exchange), 4:175, 186

Cladding, of optical fibers, 2:91

Clarke, Arthur C., 3:25

Clarke, Richard, 1:224

Classes of objects, 1:135, 2:161

Classifiers, in pattern recognition, 2:176–178

Classroom response systems, 4:105

Claymation, 1:10

Cleveland Cavaliers (basketball team), 4:69

Click enterprises, 4:99

Clickers (response systems), 4:105

Client/server technology, 2:**45–50**, *46*
databases, 2:239
FTP, 4:133–134
servers, 2:225–228

Climategate hacking scandal, 3:124

Clinton, Bill, 1:*220*

Clocks, in CPUs, 2:44

Closed Circuit Television (CCTV) systems, 4:141

Closing, of a window, 1:270

Cloud storage, 2:113, 244, 4:247

CLP (Cell Loss Priority), 4:20

Cluster analysis, 4:66–67

CMN (Common Music Notation), 3:167–168

CMOS memory, 2:137

CMOS technology. *See* Complementary Metal Oxide Semiconductor (CMOS) technology

CMYK (Cyan, Magenta, Yellow, Black) images, 4:76

CNC/NC (computer numeric control/numeric control) codes, 3:38

CNNs (cellular neural networks), 4:217

Coase, Ronald, 4:97

Coaxial cables, 1:157, 194, 2:257

COBOL (Common Business Oriented Language)
as high-level language, 1:93
history, 2:195–196
Hopper, Grace contributions, 1:101, 102
mainframe applications, 1:157
Microsoft version, 1:170
second generation computer use, 1:88

Cochrane, Peter, 4:64

Code Division Multiple Access (CDMA) networks, 1:119, 3:41, 42

Code generation, by compilers, 2:63–64

Codes, 2:**50–53**, *51*

Codes of ethics, 4:118–120

Coding techniques, 2:**53–56**, *54t–56t*

Cognitive ergonomics, 1:76

Coherent waves, 3:146

CoLab project (Xerox PARC), 3:59–60

Collaborative office automation systems, 1:198–199

Collaborative software. *See* Groupware

Collector terminals, of transistors, 1:126, 245

Colleges and universities
computer professional programs, 3:55

digital library projects, 4:81
electronic campuses, 4:103–106
learning management systems, 3:51–52, 53
proxy servers, 4:101–102
See also specific schools

Color depth, 4:77

Color display, 1:37, 2:80

Color images, 1:37, 4:76
See also Digital images

Color laser printers, 2:190

Colorado, cybercafes, 4:61

Colossus (cryptographic machine), 1:57, 61, 87, 4:57

Colossus (Jones), 4:127

Columbia supercomputer, 1:191

COM (computer output microfilm), 2:191

Comcast Communications, 2:18

Comcast Corp. v. FCC (600 F.3d 642, 2010), 2:18

"Command and Conquer" (simulation game), 1:83

Command line interfaces, 1:132, 133, 2:164, 3:249–250, 4:156, 262–263

Commercial Data Servers, 4:5

Commercial Internet Exchange (CIX), 4:175, 186

Commodore video games, 1:14–16

Common Business Oriented Language. *See* COBOL (Common Business Oriented Language)

Common Music Notation (CMN), 3:167–168

Communication channels, defined, 4:166

Communication devices, 2:**56–59**, *57*

Communication satellites, 2:212

Communications networks. *See* Networks

Communications privacy concerns, 1:209
See also Privacy

Communications protocols. *See specific protocols*

Communications servers, 2:227
See also Servers

Communications systems, speaking impairments, 4:16

Community Antenna Television (CATV) systems, 1:239

Compact disk-read-only memory (CD-ROM), 2:243–244

Compact disk-recordable (CD-R) technology, 2:244

Compact disk-ReWritable (CDRW) technology, 2:244

Companding, of sound signals, 2:234

Compass global positioning system, 4:138

Compatibility (open systems design), 2:*60*, **60–62**

Compatibility standards, 1:118

Compiler-compilers, 2:2

Compilers, 2:**63–65**
    grammar developments, 2:2
    high-level languages, 1:93
    Hopper, Grace contributions, 1:102
    minicomputers, 1:175, 176
    procedural languages, 2:192–193

Complement method, 1:208

Complementary Metal Oxide Semiconductor (CMOS) technology
    chip manufacturing, 3:47–48
    image sensors, 4:231
    mainframes, 1:156
    NASA applications, 1:191, 3:231
    overview, 1:161

Compound statements, 2:2

Compression. *See* File compression

CompuServe, 3:216

Computation. *See* Calculating machines

Computational chemistry, 4:39

Computational steering, 3:210

Computed tomography (CT), 3:65–67, 134

Computer-aided architectural design (CAAD), 3:21–22

Computer-aided design (CAD)
    architecture applications, 3:21–22
    CAM integration, 3:38–39
    computerized manufacturing and, 3:60–61
    fashion, 3:107, 108, 109
    overview, 3:37–38
    Sutherland, Ivan contributions, 3:20–21, 37

Computer-aided engineering (CAE), 3:39, 61

Computer-aided manufacturing (CAM), 3:38–39, 60–65, 4:255

Computer-aided process planning (CAPP), 3:63–64

Computer animation. *See* Animation

Computer assisted instruction (CAI), 3:**50–53**

Computer assisted reporting, 4:201–202

Computer Associates, 4:115

Computer bugs. *See* Debugging

Computer Emergency Response Team (CERT), 4:87–88, 185

Computer Fraud and Abuse Act of 1986, 1:**42–46**

Computer games. *See* Games

Computer integrated manufacturing (CIM), 3:64

Computer languages. *See* Programming languages

Computer music. *See* Music, computer

Computer Oracle and Password System (CRACK), 3:214, 215

Computer output microfilm (COM), 2:191

Computer professionals, 3:**54–57**

Computer Professionals for Social Responsibility, 4:37

Computer programming. *See* Programming

Computer Science: A First Course (Organick, et al.), 3:188

Computer scientists, 1:25, *46*, **46–48**

Computer security. *See* Security

"Computer Space" (video game), 1:79

Computer Supported Cooperative Work (CSCW), 3:**57–60**

Computer system interfaces, 2:**65–68**
    See also Input/output (I/O) devices; User interfaces

Computer vision, 4:**41–45**, 77–78

Computerized manufacturing, 3:**60–65**

Computing Scale Company, 1:107

Computing-Tabulating-Recording Company (C-T-R), 1:101, 107, 268

Conceptualization, for system analysis, 2:247–248

Concurrency control, 2:238, 239

Concurrent client server model, 2:48
    See also Client/server technology

Condensers, for memory, 1:56

Conditional statements, 2:2

Cones (speakers), 2:233

Cones (vision), 4:41–42

Conforming sessions, video editing, 3:113

Connect America project, 4:160

Connection management, 2:150

Connectivity kits, 4:*28*

Connectivity rates. *See* Data rates

Connectors, data transmission, 2:224

Conrail (Consolidated Rail Corporation), 3:207

Constant bit rate (CBR) service, 2:14

Consumer information
    privacy concerns, 1:209–211
    social media access, 3:218–219

Contemporary Legend: A Folklore Bibliography (Bennett and Smith), 4:265

Control Data Corporation (CDC), 1:175, 3:68

Control net layer (process control), 3:*194*, 196

Control units, of CPUs, 2:8, 43–44

Control Video Corp., 1:82

Controller area networks (CANs), 3:6

Convention on Cybercrime (Budapest, Hungary), 1:224

Convergence, in telecommunications, 1:239–240

Convergence Sublayer (CS), 4:22, 23

Conway, John Horton, 4:11, 12

Cook, Timothy D., 1:19, 146

Cookies, 1:210, 4:**45–47**, 225

Copernican revolution, 1:21

Copper cabling, 1:194

Cops Security Checker System (COPS), 3:214

Copy/cut and paste functionality, 3:138

Copy machines, 1:276–277

Copyright, 4:**47–52**, *48*, 161
    See also Intellectual property

Corbis, 4:146

Core memory, 3:253–254

Core, of optical fibers, 2:91

Core series microprocessor, 1:130, 4:215

Corel WordPerfect, 3:128, 262

Cormack, Allan, 3:**65–67**

Cornell University, 2:109, 4:172, 185

The Corpse in the Car (article), 4:265

Corpuses (computer programs), 1:45

Correlation analysis, data mining, 4:67

Cosmological modeling, 3:28

Cost concerns
    data mining, 4:69
    e-commerce transaction costs, 4:97–98
    e-readers, 4:95–96
    fashion design, 3:107

Counterfeiting, 3:224

Covering tracks phase, hacking, 3:122

Cowcatcher invention, 1:31

CPUs. *See* Central processing units (CPUs)

CRACK (Computer Oracle and Password System), 3:214, 215

Crackers (hackers), 4:149

Cracking, 3:225

Cranor, Lorrie Faith, 4:225–226

Crawlers, 1:116

Cray Computer Corporation, 3:69

Cray Research, 1:233, 3:68–69

Cray, Seymour, 1:175, 3:**68–70**

Cray supercomputers, 1:233, 235, 254, 3:68, 69

CRC (cyclical redundancy check) coders, 2:151

Creative Commons (CC) licensing, 3:184, 4:51–52

Creative Technology, 2:236

Credit cards
    ATMs *vs.,* 3:31
    for e-commerce payments, 1:69
    fraud, 1:70
    identity theft, 4:177
    online applications, 4:54
    online fraud, 4:54

Credit online, 4:**52–55**

Credit reports, 4:54

Crick, Francis, 4:39

Crookes, Sir William, 1:253

Crossbar switching, 4:217

Crowd Sourced Art, 4:8

CRT. *See* Cathode ray tube (CRT) displays

Cryptanalysts, 4:56

Cryptographic hash, 1:67

Cryptographic keys, 2:218–219

Cryptography, 4:*55,* **55–59**
    authentication and, 4:24, 25
    defined, 1:67
    digital signatures, 4:87
    e-commerce use, 1:67–68, 4:93
    early computers, 1:56–57, 61
    hardware, 2:218–219
    introduction, 4:185
    Kerberos authentication scheme, 4:101
    mathematical foundations, 3:158
    RSA public-key cryptosystem, 1:221, 4:58

Turing, Alan work, 1:56, 61
    VPNs, 2:270

CSCW (Computer Supported Cooperative Work), 3:57–60

CSIRAC, 2:144

CSNET, 4:174, 185

CT (computed tomography), 3:65–67, 134

Cuba, hacking into US systems, 4:150

Cuban Missile Crisis (1962), 4:142

The Cuckoo's Egg: Tracking a Spy through the Maze of Computer Espionage (Stoll), 1:223

Curiosity rover, 2:209

Cursors, 2:182–183

Curved interpolation, 1:11

Customer Information Control System (CICS), 1:157

Cut and paste functionality, 3:138

Cut prints, 1:9

CuteFTP application, 4:263

Cutout animation, 1:9, 10

Cybercafes, 4:**59–62,** *60*

Cybercrime, international treaties, 1:223–224

Cybernetics, 4:**62–64,** 142–144

Cyberpunk fiction, 4:128

Cybersecurity. *See* Security

Cybersecurity Research and Development Act (2002), 1:224

Cybertherapy, 3:161

Cyberwarfare. *See* Internet control and cyberwarfare

Cyclical redundancy check (CRC) coders, 2:151

Cylinders, on magnetic disks, 2:242

Cylindrical slide rules, 1:230, *231*

D

da Vinci Surgical System, 2:210

Daisywheel printers, 2:191

D'Albe, E. E. Fournier, 2:166

Dallas Semiconductor, 2:218–219

Dangling string network monitors, 3:100

Dark fiber networks, 2:94

DARPA (Defense Advanced Research Projects Agency), 1:97, 138, 4:44, 184
    See also ARPANET

DARPA Grand Challenge, 4:44

DARPA Robotics Challenge, 4:44

Dartmouth University, 3:141, 142

Data caches, 2:36–37

Data Definition Language (DDL), 2:238

Data Encryption Standard (DES), 4:57

Data entry, interactive systems, 1:133

Data Extraction System (Census Bureau), 1:41

Data flow diagrams (DFDs), 2:251

Data gloves, 2:67, 105, 273

Data Manipulation Language (DML), 2:238

Data mining, 4:**65–70**
    e-commerce, 4:98
    social media users, 3:218
    supercomputer applications, 1:234

Data piracy. *See* Piracy

Data processing, 1:39–42, 3:**71–72,** 4:235–236

Data rates
    ATM transmission, 2:13–14
    broadband communications, 4:29
    cable, 2:58
    fiber optics, 2:59, 93
    mobile computing, 4:208
    MPEG standards, 2:15
    network design considerations, 2:147–148, 257
    telephone lines, 2:58
    USB connections, 2:12, 67, 224
    wireless communications, 2:59, 4:208
    See also Bandwidth

Data sampling. *See* Sampling

Data structures, 2:158

Data visualization, 3:**73–75,** *74,* 209–212, *210,* 238

Data warehousing, 4:**70–73**

Database management software, 3:**75–78**
    agents, 4:1–2
    art applications, 4:9
    automatic data processing, 2:85
    chemistry applications, 4:39, 40
    data warehousing systems, 4:72
    early developments, 1:33
    geographic information systems and, 3:115, 117
    medical applications, 3:161–162
    overview, 3:71–72
    in productivity software, 3:199
    railroad use, 3:206–207
    SQL, 1:94, 2:238–240, *239,* 3:76–77

Database servers, 2:227
See also Servers
The Day the Earth Stood Still (film), 4:128
DB-25 connectors, 2:224
DDL (Data Definition Language), 2:238
DDoS (distributed denial of service), 1:224, 2:118, 3:213, 4:180–181
De facto standards, 1:119
De Forest, Lee, 1:86, 253
De jure standards, 1:119
De Morgan, Augustus, 1:151
Deafness, assistive technology, 4:16–17, 18
"Death Race" (video game), 1:81
Debit cards, 3:31
Debugging
origin of term, 1:60, 101, 255
project management, 3:204–205
DEC (Digital Equipment Corporation), 1:15, 44, 176
Decibel (unit), 2:24
Decideability problem, 1:251
Decimal number system. *See* Base-10 number system
Decision support systems (DSSs), 3:**79–81**
agriculture needs, 3:5–6
geographic information systems and, 3:115, 116
overview, 2:109
in programming, 2:201
systems design, 2:250–251
Decision trees, 2:178, 4:68
Decrypted values, 1:67
Dede, Chris, 1:257–258
Deep Blue chess competition, 1:83, 111, 3:44–45
Deep Fritz chess program, 3:45
Defense Advanced Research Projects Agency. *See* DARPA (Defense Advanced Research Projects Agency)
Defense Meteorological Satellite Program (DMSP) Operational Linescan System, 3:*210*
Definiteness, in algorithms, 2:5
Defragmentation tools, 3:129
Delagi, Greg, 2:*262*
Delay-line storage, 1:58
Dell laptops, 2:*104*
DeMarco, Tom, 2:251

Demodulation of signals, 2:57–58
DENDRAL, 3:102–103, 144
Denial of service cybersecurity attacks, 1:224, 2:118, 3:213, 4:180–181
Denning, Peter J., 4:145
Derivatives, 1:4
DES (Data Encryption Standard), 4:57
Desargues, Girard, 1:207
Descartes, René, 1:207–208
Descendants, in object-oriented programming, 2:159–160
Descriptive markup, 2:131, 3:85–86
See also Markup languages
Design tools, 2:28–29, **69–72,** *70, 71, 72*
Desktop publishing, 3:**82–86**
journalism use, 4:200–201
office automation systems, 1:197
productivity software, 3:199–200
technology, 3:241–245
word processing *vs.,* 3:82, 262
Desktop-style windows interface, 1:270
Desktop videoconferencing, 1:198
Destroy method (Java applets), 4:192
DETC (Distance Education and Training Council), 3:88
Deterministic models, political events, 4:237
Dethloff, Jürgen, 2:205
Deutsch Institute fur Normung (DIN), 1:120
Developer's office suite software, 3:137
Developing nations, information access, 4:161–162
Device managers, in operating systems, 2:162, 163
Devol, George C., Jr., 1:213
DFDs (data flow diagrams), 2:251
Dialects, of programming languages, 2:193
DIALOG information service, 1:114
Dialog-oriented systems, 1:133
Dick Tracy comic book series, 3:119
Dictation systems, 3:234–236, 4:16
Difference Engine, 1:20, 29–30, 95, 151, 152, 2:191, 3:191
Differential analyzers, 1:4, 53, 3:191
Differential equations, 1:4, 5
Differential GPS measurements, 4:137
Diffie, Whitfield, 4:58
Digital backs (cameras), 4:230
Digital cameras. *See* Cameras

Digital cash, 1:69, 4:107
Digital cellular systems, 2:40
Digital certificates. *See* Certificate Authority (CA)
Digital checks, 4:109
Digital computing, 1:**49–51**
abacuses, 1:1–2, 49–50
analog computing *vs.,* 1:2–3, 4–5
mixed systems, 1:49
physics applications, 3:192, 193
speed *vs.* accuracy, 1:50, 51
Digital divide, 4:159–162
Digital Equipment Corporation (DEC), 1:15, 44, 176
Digital filmmaking, 4:*73,* **73–76**
Digital images, 4:**76–78**
Digital integrated circuits, 1:126–127
Digital Landfill (art Web site), 4:8
Digital libraries, 3:152–153, 4:*79,* **79–83**
Digital Library Federation (DLF), 4:79
Digital Living Network Alliance (DLNA), 2:148
Digital logic design, 2:*73,* **73–78,** *74, 75, 76, 78t*
Digital Millennium Copyright Act (DMCA), 3:225, 4:50
Digital music synthesis, 1:184
Digital photography, 4:*83,* **83–86,** **229–232**
Digital rights management (DRM), 4:50
Digital signatures, 1:221, 4:58, **86–89,** *87, 88*
Digital single lens reflex (DSLR) cameras, 4:75
Digital subscriber line. *See* DSL (digital subscriber line)
Digital telephony, 1:237–238
See also Telephone networks
Digital-to-analog conversion
chip-based, 1:51
for mixed systems, 1:49
music synthesis, 1:184, 2:142–145
time lags, 1:50–51
Digital versatile disks. *See* DVDs (digital versatile disks)
Digital wallets, 1:69, 4:109
Digitizing tablets, 2:254
Dijkstra, Edsger W., 2:201
DIN (Deutsch Institute fur Normung), 1:120

Diode tubes, 1:253

Diodes
    optical communications, 1:202
    photo, 3:147
    in transistors, 1:245

Direct mail, political applications, 4:234

Direct manipulation systems, 1:133, 134–135

Director (multimedia authoring system), 1:14–15

Directories, search engines, 4:245

Disabilities
    assistive computer technology, 4:13–19, *14*
    educational virtual reality, 1:258
    keyboards, 1:150
    user interfaces, 3:251
    voice commands, 3:252
    whiteboard adaptations, 4:105

Disabilities Discrimination Act (United Kingdom), 4:13–14, 18

Disaster insurance market, 4:108–109

Discrete event simulation, 1:228
    See also Simulation

Discrete numbers, defined, 1:36

Discussion groups, e-mail, 1:73–74, 75

Disintermediation, 1:70

Disk defragmentation tools, 3:129

Disk management tools, 3:129

DiskOnKey flash drives, 2:243

Disney, Roy O., 1:12

Disney, Walt, 1:10, 11–12

Display devices, 2:**78–84,** *79,* 3:30, 4:156
    See also Graphic devices

Distance Education and Training Council (DETC), 3:88

Distance learning, 2:104, 126, 3:*87,* **87–92,** 4:103–106

Distant/asynchronous distance learning, 3:90

Distant/synchronous distance learning, 3:89

Distracted driving, 2:41–42, 3:42

Distributed authentication, 1:222

Distributed computing systems, 2:46–50
    See also Client/server technology

Distributed data warehousing systems, 4:71–72

Distributed denial of service (DDoS), 1:224, 2:118, 3:213, 4:180–181

Distributed processing databases, 2:239

Distributed system agents, 4:2, 3

District boundaries, data processing, 4:235

Division of Parasitic Diseases (CDC), 3:33–34

DLF (Digital Library Federation), 4:79

DLNA (Digital Living Network Alliance), 2:148

DMCA (Digital Millennium Copyright Act), 3:225, 4:50

DML (Data Manipulation Language), 2:238

DMSP (Defense Meteorological Satellite Program) Operational Linescan System, 3:*210*

DNA computing, 3:166, 4:128, 211–213, 217

DNA sequencing, 3:163–165

DNA structure, 4:39

DNS (Domain Name System), 1:222, 4:178, 185

Document cameras, 4:104

Document Object Model (DOM), 4:197

Document processing, 2:**85–87,** 3:82–86, 149–150

Document vectors, 1:115

Document viewers, 3:130

Documentation
    in object-oriented programming, 2:160
    open source applications, 3:186
    system analysis, 2:248

DoD (Department of Defense) firewall model, 4:130

Dodge, Charles, 1:185

DOM (Document Object Model), 4:197

Domain Name System (DNS), 1:222, 4:178, 185

Domain Wall Memory (DWM), 1:162, 2:139

Donor impurities, 1:243, 244

Dope sheets, 1:9

Doping, of semiconductors, 1:125, 165, 3:48

Doppler radar, 3:257

Dorsey, Jack, 3:217

Dorson, Richard M., 4:265

DOS operating system
    as command line system, 1:132, 3:249–250
    in IBM PCs, 1:18, 110
    MS-DOS, 1:84, 170, 171, 2:163, 4:267

Dot matrix printers, 2:188–189

Dotcom, Kim, 4:*48*

dot.coms, 1:69, 3:54, 4:247–248

Dots per inch (dpi), 2:188

Downlink data rates, 2:258–259

Download *vs.* upload bandwidth, 4:29–30

Dr. Strangelove: Or How I Learned to Stop Worrying and Love the Bomb (film), 4:127

Dragging, in windows interfaces, 1:270, 271

Dragon capsule, 3:230

DRAM (dynamic random access memory), 1:89, 2:137

Driverless cars, 4:44

Driving while distracted, 2:41–42, 3:42

DRM (digital right management), 4:50

Droids, 1:216
    See also Robotics

Drop-down menus, 1:271

Drugs, prescription, 3:162

Drum scanners, 4:231–232

Dry-erase boards, 2:254

DSL (digital subscriber line)
    bandwidth capacity, 4:29
    overview, 2:58–59
    service providers, 4:247, 248

DSLR (digital single lens reflex) cameras, 4:75, 84–85

DSSs. *See* Decision support systems (DSSs)

Dudley, Homer, 2:144

Duke University, 3:216

Dumb terminals, 1:158, 177–178, 4:207–208

Dummy statements, 2:2

Duplex cellular networks, 2:38
    See also Cellular networks

DuPont, 2:241

DVDs (digital versatile disks), 2:244, 3:113, 131

Dvorak, August, 1:149

Dvorak keyboard layout, 1:149

DWM (domain wall memory), 1:162, 2:139

DXplain decision support system, 3:81

Dye-based inks, 2:190

Dye sublimation, 2:190–191

Dynabook project, 1:95, 272

Dynamic data visualizations, 3:73

dynamic Hypertext Markup Language (dHMTL), 1:14

Dynamic links, 4:100

Dynamic random access memory (DRAM), 1:89, 2:137

Dynamic routing, 4:240–241

Dynatech Newstar, 4:200

E

E-agriculture, 3:7

E-banking, 1:70, 3:31, 4:**91–94,** *92,* 109

E-benefits Company, 4:115

E-books, 3:52, 151, 153, 4:**94–97,** *95*

E-cash, 1:69, 222, 4:107

E-commerce, 1:**67–72,** *68*
   airline reservations, 3:18
   cookies, 4:45–47
   electronic markets, 4:106–110
   public-key cryptography, 4:58–59
   See also E-banking

E-commerce, economic and social aspects, 4:**97–100**

E-journals and e-publishing, 3:153, 4:**100–102**

E-learning. *See* Computer assisted instruction (CAI); Distance learning

E-mail, 1:**72–76,** *73*
   emoticons, 1:74, 4:187
   Gopher protocol, 3:137
   groupware, 3:201
   hearing impairment benefits, 4:17
   Internet precursor network, 4:184
   in office automation systems, 1:197–198
   as primary Internet application, 4:168–169
   privacy concerns, 1:75, 223, 4:224–225
   security measures, 1:221
   urban myth circulation, 4:266

E-mail addresses, 1:72–73

E-mail discussion groups, 1:73–74, 75

E-mail servers, 2:227
   See also Servers

E-publishing. *See* E-books; E-journals and e-publishing

E-readers, 4:*95,* 95–96, 97

E-Signature (Electronic Signatures in Global and National Commerce) Act, 4:87

E-text, 4:94

EAPROM (electrically alterable programmable read-only memory), 2:138

Early computers, 1:**53–60**
   Atanasoff-Berry Computer, 1:55–56, 63, 66
   Bell Labs Model 1, 1:53–54
   Colossus, 1:57, 61, 87, 4:57
   differential analyzers, 1:4, 53
   EDSAC, 1:50, 59–60, 65, 87
   EDVAC, 1:58–59, 63, 66, 87, 2:90, 91
   ENIAC, 1:6, 50, 57–58, 63–64, 65–66, 87, 219, 254–255, 2:89–90, 3:71, 72
   first generation, 1:86–88
   Great Britain developments, 1:56–57, 59, 61–62, 64–65
   Harvard Mark I/II/III/IV, 1:54–55, 60, 62, 101, 102, 108, 268, 3:253–254
   Manchester Mark I, 1:59, 64–65
   second generation, 1:88
   UNIVAC I, 1:39–40, 87–88, 96, 102, 219, 3:68, 71
   Whirlwind, 1:60
   workplace impact, 4:255
   Z1, 1:55, 65, 2:282, *282*
   See also Generations, computers

Early pioneers, 1:**61–66**
   Aiken, Howard, 1:54, 62, 66, 268, 2:283, 3:253
   Atanasoff, John V., 1:50, 55–56, 62–63, 66, 2:90–91
   Berry, Clifford, 1:50, 55–56, 63
   Bush, Vannevar, 1:53, 61, 103–104, 3:191, 4:32, 250
   Eckert, J. Presper, Jr., 1:39–40, 50, 57–58, 63, 64, 87, 88, 2:89–91, 3:72
   Mauchly, John, 1:24, 39–40, 50, 57–58, 63–64, 66, 87, 88, 2:89–91, 3:72
   Newman, Maxwell, 1:59, 64
   Turing, Alan, 1:22–23, 24–25, 56, 61, 96, 247–250, 2:5–6, 3:45, 4:*10,* 62, 250
   von Neumann, John, 1:58–59, 66, 87, 248, 2:90, 91, 275–277, 3:141, 4:11
   Wilkes, Maurice V., 1:50, 59, 64, 65, 87, 249

Williams, Sir Frederic, 1:59, 64–65

Zuse, Konrad, 1:55, 65, 2:281–283

EARN (European Academic and Research Network), 4:174

EASSy undersea cable, 4:162

Eastman Kodak Company, 4:232

eBay, 4:53, 108, 115

EBCDIC (Extended Binary Coded Decimal Interchange Code), 1:*160,* 2:52

EBONE (European Internet backbone), 4:173, 175

eBook Reader software, 3:130

ECHO satellite, 2:212

Eckert, J. Presper, Jr., 2:**89–91**
   EDVAC development, 2:90, 91
   ENIAC development, 1:39–40, 50, 57–58, 63, 64, 87, 2:89–90, 3:72
   UNIVAC development, 1:88

Eckert-Mauchly Award, 4:5

Eckert-Mauchly Computer Corporation, 2:89

ECMA (European Computer Manufacturers' Association), 4:199

Ecology, mathematical, 3:158

Economic modeling, 3:**93–95**

Edge detection, 4:43

EDGE (Enhanced Data rates for GSM Evolution), 4:209

EDI (Electronic Data Interchange) protocol, 1:67

Edison, Thomas, 1:122, 253

EDSAC (Electronic Delay Storage Automatic Calculator), 1:50, 59–60, 65, 87

Edu-commerce, 1:71

Education
   chemistry, 4:38–39, 40
   computer assisted instruction, 3:50–53
   computer professionals, 3:55
   distance learning, 2:104, 126, 3:*87,* 87–92, 4:103–106
   educational software, 3:95–98
   electronic campuses, 4:103–106
   fashion design software, 3:109
   IEEE contributions, 1:123–124
   Logo use, 2:125–126
   mathematics learning, 3:158–159
   OMR testing scoring, 2:205

Education *(continued)*
Open Source Education project, 3:*184*
Organick, Elliot contributions, 3:187–188
virtual reality use, 1:*256, 256–260, 257*
See also Colleges and universities
Educational software, 3:**95–98**
EDVAC (Electronic Discrete Variable Automatic Computer), 1:58–59, 63, 66, 87, 2:90, 91
edX online course platform, 3:90, 4:106
EEPROM (Electronic erasable programmable read-only memory), 1:161
EGP (Exterior Gateway Protocol), 4:173
Egress/ingress (radio waves), 2:257
Egypt
Arab Spring protests, 3:219–220
cybersecurity attacks, 4:150
EIA (Engineering Industries Association), 1:120
Eich, Brendan, 4:198
8-bit code
black and white display, 1:36
color display, 1:37
800 telephone numbers, 3:246
Einstein, Albert, 2:277, 3:141
Eisenhower, Dwight, 1:87
Electrically alterable programmable read-only memory (EAPROM), 2:138
Electro-acoustic music, 1:184
Electroluminescent panels, 2:83
Electromagnetic relays, 1:65
Electromagnetic spectrum, 2:279–280
Electromechanical mouse, 1:181–182, 2:183
Electron guns, 1:255, 2:79
Electronic books. *See* E-books
Electronic calendars, 3:150
Electronic campuses, 4:**103–106**
Electronic cash (E-cash), 1:69, 222, 4:107
Electronic checks, 4:109
Electronic Data Interchange (EDI) protocol, 1:67
Electronic Delay Storage Automatic Calculator (EDSAC), 1:50, 59–60, 65, 87
Electronic Discrete Variable Automatic Computer (EDVAC), 1:58–59, 63, 66, 87, 2:90, 91

Electronic erasable programmable read-only memory (EEPROM), 1:161
Electronic Frontier Foundation, 4:37, 57, 186–187
Electronic journals. *See* E-journals and e-publishing
Electronic libraries. *See* Digital libraries
Electronic mail. *See* E-mail
Electronic markets, 4:**106–110**
See also E-commerce
Electronic meeting rooms, 3:59–60
Electronic Numerical Integrator and Computer. *See* ENIAC (Electronic Numerical Integrator and Computer)
Electronic Performance Support Systems (EPSSs), 3:52–53
Electronic purses. *See* Stored value cards
Electronic Signatures in Global and National Commerce (E-Signature) Act, 4:87
Electronic tally systems, 4:105
Electronic Visualization Laboratory (University of Illinois), 3:212
Electronic *vs.* digital signatures, 4:87
Electronic wallets, 1:69, 4:109
Elements (Euclid), 2:6
Ellison, Harlan, 4:127
Elographics, 2:254
Elxsi, Ltd., 4:5
Embedded computers, 3:62, 63
Embedded technology (ubiquitous computing), 1:136–137, 3:**98–102,** 160–161
Embedding, objects, 3:138–139
Emirati Louvre museum, 3:*20*
Emitter terminals, of transistors, 1:126, 245
Emoticons, 1:74, 4:187
Encapsulation, in object-oriented programming, 2:158–159
Encoding
information, 4:167
keyboards, 1:147–148
sound data, 2:234–235
Encryption. *See* Cryptography
Encyclopedias, multimedia, 3:130–131
End-effectors, 2:208
End-to-end architecture concept, 4:259
Enemy of the State (film), 4:127
Engelbart, Douglas, 1:104–105, 180–181, 2:186
Engelberger, Joseph, 1:213, 215

Engineering Industries Association (EIA), 1:120
England, Gary, 3:257
Enhanced Data rates for GSM Evolution (EDGE), 4:209
ENIAC (Electronic Numerical Integrator and Computer)
creation, 1:87, 2:89–90, 3:71, 72
ENIAC-on-a-chip, 1:254
general-purpose nature, 1:6, 50
history, 1:57–58, 63–64
programming, 1:65–66
security measures, 1:219
vacuum tubes in, 1:254–255
Enigma (cryptographic machine), 1:56
Enigma (rotor machine), 4:57
Enquire software program, 4:111
Enterprise information systems, 4:3
Enterprise networks, defined, 1:195
See also Wide area networks (WANs)
Entrepreneurs, 4:*110,* **110–118**
Entscheidungsproblem, 1:250, 251
Enumeration phase, hacking, 3:122
Environmental sciences, 3:35–36, 80, 124
EPC (European Patent Convention), 4:227–228
EPO (European Patent Office), 4:228
EPROM (erasable programmable read-only memory), 1:161, 2:138
EPSSs (Electronic Performance Support Systems), 3:52–53
Equation engines, 4:38
Erasable programmable read-only memory (EPROM), 1:161, 2:138
Eraserhead pointing devices, 2:186
Ergonomic keyboards, 1:149–150
Ergonomics, 1:**76–78,** 149–150, 3:251–252, 4:155–157
Ericsson smartphones, 2:180
Error correcting codes, 2:55–56, 55*t,* 56*t,* 150
Erwise (browser), 4:33
ESA (European Space Agency), 1:168
ESNET (Energy Sciences Network), 4:174, 176
Estridge, Phil, 1:110
Ethernet networks, 1:195, 278, 4:184
Ethics, 1:23, 27, 4:**118–121**
Euclid, 2:5, 6
Euclid's algorithm, 2:5

European Academic and Research Network (EARN), 4:174

European Computer Manufacturers' Association (ECMA), 4:199

European Organization for Nuclear Research, 3:216

European Patent Convention (EPC), 4:227–228

European Patent Office (EPO), 4:228

European Space Agency (ESA), 1:168, 3:229

Event analysis, 1:134, 2:158, 247

Events, JavaScript, 4:197–199

Exaggeration (animation), 1:14

Exclusive locking, 2:239

Exidy, 1:81

ExoMars program, 3:229

Expansion slots, 4:208

Expert systems, 3:**102–105**
    industrial robots, 3:63
    overview, 2:109–110
    political event simulation, 4:237
    See also Knowledge-based systems

Extended Binary Coded Decimal Interchange Code (EBCDIC), 1:*160,* 2:52

Exterior Gateway Protocol (EGP), 4:173

External storage. *See* Storage devices

Extraction and recognition, image, 4:43

Extrasolar planets, 3:28

Extraterrestrial life, SETI@home project, 3:27

F

Facebook
    Arab Spring role, 3:219, 221
    DDoS attacks, 4:181
    journalism use, 4:202
    launch, 3:216, 263–264, 4:117
    popularity, 4:257
    privacy concerns, 1:210
    scaling factors, 2:215–216

Facial recognition systems, 4:26

Facsimile (fax) machines, 1:198, 4:223

Factor analysis, data mining, 4:67–68

Fair Credit Reporting Act (FCRA), 4:54

Fair use concept, 4:49

Fairchild Camera and Instrument, 1:80

Fairchild Semiconductor, 1:88, 126, 2:22, 45

Fantasia (animated film), 1:12

Fashion design, 3:**107–109,** *108*

Fat client/server technology (FCST), 2:49
    See also Client/server technology

The Fatal Initiation (article), 4:265

Fawkes, Guy, 4:147

Fax machines, 1:198, 4:223

Fax servers, 2:227
    See also Servers

FBI (Federal Bureau of Investigation), 1:209

FCC. *See* U.S. Federal Communications Commission (FCC)

FCC, Comcast Corp. v. (600 F.3d 642, 2010), 2:18

FCRA (Fair Credit Reporting Act), 4:54

FCST (fat client/server technology), 2:49
    See also Client/server technology

FD-SOI (fully-depleted silicon-on-insulator) transistors, 1:246

FED (field emission display), 2:84

Federal Aviation Administration (FAA), 3:10, 11, 176–177

Federal Bureau of Investigation (FBI), 1:209

Federal Communications Commission (FCC). *See* U.S. Federal Communications Commission (FCC)

Federal interest computers, 1:43

Federal Internet Exchanges (FIX-E and FIX-W), 4:173

Federal Railroad Administration (FRA), 3:208

Feedback circuits, 1:4

Feeding systems, agriculture, 3:6, 7

A Feeling of Power (short story), 3:24

Feiertag, Rich, 2:218

Feigenbaum, Edward, 3:144

Fermat, Pierre de, 1:207

Fermilab, 3:193

Ferranti Mark I Computer, 1:*247*

Feurzeig, Wallace ("Wally"), 2:125

The Feynman Lectures on Physics (Feynman), 4:124–125

Feynman, Richard P., 4:**123–125,** *124*

Fiber for Communities project, 2:59

Fiber optics, 2:**91–95,** *92, 94t*
    data transmission rates, 1:194, 2:59, 92–93, 257
    developing infrastructure, 2:59
    history, 1:201–204, 2:91–95

mainframe channels, 1:157
    telephony, 1:237–238

Fiction, computers in, 1:15, 216, 3:23–26, 4:**125–129**

FIDONET, 4:174, 185

Field emission display (FED), 2:84

Field net layer (process control), 3:195

Fifth Generation Computer Systems (FGCS) project, 1:90

Fifth generation computers, 1:90

Fighting video games, 1:15

Filaments, in vacuum tubes, 1:253–254

File access controls, 1:220

File compression
    digital images, 4:77, 231
    JPEG and MPEG standards, 2:119–121, 4:77, 85, 231
    multimedia applications, 2:105
    sound data, 2:235
    video data, 2:261, 3:112

File compression utilities, 3:130

File Maker Pro, 3:77

File managers, in operating systems, 2:162, 163

File servers, 2:227
    See also Servers

File transfer protocol (FTP), 4:132–134, *133,* 186

Fill-in forms, 4:156

Film and video editing, 3:**109–114,** *110,* 4:*73,* 73–76, 201

Film photography, 4:83–84

Films, computer-related, 4:127, 128–129

Filo, David, 1:274, 275, 4:117

Filtering software, 4:36

Finance
    decision support systems, 3:79–80
    electronic markets, 4:106–109
    privacy concerns, 1:211

Fincher, David, 4:75

Fingerprint scanning, 2:118

Finiteness, in algorithms, 2:5

Firefox (browser), 2:225, 4:*31,* 31–32, 170, 172

Firewalls, 4:**129–132**
    defined, 3:123–124
    e-banking, 4:93
    home systems, 3:129–130
    intranets, 4:188–189
    origins of use, 1:223
    overview, 3:215

Firewire technology, 4:73, 74
First generation computers, 1:86–88
First generation programming
  languages, 1:91
First-person shooter video games, 1:15
First sale doctrine, 4:50–51
First Warning weather warning system,
  3:257
Fixed assets software, 3:3
Fixed-base simulators, 2:230
Flame (malware), 3:123, 4:150, 182
Flash drives, 2:243
Flash memory chips, 1:162
Flash plug-in, 1:15, 2:237
Flatbed scanners, 4:231
Fleming, John Ambrose, 1:253, 4:206
Flexible manufacturing systems, 3:62
Flight management systems (FMSs),
  1:50–51, 3:9–11, 14–15
Flight simulation, 1:227, 2:229–232,
  3:20
Flight simulator video games, 1:15, 4:157
Flight training software, 2:231–232
Flint, Charles R., 1:268
Flip-flop devices, 1:127, 2:7–8, 74
Floating-point arithmetic, 1:49
Floating-point operations per second
  (flops), 1:233, 235, 2:174, 175
Floppy disks, 2:242
Florida Virtual School, 3:87
Flow-Matic compiler, 1:102
Flowcharts, 2:69–71, 70, 201, 251
Fluxions, 1:4
Fly-by-wire navigation, 1:189–190
Flynn, Michael J., 2:172–173
FM (frequency modulation) synthesis,
  2:235, 3:171
FMSs. See Flight management systems
  (FMSs)
Focus windows, 1:271
FOIA (Freedom of Information Act),
  4:233
Follow-Through and Overlapping
  Action (animation), 1:14
Footprinting, 3:121–122
Force feedback controllers, 2:97–98
Foregrounds, animation, 1:10
Form-based programs, 1:132–133
Formatting text, word processors, 3:261
Formula Translator (FORTRAN). See
  FORTRAN (Formula Translator)
Formulas, in spreadsheet cells, 3:238

FormZ software, 3:22
Forrester, Jay W., 1:60, 2:136, 3:254
Forster, E. M., 4:126
Forsythe, A. I., 3:188
FORTRAN (Formula Translator)
  as high-level language, 1:93, 2:157
  history, 2:193–194
  Microsoft version, 1:170
  Organick, Elliot textbooks,
    3:187–188
  second generation computer use,
    1:88
Forward bias connections, 1:245
4G cellular technology, 1:240, 2:59,
  4:209
Fourth generation computers, 1:89–90
Fourth generation programming
  languages, 1:94
FRA (Federal Railroad Administration),
  3:208
Frame-grabbers, 4:42
Frame relay networking, 1:195
France
  broadband access, 4:160
  cybercafes, 4:61
  Minitel, 4:61
  Minitel network, 1:177–180, 178
  satellite programs, 3:229
  smart card use, 2:205
France Telecom, 1:177–179
Frankel, Stanley, 4:123
Franklin, Benjamin, 4:142
Frankston, Robert, 3:239
Fraud
  Computer Fraud and Abuse Act of
    1986, 1:42–46
  credit card, 1:70, 4:54
Free flight air traffic control, 3:14–15
Free Software Foundation (FSF), 3:183,
  184
Free speech. See Censorship: national,
  international
Free vs. open source software,
  3:183–185
Freedom of Information Act (FOIA),
  4:233
Freedom of speech, 4:120–121, 178
Freespace loss, 2:279
Frege, Gottlob, 1:20
Frend, William, 1:151
Frequency division multiplexing, 1:202,
  2:93, 3:41

Frequency modulation (FM)
  cell phone networks, 2:40
  radio networks, 2:38
Frequency modulation (FM) synthesis,
  2:235, 3:171
Frequency reuse, 2:39, 3:40
Frequency shift keying (FSK), 2:57, 58
Frequency sub-bands, 3:40, 41
Frisch, Otto, 3:66
FSF (Free Software Foundation),
  3:183, 184
FSK (frequency shift keying), 2:57, 58
FTP (file transfer protocol), 4:**132–134**,
  133, 186, 263–264
Fujitsu, 1:109, 155, *232*, 4:4
Full mesh topologies, 2:156
Full-motion video games, 1:15
Full-text indexing, 4:243
Full-text searching, 3:149
Fully-depleted silicon-on-insulator
  (FD-SOI) transistors, 1:246
Functional programming languages,
  2:123
    See also Programming languages
Fuzzballs, 4:173
Fuzzy logic, 3:105
Fylstra, Daniel, 3:239

G

Gaddafi, Muammar, 3:221
Gagadaily.com site, 4:148
Gale, Leonard, 2:141
Galileo Galilei, 3:211
Galileo global positioning system,
  4:138
Galileo International Inc., 3:17
Game animations, 1:15–16
Game controllers, 2:**95–99**, *96*
Game of Life (cellular automaton),
  4:11, 12
GameBoy (hand-held video game), 1:82
Games, 1:**79–83**, *80*
  animation technology, 1:15–16,
    79–83, *80*
  artwork inspirations, 4:9
  controllers, 2:95–99, *96*
  fictional depictions, 4:127–128
  home system software, 3:132
  online gaming, 2:98
  overview, 4:154
  simulation video games, 1:15, 83,
    228–229

Gaming servers, 2:227
   See also Servers
GAMS (General Algebraic Modeling System), 3:94
Gamut, of printers, 2:189–190
Gantt charts, 3:*203,* 204
GarageBand music software, 3:169
Garrison, Bruce, 4:202
Gates Foundation, 1:85–86, 172, 4:113
Gates, logic, 1:126–127, 2:73
Gates, Melinda French, 1:85, 86
Gates, William Henry ("Bill"), 1:*84,* **84–86,** 169, 172, 4:112–113, 146
Gateways, 2:33–34
Gattaca (film), 4:211
Gaussian classifiers, 2:178
GB (gigabyte), defined, 1:162
Gbps (gigabits per second), 2:17
Gemini Program, 3:227–228
Genachowski, Julius, 2:*18*
Gene sequencing, 3:34–35
Gene therapy, 3:165
General Algebraic Modeling System (GAMS), 3:94
General Electric, 3:188
General ledger accounting software, 3:1
General Motors (GM), 1:213
General Public License (GPL), 3:183–184
General purpose registers, 2:8
   See also Registers
Generations, cellular networks, 1:240
Generations, computers, 1:**86–90**
   See also Early computers
Generations, languages, 1:**91–95**
Generative computer-aided processing planning, 3:64
Generative systems, architecture, 3:22
Generic Flow Control (GFC), 4:20
Genetic sequences, 4:211–212
Genetics, computer-assisted research, 3:163–164
GEO (geostationary earth orbit), 2:211, 258–259, 4:139–140
Geographic information systems (GISs), 3:5, 6, **115–117,** 4:140
Geographical factors, scaling, 2:215
Geostationary earth orbit (GEO), 2:211, 258–259, 4:139–140
Geostationary Operational Environmental Satellites (GOES), 2:212

Germanium, as semiconductor, 1:125, 165
Gerrity, Tom, 3:79
Gerstner, Louis V., Jr., 1:110–111
GERTY (fictional robot), 4:128
Gery, Gloria, 3:52
GET command, 4:134
GFC (Generic Flow Control), 4:20
G.hn standard, 2:148
Ghonim, Wael, 3:220
GhostNet, 1:224
Giant magnetoresistance, 1:162, 2:139
Gibson, William, 1:261, 4:128
GIF animation, 1:8, 14
GIF images, 1:8, 14, 4:77
Gigabits per second (Gbps), 2:17, 4:28
Gigabyte (GB), defined, 1:162
Gigaflops (billions of floating-point operations per second), 1:233
Gilliam, Terry, 1:10
Giotto (space probe), 3:229
GISs. *See* Geographic information systems (GISs)
Glenn, John, 3:227
Global Positioning Systems (GPSs), 4:**135–138,** *136*
   agriculture applications, 3:5, 6
   development, 3:175–176
   driverless cars, 4:44
   overview, 2:213–214
   PDA and smartphones receivers, 2:180–181
   surveillance use, 4:140–141
Global surveillance, 4:**139–142**
Global System for Mobile (GSM) networks, 1:119, 3:41
Globalscape, 4:263
GLOSNASS global positioning system, 4:138
Gloves, data, 2:67, 105, 273
Glushkov, Victor M., 4:**142–144**
Gnomons, 3:173–174
Go to statements, 2:2
Goals, Operators, Methods, and Selection (GOMS) system, 4:221
Goddard Scientific Visualization Studio, 3:212
GOES (Geostationary Operational Environmental Satellites), 2:212
Goldberg, Emmanuel, 2:166
Goldfarb, Charles, 2:132

GOMS system (Goals, Operators, Methods, and Selection), 4:221
Google, 4:*242*
   driverless cars, 4:44
   Fiber for Communities project, 2:59
   founding, 4:115–116
   personalized information services, 4:164–165
   search engine approach, 4:244–245
Google Books, 2:168
Google Chrome, 1:274, 2:225, 4:31–32, 225
Google Docs, 2:168, 3:199
Google Drive, 2:168, 3:199
Gopher protocol, 3:137, 4:186
Gordon, George (Lord Byron), 1:150–151, 153
Gore, Al, 4:237
Gort (fictional robot), 4:128
Gosling, James, 4:145
Gould, Chester, 3:119
Government funding, research, 1:**95–97,** 188–193
GPL (General Public License), 3:183–184
GPO (U.S. Government Printing Office), 4:89
GPSs. *See* Global Positioning Systems (GPSs)
Gramm-Leach-Blilely Act of 1999, 1:211
Grammar, in programming, 2:2–3
Granholm, Jackson, 4:144
Graph theory, for network topologies, 2:154
Graphic devices, 2:**99–101,** 3:192–193
   See also Display devices
Graphic Interchange Format (GIF), 1:8, 14, 4:77
Graphical primitives, 3:211
Graphical user interfaces (GUIs)
   character-based interfaces *vs.,* 3:249
   evolution, 1:133, 3:250
   introduction, 1:18
   operating systems, 1:84, 2:163–164
Graphics cards, 1:15, 2:99, 3:114
Graphics tablets, 2:186
Gray, Elisha, 2:23, 24
Grayscale display, 1:36–37
Grosch, H. R. J., 4:145
Grosch's Law, 4:145

Gross, Alfred J., 3:**117–119**
Gross Electronics, 3:118, 119
Grötrupp, Helmut, 2:205
Groupware
    computer supported cooperative
        work and, 3:58–60
    for electronic collaboration, 1:198
    productivity software, 3:200–201
Groupware servers, 2:227
    See also Servers
Grove, Andy, 1:128, 130, 131
Groves, Leslie, 2:277, 4:125
Groves, Robert Martin, 1:41
GSM (Global System for Mobile)
    networks, 1:119, 3:41
Guardbands, 4:27
GUIs. *See* Graphical user interfaces
    (GUIs)
Gulliver's Travels (Swift), 4:125–126
"Gunfight" (video game), 1:80
Guns, analog-computer controlled, 1:4
Gunter, Edmund, 1:230, 231
Gurus, 4:**144–146**
Gyros (gyroscopes), 3:9

H

H. L. Hunley (submarine), 3:39
Hackers, 4:**147–151**, *148*
Hacking, 3:**121–125**
    ATMs, 3:31–32
    cookiejacking, 4:47
    Palin, Sarah e-mail, 1:75
    timeline of cybersecurity attacks,
        1:220–225
    See also Internet control and
        cyberwarfare
Haddock, Jon, 4:9
HAL (fictional computer), 4:127
Half-duplex radio systems, 2:38
Haloid Company, 1:276
Hamilton, Edmond, 4:126
Hamming code, 2:55–56, 56*t*
Hamming, Richard ("Dick"), 1:34, 2:55
Hand-drawn animation, 1:9–10
Hand-held video game units, 1:82
Handheld scanners, 2:168
    See also Scanners
Handoff, in cellular communications,
    2:39, 3:41
Handshakes, Telnet use, 4:264
Handwriting recognition, 2:167, 186
Hanging chads, 4:237

Hankey, Rosalie, 4:265
Hanna, William, 1:13
Hard copies, defined, 2:86
Hard-disk loading, 3:224
Hard drives, 2:106, 241–242, 243
Hardware authentication tokens,
    2:217–218
Hardware engineering, careers, 3:54, 55
Hardware representation, in
    programming languages, 2:1
Hart, Michael, 3:151
Harvard Cyclotron, 3:66
Harvard Mark I/II/III/IV computers,
    1:54–55, 60, 62, 101, 102, 108, 268,
    3:253–254
Harvard University
    edX online course platform, 3:90,
        4:106
    Facebook launch, 3:216, 263–264,
        4:117
    Zuckerberg, Mark affiliation, 3:263
Hashtags, 3:217
Hazen, Harold Locke, 1:53
HDLC (High-level Data Link Control),
    2:12
Head crashes, 2:243
Head-mounted displays (HMDs)
    early developments, 2:272–273
    educational use, 1:257, 259
    wearable computing, 3:100
Header data, in virtual circuits, 2:13–14
Header Error Control (HEC), 4:20,
    21–22
Headers, of packets, 2:151
Heal, Laird, 1:258
Health care. *See* Medical systems
Hearing impairments, assistive
    technology, 4:16–17, 18
Heath Robinson (cryptographic
    machine), 1:56–57
Hebb, Donald O., 3:180
HEC (Header Error Control), 4:20,
    21–22
HECC (High-End Computing
    Capability Project), 1:191
Heilig, Mort, 2:272
Hellman, Martin, 4:58
Help systems, application wizards,
    1:271–272
Henry, Joseph, 2:141
HEPNET, 4:174
Hertz, Heinrich, 2:279, 4:205

Heuristics
    artificial intelligence development,
        1:22
    defined, 1:22
    inference engines, 3:104
    knowledge-based systems, 3:143,
        144
Hewlett-Packard Company, 2:62,
    3:125–126, 4:115, *216*
Hewlett, William, 3:*125,* **125–127,**
    4:113–114
Hexadecimal number system, 1:35,
    36, 91
HIARCS (higher intelligence auto-
    response chess system), 3:46
Hidden Markov Models (HMMs),
    3:233–234
Hidden surface removal, 2:100–101
Higgs boson, 3:193
High definition television (HDTV),
    2:82, 4:153–154
High-definition video, 3:111, 114,
    4:74–75
High-End Computing Capability
    Project (HECC), 1:191
High-level Data Link Control (HDLC),
    2:12
High and low pressure areas (weather),
    3:258
High Order Language Working Group
    (HOLWG), 2:199
High order languages, 2:157–158, 199
High Performance Computing and
    Communications (HPCC) program,
    2:171
High precision/high recall search results,
    4:244
High precision/low recall search results,
    4:244
High-speed trains, 3:208
Higher intelligence auto-response chess
    system (HIARCS), 3:46
Hilbert, David, 1:251
Hiller, Lejaren, 1:185, 3:168
Hillis, W. Daniel, 2:200
Histograms, 3:75
History of computers. *See* Early
    computers; Early pioneers;
    Generations, computers
Hitachi, 1:109, 155
HMDs. *See* Head-mounted displays
    (HMDs)

HMMs (Hidden Markov Models), 3:233–234

Hodges, Larry, 2:274–275

Hoff, Marcian ("Ted"), 1:129

Hoffman, E. T. A., 4:126

Holberton, Frances Snyder, 1:66

Holey Optochip, 1:165–166

Holler, F. James, 4:40

Hollerith codes, 2:114

Hollerith, Herman, 1:39, 96, *99,* **99–101,** 107, 2:114

Hollerith tabulating machines, 1:99–101, *100,* 3:71

Holograms, 3:147

HOLWG (High Order Language Working Group), 2:199

Home entertainment, 4:*152,* **152–155**

Home location registers, 3:246–247

Home servers, 2:227
See also Servers

Home system software, 3:**128–132,** 137

Home theater systems, 4:*152*

HomePlug Powerline Alliance, 2:147–148

Honeywell, 2:90–91

Hopfield, John J., 3:180

Hopkins Beast, 1:213

Hopper, Grace, 1:60, **101–103,** *102*

Horty, John, 3:149

Host-based databases, 2:238

Host-based intrusion detection systems, 3:213–214

Host blocking, 4:36

Hounsfield, Godfrey Newbold, 3:*65,* **65–67**

HPCC (High Performance Computing and Communications) program, 2:171

HTC smartphones, 1:240, 2:181

HTML editors, 3:129

HTML (Hypertext Markup Language)
Berners-Lee, Tim contributions, 4:111, 145
browser use, 1:274, 4:31, 32
defined, 1:73
e-banking applications, 4:92
e-journal format, 4:102
e-mail use, 1:72
Java applets and, 4:191–192
JavaScript embedded programs, 4:194–199
overview, 2:*133,* 133–134

source code documentation, 2:160
XHTML development, 2:134–135

HTTP (Hypertext Transport Protocol)
Berners-Lee, Tim contributions, 4:32–33, 111, 145
browser use, 4:30–32
cookies, 4:45–47
defined, 1:67

HTTPS (Hypertext Transport Protocol with Security extension)
defined, 1:67
e-banking use, 4:93
e-commerce use, 1:67–68

Hughes, Chris, 4:117

Human brain research, 4:63

Human-computer interaction. *See* User interfaces

Human factors, user interfaces, 4:**155–157,** 256

Human Rights Watch, 4:36

Human *vs.* computer strengths, 1:76–77

Hurst, George Samuel, 2:254

Hybrid digital-analog music production, 2:142

Hydra chess computer, 3:45

HyperCard, 1:105

Hyperlinks
dynamic links, 4:100
hypertext and, 4:34
integrated software, 3:139
search engine results, 4:242, 243
sponsored links, 4:243

Hypermedia and multimedia, 1:*104,* 2:**103–107,** *104*
documents, 2:86
encyclopedias, 3:130–131
history, 1:104–105, 2:105
indexing speech recognition applications, 3:235, 236
office automation systems, 1:199
realism, 4:157
user interfaces, 3:250–251

Hypertext, 1:**103–105,** 4:32–33, 34, 111

Hypertext Markup Language. *See* HTML (Hypertext Markup Language)

Hypertext Transport Protocol. *See* HTTP (Hypertext Transport Protocol)

Hypertext Transport Protocol with Security extension (HTTPS). *See* HTTPS (Hypertext Transport Protocol with Security extension)

I

I Have No Mouth, and I Must Scream (Ellison), 4:127

I Love You virus (2000), 1:223

i-Minitel, 1:179

I/O controllers, 2:66

I/O (input/output) devices. *See* Input/output (I/O) devices

I, Robot (Asimov), 1:216, 4:127

I, Robot (film), 4:127

I, Robot (game), 1:15

IBM Corporation, 1:**107–112,** *108*
701 computer, 1:88, 108, 4:4
704 computer, 4:4
7090 computer, 1:33, 88
Amdahl, Gene Myron involvement, 4:4
Blue Gene P supercomputer, 3:46
C-T-R origins, 1:101, 107, 268
carbon nanotube development, 3:49
character code developments, 2:52
CHRISTMAS.EXE worm, 1:263
collaboration in industry, 1:170, 171, 2:62, 4:113
computer assisted instruction development, 3:50
Deep Blue chess competition, 1:83, 111, 3:44–45
flash drives, 2:243
FORTRAN association, 2:193, 194
Harvard Mark I involvement, 1:54–55, 108
Internet backbone connections, 4:175
intranet, 4:189
Lotus acquisition, 3:240
Magnetic Tape Selectric Typewriter, 3:259, 262
microcomputer development, 1:168
optical microchip development, 1:165–166
patents, 4:229
PDA introduction, 2:180
RAMAC 305 computer, 1:108
RS/4000 computer, 4:173
SGML development, 2:132
space program computers, 3:227–228
supercomputer development, 1:235, 2:175

IBM Corporation (continued)
Tabulating Machine Company origins, 1:101, 107
THINK slogan, 1:111, 267, *267*
Thompson, John W. involvement, 4:116
Wang Laboratories rivalry, 3:254, 259, 262
Watson computer, 1:23, 111
Watson, Thomas J., Jr. management, 1:108, 109–110, 268
Watson, Thomas J., Sr. management, 1:107–108, 268
IBM Lotus Freelance Graphics, 3:200
IBM Lotus Notes, 3:201
IBM mainframe computers
character code developments, 2:52
System/360, 1:88, 109, 155, 4:4, 6
System/390, 1:109, 155
zEnterprise system, 1:155–156, 2:45
IBM minicomputers, 1:*174*
IBM operating systems, 1:109, 157, 3:30
IBM personal computers
Apple competition, 1:18, 143–144
history, 1:18, 44, 110–111
Intel 8086 chips, 1:89
Intel 8088 chips, 1:127, 129
introduction, 1:170, 171
iBook computers, 1:144
iButton, 2:218–219
ICANN (Internet Corporation for Assigned Names and Numbers), 4:178
ICCA (International Computer Chess Association), 3:45
ICL Distributed Array Processor, 2:*172, 173*
Iconifying, of a window, 1:270
Identification
e-banking, 4:93
as security measure, 1:219
security software processes, 2:221
Identity theft, 4:177
Identity Theft Enforcement and Restitution Act of 2007, 1:45
IDNs (Internationalized Domain Names), 4:178
IEC (International ElectroMechanical Commission), 1:119, 120
IEEE. *See* Institute of Electrical and Electronics Engineers (IEEE)

IEEE Computer Society, 1:122–123
IEEE Internet Computing Online (online magazine), 4:3
IEEE Standards Association (IEEE-SA), 1:124
IETF (Internet Engineering Task Force), 1:120, 2:15, 4:132
Iliac Suite (music score), 1:185
iMac computers, 1:18–19, 144
Image analysis, medicine, 3:**133–136,** *134*
Image editing software
digital images, 4:77, 85, 232
fashion design, 3:107
See also Film and video editing
Image extraction and recognition, 4:43
Image pre-processors, 4:42–43
Image segmentation, 4:43
Image sensors (digital cameras), 4:231
ImmersaDesks, 1:256, 258, 259
ImmersaWalls, 1:257, 259
Immersion, in virtual reality, 2:273–274
iMovie application, 1:145
Impact printers, 1:158
In-betweening, 1:11
In the Deep of Time (Lathrop), 4:126
Inclination (satellites), 2:211
Index of refraction, 1:202
Indexed searching, 3:149, 4:243
India
Internet censorship, 4:*36*
space program, 3:230
Indiana Folklore (journal), 4:265
Inference engines, 3:81, 104–105, 143, 144
Information access, 4:**159–162**
Information aggregating agents, 4:1
Information chunking, 1:133
Information, defined, 4:166–167
Information overload, 4:**163–165**
Information privacy concerns, 1:209
See also Privacy
Information processing languages (IPLs), 4:221
Information repository construction. *See* Data warehousing
Information retrieval, 1:**112–117,** 2:108–109, 4:186
See also Search engines
Information systems, 2:**107–112**
Information technology (IT) professionals, 3:56

Information technology standards, 1:**117–121**
cell phones, 2:40
client/server systems, 2:47
compatibility, 2:60–62
computer assisted instruction, 3:51–52
computer system interfaces, 2:66–67
digital libraries, 4:82
geographic data sharing, 3:115
IEEE contributions, 1:120, 123, 124
image compression, 2:119–121, 4:77, 231
JavaScript, 4:199
magnetic stripe cards, 3:157
networking, 2:148
precision of numbers, 3:158
SCORM, 3:52, 98
SQL, 3:77
TCP/IP adoption, 4:260–261
Information theory, 2:29–30, 4:**165–168,** 223, 249–251
Infrared radiation (IR), 2:259, 279, 280
ING Direct (online bank), 4:91
Ingress/egress (radio waves), 2:257
Inheritance, object-oriented programming, 2:159–160
Init method (Java applets), 4:192
Ink Development Corp., 4:115
Inkjet printers, 2:189
Inks, for printers, 2:190
Input devices, 2:**112–115**
assistive computer technology, 4:13–18
ATMs, 3:30
joysticks, 1:79, 2:95–97, 185
keyboards, 1:147–150, *148,* 271, 2:112, 4:16
light pens, 2:113, 186
mouse, 1:18, *180,* 180–183, 2:112, 183–184, 186
pointing devices, 2:*182,* 182–187, 253, 3:146
specialized, 2:67
styluses, 2:253, 254, 255
user interfaces, 4:157
See also Touch screens
Input/output (I/O) devices, 2:65–68, 104–105
See also Input devices; Output devices

Inputs
    algorithms, 2:5
    system analysis models, 2:247
Instant messaging, 4:17, 169
Institute for Advanced Studies (IAS), 1:87, 2:275, 276
Institute of Cybernetics, 4:142–143, 144
Institute of Electrical and Electronics Engineers (IEEE), 1:**122–125**
    Amdahl, Gene Myron honors, 4:5
    Berners-Lee, Tim honors, 4:111
    digital library conference, 4:80
    ethics code, 4:118, 119
    Gross, Alfred J. honors, 3:119
    number precision standards, 3:158
    Nyquist, Harry honors, 4:223
    purpose, 1:120
Institute of Museum and Library Services, 4:80
Institute of Radio Engineers (IRE), 1:122
Institute for Social Inventions, 1:139
Insurance, catastrophe, 4:108–109
Integrated circuits, 1:**125–128**
    design principles, 2:77–78, 78*t*
    electrical *vs.* optical signals, 1:203
    fourth generation computer use, 1:89
    invention, 1:88, 126, 128
    memory devices from, 2:136–137
    NASA applications, 1:191
    space program computers, 3:228
    third generation computer use, 1:88
    transistors in, 1:242–246, 2:44
Integrated pest management (IPM), 3:5–6
Integrated services digital networks (ISDNs), 4:29
Integrated software, 3:**136–139**
Intel Corporation, 1:**128–132,** *129*
    cache memory innovations, 2:37
    founding, 1:128
    integrated circuit development, 2:45
Intel microprocessors
    4004, 1:127, 129, 167, 2:45
    8080, 1:17, 18
    8086, 1:89, 129, 2:45
    8088, 1:127, 129
    in Apple products, 1:19

Core series, 1:130, 4:215
    in IBM-compatible PCs, 1:18, 89, 110
    invention of microprocessor chip, 1:129, 167
    Pentium series, 1:89, 127, 130, 2:45
    Poulson Itanium processor, 2:37
Inteliquent, 4:176
Intellectual property
    Bell Labs royalty waiving, 1:246
    digital libraries and, 4:82
    EDVAC patents, 2:90
    ethics concerns, 4:119
    IBM ventures, 1:110, 111
    illegal music distribution, 2:236, 237
    information access and, 4:161
    open source concept and, 3:183–186
    overview, 1:44
    See also Copyright; Patents; Piracy
Intelligent CAD (intCAD), 3:39
Intelligent Network (telephone system), 3:246
Intelligent software agents. *See* Agents
Interactive systems, 1:**132–137,** *135, 136*
    See also Hypermedia and multimedia
Interactive television (ITV), 3:88, 4:105
Interfaces. *See* User interfaces
Interlace scanning, 2:80
Intermediate code generation, by compilers, 2:64
Internal storage. *See* Memory
International Business Machines. *See* IBM Corporation
International Computer Chess Association (ICCA), 3:45
International copyright, 4:51–52
International ElectroMechanical Commission (IEC), 1:119, 120
International Internet-Free Day, 1:139
International Journal of Geographical Information Science (journal), 3:117
International Morse code, 2:142
International Organization for Standardization (ISO)
    character code developments, 2:52–53
    JavaScript standards, 4:199
    purpose, 1:119, 120, 121, 2:53

International Society for Folk Narrative Research, 4:265
International Space Station (ISS), 1:168, 191, 3:229, 230
International Telecommunication Union (ITU), 2:148
International Time Recording Company, 1:107
Internationalized Domain Names (IDNs), 4:178
Internet, 1:**138–140**
    ARPANET origins, 1:138, 273, 4:184–185
    bridging devices, 2:33–34
    chemistry and, 4:39, 40
    chess-playing, 3:46
    computer assisted instruction, 3:51–53
    connectivity software, 3:131
    digital divide, 4:159–162
    disabilities benefits, 4:17–18
    document processing, 2:86–87
    expert systems availability, 3:105
    freedom of speech concerns, 4:120–121
    importance for communications, 2:59
    information overload concerns, 4:163–165
    as information system, 2:110–111
    journalism and, 4:202
    mathematical foundations, 3:159
    Minitel precursor, 1:177–180, *178*
    net neutrality concerns, 1:140, 2:17–19, 4:162, 187
    political applications, 4:234–235, 236
    security measures, 1:219, 221
    telephone system role, 3:247
    transmission, 1:195
    urban myth circulation, 4:266
    URLs, 4:30
    user interfaces, 3:250
    video games, 1:81
    Web-based animation, 1:14–15
    wireless access, 2:281
    workplace impact, 4:256
    See also World Wide Web
Internet, applications, 4:**168–172**
Internet, backbone, 4:**172–176,** 186
Internet browsers. *See* Browsers
Internet cafes. *See* Cybercafes

Internet control and cyberwarfare, 1:224, 4:**177–183**

Internet Corporation for Assigned Names and Numbers (ICANN), 4:178

Internet Engineering Task Force (IETF), 1:120, 2:15, 4:132

Internet Exchange (IX) facilities, 4:173

Internet Explorer (browser)
    antitrust case, 1:85, 172, 274, 4:172
    bundling with Windows, 1:85, 172
    cookie vulnerability, 4:47
    creation, 1:84
    popularity, 1:274, 2:225, 4:31–32, 169, 170
    release, 4:34
    SSL support, 4:225

Internet, history, 1:138–140, 239, 4:**183–187**

Internet-only banks, 4:91

Internet piracy, defined, 3:224
    See also Piracy

"Internet problem," 4:184

Internet Protocol (IP)
    ATM transmission, 2:15
    dominance, 2:47
    e-journal authentication, 4:101, 102
    gateways, 2:33–34
    IPv6 launch, 2:154
    overview, 1:139

Internet Protocol (IP) addresses, 4:131, 132, 179, 260

Internet service providers (ISPs)
    connectivity software, 3:131
    defined, 1:73
    e-mail services, 1:72–73, 74–75
    FCC oversight, 2:17–19
    Internet backbone connections, 4:173
    overview, 4:247
    services, 1:140

"Internet" worm, 1:263, 2:117

Interpolation
    animation, 1:11
    digital images, 4:232

Interpress page description language, 3:243–244

Interpreters (programs), 1:93, 2:124, 192–193

Intranets, 1:67, 195, 4:**188–190**

Intrusion detection systems, 3:124, 213–214

Invasive programs, 2:**115–119,** 3:31–32
    See also Trojan horses; Viruses; Worms

Inventory software, 3:2

Inverters, in digital logic design, 2:73

Investing, online, 4:107–108

Invisible Web, 4:245

Iomega zip drives, 2:242–243

iOS mobile operating system, 2:*162,* 4:208

IP. *See* Internet Protocol (IP)

IP addresses, 4:131, 132, 179, 260

iPad tablet computers, 1:19, 146

iPhones, 1:19, 145, 146

IPLs (information processing languages), 4:221

IPM (integrated pest management), 3:5–6

iPod portable digital audio players, 1:19, 145, 146

Iran
    cybersecurity attacks, 1:224–225, 264, 2:117, 4:150, 180, 182
    social media and protests, 3:217, 220, 222
    Stuxnet worm, 4:182
    telecommunications tower, 1:*238*

Iraq War (2003-2011), 4:86

IRC (Internet relay chat) servers, 2:227
    See also Servers

IRE (Institute of Radio Engineers), 1:122

Iridium satellite system, 2:212, 214

IS-136/IS-95 wireless standards, 3:41, 42

Isaacson, Leonard, 1:185

ISDNs (integrated services digital networks), 4:29

ISO. *See* International Organization for Standardization (ISO)

ISPs. *See* Internet service providers (ISPs)

Israel, cybersecurity attacks, 4:150, 182

ISS (International Space Station), 1:168, 191, 3:229, 230

IT (information technology) professionals, 3:56

Iteration diagrams, 2:71, *72*

Iterative client server models, 2:48
    See also Client/server technology

Iterative systems design, 2:249–250

ITU (International Telecommunication Union), 2:148

ITU-T (Telecommunication Standardization Sector of the International Telecommunications Union), 1:119–120

iTunes music store, 1:19, 145, 4:49

ITV (interactive television), 3:88, 4:105

Ive, Jonathan, 1:19

Iwatami, Toru, 1:81

Iwerks, Ub, 1:12

IX (Internet Exchange) facilities, 4:173

J

Jackson, Thomas Penfield, 1:172

Jacquard, Joseph-Marie, 1:141, 4:254

Jacquard's loom, 1:100, *141,* **141–142,** 4:254

Jaguar supercomputer, 1:235, 254, 2:172, 175

JANET, 4:174

Jannard, Jim, 4:75

Japan
    abacuses, 1:1
    cybercafes, 4:61
    Fifth Generation Computer Systems project, 1:90
    high-speed trains, 3:208
    molecular computing research, 4:212
    Purple cryptosystem, 4:57
    space program, 3:229–230
    video game development, 1:81–82

Java, 1:223, 2:161

Java applets, 1:223, 2:161, 4:**191–194**

Java Virtual Machine (JVM), 2:161, 4:191

JavaScript, 4:**194–199,** *195, 196, 197*

JCL (Job Control Language), 1:157

Jeopardy! (television show), 1:23, 111

Jerry's Guide to the World Wide Web (Yang and Filo), 1:274, 275, 4:117
    See also Yahoo! portal

Jet Propulsion Laboratory (JPL), 3:231, 232, 4:229–230

JFIF (JPEG File Interchange Format), 2:120

Joan/Eleanor project, 3:118

Job Control Language (JCL), 1:157

Job costing software, 3:2–3

Jobs. *See* Careers

Jobs, Steve, 1:**142–147,** *143*
    Apple founding, 1:17, 143
    Atari involvement, 1:82
    biographical overview, 1:18,
      4:113–114
    death, 1:146
    departure from Apple, 1:18, 144
    as guru, 4:146
    Hewlett, William influence on,
      3:126–127, 4:113
    NeXT computers, 4:33
    Pixar management, 1:13, 18, 144
    return to Apple, 1:18, 19, 145–146
    stock options controversy,
      1:145–146
Jogging, of computer memory, 1:56
John the Ripper network security
    program, 3:214
Johns Hopkins University, 1:213
Joint Conference on Digital Libraries,
    4:80
Joint Photographic Expert Group
    (JPEG). *See* JPEG, MPEG
Jones, D. F., 4:127
Journalism, 4:**199–203,** *200*
Journals, electronic. *See* E-journals and
    e-publishing
Joysticks
    defined, 1:79
    history, 2:95–97
    invention, 1:79
    as pointing device, 2:185
JPEG 2000 standard, 2:120
JPEG File Interchange Format (JFIF),
    2:120
JPEG, MPEG, 2:**119–121,** 4:77, 85, 231
JPEG XR standard, 2:120
JPL (Jet Propulsion Laboratory), 3:231,
    232, 4:229–230
JSTOR e-journals, 4:102
Julia, Gaston, 3:159
Julia sets, 3:159
JVM (Java Virtual Machine), 2:161, 4:191

K

k-nearest neighbors, 2:178
Kahn, Robert, 4:184, 260
Kaissa chess program, 3:45
Kalmár, László, 3:189
Kapor, Mitchell, 3:239, 4:114
Karpov, Anatoly, 3:45

Kasparov, Garry, 1:83, 111, 3:45, 46
Kaspersky Labs, 3:123, 4:150, 182
Katz, Phil, 3:130
Kay, Alan, 1:94, 95
KB (kilobyte), 1:34, 162
Kbps (kilobits per second), 2:17
Keenan, T. A., 3:188
Kelvin, William Thomson, 3:191
Kemeny, John G., 2:196–197,
    3:**141–142,** *142,* 4:267
Kempelen, Wolfgang von, 3:45
Kenandy Inc., 4:115
Kenya, cybercafes, 4:*60*
Kerberos authentication scheme, 4:101
Kerlow, Isaac Victor, 1:13
Kernell, David, 1:75
Kernighan, Brian, 1:34
Key generators, 3:225
Keyboards, 1:**147–150,** *148,* 271,
    2:112, 4:16
Keyframing, 1:11
Keys, encryption, 4:55, 57
    See also Public key infrastructures
    (PKIs)
Keyword blocking, 4:36
Keywords, search engines, 4:243
Kilby, Jack, 1:88, 126, 128
Kilobits per second (kbps), 2:17, 4:28
Kilobyte (KB), 1:34, 162
Kindle (e-reader), 4:95–96, 97
Kinect controllers, 2:98
King, Ada Byron, 1:**150–153,** *151*
    Ada computer language, 2:199
    Babbage, Charles collaboration,
      1:6, 20, 30, 96, 151
    music applications, 1:184, 2:143
King, Martin Luther, Jr., 4:9
King, Stephen, 4:96
Kleinrock, Leonard, 4:183–184
Kludge, as term, 4:144–145
Knowledge-based systems, 3:**142–144**
    See also Expert systems
Knowledge bases
    decision support systems, 3:81
    expert systems, 3:104
    knowledge-based systems,
      3:143–144
Knowledge manipulation, 1:21–22
Knowledge representation, 1:21
Knuth, Donald, 1:25
Kodachrome film, 4:84, 86
Kodak company, 4:86

Kodak Gallery, 4:232
Kosmos 2251 satellite, 2:214
KPMG, 4:189
Kramnik, Vladimir, 3:45
Kristol, William, 4:*110*
Kubrick, Stanley, 4:127
Kuekes, Philip, 4:*210*
Kurtz, Thomas E., 2:196–197, 3:141,
    142, 4:267
Kurtzig, Sandra, 4:114–115
Kurzweil, Raymond, 4:12–13

L

Labeled data, in pattern recognition,
    2:177–178
Labels, assembly language, 1:92
Labels, spreadsheet cells, 3:237
LaCie FastKey, 2:*240*
Lady and the Tramp (animated film), 1:12
Lady Gaga (entertainer), 4:148
Laird, John E., 4:220
Lambda calculus, 1:21, 2:123
LAMP (Linux, Apache, MySQL and
    PHP), 3:186
Landsat satellites, 2:212–213
Landscape design and construction, 3:6
Langton, Christopher, 4:11
Language models, speech recognition,
    3:234
Languages. *See* Programming languages
LANs. *See* Local area networks (LANs)
Laptop computers
    Dell, 2:*104*
    e-reader capability, 4:96
    encryption needs, 4:58
    iBook series, 1:144
    Kay, Alan contributions, 1:95
    MacBook series, 1:19, 146, 2:*79*
    ubiquitous computing, 3:99
Large Hadron Collider, 3:193
Large-scale integrated (LSI) circuits,
    1:80, 89, 175, 2:78
Laser diodes, 1:202
Laser mouse, 1:182, 2:184
Laser pointers, 2:*182,* 3:146
Laser printers
    Apple development, 3:82, 85, 243
    color, 2:190
    desktop publishing, 3:242–243
    mainframes, 1:158
    overview, 2:189
    Xerox development, 1:278

Laser technology, 3:**145–148,** *146*

Laserwriter printers, 3:82, 85, 243

Lasseter, John, 1:14

LastPass, 4:114

Lathrop, George Parsons, 4:126

Latitude lines, 3:173

Lawrence Livermore National Laboratory, 4:149

LCD. *See* Liquid crystal display (LCD)

LDP (Linux Documentation Project), 3:186

Learning Company, 3:97

Learning disabilities, assistive technology, 4:17

Learning, machine, 3:180–181

Learning Management Systems (LMSs), 3:51–52, 53, 95–97

Least significant numbers, 1:3

Lebanon, cybersecurity attacks, 4:150

Lederberg, Joshua, 3:144

LEDs. *See* Light emitting diodes (LEDs)

Legal cases

    malicious software, 2:118

    software patent protection, 4:228, 229

    Sperry-Rand lawsuit, 2:90–91

    See also Antitrust litigation

Legal systems, 3:**148–151**

Legislation

    computer fraud, 1:42–46

    disabilities, 4:13–14, 18

    driverless cars, 4:44

    hacking, 3:124

    Internet regulation, 3:222, 4:178, 179

    piracy, 3:225, 226

    privacy concerns, 1:210, 211

    telecommunications, 4:186, 246

LEGO-Logo, 2:128

Lego Mindstorms system, 2:128

Leibniz, Gottfried Wilhem von, 1:20, 4:62, 254

Leibowitz, Joe, 4:*225*

Leica (dog), 2:214

Lenses, video cameras, 4:74, 75

LEO (low earth orbit), 2:211, 258–259, 4:139–140

Level 3 Communications, 4:176

Levin, Ira, 4:126

Lex (lexical analyzer), 2:2

Lexical analyzers, 2:2, 63

LEXIS-NEXIS information service, 1:114, 3:149

Libraries, digital, 4:*79,* 79–83

Library applications, 3:**151–153,** 4:233–234

Library of Congress, 4:81

Libya, Arab Spring effects, 3:221

Licensing agreements, software, 3:223–224

Licklider, Joseph, 4:183–184

LIDAR (LIght Detection And Ranging), 4:44

Life cycle methods (Java applets), 4:192

Light emitting diodes (LEDs)

    fiber optics development, 1:202, 2:91

    infrared radiation communications, 2:259

    joysticks, 2:97

    optical mice, 1:182, 2:184

Light pens, 2:113, 186

"Like" feature, 3:264

Line printers, mainframes, 1:158

Linear encoding, 2:234

Linear integrated circuits, 1:126

Linear interpolation, 1:11

Linear Pulse Coding Modulation (LPCM), 2:234

Linear regression, data mining, 4:67

Link, Edwin, 1:226–227

Link layer, OSI Reference Model, 2:151

Linking, objects, 3:138–139

Links, hypertext, 1:105

Links, in networks, 1:193–194, 2:154

Linux Documentation Project (LDP), 3:186

Linux operating system

    development, 2:164–165

    documentation project, 3:186

    mobile applications, 4:209

    open source concept and, 3:185

    scalability, 2:216, 4:145

Lipstick Enigma (artwork), 4:8

Liquid crystal display (LCD)

    CRTs *vs.,* 1:255, 2:84

    overview, 2:81–82

    projection technology, 4:104

    touch screens, 2:254–255

LISP (LISt Processing), 2:**123–125**

List servers, 2:227

    See also Servers

Live Free or Die Hard (film), 4:128

Live Messenger, 4:169

Live streaming technology, 2:237

LivePerson, Inc., 4:189

LiveScript. *See* JavaScript

LMDS (local multipoint distribution service), 2:281

LMSs (Learning Management Systems), 3:51–52, 53, 95–97

Local area networks (LANs)

    bandwidth measurement, 2:17

    bridging devices, 2:*31,* 31–34

    computer supported cooperative work and, 3:57–60

    Internet backbone connections, 4:173

    mainframe connection, 1:158

    network design considerations, 2:147–149

    in office automation systems, 1:197

    origins, 1:239, 4:184

    overview, 1:195

    peer to peer networking and, 1:138–139

    twisted pairs, 1:194, 2:257

    wireless, 2:281

Local/asynchronous distance learning, 3:90

Local direct connection, mainframes, 1:158

Local loops, 4:28

Local multipoint distribution service (LMDS), 2:281

Local/synchronous distance learning, 3:89

Location aware mobile computing, 4:209

LOCI (calculator), 3:254

LOCK (Logical Coprocessing Kernel), 2:217

Locking, for concurrency control, 2:239

Lodge, Oliver Joseph, 4:205

Logarithms

    analog computer calculations, 1:4

    defined, 1:3

    Napier, John development, 1:230, 231

    slide rule calculations, 1:3, 230, 231

Logic

    artificial intelligence development, 1:21

    Boolean, 1:114–115, 116, 2:25–30, 4:245

    digital computing use of, 1:49

    query languages, 1:94

    Turing, Alan work, 1:251

Logic gates, 1:126–127, 2:73

Logic Theorem Machine, 4:220, 253

Logical Coprocessing Kernel (LOCK), 2:217

Logical diagrams. *See* Flowcharts

Logicon, Inc., 2:203

Logo (programming language), 2:*125–126,* **125–130,** *129*

London Grand Prix simulator, 1:*227*

Long, Edward, 1:211

Long term evolution (LTE) technology, 1:240, 2:59, 4:209

Long-term memory, 1:133–134

Longitude determination, 3:173, 174

Looping, in programming, 2:201

Loosely typed languages, 4:197

LORAN (long range navigation), 3:10–11, 175

Lorraine Motel (artwork), 4:9

Los Alamos National Laboratory, 1:235, 2:175

Lossy compression, 2:120, 235, 4:77

Lost update problem, 2:239

Lotus 1-2-3, 3:137, 239, 4:114

Lotus Corporation, 4:114

Lotus Freelance Graphics, 3:200

Lotus Notes, 3:201

Lotus Smartsuite 97, 3:138

Lovebug virus (2000), 1:223

Lovelace, Ada King (countess). *See* King, Ada Byron

LoveLetter worm, 2:118

Low earth orbit (LEO), 2:211, 258–259, 4:139–140

Low precision/high recall search results, 4:243

LPCM (Linear Pulse Coding Modulation), 2:234

LSI. *See* Large-scale integrated (LSI) circuits

LTE (Long Term Evolution) technology, 1:240, 2:59, 4:209

Lucas, George, 1:18, 4:74

Lucent Technologies, 1:33, 34

Lynx (browser), 4:33

M

MacBook laptop series, 1:19, 146, 2:*79*

Machine language, 1:91, 2:9, 64

Machine Readable Cataloging (MARC), 3:152

The Machine Stops (Forster), 4:126

Macintosh operating systems, 1:18, 19, 171, 2:265–266

Macintosh personal computers
    desktop publishing development, 3:82, 85
    innovations, 1:144–145
    introduction, 1:18, 144
    Microsoft Excel, 3:239–240
    virus attacks, 1:263
    as WIMP system, 1:133, 272

Macro viruses, 1:262–263
    See also Viruses

Macromedia, 1:14–15

MAD (Michigan Algorithm Decoder), 3:188

MAE (Metropolitan Area Exchange), 4:175

Magic mouse, 1:183

Magnavox, 1:80

Magnetic cores, 1:60, 2:136

Magnetic disks
    information retrieval systems, 1:113
    optical storage *vs.,* 1:204
    second generation computer use, 1:88
    as storage device, 1:160, 2:241–243
    virtual memory, 1:161

Magnetic drums, 2:241

Magnetic ink character recognition (MICR), 2:114, 167–168

Magnetic resonance imaging (MRI), 3:135

Magnetic stripe cards, 2:113, **3:155–157,** *156, 157*

Magnetic tape
    information retrieval systems, 1:113
    as input device, 2:113
    optical storage *vs.,* 1:204
    second generation computer use, 1:88
    as storage device, 1:160, 2:241
    UNIVAC use, 1:88
    videotape technology, 3:110–111

Magnetic Tape Selectric Typewriter, 3:259, 262

Magnetospirilllum magneticum, 4:212

Magnification programs, 4:15

Mail trap doors, 1:221

Main memory. *See* Memory; Random access memory (RAM)

Mainframes, 1:**155–159,** *156*
    Amdahl corporation, 4:4
    Andor Systems, 4:5
    communication devices, 2:56
    defined, 1:18, 79
    early networks, 1:239
    first video games, 1:79
    IBM, 1:88, 108–109, 155–156, 2:45, 52, 4:4, 5, 6
    journalism use, 4:200
    minicomputers *vs.,* 1:173, 174

Major search engines, 4:244–245

Malaria, computer modeling, 3:36

Malaysia, cybercafes, 4:61

Malware. *See* Invasive programs; Trojan horses; Viruses; Worms

Management information systems (MISs), 2:109, 110, 3:79–81

Manchester Mark I, 1:59, 64–65

Mandelbrot, Benoit B., 3:159

Mandelbrot sets, 3:159

Manhattan Project
    Feynman, Richard involvement, 4:123–124, 125
    Kemeny, John G. involvement, 3:141
    Organick, Elliot involvement, 3:187
    von Neumann, John involvement, 2:276, 277

Manipulators (robot arms), 1:215, 2:208, 3:63

MANs (metropolitan area networks), 1:195, 2:147–149

Manufacturing
    automation, 3:*194,* 194–197
    chips, 3:*47,* 47–50
    computer-aided, 3:38–39, 60–65, 4:255
    computer-integrated, 3:64
    decision support systems, 3:80
    expert systems, 3:103
    nanoscale technology, 4:217
    process control, 3:*194,* 194–197
    robotics use, 1:213, 214, 215, 2:207–208

Map overlay operations, 3:116

Map reclassification operations, 3:116

Maps
    computer generated, 3:*174*
    data visualization, 3:73
    weather, 3:257
    See also Geographic information systems (GISs)

MARC (Machine Readable Cataloging), 3:152

Marchand hand calculators, 4:123

Marconi, Guglielmo, 2:257, 279, 4:153, **205–206**

Marconi Memorial Gold Medal, 3:119

Marino, Roland, 2:205

Mark I computers. *See* Harvard Mark I/II/III/IV computers; Manchester Mark I

Mark sense (optical mark recognition), 2:114, 167, 205

Markers (computers), 1:33

Marketing
e-commerce, 1:69
privacy concerns, 1:210

Markup languages, 2:86, **131–136,** *132, 133*
See also HTML (Hypertext Markup Language)

Mars exploration, 3:229, 230–231, 232–233

Mars Pathfinder Mission, 2:209, 3:232

Maser (Microwave Amplification by Stimulated Emission of Radiation), 3:145

Mass spectrometry, 4:40

Massively Multiplayer Online Games (MMOGs), 1:16

Massively parallel architecture, 1:203

Mathematical Markup Language (MathML), 2:135

Mathematics, 3:**157–160**

Mathews, Max, 1:185, 2:144

MathML (Mathematical Markup Language), 2:135

MathWorks, 3:181

The Matrix (film series), 4:128

Matrix technology, printers, 3:242–243

Mauchly, John, 2:**89–91,** *90*
Association for Computing Machinery founding, 1:24
EDVAC development, 2:90, 91
ENIAC development, 1:39–40, 50, 57–58, 63–64, 66, 87, 2:89–90, 3:72
UNIVAC development, 1:88

Max Headroom (film/television series), 4:128

Maxim (hacker), 3:123

Maxis, Inc., 1:83

Maxwell, James Clerk, 4:205

Maze video games, 1:15

MB (megabyte), defined, 1:162

Mbps (megabits per second), 2:17

McAfee, Inc., 1:131

McCain, John, 1:224

McCarthy, John, 1:25, 2:123–125, 4:220

McConnell, John Michael ("Mike"), 4:180

McCormick, Ernest J., 1:76–77

McDonald, Aleecia, 4:225–226

Measurement standards, 1:118

Mechanical calculators, 1:61

Mechanical computers, 1:4

Mechanicals (paste-up boards), 3:84

Medical systems, 3:**160–163**
biology research, 3:33–35
cell phone concerns, 2:40–41, 3:42
computed tomography, 3:65–67, 134
data mining applications, 4:66
decision support systems, 3:80, 81
expert systems, 3:103
image analysis, 3:133–136, *134*
molecular biology research, 3:165–166
molecular computing applications, 4:212
pager use, 3:118–119
pattern recognition applications, 2:177
personal digital assistants, 2:181
robotics use, 1:214, 2:210
virtual reality-based therapies, 2:274–275

Medium earth orbit (MEO), 4:139

Medium-scale integrated (MSI) circuits, 1:175, 2:77–78

MEDLINE system, 1:114

Meeting rooms, electronic, 3:59–60

Megabits per second (Mbps), 2:17, 4:28

Megabyte (MB), defined, 1:162

Megaflops (millions of floating-point operations per second), 1:233

Meissner, L. P., 3:187

Meitner, Lise, 3:66

Melissa virus, 1:260, 261

Meltzer, Marlyn Wescoff, 1:66

Memex devices, 1:61, 104

Memory, 1:**159–163,** *160*
Atanasoff-Berry Computer, 1:56
cache memory, 2:35–37, *36*
early computers, 1:53–60

mainframe capabilities, 1:155, 156
Read Only Memory, 1:160–161, 2:138
video editing needs, 3:114
Whirlwind, 1:60
See also Random access memory (RAM); Virtual memory

Memory devices, 2:**136–140**

Memory management models, 2:*263,* 263–268, *264, 265, 268*

Memory managers, in operating systems, 2:138–139, 162, 163

Memory protection hardware, 1:220

Memory registers. *See* Registers

Menabrea, Luigi Federico, 1:152

Menu bars, 1:271

Menu-based systems, 1:132, 4:156

Menu labels, 1:271

MEO (medium earth orbit), 4:139

Mercury-Atlas (rocket), 3:227

Mercury barometers, 1:208

Merit Network, Inc., 4:175

Mesh topology networks, 1:193, 2:154, 156

Messaging, 4:17, 169

Meta-search engines, 1:275, 4:244

MetaCrawler, 4:245

The Metal Giants (Hamilton), 4:126

Metasploit network security program, 3:214

Metastable state, 3:145–146

Metric system prefixes, 2:95, 4:28

MetroPCS Communications, 1:240, 2:59

Metropolitan Area Exchange (MAE), 4:175

Metropolitan area networks (MANs), 1:195, 2:147–149

Mexico, cybercafes, 4:61

MFENET, 4:174

MFS network, 4:175

MGM (Metro-Goldwyn-Mayer), 1:13

Michelangelo (artist), 4:10

Michie, Donald, 1:249

Michigan Algorithm Decoder (MAD), 3:188

MICR (magnetic ink character recognition), 2:114, 167–168

Micro-communities, social media and, 3:218

Micro Instrumentation and Telemetry Systems (MITS), 1:169, 4:112

Microchips, 1:*163*, **163–166**

Microcomputers, 1:77, **166–169,** 173
See also Personal computers (PCs)

Microfilm, 2:191

Micromarketing, 1:210

Micropayments, 1:69

Microphones, wireless, 4:103

Microprocessors
analog-to-digital and digital-to-analog conversion, 1:51
Apple products, 1:17, 18, 19
in auto-pilots, 3:10
computer science research, 1:47
fourth generation computer use, 1:89–90
in game controllers, 2:98
invention, 1:129, 167
manufacturing, 3:*47,* 47–50
multiple, 1:47
video editing needs, 3:114
video game use, 1:80, 82
See also Intel microprocessors; Parallel processing

Microsoft Access database software, 3:77

Microsoft Active Accessibility (MSAA), 4:18

Microsoft Corporation, 1:**169–173,** *170*
Apple agreement, 1:18
compatibility priorities, 2:62
flight simulation game, 4:157
founding, 1:84, 169, 4:146
history, 1:84–86, 169–173
IBM collaboration, 1:18, 110
Live Messenger, 4:169
mobile computing operating systems, 4:208
MS-DOS operating system, 1:84, 170, 171, 2:163, 4:267
video game development, 1:82
Visual Basic development, 4:267–268
Windows Media Player, 2:237
See also Windows operating system

Microsoft Excel, 1:171, 3:239–240

Microsoft Exchange Server, 3:201

Microsoft Flight Simulator (MSFS), 2:231–232

Microsoft Information Interchange Server (IIS), 2:225

Microsoft Kinect, 2:98

Microsoft Office, 1:171, 3:128, 137–138

Microsoft Outlook, 3:201, 4:169

Microsoft PowerPoint, 1:171, 3:200

Microsoft Publisher, 3:82

Microsoft SharePoint, 3:201

Microsoft Surface tablet computer, 1:*170,* 172

Microsoft Word, 1:171, 3:82, 262

Microsoft Xbox, 1:82, 4:154

Microwave Communications Inc., 4:175

Microwave transmission, 2:258, 4:28–29

MicroWorlds, 2:127

MIDI (Musical Instrument Digital Interface), 1:185, 2:235, 3:169, 170

Military
Ada computer language, 1:153, 2:198–199
computer assisted instruction, 3:50, 51
cryptography applications, 4:56–57
educational virtual reality use, 1:259
virtual reality training, 2:274
See also U.S. Department of Defense (DoD)

Millennium bug (Y2K scare), 3:124, 4:5

Miller, Joan E., 2:144

Million Book Project, 4:81

MIMD (Multiple Instruction, Multiple Data), 2:173

MIME (Multipurpose Internet Mail Extensions), 4:168–169

Mind over Matter (artwork), 4:7–8

Minicomputers, 1:44, **173–177,** *174,* 239, 3:206

Minimax algorithm, 3:44

Minimum attribute standards, 1:118

Minimum spanning trees, 2:155

Minitel, 1:**177–180,** *178,* 4:61

Minix operating system, 2:164, 3:185

Minsky, Marvin, 4:220

MISD (Multiple Instruction, Single Data), 2:173

MISs (management information systems), 2:109, 110, 3:79–81

Missile defense systems, 4:120

MIT (Massachusetts Institute of Technology)
decision support systems development, 3:79
e-journals, 4:102

edX online course platform, 3:90, 4:106
flight simulation project, 1:227
Kerberos authentication scheme, 4:101
Multics system, 1:221, 3:188
space program computers, 3:228
video game development, 1:79
X-Windows development, 1:272

MITS (Micro Instrumentation and Telemetry Systems), 1:169, 4:112

Miyamoto, Shigeru, 2:*96*

MMOGs (Massively Multiplayer Online Games), 1:16

Mnemonics, 1:91, 2:9

Mobile agents, 4:2

Mobile computing, 4:*207,* **207–210**
See also Cell phones; Laptop computers; Personal digital assistants (PDAs); Tablet computers

Mobile phone system (MPS), 2:38–39

Mobile phones. *See* Cell phones; Smartphones

Mobile robotics, 1:215, 2:209
See also Robots

Mobile switching centers, 3:41

Mobile virtual private networks (mVPNs), 2:271

Mobility management, 3:41

Modeling
animation, 1:9, 10
cosmological research, 3:28
molecular, 4:39
system analysis, 2:247

Modems
cable, 2:58
callback, 1:222
origin of term, 2:57
telephone, 2:57–58, 4:28
wireless, 2:258

Moderation, of discussion groups, 1:73–74

Modes, in fiber optics, 2:92

Modular engineering, 4:3

Modulation
lasers, 3:147
signals, 2:57–58

Modules, in programming, 2:201–202

Molecular biology, 3:**163–167,** *164*

Molecular computing, 3:166, 4:128, *210,* **210–213,** 217

Molecular modeling, 4:39

Molniya orbit, 4:139

Monarch Marking, 2:203

Monitors
cathode ray tube display, 1:255, 2:78–81, 254–255
graphical display types, 2:99–101
liquid crystal display, 1:255, 2:81–82, 84, 254–255, 4:104
resolution, 4:76

Monochrome display, 2:80

Monolithic data warehousing systems, 4:71

Monopolies. *See* Antitrust litigation

Monte Carlo simulation, 1:228

Monty Python's Flying Circus (film), 1:10

Moon (film), 4:128–129

Moon landing program, 1:189–190, 191, 3:227–228

Moore, Edward ("Ed"), 1:34

Moore, Gordon
Fairchild Semiconductor founding, 2:22
as guru, 4:145
Intel founding, 1:128

Moore's Law, 1:130, 131, 2:44, 45, 3:49, 4:145

Moran, Thomas, 4:221

Morowitz, Harold, 3:33

Morris, Robert T., 1:45

Morris worm, 1:45

Morse code, 2:50–51, 54t, 55, 141–142

Morse, Samuel, 2:50–51, **140–142,** *141*

MOS Technologies, 1:17

Mosaic browser, 1:274, 275, 4:33

Moskovitz, Dustin, 4:117

Motherboards, 1:17

Motion-base simulators, 2:230–231

Motion Picture Experts Group (MPEG), 2:15, 119–121

Motion sensing controllers, 2:98

Motor impairments, assistive technology, 4:16

Motorola microprocessors, 1:17, 18

Mouse, 1:18, *180,* **180–183,** 2:112, 183–184, 186

Movies. *See* Digital filmmaking; Film and video editing

Mozilla Firefox (browser), 2:225, 4:*31,* 31–32, 170, 172

MP3 audio standard, 2:121, 235, 4:209

MPEG-1 standard, 2:121

MPEG-2 standard, 2:121

MPEG-4 standard, 2:121

MPEG (Motion Picture Experts Group), 2:15, **119–121**

MPS (mobile phone system), 2:38–39

MRI (magnetic resonance imaging), 3:135

MS-DOS operating system, 1:84, 170, 171, 2:163, 4:267

MSAA (Microsoft Active Accessibility), 4:18

MSI (medium-scale integrated) circuits, 1:175, 2:77–78

Mubarak, Hosni, 3:220, 221

MUDs (mult-user domains), 4:185

Muffett, Alec, 3:215

Multi-player video games, 1:81

Multi-touch interfaces
Apple innovations, 1:19, 147
magic mouse, 1:183
PDAs, 2:181
shape-shifting technology, 3:252
See also specific types

Multi-User Domains (MUDs), 4:185

Multiagent systems, 4:3

Multiconnected networks, 4:174

Multics system, 1:221, 2:217, 3:188

Multilingual keyboards, 1:149

Multimedia, defined, 2:103
See also Hypermedia and multimedia

Multiplane animation cameras, 1:12

Multiple Instruction, Multiple Data (MIMD), 2:173

Multiple Instruction, Single Data (MISD), 2:173

Multiple microprocessors, 1:47

Multiple Virtual Systems (MVS), 1:157

Multiplexing
digital logic design, 2:75–76, *76*
time division, 2:93, 3:41–42
wavelength division, 1:202, 2:93, 3:41

Multipurpose Internet Mail Extensions (MIME), 4:168–169

Multitasking, 1:168, 171, 2:48, 4:156

Multivac (short story series), 3:24

Museum of Contemporary Art (Sydney, Australia), 4:7

Music, 1:**183–185**
downloading, 2:237, 4:48–49, 264
MP3 audio standard, 2:121, 235, 4:209

Music boxes, 4:153

Music composition, 3:*167,* **167–171,** *168*

Music, computer, 2:128, **142–145,** *143,* 3:168–169

Music editors, 3:170–171

Music Instrument Digital Interface (MIDI), 1:185, 2:235, 3:169, 170

MUSIC V program, 2:144

MUSIC XI program, 2:144

Musical Instrument Digital Interface (MIDI), 1:185, 2:235

mVPNs (mobile virtual private networks), 2:271

MVS (Multiple Virtual Systems), 1:157

myApplet, 4:193

Mylar tape, 2:241
See also Tape drives

MySpace, 2:215–216, 3:216

N

N-type semiconductors, 1:126, 243

The Naked Sun (Asimov), 4:127

Namco, Ltd., 1:81

"nand" gates, 1:127, 2:75

NanoComputer Dream Team, 4:218

Nanocomputing, 4:211, **215–219,** *216*

Napier, John, 1:3, 187–188, 230, 231

Napier, Mark, 4:8

Napier's bones, 1:*187,* **187–188**

NAPs (Network Access Points), 4:173, 175

Napster, 2:237, 4:48–49, 264

Narenda, Divya, 3:263

Narrowband channels, 4:27

NAS (NASA Advanced Supercomputers), 1:191

NASA. *See* National Aeronautics and Space Administration (NASA)

NASA Advanced Supercomputers (NAS), 1:191

Nasdaq stock market, 4:107

Nassi, Isaac, 2:71

Nassi-Shneiderman diagrams, 2:71, *72*

NAT (Network Address Translation), 4:131

National Aeronautics and Space Administration (NASA), 1:*188,* **188–193**
Apollo missions, 1:189–190, 191, 3:227–228
Blue Origin collaboration, 4:112

Challenger space shuttle, 3:228, 4:125

demand for computing, 3:226–232

Goddard Scientific Visualization Studio, 3:212

mainframe obsolescence, 1:159

microcomputer use in space, 1:168

missing day urban myth, 4:266

NASA Science Internet, 4:174

photography development, 4:229–230

satellite programs, 2:211–215

National Basketball Association (NBA), 4:69

National Broadband Plan, 4:160

National Bureau of Standards, 1:119

See also National Institute of Standards and Technology (NIST)

National Cash Register Company (NCR), 1:267–268, 2:203

National Center for Atmospheric Research, 4:172

National Center for Biotechnology Information (NCBI), 3:34, 165

National Center for Supercomputing Applications (NCSA), 1:275, 4:33, 172

National Committee for Information Technology Standards (NCITS), 1:120

National Computer Security Center (NCSC), 2:217

National Crime Information Center (NCIC) database, 1:209

National Information Infrastructure Protection Act of 1996, 1:43

National Information Standards Organization (NISO), 1:120

National Institute of Standards and Technology (NIST), 1:116, 119, 4:57

National Institutes of Health (NIH), 3:34, 4:39–40

National People's Congress Web site, 4:*233*

National Reconnaissance Office (NRO), 4:139

National Science Foundation (NSF)
digital library initiatives, 4:80
Domain Name System, 4:178
Internet backbone connections, 4:173, 174, 175

NSFNET, 1:138, 139, 4:172, 173, 174, 185
research funding, 1:97, 3:187
scientific visualization research, 3:211

National Weather Service (NWS), 3:256

Natural language interfaces, 4:156

Natural language processing, artificial intelligence, 1:22

Natural language queries, 1:116, 3:149

Naur, Peter, 2:1, 195

Navajo Code Talkers, 4:59

Navigation, 1:189, 3:**173–177,** *174*
See also Global Positioning Systems (GPSs)

Navigation Satellite Timing and Ranging (NAVSTAR) satellites, 2:213–214, 4:135–136

Navigational speech recognition applications, 3:235, 236

NAVSTAR (NAVigation Satellite Timing And Ranging) satellites, 2:213–214, 4:135–136

NBA (National Basketball Association), 4:69

NBC (National Broadcasting Corporation), 4:147

NCBI (National Center for Biotechnology Information), 3:34, 165

NCIC (National Crime Information Center) database, 1:209

NCITS (National Committee for Information Technology Standards), 1:120

NCP (Network Control Protocol), 4:184, 185

NCR (National Cash Register Company), 1:267–268, 2:203

NCSA (National Center for Supercomputing Applications), 1:275

NCSC (National Computer Security Center), 2:217

Near typeset quality concept, 3:243

NEC Corporation, 3:166

Necromancer (Gibson), 1:261

Negative cut lists, 3:113

Negative scanners (photography), 4:231

Nelson, Theodor ("Ted"), 1:104, 105, 4:32, 111

Neon light, 3:145–146

Nessus network security program, 3:214

NESSY (object recognition system), 4:44

The Net (film), 4:127

Net neutrality, 1:140, 2:17–19, 4:162, 187

NET (No Internet Theft) Act, 3:226

Netcat network security program, 3:214

Netherlands, railroad management, 3:208

Netscape Communications
browser development, 4:33–34, 169, 170, 172
cookies invention, 4:45
JavaScript development, 4:198

Netscape Navigator (browser), 1:14, 274, 4:34

Network Access Points (NAPs), 4:173, 175

Network Address Translation (NAT), 4:131

Network analysis, 2:147

Network architectures, 2:148–149, 151–152

Network-based intrusion detection systems, 3:213–214

Network boards, analog computers, 1:*3*

Network Control Protocol (NCP), 4:184, 185

Network design, 2:**147–150**

Network engineering, careers, 3:54

Network layer
firewall implementation, 4:130
IP protocol, 4:259–262
OSI Reference Model, 2:151, 152

Network management agents, 4:2

Network managers, in operating systems, 2:162, 163

Network Mapper (NMAP), 3:214

Network protocols, 2:47, **150–154,** 4:19–23

Network sniffing, 1:223

Network theory, 3:159

Network topologies, 2:**154–156**

Networked windows (NeWs), 1:272

Networks, 1:**193–196**
ATMs, 3:30
classroom, 4:105
database management systems, 3:77–78
history, 1:193–196, 239
hypertext development, 1:105

Networks *(continued)*
  intranets, 1:67, 195, 4:188–190
  library applications, 3:152–153
  Minitel, 1:177–180, *178*
  NASA applications, 1:190
  office automation systems, 1:*197,* 197–200
  peer to peer, 1:138
  Telnet protocol, 4:262–264
  VPNs, 2:268–271
  workplace impact, 4:255–256
  worm attacks, 1:261, 263
  See also Client/server technology; Internet; Routers; Routing; Telephone networks
Neural Network Toolbox, 3:181
Neural networks, 2:178, 3:**177–181,** *179,* 4:44, 68–69
New York Knicks (basketball team), 4:69
New York Stock Exchange, 2:*4*
Newell, Allen, 4:*219,* **219–221,** *252,* 253
Newman, Maxwell, 1:59, 64
NeWs (networked windows), 1:272
Newspapers, computer use, 4:200–201, 202
Newton, Isaac, 1:4
Newton MessagePad, 2:180
NexGen (Next Generation Air Transportation System), 3:11, 15, 176–177
NeXT computer company, 1:18, 19, 4:33, 113, 146
Next Generation Air Transportation System (NexGen), 3:11, 15, 176–177
NextStep, 1:144
Nexus (browser), 1:274, 4:33
NIH (National Institutes of Health), 3:34
9/11 terrorist attacks, 3:18, 4:157, 266
1984 (Orwell), 4:141
Nintendo
  innovations, 1:82
  video game development, 4:154
  Wii, 1:*80,* 2:*96,* 98
Nintendo Entertainment System, 1:15, 82
NISO (National Information Standards Organization), 1:120
NIST (National Institute of Standards and Technology), 1:116, 119, 4:57
NLEs (non-linear editors), 3:111–114, 4:74, 201

NMAP (Network Mapper), 3:214
No. 1 Electronic Switching System (1E), 1:33
No Internet Theft Act (NET Act), 3:226
Nodes, in networks, 1:193–194, 2:154
Noise, in communication systems, 4:166
Nokia, 2:181
Nolan, Christopher, 4:75
Non-destructive video editing, 3:112–113
Nonlinear editors (NLEs), 3:111–114, 4:74, 201
Nonlinear quantization, 2:234–235
Nonprocedural languages, 1:94
Nook (e-reader), 4:95–96
"nor" gates, 1:127, 2:74
Norfolk Southern Railroad, 3:207
Norman, Donald A., 1:133
Norton computer security products, 4:116
"not" gates, 1:127, 2:73, *73*
NOT operators, 2:26, 27–29, *27–30*
Notation-oriented music models, 3:169
Notational music composition, 3:170
Nouvel, Jean, 3:20
Noyce, Robert, 1:88, 126, 128, 2:22
NRO (National Reconnaissance Office), 4:139
NSF. *See* National Science Foundation (NSF)
NSFNET, 1:138, 139, 4:172, 173, 174, 185
Nuclear medicine, 3:135
Numeric values, in spreadsheet cells, 3:237–238
Numerical factors, scaling, 2:215
Nutt, Roy, 2:193
Nvidia window interface, 1:*269*
NWS (National Weather Service), 3:256
Nyquist, Harry, 4:30, **222–223**
Nyquist Intersymbol Interference Theorem, 4:30

O

Oak Ridge National Laboratory, 1:224, 235, 254, 2:172, 175
OASs (office automation systems), 1:*197,* 197–200, 4:255–256
Obama, Barack, 1:224, 4:181, 234–235

Object-based programming, 1:134–135, 4:197
Object Linking and Embedding (OLE), 3:138–139
Object-oriented languages, 1:94–95, 2:**157–161**
Object-oriented programming, 1:94–95, 134–135, 2:129
Object recognition, 4:77–78
Objects *vs.* classes, 2:161
OCR. *See* Optical character recognition (OCR)
OCS (Operational Control System), 4:136
Octal (base-8) number system, 1:50, 91
"Odyssey" (video game), 1:80
OEM unbundling, 3:224
Office automation systems (OASs), 1:*197,* **197–200,** 4:255–256
Office management systems, 1:200
Office suite software, 3:128–129, 137–138, *197,* 197–202
Offline information retrieval, 1:113
Ohlhausen, Maureen, 4:*225*
OIC (Open Internet Coalition), 2:18
OLAP (On-Line Analytical Processing), 4:66
OLE (Object Linking and Embedding), 3:138–139
Olsen, James, 4:149–150
Olympia (automaton), 4:126
Omidyar, Pierre, 4:115
OMR (optical mark recognition), 2:114, 167, 205
On-demand information integration, 4:71
On-demand streaming, 2:237
  See also Streaming technology
On-Line Analytical Processing (OLAP), 4:66
One-time pads, 4:56–57
One-time use passcode/password, 4:25
1G cellular technology, 1:240
Online banking. *See* E-banking
Online credit. *See* Credit online
Online disk-based storage. *See* Cloud storage
Online education. *See* Distance learning
Online gaming, 2:98
Online privacy, 4:**223–226,** *224*
Online Privacy Alliance (OPA), 4:224
Online Public Access Catalogs (OPACs), 3:152

Online shopping. *See* E-commerce

Online trading, 4:107–108

OPA (Online Privacy Alliance), 4:224

OPACs (Online Public Access Catalogs), 3:152

Opel, John R., 1:110

Open architecture, 1:44, 110, 4:82

Open Internet. *See* Net neutrality

Open Internet Coalition (OIC), 2:18

Open Internet rules (FCC), 2:19

Open Learning Initiative (Carnegie Mellon University), 3:90

Open Pattern Recognition (OpenPR) project, 2:178–179

Open source, 3:128, **183–186**, *184,* 4:170

Open Source Applications Foundation, 4:114

Open Source Certification Program, 3:184–185

Open Source Definition, 3:184

Open Source Initiative, 3:184–185

Open systems design, 2:*60,* 60–62

Open Systems Interconnections (OSI), 4:21, 22

Open Systems Interconnections (OSI) Reference Model, 2:151

OpenNet Initiative, 4:179

OpenOffice software, 3:200

OpenPR (Open Pattern Recognition) project, 2:178–179

Operands, 1:92

Operating systems, 2:**161–166,** *162*
    accessibility utilities, 4:18
    authentication functions, 4:25–26
    early developments, 1:33
    encryption abilities, 4:58
    IBM contributions, 1:109
    mainframes, 1:157
    memory management, 2:138–139
    minicomputers, 1:176
    mobile computing devices, 4:208
    scalability, 2:216
    servers, 2:228
    speech recognition bundling, 3:250–251
    window manager functionality, 1:134
    See also specific types

Operation codes, 1:92

Operational amplifiers, 1:4, 5

Operational Control System (OCS), 4:136

Oppenheimer, J. Robert, 2:277, 4:125

Opportunity (rover), 3:232–233

Optical character recognition (OCR), 2:**166–169**
    assistive computer technology, 4:15
    history, 2:204–205
    as input device, 2:114
    post office use, 4:78

Optical communications. *See* Fiber optics

Optical computing, 2:95

Optical disks, 1:160, 204–205, 2:243–244, 3:166
    See also CD-ROM (compact disk-read only memory)

Optical fiber communications. *See* Fiber optics

Optical mark recognition (OMR), 2:114, 167, 205

Optical microchips, 1:165–166

Optical mouse, 1:182, 2:184

Optical technology, 1:**201–205,** *202*

Optimization
    agriculture applications, 3:6, 7
    code compilers, 2:63, 64
    neural network applications, 3:178–180
    search engine optimization, 4:243

Optomechanical mouse, 1:182, 2:184

Optophones, 2:166

"or" gates, 1:34, 127, 2:73–74, *74,* 77

OR statements, 2:26, 27–29, *27–30*

Oracle database software, 3:77

Orange Book, 2:219

Orbits (satellite)
    geostationary earth orbit, 2:211, 212, 258–259, 4:139–140
    low earth orbit, 2:211, 212, 258–259, 4:139–140
    medium earth orbit, 4:139
    polar, 2:211
    sunsynchronous orbit, 2:212

Orbitz.com, 3:18

Organick, Elliot, 3:**187–188**

The Organization of Behavior (Hebb), 3:180

Organizational ergonomics, 1:76

Orthogonal projection, 3:109

Orwell, George, 4:141

OS/2 Warp operating system, 3:30

OS/360 operating system, 1:109

OS/390 operating system, 1:157

Oscillators, 1:184

Oscilloscopes, 1:3

OSI (Open Systems Interconnections), 4:21, 22

OSI (Open Systems Interconnections) Reference Model, 2:151

OSX Mountain Lion, 2:*162*

Oughtred, William, 1:230, 231

Out-of-band control information, 4:133

Output devices
    assistive computer technology, 4:13–18
    ATMs, 3:30
    See also User interfaces

Outputs, for algorithms, 2:5

Outputs, for system analysis models, 2:248

Overhead projectors, 4:103, 104

Oxford University Press e-journals, 4:102

Ozma of Oz (Baum), 4:126

P

P-type semiconductors, 1:126, 243

P2P. *See* Peer-to-peer networking

"Pac-Man" (video game), 1:81–82

PacBell, 4:175

Packard, David, 3:125, *125,* 126, 127

Packet filtering firewalls, 4:130

Packet spoofing, 1:223

Packet-switched networks
    ATM support, 2:13
    defined, 1:193
    Internet Protocol and, 1:139–140, 4:183–184, 260
    transmission, 1:194–195

Packets, 2:151

Page description languages, 2:188, 3:82, 85, 243–244

Page, Larry, 4:115–116

Page layout software, 3:82–86, 241–244, 4:200

Page scanners, 2:168
    See also Scanners

Page tables, 2:267–268, *268*

PageMaker software, 3:82, 85, 242

Pagers, 3:118–119

Paint method (Java applets), 4:192

Pakistani Brain virus, 1:264, 2:116

Palin, Sarah, 1:75

PalmPilot, 2:180

Palo Alto Research Center (PARC). *See* Xerox Palo Alto Research Center (PARC)

Pandora Internet Radio, 2:237

Paper tape, as input, 2:113

Paperless society, 2:187, 191

Papert, Seymour, 2:125–127

Paradoxical Escape (short story), 3:25

Parallel algorithms, 2:173–174, 175

Parallel circuits, 2:29, *30*

Parallel communications, 2:150

Parallel data transmission, 2:222–225

Parallel optical transceivers, 1:165–166

Parallel processing, 2:**171–175,** *172*
Colossus, 1:57
distributed computing systems *vs.,* 2:46–47
Fifth Generation Computer Systems project, 1:90
introduction, 1:89
mainframes, 1:155, 156
massively parallel architecture, 1:203
molecular computing, 4:211, 212
supercomputers, 1:233–234, 235

PARC. *See* Xerox Palo Alto Research Center (PARC)

Paris in the Twentieth Century (Verne), 4:126

Parity, mainframe disk storage, 1:158

Park, Nicholas ("Nick"), 1:10

Parker, Trey, 1:10

Parkin, Stuart, 1:162, 2:139

Parnas, David, 1:189

Partial mesh topologies, 2:156

Particle collision, 3:192, 193

Partitioning, as security measure, 1:220

Pascal, Blaise, 1:50, *207*, **207–208,** 4:62, 254

Pascal programming language, 2:2, 195, 197

Pascaline calculating machine, 1:208

Pascal's theorem, 1:207

Pascal's triangle, 1:207

Password tokens, 1:222

Passwords
authentication, 4:24
e-journals, 4:101
protection measures, 1:220, 221, 222

Paste functionality, 3:138

Paste-up boards, 3:84

Patent and Trademark Office (PTO), 4:227, 228, 229

Patents, 4:**227–229**

Patriot Act of 2002, 1:45

Pattern recognition, 2:*176*, **176–179,** 3:180–181, 4:43
See also Speech recognition

Patternmaking, fashion, 3:107–108, 109

Payload Type (PT), 4:20

Payloads (robots), 2:208

Payloads (viruses), 1:262, 2:115–116

PayPal, 4:93, 147

Payroll software, 3:2

PB (petabyte), defined, 1:162

PCs. *See* Personal computers (PCs)

PDAs. *See* Personal digital assistants (PDAs)

PDF (Portable Document Format), 2:135, 3:130, 4:102

PDP-8 (Programmable Data Processor 8), 1:44

PDP-series computers, 1:176

Pearl, Judea, 1:25

Peer backbones, 4:174

Peer-to-peer networking
ARPANET, 1:138
Comcast case, 2:18
history, 1:239, 4:170–171
local area networks, 1:138–139

Peerce, Sir William, 4:206

Peering exchange agreements, 4:175–176

PEM (privacy-enhanced electronic mail), 1:223

Pen input devices, 2:186

Pencil tests, 1:8–9

Penetration phase, hacking, 3:122

Pennsylvania State University, 3:50

Pentium series microprocessors, 1:127, 130, 2:45

Pentodes, 1:253

Performance analysis tools, architecture, 3:22

Perigees (satellites), 2:211

Perlis, Alan, 2:194, 195

Permanent virtual channels (PVCs), 2:13

Personal assistants (agents), 4:1

Personal computers (PCs)
Alto, 1:251, 272, 278, 4:184

assistive computer technology, 4:13–19, *14*
classroom use, 4:104, 105
desktop publishing development, 3:241
Dynabook project, 1:95, 272
early versions, 1:18, 84
journalism use, 4:200
mainframes *vs.,* 1:156–157, 158–159
as microcomputer, 1:166
minicomputers *vs.,* 1:175–176
number in use, 1:89–90
weather forecasting, 3:256–257, 258
workplace impact, 4:255–256
See also Apple Computer, Inc.; IBM personal computers

Personal digital assistants (PDAs), 2:**179–182,** *180*
chess programs, 3:46
e-mail capabilities, 4:168
information overload concerns, 4:163
medical applications, 3:161
touch screens, 2:253–254
Web browsers, 4:170
See also Smartphones

Personal financial software, 3:128–129

Personal identification numbers (PINs), 2:218, 3:32, 4:25

Personal Software Company, 3:239

Personalization
home entertainment systems, 4:154
information services, 4:164–165

PERT (Program Evaluation and Review Technique) charts, 3:*202*, 203, 204

Pervasive computing, overview, 3:99, 101

Petabyte (PB), defined, 1:162

Petaflops (quadrillions of floating-point operations per second), 1:233, 2:174, 175

Péter, Rózsa, 3:**189–191**

Pfaff, Kurt T., 2:*60*

PGP (Pretty Good Privacy), 1:223

Philco Corporation, 1:88

PhM (physical modeling synthesis), 3:171

Phoenix (space probe), 3:232

Phosphor coatings, 1:255, 2:79, 80

Phosphorous, in semiconductors, 1:125–126

Photo diodes, 3:147

Photo-resist, 1:243, 244

Photo restoration, 4:*83*

Photocopiers, 1:276–277

Photography, 4:**229–232**
    See also Digital photography

Photolithography, 1:242, 243–244

Photomasks, 3:48

Photonic switching, 2:95

Photons
    fiber optics, 2:92, 95
    laser technology, 3:145, 146, 147

Photophone invention, 2:23

Photosensitivity, 4:41

PhotoShop image editing software, 3:22, 4:232

Phreakers, 4:148

Physical addressing, 2:*263*, 264, *264*, 265–266

Physical ergonomics, 1:76

Physical layer
    ATM transmission, 4:21–22
    network connections, 4:130
    OSI Reference Model, 2:151

Physical modeling synthesis (PhM), 3:171

Physics, 3:**191–194**

Picture lock (video editing), 3:113

Pierce, John, 2:144

Pigment-based inks, 2:190

Ping sweeps, 3:122

PINs (personal identification numbers), 2:218, 3:32, 4:25

Pioneers. *See* Early pioneers

PIPA (Protect IP Act), 3:222, 4:179

Piracy
    hackers and, 4:149
    Jacquard's loom punch cards, 1:142
    online gaming, 2:98
    peer-to-peer networking and, 4:171
    software, 3:223–226, *224*
    SOPA and PIPA acts, 3:222
    See also Intellectual property

Pittsburgh Supercomputing Center, 4:172, 185

Pixar, Inc., 1:13, 18, 144, 4:128

Pixels
    defined, 1:36, 4:76
    digital camera resolutions, 4:231
    dots per inch of printers *vs.*, 2:188
    LCDs, 2:81, 82

PKIs (public key infrastructures), 2:219, 4:88

Plan position indicators (PPIs), 3:13, 14

Plane polarized light, 2:81

Playing with Infinity: Mathematical Explorations and Excursion (Péter), 3:189, 190

Playstation, 1:82, 4:154

PLCs (programmable logic controllers), 3:6

Pleiades supercomputer, 1:191

Plessey Telecommunications, 2:203

Plotters, 2:191

Plug boards, 1:58, 87

Plummer, R. P., 3:188

Pocket Fritz 4 chess program, 3:46

Pointing cursors, 2:183

Pointing devices, 2:*182*, **182–187**, 253, 3:146

Points of interest (POIs), 3:*74*, 74–75

The Poison Dress (article), 4:265

Polar orbits, 2:211

Polarizers, in liquid crystal displays, 2:81–82

Police radio, 2:37–38

Political applications, 4:*233*, **233–237**

Political campaigns, 4:234–235, 236

Political information, computerization, 4:233–234

Polling, political, 4:236

Polonius security system, 2:217, 218

Polyalphabetic ciphers, 4:56

Polyalphabetic substitution systems, 4:57

Polymorphic viruses and worms, 1:264

Polymorphism, object-oriented programming, 2:160

Polynomials, 1:20

"Pong" (video game), 1:79–80, 83, 4:154

Pop-up dialog boxes, 4:*195*, 196

Population inversions, 3:145

Port IDs, 4:131, 132

Port scans, 3:122

Portability, of software, 2:62

Portable computing. *See* Mobile computing

Portable Document Format (PDF), 2:135, 3:130, 4:102

Position indicator cursors, 2:183

Positional notation, 1:35

Positioning sensors, for joysticks, 2:97

Positive Train Control (PTC) project, 3:208

Post, E. L., 2:2

Postscript page description language, 3:82, 85, 243, 244

Poulson Itanium processor, 2:37

Power transistors, 1:*242*

PowerMac series, 1:144

PPIs (plan position indicators), 3:13, 14

Pre-processors, image, 4:42–43

Precision, in information retrieval, 1:115, 4:164, 243–244

Predicate calculus, 1:21

Predicate logic inference engines, 3:105

Prefixes, metric, 2:95, 4:28

Prendergast, James ("Jim"), 1:122

Prescription drugs database management systems, 3:162

Presentation layer, OSI Reference Model, 2:152

Presentation software
    in office automation systems, 1:199
    political applications, 4:235
    in productivity software, 1:171, 3:200
    scientific visualization *vs.*, 3:211

President's Critical Infrastructure Protection Board, 1:224

Pressure measurement, 1:208

Pressure sensitive touch screens, 2:255

Pretty Good Privacy (PGP), 1:223

Preventing Real Online Threats to Economic Creativity and Theft of Intellectual Property Act (PIPA), 3:222, 4:179

Price, Mark, 4:69

Primary storage. *See* Memory; Random access memory (RAM)

Priming, 1:134

Primitives
    graphical, 3:38, 211
    Logo syntax, 2:127

Princeton University, 2:276, 4:172, 185

Print servers, 2:227
    See also Servers

Printing devices, 2:*187*, **187–192**
    3D, 3:62
    desktop publishing, 3:242–244
    mainframe connections, 1:158
    resolution, 4:76
    See also Laser printers

Printing press invention, 3:83

Privacy, 1:**209–212**, 4:**223–226**
 cookies, 4:45–47
 data mining concerns, 4:69
 e-commerce, 4:98
 e-mail, 1:75, 223
 legislation addressing, 1:42–46
 medical records, 3:162
 personalized information services
  and, 4:165
 surveillance concerns, 4:141–142
 VPNs, 2:268–271
Privacy-enhanced electronic mail
 (PEM), 1:223
Privacy policies, 4:224, 225–226
Private key decryption, 1:67, 4:57
Private peering exchange agreements,
 4:176
Probes (computer programs), 1:45
Procedural languages, 1:94, 2:123,
 192–199
Procedural markup, 2:131
 See also Markup languages
Procedure statements, 2:2
Process control, 1:5, 33, 3:*4, 194,*
 194–197
Process net layer (process control),
 3:*194,* 195
Process planning, computer-aided,
 3:63–64
Processor managers, in operating
 systems, 2:162, 163
Processors. *See* Central processing units
 (CPUs); Microprocessors
Prodigy, 3:216
Production systems inference engines,
 3:104
Productivity software, 3:*197,* **197–202**
 See also Office suite software
Program control switching offices,
 3:245–246
Program Evaluation and Review
 Technique (PERT) charts, 3:*202,* 203,
 204
Programmable Data Processor 8
 (PDP-8), 1:44
Programmable logic controllers (PLCs),
 3:6
Programmable read-only memory
 (PROM), 1:161, 2:138
Programming, 2:**200–202**
 analog computers, 1:164
 analytical engine, 1:6, 30

artillery firing calculations,
 1:65–66
careers, 2:202, 3:54, 55–56
design tools, 2:69–72, *70, 71, 72*
event-handling functions, 1:134
expert systems, 3:103–104
 object-based, 1:134–135, 4:197
 object-oriented, 1:94–95,
  134–135, 2:129
 ubiquitous computing needs, 3:101
 Visual Basic process, 4:268
Programming Language Structures
 (Organick, et al.), 3:188
Programming languages
 Ada, 1:153, 2:198–199
 Algol, 2:1–3, 194–195, 3:187, 188
 artificial intelligence development,
  1:21
 assembly language, 1:91–92,
  2:6–10, *7,* 63–64, 157, 3:10
 C, 1:33, 93, 2:197–198
 C++, 1:33, 2:160
 COBOL, 1:88, 93, 101, 102, 157,
  170, 2:195–196
 FORTRAN, 1:88, 93, 170, 2:157,
  193–194, 3:187–188
 functional, 2:123
 generations, 1:91–95
 grammatical constructs, 2:2–3
 Hopper, Grace contributions,
  1:101, 102–103
 Java, 1:223, 2:161
 LISP, 2:123–125
 Logo, 2:*125–126,* 125–130, *129*
 machine language, 1:91, 2:9, 64
 object-oriented, 1:94–95,
  2:157–161
 parallel processing, 2:174, 175
 Pascal, 2:2, 195, 197
 procedural, 1:94, 2:123, 192–199
 scripting, 4:194–199, 269
 Smalltalk, 1:94, 95, 272, 2:158, 160
 Visual Basic, 2:196, 4:267–269
 See also BASIC programming
  language
Progressive scanning, 2:80
Progressive streaming, 2:237
Project Gemini, 1:189
Project Gutenberg, 3:151, 4:94–95
Project management, 3:*202,* **202–205,**
 203, 204*t*
Project Mercury, 1:189, 190

Project Prospect, 4:40
Project tracking, 3:204–205
Project Whirlwind, 1:227
ProjectBank software, 3:22
Projection of images, 4:*7*
Projectors, overhead, 4:103, 104
PROM (programmable read-only
 memory), 1:161, 2:138
Protect IP Act (PIPA), 3:222, 4:179
Protecting Cyberspace Act, 4:178
Protein Data Bank, 1:234
Protocol filtering, 4:36
Protocols. *See specific protocols*
Prototyping
 computer-aided engineering use,
  3:39, 61
 rapid, 3:62
 system analysis, 2:248
Proxy servers, 2:227, 4:101–102
 See also Servers
Pseudocode, 2:71, *71,* 201
PSTN (public switched telephone
 network), 2:38–39
Psychological impact, 4:256–257
Psychotherapy, online, 3:161
PT (Payload Type), 4:20
PTC (Positive Train Control) project,
 3:208
PTO (Patent and Trademark Office),
 4:227, 228, 229
Public computer systems, touch screens,
 2:253
Public-key cryptography, 1:67, 221,
 4:58–59
Public key infrastructures (PKIs), 2:219,
 4:88
Public switched telephone network
 (PSTN), 2:38–39
Publication language concept, 2:1
Publishing. *See* Desktop publishing;
 E-books; E-journals and e-publishing
Punched cards
 analytical engines, 1:6, 30
 Atanasoff-Berry Computer, 1:55
 ENIAC use, 1:87
 hanging chads, 4:237
 Hollerith, Herman use, 1:99
 information retrieval systems,
  1:113
 as input device, 2:113–114
 Jacquard's loom, 1:100, 141–142
 tabulating machines, 1:39

Puppet animation, 1:10

Purdue University, 3:214

Purple cryptosystem (Japan), 4:57

PUT command, 4:134

Putin, Vladimir, 3:*12*

Puzzle video games, 1:15

PVCs (permanent virtual channels), 2:13

Pyrolysis mass spectrometry, 4:40

Q

QCA (quantum-dot cellular automata), 4:217

QoS. *See* Quality-of-service (QoS)

Quadtrees, 3:117

Quality-of-service (QoS), 2:271

Quantization, 1:184

Quantization, of sound signals, 2:234

Quantum Computer Services, 1:82

Quantum-dot cellular automata (QCA), 4:217

Quantum dots, 4:216–217

Queries
    Boolean logic, 2:26–27, 29–30
    information retrieval, 1:113, 114–116

Query languages, 1:94, 2:238–240, *239,* 3:76–77

Quick Time media player, 2:237

Quicktime VR, 1:11

QWERTY keyboard layout, 1:148–149

Qzone (social media site), 4:257

R

Racetrack memory, 1:162, 2:139

Racing video games, 1:15

Rack units, 2:228

Radar
    aircraft traffic management, 3:13–14
    Doppler, 3:257
    driverless cars, 4:44

Radio
    cryptography development, 4:56
    home entertainment use, 4:153
    Marconi, Guglielmo contributions, 2:257, 279, 4:153, 205, 206
    newsroom computer use, 4:201
    walkie-talkies, 3:117, 118

Radio-Frequency Identification (RFID), 2:206–207

Radio navigation, 3:9, 12–13, 175

Radio networks, 1:238–239, 2:37–38

Radiofrequency (RF) signals, 2:257, 279

RAID (redundant array of inexpensive disks) technology, 1:158

Raikes, Jeff, 4:113

Railroad applications, 1:31, 3:**205–208,** *206*

RAM. *See* Random access memory (RAM)

Ramade, Camille, 2:206

Random access memory (RAM)
    chips, 1:89, 160
    mainframes, 1:157
    memory management, 2:138–139, 162, 163
    overview, 1:160, 2:137–138
    virtual memory *vs.,* 1:161

Range images, 4:76

Ranger lunar probe series, 3:227

Ranked output, information retrieval, 1:115, 116

Rapid prototyping, 3:62

Raster data, 1:255, 3:38, 244

RAW image format, 4:85

RDBMSs (relational database management systems), 3:72, 76

RDF (Resource Description Framework), 4:34

Read Only Memory (ROM), 1:160–161, 2:138

Reading tools, 2:**203–207,** *204*

Reagan, Ronald, 3:119, 127, 4:120

Real time systems
    military applications, 2:198–199
    NASA computing, 1:189

RealNetworks, 2:237

RealPlayer streaming technology, 2:237

Reaver, J. Russell, 4:265

Recall, in information retrieval, 1:115, 116, 4:164, 243–244

Recommended Standard 232C (RS-232C) protocol, 2:11–12

Recording of music, 1:184

Rectification, 1:253

Recursive functions, 3:189–190

Recursive procedures, 2:127–128, *129*

RED Digital Cinema, 4:75

RED ONE (video camera), 4:75

Reddy, Dabbala Rajagopal ("Raj"), 1:25

Redundancy
    NASA applications, 1:190
    networks, 2:32–33

Redundant array of inexpensive disks (RAID) technology, 1:158

Reel-to-reel tape drives, 2:113, 241
    See also Tape drives

Reference language concept, 2:1

Reflective liquid crystal displays, 2:83

Registers
    CPUs, 2:7–8, 43, 44, 64
    minicomputers, 1:176

Regression analysis, economic data, 3:93–94

Regulation, 2:17–20
    See also Internet control and cyberwarfare; Legislation; U.S. Federal Communications Commission (FCC)

Reid, Harry, 4:179

Relational database management systems (RDBMSs), 3:72, 76

Relays, 1:54, 65, 4:250

Relevance feedback, information retrieval, 1:115, 116, 4:243, 244

Remington-Rand Corporation, 1:40, 2:283

Remote (app), 1:19

Remote Method Invocation (RMI) protocol, 2:49

Remote Procedure Call (RPC) protocol, 2:49

Remote surgery, 2:210, 3:162–163

Renting, unauthorized, 3:224

Renugopalakrishnan, Venkatesan, 3:166

Repeaters, 2:31–32, 257, 258

Repetitive stress injuries, 1:66, 77–78

Replicating rapid prototyper (RepRap) project, 3:62

Reporters without Borders, 4:36, 37

RepRap (replicating rapid prototyper) project, 3:62

Reproduction of documents, 2:85–86

Reputation, online, 4:53

Request for Comments (RFC), 2:15, 4:264

Research
    agriculture, 3:7
    art, 4:9
    astronomy, 3:27–28
    bandwidth, 4:30
    biology, 3:33–36
    chemistry, 4:37–41, *38*

Research (*continued*)
digital libraries, 4:80
e-journals and, 4:101
geographic information systems, 3:117
government funding, 1:95–97, 188–193
human brain, 4:63
scientific visualization, 3:211–212
Research In Motion (RIM), 2:181, 4:208
Resistive touch screens, 2:185
Resizing, of a window, 1:270, 271
Resolution
digital images, 4:76, 231
printers, 2:188, 189, 3:242–244
video cameras, 4:75
Resource allocation, by operating systems, 2:165
Resource Description Framework (RDF), 4:34
Restoring, of a window, 1:270
Retina, 4:41–42
RETRieve command, 4:134
Retrofitting systems, 2:245–246
Retroviruses, 1:264
Reverse bias connections, 1:245
Revit software, 3:22
RF (radiofrequency) signals, 2:257, 279
RFC (request for comments), 2:15, 4:264
RFID (Radio-Frequency Identification), 2:206–207
RGB (red, green, blue) images, 4:76
Rhapsody music service, 4:49, 264
Rhythm video games, 1:16
Rich Internet Applications (RIAs), 1:15
Riding the Bullet (King), 4:96
Rijndael encryption algorithm, 4:57
Ring topology networks, 2:155
Ritchie, Dennis, 1:25, 33, 34, 2:197–198
Rivest, Ron, 1:221, 4:58
RMI (remote method invocation) protocol, 2:49
Roadrunner supercomputer, 1:235, 2:175
Roaming, in cellular communications, 2:40
Roberval, Gilles Personier de, 1:207–208

Robotics, 1:**212–217,** *213*
Asimov, Isaac coining of term, 3:24–25
Asimov's three laws, 3:25, 4:127
computer science research, 1:47
computer vision and, 4:41–45, 77–78
cybernetics groundwork, 4:64
fashion design, 3:*108*
space exploration, 3:231–232
Robots, 1:*20,* 2:**207–210,** *208*
computerized manufacturing and, 3:62–63
fictional depictions, 3:25, 4:126–128
as information system, 2:110
remote surgery, 2:210, 3:162–163
The Robots of Dawn (Asimov), 4:127
Robots and Empire (Asimov), 4:127
Robots (search engines), 4:242–243, 244, 245
Robustness, of codes, 2:55
Rods (vision), 4:42
Rogers, Lawrence, 4:184
Role-playing games video games, 1:15
ROM (read-only memory), 1:160–161, 2:138
Romney, Mitt, 4:235
Roosevelt, Franklin, 2:277
Rosa, Vincenzo, 4:205
Rosenbloom, Paul S., 4:220
Rossum's Universal Robots (R.U.R.) (play), 1:216, 3:24–25
Rotational delay time, 2:242
Rothbaum, Barbara, 2:274–275
Rotor machines, 4:57
Round Earth Project, 1:258–259
Routers
as bridging device, 2:33
Internet role, 1:139–140, 4:173–174, 260
network design considerations, 2:149
Routing, 4:**239–241,** *240,* 260
Routing tables, 1:139–140, 2:33, 4:240, 260
Royal Astronomical Society, 3:26–27
Royal Society for Chemistry Publishing (RSC), 4:40
RPC (remote procedure call) protocol, 2:49

RS-232C (Recommended Standard 232C) protocol, 2:11–12, 223–224
RSA public-key cryptosystem, 1:221, 4:58
RSC (Royal Society for Chemistry Publishing), 4:40
Rule-based systems, 3:142–144
See also Expert systems
Runaround (short story), 1:216, 4:127
R.U.R. (Rossum's Universal Robots) (play), 1:216, 3:24–25
Rusch, Frank R., 1:258
Russell, Steve, 1:79
Russia
cyberattack allegations, 4:150, 180, 181
cybersecurity program, 4:182
GLOSNASS global positioning system, 4:138
Institute of Cybernetics, 4:142–143, 144
Molniya orbit satellites, 4:139
software piracy, 3:225
Soyuz space capsules, 3:229
space program, 3:232
Rybka chess computer, 3:45

S

Sabre (Semi-Automated Business Research Environment) System, 3:16–17, 18
Sachs, Jonathan, 4:114
Safari (browser), 1:274, 2:225, 4:170, 225
Salavon, Jason, 4:8
Sales orders software, 3:3
Salton, Gerard, 1:115, 2:109
Sampling
music data, 1:36, 184, *184,* 3:170–171
Nyquist, Harry theorem, 4:222–223
rates, 1:49
scientific visualization and, 3:211
sound data, 2:*233, 234*
Samsung, 1:240, 2:181, 4:229
Sandia National Labs, 3:28
The Sandman (Hoffman), 4:126
SAR (Segmentation and Reassembly) sublayer, 4:22
Sarnoff, David, 4:153
SAS software, 3:94

SATAN (Security Administrator Tool for Analyzing Networks), 3:214
Satellite technology, 2:**211–215**
    data links, 2:258–259
    European Space Agency programs, 3:229
    flight management systems, 3:11, 15
    global surveillance, 4:139–142
    railroad use, 3:207
    See also Global Positioning Systems (GPSs)
Satellite-to-satellite communications, 2:212
Satisficing concept, 4:253
Saudi Arabia, cybersecurity attacks, 4:150
Saverin, Eduardo, 4:117
Sayre, David, 2:193
Scaling, 2:**215–217**
Scanners
    digital photography and, 4:231–232
    as input device, 2:114
    optical character recognition, 2:168
Scanning codes, keyboards, 1:148
Scanning phase, hacking, 3:122
Scheduling, decision support systems, 3:80
Schlumberger Excellence in Educational Development (SEED), 4:40
Scholarly Publishing and Academic Resources Coalition (SPARC), 4:101, 102
Schreyer, Helmut, 2:282
Scientific Computing and Imaging Institute (University of Utah), 3:211
Scientific visualization, 3:**209–212,** *210*
SCORM (Sharable Content Object Reference Model), 3:52, 98
Screen readers, 4:15
Script Kiddies (hackers), 4:148
SCRIPT tags, 4:194–195
Script viruses, 1:263
    See also Viruses
Scripting
    JavaScript, 4:194–199
    Visual Basic Scripting Edition, 4:269
Scriptoria (copying rooms), 3:86
Scroll bars, in windows interfaces, 1:271
SCSI (small computer systems interface) standard, 2:66

Sculley, John, 1:144
Scullin, Frederick J., Jr., 1:45
SDNs (software-defined networks), 2:270
SEACOM undersea cable, 4:162
Seals, privacy, 4:224
Search concept, in problem-solving, 1:21–22
Search engine optimization (SEO), 4:243
Search engines, 4:*242,* **242–245**
    Boolean algebra in, 2:29–30
    digital libraries, 4:80–81
    information overload concerns, 4:163–164
    information retrieval, 1:113–116
    overview, 1:275
    Web-based, 1:116
    See also specific sites
Search expressions, 4:243
Search for ExtraTerrestial Intelligence (SETI@home) project, 3:27
Search spaces, 1:21–22
Search strategies, 1:113
Search.com, 4:245
Seaton, Charles W., 1:39
Second generation computers, 1:88
Second generation programming languages, 1:91–92
Secondary Action (animation), 1:14
Secondary storage. *See* Storage devices
Sectors, of floppy disks, 2:242
Secure Computing Corporation, 2:217
Secure Electronic Transactions (SET) protocol, 1:68
Secure Sockets Layer (SSL) protocol, 1:67–68, 4:54, 93, 225
Security, 1:**219–226,** *220*
    applications, 3:213–215
    Certificate Authority, 1:67–68, 2:270, 4:25, 99
    cookies, 4:45–47
    credit online, 4:52–55
    data mining concerns, 4:69
    database management systems, 3:77–78
    digital signatures, 1:221, 4:58, 86–89, *87, 88*
    e-banking, 4:92–93
    e-commerce, 1:67–68, 4:98–99
    e-mail, 1:75
    hardware, 2:217–219

    intranets, 4:188–189
    legislation, 1:42–46
    software, 2:219–222, *220*
    Telnet concerns, 4:263
    See also Hackers; Hacking; Internet control and cyberwarfare
Security Administrator Tool for Analyzing Networks (SATAN), 3:214
Security applications, 3:**213–215**
Security hardware, 2:**217–219**
Security software, 2:**219–222,** *220*
SEED (Schlumberger Excellence in Educational Development), 4:40
Sega video games, 1:82, 4:154
Segmentation and Reassembly (SAR) sublayer, 4:22
Segmentation, image, 4:43
Selectric typewriter, 3:259, 262
Selegue, John P., 4:40
Self-replicating systems, 2:276–277
Selfridge, Oliver, 4:220
Semi-Automated Business Research Environment (Sabre) System, 3:16–17, 18
Semiconductor lasers, 3:147
Semiconductors, 1:125–126, 128, 164–165, 242–243
Semtech, 1:165
Sendmail, 3:186
Senses, virtual reality and, 2:273
SEO (search engine optimization), 4:243
September 11, 2001 terrorist attacks, 3:18, 4:157, 266
Sequencing, in programming, 2:201
Sequoia supercomputer, 1:235, 2:175
Serial and parallel transmission, 2:**222–225**
Serial communications, 2:150–153
Series circuits, 2:29, *30*
Server file systems, 2:228
Servers, 2:**225–228,** *226*
    mainframes, 1:155–156, 158
    minicomputers, 1:173–174
    proxy, 2:227, 4:101–102
    Web servers, 2:225, 227, 4:30–31, 188
    See also Client/server technology
Service providers, 4:**246–249**
    See also Internet service providers (ISPs)

Session layer, OSI Reference Model, 2:152, 153

Set-Reset Flip-Flop, 1:127, 2:7–8, 74

SET (Secure Electronic Transactions) protocol, 1:68

SETI@home project (Search for ExtraTerrestial Intelligence), 3:27

SGML (Standard Generalized Markup Language), 2:132

Shadbolt, Nigel, 4:111

Shadow mask cathode ray tubes, 2:80

Shakey (robot), 1:214

Shamir, Adi, 1:221, 4:58

Shannon, Claude E., 4:*249*, **249–251**
  bandwidth research, 4:30
  Bell Labs involvement, 1:34, 4:250–251
  Boolean principles application, 2:26
  chess strategies, 3:45, 46
  information theory research, 4:166–167, 223
  Turing, Alan collaboration, 1:249

Shape-shifting technology, 3:252

Sharable Content Object Reference Model (SCORM), 3:52, 98

Shared locking, 2:239

Sharp Corporation, 3:237

Shaw, John Clifford, 4:220, 221, 253

Sheridan, Peter, 2:193

Shielded twisted pairs, 1:194, 2:257

Shipping costs, with e-commerce, 1:71

Shneiderman, Ben, 2:71

Shockley Semiconductor Laboratories, 1:128, 2:22

Shockley, William B., 2:*20*, **20–22**
  semiconductor research, 1:128, 164–165
  transistor invention, 1:34, 66, 88, 125, 126, 241, 2:20

Shockwave plug-in, 1:14–15

Sholes, Christopher Latham, 1:148, 149

Shooter video games, 1:15

Shopping carts (e-commerce), 1:68

Short-term memory, 1:133

Shutterfly, 4:232

Shuttleworth, Mark, 3:232

Sidewalks of America (Botkin), 4:265

Siemens Corporation, 2:254

Sierra Monolithics Inc., 1:165

SIGDA Pioneering Achievement Award, 4:5–6

Sign-bit extraction, 2:142

Signal processing, 1:126

Signal-to-noise ratios (SNRs), 2:93

Signaling System 7, 3:246

Signature-based intrusion detection systems, 3:213–214

SIIA (Software and Information Industry Association), 3:225

Silicon
  in integrated circuits, 1:125
  in microchips, 1:165, 3:48
  mining, 2:139
  in transistors, 1:242–243

Silicon Graphics, 3:257

Silicon Valley, California, 1:165

Silver, Bernard, 2:203

"SimCity" (simulation game), 1:83

SIMD (Single Instruction, Multiple Data), 2:172–173

Similarity values, information retrieval, 1:115

Simon, Herbert A., 4:*219*, 220, 221, *252*, **252–254**

Simon Personal Communicator, 2:180

Simple Object Access Protocol (SOAP), 4:170

Simple substitution (cryptography), 4:56, 57

Simplex radio systems, 2:38

Simputers, 4:209

Simulation, 1:**226–230**, *227*
  artificial life, 4:*10*, 10–13
  chemistry, 4:39
  computer-aided engineering use, 3:39
  economic modeling, 3:94–95
  human factors, 4:157
  legal applications, 3:150
  political events, 4:237
  supercomputers, 1:234

Simulation video games, 1:15, 83, 228–229

Simulators, 2:**228–232**, *229*
  See also Virtual reality (VR)

Sinatra, Frank, 1:80

Single electron devices, 4:217

Single Instruction, Multiple Data (SIMD), 2:172–173

Single Instruction, Single Data (SISD), 2:172

Single Program, Multiple Data (SPMD), 2:173

The Singularity is Near (Kurzweil), 4:12–13

SiP (system-in-package), 1:128

SISD (Single Instruction, Single Data), 2:172

Sistine Chapel, 4:10

16-bit code, 1:37

Sketchpad, 3:20–21

Slide rules, 1:3, 187, **230–232**, *231*

Slow In and Out (animation), 1:14

Small computer systems interface (SCSI) standard, 2:66

Smalltalk programming language, 1:94, 95, 272, 2:158, 160

SMART Board interactive whiteboards, 4:104, 105

Smart buildings, 3:99, 101

Smart cards
  history, 2:205–206
  magnetic stripe cards *vs.*, 3:157
  medical applications, 3:161
  password tokens, 1:222
  RFID tags vs.l, 2:207

Smart devices, ubiquitous computing, 3:99, 101

SMART (System for the Mechanical Analysis and Retrieval of Text), 1:115, 2:109

Smart Technologies, 4:104

Smartphones
  authentication functions, 4:26
  e-mail capabilities, 4:168
  encryption needs, 4:58
  generations of, 1:240
  GPSs, 3:176
  information overload concerns, 4:163
  iPhones, 1:19, 145, 146
  mobile computing, 4:*207*
  multimedia and hypermedia needs, 2:104
  origin of term, 2:180
  popularity, 3:42
  Web browsers, 4:170
  See also Personal digital assistants (PDAs)

SMIL (Synchronized Multimedia Integration Language), 2:135

Smith, David, 1:261

Smith, F. O. J., 2:141

Smith, Paul, 4:265

Smith, Will, 4:127

Snail mail, 1:73

Sniffing (networks), 1:223

Snort network security program, 3:214

Snow White and the Seven Dwarfs
(animated film), 1:12

SNRs (signal-to-noise ratios), 2:93

Snyder, Richard, 1:87

SOAP (Simple Object Access Protocol),
4:170

SOAR project, 4:220, 221

SoC (system-on-a-chip), 1:127

Social impact, 4:**254–257**

Social informatics, 4:254, 257

Social media, 3:**216–223**
journalism use, 4:202
political applications, 4:234
social impact, 4:256–257
See also specific sites

The Social Network (film), 3:263–264,
4:75

Soft copies, defined, 2:86

Softlifting, 3:224

Software
Bell Labs research, 1:33
computer science research, 1:46–48
copyright concerns, 4:50
data warehousing systems, 4:72
early developments, 1:33
ergonomic considerations, 1:78
ethics concerns, 4:119
home system, 3:128–132
human factors, 4:156–157
information technology standards,
1:120
integrated, 3:136–139
patent protections, 4:228, 229
See also specific types

Software-defined networks (SDNs),
2:270

Software engineering, careers, 3:57

Software and Information Industry
Association (SIIA), 3:225

Software piracy, 3:**223–226,** *224*

Sojourner rover, 2:209

Solar Sunrise incident (1998), 4:181

Solar time, 3:174

Solid ink printers, 2:190

Solid Logic Technology (SLT), 1:109

Solid-state drives (SSDs), 2:*240*

Solitons, 2:95

SONET (Synchronous Optical
NETwork), 4:173

Sony
Betamax VCR, 2:262
digital cameras, 4:230
e-reader, 4:*95*
video cameras, 4:73–74
video game development, 1:82,
4:154

SOPA (Stop Online Piracy Act), 3:222,
4:179

Soul Catcher project, 4:64

Sound Blaster sound cards, 2:236

Sound cards, 1:15, 2:235–236

Sound devices, 2:*232,* **232–237,** *233*

Sound editors, 3:170–171

Sound files, 2:121, 3:113–114

Sound-oriented music models, 3:169

Sound servers, 2:227
See also Servers

Soundings (weather measurements),
3:256

Source code, open source concept and,
3:183

Source documents, defined, 2:86

South Park (television show), 1:10

Soviet Union. *See* Russia

Soyuz space capsules, 3:229

Space debris, 2:214

Space Exploration Technologies
(SpaceX), 3:229, 230

"Space Invaders" (video game), 1:81

Space Launch System (SLS) rockets,
3:231

Space travel and exploration,
3:**226–233**
Apollo missions, 1:189–190, 191,
3:227–228
global surveillance, 4:139–142
space shuttle program, 1:*188,* 190,
191, 3:228–229
virtual reality training, 2:*272*

SpaceScience World, 1:257–258

"SpaceWar" (video game), 1:15, 79

Spamming, 1:75, 4:266

SPAN (NASA Space Scientists
network), 4:175

SPARC (Scholarly Publishing and
Academic Resources Coalition),
4:101, 102

Spatial query processing, 3:116, 117

Speakers, 2:233–234

Speaking impairments, assistive
technology, 4:16

Special Interest Group on Design
Automation Award, 4:5–6

Special needs. *See* Disabilities

Special purpose registers, 2:8
See also Registers

Specialty search engines, 4:244

Speech-generation devices, 3:251

Speech recognition, 3:**233–236,** *234*
assistive computer technology, 4:16
browsers and, 4:34
for input, 2:114
user interfaces, 3:250–251
voice commands, 3:252

Speedup (parallel processing),
2:174–175

Spense, Bill, 4:218

Sperry-Rand, 2:89, 90–91

Spiders, 4:242–243, 244, 245

Spielberg, Steven, 1:23

Spintronics, 1:162, 2:139

Spiral systems design, 2:250

Spirit (rover), 3:232–233

SPMD (Single Program, Multiple
Data), 2:173

Sponsored links, 4:243

Spoofing, 1:223

Sports
data mining applications, 4:69
GPS applications, 4:138
video games, 1:15

Spotify, 2:237

Spreadsheets, 3:**236–240,** *237,
238, 239*
integrated software, 3:137
invention, 1:168
productivity software, 3:198–199,
201
what-if analysis capabilities, 3:201,
238

Springer e-journals, 4:102

Sprint network, 4:175, 176

SPSS software, 3:94

Sputnik missions, 2:211, 214

SQL, 1:94, 2:**238–240,** *239,* 3:76–77

Squash and Stretch (animation), 1:14

SRAM (static random access memory),
2:137

SRI (Stanford Research Institute),
1:213–214

SSDs (solid-state drives), 2:*240*

SSL (Secure Sockets Layer) protocol,
1:67–68, 4:54, 93, 225

Staging (animation), 1:14

Stallman, Richard, 3:184

Standalone servers, 2:227
    See also Servers

Standard Generalized Markup Language (SGML), 2:132

Standard programming languages. *See* Procedural languages

Standards. *See* Information technology standards

Stanford Research Institute (SRI), 1:213–214

Stanford University, 3:90, 4:184

Stanton, Andrew, 4:128

Star topology networks, 1:193, 2:154–156

Star Wars (film series), 1:216, 4:74

Star Wars missile defense system, 4:120

StarLogo software, 2:129

StarOffice 7 software, 3:*197*

Start method (Java applets), 4:192

Stateful packet filtering firewalls, 4:131

Statements, in programming languages, 1:92, 93, 2:2–3

Static random access memory (SRAM), 2:137

Static routing, 4:240, 241

Statistical multiplexing, 2:15

Statistical pattern recognition techniques, 2:178

Statistics
    census-taking, 1:39, 40, 41
    economic data analysis, 3:93–94
    political applications, 4:236

Stealth viruses, 1:264
    See also Viruses

Steamboat Willie (cartoon), 1:12

Steiner points, 2:155

Steiner Trees, 2:155

Stenberg, W., 3:188

The Stepford Wives (novel/film), 4:126

Stibitz, George R., 1:54

Stock market
    electronic, 4:107–109
    neural network applications, 3:181

Stoll, Clifford ("Cliff"), 1:223

Stone, Biz, 3:217

Stone, Matthew ("Matt"), 1:10

Stop method (Java applets), 4:192

Stop-motion animation, 1:10

Stop Online Piracy Act (SOPA), 3:222, 4:179

Stop words, 4:243

Storage devices, 2:*240*, **240–244**
    mainframes, 1:158
    optical *vs.* magnetic, 1:203–205
    RAM *vs.*, 1:160

Storage service providers, 4:247

STORe command, 4:134

Stored-program concept
    Eckert, J. Presper, Jr. work, 2:90–91
    first generation computer use, 1:87–88
    Manchester Mark I, 1:64–65
    Mauchly, John work, 2:90–91
    von Neumann machines, 1:58–59

Stored value cards, 2:205

Storyboards, animation, 1:9

Stott, Alicia Boole, 2:26

Straight-Ahead and Pose-to-Pose Action (animation), 1:14

Strategic Defense Initiative, 4:120

Strategy to Secure Cyberspace (U.S. Department of Homeland Security), 4:180

Streaming technology
    Apple TV, 1:145
    home system software, 3:131
    music distribution, 2:236–237

Stroustrup, Bjarne, 1:33

Structural pattern recognition techniques, 2:178

Structured Analysis and System Specification (DeMarco), 2:251

Structured flowcharts, 2:71, *72*

Structured programming, 2:158, 201–202

Structured Query Language (SQL). *See* SQL

Stub networks, 4:174

Stucken, Harro, 2:283

Stuxnet (worm), 1:224–225, 264, 2:117, 4:182

Styluses, 2:253, 254, 255

Sub-bands, frequency, 3:40, 41

Submarines
    H. L. Hunley excavation, 3:39
    ultrasound location, 3:136

Substitution (cryptography), 4:56, 57

Subtractive sound synthesis, 3:171

Sudan, cybersecurity attacks, 4:150

Sun Microsystems, 1:272, 2:161, 3:*197*

Sundials, 3:173–174

Sunlight readable displays, 2:83–84

Sunsynchronous orbits, 2:212

Supercomputers, 1:*232*, **232–235**
    astronomy applications, 3:27–28
    Cray, Seymour contributions, 3:68–70
    fictional depictions, 4:127
    Internet backbone and, 4:172
    NASA applications, 1:191
    parallel processing, 2:171–175
    weather forecasting, 3:256

Surface wave touch screens, 2:185

Surgery, robotic, 2:210, 3:162–163

Surveillance, global, 4:139–142

Sutherland, Ivan, 1:25, 2:272–273, 3:20–21, 37

SVCs (switched virtual channels), 2:13

SVG image format, 4:77

Swift, Jonathan, 4:125–126

Swipe cards. *See* Magnetic stripe cards

Switchboards, telephone, 3:247

Switched virtual channels (SVCs), 2:13

Switches
    binary number system and, 1:35
    telephone switching systems, 1:33, 53–54, 237–238, 3:41
    transistors as, 1:126–127

Switching offices, 3:245–246

Swordfish (film), 4:128

Symantec, 4:116, 148

Symbolic processing, 2:124

Synchronized Multimedia Integration Language (SMIL), 2:135

Synchronous/co-located applications, 3:59–60

Synchronous Optical NETwork (SONET), 4:173

Synchronous transmission, 2:10–13, 223
    See also Serial and parallel transmission

Syntactic analyzers, 2:63

Syntax
    defined, 1:94
    Logo, 2:127
    search engines, 4:243, 244

Synthesizers, music, 1:184–185

Syria
    Arab Spring effects, 3:221–222, 4:85–86
    cybersecurity attacks, 4:150

System/360, 1:88, 109, 155

System/390, 1:109, 155
System analysis, 2:**245–249,** 250
System design, 2:246
System for the Mechanical Analysis and Retrieval of Text (SMART), 1:115, 2:109
System-in-package (SiP), 1:128
System-on-a-chip (SoC), 1:127
Systems design, 2:**249–252**

T

T1 circuits, 4:223
T1 leased lines, 4:29, 173
T3 leased lines, 4:29, 173
Tablet computers
 e-reader capability, 4:96
 encryption needs, 4:58
 GPSs, 3:176
 handwriting recognition, 2:167
 iPads, 1:19, 146
 Microsoft products, 1:*170,* 172
Tabulating Machine Company, 1:100–101, 107
Tabulating machines, 1:*100*
 Census Bureau use, 1:39, 96, 100, 101, 107
 Hollerith, Herman contributions, 1:39, 96, 99–101, 107
Tank, David W., 3:180
Tape cartridges, 2:113, 241
Tape drives, 1:158, 2:113, 241
Tapella, Robert C., 4:89
Tarski, Alfred, 1:21
Tartan Racing team, 4:44
Tax software, 2:283, 3:*2,* 201
TB (terabyte), defined, 1:162
TCP/IP (Transmission Control Protocol/Internet Protocol), 4:**259–262**
 firewalls, 4:130–132
 history, 4:184–185, 260–261
 Internet backbone connections, 4:173, 175
 intranets, 4:188
 OSI Reference Model *vs.,* 2:152–153
 overview, 1:195
 popularity, 2:149
 scalability, 2:216
TCP port numbers, 4:260
tcpdump network security program, 3:214

TCSEC (Trusted Computer Systems Evaluation Criteria). *See* Orange Book
TCST (thin client/server technology), 2:49
TDMA (Time Division Multiple Access) standard, 3:42
Technicolor, 1:12
Technology of desktop publishing, 3:**241–245**
tekGear, 2:101
Telcordia, 1:33
Telecommunication Standardization Sector of the International Telecommunications Union (ITU-T), 1:119–120
Telecommunications, 1:**237–241,** *238*
 document processing, 2:86–87
 information technology standards, 1:119
 legal applications, 3:151
 service providers, 4:246–249
Telecommunications Acts (1995/1996), 4:186, 246
Telecommuting, 1:199, 4:256
Teleconferencing, 1:198–199, 2:262
Telegraph systems
 codes, 2:50–51
 cryptography applications, 4:56–57
 history, 1:237, 2:141–142, 4:222
 railroad use, 3:205–206
 wireless, 2:257, 279, 4:205–206
Telemedicine, 3:162–163
Teleoperation, 1:213, 215
Telephone communication satellites, 2:212
Telephone networks
 analog to digital conversion, 4:28
 bandwidth capacity, 4:27, 28
 copper cabling, 1:194
 DSL development, 2:58–59
 history, 1:237
 packet switching *vs.,* 1:139
 phreaker hackers, 4:148
 video games, 1:82
Telephone relays, 1:65, 2:282
Telephone switching systems, 1:33, 53–54, 237–238, 3:41
Telephony, 3:**245–248**
 e-mail *vs.,* 1:74
 invention, 2:23
 TTYs, 4:17, 18
Teleprinters, 2:51, 57–58
Telerobotics, 1:215

Teletype machines, 2:57, 58
Television
 Apple TV, 1:19
 evolution from broadcast to cable, 1:239
 high definition, 2:82
 home entertainment use, 4:153–154
 interactive, 3:88, 4:105
 newsroom computer use, 4:200–202
 satellite broadcast, 2:212
 scanning lines, 2:82
 transition to digital, 2:261, 4:*87*
 weather forecasting, 3:*255,* 255–258
Telnet, 4:134, **262–264**
Telstar satellite, 2:212
Ten-Second Film Challenge, 4:*73*
Tenenbaum, Ehud, 3:123
Terabits per second (Tbps), 4:28
Terabyte (TB), defined, 1:162
Teraflops, 2:174
Term weighting, information retrieval, 1:115, 116
Terminal symbols, 2:2
Terminals, dumb. *See* Dumb terminals
Terminating resistors, 2:66
Terrorism
 airline passenger screening, 3:18
 anthrax scare, 3:36
 cyberwarfare, 4:179–182
 September 11 attacks, 3:18, 4:157, 266
 See also Bioterrorism
Tetrodes, 1:253
Tevatron particle collider, 3:193
Texas Instruments, 1:88, 126, 2:44
Text editing, 3:261
Text entry, 3:261
Text formatting, 3:261
Text messaging, 2:41–42
Text Retrieval Evaluation Conference (TREC), 1:116
Text telephones (TTYs), 4:17, 18
Text translation, urban myths, 4:265
Tfxidf values, 1:115
Thacker, Charles P., 1:251
Thakkar, Umesh, 1:258
Thematic mapping, 3:116
Therac-25 radiation therapy machine, 4:119

Thermal wax transfer, 2:190–191

Thiel, Peter, 4:*110*

Thin client/server technology (TCST), 2:49

Thin film transistor active matrix LCDs, 2:83

"THINK" slogan, 1:111, 267, *267*

Third generation computers, 1:88

Third generation programming languages, 1:92–93

Third-party endorsements, 4:53–54

Third-person 3-D video games, 1:15

Thompson, John W., 4:116

Thompson, Ken, 1:25, 33–34, 2:197–198

Three-body problem, 3:27

Three-dimensional animation, 1:9, 10

3D HDTV, 4:153–154

3D-ICs (three-dimensional integrated circuits), 1:128

Three-dimensional image projection, 4:*7*

Three-dimensional integrated circuits (3D-ICs), 1:128

3D interfaces, 4:156

3D mouse, 1:182, 2:184

3D printers, 3:62

Three Laws of Robotics (Asimov), 3:25, 4:127

Three-tier client server systems, 2:49

3-CCD technology, 4:73, 74

3G cellular technology, 1:240, 4:209

Throughputs, for system analysis models, 2:247–248

ThumbDrive flash drives, 2:243

Thumbnail images, 1:271

Tier 1 service providers, 4:247

TIGER (Topologically Integrated Geographic Encoding and Referencing) system, 1:41

Tik-Tok (fictional robot), 4:126

Tik-Tok of Oz (Baum), 4:126

Tiling windows interface, 1:270

Time-division multiplexing, 2:93, 3:41–42

Time-sharing jobs, 1:156

Time zones, 1:118, 3:174

Timing (animation), 1:14

Titanic (film), 4:8

Titchmarsh, E. C., 1:249

Title bars, 1:270

Tito, Dennis, 3:232

Tokens, for authentication, 2:217–218, 4:25, 107

Toll-free telephone numbers, 3:246

Top Grossing Film of All Time, 1 € 1 (artwork), 4:8

Top hats (joysticks), 2:96

Top-tier backbones, 4:176

Topalov, Veselin Aleksandrov, 3:46

Torricelli, Evangelista, 1:208

Torvalds, Linus, 2:164–165, 3:185, 4:145

Total internal reflection, 1:202

Touch mouse, 1:183

Touch screens, 2:**253–256**, *254*
    multi-touch interfaces, 1:19, 147, 183, 2:181, 3:252
    PDAs, 2:179, 181
    as pointing device, 2:185

Touchpads, 2:184–185

Toy Story (film series), 1:10, 18

Trackballs, 1:181, 182, 2:186

Trade secrets, 4:229

Trailers, of packets, 2:151

Training data, in pattern recognition, 2:177–178

Trains. *See* Railroad applications

Transac S-2000, 1:88

Transaction processing systems, 1:156, 3:16–17

Transactional speech recognition applications, 3:235, 236

Transactions, in databases, 2:239

Transatlantic transmission, 4:206

Transceivers, optical, 1:165–166

Transducers, ultrasound, 3:133

Transistors, 1:**241–247**, *242*
    defined, 1:32
    first uses, 2:22
    in integrated circuits, 1:125, 126
    invention, 1:32, 34, 66, 88, 125, 126, 2:20
    in second generation computers, 1:88

Transit exchange agreements, 4:175–176

Transit networks, 4:174

Transmedia Glide Write, 3:*260*

Transmission Control Protocol/Internet Protocol. *See* TCP/IP (Transmission Control Protocol/Internet Protocol)

Transmission Control Protocol (TCP)
    dominance, 2:47

FTP and, 4:133–134
history, 4:184–185
overview, 1:139
Telnet and, 4:134

Transmission convergence sublayer (ATM transmission), 4:21–22

Transmission lines, 2:256

Transmission media, 2:**256–259**

Transmissive liquid crystal displays, 2:83

Transponders, railroad use, 3:206

Transport layer
    firewall implementation, 4:130–131
    OSI Reference Model, 2:151–152, 153
    TCP protocol, 4:259–262

Transportation Security Administration (TSA), 3:18

Transposition (cryptography), 4:57

Transreflective liquid crystal displays, 2:83

Traveling salesperson problem, 3:180

Travelocity.com, 3:18, 4:99

Travelport, 3:17

Treatment (animation), 1:9

TREC (Text Retrieval Evaluation Conference), 1:116

Tree topology networks, 1:193, 2:155, 156

Trek Technology, 2:243

TRI-X film, 4:84–85

Trigonometric functions, 1:3, 4

Trilogy Systems Corporation, 4:4–5

Triodes, 1:164, 253

TRIPS (Agreement on Trade Related Aspects of Intellectual Property Rights), 4:228–229

Tripwire, 3:213

Trojan horses, 1:44, 223, 261, 262, 2:117–118

Tron (film), 4:128

Trusted Computer Systems Evaluation Criteria (TCSEC), 2:219

Truth tables, 2:27–29, 27*t*–29*t*

TSA (Transportation Security Administration), 3:18

TTYs (text telephones), 4:17, 18

Tunisia, Arab Spring beginnings, 3:219, 220

Tunneling, VPNs, 2:270

TurboTax, 3:*2*

Turing, Alan M., 1:*247*, **247–250**
    ACM involvement, 1:24–25
    algorithm development, 2:5–6
    artificial intelligence test, 1:22–23
    chess programming, 3:45
    cryptography work, 1:56
    cybernetic tortoise, 4:*10*
    cybernetics groundwork, 4:62
    funding sources, 1:96
    as pioneer, 1:61
    Shannon, Claude collaboration, 4:250
Turing Award, 1:24, 25, 248, 251
Turing Machine, 1:248, **250–252**, 2:6, 4:11, 62
Turing test, 1:22–23, 249
Turtle graphics, 2:126, 127
Twisted pairs, 1:194, 2:257
Twitter
    Arab Spring role, 3:219
    DDoS attacks, 4:180, 181
    hacking incident, 4:147
    journalism use, 4:202
    launch, 3:217
    popularity, 4:257
    scaling factors, 2:216
Two-factor authentication, 4:24
2G cellular technology, 1:240
2001: A Space Odyssey (film), 4:127
Tymnet, 3:153
Typewriters, 1:149
Typographics, 2:85–86

U

UARTs (universal asynchronous receiver transmitters), 2:223
Ubiquitous computing (embedded technology), 1:136–137, 3:98–102, 160–161
UBR (unspecified bit rate) service, 2:14
UCSD Pascal, 2:197
UGPIC (Universal Grocery Products Identification Code), 2:203
UIA (User Interface Automation), 4:18
Ultra-large-scale integration, 1:127
Ultrasound imaging, 3:133
Unauthorized renting, 3:224
Uniacke, Mark, 3:46
Unicode Consortium, 2:53
Unicode standard, 1:121, 2:53, 4:94
Uniform resource locators (URLs), 4:30, 111, 145

Unimation Corporation, 1:213
United Airlines, 3:17
United Kingdom
    cybercafes, 4:59, 61, 62
    data.gov.uk project, 4:111
    JANET, 4:174
    molecular computing research, 4:212
United States Patent and Trademark Office (USPTO), 4:227, 228, 229
Units, prefixes, 2:95, 4:28
UNIVAC I (Universal Automatic Computer I), 1:39–40, 87–88, 96, 102, 219, 3:68, 71
Universal asynchronous receiver transmitters (UARTs), 2:223
Universal Grocery Products Identification Code (UGPIC), 2:203
Universal Product Codes (UPCs), 2:167, 203
Universal Resource Identifiers (URIs), 4:33
Universal Serial Bus (USB) protocol, 2:12, 66–67, 224
Universal Turing machines, 4:11
Universities. *See* Colleges and universities
University of Alberta, 3:50
University of Bielefeld, 4:44
University of California system, 4:81, 106, 172, 184, 185, 261
University College, London, 4:184
University of Illinois, 1:258, 3:212, 4:33, 172, 185
University of Kansas, 4:33
University of Michigan, 3:187, 188
University of Minnesota, 3:137
University of North Carolina, 3:216
University of Pennsylvania, 3:191
University of Phoenix, 3:51
University of Pittsburgh, 4:105
University of Utah, 3:211, 4:184
University of Wisconsin, 4:4
Unix operating system
    Bell Labs research, 1:33, 34
    Berkeley version, 4:261
    as command line system, 1:132
    event-driven functionality, 1:134
    Mac OS X based on, 1:19
    TCP/IP incorporation, 4:261
    Viola-WWW browser, 4:33
    windows interfaces, 1:272

    See also Linux operating system
Unix-Unix System Mail (UUCP), 1:221
Unshielded copper cabling, 1:194
Unspecified bit rate (UBR) service, 2:14
UPCs (Universal Product Codes), 2:167, 203
Upload *vs.* download bandwidth, 2:258–259, 4:29–30
Ur (King), 4:96
Urban myths, 4:**264–267**
URIs (Universal Resource Identifiers), 4:33
URLs (uniform resource locators), 4:30, 111, 145
U.S. Census Bureau. *See* Census Bureau
U.S. Centers for Disease Control and Prevention (CDC), 3:33–34, 36
U.S. Department of Defense Advanced Research Projects Agency (DARPA), 1:97, 138, 2:274
U.S. Department of Defense (DoD), 1:97, 2:198–199, 4:181, 260, 261
U.S. Department of Energy, 4:176
U.S. Department of Transportation, 3:208
U.S. Federal Communications Commission (FCC)
    bandwidth oversight, 2:17
    Carterfone case, 2:39
    digital television mandate, 4:153
    frequency band regulation, 2:280
    Internet openness regulation, 4:187
    National Broadband Plan, 4:160
U.S. Fish and Wildlife Service, 3:35
U.S. Geological Survey (USGS), 2:213
U.S. Government Printing Office (GPO), 4:89
U.S. Library of Congress, 3:152
U.S. National Library of Medicine, 3:210
U.S. National Science Foundation. *See* National Science Foundation (NSF)
U.S. Navy, 3:20
U.S. Postal Service, 4:78
U.S. State Department, 2:271
USAN (Satellite Academic Network), 4:175
USB flash drives, 2:243
USB (Universal Serial Bus) protocol, 2:12, 66–67, 2:**65–68**, 224
USENET, 3:216, 4:175
User Interface Automation (UIA), 4:18

User interfaces, 3:*248*, **248–252**
    human factors, 4:155–157, 256
    knowledge-based systems, 3:143
    operating systems, 2:162, 163–164
    software design, 1:78
    virtual reality, 3:251, 4:156
    Visual Basic programming, 4:268
    See also Graphical user interfaces
       (GUIs)
Userid/password authentication, 4:24
USGS (U.S. Geological Survey), 2:213
USPTO (United States Patent and
    Trademark Office), 4:227, 228, 229
USS *Yorktown,* 3:136

V

Vacuum tubes, 1:53, 86–88, **253–256,**
    254, 2:136
Vacuums, wireless data transmission,
    1:208, 2:258, 259
Vail, Alfred, 2:141
Valiant, Leslie, 1:23
Valotta, Rosario, 4:47
Van Arman, Pindar, 4:8
The Vanishing Hitchhiker (legend),
    4:265
Vardi, Moshe, 1:*24*
Variable bit rate-non-real time (VBR-
    NRT) service, 2:14
Variable bit rate-real time (VBR-RT)
    service, 2:14
Variables, JavaScript, 4:196, 197
Variant computer-aided processing
    planning, 3:64
VAX series computers, 1:176
VBA (Visual Basic for Applications),
    4:268
vBNS (very high-speed Backbone
    Network Service), 4:186
VBR-NRT (variable bit rate-non-real
    time) service, 2:14
VBR-RT (variable bit rate-real time)
    service, 2:14
VBScript (Visual Basic Scripting
    Edition), 4:269
VCCs (virtual channel connections),
    2:13, 4:21
VCI (Virtual Channel Identifier),
    4:20–21, 22, 23
VCRs (videocassette recorders), 2:262,
    4:103
VCs (virtual circuits), 2:13

Vector graphics display, 2:100–101,
    3:38
Vector processing, supercomputers,
    1:233–234, 3:68
Vector space model, 1:115
Vehicle-based video games, 1:15
Vercoe, Barry, 2:144
VeriSign Secured Seal, 4:224
Verizon Wireless, 1:240, 4:176, 209
Vernam, Gilbert, 4:56
Verne, Jules, 3:24, 25, 4:126
Verniero, Peter, 1:*260*
Veronica (Internet index), 4:186
Very high-speed Backbone Network
    Service (vBNS), 4:186
Very large-scale integrated (VLSI)
    circuits, 1:89, 175, 2:78
VIBE (Visual Information Browsing
    Environment), 3:*74,* 74–75
Video cameras, 2:262, 4:73–74, 85
Video cards, 1:15, 2:99, 261, 3:114
Video co-processors, 2:100
Video compression standards, 2:15
Video devices, 2:15, 119–121,
    261–263, *262,* 4:*73,* 73–76
Video display, 8-bit *vs.* 16-bit,
    1:36–37
Video editing. *See* Film and video
    editing
Video games. *See* Games
Video masters, 3:113
Video output cards, 2:261
Videocassette recorders (VCRs), 2:262,
    4:103
Videoconferencing, 1:198–199, 2:262
Viking (lander), 3:231
Viola-WWW (browser), 4:33
Virgin Galactic, 3:230
Virtual Address eXtension (VAX) series
    computers, 1:176
Virtual addressing, 2:*263,* 264–265,
    265, 266–268, *268*
Virtual channel connections (VCCs),
    2:13, 4:21
Virtual Channel Identifier (VCI),
    4:20–21, 22, 23
Virtual circuits (VCs), 2:13
Virtual communities, 1:71
Virtual libraries. *See* Digital libraries
Virtual memory, 2:*263,* **263–269,** *264,*
    265, 268
       defined, 1:161, 2:139

Denning, Peter J. contributions,
    4:145
    as security measure, 1:220
Virtual path connections (VPCs), 4:21
Virtual Path Identifier (VPI), 4:20–21,
    22, 23
Virtual private networks (VPNs),
    2:**268–271**
Virtual reality animation, 1:9, 10–11
Virtual reality in education, 1:*256,*
    256–260, *257*
Virtual Reality Modeling Language
    (VRML), 1:10, 11
Virtual reality (VR), 2:*272,* **272–275**
    defined, 1:9, 2:272
    research, 1:135–136
    simulation and, 1:228, 2:228–232,
       229
    user interfaces, 3:251, 4:156
    video game contributions, 1:79
Virtual systems research, 1:135–136
Virtualization, 1:133
Viruses, 1:*260,* **260–265**
    detection programs, 3:214
    first cases, 1:222
    overview, 1:44, 2:116
    payloads, 1:262
    types, 1:262–263
    via e-mail attachment, 1:75
Visi-Calc spreadsheet software, 3:198,
    239
Visible Human Project, 3:210
Vision, computer, 4:41–45
Vision impairments, assistive
    technology, 4:15, 33, 34, 43
Visitor location registers, 3:246–247
VisTrails software, 3:211
Visual Basic, 2:196, 4:**267–269**
Visual Basic for Applications (VBA),
    4:268
Visual Basic Scripting Edition
    (VBScript), 4:269
Visual Information Browsing
    Environment (VIBE), 3:*74,* 74–75
Visualization systems, 1:135,
    3:192–193, 209–212, *210*
VLSI (very large-scale integrated)
    circuits, 1:89, 175, 2:78
Vocoder, 2:144
Voice-coding devices, 2:144
Voice coils, 2:233–234
Voice commands, 3:252

Voice-driven applications, 4:169

Voice mail, 1:74, 198

Voice-over-Internet-protocol (VoIP), 3:247, 4:248

Voice recognition. *See* Speech recognition

Volatility of RAM, 1:160

Volume software licenses, 3:223–224

von Neumann, John, 2:**275**–**277**, *276*
  artificial life model, 4:11
    EDVAC development, 1:58–59, 66, 2:90, 91
    Kemeny, John G. collaboration, 3:141
    stored-program concept development, 1:87
    Turing, Alan collaboration, 1:248

von Neumann machines, 1:58–59, 87

Voting, data processing, 4:236, 237

Voting districts, data processing, 4:235

Voyager (space probe), 3:231, 232

VPCs (virtual path connections), 4:21

VPI (Virtual Path Identifier), 4:20–21, 22, 23

VPNs (virtual private networks), 2:268–271

VR. *See* Virtual reality (VR)

VRML (Virtual Reality Modeling Language), 1:10, 11

Vulnerabilities, security software and, 2:220, 3:124

W

W3C. *See* World Wide Web Consortium (W3C)

WAAS (Wide Area Augmentation System), 4:137–138

Wafer-scale integration (WSI), 1:128

Wafers, 3:48

Wal-Mart, 4:69

Walkie-talkies, 3:117, 118

WALL-E (film), 4:128

Wallace and Gromit (animated characters), 1:10

Walt Disney Studios, 1:12–13, 14, 3:126

Walters, Grey, 1:213

Wang, An, 3:**253**–**255**, 262

Wang, Charles, 4:115

Wang Computer System, 3:262

Wang Laboratories, 3:253, 254

Wang Word Processing System, 3:254, 259, 262

Wannabes (hackers), 4:148

WANs. *See* Wide area networks (WANs)

"Warcraft" (simulation game), 1:83

Warez Dudez (hackers), 4:149

WarGames (film), 4:128

Warnock, John, 3:243–244

Waterfall paradigm, 2:249, 251

Watson (IBM computer), 1:23

Watson, James, 4:39

Watson, Thomas A., 1:240, 2:23

Watson, Thomas J., Jr., 1:108, 109–110, 268

Watson, Thomas J., Sr., 1:107–108, *267*, **267**–**269**

Wave interruption touch screens, 2:255

Wave table synthesis, 2:235

Wavelength division multiplexing (WDM), 1:202, 2:93

Wearable computing, 2:101, 3:100, 101

Weather forecasting, 3:210, *255,* **255**–**259**

Weather monitoring, 2:212, 3:119

Web. *See* World Wide Web

Web animation, 1:14–15

Web browsers. *See* Browsers

Web servers, 2:225, 227, 4:30–31, 188

Webb, Jim, 4:234

Webphone, 1:179

Web sites
  as art, 4:8
  intranets, 1:67, 195, 4:188–190
  journalism, 4:202
  political applications, 4:233, 234, 235

WebStar server program, 2:225

Wei, Pei, 4:33

Weighted information retrieval, 1:115, 116

Weiser, Mark, 3:101

Wells, H.G., 3:24, 25

Werbos, Paul J., 3:180

Wergo Records, 1:185

West Publishing Company, 3:149

Western Electric Company (WECo), 1:31–32, 33

Western Music Notation, 3:168

Westlaw, 3:149

Westworld (film), 4:128

What-if analysis, 3:201, 238

Wheatstone, Charles, 1:152, 2:113, 114

While Rome Burns (Woollcott), 4:265

Whirlpool project, 3:20

Whirlwind computer, 1:60

White Hat hackers, 4:148

Whiteboards, interactive, 4:104, 105

Wi-Fi (Wireless Fidelity), 4:209

Wide Area Augmentation System (WAAS), 4:137–138

Wide area networks (WANs)
  Internet backbone connections, 4:172–173
  mainframe connection, 1:158
  network design considerations, 2:147–149
  origins, 1:239
  overview, 1:195
  VPNs *vs.,* 2:268

Wiener, Norbert, 4:62–63

Wii, 1:*80,* 2:*96,* 98

Wilkes, Maurice V., 1:50, 59, 64, 65, 87, 249

Williams, Evan, 3:217

Williams, John, 4:69

Williams, R. Stanley, 4:*210*

Williams, Sir Frederic, 1:59, 64–65

Wily Hacker attack (1986), 1:223

WIMP (windows, icon, menu, and pointer) systems, 1:133, 3:241
  See also Graphical user interfaces (GUIs)

Window interfaces, 1:*269,* **269**–**273,** 2:86

Window manager functionality, 1:134

Windows Media Player, 2:237

Windows operating system
  accessibility utilities, 4:18
  creation, 1:84
  encryption abilities, 4:58
  GUIs, 2:163–164
  Internet Explorer bundle, 1:85, 274, 4:172
  introduction, 1:171
  Microsoft Excel performance, 3:240
  multitasking capabilities, 1:171
  Visual Basic programming, 4:268
  windows interfaces, 1:272

Windows Phone mobile operating system, 4:208

Windows technology, 1:95

Winklevoss, Cameron, 3:263

Winklevoss, Tyler, 3:263

WIPO (World Intellectual Property Organization) Copyright Treaty, 3:225

Wire frames, 2:100
Wired control switching offices, 3:245
Wireless communications
    AirPort technology, 1:144
    Apple TV, 1:145
    Gross, Alfred J. contributions,
      3:117–119
    mobile computing devices,
      4:207–210
    mobile virtual private networks,
      2:271
    portable devices, 1:240
    See also Broadcast
      telecommunications; Cell phones;
      Smartphones
Wireless lavaliere microphones, 4:103
Wireless local area networks (WLANs),
  2:281, 4:209
Wireless local loops (WLLs), 2:281
Wireless modems, 2:258
Wireless mouse, 1:183
Wireless technology, 2:**279–281,** *280*
Wireless Telegraph and Signal Company
  Limited, 4:206
Wireless telegraph systems, 2:257, 279,
  4:205–206
Wireless transmission, 2:258–259
Wireshark network security program,
  3:214
Wirth, Niklaus, 2:1, 195, 197
Wisconsin Integrally Synchronized
  Computer (WISC), 4:4
Wizards, application, 1:271–272
Wizards, gurus *vs.,* 4:146
WLANs (wireless local area networks),
  2:281, 4:209
WLLs (wireless local loops), 2:281
Wolfram Mathematica, 3:94
Women
    Association for Computing
      Machinery chapters, 1:26
    early programming, 1:65–66
    See also specific women
Wong, Ray, 2:218
Woodland, Joseph, 2:203
Woollcott, Alexander, 4:265
Word processors, 3:**259–262,** *260*
    desktop publishing *vs.,* 3:82, 262
    integrated software, 3:136–139
    office automation systems, 1:197
    productivity software, 3:197–198
    Wang systems, 3:254, 259, 262

WordPerfect software, 3:128, 262
WordStar software, 3:139
Work prints (animation), 1:9
Workplace impact, 4:255
Worksheets, in spreadsheets, 3:236
World Intellectual Property
  Organization (WIPO) Copyright
  Treaty, 3:225
World Trade Center, 4:157
World Trade Organization (WTO),
  4:51, 228–229
World War II (1939-1945)
    computer development, 1:53–58,
      61–62
    cryptography use, 4:57, 59
    radio communications
      development, 3:118
World Wide Web, 1:**273–276**
    Berners-Lee, Tim contributions,
      2:226, 4:32–33, 111, 145, 186
    hypermedia model, 2:105
    Internet flexibility and, 1:239
    invisible Web, 4:245
    servers, 2:225, 227, 4:30–31, 188
    standards, 1:121, 2:47
    See also Browsers; Internet; Search
      engines; *specific sites*
World Wide Web Consortium (W3C)
    Berners-Lee, Tim contributions,
      4:111, 169–170
    browser development, 4:34,
      169–170
    information technology standards,
      1:120
    XML coordination, 2:134
Worldspan LP, 3:17
WORM (write once/read many),
  2:244
Worms
    first cases, 1:222
    Morris worm, 1:45
    overview, 1:44, 263–264, 2:117
    payloads, 1:262
    via e-mail attachment, 1:75
    viruses *vs.,* 1:261, 263
Wozniak, Stephen
    Apple founding, 1:17, 18, 143
    Atari involvement, 1:82
    biographical overview, 1:19
    departure from Apple, 1:18
    Jobs, Steve collaboration, 1:142,
      4:113

Wright, S. Fowler, 4:126–127
Write once/read many (WORM),
  2:244
Writing, history, 3:82–83
WSI (wafer-scale integration), 1:128
WTO (World Trade Organization),
  4:51, 228–229
WYSIWYG
    desktop publishing development,
      3:82, 84–85, 241–242
    word processors, 3:198, 261

X

X rays, 3:134
X-Windows system, 1:272
X3D (modeling language),
  1:10–11
Xbox console series, 1:82, 4:154
Xenakis, Iannis, 1:185
Xerography, 1:276, 278, 2:189
Xerox 800 word processor, 3:262
Xerox 8010 Star computer,
  1:137
Xerox 9700 printer, 3:242–243
Xerox Corporation, 1:133, 137,
  276–279, *277*
Xerox Palo Alto Research Center
  (PARC)
    Alto computer, 1:251, 272, 278,
      4:184
    CoLab project, 3:59–60
    computer research, 1:278
    desktop publishing development,
      3:82, 244
    inadvertent worm creation, 1:263,
      2:117
    Interpress page description
      language, 3:243–244
    mouse development, 2:186
    windows interfaces, 1:272
Xerox Star computer, 1:133, 278
XHTML (eXtensible hypertext markup
  language), 2:134–135
Xmarks, 4:114
XML (eXtensible markup language),
  2:*132*
    browser development, 4:34
    desktop publishing use,
      3:86, 244
    music applications, 3:169
    overview, 2:134–135
    Web browsing and, 4:170

Y

Y2K scare, 3:124, 4:5

Yacc (Yet another compiler-compiler), 2:2

Yahoo! portal, 1:274, 275, 4:117, 245

Yamaha, 3:171

Yang, Jerry, 1:274, 275, 4:116–117

Yield, LCD manufacturing, 2:83

Yin/yang concept, 1:37

York, Jillian, 3:221

YouTube, 3:217

Z

Z Machine, 3:28

Z1 (early computer), 1:55, 65, 2:282, *282*

Z2 (early computer), 1:65, 2:282

Z3 (early computer), 1:65, 2:282

Z4 (early computer), 1:65, 2:282–283

Zero meridian, 3:173, 174

Zeus (Trojan horse), 2:118

Ziller, Irving, 2:193

Zip disks, 2:242–243

Zip drives, 2:242–243

.zip files, 3:130

Zombie Trojan horses, 2:118

ZTE, 2:181

Zuckerberg, Mark, 3:216, **262–265,** *263,* 4:117

Zuse, Konrad, 1:55, 65, 2:**281–283,** *282*

Zweig, Janet, 4:7–8